AN INTRODUCTION TO LAW

LAW IN CONTEXT

Editors: Robert Stevens (Covington & Burling, London)
William Twining (University College, London) and
Christopher McCrudden (Lincoln College, Oxford)

PUBLISHED TITLES INCLUDE:

Atiyah's Accidents, Compensation and the Law (Fifth Edition), Peter Cane
Karl Llewellyn and the Realist Movement (reissue), William Twining
Cases and Materials on the English Legal System (Sixth Edition), Michael Zander
How to do Things with Rules (Third Edition), William Twining and David Miers
Evidence, Proof and Probability (Second Edition), Richard Eggleston
Family Law and Social Policy (Second Edition), John Eekelaar
Labour Law (Second Edition), Paul Davies and Mark Freedland
The Law Making Process (Third Edition), Michael Zander
An Introduction to Law (Fourth Edition), Phil Harris
Law and Administration, Carol Harlow and Richard Rawlings
Legal Foundations of the Welfare State, Ross Cranston
British Government and the Constitution (Second Edition), Colin Turpin
Sexual Divisions in Law, Katherine O'Donovan
The Law of Contract (Second Edition), Hugh Collins
Regulation and Public Law, Robert Baldwin and Christopher McCrudden
Freedom of Information, Patrick Birkinshaw
Remedies in Contract and Tort, Donald Harris
Trusts Law, Graham Moffat and Michael Chesterman
Courts and Administrators, Michael Detmold
Consumer Protection, Iain Ramsay
Subjects, Citizens, Aliens and Others, Ann Dummett and Andrew Nicol
New Directions in European Community Law, Francis Snyder
Languages of Law, Peter Goodrich
Reconstructing Criminal Law, Nicola Lacey, Celia Wells and Dirk Meure
Analysis of Evidence, Terence Anderson and William Twining
International Business Taxation, Sol Picciotto
Sentencing and Criminal Justice, Andrew Ashworth
Investor Protection, A. C. Page and R. B. Ferguson

An Introduction to Law

Fourth Edition

PHIL HARRIS

Senior Academic in Law at Sheffield Hallam University

BUTTERWORTHS
London, Dublin, Edinburgh

United Kingdom	Butterworth & Co (Publishers) Ltd, Halsbury House, 35 Chancery Lane, LONDON WC2A 1EL and 4 Hill Street, EDINBURGH EH2 3JZ
Australia	Butterworths, SYDNEY, MELBOURNE, BRISBANE, ADELAIDE, PERTH, CANBERRA and HOBART
Belgium	Butterworth & Co (Publishers) Ltd, BRUSSELS
Canada	Butterworths Canada Ltd, TORONTO and VANCOUVER
Ireland	Butterworth (Ireland) Ltd, DUBLIN
Malaysia	Malayan Law Journal Sdn Bhd, KUALA LUMPUR
New Zealand	Butterworths of New Zealand Ltd, WELLINGTON and AUCKLAND
Puerto Rico	Butterworth of Puerto Rica, Inc, SAN JUAN
Singapore	Butterworths Asia, SINGAPORE
USA	Butterworth Legal Publishers, CARLSBAD, California, and SALEM, New Hampshire

Reprinted December 1993, January 1995

A CIP Catalogue record for this book is available from the British Library.

ISBN 0-297-82122-9

Typeset by Deltatype Ltd, Ellesmere Port
Printed in England by Clays Ltd, St Ives plc

CONTENTS

TABLE OF CASES

TABLE OF STATUTES

PREFACE TO THE FOURTH EDITION

This book has been written as an introductory text, mainly for students who are studying law at A-level, AS-level, on BTEC courses, and on degree courses (particularly mixed or integrated courses where law is taught alongside other subjects).

It is not necessary, however, to enrol on a course of study before undertaking an exploration of English law. We live in a society in which everyday life in all its aspects is touched by legal regulation and rules more than at any other period in history. This, indeed, is one of the truisms underlying the approach taken in this book, the other important truism being that law cannot properly be understood, and certainly ought not to be studied, in a manner which fails to take account of the social, economic and political contexts and formations out of which the law arises and in which it operates.

Consequently, the reader will find, it is hoped, that the approach taken here is rather different from that of most other law texts. I have tried to locate legal rules and institutions within the contexts of their historical background, taking into account the economic and political forces which have shaped – some might even say distorted – English law. To do this, I have tried to incorporate, where appropriate, materials from disciplines other than that which is conventionally regarded as law. This approach, together with the inevitable constraints of space and time, has necessitated a considerable degree of selection as to the topics covered. Within these constraints, I have concentrated on those areas of law – contract, tort, property, crime, administration and aspects of the legal system – which are the main concerns of students taking the kind of course indicated above.

It is hoped that the result is a discussion of legal phenomena which treats law as a *social* construct, created and implemented by people living in a society which is undergoing continuous change, rather than something akin to what the famous American judge and legal writer Oliver Wendell Holmes (1841–1935) called a 'brooding omnipresence in the sky' – existing independently of the deeds and consciousness of men and women in society, regulating their conduct but beyond their control.

For if we are to have law at all (and every known social group has had codes approximating to what we would recognize as law) then it must be responsive to the needs of society. If the law, or any legal institution, fails to respond to those needs, then it clearly becomes open to criticism. I see neither use nor virtue in presenting or studying law as if it were merely a package of rules; or in a way which suggests that there is nothing wrong with it. And if criticisms of the law lead to criticisms of the society whose law it is, then so be it. Laws are the expressions of historical processes and contemporary policies; those processes and policies, controversial though they often are, are themselves fascinating and rewarding areas of study, and they serve to help us understand *why* the law takes the form that it does. If the critical comments in this book have the effect of stimulating further thought and discussion on the part of the reader, then one objective, at least, will have been achieved.

It is worth repeating that this is an *introductory* text. The reader is warned that he or she will search in vain for the outcome of painstaking research, new theoretical formulations or even original insight. Rather, I have tried to draw together various strands of development, debate and controversy, and to present them within a framework of 'law in context'. This fourth edition generally follows the structure of the third; within that structure, I have added a new chapter designed to introduce the student to European law and institutions, and there are sections on new areas of legal regulation (for example, intellectual property law and product liability) and current issues concerning law and the legal system are discussed – two examples are environmental protection, and the recent debates concerning changes in the work of the legal profession and the government's concern over the rising cost of legal aid. Naturally, the contents have been updated throughout.

My debts to students, colleagues and friends who have – however unconsciously and in some cases involuntarily – assisted in the preparation of this book continue to accumulate. For this edition, I was deprived of the help of one or two of them who have gone on to pastures new, though their influence remains in evidence. Among the contributors to this edition are Pete Alcock, Rhoda James, Nigel Johnson, Peter Vincent-Jones, Paul Lawless, Richard Grimes, David Woodhill, and Alison Ward – all at Sheffield Hallam University; special thanks to Chris Roberts and Su McCaughan; to Andrea Nollent at S.H.U. for her advice and suggestions for the drafting of chapter 8; to Marianne Giles at the University of Kent at Canterbury for scrutinizing and commenting on the whole manuscript – a daunting task which was once again carried out with stunning efficiency and speed; and, last but certainly not least, to Sue and Dominic, without whom this book would probably have been written, but would not have been half as much fun. Although, like all authors, I wish I could blame someone else, errors which remain are, of course, my own responsibility.

I
Law and society

One of the many ways in which human societies can be distinguished from animal groups is by reference to social *rules*. We eat and sleep at certain intervals; we work on certain days for certain periods; our behaviour towards others is controlled, directly and indirectly, through moral standards, religious doctrines, social traditions and legal rules. To take one specific example: we may be born with a 'mating instinct', but it is through social rules that the attempt is made to channel this 'instinct' into the most socially acceptable form of relationship – heterosexual marriage.

Marriage is a good example of the way in which social rules govern our lives. Not only is the monogamous (one man/one woman) marriage supported by the predominant religion in our history – Christianity; it is also maintained through *moral* rules (hence the idea of unmarried couples living together being 'wrong') and by the operation of rules of *law* which define and control the formalities of the marriage ceremony, lay down who can and who cannot legally marry, specify the circumstances whereby divorce may be obtained, define the rights to matrimonial property upon marital breakdown, and so on.

Marriage is only one example of social behaviour being governed through rules. Legal rules are especially significant in the world of business, with matters such as banking, money, credit and employment all regulated to some extent through law. Indeed, in a complex society like our own, it is hard to find any area of activity which is completely free from legal control. Driving, working, being a parent, handling property – all these are touched in some way by law. Even a basic activity like eating is indirectly affected by law, in that the food we eat is required by legal rules to meet rigorous standards of purity, hygiene and even description.

In this introductory chapter, attempts by various writers to analyse and explain law will be examined. We shall also consider some important social, economic and political developments over the past century or so which have profoundly affected the nature and extent of the regulation of social life by means of legal rules and procedures. In addition, some of the important themes running through this book will be introduced, such as the proposition that the law is never static; it is always changing, being reinterpreted or redefined, as legislators and judges strive, with varying degrees of success, to ensure that the law constantly reflects changes in society itself. This, in turn, leads to a second important theme: that law can be properly understood only by examining the ways in which it actually operates in society, and by studying the often extremely complex relationship between a social group and its legal code.

Analysing law

Most of us, if asked to define law, would probably do so in terms of rules: for instance, we understand criminal law, forbidding certain activities, as a set of rules defining the types of behaviour which, if indulged in, result in some form of official 'retaliation' through police intervention, the courts and some form of criminal *sanction* such as imprisonment or a fine. Criminal law and the notion of legal sanctions will be examined in a later chapter. For the moment, the fundamental notion for us is that of a 'rule'.

In their work on the subject, Twining and Miers offer a wide definition of a rule as 'a general norm guiding conduct or action in a given type of situation'.[1] A rule prescribes what activity may, should or should not be carried out, or refers to activities which should be carried out in a specified way. Rules of law may forbid certain activity – murder and theft are prohibited through rules of criminal law – or they may impose certain conditions under which activity may be carried out (car drivers and television-set users must, for example, have valid licences for those items before they can legally drive or use them). Again the law contains some rules which we might call 'power-conferring' rules: rules which enable certain activities to be carried out with some form of legal backing and protection, the best example of which is perhaps the law of contract, which provides rules which, among other things, guide us in the manner in which to act if we wish to make a valid contract.[2]

Because a rule guides us in what we may, ought or ought not to do, it is said to be *normative*. We can best grasp the meaning of this term if we contrast a normative statement, telling us what *ought* to happen, with a *factual* statement, which tells us what *does* happen. For instance, the statement 'cars must not be driven except on roads' is a normative, 'ought'-type statement, whereas 'cars are driven on roads' is a factual, 'is'-type statement. All rules, whether legal, moral or just customary, are normative, laying down standards of behaviour to which we *ought* to conform if the rule affects us.

Although the notion of a 'system of rules' probably corresponds closely to most people's idea of law, we can soon see that this is not sufficient by itself to be an accurate or adequate account of law, because there are, in any social group, various 'systems of rules' apart from law. How do we distinguish, for example, between a *legal* rule and a *moral* rule? In our society, though we consider it immoral to tell lies, it is not generally against the law to do so.[3] Of course, some moral rules are also embodied in the law, such as the legal rule prohibiting murder. This does not mean, however, as we shall see in chapter 2, that law and morality *always* correspond. It would take a very wide definition of 'morality', for instance, for the idea to be accepted that a driver who exceeds the speed limit by only two miles per hour (a criminal offence) would thereby be acting *immorally*!

Again, how do we distinguish between a legal rule and a rule of custom or etiquette? What is the difference between a judge's ordering a convicted person to pay a fine for breaking a criminal-law rule and a father's ordering his son to forfeit his pocket-money for disobeying him? Clearly, there *are* differences between these types of rule, and perhaps the only feature which they all have in common is their normativeness. But where do these differences lie?

The analysis of law, and the specification of the distinctions between law and other rules, have proved surprisingly difficult to articulate. Writers have, over the years, adopted various perspectives on legal analysis, sometimes concentrating on law as a system of rules of an official nature (as in the work of H.L.A. Hart), sometimes focusing upon individual legal rules, their origin and their operation as part of an overall system (as can be seen in works within the sociology of law).[4] Some writers have analysed law as if it were a 'closed' system, operating within its own logical framework, and divorced in important ways from the wider social context. John Austin, writing in the nineteenth century, is an example of such writers. Others have insisted (especially in recent years) that law and the legal system can only be analysed by considering them in relation to the other processes and institutions within the society in which they operate – as stated above, such is the perspective within this book.

Still other legal writers have provided accounts of law which take as their central issue the various functions which law is supposed to perform in a society. Two examples of this approach are worthy of note here. First, the American writer Karl Llewellyn expounded his 'Law-Jobs Theory',[5] which is a general account of the functions of legal institutions in social groups of all kinds. Llewellyn argued that every social group has certain basic needs, which are catered for by the social institution of law by helping ensure that the group survives as such, and by providing for the prevention of disruptive disputes within the group. Should any disputes arise between members, the law must provide the means of resolving them. The law must also provide the means whereby the authority structure of the group is constituted and recognized (such as a constitution) and, finally, the law must provide for the manner and procedures in which the above 'law-jobs' are carried out.

A second example of this approach is that of Robert Summers.[6] He identifies five techniques of law, which may be used to implement social policies. These are, first, the use of law to remedy grievances among members of a society; second, the use of law as a penal instrument, with which to prohibit and prosecute forbidden behaviour; third, law as an instrument with which to promote certain defined activities; fourth, the use of law for managing various governmental public benefits, such as education and welfare policies; and fifth, the use of law to give effect to certain private arrangements between members of a society, such as the provisions of the law of contract in our own legal system.

We can contrast the analyses of Llewellyn and Summers with those of writers such as Austin, in that their accounts relate the law to its social context, whereas Austin treats rules, including legal rules, as though they were amenable to analysis 'in a vacuum', so to speak, or, put another way, in a manner divorced from social contexts or settings. For Austin, the hallmark of a legal rule (which he terms 'positive', or man-made, law) lies in the manner of its creation. He defined law as the *command of the sovereign body* in a society (which may be a person, such as a king or queen, or a body of elected officials such as our own law-making body which we refer to formally as 'the Queen in Parliament'), and these commands were backed up by threats of sanctions, to be applied in the event of disobedience.

A major problem with Austin's analysis concerns his use of the idea of the 'command'. Although the rules of criminal law, mentioned above, may perhaps approximate to the idea of our being 'commanded' by the law-makers not to engage in prohibited conduct, on pain of some criminal sanction, there are very many rules of law which do not 'command' us to do things at all. The law concerning marriage, for example, never commands us to marry, but merely sets out the conditions under which people may marry, and the procedure which they must follow if their marriage is to be valid in law. Similarly, the law does not command us to make contracts, but rather lays down the conditions under which an agreement will have the force of a legally binding contract. This type of rule may be termed a 'power-giving' rule, and may be contrasted with the duty-imposing rules which characterize criminal law. As Hart, among others, has pointed out, there are many other instances in law where the legal rule in question cannot sensibly be described as a form of 'command': 'Is it not misleading so to classify laws which confer powers on private individuals to make wills, contracts, or marriages, and laws which give powers to officials, e.g. to a judge, to try cases, to a minister to make rules, or a county council to make by-laws?'[7] The law, then, is far too complex, and contains far too great a variety of *kinds* of legal rules, for it to be reduced to the simple proposition that 'laws are commands'.

What other formulations and classifications of law may be offered by legal writers? One significant attempt in recent years has been Hart's own theory, contained in his book *The Concept of Law*, in which he sets out, first, the basic legal requirements, as he sees them, of any social group which is to be more than a 'suicide club'. Every such social group, Hart suggests, must have certain rules which impose duties upon the members of the group concerning standards of behaviour. These 'primary' rules, which might contain rules approximating to basic criminal-law rules but which might also impose what we would call civil-law duties (akin to duties contained in the law of tort – see chapter 9), could conceivably comprise the *only* rules within a social group; but, Hart argues, in a developed and complex society, these 'primary' rules will give rise to certain problems which will have to be dealt with by means of additional, 'secondary' rules. The first problem with such a simple code is that there will be no settled procedure for resolving doubts as to the nature and authority of an apparently 'legal' rule. To remedy this, the introduction of 'rules of recognition' is needed: these rules will constitute the hallmark of what is truly a *law*, and may do so by reference to a set of other rules or institutions, such as a constitution, a monarch or a representative body, such as Parliament.

A second problem will be that the primary rules will be static: there will be no means of changing the rules in accordance with changes in the circumstances of the social group. The remedy for this defect, says Hart, is a set of 'rules of change', enabling specified bodies to introduce new rules or to alter existing ones. Third, the primary rules will be inefficiently administered, because their enforcement will be through diffuse social pressures within the group. The remedy for this, says Hart, is the introduction of 'rules of adjudication', which provide for officials (judges) to decide disputes authoritatively. It will be appreciated that these secondary rules are really 'rules about rules', and Hart argues that the characteristic feature of a modern legal system is this *union* of primary and secondary rules.

Interesting though this approach is, it has suffered at the hands of critics. To begin with, some commentators have argued that Hart's reduction of all duty-imposing rules to a category which he calls 'primary' rules is far too great a simplification. Can this category really usefully embrace areas of law, all of which impose duties of various kinds and with various consequences, as diverse in content and objectives as contract law, private property law, family law, criminal law, tort law and labour relations law? It may be argued that a much more complex classificatory scheme is required in order for such differences to be adequately analysed and understood.

Another criticism is that Hart's treatment of a legal system as a 'system of rules' fails to take into account the various other normative prescriptions contained within a legal system which affect the course, development and application of the law, but which are not 'rules'. In particular, Dworkin has argued[8] that Hart fails to take account of the role of *principles* in the operation of the law. Principles, he maintains, differ from rules in that, while the latter are applicable in an all-or-nothing manner, the former are guidelines, stating 'a reason that argues in one direction, but [does] not necessitate a particular decision'.[9] Thus, suppose that a man murders his father in order to benefit from the father's will which, as he knows, provides that all the father's property will come to him upon the father's death. Irrespective of the liability of the man for murder, the question will fall to be considered whether he will ultimately acquire that property. Normally, the law attempts to give effect to the wishes of the maker of a will, but here the outcome may well be affected by the *principle* that 'no man should profit by his own wrong' and the result may well be that, through the operation of this principle, and *despite the existence of legal rules* which would otherwise have operated in the son's favour, the murderer does not receive the inheritance.[10] Whether or not this type of principle is *part of* the fabric of legal rules, as Dworkin argues, is a difficult question: all parts of the law contain principles as well as 'hard rules' – an example might be principles of public policy which affect judicial deliberations concerning the law of negligence, which we shall consider in chapter 9 – but for the moment, it can be appreciated from the above discussion that there is much more to law than merely legal rules.

A more general point which must be made here is that, although the 'law as rules' approach has, through the work of writers such as Austin and Hart, greatly influenced patterns of legal thought in this country and elsewhere, it is by no means the only approach which may be taken in legal study. Already we have mentioned the approach which looks at law in terms of its functions within society. Other writers have taken the view that law is best understood by examining the actual *operation* of the legal system in practice, and by comparing the 'letter of the law' with the way it actually operates. Such an approach is taken by those writers whose work is usually categorized as 'Legal Realism' – principally, Karl Llewellyn, Jerome Frank and Oliver Wendell Holmes. Other writers, at various times, have analysed law in terms of a society's cultural and/or historical background, while still others, adopting an anthropological approach, have argued that the idea of a legal system may be illuminated by considering and comparing modern legal systems with the systems of small, technologically less developed societies.

Authority and obedience to law

Another important aspect of rules in general, and legal rules in particular, is the phenomenon of obedience to those rules, and the acceptance that those rules are both legitimate and authoritative. Again, there are many analyses of these issues, one or two of which may be briefly considered here.

For example, Austin's idea of why we obey law is found in his notion of the 'habit of obedience' to the sovereign body in a society, which, together with the ever-present threat of sanctions, explains obedience to law. Few, however, would accept this idea as an adequate explanation. It is a questionable assumption that we obey law out of habit or for fear of official reprisals. Do we really go through our daily law-abiding lives with such things kept in mind? Surely not. Rather, as Hart[11] argues, most of us conform to law because of more complex social and psychological processes. Hart's own explanation of obedience to law lies in the idea of some inner psychological inclination whereby we accept the *legitimacy* or *authority* of the source of the law; we obey because we consider it 'right and proper' to do so. Hart calls this acceptance the 'internal' aspect of obedience to law, and argues that people usually obey because of such acceptance.

Of course, as Hart acknowledges, there are exceptions. Some might obey out of a genuine worry about the consequences of disobedience; others might disagree with the entirety of the legal and social arrangements in our society, but obey the law out of sheer convenience. Everything depends, of course, upon the kind of society and legal system in question, for an extreme and oppressive regime might deliberately obtain obedience to its dictates by instilling terror into the population. In our own society, however, few of us would seriously dispute the idea that most people accept the legitimacy of existing legal, social and political authority, as defined through constitutional doctrines and principles, and our everyday 'common-sense' notions of legal authority.

This question of the idea of authority in society is worthy of closer attention, however. One sociologist who wrote extensively about law, Max Weber, identified three *types of authority* in social groups.[12] First, he argued, the authority of a leader or ruler may be the result of the personal, individual characteristics of that leader – his or her *charisma* – which sets that person apart from the rest. Examples might be Jesus, Napoleon and, more recently, Hitler in Nazi Germany, Eva Peron in Argentina and Winston Churchill in Britain, all of whom, it might be said, to some extent and to varying degrees, rose to their exalted positions and maintained those positions as leaders through their extraordinarily strong personalities.

A second type of authority, according to Weber, is *traditional* authority, where obedience to the leader or regime is sustained because it is traditional: 'it has always been so'. Third, Weber identifies in modern Western societies a form of authority which he calls *rational-legal* or *bureaucratic*, where the authority of the regime is legitimized not through personal charismatic leadership, nor through pure tradition, but through rules and procedures. Although such a type may correspond roughly to authority in our own society, where the system of government and law-making depends upon a constitution providing formal procedures for law-creation and the business of government by Parliament, Weber's three types of authority have rarely, if ever, existed in reality in their *pure* form. Most societies have elements of more than one type. Our own society has elements of all three – the traditional (as seen in the ceremonies surrounding, say, the formal opening of Parliament), the charismatic (such as the leadership of Churchill during the last war) and the rational-legal (as in bureaucratic political and legal institutions such as the civil service). The issues raised by notions such as 'obedience to law' and 'sources of authority', then, are clearly much more complex than Austin's simple idea of a 'sovereign' might suggest.

Law and society

We have seen that there is no one way of undertaking legal study; while all the various approaches may well have something useful to offer, none has yet managed to produce an analysis of law and legal systems which answers all the many and varied questions which students and researchers might want to ask about this complicated and fascinating subject. The perspective taken in this present book is that an understanding of law cannot be acquired unless the subject matter is examined in close relationship to the social, economic and political contexts in which it is created, maintained and implemented. To equip us for the task of understanding something of the *society* in which the law operates, as well the law itself, we must turn our attention to some analyses which take law as but a part (albeit an important part) of the wider social arrangements.

When a lawyer uses terms such as 'society', the picture often conjured up is of a rather loose collection of people, institutions and other social phenomena in the midst of which law occupies a central place, holding these social arrangements together in an orderly fashion. But if law were suddenly relaxed, would society immediately plunge into chaos and disorder? Most of us doubt that this would happen. One reason why it would not happen is that society is not just a loose group of independent units, but rather exhibits certain regular patterns of behaviour, relationships and beliefs. What gives a particular society its uniqueness is the way in which these patterns interrelate at any given time in history. Law, far from being a kind of social glue holding us all inside a boundary of legality and punishing those who try to extricate themselves, is but one component of the overall *social structure*, having links and dependencies with other social elements and forces. We can identify various social phenomena which constitute parts of the overall structure of a society, including, in addition to law, political institutions

(Parliament, political parties), economic and commercial institutions (trade unions, manufacturers' associations, patterns of production and trade, and so on), religious institutions, institutions concerned with the teaching of social rules and standards (such as schools and the family) and cultural institutions (such as literature and the arts, the press, television and radio). We shall, at various points in our examination of the place of law in society, refer to these other facets of the social structure.

It we imagine a society as a complex network of the kinds of institutions and social forces mentioned above, we could map out the ways in which they relate to each other without too much difficulty. But some institutions and social groups are more important than others; some groups have more political power, or more economic influence, than others. Some groups may enjoy considerable prestige, whereas others may be thought of as less worthy. Within a society, therefore, groups and individuals may be differentiated, or *ranked*, by their place on a 'ladder of influence', with some ranking higher in terms of power, prestige, wealth, or some other criterion, than others. Sociologists use the term *social stratification* to express this idea, and there are many ways in which social stratification may be analysed. If we are interested in prestige groups in India, for instance, we may look at the stratification of groups in terms of the caste system, in which some groups, or 'castes', are regarded as higher in status than others. In a simple tribal society, stratification may occur through a ranking system descending from king, or chief, at the top, through, perhaps, village elders and religious officials, down to the ordinary family unit, which may itself be stratified in terms of power (male elders frequently being the heads of households). Or, taking our own society, we may classify people in terms of social class – a very important aspect of our society, particularly when we come to consider political and economic power and position.[13]

Some sociologists would go on to analyse social institutions and processes in terms of their *function* in society; we noted above how such an approach might be applied to an analysis of law. Put simply, the 'function' of a social institution or process is the contribution it makes to the overall social structure and its maintenance. We may say, for example, that the function of the family unit in our society is to ensure continued procreation, to ensure socialization, and to bolster the economic base of the society through its activities as a consumer unit.

Armed with these concepts of social structure, social stratification and social function (none of which, for reasons of space, we are able to explore further here), we can begin to examine some approaches to law in society taken by sociologists. One of the most influential writers in this field was the French sociologist Émile Durkheim, whose major works appeared at the end of the nineteenth century. One of Durkheim's main concerns was the problem of social cohesion: what is it that keeps a society together? We noted above the fact that societies exhibit regularities, and patterns of behaviour and attitudes. What provides this cohesion?

Durkheim, in trying to resolve this problem, presented two contrasting 'types' of society[14] – an analytical device frequently used by social scientists to enable us to draw contrasts. The first type discussed by Durkheim is a relatively simple, technologically undeveloped society; the other type being 'advanced' in terms of technology and social structure. He argued that the primary characteristic of the first type will be that the whole group exists and acts collectively towards common aims, the moral and legal code (the 'collective conscience') being acknowledged and accepted by the whole group and keeping the group together. This is called 'mechanical solidarity'. In the event of any deviance from these collectively held norms of the groups, sanctions are brought to bear on the offender through *repressive* (criminal, or penal) law, which expresses the community's anger and avenges the offence against the collective moral sentiments of the group. Not only does this repressive law serve to identify and punish the deviant, however; it also fulfils the function of maintaining the boundaries between acceptable and unacceptable behaviour, thus helping maintain the collective conscience, and hence the cohesion of the group. Central to Durkheim's thesis is the proposition that the interests of any one individual in such a group are identical to those of the group as a whole; there is no room for the expression of individual creativity or dissent from group norms.

As the social group becomes more complex (larger, with increasing economic and other ties between social units and with other social groups) there occurs, argues Durkheim, increasing *occupational specialization*, or *division of labour*, where no single individual occupies a self-sufficient position as both producer and consumer of his or her everyday needs. Instead, tasks become divided among members of the society. The making of bread, for example, becomes no longer a task undertaken by each family for its own needs, but is rather a series of tasks, divided between farmer, flour mills and bakeries. Each, therefore, is occupationally specialized. But more than this: in the complete bread-production process, the bakery is dependent on obtaining supplies of flour from the mill, and the mill is in turn dependent upon the farmer for the supply of corn. The farmer is dependent on the flour mill for payment for the corn; and the flour mill is similarly dependent upon income from sales of flour. Each of these units, then, is not only occupationally specialized, but *economically dependent* upon the others involved in the process.

It is precisely this interdependence, argues Durkheim, that is the keynote of social solidarity in advanced industrial society. There is a radical change in the nature and range of the collective conscience, in that the individual takes on a new social importance in his or her own right, rather than occupying a social position simply as one member of a collective. The individual, encouraged socially to develop and realize talents, skills and potentialities, is elevated to quite a different status.

These changes are accompanied by a corresponding change in the type of law present in the society. Whereas law in the 'simple' type of society is, according to Durkheim, repressive or penal law, in the 'advanced' type of society it takes on the form of *compensatory* rules, where the object is not to punish, but to solve grievances by trying to restore the aggrieved person to the position he or she was in prior to the dispute. The disputes dealt with through the law in such a situation are not those between, so to speak, the group and the individual deviant, but rather those which occur between individuals or between groups, within the society.

Durkheim's analysis has been very influential; nevertheless many have found problems with his work. He greatly overestimated the extent to which repressive law would decline and give way to compensatory law in an industrialized society. He himself explained the continued existence of repressive, criminal-type rules in modern society as being due to the incomplete, defective or 'pathological' forms of the division of labour to be found in existing industrial societies, and put forward suggestions as to how these 'pathological' forms of the division of labour might be remedied to facilitate the development of a pure or 'spontaneous' form of division of labour where repressive law would decline much further. Yet today we have as many criminal-law rules as ever.

Also, it is clear from later research that Durkheim underestimated the degree to which compensatory, or *civil*, law already exists in 'simple' societies. Many tribal groups, for instance, have firm relationships within and between families and other groups, giving rise to patterns of mutual dependency ties having the force of legal obligation; many have clearly discernible political and legal structures, and property relationships involving obligations and rights similar to those existing in our own law. While there may well be certain differences in the manner in which disputes are solved (we shall come to this issue later), it is clear that Durkheim's twofold classification of types of society, though containing useful insights, will not do the analytical job for which he fashioned it.

The researches of social anthropologists, studying simple societies, have also provided us with useful information concerning law in society, although we must always be careful not to assume that what may hold for a technologically undeveloped group will necessarily be applicable to a complex and advanced society. We referred above to the American writer Llewellyn: with an anthropologist, Hoebel, Llewellyn studied American Indian groups and based his ideas as to the social functions of law on their researches. It is interesting that similar conclusions as to the functions of law have been reached by Hart (a lawyer and philosopher), by Talcott Parsons (a sociologist)[15] and by Hoebel in his own work *The Law of Primitive Man*.[16] As Schur points out:

However their terminology may differ, anthropologists, legal philosophers, and sociologists are in general agreement that a legal order must, at the very least, provide for the authorisation and recognition of legitimate authority, provide means of resolving disputes, and provide mechanisms for facilitating interpersonal relationships, including adaptation to change.[17]

To what extent, then, can such functions be identified in our own society?

Law plays an important part in the definition and regulation of all kinds of social relationships, between individuals and between groups. Thus, for example, the basic social unit in our society, the family, is defined and protected through legal rules and institutions. The marriage bond is created partly through deference to religion, partly through the necessity for legal formalities. Divorce, too, can only be obtained through legal channels, and the law also contains provision for ensuring that the monogamous relationship is preserved through prohibitions on bigamy. The rights and obligations of members of the family, as spouses and parents, are defined through law, and there is provision through the Children Act 1989 for removing children from unsuitable homes with their natural parents and placing them in the care of local authorities or with foster parents. In the business world, too, the law regulates the activities of the limited company, the partnership and the trade union. Financial deals between people in business are subject, normally, to the law of contract, at least in theory,[18] and there are many obligations contained in Acts of Parliament such as the Companies Acts, with whose regulations all companies must comply.

Regarding the identification and allocation of official authority, it is through legal rules that specific powers are vested in Parliament to enact new laws, and in the courts to administer the law and to mete out sanctions and remedies in criminal and civil cases. This body of law, known as *public law*, deals with constitutional rules, the authority of elected representatives such as councillors, or members of Parliament, and the powers of bodies such as the civil service, the courts, tribunals, the police, local authorities and nationalized bodies such as the Post Office and the National Health Service. We shall examine various aspects of all these matters later, and we shall look in particular at the relationship between law and public administration in chapter 12.

It is by means of such constitutional rules that social changes may become reflected in, or in some cases encouraged by, changes in the law. One of the most important facets of law, as we noted earlier, is its *dynamic* character; social conditions, and hence law, change all the time. Some changes are little more than passing fads, and make little impact upon the legal structure. But others bring with them permanent and far-reaching effects, and such developments usually result, sooner or later, in changes in the fabric of legal rules. The development and increased use of the motor car in the twentieth century is a good example. Given the proliferation of cheaper, faster and more reliable cars, it is not altogether surprising that the legal code responded by the enactment of numerous rules designed to protect both car-drivers and others, through the regulation of car safety, speed and driving skills – a far cry from the somewhat crude device of having someone carrying a red flag walk in front of the slow-moving early mechanical vehicles! This example illustrates not only the reflection in the law of these developments, but also the way law may be, at least partially, used as an *educative* instrument. Road safety and motor-vehicle law may be viewed as a means of inculcating public awareness of the dangers of modern road conditions, thus encouraging the development of attitudes of safety-consciousness. Other similar instances are the use of law in race relations and equal opportunities (currently through the Race Relations Act 1976 and Sex Discrimination Act 1975) not only to outlaw discrimination on the grounds of race or sex in the workplace, in the provision of goods and services, and elsewhere, but also to play a part in changing people's attitudes and, arguably, to help to create a social environment in which prejudice diminishes and, hopefully, disappears.

The changing nature of law is seen in all aspects of the legal system, not least in those areas concerned with one more 'function' of law: dispute-settlement. Now, while most studies of law in various types of society have revealed the existence of more or less formal mechanisms of dispute-settlement, it is possible to see, as Chambliss and Seidman argue, certain differences between advanced and undeveloped societies in the way that the legal system goes about this task: 'The dispute-settlement systems of simple societies tend toward compromise, or "give-a-little, get-a-little"; the official dispute-settlement systems of most complex societies tend toward "winner-takes-all".[19] This distinction, say Chambliss and Seidman, is connected with certain factors about the types of society in question. Simple societies, as we noted above when discussing Durkheim's work, tend to be community-based, relatively self-sufficient, and with low degrees of technology and division of labour. It is this type of society which some writers have called *Gemeinschaft*, or 'community', as distinct from *Gesellschaft*, referring to a more complex, differentiated society.[20] In societies approximating to the community-type (these terms referring, like Durkheim's types, to hypothetical models, or 'ideal types' which never actually occur in reality in their 'pure' form), social relations tend to be fairly permanent; indeed the continued existence of the community group depends upon the continued existence of social ties, and consequently in such groups the type of dispute-settlement is often *compromise*.

In a modern, differentiated society, on the other hand, there are many disputes involving no desire or need by the parties to continue their relationship; the example given by Chambliss and Seidman is a typical personal injury claim: 'When a person gets injured in an automobile accident, usually he had no prior relationship with the other party and anticipates no future relationship. In such cases, the parties typically expect in the end that if necessary they will settle their dispute in court on a "winner-takes-all" basis.'[21] Nevertheless, in such situations negotiations and compromise may well take place. As we shall see in a later chapter, bargaining and negotiations through insurance companies, and between the parties' lawyers, will more often than not result in the settlement of disputes outside courts of law. But, as Chambliss and Seidman point out, such negotiation is mainly to save time, trouble and, in particular, expense: 'They bargain, not in an effort to make possible a future relationship, but in light of their estimates of the probabilities of a favourable outcome of the potential "winner-takes-all" litigation.'[22] Only in cases where the parties *do* anticipate future relations is there any genuine attempt to 'give a little, take a little'. Such cases would include those discussed by Macaulay,[23] where business firms negotiate with a view to *avoiding* disputes, or, where disputes arise, to *compromise* rather than take the dispute to court, because good business relations are essential if a business is to continue to flourish.

From the foregoing discussion, certain additional features of law, particularly that of modern Western societies, may be identified. Whereas, for instance, law may be used to provide an institutional setting for the resolution of disputes between private individuals, as discussed in the last paragraph, the use of law to achieve certain *positive objectives of social or economic policy* may be, by contrast, a somewhat different function for the law to perform. State intervention in the sphere of motor-vehicle use, or in the field of race relations, expresses such general policies, which are of clear benefit to the community. Other examples of state intervention usually brought about through the use of law would include the development of the welfare state, the nationalization of the coal industry, the railways and the health service, and the provisions and regulations constituting town and country planning. Significantly, all these areas of regulation were, prior to intervention by the state, left to private enterprise or individual discretion.

Such intervention by the state, usually presented by governments and by politicians as being 'in the interests of the community as a whole', is often the expression and attempted realization of the political convictions of those governments and politicians. In Britain in the 1980s and early 1990s, for example, we might note the Conservative governments' policies of denationalizing industries such as telecommunications, oil, water, electricity and gas in line with their commitment to a return to a national economy based substantially upon free private enterprise. In such circumstances, it is not altogether surprising that state intervention in particular fields of social or economic activity is often highly controversial. The twentieth century has, none the less, seen unprecedented increases in interventionist regulation, often expressed through legal rules and procedures. Such regulation, affecting many of the areas discussed in this book, raises important questions about the relationship between the state and private individuals and groups, and about the appropriateness or otherwise of using *legal* mechanisms for the realization of political policies and objectives. It is vital, therefore, to appreciate the historical, social and political context of these developments – a context which requires examination of the far-reaching changes which were subsequent upon rapid industrial advances taking place within an economy based upon capitalism. Some aspects of these developments – affecting, for instance, the world of commerce – are discussed in later chapters. For the moment, it is useful to examine briefly the ways in which developing industrialization brought changes in employment relationships, and in more general *social* relationships within the developing economy.

Industrialization and the role of law

Although the eighteenth and nineteenth centuries are usually regarded as the most important period for the growth of industry and commerce, the period does not mark the *origin* of industrial or commercial development: Britain's economy had long been tied to trading at home and abroad. What the period does signify is a change in the *scale* and *nature* of industry and trade – the emergence and consolidation of *capitalism* as the basis for the economic system. By 'capitalism' we refer to the mode of production which is geared to the making of private profit, and it is no accident that this mode of production flourished in Britain during the period of the eighteenth and nineteenth centuries.

Many factors contributed to the expansion of manufacturing industries, among them the availability of natural resources (notably coal) and the suitability of certain areas for the use of water- and steam-powered machines. More important, the acquisition by Britain of overseas colonies not only yielded an abundance of raw materials but also provided a market for goods manufactured in Britain.[24]

Another supremely important factor was the existence of a *free market in labour*. This refers to a situation in which workers 'sell' their labour in exchange for wages, as opposed to being 'tied' to farms, estates and small, family-run manufacturing concerns. Prior to the industrial revolution, when the economy was primarily, though not exclusively, dependent upon agriculture, the dominant mode of production was feudalism. This gave rise to social relations in which agricultural labourers or peasants were tied to, and economically dependent on, the land-owning gentry and nobility (their lords and masters); for upon the feudal relationship between lord and servants depended the latter's livelihoods and homes. From the mid-1700s, however, the enclosure movement, whereby land – including land previously regarded as 'common' land – was parcelled up and acquired by landlords, had the effect of forcing many farm labourers, many of whom had depended for their survival upon the old traditional rights to the common land, out of their agricultural settings and, for many, into the expanding new towns to become workers in the developing factory industries.

These factories were owned and run by those 'captains of industry' who had invested their capital in the new machines, many powered by the recently invented steam-engine (another factor contributing to the rapid industrial development of the period), which required industrial workers to operate them. The factory system thus helped crystallize the new formations of social class. No longer could the population be divided only into agricultural peasants and powerful land-owners, with a sprinkling of tradesmen and artisans, for now the industrial revolution had brought two new classes: the industrial working class and the industrialists who employed them, paid their wages and frequently provided them with housing. Together with the commercial entrepreneurs who traded in the manufactured goods and brought raw materials to be worked in the factories, these constituted the rising new 'middle classes', the 'bourgeoisie', a social class distinct from the landowners who had traditionally possessed the wealth and political power and who had until then been the sole 'ruling class' in England.

Such class formations brought tensions. Not only did the middle classes make demands for a greater political voice in Parliament (something they felt was their due, given their developing key role in the country's economic affairs),[25] bringing them at times into conflict with the established landowning class, but also many of the working classes, conscious of the iniquities of the factory system (low wages, appalling working conditions, long hours, bad housing and the systematic exploitation of women and children), were beginning to make demands for improvements in their working conditions, and for a political voice. Hence, we see many cases of attempts by workers to form themselves into associations – what we would now recognize as trade unions – in order to press collectively for better pay and conditions. And there were movements, such as Chartism in the 1840s (a working-class campaign for more political involvement), which involved demands for universal male suffrage, removal of the property qualification for members of Parliament and the holding of annual general elections.

It is easy to see in these latter developments the basis of what we would today call industrial relations problems, but the period was not, in fact, the beginning of such potential or actual conflicts. Legal controls of employment relations date back to periods long before the industrial revolution, and one or two brief instances reveal the repressive attitude of law-makers and judges to any attempt by working people to improve their lot by collective action. In 1563 the Statute of Artificers gave power to justices of the peace to fix wages; in 1698 a body of journeymen was successfully prosecuted for having 'combined' to negotiate with their employers over wages; the Master and Servant laws of 1823 provided for the imprisonment of any workers who 'broke their contracts of employment' by going on strike; and various statutes outlawed 'combinations of workers' – the forerunners of trade unions – throughout the eighteenth century.[26]

These early laws regulating wages and prohibiting 'combinations' are, of course, examples of direct state intervention which, though no doubt legitimated as being in the interests of the national economy, nevertheless clearly operated to the advantage of employers and to the detriment of employees. The effect of these restrictions was, moreover, to enhance the conflicts inherent in the employment relationship – conflicts which become clearer when we examine the relative positions of *power* between them.

Then, as now, recurrent unemployment was a problem for many, and if people wished to work for an employer, they had little choice but to accept employment on the terms dictated by that employer. Workers were in no position to argue or negotiate, for they had little or no bargaining power. The strike (that is, *collective withdrawal of labour*) was one of the few means of bringing any kind of pressure to bear on employers for improvements in pay and conditions, and it is not altogether surprising that the law was one of the principal weapons used to try to prevent any such disruptions which might damage employers' business, and perhaps ultimately the whole fabric of trade and industry upon which the national economy had come to depend. Even when these Combination Acts were repealed, the judges were still able to interpret strikes as 'conspiracies to injure' the employers' interests. The turbulent events of the French Revolution at the end of the eighteenth century caused many members of the English ruling classes to fear lest similar troubles should occur on this side of the Channel; indeed, the period saw frequent uprisings by ordinary working people: food riots, and of course the machine-breaking riots and the Luddite movement in the early nineteenth century, directed against the use of machines which threatened the jobs of skilled workers in some parts of the country.[27] These were reasons why every sign of workers' resistance to the existing and developing economic and political order was severely repressed. It was not until well into the second half of the nineteenth century that the beginnings of trade union activity, especially free collective bargaining over terms and conditions of employment between workers and employers, began on a legal, organized basis. Even then (some would argue, even now) the attitude of the judges, when disputed cases came before them, was typically one of conservatism and anti-trade unionism. The landmark cases are recounted in all the major works on labour law,[28] especially those cases dating from the turn of the century to the present day, in which the judges have consistently interpreted the law in a manner against the interests and activities of the unions.

The relationship between employer and employee is, in law, one of *contract*: that is, a legally binding agreement made by two parties, containing the agreed rights and obligations of each party, any breach of which entitles the aggrieved party to a legal remedy for *breach of contract*. This idea of the contract, discussed here in the context of the employment contract, applies to many other situations, notably, as we shall see in chapter 11, to the buying and selling of goods and services. Ideas of social relations based on the contract were particularly prevalent during the nineteenth century, when the dominant social and economic philosophies were those of 'freedom of contract' and *laisser-faire* individualism. By this was meant that each individual in society should be left free to regulate his[29] own affairs with as little interference as possible by the state. Relationships between people in business and employment were regarded as best left to the parties concerned, to drive as good a bargain as they could get for their goods or services. Consequently, in line with this dominant ideology, there was relatively little state intervention through legal controls over, or restrictions upon, business, industry or employment, although piecemeal legislation in the nineteenth century did begin to lay down minimum standards of working conditions: for example, by means of the Factory Acts.

Laisser-faire involved the assumption, then, that all members of society were free and able to regulate and arrange their affairs with others (including their employers), and that all were equal in terms of their bargaining positions. If people were to be left free and equal then, according to dominant social and economic philosophies, competitive trade and industry would flourish, and the nation would thrive. In fact, as we have noted, there was, and still is, a fundamental *in*equality in terms of wealth, social position and bargaining power between people of different positions within the social structure. Two business representatives, negotiating over, say, the sale of goods, might have been in more or less equal bargaining positions; but the same was certainly not true of the relationship between most employers and employees. Nevertheless, the employment contract (supposedly freely made between employer and employee) was deemed to be made between people of equal standing, and even today the expressions 'freedom' and 'equality of contract' remain the basis for many areas of law involving contractual agreement. Given the predominance of these ideas about freedom and equality of contract, what particular problems confronted the parties to an employment contract in the nineteenth century, and to what extent has subsequent state intervention successfully tackled them through legislation?

To begin with, the fact that the terms of an employment contract might be oral, coupled with the frequently vague and complex nature of the terms of such a contract, led to the law being called upon to settle the many and varied disputes arising from employment situations. For example, an employee who was injured at work might claim compensation (see chapter 9); or an employee who was dismissed might bring a claim against the ex-employer alleging that the dismissal was unlawful. The difficulty is that many legal rules and remedies are only applicable if there is a proper 'employment contract' as opposed to other situations where one person does work for another: if I call a taxi which carries me to my destination, the driver may be said to be doing work for me, but is hardly to be called my 'employee'.

The old legal test for ascertaining whether an employment relationship existed was the 'control' test, expounded in the case of *Yewens* v. *Noakes*[30] in 1880, and formulated in terms of the extent to which the employer exercised effective *control* over the workers. However, the growth of specialized and highly skilled occupations led to many cases where the employer could not sensibly be said to be 'in control' of the activities of the employee, and this test has been discarded. Unfortunately, no acceptable substitute test has yet found full favour with the judges. In *Short* v. *Henderson*[31] in 1946, one judge referred to the need to take into account a multiplicity of factors in deciding the issue, and in 1953 Denning L.J. observed that 'the test of being a servant does not rest nowadays on submission to orders. It depends on whether the person is part and parcel of the organization.'[32]

This 'organization' test, like all other tests resting upon single factors, has been found unworkable in practice. The modern approach to the problem has been to consider many factors, notably the power to appoint and dismiss, the mode of payment and the making of deductions for national insurance and income tax, the organization of the workplace, and the issue of who provides the tools for the job.[33] This is the 'multiple' or 'mixed' test – still of practical importance since in English law the status of the worker is still the basis of most employment protection rights.

It is noteworthy, however, that today many employers are using labour much more flexibly than in the past: more use is being made, for example, of part-time workers and short-term contract workers, and the European Community is seeking to protect the rights of such workers. Interestingly, although the British government is attempting to resist such moves, recent English legislation has tended to blur the old distinction between a contract of employment and other types of working relationship. The Wages Act 1986, s.8, for example, extends employment rights somewhat by providing a rather broader definition of 'worker' than simply one who is in a contract of employment.

Of course, once the relationship has been established as one of employment, there will remain the substantive issue of the case, which may be over a dismissal, a redundancy, or some alleged breach of the contract by either employer or employee. The infinite variability of terms of employment contracts, coupled with the fact that in many cases employees suffered the double disadvantage of inability both to negotiate those terms and readily to ascertain the terms as dictated by the employer, has led, over the years, to a large number of instances of state intervention, through a series of statutes, in the field of employment. Changed philosophies about 'state interference', the reforming zeal of individual politicians and campaigners and, most important of all, the gradual absorption of working-class interests into the political process – through the widening of the franchise, the emergence of the trade union movement as a vociferous pressure-group, and the development and electoral success of the Labour Party – have all played their part, at different times, in furthering such legislative intervention. Work conditions, the existence of hazards, hidden and apparent, and insecurity of employment, have long been regarded as worthy of legal intervention. A number of separate Acts of Parliament have provided, for example, for the physical protection of workers. Today the Health and Safety at Work Act 1974 lays legal duties upon employers, employees, sub-contractors, manufacturers and others to observe due care in installing, using and maintaining equipment and premises; the Act provides various administrative sanctions for the enforcement of its provisions, and contains a legal framework for worker-participation in safety at work.

With regard to terms and conditions of employment, the Contracts of Employment Acts 1963 and 1972, and the Employment Protection (Consolidation) Act 1978, provide that the employee must be given notice of the main terms of the contract of employment. The latter Act also contains provision for increased protection for employees in most industries by providing for redundancy payments (paid out when there is no longer any work for an employee to do, and first introduced in 1965); and for unfair dismissal (first introduced in 1971), whereby an employee who successfully alleges, before an Industrial Tribunal, that he or she was unfairly dismissed may be offered reinstatement (the same job with the same employer), re-engagement (a different job with the same employer) or compensation (the remedy which is most frequently sought).

Protective legislation affecting work and working conditions is only one important area in which state intervention has taken place – often on the grounds of benefit to the community. The nineteenth century saw the beginnings of local government services, in fields such as public health, urban amenities and improvement, and, later, slum-clearance programmes which would, in time, sweep away the foul and inadequate housing stock which had characterized many industrial towns. These beginnings prefaced the acceleration of central and local government intervention in areas of social life which had previously been private, not public, domains; and the twentieth-century 'welfare state ethic' of state intervention (ostensibly) for the benefit of the community stands in direct contrast to the nineteenth-century individualist *laisser-faire* ideal of leaving people alone to manage their own affairs as best they could, without state help or 'interference'. During this century, the state has played a significant role in all aspects of everyday life, especially in the context of various schemes which we associate with the term 'welfare state' – social security, supplementary benefit, unemployment and sickness benefits, old-age pensions, social services and so on. Other aspects of the welfare state are the state-run education system, the health service, and local authority services ranging from refuse disposal to the provision of housing, and from street lighting to the maintenance of highways. These examples are clear cases where the state has accepted a large measure of social responsibility for providing for the *whole* community in key areas.

It should not be assumed from this, however, that interventionist policies are invariably seen as operating for the benefit of all, or that 'welfare statism' has met with support from all government administrations. The Conservative adminstrations under Margaret Thatcher during the 1980s, and the ideas of 'Thatcherism', were highly critical of what became derided as the 'nanny state', with a large measure of approval of old ideas of self-determinism for the individual. And apart from the fact, noted above, that party-politically inspired measures will attract party-political opposition both inside and outside Parliament, there are other levels at which doubts, fears or anger may result from policies introduced by particular governments, which may be seen as operating *against* the interests of certain sections of the community. Private landlords, for example, may oppose the legal protection of tenants against eviction; property-developers may resist the introduction of legal requirements for satisfying conditions imposed by planning or building regulations; trade unions may oppose legislation designed, directly or indirectly, to impose new obligations upon unions or their members; and so on.

In assessing the strengths and weaknesses of arguments for or against such measures, and indeed *any* legal rule, procedure or institution, we need, at a more general level, to be able to make analytical and theoretical connections between law and the various aspects and components of modern social structure. By what means can such an analysis be carried out?

Law and society: consensus or conflict?

Law may be regarded as a benign facilitating mechanism, making transactions possible between men and solving awkward problems as they arise; it may, alternatively, be seen as a mechanism of social control, regulating activities and interests in the name of either the community, a ruling class or the state. The state itself may be defined as either 'neutral arbiter' or 'interested party' in the solution of disputes and the balancing of interests. Again, law may be seen as an institution for the furtherance and protection of the welfare of everyone, or it may be seen, crudely, as an instrument of repression wielded by the dominant groups in society.[34]

The above alternative standpoints are simplified statements of what are usually extremely complicated political views and positions, but the point is that people do have very different views as to what law, in general or with regard to specific rules, is for.

Within the field of legal and social study, there may be discerned a whole range of alternative or competing viewpoints about law and society, which at its simplest may be presented as debates as to whether our society and its legal system are representations or reflections of social *consensus* or social *conflict*. The former position perceives law as protecting social values to which everyone subscribes; the latter holds that there is no such single, universally agreed set of social values, but rather a whole variety of different social values, certain of which are protected by a less-than-neutral legal system in order to protect some interests as against others.

One important sociologist adhering to the 'consensus' view of society was Talcott Parsons. His view of society as a 'system' comprising actions and institutions, each functioning to maintain social stability and order, has been frequently criticized, not least because of its assumption that society is indeed characterized by a shared consensual value-system. One critic has pointed out,[35] for example, that Parsons' analysis concentrates on examining those elements within society which tend towards the maintenance of order and equilibrium, at the expense of considering those elements which tend towards social conflict and instability – elements which must be accounted for in any theory of social order.

Another basic criticism of the Parsonian functionalist position is that there is very little evidence of a monolithic, universally shared value-system within society. We shall see many examples of this assertion in due course, especially in chapter 2, but drawing on material presented so far in this chapter, the existence of disputes and the necessity of providing, through law, the means of dealing with them, indicates the presence of conflict between individuals and groups within society. The very creation of a legal rule implies that some people may well be inclined to engage in the behaviour it prohibits, suggesting that those persons may well disagree with the content of the rule. Conflicts are resolved through law; as White has put it: 'The consensus model views society as basically unitary. Parliament represents us all; the executive acts in the common interest . . . the law is equal and just to all and is administered without fear or favour for the common good . . . Conflicts that there are will be on a personal level.'[36]

Opposing ideas about the nature of society may be classified as falling into some form of 'conflict' or 'pluralist' theories of society and the social and legal order. Both types of theory take for granted the fact that there is *no* 'shared value-system' in our society. The pluralist view, in its 'pure' form, accepts the existence of conflicting groups and interests, but maintains that the constant interaction and negotiation between conflicting groups, all of which are assumed to have more or less equal bargaining-power, helps maintain social stability and equilibrium. The role of the law and the state is portrayed as 'neutral arbiter', or 'honest broker' – taking no sides in these conflict situations, but providing the machinery of conflict-settlement either through law or through political debate and policy-making by government.

The trouble with such a view is that the multitude of interest-groups in society do not possess equal power, in either political, legal or economic terms. Some groups have the power to influence law-making and the implementation of those laws; others do not. In general, the stance taken in this book accepts as accurate the proposition that those interest-groups possessing political and economic power and control of key institutions in society will be found to exert the most profound influence over the making and the implementation of law.

Given that this is the case, does this imply some sort of political conspiracy, in which the powerful groups in society impose their policies, and laws for the protection of their interests, upon the less powerful groups and social classes? Most people would find such a sinister notion rather extreme and lacking in credibility when applied to our own liberal-democratic society. How, then, do the less powerful come to accept the views and policies of the ruling groups? How do we identify those ruling groups, and what are the relationships between these various groups and between law, state and society?

There have been many answers put forward to questions such as these. Some writers have questioned the extent to which social conflict pervades society, and have argued that propositions as to degrees of social consensus have been too easily dismissed by writers taking a 'conflict' perspective. Some of these writers have presented analyses which are highly complex, while others have taken a stance which may be termed a basic 'liberal-democratic' viewpoint, involving the acceptance of social conflict whose manifestations are played out within boundaries of socially accepted norms in terms of the legitimacy of official legal and governmental authority, whose concerns are the resolution of such conflicts. White, for example, discusses not only the basic 'consensus' and 'conflict' theories, but also presents a third model of society, which he calls an 'open' model, where

Conflict is expected to continue in different forms between interest groups but it is assumed that these conflicts can be resolved through a legitimate process. There will be basic agreement that conflict-resolution can be achieved within a framework of negotiation, arbitration, judicial decision and electoral battle, backed up by strike or rent strike but without resort to revolution.[37]

Before drawing our own conclusions as to the appropriateness or otherwise of such a model of society, it is pertinent here to consider, albeit in very simplified form, the work of the nineteenth-century German philosopher and social scientist Karl Marx, whose work has been very influential both in terms of political developments in various parts of the world, and in terms of later academic debates.

Marx was concerned with the analysis of capitalist societies, though he wrote at a time when capitalism in Europe was less developed than it is today. Capitalism, according to Marx, involves the exploitation of the working classes by the capitalist class. The exploitation springs from the fact that, in order for any employer (capitalist) to make profit, the workers must be paid less, in wages, than the value of the goods they produce, hence producing 'surplus value', or profit. Marx distinguished between the working class ('proletariat') who possess the labour power; the capitalists ('bourgeoisie') who own the capital and means of production (factories, business concerns and so on); and the landowners, who derive their income from the rent of their land. The latter two classes occupy the powerful economic and political positions in society through the exploitation of the working class, and the relationship between the classes clearly cannot be one of equality, since exploitation necessarily involves the subjugation of one class to the interests of another.

How, then, does Marx explain the continued exploitation by one social class of another? Marx recognized that exploitation could continue only as long as bitter revolutionary confrontation could be avoided, and the most effective way of avoiding this was, according to Marx, for the capitalist classes to maintain control of the official state institutions. For Marx, the state was 'the form in which the individuals of a ruling class assert their common interests';[38] by control of state apparatus (government, law, police and so on), the interests of the dominant classes could be protected and perpetuated through the continued oppression of the working class.

But how is it that so many 'exploited' people in a capitalist society accept the fact of political and economic domination? One reason, according to Marx and other marxist writers, is that the ruling classes have control of those state institutions which give expression, when the need arises, to *forceful* repression: the army, the police and the law. But apart from these 'repressive state apparatuses',[39] the ruling classes also control, through various public and private institutions, the dominant ideas, opinions and attitudes about how society operates: 'the ideas of the ruling class are in every epoch the ruling ideas: i.e. the class which is the ruling *material* force of society is at the same time its ruling *intellectual* force'.[40] This collection of ideas, values, standards and beliefs – this *ideology* – finds expression, according to later marxist writers such as Gramsci[41] and Althusser,[42] through social institutions such as the school, the family, political (including trade union) organizations and, importantly, *law*. The marxist views law as an important means whereby the interests and values of capitalism are protected and maintained, and sees the legal system as part of what Althusser termed both *repressive* and *ideological* state apparatuses. In terms of capitalist ideology as expressed through law, private property is regarded as fundamental to social and economic stability; the values of justice and legal neutrality are presented as endemic in our legal system (obscuring the 'reality' that law is, in fact, operated for the protection of the interests of powerful capitalism); and the legal system is presented by lawyers and politicians as providing justice for all.

Now while it is vital to recognize that this brief and simplified sketch of the implications of marxist writers cannot possibly reflect the richness and complexities of the analyses of both Marx himself and later writers who have developed Marx's ideas,[43] it is believed that enough has been said to indicate that the liberal-democratic, 'neo-consensus' theories about the legal and social order can themselves be accommodated within marxist analysis. Beliefs concerning the 'agreed' values as to the legitimacy, equality and justice of law and government may *themselves* be ideological constructs serving to bolster and justify capitalist institutions and processes. The question then becomes not whether there *is* any basic consensus within society on any given issue, but rather why, how and when such consensus occurs, how it is maintained, and how deeply any such consensual ideas are held by the members of the society in question. Some areas of apparent consensus may, in fact, hide the process whereby sectional interests, inherently oppositional to other groups' interests, become defined and presented as 'basic' interests, or interests which are 'in the national interest' or 'for the common good'. Examples of such processes will be discussed presently. Other areas of apparent consensus may be the result of complex historical processes whereby certain interests come to be embodied in legal and other social institutions because of their fundamental importance to the economic or political structure. The outstanding example of such a process is the development of the social value attached to private property, as reflected in both law and everyday social practice. In chapter 5, we will see how the *particular* institutions of private property in our society have their roots in the economic and political changes which took place hundreds of years ago.

The theme to be developed in this book, therefore, is not that of a simple denial or assertion of consensus or conflict, but rather the exploration of basic questions regarding the roots of such consensus or conflict, the ways in which social conflicts are manifested and controlled by law and other agencies, and the manner in which areas of apparent consensus are maintained through legal and other social institutions and processes. In particular, a sense of history is vital for the understanding of these questions, for, as shall see time and again in the course of this book, legal rules and institutions can only be fully understood by perceiving them in the context of the social structural formations and arrangements, at any given historical period, in which they arose.

2
Law and morality

In this chapter we examine the relationships between law, society and morality. A society's 'code of morality' may be defined as a set of beliefs, values, principles and standards of behaviour, and such codes are found in all social groups. We noted in chapter 1 how the sociologist Émile Durkheim presented a theory of social cohesion, part of which rested on the notion that in technologically undeveloped societies, such as small tribal groups, there tends to be a single, consensually held moral code (the 'collective conscience') to which all members of the group subscribe. In a technologically advanced society such as our own, however, with immense differentiation in terms of social status, income, occupation, ethnic background and so on, it is unlikely that we will find such a monolithic moral code. Rather, as will be argued later in this chapter, there is diversity of moral attitudes on all kinds of social and personal issues.

Most of us, if asked to give an example of an area of moral rules in our society, would probably think of sexual morality, or perhaps acts of violence against the person. It is important to emphasize, however, that morality embraces much more than sex and violence; it is part of dominant ideological currents,[1] whereby dominant beliefs and attitudes conducive to the maintenance of the overall status quo are 'translated' into a positive general code involving social attitudes to property, politics and social relationships in general. And, as we shall see, a moral code may not be wholly without its inconsistencies and contradictions: established institutions such as the Church, for example, may condemn apartheid, or racial segregation, on moral grounds, while other established institutions, notably at government level, may nevertheless maintain commercial and political relations with states which are structured around policies of apartheid, as was seen for many years in the attitudes of various Western countries, including Britain, towards South Africa – which has only recently begun to dismantle the machinery of apartheid and systematic racial oppression.

We noted in chapter 1 some general features of law and morality: we saw that, though having much in common, law and morality have important points of divergence. Legal rules, for instance, are backed by official state sanctions and procedures, whereas moral rules, if they involve any sanctions at all, rest upon more diffuse and generalized *informal* sanctions – we might call this 'social disapproval' – as where, for example, neighbours may shun a person whom they have discovered to be engaging in prostitution. In some instances, particular behaviour may offend both legal and moral codes, such as the commission of murder, but in other cases, behaviour may be defined by some people as immoral, though that behaviour is not unlawful. Examples are telling lies, or committing adultery. In yet other cases, social behaviour may be unlawful even though no moral disapproval attaches to the action in question – the example used in chapter 1 was the criminal offence of exceeding the speed limit by only two miles per hour.

Morality is connected with the law in many ways. To begin with, the conditions under which a person may be held liable in law may be seen as based on the moral idea of 'blame' or 'fault'. Although liability in law is examined in more detail in later chapters, it is useful at this point to outline some general considerations.

'Conditions of liability' may conveniently be divided into 'general' and 'specific' conditions. Specific conditions of liability will depend upon the precise scope of a given legal rule or set of legal rules, each of which will be different according to the context of the rules, their history and their objectives. For example, in criminal law (see chapter 10) the definition of 'theft' is the dishonest appropriation of property belonging to another with the intention of depriving the other of it (Theft Act 1968, s.1 (1)), while the definition of murder is accepted as 'when a man of sound memory, and of the age of discretion, unlawfully killeth within any county of the realm any reasonable creature . . . under the king's peace, with malice afore-thought . . .'. These two legal rules clearly lay down different conditions which must be proved by the prosecution before liability can follow. The same variety will be found in the body of law we know as the law of *tort*, or civil wrongs (see chapter 9), which includes rules specifying the conditions under which a defendant will be liable to a plaintiff for wrongs such as assault and battery, trespass to land, nuisance, defamation, negligence and various others; and yet other conditions of liability are found within the law of contract (see chapter 11).

Apart from the specific conditions of liability contained within individual rules, however, there are, underlying the idea of liability in law, certain general principles perceived by judges and legislators alike as being fundamental to liability in any branch of the law. These principles are rooted in conceptions of morality (of which the notion of justice is one of the most important), and the way in which these moral principles are incorporated into the law may best be appreciated by means of the criminal law examples cited above. It will be noted that before a person can be convicted of theft, it must be established not only that the accused person 'appropriated property belonging to another', but also that this appropriation took place 'with the intention of depriving the other of it'. Again, a conviction for murder can occur only if it is established not simply that the accused brought about the death of another, but also that this was done 'with malice aforethought'.

It follows that if someone takes another's property in the belief that it is his or her own, or that if someone causes another's death by accident, then convictions for theft or murder cannot follow. In general, then, it is not considered acceptable in English law to subject a person to legal sanctions unless it can be shown that that person did the act in a 'blameworthy' manner, since we do not normally attribute blame in situations where injury occurs accidentally, or by reason of an honest mistake, or where the person concerned cannot be said to have been responsible for his or her actions. This means, then, that 'blameworthiness' – a moral principle – is normally required before we consider it acceptable to subject a person to legal sanctions. By way of illustration of this point: it is a defence in criminal law to show that the accused was, at the time of the commission of the alleged offence, suffering from some mental illness, or was for some other reason not in control of his or her actions. If X is hammering a nail, and D comes along, seizes X's wrist and uses it to strike P with the hammer which X is holding, it will be D, not X, who will be liable for that injury.

Similarly, in the law of contract, special legal rules apply regarding the capacity to make contracts of minors (persons under eighteen years of age), mentally disordered persons and drunken persons. Where contracts are made by minors, the law presumes insufficient maturity to appreciate fully the contractual bond, although there are exceptions to this: it has long been held that minors may be held bound by the terms of contracts for 'necessaries' (food, clothing and other items deemed essential). With regard to the other exceptional cases, their state of mind is likely to be such as to affect their capacity to understand what they are doing and the contractual obligations which they are taking on.

These general principles may be summed up in two propositions: first, the law holds liable, as a general rule, only the actual wrongdoer, and second, the law insists, as a general rule, that liability is contingent upon a context in which the person concerned may be said to be morally blameworthy. These underlying general principles, referred to by such phrases as 'individual responsibility' and 'no liability without fault', have long been at the root of liability in English law, and are, despite certain exceptional situations discussed in later chapters, still regarded as fundamentally important.

In examining more closely the relationship between law and morality, we begin by discussing some philosophical ideas about this relationship, and the ways in which such ideas have found their way into the law; we then discuss the social basis and definition of moral ideas, and how the social and economic structure of a given period can generate moral, as well as legal, attitudes and norms which may not necessarily be accepted by all sections of a society. It will be argued that morality, and especially specific ideas within a moral code (such as definitions of what constitutes 'deviant' behaviour), are *relative* concepts. By this we mean to emphasize not only that different individuals and groups often have different ideas about the rightness or wrongness of particular forms of behaviour, but also that moral climates shift over periods of time, and that these changes have corresponding shifts in the nature and extent of formal regulation through legal rules.

We shall consider presently how moral standards, values and rules are created, and frequently embodied within the law; but first we must consider how very closely law and morals have been connected throughout history, principally because of the historically important and close relationship between religious doctrine and political structures in the Western world. In particular, we must consider the impact on law and state of the long-established philosophies of *natural law*.

The early natural-law philosophers enquired into the 'essential nature' of human beings and their relationship with other phenomena occurring in the natural world. For the Greek philosopher Aristotle, writing in the fourth century BC, people were as much a part of nature as trees, rocks and birds, the only differentiating feature being the human capacity to *reason*, through which people formulate their will and direct their activities towards the attainment of their desires. Moreover, men and women are, according to Aristotle, *political* beings, in that they live, by nature, in social groups. The laws of nature thus create the community, or state, the laws regulating people's behaviour being made by men and women through the exercise of reason. Just as the trees are there 'because nature decrees it', so the 'state' (which at various periods in the history of many societies has involved institutions for which we could today find no moral justification, such as slavery) is there because nature has decreed that it 'ought to be there'.

This connection between fact and value, between what 'is' and what 'ought to be', can be traced through all natural-law ideas, and in its later formulations the philosophy is accompanied by strong theological connotations. The history of natural law is long and complex, with various schools of thought emerging at different periods in different parts of the world. Over the centuries, and certainly by the Middle Ages, the notion of the 'law of God' came to replace the Aristotelian conception of the 'law of nature' as the *ultimate criterion* whereby society, law and human existence might be evaluated. One reason for this link between religion and philosophies of law and state was that, as European societies developed and the struggle between the traditional power of the Church and the new and increasing political power of emerging nation-states and rulers became more pronounced, natural-law philosophy, which could be seen as often, though not invariably, having conservative overtones ('what is, ought to be, because nature has decreed it'), came to be a useful weapon for the justification of the existing political and social institutions and the resistance of radical change. In the course of this historical process, over many centuries, natural-law philosophies became closely and inextricably tied to morality and to religious doctrine.

This connection between natural law, human law and society was crystallized into the classical formulation of natural-law theory as we know it today (despite the many guises it may take) through the writings of St Thomas Aquinas in the Middle Ages. Aquinas related 'Divine' law to human or 'positive' law, and acknowledged the role of the latter in social and political affairs:

It was not the least of Aquinas' contributions that, in his synthesis of Aristotelian philosophy and Catholic faith in a universal divine law, he rejected the idea that civil government was necessarily tainted with original sin, and argued for the existence of a hierarchy of law derived ultimately from God, and in which human or positive law had a rightful though lowly place and was worthy for its own sake.[2]

Human law derived ultimately from God's law. Since it was perceived as obvious that God's law constituted the ultimate and absolute criterion of good and evil, right and wrong, human law, in general, was such that it was beyond criticism. The conformist and conservative uses to which this doctrine could be put are clear, as is the foundation for the notion of morality, being derived from religious principles of right and wrong, as an all-embracing, universally applicable set of values and rules.

But natural-law arguments were by no means always limited to attempted justifications for the social or political *status quo*. The idea that there existed a body of values higher than those contained in the practical social arrangements of a society contained the potentialities for *revolutionary* arguments, used to justify radical change in social and political structures, through the notion of universal and inalienable *human rights*. Here the argument is, at its simplest, that everyone has, or should have, certain basic human rights which civil government should respect. In the event of particular social and political arrangements which do not respect and guarantee these 'human rights', people are justified in struggling against such regimes in order that their human rights may be recognized.

History has seen many examples and many variants of this basic argument. The French Revolution, for instance, was influenced to an extent by the arguments of philosophers such as Rousseau; the United States Constitution, providing and guaranteeing certain rights for every individual, is regarded by many as embodying natural-law principles. More recently, we have seen codes such as the Universal Declaration of Human Rights in Europe, and similar codes in West Germany, Canada and elsewhere; there have been many movements throughout the world campaigning for more protection for 'civil rights', and demonstrating their opposition to groups and political regimes thought to be guilty of infringements of 'basic human rights'. For example, there were mass demonstrations during the 1960s in the United States against racial discrimination and segregation; in Poland in the early 1980s the workers engaged in struggle, through the trade union 'Solidarity', for the rights of the individual against an oppressive state; the South African government policy of apartheid brought reactions of condemnation and economic sanctions from many Western countries, and among the 'communist' east European regimes that collapsed at the end of the 1980s, perhaps none was more dramatic than that of Romania, where the repressive regime was toppled and the dictatorial ex-President Ceaucescu deposed and shot. The 1980s saw energetic efforts by campaigners against nuclear arms, notably, in England, the Campaign for Nuclear Disarmament and the active opposition by many thousands of women to the installation of American nuclear missiles on British soil. In all these and many other campaigns and incidents, it is possible to discern strong natural-law themes invoking respect for human life and liberty.

The aims of such campaigns are not, of course, *necessarily* based on idealistic conceptions of human rights: it is perfectly feasible for campaigners aiming to improve the lot of a group, or of a nation, to base their arguments on purely political grounds, although the two frequently merge so that the idealism obscures the political realities of specific situations. After the Second World War, for example, there took place at Nuremberg the 'war crimes trials', where the victorious allied forces took on the task of trying individuals who had done various acts under the Nazi regime in Germany, using charges such as 'crimes against humanity'. Critics have suggested that, although these trials may have been perceived as necessary in order to avoid unofficial reprisals against the perpe-trators of the horrors of the Nazi regime, to dress up what was essentially a political act by the victors as 'law' obscures the true nature of that act by introducing legal form and terminology into a setting where no precedent for such trials, or for such charges, had previously existed.

Nevertheless, the concept of 'crimes against humanity' has persisted, with arguments based on such notions used against the United States over its involvement in South-East Asia (the Vietnam war) in the 1960s, against Israel over its treatment – political and military – of the Palestinian people, and against President Saddam Hussein's regime in Iraq for its treatment of – in particular – the Kurdish people there.

Whatever the political uses to which natural-law doctrines may be put, the basic combination of law and morality within those doctrines is an invariable feature. The 'higher truth' or 'ideal' is presented as the highest moral authority for all human actions: as the ultimate criterion whereby we identify the good and the evil, and as the yardstick whereby we assess the morality or otherwise of human laws and human political actions. And, according to the classic formulation of the doctrine as propounded by Aquinas, if human law is found not to coincide with the principles of the 'ultimate' (in Aquinas's terms, 'Divine') law, then *it is not to be accorded the status of 'law' at all*. Such an analysis of law, which stresses the importance of the *substance* of law, and insists on the connection between law and morality, may be contrasted with some of the theories of law discussed in chapter 1, which concentrate upon the *formal* aspects of legal rules, paying much less attention to their *content*.

In this classical form, natural law is no longer given much credence by legal philosophers or political theorists, at least in most of the English-speaking world. The hold which the Church once had over political life has long ceased to grip very strongly: the age of religious supremacy gave way in the period of the industrial revolution to an era of scientific rationality, in which the dominant philosophers of the eighteenth and nineteenth centuries, such as Jeremy Bentham, scorned natural law for its metaphysical, unprovable principles. In today's secular, technologically advanced society where the role of the Church has decreased considerably in the lives of many people, natural law and its premises appear to many to be strangely irrelevant and too far distanced from the material and political claims and needs of the majority of the population. In short, too many criticisms have been levelled at the classical natural-law position for it to remain unscathed, although the equation of law with morality, and occasionally with religious notions, is still discernible in many modern ideas about law. And to be sure, some modern writers have presented newer variants of natural law, among them Lon Fuller and John Finnis.

Fuller was far less concerned with 'absolute values' than with the *procedural* aspects to a legal system. Referring to what he termed the 'inner morality of law',[3] Fuller argued that in order to create and maintain a system which can properly be called a 'legal system', certain procedural requirements should be satisfied. These are (i) that there should be rules in the first place, as opposed to a series of *ad hoc* judgments; (ii) those rules must be made known to all those affected by them; (iii) rules should not have retrospective effect; (iv) the rules should be understandable and (v) consistent, and (vi) should not require the impossible of people; (vii) the rules should not be changed so frequently that people cannot orient their actions by them; and (viii) the rules as announced should coincide with the actual administration of those rules.

Fuller claims that 'a total failure in any one of these eight directions does not simply result in a bad system of law; it results in something that is not properly called a legal system at all'.[4] The 'natural law' element in Fuller's writings tends to be reflected in this concern with *legality*, or due process, rather than in a concern with the substance, or content, of laws; this 'internal morality' of law – a set of criteria whereby a legal order may be evaluated – constitutes a series of guidelines, or ideals, to which a legal system should *aspire*.

This modern variant of natural law has met with various criticisms. Why, it has been asked, should a legal system that adopts Fuller's eight procedural requirements necessarily be a 'good' legal system? As Lloyd has said, 'the Nazi legal system was faithful, with one possible exception,[5] to Fuller's standards, yet it was able to promulgate laws contrary to the most fundamental principles of humanitarian morality'.[6] Finnis has countered this objection with the observation that a tyrannous regime is usually founded upon either the rulers' self-interest or a fanatical pursuit of some ideological goal which they consider good for the community; either way, tyranny is inconsistent with the values of reciprocity, fairness and respect for persons which Fuller's criteria rest upon. Moreover, 'Adherence to the Rule of Law . . . is always liable to reduce the efficiency for evil of an evil government, since it systematically restricts the government's freedom of manoeuvre.'[7]

Finnis himself develops[8] a theory of natural law which rests upon the idea of a set of basic principles of human existence which are *good in themselves*: that is to say, they are not 'good' because they are thought 'morally good'. Rather, they are 'good' because they constitute the 'basic values' of all human existence which in turn underlie both human activity and, indeed, subsequent moral judgments. In other words, these 'basic values' are 'obvious' and 'even unquestionable'.[9] The point about these values is, argues Finnis, that *no one can deny them*: every social group accepts and adopts them.

What, then, are these 'basic values'? Finnis argues that there are seven:[10] life, knowledge, play, aesthetic experience, sociability, practical reasonableness and 'religion' ('questions of the origins of cosmic order and of human freedom and reason').[11] They relate to the concept of law and legal systems in so far as human beings live in social groups, and only in this context can these basic goods be pursued; a legal system is required to achieve these ends, and so law should strive to maximize the achievement, or satisfaction, of these basic goods for the benefit of the community.

Now, it must be admitted that at the end of the day Finnis' conclusions may seem rather vague: it may be thought that his list of seven basic goods is highly subjective, in that other thinkers might offer a longer, a shorter or a quite different list; and as Lloyd says, 'as with much natural law theorising, we are left . . . not with a blueprint for legal and political action, . . . but with hints, no more, of how to better ourselves and the communities within which we live'.[12]

Although natural-law theories are open to the criticisms of vagueness and inconclusiveness, there is no doubt that many still insist on a connection between law and morality. In particular, many judges still hold that the foundations on which law (especially criminal law) is based are those of religious morality. To take one example, Lord Devlin has written: '[I feel] that a complete separation of crime from sin . . . would not be good for the moral law and might be disastrous for the criminal.'[13]

Lord Devlin argues that there are ultimate moral principles and criteria whereby social behaviour must be judged, though he acknowledges that the principles of Christianity upon which these principles are based no longer constitute the foundation of moral attitudes in our secular society. Nevertheless, Lord Devlin holds that ultimate standards of right and wrong *do* exist, and bases this notion upon the necessity for a binding moral code – a 'public morality' – which serves to hold a society together; without such consensual moral beliefs, he says, 'the society will disintegrate. For society is not something that is kept together physically; it is held by the invisible bonds of common thought. If the bonds were too far relaxed the members would drift apart'.[14] This argument is another modern version of natural-law theory, and as such is vulnerable to the criticisms which have been mentioned above. The idea of 'invisible bonds of common thought' is not susceptible to any empirical or rational analysis of morality and law: *which* bonds of thought? *How* 'common' must they be? Exactly *how* would this 'drifting apart' take place? Some other implications of Lord Devlin's attitude (which is not uncommon among members of the judiciary) are discussed in chapter 14, but at this point we must ask some important questions about law, society and morality which are raised by natural-law philosophy in general, and by the views of writers such as Lord Devlin in particular.

The social definition of law and morality

To begin with, both 'classical' natural-law ideas, based upon religious doctrine, and modern variants (such as those of Finnis, or Devlin), based upon more 'secularized' criteria, suffer from the fact that it is not possible to demonstrate empirically and scientifically the existence of such values. More than this, there is little agreement among natural-law scholars about the precise *content* of any absolute moral code. It was argued in chapter 1 that, contrary to the premises of natural-law philosophy, societies, especially modern industrialized societies, show far more divergence than convergence where moral values are concerned. To take the example of the controversy surrounding abortion: the attitudes towards this subject range from the strong anti-abortion stance based on the view that all taking of life is wrong, through the 'medical stance', whose adherents argue that abortion is justified if the medical condition of the mother or the foetus warrants it, to the view taken by many feminists that abortion should be available 'on demand' – a view based on the idea of 'a woman's right to choose'. Can any of these be shown to be the 'right' view?

The Abortion Act 1967 provides that abortion may be lawful if it is certified by two medical practitioners that to continue the pregnancy would involve risk to the life of, or injury to, the pregnant woman or her existing children, and that that risk is greater than if the pregnancy were terminated; or that there is a substantial risk that if the child were born it would suffer serious physical or mental handicap. In considering the matter, it is permissible for the doctors to take into account the pregnant woman's 'actual or reasonably foreseeable environment' (the 'social clause'). It should be noted that this Act does not affect the provisions of the Infant Life (Preservation) Act 1929, which makes it a criminal offence to terminate a pregnancy when the child is 'capable of being born alive' (s.1(1)) – normally after twenty-eight weeks or more of the pregnancy. In fact it has been held that abortions carried out before that time may be unlawful.[15]

Sincle 1967, a number of attempts have been made by means of private members' bills to amend the Act and to restrict the availability of abortions. So far these bills have not been successful. The most recent was a bill sponsored by David Alton MP which sought to limit the period within which abortions could lawfully be carried out to eighteen weeks. Opponents of this bill argued that this would mean that babies might be born with handicaps which could not be detected until after eighteen weeks of pregnancy, and that the time-limit in the 1967 Act enabled pregnancies involving serious deficiencies or handicaps to be aborted. Supporters of the bill argued that the reduced time-limit would result in fewer abortions, which they felt had been too easily available under the 1967 Act.

The latest statutory provision in this controversial area is s.37 of the Human Fertilisation and Embryology Act 1990, which provides, among other things, that a pregnancy which has not gone beyond twenty-four weeks may be terminated if its continuance would involve risk, greater than if the pregnancy were terminated, of injury to the physical or mental health of the pregnant woman or any existing children of her family, but no time-limits are imposed in cases where termination may be necessary to prevent 'grave permanent injury to the physical or mental health' of the pregnant woman, or risk to her life, or 'if there is a substantial risk that if the child were born it would suffer from such physical or mental abnormalities as to be seriously handicapped'. Department of Health figures reveal that in the first year after the implementation of these provisions, the number of late abortions (that is, after twenty-four weeks or more of pregnancy) rose considerably from around twenty-four to sixty, although all these cases involved diagnosis of severe abnormalities such as spina bifida, genetic abnormality and renal and heart conditions.

Despite these legal developments, many people feel that the Abortion Act should be repealed altogether, and that *all* abortion should be unlawful; others still feel that the law does not go far enough. The point is that none of these views can be justified by means of any *uncontested* moral principles. The anti-abortion lobby may introduce moral arguments based on religion, or the 'rights of the unborn', but the pro-abortion lobby may produce equally strongly held arguments based on conceptions of women's rights, and the importance of recognizing a woman's personal integrity and independence in treating her own body as she wishes. The debates over embryo experimentation, surrogate motherhood and the sterilization of the mentally handicapped also raise difficult and sensitive issues of law, morals, and medical and scientific ethics.

In 1986 the question as to whether contraception advice and facilities should be available to girls under sixteen without parental consent was brought into public debate by the *Gillick* case,[16] where the plaintiff sought a declaration from the court that guidance from the DHSS to area health authorities, which contained advice as to the provision of advice on contraception to young people under the age of sixteen without parental consent, was unlawful and wrong in that it undermined parental rights and duties. The House of Lords held that the guidelines concerned essentially medical matters, and that in such matters girls under sixteen had the legal capacity to consent to medical examination and treatment, including contraceptive treatment, as long as they are sufficiently mature and intelligent to understand the nature and implications of the proposed treatment.

Consent to the medical treatment of people aged between sixteen and eighteen may be given by the patients themselves: the Family Law Reform Act 1969 provides that such young people may give their consent 'as if they were of full age'. However, a case in 1992 involved a seriously anorexic sixteen-year-old girl, referred to throughout the proceedings simply as 'J', who had repeatedly refused to undergo treatment for her illness.[17] The question arose as to whether J could continue to refuse treatment or whether she could lawfully be compelled to undergo that treatment against her will. The Court of Appeal ruled that, notwithstanding the Act of 1969, a court of law could override a young person's consent to or refusal of treatment; and, furthermore, that parents or (for children in care) local authorities could override a young person's refusal (though not consent). The Master of the Rolls, Sir John Donaldson, stated that J's wishes were 'completely outweighed by the threat of irreparable damage to her health and risk to her life'. It has been suggested that this judgment 'completely restates the rights of adolescents and is entirely out of line with national and international thinking about the place of adolescents in our society'.[18]

It seems that the more medical science progresses, the more controversial the issues of ethics and law become. These examples illustrate graphically the basic point that, despite what Lord Devlin would like to believe, there is very little consensus in our society over particular moral issues, or over the extent to which law should be used to enforce moral principles other than the basic prohibitions on violence which are clearly necessary for any social group to survive.

The argument which is put forward here is that both law and morality, far from having their origins in mysterious revelations through religious visionaries or other mystical sources, are firmly rooted in social conditions and practices. Law and morality are human constructs, having their foundations in scriptures as written and interpreted at various times, in traditions or cultural patterns, or in the conditions of social life prevailing at different periods, which are informed and underpinned by historically specific economic and political formations. The diversity of moral values which we observe in discussions of law and morality is therefore to be seen as a reflection of the diversity of economic and political interests existing in a society at any given time. In matters in which the state intervenes to prohibit or control moral behaviour through law, we find, as we shall see, that such intervention is usually the outcome of the workings of an intricate complex of pressure-groups, political parties and other interested individuals and groups who possess the *power* to influence the creation of legal rules.

Rules, both moral and legal, arise as responses to social or political problems and crises. Even our most basic rules forbidding the taking of human life extend far back into early history, for such rules are clearly a fundamental prerequisite for the continued existence of any stable social group. Again, rules and values which uphold the family unit – whichever form it may take[19] – are found in most societies at most periods, because of the importance of ensuring reproduction and survival of the social group, as well as because of the economic importance as a productive and consumer unit which the family has in a social structure.

Another example of the social origin of moral and legal values and rules is the position in Western societies of the social institution of *property*. Private property is so basic to our society that we readily condemn any infringement of our rights – legal and moral – to acquire, possess and enjoy our personal property. But in a society where property is held *communally*, such a value as the 'sanctity of private property' can have little or no meaning.[20] In such a social setting, any attempt by one individual in the group to treat property as his or her own 'private' possession would be regarded as an affront to the entire community. The value we place upon private property in our own society must therefore have its origins in the social and economic structure, at various periods in history, whereby the development of an economy dependent upon the acquisition, accumulation and transfer of property from one private individual or group to another (that is, trade and commercial dealing) was taking place. Thus, the development of the modern law of theft can be seen as a response to the growing needs of commercial interests, from about the fifteenth century onwards, which demanded adequate legal protection from unauthorized incursions upon property belonging to others.[21] Hay, writing about the criminal code of the eighteenth century, notes:

As the decades passed, the maturing trade, commerce and industry of England spawned more laws to protect particular kinds of property. Perhaps the most dramatic change in the organisational structure of British capital was the growth of promissory notes on banks as a medium of exchange, and the increase in negotiable paper of all kinds. This new creation was exposed to fraud in many ways never foreseen by the ancient criminal law. The result was a rash of capital statutes against forgeries and frauds of all kinds, laws which multiplied towards the end of the century.[22]

And Hay notes also how the 'sanctification' of property was almost complete by the eighteenth century, citing Blackstone, a well-known writer on the law of that time, who wrote that 'there is nothing which so generally strikes the imagination, and engages the affections of mankind, as the right of property'.[23]

Property, then, and the moral and legal codes which justify and protect it, must be seen as developments arising from economic bases; we shall see the connection between *landed* property and capitalism in chapter 5. In the above mentioned context of the growth of moveable and negotiable property in the period of developing capitalism, the 'rash of capital statutes' can be seen as a consequence of the needs of the propertied classes to protect their wealth against the frauds and other encroachments of the property-less. The elevation of property and wealth to one of the highest social and moral values belongs only in a society based on material gain; it certainly has little place in the more traditional and orthodox sources of our moral code: 'It is easier for a camel to go through the eye of a needle, than for a rich man to enter the kingdom of God' (Matthew 19:24).

These connections between law, morality and the social and economic structure are intricate and complex. The ideological function of the socially defined codes of law and morality is the underpinning of particular social structural processes, relations and institutions (law, state, capital, the social order and so on) by means of providing 'master definitions' of beliefs and ideas, inculcated through various socialization processes (family, school, the mass media) and the legitimized sanctions of the law. Because of the divided and diverse nature of our society, however, it is inevitable that clashes will occur, at various levels and in various institutions, between the adherents of *differing* moral values and views. Returning to the earlier example of the abortion controversy, we have seen several such clashes between, specifically, those wishing to repeal the existing law, and those wishing to extend that law to permit abortions in more, or even all, cases where the pregnant woman desires it. It would be easy to catalogue many other such instances. The point, however, is not simply that such pluralities of moral values exist – this has been stated already – but rather how we analyse and understand the different and complex moral stances on these and many more issues; the shifting terrain of allegiances and opposition to proposals for change; the ways in which some, and not other, interest-groups succeed in getting *their* definitions of morality accepted, enacted and enforced through the legal process; and the ways in which moral viewpoints, state responses through law, and the wider processes and institutions of the social structure are interrelated.

Morality and the law

'Social groups create deviance by making the rules whose infraction constitutes deviance, and by applying those rules to particular people and labelling them as outsiders.'[24] This well-known and often-cited statement by Becker highlights the crux of our concern with law and morality. Given that rules are social constructs, it is vital to appreciate the social context in which particular rules are created, especially when we are faced with situations where persons falling foul of such rules are being processed through official machinery such as the legal system and courts of law. At the same time, we must keep in mind the *reality* of moral codes. Moral codes exist, for whatever reasons, and the object of discussion here is not the denial of this fact: indeed, some have argued that the creation of deviance as such through the making of rules fulfils an important social function. As Durkheim wrote, the social condemnation of the deviant by other members of a community serves to maintain and reinforce the values against which the deviant has offended, and so plays an important part in the maintenance of the social order. Moral and legal codes mark the boundaries of the acceptable and the unacceptable. But given that conflicting moralities may surround a given social activity, we are concerned to examine by what processes and with what consequences a *particular* moral attitude may become embodied in law, to the exclusion of any other competing or clashing moral stance.

It is instructive to examine such processes in the context of particular legislative activity, and in England perhaps the best examples of moral reformism through legal change were the reforms of the 1960s. Thought by many critics to symbolize the high-water mark of the 'permissive society', the 1960s saw a number of Acts of Parliament whose effect was to relax, in many areas of social life, the rigidity of what many regarded as an outmoded moral code, much of it embodied within the law. Let us examine briefly some of the more striking reforms of that period.

'Crimes without victims'

Schur[25] uses the term 'crimes without victims' to refer to certain activities which were all, at the time of his writing, criminal offences. The examples he discusses are drug-use, homosexuality and abortion. The common characteristics of these crimes, argues Schur, are that, first, they are activities which involve no harm to anyone except the participants; second, they occur through the willing participation of those involved, with the result that, third, there is no 'victim' of the crime to register complaints to the law enforcement agencies, and so (fourth) the law is very difficult to enforce. Schur argued that given the existence of a social demand for consensual (as between the participants) activities such as these – a demand, moreover, which continues to be met, despite prohibition, in the form of back-street abortions, clandestine drug supply and use, and so on – and in the absence of any demonstration that prohibition brings greater social benefit than de-criminalization, such prohibitions as existed should be abolished.

It is possible, of course, to take issue with Schur on a number of points. Is it true that drug-use and abortion only harm the participants, and no-one else? What of the argument that some may be 'corrupted' into using illicit drugs? Or that the social cost of drug addiction (medical care, rehabilitation programmes) is such as to affect the community as a whole? What of young people, who may not appreciate the dangers of drug-use? And what difference to Schur's arguments is made by the fact that illicit intravenous drug-use carries the serious risk of HIV infection and potential full-blown AIDS?

And is there really no 'victim' of an abortion? What are we to make of the argument presented by organizations such as the Society for the Protection of the Unborn Child, that abortion is equivalent to murder of the unborn human being? And how much force is there in the point that laws against 'victimless crimes' are difficult to enforce? Some other offences, notably burglary, involve extreme difficulty in enforcement and apprehension of offenders: few would argue that burglary should, therefore, cease to be an offence.

We shall return to some of these problems presently. For the moment, however, let us note that reforming legislation in two of these areas – homosexuality and abortion – was passed during the 1960s. In 1967 the Sexual Offences Act provided that homosexual acts between two consenting male adults[26] in private should no longer be criminal offences (there remain a number of offences concerning homosexuality, notably those prohibiting acts done in public, or when more than two are involved, or acts involving persons under twenty-one). In the same year, the Abortion Act, discussed above, was passed as a private member's bill (see chapter 7) introduced by David Steel MP.

It has been suggested that the starting-point for the process of moral reformism during the 1960s was the *Report of the Committee on Homosexual Offences and Prostitution* (the Wolfenden Committee) in 1957. This report, and the philosophical/ ideological moral stance running through it, arguably 'articulate[d] the field of moral ideology and practice which defines the dominant tendency in the "legislation of consent" '.[27] Two passages from the Wolfenden Report indicate the line of thought adopted by the committee. Referring to prostitution and homosexuality, the report states:

In this field [the function of the criminal law] as we see it, is to preserve public order and decency, to protect the citizen from what is offensive or injurious, and to provide sufficient safeguards against exploitation and corruption of others, particularly those who are specially vulnerable because they are young, weak in body or mind, inexperienced, or in a state of special physical, official or economic dependence. It is not, in our view, the function of the law to intervene in the private lives of citizens, or to seek to enforce any particular pattern of behaviour, further than is necessary to carry out the purposes we have outlined.[28]

The proper role of the law in preventing the *public* expression of private morality is stressed; in relation to prostitution, says the report, the law should confine itself to

Those activities which offend against public order and decency or expose the ordinary citizen to what is offensive and injurious; and the simple fact is that prostitutes do parade themselves more habitually and openly than their prospective customers, and do by their continual presence affront the sense of decency of the ordinary citizen. In doing so they create a nuisance which, in our view, the law is entitled to recognise and deal with.[29]

The Wolfenden recommendations on homosexuality were incorporated, ten years after the report, in the Act of 1967 noted above. On prostitution, the report felt that, though prostitution itself should not be made a criminal offence, public manifestations of prostitution (street-walking and brothel-keeping) should remain criminal offences. Though much of the law relating to prostitution and related offences is contained in the pre-Wolfenden Sexual Offences Act 1956, the 'public nuisance' aspects were embodied in the Street Offences Act 1959, designed to 'clean up the streets' by prohibiting 'common prostitutes' from loitering or soliciting in a street or public place for the purposes of prostitution.

The Wolfenden recommendations met with a considerable degree of opposition, of which the best known is perhaps the argument presented by Lord Devlin, writing extra-judicially in 1959 about the enforcement of morality through the law. Criticizing the reasoning in Wolfenden Report, Lord Devlin had this to say:

Societies disintegrate from within more frequently than they are broken up by external pressures. There is disintegration when no common morality is observed and history shows that the loosening of moral bonds is often the first stage of disintegration, so that society is justified in taking the same steps to preserve its moral code as it does to preserve its government . . . the suppression of vice is as much the law's business as the suppression of subversive activities.[30]

Devlin's views were, in turn, responded to by Hart,[31] who relied heavily upon the writings of the nineteenth-century philosopher John Stuart Mill, who, in his essay *On Liberty*, made his position on such issues perfectly clear: 'The only part of the conduct of anyone, for which he is amenable to society, is that which concerns others. In the part which merely concerns himself, his independence is, of right, absolute. Over himself, over his own body and mind, the individual is sovereign.'[32]

Lord Devlin's views, although out of step with parliamentary reforms, were, and remain, fairly typical of those of the officials charged with the administration of the law in these areas (the police, and more especially the judges), who have shown little tendency to countenance the relaxations of the legal controls of sexual deviance despite the undoubted changes in social attitudes towards various forms of sexual expression.

In 1962, for example, the case of *Shaw* v. *Director of Public Prosecutions*[33] came on appeal before the House of Lords. Shaw had published a booklet entitled *The Ladies' Directory*, which listed and advertised prostitutes, together with photographs and descriptions of their particular sexual predilections and practices. Shaw was successfully convicted of the offence of 'conspiring to corrupt public morals' (an offence last heard of in the eighteenth century), and the conviction was upheld in the House of Lords. Regarding the jurisdiction of the court to uphold the recognition of such an antiquated offence, Viscount Simonds said: 'In the sphere of criminal law I entertain no doubt that there remains in the courts of law a residual power to enforce the supreme and fundamental purpose of the law, to conserve not only the safety and order but also the moral welfare of the State'.[34] Having established this jurisdiction, his lordship went on to make a remarkable prediction: 'Let it be supposed that at some future, perhaps early, date homosexual practices between consenting adult males are no longer a crime. Would it not be an offence if, even without obscenity, such practices were publicly advocated and encouraged by pamphlet and advertisement?'[35]

In 1967 the Sexual Offences Act was passed, which provided, among other things, that homosexual acts between consenting adult males in private were no longer a criminal offence. And in the case of *Knuller* v. *Director of Public Prosecutions*[36] in 1973, the exact situation envisaged by Viscount Simonds came before the House of Lords. The defendants were prosecuted for having published, in their magazine *International Times*, advertisements placed by readers inviting others to contact them for homosexual purposes. The charge was again conspiracy to corrupt public morals. Lord Reid, who had dissented from the majority decision in *Shaw*'s case, felt that *Shaw* should none the less be followed in order to ensure certainty in the law. He acknowledged the passage of the 1967 Act, but said this:

I find nothing in that Act to indicate that Parliament thought or intended to lay down that indulgence in these practices is not corrupting. I read the Act as saying that, even though it may be corrupting, if people choose to corrupt themselves in this way that is their affair and the law will not interfere. But no licence is given to others to encourage the practice.[37]

The accused were unsuccessful in their appeal against the conviction for conspiring to corrupt public morals.

The question as to whether the law should interfere in the private affairs of adult individuals who consent to certain sexual practices was considered once again by the Court of Appeal in 1992 in the extraordinary case of *R.* v. *Brown and Others*.[38] Although the facts of the case raise, albeit rather indirectly, issues which strictly speaking go further than that of sexual practices between consenting adults,[39] our discussion will concentrate on this aspect of the facts. The six appellants were convicted of a number of offences under the Offences Against the Person Act 1861. They had belonged to a group of homosexual men who had willingly participated in the commission of acts of sado-masochistic violence against each other involving the use of, among other things, heated wires, map-pins, stinging nettles, nails, sandpaper and safety-pins. The evidence showed that the various activities had been videotaped by the participants, though not for any profit or gain; that the injuries inflicted were not permanent; that no medical attention had been sought; and that none of the 'victims' had complained to the police. It was clear that this was a group of individuals who had all consented to a series of bizarre sexual practices, carried out in private, over a substantial period of time.

The men were charged with the offences of assault occasioning actual bodily harm contrary to s.47 of the Offences Against the Person Act 1861, and unlawful wounding, contrary to s.20 of the same Act. For Lord Lane, the Lord Chief Justice, the crux of the matter was whether the victims' consent to these activities negatived the charge of assault, given that assault may be defined as 'the unlawful touching of another without that other's consent'.[40] Lord Lane referred to situations in which the consent of a victim would certainly not prevent criminal liability, as where a victim consented to be killed; and to those situations such as sporting events where consensual physical contact is made (such as at a boxing match) and where consent *would* normally prevent any criminal assault being committed. Lord Lane discussed several cases where the issue of consent had arisen, including *R.* v. *Donovan*[41] in 1934 in which the court stated that

'bodily harm' has its ordinary meaning and includes any hurt or injury calculated to interfere with the health or comfort of the prosecutor. Such hurt or injury need not be permanent, but must, no doubt, be more than merely transient and trifling.[42]

Ultimately, however, Lord Lane based his judgment in the present case not so much on precedent as on grounds of public policy. He cited a case in 1981 in which two youths had met in a street and had decided to fight each other,[43] and in which it was stated that

it is not in the public interest that people should try to cause or should cause each other actual bodily harm for no good reason. Minor struggles are another matter. So, . . . it is immaterial whether the act occurs in private or in public; it is an assault if actual bodily harm is intended and/or caused. This means that most fights will be unlawful regardless of consent.[44]

Lord Lane continued:

What may be 'good reason' it is not necessary for us to decide. It is sufficient to say, so far as the instant case is concerned, that we agree with the learned trial judge that the satisfying of sado-masochistic libido does not come within the category of good reason nor can the injuries be described as merely transient or trifling.[45]

The convictions against all the accused were upheld.

From the point of view of our discussion as to whether, and in what circumstances, the law should intervene to control such sexual behaviour, the case raises interesting questions. Bearing in mind that none of the injuries sustained by the 'victims' in *R*. v. *Brown* was serious or of a lasting nature, on what grounds should the law now *not* declare the 'sport' of boxing to be unlawful, especially when we take into account the medical evidence to the effect that boxing can lead to serious and permanent physical damage? If consent cannot make lawful a fight in the street, why should it make any difference to a fight in the boxing-ring, which is, moreover, undertaken with a view to financial gain?

Again, leaving aside any revulsion that the particular activities involved in *Brown* might cause us to feel, what implications does the decision have for other, perhaps less bizarre, consensual acts carried out in private in the course of sexual relationships? Counsel for one of the defendants in the case asserted that 'a youth who gave a girlfriend a love bite would fit exactly'[46] into the definition of unlawful assault given by the judge at the original trial of the men, and that 'love bites caused longer lasting bruises than the cuts and bruises the men in the group had received'.[47] Presumably such an act would be 'for no good reason'?

And what of the civil liberties of the individual? Although there are situations, easily imaginable, where the state, through the law, ought properly to put individual health or well-being or public safety before the untrammelled freedom of the individual, it is arguable that cases such as *Brown*, involving consensual if distasteful activity, are at least borderline. Article 8 of the European Convention on Human Rights states that everyone has the right to respect for his private life, and that there should be no interference with the exercise of this right except where it is necessary in the interests of national security, public safety or the economic well-being of the country, for the prevention of disorder or crime, for the protection of health and morals, or for the protection of the rights of others. Does *Brown* fall within any of these exceptional cases, or was this prosecution an unjustifiable breach of Article 8?

Certainly, in *Dudgeon* v. *United Kingdom*,[48] in 1981, the European Court of Human Rights held that the prohibition in Northern Ireland of homosexual acts between consenting males was a breach of Article 8, in response to which the law was changed. The Court recognized that some degree of regulation of sexual activity – whether homosexual or heterosexual – through the criminal law was justified, but denied that any perceived social need to criminalize consensual homosexual activity in private outweighed the detrimental effects which prohibition had on the life of the individual. Could similar arguments not be made out in respect of situations like that in *Brown*? Who benefits from such prosecutions? Was the prosecution in *Brown* justified on grounds of public safety, health or morals?

Surely no one could seriously argue that the public might be tempted to indulge in sado-masochistic activities, were the accused in *Brown* to go unpunished? One commentator has argued that

benefits from the legal enforcement of morality have to be weighed against the misery caused directly and indirectly by legal punishments and by the consequent infringement of human freedom. Hart would surely argue that there is no public interest in prosecuting in a case such as *Brown*. The benefits from the enforcement of morality in cases of consensual sexual activity are, at the least, unclear.[49]

Leave to appeal to the House of Lords was given by the Court of Appeal in *Brown*; at the time of writing it remains to be seen what, if any, clarification of the matter will be provided through the judgment of that court.

Censorship

The cases of *Shaw* and *Knuller*, in particular, lead us to consider a rather different aspect of the relationship between law and morals. It is one thing for the law to withdraw from control over various activities done consensually in private; it is quite another when such activities are brought into the public gaze by means of the written word, photographs and films, and theatrical and television productions. There have been organizations such as the National Viewers and Listeners' Association, and individuals such as Mary Whitehouse and Lord Longford, who have rarely been slow to seek publicity for their deep concern about the 'permissive society'. It was Mary Whitehouse who initiated the successful prosecution, for the little-used offence of blasphemous libel, of the editor of the newspaper *Gay News* in 1978, for the alleged blasphemous content of a poem published in the paper;[50] she was also responsible for starting proceedings (subsequently dropped) against the play *The Romans in Britain* in 1981, again invoking what many thought to be an inappropriate offence: that of procuring others (in this case, actors) to commit homosexual acts (though in this case, simulated). The view of Mrs Whitehouse[51] and others like her is that the existing law relating to obscenity and pornography is too weak, and is in need of strengthening.

Ranged against such positions, of course, are the arguments of writers, journalists, producers and many others[52] who argue the case for less, not more, censorship on the grounds of freedom of expression and freedom on the part of citizens to choose whether to read books or view films or television for themselves. Recently, a significant new dimension to debates about pornography has come from the feminist movement, arguing against pornography not on the ground of 'excess permissiveness', but rather on the ground that pornography exploits, and thereby oppresses, women depicted within it, and women in general. The feminist criticism extends beyond the explicit portrayal of sex, and covers major films on general release which show, and in the feminist view glorify, male violence against women.[53]

Blasphemous libel, the common-law offence which was successfully charged against *Gay News* in 1978, reappeared in 1991 in an attempt to convict the writer Salman Rushdie, author of the book *Satanic Verses*, and his publishers, of the offence. The furore triggered by the publication of this book, which Muslims in many countries regard as deeply offensive to the religion of Islam, reached its climax when Iran placed Rushdie under what was, and remains, literally a sentence of death for having written and published the book. The author has since then remained in hiding, and diplomatic relations between Britain and Iran have been somewhat difficult. Against this background, consider *R*. v. *Chief Metropolitan Magistrate, ex parte Choudhury*,[54] in which the applicant sought summonses against Rushdie and his publishers accusing them of blasphemous libel. The Queen's Bench Division of the High Court, after carefully reviewing the history of this offence, concluded that the common-law offence of blasphemous libel was confined to protecting only the Christian religion; the court would not extend the law to cover other religions:

The mere fact that the law is anomalous or even unjust does not, in our view, justify the court in changing it, if it is clear. If the law is uncertain, in interpreting and declaring the law the judges will do so in accordance with justice and to avoid anomaly or discrimination against certain classes of citizens; but taking that course is not open to us, even though we may think justice demands it, for the law is not, we think, uncertain.[55]

Furthermore, the court pointed out that, even had it been open to the court to extend the law, it would not have done so, since, among other problems, the boundaries would be too difficult to draw as to what might constitute a religion.[56] The court asserted that such a change in the law was properly a matter for Parliament. It is difficult not to be sympathetic to the court's stance in this matter, since religious affairs may be a matter of deeply felt sensitivity to many people: but none the less it may be thought disturbing to note that the review of the history of the offence of blasphemous libel in the judgment of Watkins L. J. reveals that this offence fails to protect not only the religion of the many British people of the Muslim faith, but also, apparently, *any* religion other than that of the established Church of England.

If we now consider in more detail the law relating to obscenity and pornography, we find that the relevant statutes stem from 1959 to 1968. In 1959 the law relating to obscene publications, until then confusing and unsatisfactory to libertarians and would-be censors alike,[57] was reformed in the Obscene Publications Act. This Act was amended in 1964 by the Obscene Publications (Amendment) Act. In 1968 the Theatres Act ended the system whereby *any* play could be banned by the Lord Chamberlain, one of whose functions was to censor theatrical productions prior to their public performance. Theatrical productions, with the curious exception of strip-tease shows and the like, are now subject to the Obscene Publications Act. Strip-shows are dealt with, where appropriate, by the common-law offence of conspiracy to corrupt public morals.

The Obscene Publications Act 1959 recognized that there was a difference between sheer pornographic representation, and works of art, literature or learning which may necessarily contain material which some people do not consider to their taste. Section 1 of the Act provides that an article is obscene if, *taken as a whole*, 'its effect is to tend to deprave and corrupt persons who are likely, having regard to all relevant circumstances, to read, see or hear the matter contained or embodied in it'. It is clear from this section that it is no longer possible for prosecuting counsel simply to select for the jury those portions of a work which might be deemed obscene; rather, such passages must be presented in the overall context of the entire work. Section 4 embodies the distinction referred to above. It provides that no offence under the Act is committed if 'it is proved that publication of the article in question is justified as being for the public good on the grounds that it is in the interests of science, literature, art or learning, or of other objects of general concern', and the section further provides that expert opinion as to the scientific, literary or other merit of the work is admissible in evidence. It is *not*, however, permissible to introduce expert evidence as to the issue of obscenity – that is for the 'ordinary men and women' of the jury to decide for themselves. The Obscene Publications (Amendment) Act 1964, which was introduced in the attempt to control what was regarded as a worrying increase in the importation of pornographic literature from other countries, created a new offence of being in possession of an obscene article for publication for gain – an offence which may be committed before there is any actual publication of the material.

What the 1959 and 1964 Acts failed to do, however, was to throw any light on the precise meaning of the word 'obscene'. They maintained the pre-existing definition – 'that which tends to deprave and corrupt' – without any further help for judges or juries as to what these words entail.[58] It is clear that 'obscene' refers to material of a higher degree of unacceptability than does the word 'indecent' (a term used in legal provisions relating, for example, to the sending of obscene *or* indecent matter through the post),[59] which has been held to mean material 'which an ordinary decent man or woman would find to be shocking, disgusting or revolting'.[60] The law relating to indecency, rather like that relating to street offences, discussed above, is concerned to prevent the 'nuisance aspect' of material which might otherwise come before an unwitting public gaze. The law relating to 'obscenity', on the other hand, would seem to refer to the need to control material of a much more positively dangerous nature – that which 'tends to deprave and corrupt'. The difficulty lies in explaining exactly what it is to be 'depraved and corrupted', how these states identify and manifest themselves, and how to assess the vulnerability of those who might come into contact with such material.

In practice, much material suspected by the police as being obscene, and kept in any premises for publication for gain, is dealt with by means of a procedure laid down in s.3 of the Act of 1959, whereby such material may be brought before any magistrate; if the magistrate decides that the material is obscene, and kept for publication for gain, then the material must be forfeited; the 'public good' defence is available, but the significance of this procedure is that the defendant is deprived of a jury trial: the decision as to whether or not the material is obscene is in the hands of magistrates. Not surprisingly, perhaps, many have criticized this procedure for this very reason.

The Home Office Committee on Obscenity and Film Censorship, chaired by Bernard Williams, which reported in 1979,[61] realistically confronted these and many other problems, remarking laconically that the law was 'in a mess'. Their report proposed the abolition of all the existing law in this area, replacing it with a single statute in which prohibition would depend on the likelihood that the material in question would harm someone. Such harm would include the fact that children had been exploited for sexual purposes, or that physical violence appeared to have been perpetrated and recorded on film or photograph. Pornography would be available only in shops specializing in such material, where people under eighteen would be denied access, and whose contents were made the subject of a warning notice. To date, no legislative activity has been directed towards reforming the obscenity laws themselves, though several recent statutes in this area should be noted. The first is the Indecent Displays (Control) Act 1981, which originated as a private member's bill, and which prohibits the display of indecent material in public places. Second, local authorities may now, by virtue of the Local Government (Miscellaneous Provisions) Act 1982, require sex shops and cinemas to operate only with a licence from the local authority, and may refuse such a licence. An applicant who has been refused such a licence may, however, appeal against such a refusal to the magistrates' court.

More recently, the Video Recordings Act 1984 (once again, a measure which began as a private member's bill) introduced what has been called 'the most stringent form of pre-censorship this country has ever known'.[62] Ostensibly designed to control and curb the supply to the public of videotaped films portraying explicit sex and violence, the Act arguably goes much further in requiring *all* videotaped films and other programmes to be 'classified' (that is, censored) before being supplied to the public in shops or video libraries. Certain types of programme are exempted from the Act (works designed to provide information, education or instruction, or concerned with sport, religion or music), although even these exempted materials must be submitted for classification if 'to any extent' they portray any of the prohibited acts or images, which include human sexual activity, mutilation, torture or acts of force or restraint associated with sexual activity. The censoring authority has the responsibility of classifying videotapes as suitable (or not) for home viewing, and if the authority considers the material unsuitable for viewing, no classification certificate will be granted. In such cases, the video will be prohibited from supply, or may be limited for supply by licensed sex shops only. Any person supplying or offering to supply an unclassified videotape to the public (and not fulfilling the sex-shop condition, if it applies) may be fined up to £10,000. Critics of this wide-ranging Act argue that the provisions will apply not only to the 'video nasties' which the Act ostensibly controls, but also to 'news contained on videos of war . . . videos of childbirth . . . videos dealing with serious subjects . . . would similarly be open to censorship . . . [and] even films that have been shown already in cinemas or on television must be resubmitted for classification and possible censorship before they may be distributed in video form'.[63] More recently, extensive coverage of serious crimes of violence in the media, such as the shooting of fourteen people in the village of Hungerford in 1987, has led many to question whether the portrayal of violence on television may, in some way, lead to violent behaviour on the part of certain individuals, although extensive research carried out over the years has failed to establish any such causative link.

The passage of the Video Recordings Act, and the proposed curbs on broadcast material, would seem to constitute evidence of what many have seen as a new authoritarianism in the British state, replacing individual choice, responsibility and integrity by centralized controls. It seems certain that the controversies over obscenity and censorship will continue, with fears of corruption and decline of moral standards expressed by one lobby being met with equal and opposite indignation from the other, claiming the paramount freedom of the individual, both of expression and of choice in what and what not to read, see or hear. Perhaps the solution, at least as far as blatant pornography is concerned, will come not from mere law reform; as Robertson suggests, 'it may be that much of the leering salacity dispensed on street corners will prove unacceptable when society becomes genuinely concerned to uphold the dignity of women'.[64]

During 1987 the controversy over censorship moved significantly from the arena of pornography and sexual morality to that of *political* censorship. Though the government had invoked the much-criticized s.2 of the Official Secrets Act 1911[65] unsuccessfully in the prosecution of the civil servant Clive Ponting, its determination to suppress any publication of what it regarded as 'sensitive' information persisted. Injunctions were obtained by the government in 1987 to prevent the broadcast of a series of television programmes called *The Secret Society*, and a three-part radio series, *My Country: Right or Wrong*, which examined the role of the security services. In 1988 directions were issued by the Home Secretary to the BBC and the IBA stating that they were not to broadcast anything spoken by any representative of Sinn Fein, Republican Sinn Fein, and the Ulster Defence Organization, despite the fact that none of these organizations are illegal bodies. Various television journalists unsuccessfully brought an action challenging the validity of this directive,[66] the Court of Appeal being of the opinion that it was not open to the court to intervene in the Home Secretary's decision: the court's view was confirmed in the House of Lords in 1991.

In 1986, when *Spycatcher*, the memoirs of an ex-security services official, was pending publication in Australia, the British government attempted unsuccessfully to prevent its publication in that country by legal action. That failure, and the book's subsequent appearance, did not prevent the government from taking legal action in other countries to prevent its publication in those countries, nor from taking steps to persuade the British courts to prevent British newspapers from publishing extracts from the book. The House of Lords, to the utter astonishment of many observers, the sharp criticism of ex-judges such as Lord Scarman and Lord Devlin, and the distaste of dissenting judges in the case, upheld the government's attempt to suppress publication of these extracts on the ground that the importance of state security outweighed that of the freedom of the press – despite the fact that the book could readily be imported into Britain and its contents perused by any individual choosing to track it down. It is hard to identify any rational justification for either the government's or the courts' behaviour in this case, which seems to restrict freedom of the press, and indeed of information, to a degree which must surely be inexcusable in any democratic society.

The legislation of morality

Above, we looked at the issues of 'victimless crimes' and censorship in the light of law reforms occurring during one period of 'reformism', the 1960s. During that period, however, various other reforms in areas pertaining to law and morality were enacted. Capital punishment was suspended in 1965, and abolished altogether in 1969;[67] the law relating to young offenders was changed in 1969 in the attempt, among other things, to 'decriminalize' juvenile court proceedings in such cases, and thus try to reduce what many felt was the harmful stigmatizing effect upon a juvenile of appearing before a criminal court.[68] In 1969, too, the Divorce Reform Act was passed, which, when implemented in 1971, led to the easier availability of divorce following marital breakdown. In other related fields, however, despite attempts by pressure-groups to change the law, proposals for reform on moral issues failed – examples are proposals to permit euthanasia[69] and proposals to relax the penalties for certain offences connected with cannabis use, the latter being noteworthy for their embodiment in an official report of a committee chaired by Lady Wootton.[70]

On all these issues, there was considerable public debate during the 1960s. Regarding capital punishment, the debates generally comprised abolitionist arguments questioning the morality of 'a life for a life', and denying the effectiveness of the death penalty as a deterrent, backing up the latter arguments with evidence and experience from other countries. Those wishing to retain the death penalty were 'disposed to rely more on psychological arguments (based presumably on introspection) as to how a criminal would be likely to react to abolition'.[71]

The debates as to the effectiveness and appropriateness of the juvenile court system, during a period in which juvenile crime was seen by many as an increasingly serious social problem, drew on a number of crucial matters, including the problem of stigmatizing juveniles and branding them as 'criminals'; the question as to whether juveniles are best dealt with by punishment or treatment, given that in many cases young offenders come from similar home backgrounds of deprivation and inadequacy as do children who commit no offences, but who are taken into local authority care by reason of neglect, deprivation or parental cruelty; and whether a court of law having criminal jurisdiction is the best forum for dealing with juvenile offenders.[72] The culmination of a decade of public debate on these matters was the Children and Young Persons Act 1969.

With regard to marriage and divorce, the factors informing the controversies over proposed divorce law reform were many and varied. The very nature of the basic social institution of the family was thought by many to be endangered by such trends as increasing numbers of illegitimate births and of one-parent families, and the growing numbers of women who, especially since 1945, choose to earn an independent income through paid employment, usually as well as fulfilling the 'traditional' woman's role of wife, housekeeper and mother.[73] More specifically, reformists based their arguments upon the proposition that the existing law relating to divorce was out of step with social trends and changed attitudes towards divorce, and that the number of marriages ending in divorce under the old law did not reflect the actual number of marriages which had broken down.[74]

Moral climates change over time: some observers perceived a significant shift away from the social and political milieu of reformism in the 1960s, to a much more rigid and authoritarian atmosphere in the 1980s.[75] It remains to be seen how the 1990s will be characterized, but over the last few years there have been attempts, through campaigns initiated by the police and through individual MPs, to restore capital punishment, at least for certain forms of homicide such as terrorism and the killing of police officers; and many have pointed to the weaknesses in the law relating to young offenders. The moral panics during the last five years or so regarding child abuse, especially the sexual abuse of children, have served to concentrate the issues and bring them dramatically into the public eye. Such observations and events lead us to ask a number of difficult questions about reformism, and about the relationship between legislation and morality. To what extent did the legislative changes in the 1960s *reflect* general social attitudes (if such can be measured), as opposed to *generating* changes in attitude? Were the reforms the outcome of diffuse social pressures, or were they the result of proposals by specific organizations and groups, possessing different degrees of political influence? To what extent do the mass media, especially the less responsible daily newspapers but also the reporting practices of the 'respectable' press, play a part in *creating* public attitudes and *generating* public reactions towards these issues? Can it be said that any perceptible shift towards a more rigid moral code constitutes a *reaction against* the 'permissiveness' of the 1960s and, as claimed by some critics mentioned above, the consequent 'decline in standards' of morality in Britain? How do we explain the success of some reform campaigns, and the failure of others? On a somewhat different level, we might ask how appropriate are *legal* controls in areas of morality; and is it possible to 'legislate morality'?

With regard to the influence of individual campaigning pressure-groups, the intricate relationship between these and the eventual creation or repeal of legal rules has been studied in detail by Pym.[76] Such groups were actively campaigning (particularly during the 1950s and 1960s) for changes in the law relating to abortion, divorce, homosexuality, capital punishment and euthanasia, and worked to acquire public support for their causes together with parliamentary support which would result in new legislation. Pym found that analysing the intricacies of the various relationships between the campaigning bodies, parliamentary and other institutions, and the eventual outcome of the campaigns was extremely complex: 'Intuitively, we would recognise as a successful group, one which emerges from nowhere, produces a Bill, persuades everyone to vote for it and generally carries through the whole campaign. This vision of "Do-it-Yourself democracy" is far from reality.'[77] Pym found that the groups themselves played a relatively minor role in the production of each bill that came before Parliament on these various issues; the precise content of each bill was determined far more by behind-the-scenes discussion and compromise between parliamentary draftsmen, political figures (such as the Lord Chancellor) and official bodies (such as the Church of England and the Law Reform Commission) than by active and influential participation by the members of the pressure-groups under examination.

Apart from Pym's work, there have been many studies of the origins of legislation in the field of morality, and of the activities of what have been called 'moral crusaders', where the protagonists of legal and moral reform

typically want those beneath them to achieve a better status. That those beneath them do not always like the means proposed for their salvation is another matter. But this fact – that moral crusades are typically dominated by those in the upper levels of the social structure – means that they add to the power they derive from the legitimacy of their moral position, the power they derive from their superior position in society.[78]

Thus, one study discusses the creation of the laws outlawing alcohol in the United States in the 1920s.[79] This study of Prohibition illustrates some of the points raised earlier: that consensus about the 'wrongness' of a given activity often does not exist, and that support for particular causes from influential political and legal institutions must often be fought for through publicity campaigns and intensive lobbying. The acknowledged failure of the American Prohibition laws, and the fact that a large number of American citizens managed to obtain unlawful liquor during the Prohibition era, illustrate the former point, while the latter proposition is illustrated by the existence of the different kinds of group who argued in favour of Prohibition. We see that it is not always only the centrally committed members of pressure-groups who campaign for change, for the Prohibition campaign was supported not only by temperance and religious groups, and others concerned with what has been termed the 'legislation of morality',[80] but also by industrialists and employers, who favoured the movement in the belief that sober workers would be more manageable and productive.

The diversity of groups and individuals prepared to campaign for legal change is shown also by studies which have pointed out that, once *some* legal regulation exists in a given area, it can occur that the agencies entrusted with enforcing that legal regulation can themselves engage in subsequent campaigns as supporters of *further* legal intervention. Thus, Becker's study of the Marijuana Tax Act in 1937 in the United States[81] reveals how the Bureau of Narcotics was instrumental in extending its control over drug-use; Paulus's account of the development of laws controlling the purity of food and drugs[82] includes the point that the inspectors and analysts involved in the enforcement of existing laws raised substantial opposition to later attempts by manufacturers to avoid the law; and Gunningham makes a similar point with regard to the development of anti-pollution legislation[83] – that once created, the bureaucratic agencies of control comprise in themselves an interest-group who attempt to *increase* that control.

Several other aspects of the 'legislation of morality' emerge from the considerable number of studies of drug-use – one of the 'victimless crimes' which, despite pressure-group and other efforts, has consistently failed to attract relaxation of legal controls in Britain.[84] One writer has explained that this area is significant because 'more than any other form of deviance, the history of drug-use contains an abundance of material on both questions of legislation and morality, and of the relationship between them'.[85] Duster traces the history of drug-use and its legal control in America around the turn of the last century. In 1900 most drug-addicts in the USA were from the middle and upper classes, who had become addicted to morphine through the use of lawful 'patent medicines', many of which contained this drug. The shift in the pattern of the social status of the addict came to the fore when the Harrison Act of 1914, prohibiting 'dangerous drugs', opened up the way for the black market, operating from the 'criminal underworld'. It tended to be the lower classes who had the most contact, relatively speaking, with the underworld, and this meant that drug-addiction came rapidly to carry the same moral stigma as crime, which had certainly not been the case prior to the legislation when addiction carried little or no moral stigma. Thenceforward, the equation of drug-addiction with criminality, explicit in the 1914 Act, came to dominate thinking in this field. It is not, therefore, surprising that by the 1960s, when prohibited *non-addictive* drugs (notably cannabis) were becoming increasingly used, in the main by young people, this development easily inherited the moral stigma which had, arguably, been at least partly created by the introduction of legal controls fifty years earlier.

Addressing the British situation regarding the control of drug use, Young[86] has pointed out that much depends on the standpoint of the observer: from the point of view of those who believe in a 'moral consensus' view of society, the drugtaker operates outside that moral consensus, and is therefore 'maladjusted' and 'sick'. To those who consider that 'one can only judge the normality or deviancy of a particular item of behaviour *relatively* against the standards of the particular group you choose as your moral yard-stick',[87] however, 'Drugtaking ... is not necessarily deviant nor essentially a social problem; it is deviant to groups who condemn it and a problem to those who wish to eliminate it.'[88]

According to Young, it is the former view which dominates everyday definitions of the nature of drug-taking, represented by politicians, medical practitioners and, in particular, the media and the police. It is this clash of values, epitomized in encounters with the police but generally dominating the attitude towards drug-users held by many others in society, which enhances the strong *moral* connotations of the issue. In other words, it is not simply the condemnation of drug-use because it is *medically* harmful; the issue is infused with value-judgments about drug-use so that the user is seen as socially, or morally, 'sick'.

Acknowledging the fact that certain aspects of these studies (such as the role of the official agencies of enforcement) may be applicable *generally* in any discussion of the legislation of morality, certain questions remain about the wider social and political contexts in which state intervention through law takes place. To restate some of our earlier problems: how do we explain the general shifts in social climate between periods of liberalism, toleration and reform, and periods of rigid moral codes and authoritarianism? Does the legal control of morality *reflect* or *generate* changes in attitude within the various communities in society?

Hall, in an interesting analysis of periods of reform,[89] points out that during the two 'reformist' periods under discussion (1957–61 and 1965–8) the emergence of reforms in the law cannot be explained by any party-political commitment, as 'the reformist impulse ... cut across formal party alignments';[90] neither can they be explained by the existence of any general social agitation around the relevant issues, for although there were, as we have seen, a number of active pressure-groups at work, these groups were not the outcome of any manifestation of popular concern, and therefore 'cannot explain why these issues became socially pertinent in the first place'.[91] On the other hand, Hall finds that the influence of religious bodies cannot be discounted, for religious sentiments, or echoes thereof, can be seen in many of the campaigns of the periods, and indeed may be discerned in various aspects of the reformist legislation which emerged. More perplexing, perhaps, is the fact that, according to Hall, the period which saw the publication of the Wolfenden Report, discussed above, also saw widespread public 'moral panic' about the supposed increasing extent of such 'problems' as prostitution and homosexuality, which of course makes subsequent relaxation of legal controls even more difficult to explain.

Noting that each of the particular areas of reform arose from different causes and origins, Hall perceives a unifying thread which permeates the major legal reforms in the field of morality during the period we have been discussing. This unity, apparently at odds with the more usual ideas of the 'permissive sixties', is constituted by the tendency, in all the legislative reforms affecting prostitution, homosexuality, abortion, divorce and others, to *strengthen* state control while *at the same time* placing certain aspects of the 'problem' outside legal controls. Thus, prostitution itself remained lawful, being a matter left to 'private morality', but at the same time Wolfenden recommended increases in legal penalties for public manifestations of prostitution, street-walking and living on the earnings of prostitution. Homosexuality between adults in private was rendered legal, but again, penalties for soliciting and male importuning were increased. The changed law on divorce nevertheless 'did not shift an inch from the orthodox defence of the institutional basis of marriage and the regulation of sexuality by marriage'.[92] And Hall maintains that the 'social clause' in the Abortion Act allowed personal criteria to be used in some cases while the general tenor of the Act was to *tighten up* the availability of abortion by laying down strict medical criteria and placing it in the hands of the medical profession. Thus, Hall argues,

in each domain there is an increased regulation by the state, a greater intervention in the field of moral conduct – sometimes making more refined distinctions, and often taking a more punitive and repressive form than previously existing mechanisms of regulation and control. At the same time, other areas of conduct are exempted from legal regulation – and, so to speak, from the gaze of public morality, the yardstick of respectable, 'right-thinking' man – and shifted to a different domain, to be regulated by a different modality of control: that of freely contracting private individuals. This is the core of the tendency: increased regulation coupled with selective privatization through contract or consent . . .[93]

What part did the main political parties play in the reformist era? Hall doubts that Labour was the 'party of moral reform', or that the Conservative Party was necessarily against such reform. Rather, he argues, the period of moral reform was characterized by divisions *within* each of the two major parties. In the Conservative Party, the division was between the older, traditional social and political values, and a newer, more adaptive wing, which, in a period in which inflation and other economic forces were threatening the status of the middle classes, recognized the need for a progressive reformist outlook. Within the Labour Party, the reformist current also broke away from the traditional party outlook and, according to Hall, took its cue from the view that the basic economic problems of post-war capitalism had been essentially solved: 'its aim was nothing short of bringing into line and formalising social, moral and ethical trends already set in motion by the reformation of classical capitalism. And the motive and mechanism of this reformism was to "de-regulate" moral conduct, to "liberate" it from the compulsions of legal and state regulation'.[94] And, in turn, the presence of countervailing forces within the major parties facilitated a reaction against moral reformism and 'permissiveness' when, by the 1970s, the economic crises – manifested in rising inflation, problems of industrial relations, and other factors – indicated that the economic and moral 'boom' of the 1960s was over. Thus, says Hall, 'If . . . the emergent state capitalism of the "boom" period seemed to find a sort of expression in a more fluid and "liberalised" personal and moral regime, this same capitalism, under conditions of world recession, seemed to require a return to moral and ideological orthodoxy and authority.'[95] Arguably, it is this same 'moral orthodoxy and authority' which, on one view, characterized the Conservative government elected in 1979, which encouraged the 'traditional' moral virtues of discipline, work and respect for established institutions (law and order, the family), and which thus may represent a continuing reaction against the liberalism and moral reformism which marked the 1960s.

Hall's account, drawing upon the analytical tools of Marxism (the centrality of economic forces, the changing nature of the social class structure and so on), is of course only one of a number of possible explanations for the shifts in moral climate in Britain, frequently accompanied, as we have seen, by changes in the law. But our discussion of Hall's study serves to highlight a number of important aspects of the relationship between law and morality. First, phrases like 'changes in public opinion' can mask the extremely complex and subtle social, economic and political forces which, taken together at any historical moment, form the moral and ideological framework within which legal change may take place. Second, far from resting upon the kind of absolute and ultimate moral values presented, in particular, by natural-law philosophy and its variants, it seems that moral values and codes must be characterized by a dynamism and relativity which reflect the fact that such codes, and indeed the legal rules embodying them, are subject to different perceptions and definitions, and that often it is the possession of effective political *power* which finally determines which and whose definition of morality is reflected within the law. Thus, in conclusion, the complex and dynamic interplay of party politics, pressure-group activity, religious and philosophical debates, and judicial interpretation of thorny problems of law and morality will all, in various ways, affect the legal system, its rules and procedures. We might go further and assert that, far from being restricted to rules about individual 'immorality' of the kind noted above, there is very little about our legal system which is not coloured by the moral and ideological overtones and assumptions of powerful social and political groups throughout the long period of development of English law. How the legislative and judicial developments of the 1980s and 1990s will be viewed twenty years on remains to be seen, but despite Hall's reservations about the reforms of earlier periods, it seems unlikely that the period will be characterized by anything resembling the liberal reformism of the 1960s.

At various points in our discussion so far, we have noted the often close connections between law and the economic environment which, according to some commentators and critics, characterize many legal rules, institutions and procedures. In the next chapter, we turn our attention to these complex and often difficult questions surrounding law and economic activity.

3
Law and the regulation
of economic activity

It is a commonplace assertion that the twentieth century has witnessed state intervention, especially in affairs involving economic activity, on a scale greater than at any other period in history. In chapter 1 we noted some examples of this phenomenon and discussed some of its basic aspects. But if we now pursue the matter, and ask exactly what is meant by the term 'state intervention', we find that this expansion of intervention has not come about in a straightforward fashion but has occurred, over the last hundred years or so, through complex changes in the structure of society and the economy, and in the very nature and role of the state itself. As we shall see presently, the notion of 'the state' is itself surrounded by problems of definition, and by controversy both as to the precise nature of the modern state and as to what the most appropriate role for the state should be in advanced capitalist society. Of course, state intervention is by no means confined to the economic sphere: the state has taken on a more active role with respect to many other areas of social life, such as public administration and the growth of what is usually termed the 'welfare state'. We shall discuss these developments presently, but for the moment we examine some of the main issues concerning state regulation of economic activity – a sphere of social life which is central to the existence of any social group.

What do we mean by 'the state'? Many writers and theorists have expounded theories and critical accounts of the state, and we invariably find that the approach taken to this difficult topic reflects, or is closely bound up with, their general perspectives on and theories of society.[1]

From the various propositions argued, however, we can identify several persistent issues relating to analyses of the modern state. Does the state act in the interest of the whole population, or does it act principally in the interests of certain *sections* of the population? Does the state play an active, directive part in the social and economic affairs of a society, or does it take a more passive, supportive role, in particular in relation to economic life?[2] To what extent is the notion of the state bound up with the monopoly of legitimate recourse to force, and in what circumstances will, or should, such force be utilized?

The traditional legal approach to the analysis of state activity, especially when that activity takes place by means of the use of law as an instrument of control or regulation, tends to ignore these basic questions. Most texts on public or constitutional law concentrate on issues such as the nature of the constitution, analyses of various organs of public administration and government, and descriptions of the various legal and conventional practices, powers and duties of the different components and agencies of the state. Unfortunately, such analyses tend, on the whole, to adopt a traditional constitutional perspective on the composition of the state, informing us that the three 'arms of the state' are the executive (the government), the legislature (Parliament) and the judiciary. The constitutional doctrine of the 'separation of powers' (see chapter 6) tells us that these three 'arms of the state' each exercise different functions, and are possessed of powers and duties whereby each 'arm' effectively serves to 'check and balance' the powers of the other two, thus ensuring that no single state institution accedes to a position of exclusive or arbitrary political power. As we shall see later, this notion of the 'separation of powers', at least as applied to modern Britain, is largely fallacious, in that there is considerable overlap between the functions of these three institutions. The doctrine of the 'separation of powers' is, moreover, bound up with the principle of the 'rule of law'. This idea was discussed and defended at length by the influential English constitutional lawyer A.V. Dicey, towards the end of the last century,[3] who argued that in Britain we live under a government of laws, and not of the arbitrary whim of individual rulers. The principle of the 'rule of law' requires that every government action must be justified by legal authority, and that the operation of government itself is carried out within a framework of legal rules and principles.

We shall discuss these issues in more detail later, but for the moment we can see, after some reflection, that the composition of what we ordinarily understand as the state is rather more complex, and its definition rather more elusive, than these conventional constitutional-law propositions would lead us to believe. We would probably include as part of the category of 'state agencies' such institutions as the police, the judges, the prisons, the apparatus of the political establishment (government, Parliament, the monarchy), the armed forces and perhaps the established Church. But some would go further and include as part of state 'apparatuses' the media, business and trade, the trade union movement, and the various educational and cultural institutions in our society, operating, to be sure, predominantly through the dissemination of 'dominant ideology' rather than through any overt coercive measures.[4] Others view 'the state' not as a series of institutions, nor as an apparatus, but as a form of *activity* – in other words, they define the state not in terms of what it *is*, but rather in terms of what it *does*.[5]

Some advocate what might be termed a minimal role for the state: that the state in any society should carry out certain basic functions to ensure the stability of that society. Through the state, it is often said, social order and national security are maintained, as is the system of defence against aggression from foreign powers; domestic stability is assured through the balancing of interests of competing groups within society. Though there are problems in analysing even these basic functions, the difficulties of analysis are compounded when we consider other, additional functions taken on by the state in the social, political or economic sphere. Again, it may be generally agreed that one characteristic attribute of the state is its monoply of the legitimate use of coercive power, through agencies such as the police, the courts and the prisons. While recourse to such physical coercion may be rare, as we have suggested, the fact remains that coercive power by the state is unhesitatingly used where circumstances are deemed to warrant it. The presence of the armed forces in Northern Ireland is one example of this; and we might also note the readiness to use imprisonment as a sanction in the United Kingdom; or the apparent readiness on the part of security forces to fire on anti-nuclear weapons demonstrations in the vicinity of military bases.[6] In none of these cases can it be said that the tactics involved are uncontroversial, nor that they necessarily meet with the approval of the population at large. To say this is, of course, to reiterate the point made in chapters 1 and 2: that in a society such as ours, relatively few social, political or economic activities or attitudes can be regarded as reflecting any kind of universal social consensus as to their rightness or otherwise.

For the time being, let us adopt a fairly uncontentious working definition of 'the state'. We will proceed on the basis that the state comprises *those elements in a society which, taken together, represent the central source of legal, political, military and economic power*. This definition will hold for all periods in British history although, as we shall see in exploring more rigorously the relationships between law, state and economic activity, the precise form, or guise, which the state adopts will depend upon the historical period under examination. To begin an investigation of the legal regulation of economic activity, we will return to a distinction made earlier between, on the one hand, a *passive, supportive* role for the state, and on the other hand, an *active, directive* role. The argument will be presented that, over the last century or so, the state in Britain – which could once be fairly accurately characterized as having a passive role – has moved towards the adoption of a much more active role.

Our starting-point once again is the period we have already identified as the great period of increased commercial and industrial activity, and *laisser-faire* attitudes held by the middle classes towards official regulative activity: the eighteenth and nineteenth centuries. As we saw in chapter 1, this period can be regarded as the high-water mark of economic *laisser-faire* philosophy. The dominant ideas of 'free trade' and freedom of competition in the marketplace carried with them the corollary that the economy was best left to regulate itself, unimpeded by any form of directive regulation by the state. This is not to say, however, that *no* regulatory measures were taken. If the role of the non-interventionist state in this period was to adopt a non-directive position with regard to the economy, it certainly had a part to play in supporting that economy. This supportive role can be seen both in the creation, often through law, of an economic environment conducive to trade and industry in a capitalist economy, and in the various measures which were taken to protect the economic interests of the business community. Generally, such measures were responses to the calls of private business interests, and it has been noted that, far from being an absolute and unshakeable creed, *laisser-faire* had its limitations as well as its uses:

Most businessmen . . . feared radical and socialist reformers who wanted to use the government as a means of achieving greater equality and they welcomed any theory that concluded that the government should not intervene in the economic process. Even though they themselves used the government extensively to promote their own interests (through special tariffs, tax concessions, land grants, and a host of other special privileges), they relied on *laisser-faire* arguments when threatened with any social reform that might erode their status, wealth or income.[7]

Government policy regarding foreign affairs also supported the growth and consolidation of the industrial and commercial economy, particularly during the eighteenth-century period of rapid economic expansion. As Hobsbawm points out,

> British policy in the eighteenth century was one of systematic aggressiveness . . . Of the five great wars of the period, Britain was clearly on the defensive in only one. The result of this century of intermittent warfare was the greatest triumph ever achieved by any state: the virtual monopoly among European powers of overseas colonies, and the virtual monopoly of world-wide naval power. Moreover, war itself – by crippling Britain's major competitors in Europe – tended to boost exports . . .[8]

Support for free, competitive trading also came from the judiciary, engaged, particularly during the nineteenth century, in constructing the legal framework within which business affairs could operate smoothly and predictably. The legal notion of the *contract* (see chapter 11) was, and still is, the essence of the relationship between buyers and sellers of goods and services, and the basic legal rules concerning contract and remedies for breach of contract spring almost wholly from cases decided by the superior courts during the nineteenth century. The insistence by nineteenth-century judges on deciding cases and creating legal contractual rules on the basis of the juristic equivalent of *laisser-faire* economics – the notions of freedom and equality of contract – led eventually to legislative intervention during the course of the twentieth century, especially in the area of consumer protection. The common-law rules of contract (that is, rules developed by the judges – see chapter 7) afforded no special protection to the ordinary consumer: the maxim *caveat emptor* – 'let the buyer beware' – applied, so that the consumer was expected to look out for his or her own affairs as a 'free agent' in the marketplace, and presumed to operate on an equal footing with traders and substantial businesses (see chapter 11). The same notions were applied to the contractual relationships between employers and employees, as noted in chapter 1, and this particular area is perhaps especially significant as one in which direct state regulation, in the form, originally, of prohibitions, was regarded by business interests (though not by groups of workers) as legitimate for the protection of the best interests of trade and industry. Less obviously, but equally importantly, the nineteenth century also saw the development of legal rules pertaining to the *form* which business enterprises might take, and to the legal protection which particular types of enterprise enjoyed.

The form of the business enterprise

The most common forms of business enterprise were, and still are, the *limited company* and the *partnership*. Taking the limited company first, if we examine the history of the company, we see that ventures in the form of 'joint stock' companies, where several members put their individual resources together for the running of a single enterprise, can be traced back many hundreds of years, though the 'limited liability company' was expanded and consolidated in business practice and the law during the eighteenth and nineteenth centuries.

The advantages of forming a business into a limited liability company are, first, that by dividing the business into shares, which are then sold to persons wishing to purchase a stake in the enterprise, it is possible to secure the release of large amounts of capital finance from shareholders, which enables the business to proceed on a more ambitious footing than it could if the available capital were restricted to, say, that of one man and his immediate associate who together run the business. Second, the term 'limited liability' means that the liability, in law, of each shareholder to the company's creditors is limited to the amount which the shareholder has agreed to invest in the company: that is, to the value of the shares held. This provides protection for the shareholder, and also constitutes a clear incentive for potential shareholders to invest money in the business. The company, like the contract, is the creation of law, and as Hadden has put it, 'Company law is about capitalism. It provides the formal legal structure necessary to the operation of the capitalist system.'[9]

As can be appreciated, the above advantages make the limited liability company an attractive form of business enterprise. We shall see in more detail later some of the ways in which the law regulates the company and its affairs, but we may note at this point one striking feature of the legal attitude towards the company: once it has been properly formed, the company is regarded in law as if it were a *person*. Even though the company has no 'real' physical existence apart from the personnel who run it and own it (directors and shareholders), it is, in law, a *corporate body*, an entity quite separate from these persons, and can therefore be said to be an 'artificial legal person'. The company can thus enjoy various rights, and can labour under various legal duties: it can own and transfer property, it can enter into contracts, it can sue and be sued in court, and can be prosecuted for criminal offences, though in the last case the only penalty normally used is the fine, paid from the company's assets.[10]

This legal device clearly forms an important component of the regulatory framework of state support for certain forms of economic activity. By treating the company as a person, having ownership of corporate assets, the law not only allows the relatively free use of those assets in the running and expansion of the business, but also provides significant protection for individual shareholders. The regulatory framework of company law amounts, in effect, not to the proposition 'you must not do this', but rather to the proposition 'if you wish to do this and to enjoy the protection of the law, then this is the way in which you must do it'. The mechanism of the limited company has had, at times, somewhat startling consequences. In the case of *Lee* v. *Lee's Air Farming Ltd* in 1961,[11] for example, Mr

Lee, who had formed, and who was the majority shareholder in, Lee's Air Farming Ltd, was killed in an air crash while working. His wife claimed compensation from the company in respect of his death, and the court decided in favour of her claim on the basis that at the time of the accident Mr Lee was working for the company as its employee – even though in every sense except the legal, Mr Lee and Lee's Air Farming Ltd were one and the same physical entity.[12]

Apart from enjoying legal powers to enter into contracts and so on, the company also labours under special legal *duties*. It is obviously reasonable, given that a company invites others to invest in it, to try to guard against fraud, misuse of company funds, or misrepresentation as to what the enterprise is worth or what its business activities are. The law therefore requires, through a series of Companies Acts (the main one now being the Companies Act 1985, a consolidating Act bringing together the provisions of a number of previous statutes), that certain formalities be observed by those intending to bring the company into being. All companies must register a Memorandum of Association with the Registrar of Companies, which contains information regarding the company's intended activities. The 'objects clause' of this Memorandum must state the purposes for which the company has been formed. This represents, in theory, an important mode of regulation of a company's activities for, given that the company is able to enter into legally binding contracts in its own name, those contracts (or any other activities) must pertain only to the purposes set out in the objects clause. If the company purports to act in a way inconsistent with these stated objects, the position prior to 1972 was, again in theory, that the company could not be bound to fulfil any contractual obligations so made, as they would be *ultra vires*, or *beyond the powers of* the company. The doctrine of *ultra vires* is found in other areas of law, but in this context the leading case is *Ashbury Railway Carriage and Iron Co.* v. *Riche*[13] in 1875. In this case, the company's stated objects were the manufacture and sale of railway plant, machinery and rolling stock; the business of mechanical engineering; and the purchase and sale of mines, minerals, land, buildings, timber, coal, metals and other materials. The company entered into a contract to finance the construction of a railway in Belgium, and later, when the agreement was repudiated by the company, the other party sued for breach of contract. The House of Lords held that the agreement did not fall within the stated objects of the company, was *ultra vires*, and that therefore the company could not be held liable for breach of contract since there was no legally valid contract to be breached.

Such a doctrine restricting the legal rights and duties of the company may seem hard on the party with whom the company is purporting to do business, as it would seem unable to recover compensation for such an alleged breach of contractual agreement. To a large extent, however, this result has in practice long been avoided by the use of very wide objects clauses in Memoranda of Association. Such a wide clause was approved by the Court of Appeal in *Bell Houses Ltd* v. *City Wall Properties Ltd*,[14] and now s.9(1) of the European Communities Act 1972 changes the position regarding the formal doctrine of *ultra vires* in this context. This provision enacts that any transaction of a company 'decided upon by the directors' with other people who are dealing with the company in good faith (that is, with no knowledge that the company might be exceeding its stated objects), shall be 'deemed to be one which it is within the capacity of the company to enter', even though technically it may be *ultra vires*. Connected with this issue is the situation where a person acting as agent[15] of an *as yet unformed* company enters into contracts with others on behalf of the unformed company. Legally, until the company has full legal existence, it cannot make contracts, or ratify those made in its name prior to that existence. On this point, s.9(2) of the European Communities Act 1972 gives statutory force to the pre-existing common-law position, which was that in such a case, the agent, and not the company, is personally liable for any breaches of contracts thus made. The changed position with respect to the *ultra vires* rule in the 1972 Act arguably improves the legal position, both with regard to creditors who might otherwise lose out by a strict application of the rule, and by giving legal effect to the economic reality of business transactions as opposed to an over-insistence upon legal formality at the expense of the true business intentions of the directors of the company.

In addition to the 'objects clause', the Memorandum of Association must also contain details of the company's name (which, if a private company, must end with the word 'limited', and if a public company, must end with the words 'public limited company': the distinction between private and public companies is explained below), and information as to whether the company's registered office is in England and Wales or in Scotland, and as to whether the liability of members is limited by shares or by guarantee. A company limited by guarantee is one in which the members guarantee to contribute specific amounts to the company's assets in the event of the company being 'wound up': that is, terminating its existence as a corporate body by reason of its insolvency, or by reason of a desire on the part of its members that it should cease to operate.

The distinction between a public and a private company was first introduced into the law in 1907. A private company was defined as one in which there were at least two, but not more than fifty, members; in which the transfer of shares was limited (perhaps in order to keep the control of the company within a family or some other such exclusive group); and which could not offer its shares to the public. The position is now governed by the Companies Act 1980, a private company being defined as one which does not meet the legal requirements of a public company. Section 1 of the Act of 1980 provides that, in order to be a public company, the enterprise must use the words 'public limited company' (or the letters PLC) after its name; it must comprise at least two members; it must have a minimum share capital of £50,000, of which at least one quarter of the nominal value of each share has been received by the company; it must state in its Memorandum of Association that it is a public limited company; and finally it must be registered under the provisions of the Act. Any company which does not meet these requirements is a private company.

Apart from the Memorandum of Association, the company must also lodge with the Registrar of Companies a document called the Articles of Association. This contains details of the company's rules and structure, and also constitutes a contract between the shareholders and the company. The Articles may be individually drawn up by the company, or the specimen Articles now contained in the Companies (Tables A–F) Regulations 1985 (S.I. 1985 No. 805) may be adopted. Once the Memorandum and Articles of Association, along with various other documents and items of information, have been deposited, and the Registrar of Companies is satisfied that all the statutory requirements have been met, a Certificate of Incorporation is issued and the company can begin its activity. It should be noted that in the case of a public company, a second certificate must be issued, this being evidence that the statutory requirements as to nominal capital, nominal value of shares and so on have been complied with (Companies Act 1980, s.4).

The main impetus for the recent companies legislation was the need to harmonize the relevant companies legislation of the EEC countries, and the Companies Acts of 1980 and 1981 are in fact implementations of EEC Directives.[16] The intention behind the 1980 Act is to ensure uniformity among public companies in terms of share capital, and to deal with certain malpractices among company directors, such as 'insider dealing', whereby a director makes use of the inside knowledge of the company to make personal profit or gain. The Companies Act 1981 deals with matters pertaining to the publication of companies' accounts, and the disclosure and display of the full name of the company and the address of the registered office on all business documents and in places where the business is carried on. This Act also provides that the name of the company need no longer meet with the approval of the Registrar of Companies, although new companies must not take the same name as any existing company, and must not adopt names which are offensive or which suggest government approval.

Apart from the provisions already noted, the law also contains a host of other regulatory provisions. Types and transfer of shares, company borrowing, the frequency, composition and procedure of meetings, the procedure and consequences of winding-up, and the rights and duties of directors: all are within the ambit of legal regulation. Space does not allow further detailed consideration of all these rules,[17] but enough has been said to show how, as long as the various legal formalities are complied with (and so long as no other legal rules are breached), a company can continue its affairs in its own name in whichever way it pleases.

A business enterprise does not have to be formed into a limited company in order to engage in group activity in the business world. The major alternative to the company is the *partnership*, which is an *un*incorporated association (that is, it is not treated in law as a 'person') and which is defined by the Partnership Act 1890 as a relationship between persons 'carrying on business in common with a view to profit'. Usually, partnerships come into existence by explicit agreement between the partners in the *firm*, and because the firm is not a corporate entity in law, the partners themselves act in the furtherance of the business as *agents* of the other partners. This means that if one partner enters into a business transaction relating to the firm's business with X, then that transaction (or contract) is regarded as made with *all* the other partners; in the event of the firm being in breach of that contract, then all the partners will be equally liable. The only exceptions to this will be in cases where X does not know that the contract was with a partnership, or where X knows that the partner who made the contract had no authority to do so. Note that the transaction must concern the firm's normal business: if it does not, then only the contracting partner will be liable unless the other partners agreed to the particular transaction.

Other important differences between partnerships and limited companies include the fact that, unlike that of shareholders in a company, the liability of the partners for the firm's debts is generally unlimited; there is, however, provision in the Limited Partnership Act 1907 for partnerships registered under the Act to comprise two types of partner: *general* partners who are fully liable for debts of the firm, and *limited* partners who contribute a specified amount to the firm and who are liable only for debts up to that amount. Limited, or 'sleeping', partners must not, however, participate in the running of the firm, otherwise they will become fully liable for the firm's debts just like the general partners.

Of course, in order to set up in business it is not essential to form the enterprise into either a limited company or a partnership. It is true that, as can be seen, there will be certain advantages in many cases in doing so, but it may well be that for many enterprises neither form of business is appropriate. Many small businesses, for instance, operate as *sole traders*. This simply refers to a business which is run by a person in his or her private capacity, such as a small corner shop or a building or plumbing business. No special rules apply to such cases: liability is unlimited, the enterprise has no corporate status, and there are no special devices for raising money with which to operate the business.

A final alternative method of forming a business enterprise is to structure the business as a *co-operative*. This form of business has increased in popularity in recent years, though it is still not as widespread in Britain as in certain other European countries. Some co-operatives were formed by groups of employees effectively taking over a non-viable business for which they had previously worked, and running it themselves (often by modifying or diversifying the business operation). This frequently meant, however, that they were also taking over the ailing business's problems, and many such co-operatives failed. Today, many groups of workers initiate the business enterprise by forming a co-operative, and, with appropriate commitment, finance and advice, many such co-operatives are succeeding. The essence of a co-operative is that the management of the enterprise is in the hands of the workers themselves, who make decisions as to the operation of the business, make appointments to managerial posts, and control the finances of the business; and, most important, all profits made are retained within the business, rather than being distributed as dividends to members. Furthermore, if the co-operative registers under the Industrial and Provident Societies Act 1965, the enterprise can enjoy the benefits of corporate status and limited liability, as long as the basic requirements for a co-operative (especially with regard to profits, and to control of the enterprise) are satisfied.

Given this range of forms of business enterprise, it will be appreciated that it is very important for any business to adopt the form which will be most appropriate in the circumstances, and which will provide optimum benefits and flexibility (especially with regard to the possibilities of expanding the business, raising capital or protecting individuals' financial interests) for the personnel involved.

If we now turn to other aspects of the business environment, we can identify a number of ways in which the state, through law, helps provide a supportive, and in many ways protective, milieu within which economic activity can be profitably pursued. To begin with, the law of contract itself (discussed fully in chapter 11) can be seen as a framework within which businesses can conduct their affairs on a stable and predictable footing, although there is evidence that, in practice, people in business tend to avoid close entanglement with the law and with legal actions, preferring to settle their disputes in other ways such as arbitration (see chapter 6). And the law relating to cheques and other negotiable instruments (discussed in chapter 5) provides an important framework for the execution of convenient, flexible and legally protected business transactions.

Another important aspect of law which has special relevance for economic activity is that relating to *insurance* (see chapter 9). While every business venture clearly involves a degree of risk (for example, as to whether there is a viable market for the goods which a company produces, or whether the goods produced are priced in a way which reflects customer demand), there are some eventualities which can be anticipated, and their effects offset or mitigated. Suppose that a factory is burned down, a shop is ransacked by burglars, an employee is injured at work and sues for compensation, or goods are destroyed or lost in transit by road, air or sea. It is clearly wise to try to guard against the losses thus incurred by taking out insurance policies to cover these and similar risks.

The law relating to insurance is governed partly by common law and partly by statute. An insurance agreement is a contract, and as such is subject to the ordinary legal rules relating to contracts. In addition, however, it is firmly established at common law that insurance contracts are contracts *uberrimae fidei* ('of the utmost good faith'), which means that the person wishing to take out the insurance policy (the proposer) is under a strict legal duty to disclose, truthfully and accurately, all material facts to the insurance company. Failure to do this will enable the insurer to avoid all liability under the insurance contract. This rule applies to all insurance contracts, though what constitutes a 'material fact' in any given case will of course depend upon the circumstances: in essence, the insurer will want to know of any fact which might affect the decision to take on the risk, and invariably will require answers to questions put to the proposer which the insurer considers significant in assessing that risk. This information is vital, because of the very nature of an insurance contract, which is basically an agreement whereby the insurer undertakes to indemnify or compensate the proposer for any loss sustained by the latter which is covered by the terms of the agreement. Usually, business enterprises insure against the kind of losses mentioned above. We might also note that car-drivers *must* insure against (at the very least) injury to third parties[18] and passengers, this being required by statute,[19] and prudent householders will normally insure against damage both to the house itself and to the contents of the house.

It is important to appreciate that the insured person or business will only be covered for risks specified in the insurance policy, and there will invariably be certain specified eventualities which are *excluded* from the cover. For example, a typical motor insurance policy will exclude any claim arising from accidents while the car is being used for racing or other sporting purposes. In exchange for the insurance cover, the proposer pays a *premium*, usually annually, which is payment for that cover. The amount of the premium will depend upon the nature of the insurance taken out, and on the extent of the risk being undertaken by the insurer. For instance, if a racing-driver wishes to insure against injury arising from racing, then, given the very high risks involved in that activity, the driver must expect insurance premiums to be extremely high – if, indeed, an insurance company can be found which is prepared to take on so great a risk.

The attractiveness of insurance to business enterprises is clear. It is a means of protection against losses arising from certain kinds of risk, and thus provides a degree of security for the enterprise. In addition, however, there are certain statutory requirements relating to insurance in business, notably the requirement contained in the Employers' Liability (Compulsory Insurance) Act 1969 that employers take out insurance to cover themselves against claims by their employees who suffer illness or injury arising out of the course of their employment. This requirement not only protects the business enterprise, but also clearly offers protection to the employee who, in the absence of such insurance, may find that the employer (especially if the business is a small one) is unable to meet the compensation claim.

The last-mentioned statute is a good example of the state's intervention, through the use of law, in a situation where the common law is held to be inadequate to deal with a particular matter, or where law-makers take the view that public policy requires that a particular risk (in this case, to employees) is too important to be left to the individual concerned (in this case, the employer's choice as to whether or not to insure against liability to employees). It is thus one instance of the state, acting through law, stepping into a situation with a *positive direction* to the person or group affected: here, the law does not say 'do this if you wish, but follow this procedure if you wish to enjoy the protection of the law', but rather, simply, 'you *must* do this'.

The state has increasingly intervened, often through the use of law, in many areas affecting economic activity, and has done so, moreover, in ways which can be described as *directing* economic behaviour. This intervention can operate on a number of levels. At one level, the state may impose a duty on all employers to insure, as in the example just noted. At a more general level, the state may involve individual enterprises in national economic planning, with a view either to combating particular problems, such as inflation, or to directing the economy towards an improved 'state of health', such as through the encouragement of enhanced levels of export of goods. In considering such developments, we must now address ourselves once more to an earlier theme – that of the changing role of the state – and try to identify those areas of legal regulation which may be said to have a much more positive and directive thrust than the nineteenth-century pattern of relatively passive support for economic activity.

The changing functions of state and law

During the last few centuries the modern national state has had an increasing tendency to become the Leviathan of which Hobbes wrote, not only the repository of physical and legal restraining power and the protector of the nation against an external enemy, but also the main directive force in the shaping of the economic and social life of the nation.[20]

In order to understand something of the changing function of the state with regard to the regulation of economic activity, we must examine two closely related problems of analysis. The first concerns the nature of a country's economy, and the second concerns the nature and function of the state and its relationship to that particular economic structure.

Capitalism in its 'purest' form involves, among other things, an economic structure which is responsive only to the forces of free competition in the marketplace. The ideas of free trade and competition, the economic idea of the 'law of supply and demand', the absence of state interference or guidance, and the uncontrolled accumulation of private property and of profit would characterize an economic system which we would term a *private enterprise economy*. Britain in the nineteenth century and the United States in the twentieth are probably the instances which come closest to this 'pure' model, although in both cases the uncontrolled forces of the free competitive market have been subject to some state regulation through law. In the twentieth century in particular, the purity of the private enterprise economy, though still regarded by many as the ideal economic system in a 'free world', has been diluted by the perceived necessity by governments throughout the Western world to intervene more and more in order to try to offset some of the economically damaging consequences of unbridled freedom of competition.[21]

At the other end of the spectrum, there have emerged during this century national economies based on the ideals of socialism, in which private enterprise is replaced by *public* ownership and control, through the state, of the national economy. By means of the nationalization of industries, central economic planning and rigorous regulation of nearly all aspects of economic activity, the state endeavours to maximize economic efficiency in the interests, not of private companies and individuals, but of the whole community. It is this type of economy, whose principles were so deeply embedded in the political systems and ideologies of the 'communist countries' of eastern Europe, which has collapsed in the recent massive political and economic upheavals in those countries.

In practical terms, most Western countries, including Britain, operate with economic systems which fall between these two 'pure' types – systems which we usually call *mixed economies*. Here, private enterprise operates side by side with some degree of public ownership and control, and though the precise 'mix' will vary from country to country, the tendency has been for public utility industries (power, communications and transport), coal and steel to be taken over by public corporations. This is partly because of the central importance of these industries to the national economy, and partly because they involve matters of national rather than local or sectional development and policy. Of course, the divergent economic philosophies of successive governments within any particular country can mean that the 'mix' of public and private sectors will change over time. In Britain the Conversative administrations of the 1980s and early 1990s, wedded to ideals of free private enterprise and hence denationalization, have returned certain industries, at least partially, to private hands. British Telecommunications, the gas industry, the water authorities and British Airways have been subject to legislation bringing about a considerable degree of privatization, and the Conservative government elected in 1992 stated its intention to extend privatization to other industries. Labour governments, on the other hand, have tended to be more or less committed to programmes of nationalization and *public* ownership and control, although it remains to be seen whether future Labour administrations will place re-nationalization of these industries on its political agenda. In making these observations, we are, of course, referring to the relationship between state and economy, and this brings us to our second problem: the changing nature and function of the state itself in modern Western society.

As we have seen, there are various perspectives which can be taken on the 'state', especially when we begin to delve more deeply into the issues which our simple working definition raises. Broadly speaking, however, the most widely held view of the modern British state is that which we would term 'pluralist'. There are many definitions of this term, but the following are offered as principal defining characteristics of the 'pluralist' perspective.

First of all, pluralism assumes that the role of the state is *supportive*, and not *directive*, of social and economic affairs. Its functions as regards the economy are therefore akin to those discussed earlier – the maintenance of a social, political and economic environment which is conducive to the smooth running of society's affairs, the provision of machinery for the resolution of disputes and conflict, and the provision of protection – legal and otherwise – for legitimate economic interests. Second, the pluralist view, whilst recognizing the existence of diverse and often conflicting interest-groups in society, holds that despite the differential possession of political and economic power among such groups, a kind of equilibrium is none the less maintained through the democratic political process, so that no single interest-group can dominate politically or economically. Third, the state has, as a major function, an important part to play as *mediator* between competing groups, favouring no particular group but negotiating compromises as solutions to conflicts of interest between them. Fourth, this political and economic edifice stands on a bedrock of *value-consensus*; the assumption that agreement exists, broadly speaking, within society as to its political, social and economic institutions and policies, and also as to the legitimacy of those institutions and policies – a legitimacy which in turn springs from the democratic right of all individuals and groups to involve themselves and have their say in the political processes of society (see chapter 1).

Standing in direct opposition to the pluralist perspective is the marxist model of capitalist society. This view holds that the state acts in the interest of capital (that is, of powerful economic interests) which it strives to maintain and protect against the opposing interests of the working class; far from being democratic, the capitalist political structure reflects, and is responsive to, the needs and dictates of capital. In reality, according to marxism, the 'democratic' nature of that political structure is an ideological construct serving both to obscure the 'real' social relations of capitalist production and to maintain an essentially exploitative economic system. Marxist views, while differing from the pluralist perspective in crucial respects, may none the less acknowledge a relatively passive, supportive role for the capitalist state – indeed, the state in Britain maintained this role during the very period of which Marx was writing. Such views may be contrasted with those perspectives on the state which are usually termed *corporatist*, and which present a radically different function for the state in this particular respect.

Although there have been many contributions to the analytical literature on the growth of the corporate state, there would seem to be considerable diversity of views as to the precise definition and delineation of the term.[22] Essentially, corporatism refers to a *mode of participation* by the state, and to the proposition that the state in modern Western society has taken on, and continues to take on, a high degree of centralized, *direct control* of national economic affairs. Some writers contrast 'liberal' with 'state' or 'authoritarian' corporatism: the former arising within liberal-democratic societies, and usually co-existing with the social and political mores of liberal democracy, while the latter tends to be associated with totalitarian regimes of, say, Hitler's Germany or the old Soviet Russia. Liberal corporatism, growing as it does out of systems of mixed economy, thus 'combines *private ownership* and *State control*. It contrasts with capitalism's private ownership and private control and with State socialism's State ownership and State control.'[23] The liberal corporatist state, then, reaches into private enterprise in an active, positive way, involving it in exercises of economic policy and planning and in the regulation of industrial relations through negotiations between trade unions and employers, requiring it to conform to state-defined economic guidelines, and generally adopting a much more directive role in economic activity at a number of levels.

Can the term 'corporatist' be applied to the state in modern Britain? It is true that, at a number of levels and in a variety of ways, positive and directive state intervention in economic activity has occurred, and interventionist policies have frequently, though not invariably, been implemented through law. The last thirty years or so have seen many examples. In 1962 the National Economic Development Council (NEDC) was created as a means of involving leaders of industry, trade unions and ministers in discussions on the national economy. The Prices and Incomes Act 1966 and the 'freezes' on wages and prices imposed by the 1970–4 government were attempts to impose curbs on rising wage and price levels in the effort to control rising inflation and other economic problems; another example might be the Industry Act 1975, which created the National Enterprise Board, whose terms of reference included the development and assistance of the United Kingdom economy, the promotion of industrial efficiency and competitiveness, and the extension of public ownership in profitable areas. Another function of the NEB was stated to be the securing of 'large scale sustained investment to offset the short-term pull of market forces'.[24] The more recent Industrial Development Act 1982 dealt, among other things, with the creation of special areas for industrial development, and the provision of financial incentives for businesses to set themselves up in those areas; financial help for industry, which may involve reciprocal agreements and the imposition of conditions upon industries obtaining such aid; and the creation of the Industrial Development Advisory Board, comprising the Secretary of State and a number of members with wide experience of industry, banking, accountancy and finance. Other interventionist measures would include the control of anti-competitive business activity through the Fair Trading Act 1973 and the Competition Act 1980.

The ideology of Thatcherist policies during the 1980s, with their stated objectives of returning the economy to private hands, reducing the influence of government, and returning to a system of competitive market controls, did not in fact result in much more of a 'hands-off' approach by government. Although in June 1992 the Chancellor of the Exchequer announced the demise of the NEDC, stating that the 'era of corporatism' had long passed, new institutions have recently been created by statute, charged with the regulation of various sectors of the economy: the Financial Services Act 1986 is a good example. This Act includes powers to license and monitor financial organizations and creates new criminal offences (notably carrying on an investment business without authorization). Government involvement is written into the Act by means of the participation of the Secretary of State for Trade and Industry. Similarly, regulatory systems are in place regarding the part-privatized telecommunications and gas industries. It would seem that one of the essential characteristics of corporatism – active state involvement in the management of industry, commerce and business in general – will remain a feature of government in Britain at least until well into the 1990s.

One feature of liberal corporatism, however – the involvement of the trade unions in the management of the economy – has virtually disappeared, largely, it cannot be doubted, because of the decline in the influence of trade unions brought about by a series of statutes passed during the 1980s. Attempts to control the activities of trade unions, as we have already seen, are by no means new. The long struggle by unions to achieve legal recognition, and the various devices by which the courts, in particular, tried to curb industrial action, taught the trade union movement long ago to regard the law with some suspicion.

None the less, both Labour and Conservative governments in post-war Britain perceived trade union activity as potentially and actually disruptive of the smooth running of the economy, and in their different ways sought to regulate trade union activity more closely. The Labour government during the 1960s introduced plans to legislate to control trade unions, though it was the Conservative government which came to power in 1970 which finally introduced legislation in the form of the ill-fated Industrial Relations Act 1971, in response to what many saw as a continuing crisis in industrial relations manifested by a series of strikes in a number of industries. This Act dealt with the regulation of various aspects of union activity, and was unpopular with trade unionists and many employers. Critics regarded the Act as a clumsy and inappropriate means of dealing with situations which often needed a more delicate touch, especially over collective bargaining between unions and management.

The 1971 Act was repealed in 1974, when Labour was again returned to power, and there followed a period during which the government tried to base its dealings with the trade union movement on a more informal *voluntary* basis through, first, the 'social contract' and then the 'social compact'. These were agreements between government and the TUC which promised closer involvement for the latter in matters of economic policy, in exchange for the TUC's undertaking that matters such as bargaining over wage increases would be handled in a voluntary though 'responsible' way. In addition, the Labour government undertook in 1974 to investigate ways in which employees, through their trade unions, might play a more active role in negotiation and company planning through representation on company boards. This proposal (which some would regard as a typical corporatist-state development) led to the establishment of the Committee of Inquiry on Industrial Democracy (the Bullock Committee), which reported in 1977.[25] The report contained recommendations that union representation should be introduced as an extension of collective bargaining, though the government's White Paper which followed the report fell short of the full Bullock proposals,[26] and of course the Labour government itself was defeated in the general election of 1979.

The Conservative governments of the 1980s and early 1990s, not surprisingly, showed rather different attitudes to industrial relations, and a series of statutes concerning trade unions was enacted between 1980 and 1990. These statutes were ostensibly inspired largely by the then governments' conviction that the rights of the individual worker – whether a member of a trade union or not – needed strengthening, not in relation to the power of employers, but rather in relation to the collective power of the trade unions themselves. The Employment Acts of 1980, 1982, 1988 and 1990, and the Trade Union Act of 1984, provided, among other things, for the holding of secret ballots prior to industrial action, and the removal of legal protection for closed-shop agreements and to a large extent picketing during industrial action; 'secondary' industrial action (that is, the extension of industrial action against one employer to another employer not primarily involved in the original dispute)[27] has virtually become unlawful, as is industrial action inspired by alleged 'political' motivation as opposed to a genuine dispute with an employer. The individual worker's right *not* to join a union without incurring the risk of dismissal – a risk which is clearly present in the case of a closed-shop agreement – is now protected in a number of ways, though of course this particular development runs against the ideological commitment of many trade unionists to the proposition that only by uniting and acting collectively can parity with management in terms of bargaining power be achieved; the closed-shop agreement, it may be argued, is a logical consequence of this view. The government's position on this matter, however, has remained firm.

The Trade Union Act 1984 provided that periodic ballots of the members of unions must be carried out to ascertain whether members wish a portion of their subscriptions to be given to the Labour Party: the so-called political levy. Although there was considerable concern about the effect this might have upon Labour Party funds it is the case that the majority of trade unions have now carried out such a ballot, and the majority of members in all such ballots have voted to retain the political levy.

Taken as a whole, there can be no doubt whatever that this series of statutes has seriously weakened trade unions' legal powers and protections, and this systematic undermining of unions' previous legal position has been accompanied by an almost complete refusal to include trade unions in discussions on the national economy at government level. According to a major study (sponsored by, among others, the Department of Employment and the Advisory, Conciliation and Arbitration Service), whose findings were published in 1992,[28]

in 1980, two-thirds of workplaces were covered by a union agreement, but by 1990 the proportion was just over half. The number of dismissals per 1,000 workers rose from 9 in 1984 to 15 in 1990 ... the study shows that, contrary to the views of some commentators, there were 'major – and probably irreversible – changes' in employee relations in the 1980s, with the pace quickening towards the end of the decade ... The proportion of employees in union membership was down from 58 per cent by 1990 ... The sponsors [of the study] believe the report that collective bargaining between management and unions 'may no longer be characteristic of the economy', because of restructuring, privatisation and developments in the law.[29]

In a wholly different context, there has been a gradual development of direct regulation of business enterprises in a number of ways. The general picture of industrial and commercial activity in the private sector in Britain has changed radically over the years. Today, Britain's major industries revolve not so much around large numbers of small concerns, as was the pattern in the nineteenth century, but rather around huge multinational organizations which dominate the economic scene and exercise considerable economic and even political power.

We know that in Britain the big cigarette manufacturers account for over 80 per cent of production, that the big two electrical lamp manufacturers produce 65 per cent of the electric bulbs sold in Britain, that the three leading oil companies account for over 80 per cent of all petrol sold in the UK, and that one firm makes 80 per cent of all dry batteries sold.[30]

The growth of near-monopoly trading and certain other practices which have the effect of restricting freedom of competition is clearly antagonistic to any economic system based upon free private enterprise. In the United States, anti-monopoly ('anti-trust') legislation was first introduced at the beginning of this century, but the first British controls on mergers, through legislation, were introduced in 1965, the present law being contained in the Fair Trading Act 1973. This Act provides that the Director-General of Fair Trading must be informed of any merger (actual or intended), and may make recommendations about that merger to the Secretary of State. The latter may refer the matter to the Monopolies and Mergers Commission, a body charged with the responsibility for investigating whether or not the merger in question is against the public interest. If the commission is of the opinion that the merger does (or would) operate against the public interest by restricting competitiveness, then the Secretary of State may order that the merger does not take place, or if it has already done so, that the merged companies separate once again.

Apart from mergers and take-overs, it may happen that two or more enterprises, engaged in the same type of business, join together to agree between themselves on matters such as the price of the goods or services they produce, or the terms and conditions on which, or the people to whom, or the areas where, such goods and services are sold. Such agreements may be regarded in law as 'restrictive trade practices', tending to reduce freedom of competition, and may be referred, by virtue of the Restrictive Trade Practices Act 1976 and the Competition Act 1980, to the Director-General of Fair Trading and thence to the Restrictive Trade Practices Court. This area of law is complex and, in the opinion of one commentator at least, 'competition and consumer law are new and growing subjects, each taking up ground previously occupied by contract law, whilst growing away from it as successive statutory measures seek to serve the public interest better than was the case under the old regime'.[31] It is an area, too, where the complexities are multiplied by the impact of Britain's membership of the European Community, whose competition rules apply to all member states (see chapter 8). It is inappropriate to expand in detail on this part of the law, though it must clearly be recognized as another sphere of economic activity in which the state has intervened directly, providing for restrictions and controls 'in the public interest'[32] and in the interests of maintaining a competitive economic system.

In a period of sustained recession, with problems over the balance of payments, falling rates of profit and high levels of unemployment, many companies both large and small have experienced serious financial problems. Some larger companies may be able to put pressure on banks and other sources of borrowing (including the government) for aid, while many others, especially small businesses have simply gone into liquidation. High rates of inflation, fluctuations in the price of oil, on the international market, and pressure from international bodies such as the international Monetary Fund in the 1970s, gave way to a period of growth in the 1980s, which were indeed boom years for some, though the end of that decade and the early 1990s saw the onset of a deep recession, with the usual accompaniments of high rates of unemployment, fluctuations in interest rates, and lower consumer spending power. Although the main theme of this chapter has been the examination of the expansion of direct state regulation of economic activity, it must not be forgotten that economic policies have repercussions on other spheres of social life. Indeed, it is with respect to the *social* consequences of economic policy that many people were deeply critical of the post-1979 governments. Curbs on public expenditure have inevitable implications for the provision of welfare services – housing, health, social security and other benefits, pensions, and the education and social services. In all these areas, it seems that a strong central government is able effectively to subordinate the needs of the sick, the elderly, the young and the poor to what it sees as a higher commitment to saving and regenerating an ailing capitalist economic structure. These economic policies have also brought massive unemployment, which in turn generates serious social problems arising from the effects of redundancy and the presence of a large population, of young people in particular, with little prospect of jobs, despite a series of government-run schemes for youth training. It seems certain, however, that for the foreseeable future the state will retain its hold on the active direction of the economy, whichever government may be returned to power in the years to come.

Summary

In this chapter we have explored something of the transition through which our society has gone over the last hundred years or so with regard to the relationship between law, state and economy. In particular, we have seen how the nineteenth-century emphasis on *laisser-faire* ideas, carrying the implications of freedom from state intervention and control in economic life, has given way to a context in which the state, through various government policies, enters into the economic life of the country in a much more active and directive way. These changes have not been without their accompanying problems and tensions, most of which have yet to be resolved. Many of the changes are the outcomes of political programmes pursued by successive governments, against a background of many different groups competing for a voice in the economic affairs of the country. Often, such groups call upon the use of the law and the legal system, either as a force for change, in their attempts at reform, or as a force for conservatism, in their attempts to resist further change which, in their view, might be to their disadvantage. It is hard to resist the conclusion that, contrary to the pluralist view of the state, it is the demands of the powerful that are most readily heard, but we shall examine the strength of such a conclusion in more detail as we explore other contexts involving legal regulation in later chapters.

4
Some important legal concepts

The importance of legal concepts will already be appreciated from the preceding discussions, in which we mentioned such notions as 'freedom' and 'justice' and their role within the legal system. Apart from these concepts, however, which play a part in influencing the content and operation of the legal system, there are other fundamental concepts *within* the law itself, whose significance must be understood. Such concepts as 'ownership' and 'possession', for example, referring to what may be quite complex relationships between individuals and concrete things, are basic to the notions about property embodied in law; these particular ideas are dealt with in chapter 5. At a rather more fundamental level are concepts of 'rights', 'duties' and 'persons', which are so basic to the operation and implementation of rules of law that we can think of them as the 'units of legal currency' whereby rules become 'translated' and applied to specific social activities. If we say, for example, 'Jones owns a car', then in the event of Smith, another car-owner, driving his vehicle so that it collides with Jones' car, the fact that Jones' interest in her car is one of 'ownership' will give rise to all kinds of possible relationships between Jones and Smith, turning on the questions as to what rights Jones may have in law against Smith, and what *duties* Smith may have infringed in respect of Jones and her damaged car. In this chapter, these basic legal concepts and the various attempts made by legal writers to analyse and classify them will be examined critically; in the second part of the chapter, the idea of 'legal personality', or what constitutes a 'person' in the eyes of the law, will be considered with various examples.

Rights and duties: problems of analysing legal concepts

... the law consists of certain types of rules regulating human conduct and ... the administration of justice is concerned with enforcing the rights and duties created by such rules. The concept of a right is accordingly one of fundamental significance in legal theory ...[1]

What do lawyers mean when they speak of 'legal rights'? We have seen the difficulties of analysing the idea of 'rights' in the general context of 'human' or 'civil' rights in chapter 2, and we may stress once again here that the fact that a social group might recognize something as a 'moral right' does not necessarily imply that it is a *legally protected* right; furthermore, when speaking of such 'human rights', we are making statements about a social group's adherence or non-adherence to a particular moral and political code which contains such principles. Such a code may or may not be applied, or even recognized, in any given social group or society.[2] In Britain, for example, considerable social and political value is placed on the idea of 'freedom of speech'. The extent to which we enjoy such a freedom might, according to some critics, be contrasted with the relative absence of such a freedom in states such as China or in other countries governed by totalitarian regimes. Ideas such as freedom of speech, of movement, or of religion are inevitably aspects of a nation's political and cultural make-up; changes in the social and political structure will almost invariably be accompanied by changes in the ways in which, and the extent to which, various human or civil rights may be enjoyed. The major changes which have taken place in recent years in eastern European countries provide clear evidence of the extent to which individual rights are inextricably connected to the apparatuses of state.

Our concern in this chapter is with the much more specific issue of the acknowledgement and protection of *legal* rights: what does it mean when we speak of X as 'having a right to be paid a debt owed by Y', or of A as 'having a right to compensation in respect of injuries caused by B'?

Legal writers have at various times offered different analyses of the concepts of 'rights' and 'duties'.[3] Few of these analyses have met with unqualified acceptance by critics, but they have provided us with useful insights into the analytical problems involved. Let us look briefly at some of the many approaches to the problem in order to appreciate both the insights and the difficulties.

Salmond, whose *Jurisprudence* was first published in 1902,[4] regarded legal rights as being essentially connected with the idea of 'interests', which he defined as 'things which are to a man's advantage'. He pointed out that rights and interests are separate but connected: a right protects the interests, 'which accordingly form the subject matter of [a man's] rights but are different from them'.[5] Certainly, it is easy to think of legal rules which appear to embody rights protecting interests – the right to defend oneself and one's property from attack and intrusion (the right to self-defence) may be seen as protecting one's interests in life and property, for instance. But Salmond himself admitted that not all interests are protected by legal rights (it may be in my interest to accumulate wealth by appropriating yours, but the law of theft prohibits my doing so). Moreover, the *trust* is an illustration of a case where a person may be able to exercise legal rights (as where trustees administer and manage property entrusted to their care) despite the fact that the person has no *personal* interests protected by those rights: where there is a trust, the interest in the property remains at all times in the beneficiary, on whose behalf the property is managed. The only way in which we can ascertain whether a particular interest is protected by a legal right, then, is to determine whether a legal rule affecting that interest exists at all, and then to discover the way in which that legal rule, if it exists, actually operates in relation to the particular interest in question.

Sometimes it has been argued that legal rights exist only where the holder of the right can enforce it by bringing an action in law. The fallacy of this argument is shown by Hart,[6] who points out that a person may be physically incapable of preventing the unauthorized taking of his property; we do not conclude, however, that the person therefore has no legal right to the property. Similarly, if we take an example of an absence of legal, as opposed to physical, power to enforce the right: the possibility for an aggrieved party to bring certain legal actions only remains open for a limited period, after which time that party cannot sue the other person. Some debts are subject to this rule, and the effect is that after the given time-period has expired, the action in law is said to be 'statute-barred'. If Jones owes Smith money, and Smith is unable to bring a legal action against Jones to enforce his legal right to be repaid because the time-period has elapsed, then we may say that Smith's 'remedial right'[7] (the procedural right afforded in law for the provision of a legal remedy) is no longer available. This limitation does not, however, affect Smith's 'primary right' to be paid by Jones. This right will continue to exist despite the absence of a legal power by Smith to *enforce* that primary right. It would seem, then, that the connection between having a legal right and the power (physical or legal) to enforce it does not provide us with a key to understanding and analysing the concept of legal rights.

A number of writers have linked the idea of 'rights' with that of 'duties'. To return to our example of the debt owed by Jones to Smith: if Jones owes Smith £100, then we say that Smith has a legal *right* to be paid £100 by Jones, and that Jones is under a corresponding legal *duty* to repay the money. The 'right' and the 'duty' in this case are, so to speak, opposite sides of the same coin. But does this necessarily mean that *all* legal rights imply corresponding legal duties, and vice versa? Certainly this was the view taken by Salmond: as the current editor of Salmond's *Jurisprudence* explains the position, 'on this view, every duty must be a duty *towards* some person or persons, in whom, therefore, a corresponding right is vested. And conversely every right must be a right *against* some person or persons, upon whom, therefore, a correlative duty is imposed.'[8]

The contrary view, that duties do *not* necessarily imply corresponding rights, was taken by Austin, among others, writing in the nineteenth century. He distinguished between *relative* duties, which, as in our example of the debt, involve corresponding rights, and *absolute* duties, which are imposed by law without any corresponding rights being implied or involved. Examples of absolute legal duties may be found within the area of criminal law. We are all under legal duties not to commit crimes, but it is not easy to identify the subject of corresponding 'rights'. To the argument, 'it is the community, through the agencies of prosecution, which holds and exercises the right to deal with the offender', it may be replied that the prosecution of an offender may well be regarded as a *duty* rather than a right; and a criminal prosecution does not of itself present the victim of the crime, still less the community in general, with any form of *remedy* in recognition of any infringed right. Moreover, assuming that the criminal offender is caught, prosecuted and convicted, many would assert that the sentencing judge is under a legal duty to pass an appropriate sentence. Surely this cannot force us to the conclusion that the offender has a corresponding legal *right* to be fined or imprisoned?

Even if we accept the distinction between relative and absolute duties, we are left with the difficulty of ascertaining whether legal rights imply corresponding duties. It is here that the term 'rights' is perhaps at its most inadequate: one term cannot possibly accommodate the complex and varied situations within the law where a particular relationship between persons needs to be analysed. The problems of analysing such cases, and specifying appropriate terms to describe such relationships, were confronted, in particular, by Hohfeld, an American legal writer whose *Fundamental Legal Conceptions* appeared in 1913.[9] After pointing out the analytical dangers of using phrases such as 'rights' and 'duties' indiscriminately, and of attempting to reduce all legal relationships to these unit-terms, Hohfeld proceeded to elucidate his own classification of 'jural opposites and correlatives'. He substituted for the general terms 'rights' and 'duties' a set of alternative terms referring to legally specific relationships. These jural correlatives and opposites have been presented diagrammatically[10] as follows:

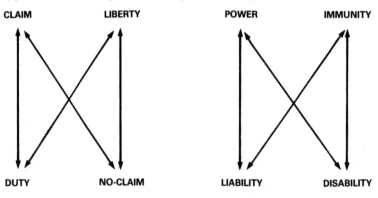

The *vertical* arrows link jural correlatives. This idea may be stated thus: 'the holding by X of a *claim* to be repaid money which s/he has lent to Y implies the presence of a *duty* in Y to repay the money to X'. The second pairing may be illustrated by the statement 'the holding by X of a *liberty* to enter and remain on his own land implies a *no-claim* in Y, who has no such liberty to enter and remain on X's land'. The correlatives 'power' and 'liability' are shown in the example of a power held by a local authority to purchase property compulsorily (provided by various legal enactments). The authority may be said to hold a *power*, while the landowner whose property is being purchased (whether s/he likes it or not) is said to be under a legal *liability* to have the land so purchased. The fourth pair of correlatives may be seen in the example of the defence of 'privilege' in that part of the law of tort relating to defamation (libel and slander). It has been the case since the Bill of Rights 1688 that if a member of Parliament makes a defamatory statement in the course of parliamentary debate, the person defamed may not bring an action for defamation against the MP, who may, in Hohfield's terminology, be said to enjoy an *immunity* from that legal action, while the aggrieved person is under a legal *disability* in respect of that action.

The *diagonal* arrows connect jural opposites: this idea is somewhat simpler. If X has a *claim* in relation to a person in respect of some matter, then X cannot at the same time have a *no-claim* in respect of that person or subject-matter; if Y is *liable* in respect of a given legal rule, then Y cannot at the same time be *immune* from falling under that legal rule, and so on.

Not even this complex classification, under which many legal relationships may be successfully pigeon-holed, has been immune from criticism. The terms used in the schema are in some cases (such as the idea of 'no-claim', or 'no-right') not legally recognized or used; and it may be argued that the seemingly simple notion of the 'legal power' may in fact denote quite different ideas. The 'legal power', or capacity, of the ordinary individual to marry, make a will or make contracts, none of which require any special status, may be contrasted with the 'legal powers' of specific officials or institutions, such as government ministers or local authorities, which may be better thought of in terms of 'authority'.[11] The same kind of objection may be made concerning the single category 'duty': civil-law duties differ in various ways from those of criminal law, for example, and arguably require a much more detailed analysis than Hohfeld provides.[12]

Despite these and other analytical problems, many of which might be remedied by elaboration of the original schema, Hohfeld's work does throw valuable light on the problems of trying to elucidate 'legal rights' and 'legal duties'. So great have these problems proved, in fact, that the modern tendency is to reject the quest for an all-embracing catalogue or definition of the terms, and to turn instead to the exploration of the proposition that the meanings of these general terms will differ according to the contexts in which they are used.

This, broadly, is the argument put by Hart.[13] He tries to show how words such as 'rights' and 'duties' are simply not amenable to definition through mere synonym, but must be examined in the specific legal contexts in which they are commonly used, in order for their meanings in those contexts to be understood.[14] Hart has not been alone in pointing to the dangers of ambiguities of terminology. Glanville Williams has shown[15] how words in common legal use, such as 'possession' and 'ownership' (both having provided headaches for would-be definers), are often used in different ways in different contexts. Lloyd, in the original Preface to his *Introduction to Jurisprudence*,[16] explained his own attraction to approaches which are sensitive to the importance of linguistic accuracy.

Taking Hart's approach as an example: he attempts to introduce a mode of elucidation of legal concepts by specifying particular contexts and conditions in which words such as 'right' and 'duty' are characteristically used. Thus, rather than seeking a simple synonym for the word 'right', Hart instead presents the following as an elucidation of the expression 'a legal right';

(1) A statement of the form 'X has a right' is true if the following conditions are satisfied:

    (a) there is in existence a legal system.

    (b) under a rule or rules of the system some other person Y is, in the events which have happened, obliged to do or abstain from some action.

    (c) This obligation is made by law dependent on the choice either of X or some other person authorised to act on his behalf so that either Y is bound to do or abstain from some action only if X (or some authorised person) so chooses or alternatively only until X (or such person) chooses otherwise.

(2) A statement of the form 'X has a right' is used to draw a conclusion of law in a particular case which falls under such rules.[17]

This formula helps us fill in something of the formal legal contextual background to the statement 'X has a right', although it does presuppose the existence of a clear legal rule under which the rights and obligations can be seen to apply. Unfortunately, as Hart himself emphasized in another article,[18] there are many legal rules which are not, at any given moment, clear-cut as regards their application. Such a rule, to adopt Hart's own example, may forbid you to take a vehicle into a public park: 'Plainly this forbids an automobile, but what about bicycles, roller skates, toy automobiles? What about aeroplanes? Are these . . . to be called "vehicles" for the purposes of the rule or not?'[19] There is, within any given rule, a 'core' of plain and settled meaning; in such a case, Hart's formulation of the idea of 'a legal right' will be fitting. But what of the doubtful cases – those cases which, as Hart puts it, fall into the area of the 'penumbra' around the 'core' of meaning? There are many such 'grey areas' involved in legal rules where we cannot, with any certainty, make sense of the case by using Hart's elucidation; and where the scope of a rule is unclear then the scope of relations falling under that rule is also unclear.

When a new legal rule is created, for instance (either by Parliament or through judicial law-making in deciding cases), it is not immediately clear what the limits of the applicability of the rule are. Take the well-known case of *Donoghue* v. *Stevenson*[20] in 1932, for example.

In this case, the plaintiff, Mrs Donoghue, had been bought a bottle of ginger-beer by a friend in a café. The ginger-beer, unknown to anyone, contained a decomposing snail which could not be detected by visual examination because the bottle was made of dark glass. The plaintiff had drunk some of the liquid, and then poured out the remainder, on doing which she saw the snail's remains, which floated out of the bottle. As a result of seeing this, coupled with the fact that she had already consumed part of the contents, she suffered shock and gastro-enteritis. She sued the manufacturer of the ginger-beer, Stevenson, on the ground that he owed consumers in her position a duty to ensure that such contamination did not occur, and that she therefore had a right to compensation in respect of her illness. Outside the law of contract (and there was no contract entered into by the plaintiff in this case) there was no clear ground on which such a legal action, in the tort of negligence, could be brought. The court decided that, on these facts, there *was* a good cause of action which might be brought against the manufacturer; but prior to that decision, if we asked, 'Has the plaintiff a right to compensation?' then, if we applied Hart's formula, the answer would have to be, in such an unclear area of law, 'Perhaps; perhaps not. It is not possible to give a firm answer.' Even after the decision in *Donoghue* v. *Stevenson*, which decided that a manufacturer owes a duty to the ultimate consumer to take reasonable care over the preparation of the goods which he produces, it was not always possible to give a clear, unequivocal answer to a case where a consumer was asserting a claim of right against a manufacturer;

for the law does not stand still, and legal rules are changed, extended, limited or modified in the course of future disputes which are decided by the courts.

Hart's analytical device, then, only takes us so far in understanding the nature of 'rights' in law. It does not explain the dynamic quality of legal rules (and hence of legal rights created through those rules). It does not explain the conditions under which new or modified rules may emerge.[21] Hart's contribution in his elucidation of the phrase 'a legal right' lies in the emphasis that words and phrases referring to legal concepts must be examined in their particular contexts and usages. These contexts, however, are constituted not only by the *formal* conditions of legal rules and the framework of legal institutions, but also by *their* contexts in turn: the structure of legal, social, economic and political events, circumstances and developments. Here, we must ask a rather different kind of question from the ones to which Hart's formulation is addressed.

To understand what is meant by such terms as 'rights' and 'duties' in law, it is suggested that an approach is needed which takes into account certain fundamental requirements or conditions. In addition to considering the part played by *interests*, and by the possession or otherwise of physical or legal *power* to enforce rights, it is surely also important to clarify the relationship between the *legal* structure of rules, rights, duties and other legal phenomena, and the *social* and *political* settings from which these legal phenomena emerge. The approach taken here attempts to take account of these relationships, and of the dynamic aspect of laws, rights and rules. Rather than viewing rights, duties and rules, then, as static, presupposed phenomena, the changing nature of law and society is considered, and rights and duties are seen as part of a *continuing process* of legal regulation, during which those rights and duties will emerge, undergo modifications or extensions, or may, in time, be extinguished altogether. The 'legal right' is, after all, merely a symbolic term, referring to a continuing process of legal regulation of a given social activity, and it is this legal regulation, together with the legal relationships which arise from that regulation – relationships which we speak of as involving 'rights' and 'duties' – which is the focus of our enquiry.

The adoption of this processual approach opens up three distinct stages in that process. First, there is the claim of right: when Mrs Donoghue, in the case discussed above, brought her legal action against the defendant Stevenson, she was in effect arguing that 'she ought to be accorded a right' in respect of her injuries. Note the two aspects to this claim: the plaintiff was claiming a right to a legal remedy (a 'remedial right') which, she argued, rested upon a basic right not to be injured through manufacturers' negligence (a 'primary right'). Such a primary right was previously unknown in law.[22] This plaintiff was therefore inviting the court to recognize her claim, and the House of Lords, by a majority of three judges to two, duly did so. *Why* did the court accept that Mrs Donoghue's claim was legitimate? In the absence of any general laws protecting the consumer in such situations as this, the court felt, as can be discerned from various passages in the leading judgment of Lord Atkin in the case, that the law *ought* to provide a remedy for such loss or injury:

It is said that the law . . . is that the poisoned consumer has no remedy against the negligent manufacturer. If this were the result of the authorities I should consider the result a grave defect in the law . . . I do not think so ill of our jurisprudence as to suppose that its principles are so remote from the ordinary needs of civilized society and the ordinary claims it makes upon its members as to deny a legal remedy where there is so obviously a social wrong.[23]

The court was, as can be seen, recognizing the general social need for some form of remedy for aggrieved consumers who suffer loss through negligence by manufacturers, and thus recognizing Mrs Donoghue's claim of right as worthy of protection in law. This first stage, the *claim of right*, is invariably the start of the process whereby rights become embodied in legal rules. Such a claim may be brought before a court, as in this case, through litigation; or it may be presented before Parliament,[24] the objective being to secure new legislation which will recognize and protect the interests concerned through the provision of new rights and duties. Even when a legal rule already exists, a plaintiff who brings an action based upon that rule will also be exerting a claim of right, for, as we shall see in chapter 7 when we consider the operation in law of the doctrine of precedent and the problems of statutory interpretation, the courts are continually being invited by plaintiffs and by prosecutors to bring a novel situation within the ambit of an existing legal rule. Indeed, this is the one way in which the law changes and is brought into line, where the judges think it appropriate, with changing social conditions.

The case of *Home Office* v. *Dorset Yacht Co Ltd*[25] in 1970 serves to illustrate the point. Although many cases decided since *Donoghue* v. *Stevenson* had widened the basic principle contained in that case so as to encompass situations involving relationships between persons other than just manufacturers and consumers,[26] this case raised an entirely novel proposition. A group of borstal trainees had been taken on a training exercise to an island in Poole harbour. They were supervised by three borstal officers who, in breach of their instructions, went to bed one night and left the trainees unsupervised. Seven of the boys escaped and went on board a yacht, which collided with the plaintiffs' yacht. The trainees then boarded the plaintiffs' yacht and caused considerable damage. The plaintiffs sued the Home Office, the supervisors' employer, claiming compensation for the supervisors' alleged negligence which, they argued, was the cause, in law, of the damage.

Among the various questions for the House of Lords was whether there was any duty owed by the defendants towards the plaintiffs, and as Lord Diplock put it, 'this is the first time that this specific question has been posed at a higher judicial level than that of a county court'.[27] Although clearly far removed from the *Donoghue* situation, the House of Lords held, by a majority, that the Home Office was under a duty of care towards the plaintiffs. In the words of Lord Reid,

where negligence is involved the tendency has been to apply principles analogous to those stated by Lord Atkin . . . [and] . . . I can see nothing to prevent our approachng the present case with Lord Atkin's principles in mind.[28]

Now, in terms of the first stage of the 'rights process', the plaintiffs were presenting a claim of right in a context in which the court, if it recognized and accepted that claim, had to apply the law of negligence to a situation in which it had not been applied before.[29] The fact that the court in this case was prepared to accept the validity of the plaintiffs' claim, and decide that on the alleged facts of the case there *could* be a duty owed by the defendants to the plaintiffs, brings us to consider the second stage in the process: that of legal *recognition* of the claimed rights. As implied above, such recognition will usually take the form of either a successful outcome for the plaintiff in a case brought before a court, or a new Act of Parliament which embodies the claimed rights in new legal rules. It must be said, however, that in the former case a court might recognize a claim of right without necessarily proceeding to the next stage in the process – that of *protection* of the primary right by the provision of a legal remedy in the case before the court.

A classic example of this was the case of *Hedley Byrne and Co. Ltd* v. *Heller and Partners*[30] in 1964. This was a decision of the House of Lords, and was the culmination of a long and complicated series of cases in the law of tort which concerned the question as to whether, and in what circumstances, a plaintiff might recover compensation in respect of financial loss suffered as a result of relying on a negligently-made statement by the defendant. In the case itself, the plaintiffs were advertising agents who wished to ascertain the credit-worthiness of a potential client. They enquired about this matter of the client's bankers (the defendants), who replied that the client company was financially sound. Relying on these references, the plaintiffs spent a considerable amount of money on behalf of the client, and when the latter went into liquidation they suffered a substantial loss. The statements made by the defendants had been untrue, and had been made negligently, although the defendants had made it clear that they accepted no responsibility for the statements they had made. The House of Lords acknowledged that in such (limited) circumstances, where there is a 'special relationship' between plaintiff and defendant (such as that between banker and legitimate enquirer), there *may* be liability for negligent misstatement: that is, the plaintiffs' *claim of right* was *recognized* by the court as capable of protection. On the specific facts of the case, however, the plaintiffs obtained no legal remedy (that is, no legal *protection*) because the defendants had explicitly denied any responsibility for the statements they had made.

It is necessary to bear in mind the possibility of a plaintiff's failing to obtain the protection, through a remedy, of a recognized right through legal technicalities or by reason of some other material factor in the case. In general, however, when we analyse a case in which a plaintiff is successful and obtains a legal remedy (be it compensation, an injunction restraining the defendant from pursuing particular activities, or some other form of redress) we shall see these stages in the 'rights' process: the initial claim of right, the recognition that the claimed right is capable and worthy of legal protection, and the provision of that protection through a remedy. Of course, in many cases a plaintiff will fail to convince the court that the claim involved is one which should result in legal rights and remedies. And it is also true that many interest-groups fail to secure the legislative enactments which they desire. Such failures indicate that, for some legal or political reason, the judges or legislators do not accept the claims of right, and do not therefore recognize or protect those claims through legal rules.

We may see something of this process in more detail when we turn to consider the important question of *who* may claim, possess and enjoy legal rights. It is by no means the case that the law, through its various regulatory and facilitative channels and mechanisms, treats everyone in exactly the same way. It may be that no distinction is made between one human being and another for the purposes of, say, the protections afforded through the criminal law; but in other respects, the law proceeds frequently upon the basis that people in society are treated according to the particular category in which, for many legal purposes, they fall.

Legal personality

The 'human being' is, of course, the most obvious entity to which legal rights and duties may be ascribed. The law, as we shall see presently, does treat other, non-human, entities as 'legal persons', but to begin with it is important to realize that even the 'basic unit' of the human being is a matter not wholly devoid of legal problems. The fundamental factors pertaining to human existence are, of course, life and death. It is crucial for the law to contain within it some form of test whereby the living existence of a human being may be definitely ascertained, for the most basic rights we enjoy may be affected. In the past, for example, the 'moment of death' has been, in law as elsewhere, accepted as the moment when the heart ceases to beat. But the development of advanced techniques in medical science have brought delicate problems: today, most of the body's functions, including the heartbeat, can be sustained by means of mechanical and electronic life-support systems. There have been cases in this country and elsewhere which have centred on the victims of tragic accidents which have resulted in comatose patients being, literally, kept alive by means of life-support systems. If such a patient can, in the opinion of medical experts, never be expected to regain consciousness, and life-functions could not continue independently of the support system, can that patient be said to be 'alive'? If the life-support system is switched off by doctors, even with the consent of the patient's relatives, are those doctors guilty of murder? Such ethical and legal problems may, in fact, have been resolved in most such cases by the recognition of the medical conception of 'brain-death': it is generally accepted that, though bodily functions may be maintained by life-support systems, the best test of whether life is present in the patient, independently of the support system, is the presence or absence of electrical activity in the brain. If there is none, then the patient is in effect already dead, for no life-supporting functions can operate independently of the support apparatus.[30a]

If the ethical problems of life-support are difficult enough, then those surrounding the moment at which the embryonic human being becomes defined as having a sufficiently independent and formed existence to be treated as a person, with all the rights which a person enjoys, are even more complicated.

One example in recent years where this issue arose was the Thalidomide tragedy. The drug Thalidomide had been introduced as a 'safe' sedative, and had been prescribed for many pregnant women to help deal with the tension which often accompanies pregnancy. Between 1959 and 1962, however, and (as it was later established) as a result of their mothers taking the drug, many children were born with severe deformities. The ensuing years saw a protracted out-of-court battle between Distillers Ltd, who had manufactured Thalidomide in this country, and the parents of the children who had suffered the handicaps. The liability of Distillers (which was, in the event, never tested before a court of law) depended upon the applicability or otherwise of the tort of negligence, which in turn raised many difficult questions. Among these questions was the extent to which, if at all, the manufacturers owed a duty of care to the unborn children – a difficult issue, given that many of the affected children were not even conceived at the time of the alleged negligence: how can a duty of care be owed to someone who does not yet exist?[31]

As a matter of policy, of course, there is no reason why such liability might not be imposed in such situations, but the attempt to solve such questions by the application of existing legal concepts of personality would raise problems which are virtually insoluble. This particular situation has now been clarified somewhat by the Congenital Disabilities (Civil Liability) Act 1976, which provides that if the parent of a child is affected by an occurrence which results in the child being born disabled, then the perpetrator of that occurrence will be liable to the child *if* he would be liable in tort to the parent concerned.

Another problem which is centrally related to the issue of the unborn child is that of the acceptability or otherwise of abortion (see chapter 2). The law permits abortion in special, and limited, circumstances: on one side of the law there stands the lobby which argues for the extension of the right to an abortion, and on the other side is the lobby holding the firm belief that all abortion, at whatever stage of development of the foetus, is morally wrong. It is not easy to see how this particular problem will, if ever, be resolved.

In recent years the law has had to confront another difficult area: the question of sex. The possibilities now exist for sex-change operations, due to advances in medical science and a growing awareness, at least in some quarters, of the fact that a person who, for instance, is biologically male may nevertheless regard him/ herself subjectively (that is, in terms of emotions, and cultural and sexual predilections) as female. Here the law, as represented at least by the opinion of the court in the case of *Corbett* v. *Corbett*[32] in 1971, appears to take a strictly limited and narrow view. The case involved the validity of a marriage ceremony between a man and a person who had been born a biological male, but who had undergone a sex-change operation in order to become female. The court considered various aspects to the problem, and decided the issue on narrow biological grounds, holding that the person in question, despite the operation, was, and at all times since birth had been, male. Since neither English law nor the Church recognizes the possibility of homosexual marriage, the result was that the marriage ceremony in question had not resulted in a valid marriage tie.

It should be pointed out that, important though biological criteria may be, there are groups in society who consider that a person's gender is as much a matter of personal identity and subjective feelings of alignment to a particular sex-role (irrespective of biological 'signposts') as it is a matter of biology: as yet, there are few signs that the law will take such arguments into account when called upon to resolve these (admittedly very rare) problems. The same conclusion as that reached in *Corbett* was reached by the court in the criminal case of *R.* v. *Tan* in 1983,[33] and although the European Court of Human Rights has recently considered the question as to whether the British government's refusal to alter the details of a person's birth certificate in order to register a change of sex was an infringement of Article 8 of the European Convention on Human Rights (guaranteeing respect for private and family life), the court's decision was that in the circumstances the government was not in breach of the Convention.[34]

The above examples show that, as far as legal definitions of situations are concerned, not even the most basic propositions about human beings can be taken for granted: questions as to what constitutes a human being may present difficult questions for the law to resolve. In the vast majority of cases, of course, there are no such problems for courts or legislators to resolve. More often, the issue concerns the *status* of a particular person, and the extent which rights and duties attach to that person as a consequence of belonging to a particular class, group or category which is legally significant.

A person may, for the purposes of the law, perform a whole variety of social roles, any of which may or may not be legally significant. A person may be an employer or employee; a householder, a voter and a trade unionist; a husband, a father, a pensioner or a consumer; he or she may be anti-vivisectionist or gambler, crippled or blind, drug-addict or alcoholic. Each of these categories may or may not have legal rules associated with it, and the rules pertaining to a person's status as a member of one of these groups may be, and frequently are, legally unrelated to other aspects of that person's life. The role of 'father', for example, involves various rights and duties which are wholly unconnected with the same person's activities as a trade unionist or a member of a political party. On the other hand, one aspect may affect others. A parent's claim to state welfare benefits and allowances may well depend upon that person's status as 'employee'. The point to be stressed is that, for legal purposes, the law *classifies* people: the response by the law to claims of right may depend upon race, occupation, sex, income, nationality, age *or any other individual or group characteristic perceived by lawmakers as relevant.* The identification of individual or group characteristics in law will normally be followed by the provision of rules stating the conditions under which these categories of people will or will not be protected or made liable through the operation of those rules and the legal rights and duties embodied in them.

The fluctuations and complexities of the legal definitions and treatment of people falling into various categories will often be quite striking. The law has, for example, for many years recognized the categories 'landlord' and 'tenant' and, as we shall see in chapter 5, various items of parliamentary legislation have provided explicitly for the regulation through law of the landlord–tenant relationship. During the last century, there was little or no legal control over the rights of landlords to lay down the terms on which they let their premises to tenants: they could charge whatever rent they liked, could evict tenants if they so desired, and could impose all manner of other, frequently oppressive, contractual terms upon their tenants. Over the years, however, the pendulum of legal protection has swung (albeit gradually and with some fluctuations) in the direction of providing legal protections for tenants through the passage of housing and rent legislation.

Nowadays, most tenancies may be subject to 'fair rent' provisions, and, except in specific and well-defined situations, a tenant may not be evicted from rented accommodation. Any attempt by the landlord, moreover, to secure eviction through any form of harassment is now a criminal offence. This example shows how the interests of one category of person ('landlords') may at one time be recognized and protected through law by certain legal rights (or, more accurately in this case, by the absence of any regulatory or controlling legislation) and may at another time lose their dominance to the interests of another category ('tenants') who come to enjoy legal protection through various legal rules embodying new legal rights.

The way in which the law is used to embody rules involving rights and duties in such cases as this is, of course, a matter of policy as decided by Parliament, ministers, judges or subordinate lawmakers. In the first case, it usually happens that important legislative enactments reflect government policies; political considerations can and do influence the content of the law. This becomes clear when we consider the ways in which the law has been used, at various times, to regulate group activity. Groups of people may be formed as a deliberate act by those people; or they may comprise diverse persons linked only by the ascription to them of certain rights or obligations. Some groups, like cricket clubs or rock bands, attract little or no legislative attention. Other groups and their activities, however, have often attracted the attention of governments, which have responded to the group and its activities in various ways. Obviously, whether or not there will be a response, and, if so, what form that response will take, are not legal but political questions whose answers will depend on the way in which particular governments perceive and define the group in question. There have been instances in history when the official response to a group and its activities, for instance, has been to declare that group an unlawful organization. Such was the fate of the early organized groups of workers, the forerunners of our own trade unions, which, as we saw in chapter 1, were unlawful for many years, as were any forms of collective action by workers such as strikes or other pressures placed upon employers.

In 1854, for example, more than three thousand workers were imprisoned for 'leaving or neglecting their work',[35] and although collective action was made lawful during the nineteenth century, many judges' attitudes remained hostile to unions and their activities well into the twentieth century. A more recent example of the prohibition of an organization is, of course, the outlawing of the Irish Republican Army, a move by the British government which has been part of its attack on IRA violence since the 1970s.

Finally, another important way in which the law can be used to regulate group activity is for the group to seek and receive some form of special legal recognition. The best example of this is the legal device of *incorporation*, whereby a group is treated, in law, *as if it were a person*. Such treatment will often serve as a mechanism which facilitates certain activities by the group, as well as a form of regulation and control of those activities. We noted in chapter 3 the best-known example of the corporate body – the limited company – but there are many other examples of corporate bodies in existence. The British Broadcasting Corporation and local government bodies are but two other instances. Yet another special case involving 'artificial' legal personality is the trade union, which has a kind of 'hybrid' legal status. A union possesses certain benefits and liabilities which accrue to corporate bodies, but it is not treated in law as a fully corporate entity. The Trade Union and Labour Relations Act 1974 provided that a trade union is not a corporate body, but also provided that a union has the power to enter into contracts, to sue and to be sued, in its own name. Before 1982 the trade union enjoyed a certain degree of immunity from liability in tort in respect of acts done in contemplation or furtherance of a trade dispute, but s.15 of the Employment Act 1982 (see chapter 3) provides that this immunity is largely removed, and the trade union now stands in the same position with regard to tort liability as an ordinary individual. Employers' associations have a similar legal status (as provided by the 1974 Act), except that such an association may choose for itself whether to remain an unincorporated association or to become a corporate body by registration as a company.

Summary

In this chapter it has been argued that legal concepts (especially those of 'rights', 'duties' and 'personality') which are frequently used in everyday legal practice are rarely simple to elucidate. In offering criticisms and limitations of some of the many contributions to the analysis of these concepts, we have suggested that these terms are best understood not by seeking alternative words or phrases to express different legal meanings, but rather by close examination of the social, economic and political contexts in which are created the legal rules which express certain relationships in terms of these concepts. 'Rights', 'duties' and so on, it is suggested, are shorthand symbolic expressions of legal relationships which are subject to change and modification. In our next chapter we will see how one such concept has gradually been accorded a place of primacy in English law, and in the legal regulation of certain social and economic relationships. This is the concept of 'property' and the accompanying structure of legal rules which create 'property rights'.

5
Law and property

Legal norms are invariably related to social and economic conditions prevailing at a given period, and so we find that the legal normative expressions of the relationship between the holder of property rights and the objects of those rights have their basis in social and economic practice. We saw in chapter 3 the extent to which the law relating to business concerns itself predominantly with business property, and the regulation and transfer of that property, in accordance with the economic structure within which business operates, and we noted in chapter 2 the relationship between the law of theft and the demands of propertied classes for adequate legal protection of their property. Similarly, property concepts such as ownership and possession, leases and mortgages, contracts and trusts, are legal normative reflections of the economic activities and demands of individuals and classes at different periods.

In considering law and property, we must also bear in mind two further points. First, in our economic system, property rights are related to wealth, and when we speak of wealth and property we are usually implicitly acknowledging the unequal distribution of property and property rights among social classes. Second, property is not treated in law as a homogeneous category. Because property objects have taken different forms and have represented differing degrees of value at different times, the law has developed a fairly specific classification of property, each type of which has particular legal rules attached to it. The most obvious form of property is land: it is the oldest and most permanent form of wealth and, as we shall see, the various rights which may exist with regard to land and its use may be traced back to feudal times. The emergence of legal rules pertaining to material, moveable objects (such as furniture, books or manufactured goods) may be seen as the reflection of developing capitalism, when such goods became increasingly important in an economic system which was coming to depend more and more upon manufacture and commerce: it is in the light of these economic developments, for example, that we may understand the development of the law of theft as we know it today. And a third legal category of property-objects, called 'choses in action', refers to a type of property which is intangible, and which only exists in some symbolic form, such as bank accounts, copyright and negotiable instruments, which will be considered presently.

The legal system of a capitalist society will inevitably exhibit a comprehensive set of rules and rights concerning private property, because private property is of basic importance to such a society. The economic system depends upon the acquisition of private personal wealth, and so we may expect the legal system to be concerned to a large extent with the protection of that wealth, and with the framework within which such wealth can be invested, transferred and consolidated. The law purports, of course, to afford equality of treatment to everyone in society, regardless of social class, wealth or poverty; but it must be borne in mind that in a society where 'the share of all personal wealth owned by just the richest 1 per cent of the adult population was probably near 30 per cent around 1970',[1] the law is used for the protection and transfer of property by only a very small proportion of the population. Similarly, with regard to transactions involving land: the law concerning land may be thought of as affecting a large number of transactions over a considerable quantity of houses, building land, industrial land and so on, but it is worth remembering that the total proportion of *urban* land in Britain is only about 8 per cent of the whole, the remainder comprising agricultural land and a much smaller proportion of forest and woodland.[2] About half the agricultural land is owned by private individuals and concerns, the remaining half being owned by central and local government, the Church, the monarchy, and so on; such land will relatively rarely change hands. Of the 8 per cent of urban land, a considerable proportion is taken up by uses other than housing (such as manufacturing, transport and amenities),[3] so, although land law is of great significance in the management of, and transactions relating to, landed property, such transactions affect only a small proportion of the total acreage of Britain.

The function of private property in capitalist society

It is illuminating at this point to consider something of the wider aspects of property and property rights in a capitalist society such as Britain, and to examine some of the views advanced by theorists in explaining the relationships between the economic system, property and law. Marx sought to show how civil law has developed side by side with the development of commerce and industrialization,[4] and how various nations faced with new problems associated with these developments often adopted the civil law of ancient Rome as the basis for their own legal systems. Roman law was appropriate, argued Marx, because its legal system reflected its complex and rigid hierarchical 'class' system, which centred on the distinction between the property-owners and the property-less.

Durkheim, too, was critical of private property in 'advanced' societies. Unlike Marx, he did not regard property as intrinsically productive of conflict and exploitative forces, but viewed certain forms of private property as tending to obstruct the realization of a truly integrated society (that is, one having 'organic' solidarity). In particular, he was concerned to show how the continued presence of hereditary transmission of private property served to impede genuine equality of opportunity, which would otherwise allow people to occupy positions in society commensurate with their abilities:

If one class of society is obliged, in order to live, to take any price for its services, while another can abstain from such action thanks to resources at its disposal which, however, are not necessarily due to any social superiority, the second has an unjust advantage over the first at law. In other words, there cannot be rich and poor at birth without there being unjust contracts. This was still more the case when social status itself was hereditary and law sanctioned all sorts of inequalities.[5]

In Durkeim's general theory – especially on the impact of the division of labour, with the accompanying growth of civil law having the aim of restitution (compensation) – property occupies a central place.[6] Restitutive legal norms rest, by definition, upon the assumption that compensation awarded through law puts the aggrieved person, as far as practicable, in the position he or she would have been in if the transaction complained of (for example, a contract which the other party has breached) had not taken place. Compensation is peculiarly apt in cases of *material* losses – property damage, unlawful possession of another's goods, or failure to deliver goods specified by a contractual agreement – though the device is also used, albeit somewhat clumsily, for injuries of a *personal*, or bodily, nature.

The precise function of private property in Western society was the concern of the Austrian legal theorist Karl Renner, writing in the early years of this century. He sought to show how the social institution of 'private property' can undergo striking transformations in its features and functions, without any radical change in the original *form* of the legal norms concerning property-ownership. Writing from a marxist perspective, Renner argued that in a capitalist system 'property, from a mere title to dispose of material objects, becomes a title to power, and as it exercises power in the private interest, it becomes a title to domination'.[7] How does this occur? Building on Marx's theoretical foundations, Renner explained that the original social function of private property in a pre-industrial society was merely to allow the owner to live, by using, exchanging or disposing of his own property – uses of property which were supported by legal norms. But, argued Renner, when private property developed into *capital*, which was used to set up enterprises in which the property-owner became the employer of workers, this original control of property became control over *people*: the owner/employer controlled the activities and tasks of his wage-labourers and supervised the execution of his commands as to the work to be undertaken.

The transformation of the function of property occurred, however, with no changes in the legal norms pertaining to property and ownership. In fact, said Renner, these developments, which led to domination over workers, took place regardless of legal rules and assumptions about 'freedom of contract' and 'contracts of employment' (see chapter 1). The reality is that the worker has choice only over *which* master is to dominate him; he cannot escape having to work for *someone*.

So, for Renner, legal norms continue basically unchanged, while the real nature and function of property become transformed. The law, Renner suggested, is in reality as irrelevant as the lawyers' assumptions about freedom of contract and of employment are illusory.

The right of ownership . . . assumes a new social function. Without any change in the [legal] norm . . . a *de facto* right is added to the personal absolute-domination over a corporeal thing. This right is not based upon a special legal provision. It is the power of control, the power to issue commands and to enforce them.

. . . This power of control is a social reality, but at the same time it is profitable to the owners – it establishes a rule not for the purposes of protection but for the purposes of exploitation, of profit.[8]

With the advantage of the ability to analyse social and economic developments in the period after Marx's work was done, Renner went on to argue that there has been, since the early stages of capitalism, a gradual but increasing transformation of private property into 'public utility', in the form of privately offered services, transport facilities, shops and so on: 'Private property has now become accessible to everyone, it is put at everybody's disposal . . . The sovereign power of private property has suddenly . . . been converted into a subject who has public duties',[9] although these changes have been accompanied by legal changes as well. Still the basic legal assumptions about ownership and contract linger on, argued Renner, with lawmakers and judges affording as much, and the same, protection through law to property interests as they ever did.

Renner's analysis has been criticized on several grounds. It has been suggested that he neglected the fact that, in modern capitalism, 'in the overwhelmingly important field of corporate enterprise, the nominal owner, that is the shareholder, is becoming more and more powerless. He turns into a mere recipient of dividends',[10] while effective power is possessed by persons other than the legal owner.[11] This point refers to the developments in modern capitalism whereby there is, it is argued, an effective separation between *ownership* of property and *control* of that property. This argument has been outlined thus:

Growth in scale has necessarily entailed the rise and predominance of joint stock enterprise. Large business is typically owned, not by single individuals, families or partners who themselves run the enterprise, but by a multitude of shareholders. The shareholders are far too many and too scattered to exercise control . . . So, in the place once occupied by owner-entrepreneurs, there is now a power vaccum. Or there would be, were it not filled by those who *are* in position to exercise control: the 'managers'. Constitutionally only salaried officials – agents responsible through the board to the legal owners – in fact they acquire real power.[12]

This argument is frequently used to support the contention that in such a context of changes within capitalist structure, the older, marxist argument that 'property equals power' falls down. The details of this particular debate are well outside the scope of this book, although we should note Westergaard and Resler's point that these changes are more apparent than real. In particular, they argue that 'middle management' may indeed have effective 'operational' control of the enterprise, in that this group takes day-to-day decisions in the running of the business (especially the larger corporate business structures), but when it is a matter of 'strategic' policy-making concerning questions of profitability and growth, investment, mergers, labour relations and relations with government, we find that these decisions are invariably taken at the top levels of the organization – by the members of the boards of directors, who are themselves large *owners* of share capital in business organizations. The apparent division, then, between ownership and control is seen to be only partial, effective power still being concentrated in the hands of the few who usually own large slices of the organization.[13]

As we saw in chapter 2, the centrality of the institution of property in our economic and political structure constitutes not only the criterion for possession of effective power, but also a criterion for the *legitimization* of that power. Property has long been clothed with moral value: the ruling class in pre-industrial society ruled by virtue of its land-ownership, and this class widened out after the industrial revolution to include manufacturing and commercial classes whose claims to a legitimate role in government rested on *their* property-owning status. Essentially, the developing propertied middle classes claimed the right to a say in political affairs; it was upon them and their economic role that Western societies were becoming increasingly dependent with industrialization, and so, as Gouldner explains, 'the new middle class held in highest esteem those talents, skills and energies of individuals that contributed to their own individual accomplishments and achievements. The middle-class standard of utility implied that rewards should be proportioned to men's personal work and contribution.'[14] The middle-class men of property, then, equated their accumulation of wealth from rents and profits with social and economic 'usefulness', a stance from which their claims to political status and participation were made and fought for: 'The middle class insisted that property and men of property were useful to society and deserving of honour and other rewards because of this'.[15]

The law of property

Because the legal right is separate from the thing which is the *object* of that right, it is possible for all kinds of legal relationships between the property right and the property-object to exist. The most basic of all the various property rights is *ownership*, described by Lloyd as 'not a single category of legal "right" but . . . a complex bundle of rights'.[16] The concept of ownership has proved difficult to elucidate. Clearly, the owner of goods or land has a greater degree of legal right to deal with those goods or land than someone who is not the owner, but there are many common situations where the owner may not, in fact, be in a position to enjoy the property-object in question because the right to *possession* of that object has been voluntarily given up. A car-hire company, for example, enters into agreements with its customers to hire out cars to them. Here, the customer is lawfully in possession of the car for the period of the hire, and the car-hire company may not, for that period, take back possession of the car without the consent of the customer, or unless the customer has broken the terms of the hire agreement. In the absence of either of these factors, the company itself will be in breach of the hire contract (see chapter 11) if it retakes possession during the period of the hire. Despite this voluntary waiving of ordinary owner's rights to possession, however, the company remains at all times the legal *owner* of the car.

There is, then, a distinction in law between ownership and possession of property-objects. Although 'ownership' usually implies exclusive right to use and control the property-object, there are cases where 'possession' entitles the possessor of the property-object to exclude the legal owner, albeit for a limited period. A tenant of a flat, for instance, is usually entitled to exclusive possession of the flat for the period of the lease, during which time the tenant is legally entitled to exclude everyone, including the owner of the flat, from taking possession, subject to the terms of the lease.

Despite the importance of the idea of possession in law, however, the many and varied contexts in which the term is used make it impossible to define in a precise manner. Like the concepts of 'rights' and 'duties' discussed in chapter 4, we must examine what is meant by this term 'possession' by taking into account the specific situations in which the word is used. In the case which is regarded as the basis for our modern law of theft, the *Carrier's Case* in 1473, a carrier of goods was held by the court to have come into possession of those goods only when he broke open the bales which he was carrying on behalf of the owner, and appropriated the contents for his own unlawful purposes, although as a matter of common sense we would consider the carrier to have been in possession of both bales and contents from the moment of the giving over of them to him by the owner for the lawful purposes of carriage.

Again, in *Warner* v. *Metropolitan Police Commissioner*,[17] a much more recent case involving the offence of possession of prohibited drugs, the problem of possession was the central issue. Warner's defence was that, although he had known that two boxes in his possession contained something, he did not know that those contents were prohibited drugs; and that he had believed them to contain scent. Now, although the offence of unlawful possession of a prohibited drug has long been held by the courts to be one of *strict liability*, involving no requirement that the prosecution establish intention or even knowledge on the part of an accused (a policy issue, justified by the courts by reason of the perceived seriousness of the 'drug problem'), the House of Lords in *Warner* nevertheless thought that the notion of 'possession' in this context *itself* required an element of knowledge on the part of the accused: he must at least know that he possesses *something*. You are not 'in possession' of a cigarette containing cannabis if someone slips it, unnoticed by you and without your knowledge, into your pocket. But could Warner be said to have been 'in possession' of the drug, if he thought that the contents of the boxes were scent? The House of Lords, in a somewhat confusing series of judgments, affirmed Warner's conviction on the grounds that, in the words of Lord Pearce, 'the term "possession" is satisfied by a knowledge only of the existence of the thing itself and not its qualities, and . . . ignorance or mistake as to its qualities is not an excuse'.[18] Warner, on this reasoning, was in possession of the contents of the boxes, *whatever those contents might turn out to be*. The decision, which does not now reflect the law,[19] is none the less useful in illustrating the problems posed in law by the notion of 'possession'. It may be that in Warner's case itself, the court was making a policy decision regarding the presence or absence, in law, of the defendant's 'possession' of the contents of the boxes; it is easy to appreciate that, had the decision been otherwise, the way would have been open in later cases for defences – perhaps spurious ones – to have been raised along the lines of asserting ignorance of the contents of containers,[20] leading, some might think, to the increased difficulty of controlling the use of prohibited drugs. Be that as it may, the case shows that the concept of 'possession' must be examined in specific legal contexts where it is used, and cannot be regarded as susceptible to an overall general definition.

In most everyday situations where the concepts of ownership and possession are significant, however, these technical problems rarely arise. There are some very common transactions which involve this distinction – the case of the car-hire was mentioned above, and other examples are hire-purchase contracts (where the trader remains the legal owner until all instalments are paid, even though the customer enjoys possession of the goods – see chapter 11), and agreements between landlords and tenants for the lease of property, which we will consider later.

As noted above, the law classifies various forms of property-objects, and specific legal rules may or may not attach to these objects according to their classification. Tangible objects, such as the things we own and usually possess as part of our everyday life (furniture, books, food, cars and clothing, for instance) are termed, in law, 'personal property'. Such property is not generally subject to special bodies of legal rules. We buy and sell articles and goods through the ordinary law of contract, and these objects (or, rather, our rights in them) are given legal protection through the various criminal-law rules (forbidding theft, criminal damage and so on) and rules in the law of tort (providing civil remedies in the event of trespass to our goods, or of someone unlawfully keeping or selling those goods).[21]

The category 'personal property', however, includes not only these tangible property-objects, called *choses in possession*, but also property-objects which cannot be seen or carried away: these objects of personal property, called *choses in action*, include such things as company shares, copyright, patents, debts and negotiable instruments (cheques, bills of exchange and promissory notes). In a material sense, these property-objects exist only as pieces of paper; but they represent assets which are clearly of value to the owner. There are other important differences between choses in possession and choses in action, however. We may understand readily everyone's need for items which are basic to our very existence: we all need food, clothes, and the means whereby we may cultivate our food, make our clothes and so on. Choses in action, however, can be seen to originate not from such basic needs, but rather from pressure and problems within specific economic systems. Of course, many tangible objects cannot be said to be necessary to our existence – cars, furniture and television sets are examples of such objects – but choses in action are particular *forms* of property-object, created as responses to perceived problems of property and property transfer at specific periods.

In particular, negotiable instruments (one of the most important kinds of chose in action) may be traced back to the appearance of banks during the sixteenth and seventeenth centuries, and the growing importance of money (rather than land) in a developing commercial economy. A negotiable instrument *represents* money or money's worth, but has none of the drawbacks which can attach to the use of money in business transactions; money is bulky, it is highly attractive to thieves and it has an anonymous quality – one banknote is similar to another banknote, and it may be difficult to establish that the possessor is truly entitled to it. Negotiable instruments, on the other hand, are convenient to despatch and handle, and they contain specific details as to the identity of the intended recipient. The definition of negotiable instruments may, then, be stated as 'written promises to pay money (or money's worth) to the holder, which can be freely transferred between individuals'. If A owes B money, and pays him by means of a cheque ('a bill of exchange drawn on a banker payable on demand'),[22] then B may transfer that amount to C by *endorsing* the cheque: that is, by writing on the back of the cheque 'please pay to C', signing his own name and delivering the cheque to C. C may use the same cheque to pay a debt to D, by means of a new endorsement, and so on.

Because of the somewhat complicated nature of negotiable instruments, and also because of the possibilities for fraud, the law was used to provide the framework within which these devices could be used to greatest advantage and with adequate security. Most of the relevant law is still contained in the Bills of Exchange Act 1882, but more recently the Cheques Act 1992 places restrictions on the transferability of cheques produced by banks, with the effect that crossed cheques bearing the phrase 'account payee' cannot be transferred simply by endorsement. They can only be paid into the account of the payee – the person originally named on the front of the cheque.[23] This measure was enacted as part of the efforts to prevent fraud. The continuing development of the law relating to these property-objects and property rights reflects the significance of choses in action in commercial transactions, and the way in which the law is adapted to try to resolve novel problems.

Intellectual property and data protection

In recent years, developments in advanced electronics and information technology have brought new problems concerning *intellectual property* which the law has been called upon to help resolve. To begin with, the huge increase in popularity of home computers, and the accompanying development and sales to consumers of commercial computer programs (notably, of course, computer games), has resulted in illegitimate copies of copyrighted programs being made; similarly the illicit 'pirating' and resale of videotaped films by entrepreneurs, and the far more commonplace but equally unlawful video- or cassette-taping of television broadcasts and records in the home by private individuals, have given rise to widespread concern among the owners of copyright in these materials.[24] Book-publishers have gone so far as to take legal action against institutions such as schools and colleges where unauthorized photocopying of books has taken place. The law concerning copyright, trade marks and patents – all choses in action – is clearly designed to protect the rights and interests of the *creators* of these materials – authors, computer-program writers, composers, artists, inventors and designers – and the current law is contained principally in the Copyright, Designs and Patents Act 1988.[25] The law on this subject is extremely complex, and what follows is a necessarily abridged and simplified account of the main provisions of the Act concerning copyright, in order to indicate the ways in which the law defines and regulates this type of property right.

Based on a government White Paper published in 1986,[26] and part of a complex web of international agreements and treaties, the Act of 1988 attempts to bring the law up to date and into line with modern developments. The Act deals with the rights of those who create original works, which may be protected by means of copyright, patent rights or design rights, depending on the nature of the work or object in question. The basic difficulty is that the proposition that the creator of innovative works should be entitled, whether through copyright, patent law or design rights, to legal protection through the exclusive right to exploit that work commercially is essentially anti-competitive. The logical result of unrestricted or unqualified protection, provided first to the creator and after that to the creator's estate, would be the legal creation and maintenance of a monopoly in that work, invention or design. As we saw in chapter 3, our economic system and indeed those of other European countries are predicated on the idea that monopolies are damaging to national economies because they restrict competition.

The law's response to this paradox is to grant the right of exclusivity to the creator of a legally protectable work, but only for a fixed time-period, and subject to some qualifications. At the end of the time-period, anyone may exploit the work for commercial purposes. Copyright cannot exist until the work has taken on some tangible form – there can be no copyright in mere ideas. But once the created work is recorded in some tangible form, copyright in that work automatically exists: there is no requirement that the author takes some further action to register the claim.

The 1988 Act identifies three categories of material which are protected by copyright – the property right which exists in relation to works created by authors. These categories are first, original *literary, dramatic, musical or artistic works*, second, *sound recordings, films, broadcasts or cable programmes*, and third, *typographical arrangements of published works*. Copyright in the first two categories lasts for fifty years after the year of the author's death; and in the third category, where the copyright is owned by the publisher of the work, the period is twenty-five years from the year of first publication. During these periods, the protected copyright interest is such that no one except the copyright owner may copy, publish, perform, show, broadcast or adapt the work without the owner's express permission. That permission may be given by means of a licence, or by means of assigning the entire right – like any property right, copyright may be disposed of to another person by means of, for example, a contractual agreement. There are many examples in everyday life of situations in which copyright permission is routinely obtained for what would otherwise be cases of infringement – where a hit record is briefly heard during a scene in a television play or film; wherever background music is played in a public place such as a hotel or airport; whenever a local video shop hires out a videotaped movie; when a well-known rock band plays in public its own version of another band's hit song; and so on. Note that the user of copyrighted material does not have to *intend* to breach the copyright: it is sufficient that the use is made of the protected material without the permission of the copyright owner. Infringement of copyright is a civil wrong, and remedies for infringement include compensation and injunctions to restrain further infringement.

The Act provides that home-taping of a broadcast programme 'solely for the purpose of enabling it to be viewed or listened to at a more convenient time' (the concept of 'time-shifting') does *not* constitute an infringement of copyright, though this still leaves unanswered the problem, taken very seriously by record and film publishers, of illicit taping for other purposes than simply time-shifting. Taping a friend's compact disc, for instance, or copying a hired video-film on to a blank video-tape, still constitute copyright infringements, since these situations do not fall into the categories of either 'broadcasts' or 'time-shift purposes'. Various ways of protecting the economic interests of music and film publishers have been considered, ranging from the proposed imposition of a levy on blank audio and video-tapes to the installation of anti-copying technology within hi-fi and video hardware. The latter solution has so far proved impracticable because of the availability of methods of counteracting the anti-copying technology, although the 1988 Act provides that anyone who makes counteracting devices available may be proceeded against as a copyright infringer. The government actively considered the blank-tape levy, but no such provision was included in the 1988 Act. A complete and satisfactory solution to the problem remains to be found.

The copying of material for educational use is dealt with by the Act through a provision that, in the absence of any licensing agreement, multiple copies of up to 1 per cent of any literary, dramatic or musical work may be made in any three-month period by an educational institution for educational purposes. In practice, it is likely that licensing agreements will regulate such copying, rather than the statutory provision; disputes concerning such licensing agreements and schemes are heard and resolved by the Copyright Tribunal, a body created by the Act which is given the task of determining proceedings involving licences, royalty payments and various other aspects of copyright.

If the rapid development of technology has created problems for the copyright owner, then the same may be said of the ordinary citizen whose personal details may, through computer data files, be easily communicated to others for all kinds of reasons and purposes. The interest at stake here is a person's interest in information about themselves and what may be done with it, and, we might say, an interest in personal privacy. The Data Protection Act 1984 represents an attempt to recognize and protect people's interests in *personal information* relating to them. There are many situations in which data concerning private individuals are filed on computers by both public and private organizations. This may be done for commercial purposes (as where a person's credit-worthiness is assessed and filed by a bank or finance company) or administrative purposes (as where a government department retains data relating to tax, motor vehicles or television licences). Problems which have arisen over such computerized records include the difficulty for the citizen in gaining access to these records; the possibilities of erroneous or out-dated information being retained; and the general threat to individual privacy posed by the collection, processing and transferring of personal information. Once again, we are dealing here with a statute of considerable complexity, but the main legal provisions may be discussed briefly.

The Act was passed in pursuance of ratification by the UK of the Council of Europe Data Protection Convention 1981, which contains the basis for the eight 'data protection principles', described below, on which the Act is based.

Essentially, any person or organization (the *data user*) collecting and processing personal data (that is, information of a *factual* or *judgmental* nature about an *identifiable* individual) by means of automatic (that is, computerized) systems must register with the Registrar of Data Protection, and the various items of information about those data, and the uses to which they will be put by the user, must be specified when registering.

The principles on which the Act is based are that (i) personal data should be obtained fairly and lawfully; (ii) such data must only be held for specified purposes, such purposes to be notified to the Registrar of Data Protection; (iii) the data may be disclosed only to specified persons, such persons to be identified when registration takes place; (iv) the data held must be adequate, relevant and not excessive, given the purposes for which the data are held; (v) the data must be accurate, and appropriately amended to maintain their accuracy; (vi) the data must not be kept for longer than they are needed; (vii) the person whom the data concern (the *data subject*) shall have the right to know if personal data are held, and also the right of access to those data. Such a person can have data corrected if inaccurate, or removed from the file; (viii) there must not be unauthorized access to, or alteration, loss or disclosure of such personal data.

Perhaps not surprisingly, although it applies to both private commercial enterprises and public bodies, including government departments, the Act contains certain exemptions. Principally, computerized data pertaining to the prevention or detection of crime, the prosecution of offenders and the assessment or collection of taxes or duty, and data relating to national security (as identified by a minister of government), among other matters, are exempt from the provisions of the Act. Although it may be thought sensible to exclude police information and some security information from free access to private individuals in the interests of national security or crime prevention and detection, it is clear that a general right of freedom of access to information held by certain government departments (the objective of campaigners for more open government)[27] will not be a side-effect of the Data Protection Act, especially since the Secretary of State is given considerable powers under the Act to grant various exemptions from the provisions of the Act.[28]

Land and the law

So far we have discussed the two legal categories of *personal* property: choses in possession and choses in action. In both cases, the law has been used, wherever it was thought appropriate, to regulate and protect the interests of property-holders by means of legally enforceable rights, and by means of a protective code of legal rules contained in the general criminal and civil law. In general, it is true to say that, apart from intervening in the ways just described, the state has never found it necessary to interfere in a *restrictive* manner in the field of personal property; rather, it has left individuals and business organizations relatively free to enjoy and dispose of their personal property in whichever ways they wish, and this is, of course, quite consistent with the demands of a free market economy and the competitive *laisser-faire* philosophies which underpin our economic structure.

When we turn our attention to the law relating to land, or *real property*, however, we see that it is quite a different matter. We have seen at various points the clear historical relationship between land-ownership and the possession of effective economic and political power; the traditional ruling class in England has long been the landowning class. The extremely complicated structure of land law cannot be understood without an appreciation of both the peculiar nature of land itself and the connections and tensions between land-ownership and use, and economic interests and inequalities.

Land, unlike goods, is immoveable, permanent and indestructible. It cannot be taken away by thieves, and it cannot be protected by locking it away in a bank vault. Moreover, it may be said to be the sole and original form of wealth, not least because it is a fixed and *limited* commodity. The control of land brings with it considerable social and economic power, for its very scarcity, coupled with the fact that everyone must, in order to live, have access to some land, however small, means that the landholder has the power to turn that land to substantial beneficial use by, for example, granting others certain rights over it in exchange for rents.

These characteristics of land have given rise to specific forms of social and political relations and institutions over different periods in history, although English land law still bears traces of the extremely complex social relations of feudal England. Under feudalism in the Middle Ages, land was ultimately owned by the sovereign (technically this is still the case, though of no practical significance today), and portions of land were given into the possession of those who served the king, typically by rendering military services, in return for those services. At the time of the Norman Conquest, these rewards to knights and followers meant that a new political order was imposed on the pre-existing structure whereby peasants lived on the land and worked the soil for the benefit of Saxon lords. As Simpson points out, however:

In general the effect of the Norman Conquest was only to substitute a new, alien lord for his Saxon predecessor. What a tenant in chief acquired by the King's grant was not the enjoyment of land so much as the enjoyment of rights over land and services due from peasants who cultivated that land; to the peasant it may not have seemed that anything very momentous had occurred.[29]

The structure of rights and titles whereby land was held by various individuals was very complex, involving many different forms of *tenure* based on the particular form of service rendered to the king. 'Tenure signifies the relation between lord and tenant, and what it implies is that the person whom we should naturally call the owner does not own the land, but merely holds it as tenant of the Crown or some other feudal superior. But if he is not owner of the land, what is the nature of the interest that he holds?'[30] The answer to this is found in the doctrine of *estates*. An estate is the specific type of interest which the landholder has, and which the law recognizes and protects. The feudal system of land law recognized a bewildering and complex array of different types of estate, on to which the jurisdiction of the Court of Chancery, administering rules of equity (see chapter 7), grafted a number of separate *equitable* interests. At common law, there were two types of landholding:

the *term of years* (the original version of the modern *lease*) – whereby land was granted to someone for a specific period, which was not really regarded as a form of estate at all – and the *freehold*. Freehold estates were of three types: the *fee simple estate*, which approximated to ownership, subject to the limitations of the principle of tenure; the *estate in fee tail*, whereby land could be passed on to the male heirs of the landholder; and the *life estate*, whereby land was held by a person for life, or during the life of another. Equity recognized a number of interests in land which the common law did not, most of which were connected with the *trust*, whereby land was held by one person (the *trustee*) on behalf of and for the benefit of another (the *beneficiary*). Landholding was thus structured upon a complicated system of legal rules and concepts under feudalism, and although important developments took place over the years, the basic scheme endured until the important land legislation of 1925.

Three conclusions follow from this structure of landholding under feudalism. First, there was nothing equivalent to our system whereby land and houses might be bought and sold. Landholding rights sprang from tenure, and the multiplicity of services (both already rendered and continuing as conditions of tenure)[31] were usually of a *personal* nature not easily transferred from one person to another. Second, the social relations of the feudal structure were static: peasants were tied to the land held by their lord, and in exchange for services and produce from the land they were allowed by that lord to eke out their own living. Social status was not so much a matter of personal industry, talent and competitiveness as a question of accident of birth. The feudal system is, then, the basis of the landed aristocracy in England as we understand the term in more modern times.

Third, the morass of technicality which comprised feudal land law plagued English law for the next eight or nine hundred years, a long period which saw the decline of feudalism and the rise of commerce and industry culminating in the period we know as the industrial revolution. It was not until the landmark Law of Property Act 1925 that the old system of tenure was removed from the rules and principles of English land law. As Cheshire says, 'The real property law as it existed in 1922 might justly be described as an archaic feudalistic system which, though originally evolved to satisfy the needs of a society based and centred on land, had by considerable ingenuity been twisted and distorted into a shape more or less suitable to a commercial society based on money.'[32]

The legislation of 1925 did much to simplify and bring up to date the law relating to real property. Much still depends upon the distinction between legal and equitable interests and remedies, however, and the legislation is still far from straightforward. The essential point of the reforms of 1925, however, apart from simplification, was to render the *transfer* of land easier by reducing the number of separate interests which might exist in a given piece of land. The old doctrine of tenure had long since fallen from use, thanks to earlier statutory reforms, but the classification of estates was still extremely complicated. In an economy which by the twentieth century had come to rest predominantly upon industry and commerce, with the attendant fluctuations in national and personal fortunes, it was clearly of the utmost importance to seek as high a degree of flexibility as possible in matters concerning land and its transfer.

The remaining equitable remedies are mainly to do with the hereditary transmission of property, through devices such as the trust, the strict settlement and other interests recognized in equity. Space does not permit a detailed examination of these equitable interests, and the reader is referred to materials providing full coverage of these matters.[33] What is more important for our purposes is the discussion of the *legal* estates in land: the fee simple, the holder of which is for all practical purposes the owner of the land; and the lease, whereby a landlord lets the land to a tenant in exchange for rent. Something must be said about these forms of legal estate, and the developments which have taken place around them.

Land and its use: private or public control?

One of the recurring themes of legal development during the twentieth century is that of increasing state intervention, through legal machinery, in areas of social and economic life which in previous times were the sole preserve of the private individual. Under the all-embracing banner of the 'welfare state', we have witnessed in this country a cascade of legislative provisions concerning all aspects of our lives, frequently providing the citizen with new rights, such as social security and unemployment benefits, but equally often imposing new responsibilities and legal duties. In few areas is this interventionist current revealed more clearly than in the law relating to land-use.

Planning

The adage 'an Englishman's home is his castle' may once have had real, and for some Englishmen literal, meaning. There was a time, up to the introduction of the first planning controls, when owners of land could do much as they pleased with it. They could build upon it, demolish existing structures, or let it out by means of the lease to tenants and receive income in the form of any rent they cared to charge. Today, the holder of land will find that before any alteration can be made to the land or to the buildings on it, planning permission must be granted by the local authority; and if the land or buildings are let out to tenants, then, subject to certain exceptions contained in the current rent legislation, the landholder will encounter close controls in the matters of the amount of rent that may be charged, and the possibility of evicting those tenants should he or she so desire.

The public control of land-use through town and country planning legislation is a creature of welfare state philosophy. The first major planning legislation was the Town and Country Planning Act 1947, directed towards the need to remove the slum housing which dated back to the nineteenth century (built in many cases by factory-owners as cheaply as possible to house their workforce and their families), the necessity of redeveloping property damaged by wartime bombing, and the importance of providing new buildings and roads while at the same time preserving the 'green belt' land and countering the urban sprawl which threatened to envelop the countryside in many areas. These regulative developments gave public sector authorities a vital role from the very beginning, and later legislation, notably the Town and Country Planning Act 1971 (as amended in 1972), required local authorities to prepare and submit to the ministry for approval 'structure plans' and 'local plans' – forming a *positive* aspect to planning policy in contrast to the more negative regulatory requirements for the acquisition of planning permission for changes in land-use or building structures.

The current law is contained principally in the Town and Country Planning Act 1990, as amended by the Planning and Compensation Act 1991.[34] In essence, local authorities draw up development plans for their area, setting out general strategy; these plans will be affected by government policy as it affects land-use planning. Individual developers must then apply for planning permission for any new development, including changes in use of land, and permission will be granted (often with conditions attached) or refused, depending on how the proposed development fits in with, or affects, the general plan. Breaches of any of the conditions, or more generally breaches of the law concerning what is done on the land by the developer or occupier, are regulated by means of the local authority's serving of an enforcement notice, and it is a criminal offence not to comply with such a notice.

If an application for planning permission is refused, there is a right of appeal to the Secretary of State, who makes the final decision. Interestingly, there is no similar right of appeal against a grant of planning permission. The decision of the Secretary of State is subject to the supervisory jurisdiction of the courts, though this jurisdiction, as we will see in chapter 12, is confined to an inquiry into the correctness of the *procedures* adopted by the minister, and does not extend to questions of fact or indeed of policy.

It has recently been suggested that

The traditional conflictual model of a regulatory body regulating the applicant by granting or refusing permission is currently breaking down. Modern town planning may be seen as a negotiative process in which consultation between the prospective developer and the local planning authority in advance of the application is the norm, and in which proposals are both made and considered in the light of local and national policies. The local planning authority and the developer often have a community of interest in carrying out a particular development; the developer gets its proposal granted and the local authority obtains the revitalisation of the economy of an area, or the creation of jobs, or some other economic benefit.[35]

The relentless pursuit in the 1980s and 1990s of the governmental aims of deregulation and privatization has been particularly felt in the area of planning and development controls. The recent legislation, and the many government administrative Circulars relating to planning policies (arguably the planning process is far more closely regulated by administrative mechanisms than through statutory provisions themselves) have been designed to streamline the processing of planning applications and to favour the private developer. The number of appeals against local refusals has substantially grown:

In the early to mid-1970s the success rate of appeals against refusal of permission was in the region of 20%. This had grown to 32% by 1984 and 40% in 1986/7, at which level it has stayed. Not surprisingly, the number of appeals also rose sharply, from around 8,000 in the mid-1970s to almost 30,000 each year at present ... A similar story is apparent in relation to appeals against enforcement notices.[36]

It is a paradoxical feature of the 1980s and 1990s that, under the guise of deregulation and privatization, central government control seems inevitably to *increase* rather than diminish. For example, direct government intervention resulted in the creation of 'Enterprise Zones' in 1980, which effectively meant that virtually any development proposal for an area designated as an Enterprise Zone was free from the usual planning controls. Government policies enshrined in the Local Government, Planning and Land Act 1980 similarly took away the conventional planning role of elected local authorities in some urban areas, and placed considerable powers relating to land development in the hands of non-elected, central-government-appointed Urban Development Corporations. Although there is some evidence that the role of local authority planning is re-emerging, there can be no doubt that the general trend in recent years has been towards the centralization of planning policies and decisions.

Many critics have pointed to other problems associated with planning legislation. First, as with nearly all interventionist legislation, the point of greatest tension is the point at which individual wishes encounter official policies. In planning, as elsewhere, mechanisms have always been provided within the legislative and administrative structure for both public consultation and individual dispute-solving. The Act of 1990 provides, for example, for drafts of local plans to be publicized and for objections to be formally made by members of the public; in the event of such objections being made, the local authority must hold a public inquiry, at which objectors have the right to appear. Similar inquiries may be held to deal with objections to specific proposals for development.

Another possibility is to channel a complaint, normally through a local councillor, to the 'local Ombudsman', or Commissioner for Local Administration. This possibility will only arise, however, if a citizen wishes to complain about alleged maladministration by a local planning department within a local authority: the ombudsman does not act as a court of appeal and has no power to assess a planning decision on its merits or demerits. In the event of maladministration by a planning authority at *central* government level, the Parliamentary Commissioner for Administration (the Parliamentary 'Ombudsman') has power to investigate complaints alleging such grievances, although this power is circumscribed by the procedures for instigating such an inquiry (he may only be approached through an MP), and by limitations upon the action he may take (he cannot alter decisions, but may only submit a report on the problem to Parliament if he finds that an injustice has been caused by maladministration).[37]

Another means of resolving individual disputes is the provision, in many areas of planning, for appeal to a higher authority (we have already noted the example of an appeal to the minister against a planning decision by a local authority planning department): in some cases, there may also be grounds for bringing an action in court if the problem falls within the supervisory jurisdiction of the courts, as, for example, in the case of an alleged breach of natural justice (see chapter 12), or where the complainant alleges that the planning authority has exceeded its statutory powers (acting *ultra vires*).[38] The difficulties with this course of action are considerable, however, not least because of the delay and expense of litigation, but also because of the cumbersome and out-dated procedural and remedial aspects of this particular procedure.

Individual and group involvement in planning decisions, whether at the level of prior consultation or in the form of objections to proposed plans, has been criticized by those who are of the opinion that the planners know best; Ambrose and Colenutt[39] note the view of one surveyor in 1973: 'One thing I think we shall all be spared is planning control by the public. Let us hope that there will not be a proliferation of exhibitions of new projects on which the public are invited to air their views. What a futile waste of time I suggest this can be.' The view of Heap, in a lecture in 1975, is similar: 'The training of a town planner takes years and years like the training of any other professional person and it must come as a bit of a bore to him to learn that he must, when seeking to exercise his expertise, constantly be asking John Citizen about what he, the planner, ought to be adoing of.'[40] Apart from the reluctance with which such planners regard public participation in decision-making, it is the case that there is little or no consultation over large-scale developments. Ambrose has recently argued,

As the development system becomes more complex, powerful and internationalized, so it becomes more difficult for people not directly connected with it either to comprehend its workings or, as a logical consequence, to affect them. As the issues become defined more in terms of professional jargon, technical models and computerized data, and less in terms of plain English, so the politics of choosing between options becomes obscured and the issue is made to appear more as a matter for the planning 'expert' to decide.[41]

This statement highlights another problem which affects almost all planning (and many other) policies in the field of state intervention, and that is the problem of bureaucracy. Many people find the world of bureaucratic officialdom, at both local and national level, overbearing, unsympathetic and unapproachable. The strong paternalistic creed with which welfare state institutions are imbued is anathema to many ordinary people, and many find unacceptable the idea that the planners 'know what is best'. Critics include not only citizens directly affected by state interference (through, for example, compulsory purchase of their property or refusal of permission for land development), but also those who feel that the environment is being harmed by such proposals as new motorways, airports, nuclear power stations or nuclear waste sites, and who form themselves into pressure-groups to try to combat the proposed developments. Although planners themselves are often cast in the role of scapegoat, taking the blame if development-schemes prove to be unsafe, or fail to make a return on investment,[42] in fact it may well be others (for example, developers or architects) who are responsible.

It should not be thought, on the other hand, that the field of planning is a kind of official bureaucratic conspiracy against ordinary citizens. Despite the doubts of some planners about public participation, reflected in the passages quoted above, the picture is not one of planners, builders and developers pursuing a common path towards agreed goals. Rather, as McAuslan points out, 'the planning process is not solely a matter of concepts, procedures and structures but it is also a matter of planners, lawyers and developers, their ideas, their interaction and the use they make of concepts, procedures and structures'.[43]

These debates about planners and their relationship with the citizen raise much wider questions about the extent to which government bodies (both central and local) should be accountable to the public, or to the local community. In the planning field, the argument in favour of greater, not less, community involvement in planning decisions has been outlined thus:

> The right to challenge and question official policies and put alternatives should not be based on the ownership or possession of property but should be seen as a right of citizenship and the law should provide accordingly. Furthermore, the law should also facilitate or require the taking into account of social and community considerations as well as property and economic ones in deciding issues of land use planning . . . finally the law should provide more opportunities for people's views on their own environment to be decisive and for them to be able to act on those views.[44]

This view runs directly against the attitudes towards public participation held by many professional planners, as we have seen, and may reflect a more generally held concern among some members of the community that professional expertise in matters affecting ordinary people should not be permitted to imply the exclusion of citizens' own views.

Connected with many people's fears about bureaucracy and 'planners' paternalism', however, is another area of controversy: the suspicion in some critics' minds about whose interests are being best protected by certain manifestations of state control. When considering the important issue of the impact of interest-groups, it is instructive to bear in mind the question of the balance between the role of public-sector authorities (especially central government) and private-sector industries and organizations which clearly have a direct interest in governmental or local authority policies. These – often very powerful – forces are able to influence policy-making levels of the civil service, whereas the opposing forces (local residents in affected areas, conservationist groups and so on) must resort to rather more lowly, and certainly less direct, tactics such as media campaigns, demonstrations and a vociferous presence at local inquiries. Similar influential forces outside of central and local government, some of them at first sight somewhat unexpected, are at work in the area of planning and development: insurance companies, banks, the construction industry and building societies.

Regarding property development in general, it has been argued[45] that planning controls operate to the advantage of the property-owners, in that the planning system is concerned only with *physical* control of the environment, and not with social or economic implications of proposed developments; the way is open to property-developers and speculators to obtain planning permission for proposals whose only function is to bring a high rate of financial return for the property-developer: 'The developer . . . need only justify his proposals in pure physical planning terms. In addition, he will have employed a team of surveyors, and valuers and ex-local authority planners who are experts at presenting their schemes to planners and councillors.'[46] Additionally, planners 'spend a lot of time assessing, for example, the retail shopping floorspace requirements to serve the needs of proposed residential developments of given size. The retail and service centres to serve these needs are rarely carried out by public sector initiatives',[47] but rather by private-sector developers who have access to this information and use it to prepare appropriate schemes which are likely to gain planning consent.

It was the property-development boom of the 1960s which saw so many towering blocks of offices appear in towns and cities all over the country (many of them remaining unoccupied for long periods, though still bringing in, potentially, enormous amounts of money through rents or sales). This was the result of the intricate interplay between property-developers, local authority planning departments and somewhat myopic legislation which enabled such development to take place, and it was noted in 1975 that

in contrast to the rate of house building, office development has been going ahead strongly in the past five years. The total national stock of office space increased . . . [by] about 21 per cent in five years. An increase of 21 per cent in the total housing stock over the period would have been more than enough to solve our housing problem several times over.[48]

A significant part of the explanation for this preference by developers for office and other commercial developments rather than housing is found in the fact that the former involve much higher rates of financial return than the latter. The critics of the existing planning procedures and legislative provisions argue that the present arrangement for planning and developing is not achieving what the Minister of Town and Country Planning in 1947 called a 'proper balance between the competing demands for land, so that all the land of the country is used in the best interest of the whole people'. The administrative and decision-making structure of planning is unwieldy and bureaucratic, and it is possible for property-developers with adequate resources to further their own economic interests by manipulating this machinery. Moreover, it has been forcefully argued that, through government policies over the last decade, the extension of privatization has resulted in a diminished role for local authority planning, with an accompanying decrease in opportunities for public participation in planning decisions. Furthermore, the overall picture has changed quite dramatically since the 1960s, with many large developments now being carried out not by individual property-developers, but by large combines with international connections. The international dimension, it has been argued, is highly significant: in order to attract international funds to Britain, for example, the domestic interest rates are periodically increased. This supports the pound, but at the same time inhibits new home investment through the raising of mortgage interest rates (that is to say, the cost of borrowing money also increases). It would seem that today, just as in feudal times, property is wealth, which is the foundation for accumulating yet more wealth, and with it the influence and status with which wealth has always been associated; we must also acknowledge, however, the influence upon planning, development and investment patterns of multinational and powerful private financial and industrial concerns.

Pollution control

Closely linked to the issue of planning, and possibly one of the most significant developments over the past twenty years, the growing concern over pollution and its effects on the environment is causing governments all over the world to rethink their policies on pollution control. Depletion of the ozone layer, poisonous waste, global warming, the effects of acid rain, threats to the rain forests and to the survival of many species of animal, bird, marine and plant life, and many other harmful consequences of both industrial and domestic pollution, have been at the forefront of such developments as the emergence of the Green Party in the UK, the activities of organizations such as Friends of the Earth and, in particular, Greenpeace in various parts of the world, the formulation of policy statements at national and international conventions, and the various stated commitments of domestic governments worldwide to tackle the problems of pollution.

In this country as elsewhere, there have been a number of recent attempts to control pollution and its effects, and these are largely, but not exclusively, incorporated in legal provisions. It should not be assumed, however, that concerns about pollution, and attempts at its control, are wholly new: as far back as the nineteenth century, statutes such as the Public Health Act 1848 were designed to confront and control the environmentally (and personally) damaging effects of industrialization. It is true to say, however, that statutory controls over more aspects of environmentally-damaging industrial and domestic practices have accelerated in recent years, as more and more evidence has emerged of the potentially devastating effects of uncontrolled pollution, and as technology has produced increasing amounts of toxic and radioactive substances and applications.

The law on environmental control is vast, complex, piecemeal and uncoordinated. It would be impossible here to detail the many legal provisions, though many attempts have been made over the years to combat individual problems through the use of law (see, for example, the Sea Birds Protection Acts 1869–80, the Protection of Birds Act 1954, the Conservation of Seals Act 1970 and the Badgers Act 1973), and once again the reader is referred to specialist texts in the area.[49] Our purpose here is to explore briefly some of the problems and evaluate the ways in which those problems have been dealt with, frequently through law.

To begin with, many questions arise when any individual pollutant, or polluting activity, is under discussion. What evidence is there that the activity in question *does* lead to the environmental damage which is alleged? How serious is that damage and its consequences, assuming that the causal link is established? What should be the balance between the conflicting public interests in, on the one hand, controlling or preventing the polluting activity and, on the other, the economic advantages of allowing that activity to continue? What *level* of pollution is deemed unacceptable? Who decides? Should the law be used, or could the industry in question effectively police itself? Who should enforce pollution control legislation, and by what mechanisms? Who should pay for the effects of pollution? And ought Britain to control a particular polluting activity if other countries do not?

Clearly, many of these are political and economic, not legal, questions, and require consideration of complex technical scientific data. Although space does not allow consideration of all the various forms of pollution, and the ways in which controls have been attempted, it is possible, by focusing on one aspect of the problem – atmospheric pollution – to gain some understanding of the difficulties in this field. A number of general propositions are explored below with particular reference to air pollution, though the point must be stressed that these propositions are equally applicable to water, land and other types of pollution.

Pollution can take many forms and result from many types of activity. The law was first used to combat air pollution as early as 1273, when a law was passed to control the emission of smoke in London, though it was not until the development of the various processes used in the manufacturing industries, and the widespread use of coal-burning fires and furnaces in the eighteenth and nineteenth centuries, that attempts to control smoke pollution became more widely used. Apart from smoke, the common use in industry of a process which produced soda, but which caused the emission into the atmosphere of hydrogen chloride gas became a serious problem: the gas, when combined with rain, formed hydrochloric acid: acid rain. The Alkali Acts of 1863 and 1874 were passed to try to combat this problem by requiring that factories prevented any hydrogen chloride emissions in excess of 0.2 grains per cubic foot, which remains the present legal limit. The consolidating Alkali, etc. Works Regulation Act 1906 required the 'best practicable means' to be taken to prevent the escape of these gases.

Smog is yet another form of seriously damaging air pollution:

On 5 December 1952 unusual climatic conditions produced fog over London. This was thickened by smoke, soot, carbon dust and gaseous waste. Visibility became nil; air could hardly be breathed. This lasted for five days. The 'smog' was alleged to have caused 4,000 deaths.[50]

The resulting inquiry led eventually to the passage of the Clean Air Act 1956, which was followed in subsequent years by further legislation regulating smoke and other emissions from the country's factory and domestic chimneys. The height of factory chimneys, in particular, is seen as critical: the theory is that the higher the chimney, the more widely the gases are to be dispersed, and the more diluted the pollutant when it finally falls – in whichever form – to earth. A side-effect of this policy, however, is that gases produced from factory chimneys in England can be carried long distances, causing pollution problems elsewhere: the Scandinavian countries in particular have suffered from deposits of sulphur dioxide and acid rain originating in Britain, and this is the subject of a continuing international dispute.

Despite the controls mentioned so far, the continuing use in industry of processes which lead to the emission of carbon dioxide (from fossil fuel burning) and other 'greenhouse gases', coupled with the contribution to the levels of these gases from car exhausts, has led to international concern about the 'greenhouse effect' leading to higher temperatures – global warming. This, it is thought, could spell worldwide disaster in many forms: melting ice-caps, rising sea-levels, unpredictable weather patterns, and the loss of homes, jobs and food-production capacity. Linked to this problem – and also caused by the emission of gases (in this instance, chlorofluorocarbons, or CFCs) – is the depletion of the ozone layer of the earth's atmosphere. This layer absorbs ultra violet radiation from the sun's rays, and massive holes in the ozone layer have the result that more UV radiation reaches the earth, leading to, among other problems, an increase in the number of cases of skin cancer.

We can add other atmospheric pollutants to this depressing list: airborne lead particles from vehicle exhausts, for example, leading to lead poisoning, which has led to the widespread use of vehicle engines designed to use unleaded fuel; and smoke produced by means other than factory and domestic chimneys, such as stubble-burning by farmers, which is now controlled by the Environmental Protection Act 1990.[51]

Attempts to control pollution have been piecemeal and complex, and a number of different agencies have been charged with enforcing control measures. Generally speaking, the pattern has been for new measures to be introduced as and when new pollution-related problems have arisen or, more accurately, have been perceived by government as sufficiently serious to warrant some form of control. Since the Alkali Act 1863, no fewer than nine separate Acts have been passed, along with innumerable regulations which provide detailed guidance, for instance about permitted levels of pollution, and which often specify the various activities which are wholly or partially exempted from controls. To take just one or two examples: the Clean Air Acts empowered the Secretary of State to make regulations concerning the emission of smoke and other substances from chimneys. Among the regulations made were the Dark Smoke (Permitted Periods) Regulations 1958, which provide for specific periods of time during which dark smoke may be emitted from factory chimneys; and the Clean Air (Emission of Grit and Dust from Furnaces) Regulations 1971, which incorporate the definition of 'grit', as distinct from 'dust'. The problems caused by emissions from vehicle exhausts were tackled in the Road Traffic Act 1988, together with amendments to the Construction and Use Regulations to take in European Community initiatives.

Not only are the legislative provisions, and regulations made thereunder, extremely detailed, technical and complex: a number of separate agencies have, over the years, been charged with the enforcement of these controls. The Alkali Acts created the Alkali Inspectorate to enforce the law relating to chemical emissions from factory chimneys. This body is now incorporated into the Health and Safety Executive. But smoke controls, provided in public health legislation from 1875 onwards and the Clean Air Acts of the 1950s, were placed in the hands of local authorities, which may be involved in their role in planning and development control, and/or their role in environmental protection. From the point of view of someone wishing to complain about a problem involving air pollution, it may not be clear as to which is the appropriate body to approach.

Controls have, to date, met with differing degrees of success in tackling pollution. There are many reasons why attempts through law to combat pollution may not be successful. First, the law may not be regarded as an appropriate method of control, though other methods may not be particularly effective. There has been no attempt, for example, at legal control regarding the ozone layer problem. Instead, there has been some progress by means of international agreements, and by the rapid phasing-out by some manufacturers of the use of CFCs – most notably perhaps the reduction in the number of domestic aerosol products using CFC gases. Second, a particular legal provision may turn out to be inadequate because it is found not to cover a particular activity. For instance:

Attempts were made to control the emission of smoke through such Acts as the Public Health Act 1875, the Public Health (Smoke Abatement) Act 1926 and the Public Health Act 1936 but these generally dealt with smoke nuisances. These powers could not rid industrial cities of the problems of smoke pollution. The physical evidence of this pollution could be seen on blackened buildings, and by the frequency of smog . . .[52]

Third, as we have seen in the case of acid rain, solving a problem in one locality could really mean only shifting it to somewhere else. Fourth, there may be resistance to proposals for change, particularly from manufacturers who deny that their activity causes pollution, and from politicians who may place pollution and the need to control it fairly low on their list of priorities: legislation may in such cases be slow to appear, and in the event may prove inadequate. Fifth, the technical nature of the problem, and of the industrial processes concerned, means that industry itself will be involved in the negotiations concerning controls: solutions which identify an 'acceptable' level of pollution and prohibit any excess over that level may fail to be effective if the 'acceptable' level fails to prevent further pollution. Finally, there are inherent difficulties in imposing liability on companies for pollution offences. As corporate bodies, the only available criminal sanction is the fine, and this may not be sufficient to deter companies from further offences. As regards criminal liability, if an offence may be committed without proof of knowledge or intent by the polluter ('strict' liability: see chapter 10) then there may be few problems in securing a conviction. Where, however, liability for a criminal offence depends on proof that the polluter intentionally, or at least knowingly, carried out the polluting activity, it may be extremely difficult, if not impossible, to prove that the persons who control the company – nowadays regarded as the human embodiment of the corporate 'will' – possessed the relevant degree of knowledge or intent.

Pollution control measures have recently been modified in a number of recent statutes, designed to achieve a more integrated system of control. The recent changes have been heavily influenced by public concern, media attention to environmental issues, the international community and, most especially, European Community initiatives (see chapter 8). There have so far been four major recent Acts: the Town and Country Planning Act 1990, the Wildlife and Countryside Act 1981, the Environmental Protection Act 1990, and a number of statutes concerning water in 1991. Noise pollution continues to be dealt with for the moment by the Control of Pollution Act 1974 (Part III), along with the Noise at Work Regulation 1989, though further legislation on noise pollution is likely.

Atmospheric pollution, along with that of water and land, is dealt with by the Environmental Protection Act 1990, although the control of smoke continues to be provided for by the pre-existing Clean Air legislation. Part 1 of the 1990 Act deals with what is termed 'Integrated Pollution Control (IPC) and Air Pollution Control by Local Authorities (APCLA)', and these constitute two separate systems of control. Both systems have in common provision for certain prescribed industrial processes to take place only if authorized by a new agency – Her Majesty's Inspectorate of Pollution – in the case of IPC, and local authorities in the case of APCLA.

The Act provides very considerable powers of enforcement regarding air pollution control. Conditions may be attached to authorizations, and the enforcement agency may vary or revoke authorizations, or issue enforcement or prohibition notices. It is provided with powers of entry, search and seizure, and has the power to take legal proceedings to secure compliance with notices. The Secretary of State also has an enormous range of powers under the Act, ranging from the power to prescribe the processes and substances to be controlled, to establishing standards and directing the enforcement agencies as to the exercise of their powers. All authorizations will be subject to a general provision that 'best available techniques not entailing excessive cost' (a phrase now in common use, usually abbreviated to BATNEEC) should be used.

As to which industrial processes are authorized and controlled by which agency, two lists of processes will be drawn up, according to whether the processes in question are felt by the minister to warrant central or local control. It is estimated that around 5,000 individual industrial plants will be brought under central (HMIP) control, and around 27,000 under local control.

Aspects of the Act are derived from European Community initiatives: the BATNEEC formula, for example, comes from a number of EC Directives, and the Act itself – especially Part 1 – constitutes the writing into English law of EC Directives, including the specification of emission limits. Other influences on the Act include various internationally agreed Conventions and Protocols on such aspects of atmospheric pollution as sulphur dioxide emissions and ozone layer depletion.

The modern tendency is for controls to be less *reactive* and more *positive* – for example, to lay down standards to be adhered to in the future, rather than waiting until a problem reaches crisis proportions before tackling it. It remains to be seen how effective all these measures and new initiatives will prove in the long run. While the European Community is dedicated to increasing pollution controls, some regard the progress made by the international community on issues such as toxic waste and the ozone layer problem as worryingly slow. Whether the environment is to be better protected through law or through international agreement, it remains the case that environmental protection is essentially a political matter: no doubt governments will need to be continuously pressed into further action, continuously reminded of the threat to the world we live in, and continuously urged to rethink political priorities so that better and more effective environmental protection remains high on their political agendas.

Housing

The fact that private property-developers have chosen to deal in terms of commercial developments rather than house-building is reflected in the diminished rate of house-building over the years. The number of public and private housing units completed in Great Britain in 1965 was 382,000;[53] in 1990 this was reduced to 184,100. The greatest proportion of these – 153,100 – were private enterprise developments. Of the remainder, 14,600 were built by housing associations, and only 16,400 by public-sector bodies (local authorities, new towns and government departments).[54]

The legal device whereby the rents from office blocks and other commercial property are derived is, of course, the *lease*. The lease, it will be recalled, creates a tenancy which is the only legal estate in land apart from the fee simple. The use of the lease enables the property-owner to render the land profitable by contracting with the tenant so that the latter enjoys possession of the land in exchange for the payment of rent to the land-owner.

One of the major areas where the lease has been widely used is housing, where many people occupy rented property which is owned by other private individuals. The precise rights and obligations of the landlord and the tenant will depend upon the terms of individual leases, subject to the conditions which have been imposed by statute (such as those provisions in the Rent Acts which provide tenants with rent control and security of tenure, making it difficult for the landlord to evict them). Here again, the intervention of the state in the hitherto private area of rented housing has made a considerable difference to housing and property-owning patterns in Britain.

In the nineteenth century and before, the vast majority of houses were privately owned by landlords and rented out. In the twentieth century, there has been an enormous decrease in the proportion of privately rented accommodation. Why has this decrease come about?

In the first place, there has of course been a huge increase in the number of people who are in a position to buy their own home. Owner-occupiers account for well over half the total number of householders today, and this increase has been due to factors such as the rise of building societies, and the coming of the 'affluent society', in which increased income and improved standards of living have created situations in which people are financially able to accede to the cultural conditions of our society, which prizes home-owning so highly. Building societies are politically and economically very powerful (hence the existence of income tax relief on loans for house-purchase, a considerable inducement to obtain such loans). Locally, building societies may be unwilling to advance loans for property in certain deteriorating parts of a town or city, or areas which are predominantly commercial in nature, and may on the other hand be keen to invest in other, more 'up-market' areas. In this way, building societies, which it should be remembered are private- not public-sector organizations, may dramatically influence local development patterns.

Although there has been a massive increase in home-ownership through mortgage loans with building societies, it should not be forgotten that homes can be repossessed by the lenders in the event of failure to maintain mortgage repayments. In the long period of recession at the end of the 1980s and continuing into the 1990s, with its usual accompaniments of high rates of redundancy and unemployment, repossessions of houses have reached record levels – in 1990 there were no fewer than 43,900 repossessions, causing untold misery for many families facing, in many cases, the prospect of having no roof over their heads.

Apart from the growth in owner-occupation, two other crucial developments – public-sector housing provision and the legal protection of tenants in the privately rented sector – have changed the pattern of residential accommodation over the last seventy or eighty years, and both these developments are part of the movement towards state intervention in the realm of property and property rights.

Council housing

In 1914 local authority rented housing accounted for only 1 per cent of residential accommodation, whereas in 1974 the figure was 33 per cent. This figure has fallen in recent years, however, to around 27–30 per cent.[55] The social class background of most council house tenants is working class – the very class for whom privately rented accommodation was usual in the last century. This factor clearly accounts to some extent for the decline of the private landlord; it may be seen as one very important aspect of welfare state philosophy, whereby housing has been recognized by state institutions as a basic necessity and taken on by successive governments' policies as part of beneficent welfare state provision.

It must be borne in mind, however, that council house building programmes are subject, like every other local authority commitment, to fluctuations in the economic tide; since the 1970s we have seen strong and continuous pressure on, and from, central government to curb public spending, and it is to be expected that cuts in expenditure by local authorities will be reflected in projected housing programmes. In addition, the Conservative government's Housing Act 1980 was designed to make a considerable impact upon the council housing sector. The current law is contained in the Housing Act 1985, largely a consolidating measure though with some changes in the law. To begin with, the 1980 Act introduced the 'tenants' charter',[56] which provides, in essence, the same protections against eviction that are enjoyed by private tenants by virtue of the Rent Acts, and additional rights such as the right to carry out minor repairs and improvements and the right to take in lodgers. The council house tenant thus enjoys *security of tenure*. The Act further provided for the 'right to buy'. Now, under the 1985 Act, all secure tenants who have been public-sector tenants for two years or more have the right to purchase their house (or, in the case of council flats, the long leasehold) from the council. There is also the statutory right to a mortgage (Housing Act 1985 s.132), provided by the council if necessary; and although the property will be valued at its market price, tenants of under three years' residence are entitled to a discount of 32 per cent on that price, the discount rising for each additional year of residence in the property up to a maximum of 70 per cent (Housing and Planning Act 1986).[57]

These provisions met with a considerable degree of criticism and opposition. They were based upon the government's assumption that owner-occupation is a status to which everyone aspires, and that the public housing sector is over-subsidized by central government. Originally, the Labour Party opposed the introduction of the 'right to buy' provisions, and some Labour-controlled local authorities resisted the implementation of the sales provisions of the Act.[58] Since the Act reserved to the Secretary of State wide powers to do 'all such things as appear to him necessary or expedient' (now contained in s.164(5) of the 1985 Act), protracted battles between recalcitrant authorities and the Secretary of State would seem to lead inevitably to a defeat for the reluctant local authorities, and in any case Labour has changed its policy to support a limited right to buy.[59]

It was strongly argued by supporters of the legislation that selling council houses would reduce public expenditure by increasing revenue to local councils through mortgage repayments and through councils being relieved of the costs of maintenance. It has been argued, on the other hand, that public money will *not* be saved in this way, because whereas rents can be increased to take account of inflation, the real value of mortgage repayments actually falls over a period of time.[60] As far as the individual purchaser is concerned, it may well be that mortgage repayments will exceed the amount otherwise payable as rent, and in many cases this will be a disincentive for tenants to buy their homes, especially with the present uncertainties about possible redundancy and the prospect of unemployment which faces many potential buyers.

In connection with the latter point, it was argued that only the better-off council tenants, in the more desirable houses on popular estates, would find the purchase of their house an attractive proposition, leaving a considerable amount of council housing stock on poorer estates and unpopular sites such as high-rise flats, containing tenants too poor to purchase, and consisting of property which tenants do not find particularly desirable anyway.[61] With reductions in council house building programmes as a result of public expenditure cuts, this may exacerbate existing housing problems, such as availability of housing stock, long waiting lists, homelessness and so on.

The 'right to buy' provisions came into force in October 1980, and by the end of March 1982 more than 400,000 claims from about 9 per cent of council tenants had been received. However, there is considerable regional variation in this overall figure: the more urbanized the area, and the greater the proportion of high-rise flats, the lower the proportion of tenants claiming the right to purchase their houses. These considerations mean that care must be taken when considering overall figures, but it seems indisputable that since the initial surge in council house sales, there has been something of a levelling-off. To date about 1½ million council houses have been sold.

Rent legislation

The legislation affecting tenants in the private housing sector is extremely complex, affecting various types of tenancy held through private leases to which somewhat different sets of rules apply. The differential positions of landlord and tenant in terms of their respective bargaining power, together with the various manifestations of that differential power, such as high rents, have been recognized by legislators for many years, and some form of rent control has been in force, through a long series of statutes, since 1915. The area had been fertile ground for party-political battles, with Conservative governments tending to attempt to restore protection and freedom to private landlords, whom Labour governments have tried to place under legal controls and restrictions. The more recent in this series of enactments, the Rent Acts of 1968, 1974 and 1977, and the Housing Act 1980, provide considerable protection for the private tenant through what is, generally speaking, a system of rent regulation ('fair rents' being fixed, on application by landlord or tenant, by rent officers, their decisions being subject to appeal to rent assessment committees) and a system of security of tenure, whereby the tenant enjoys, by virtue of the protection provided by the Acts, possession of the property without danger of eviction save in a number of specified circumstances. Recent changes in the legislation – in particular the Housing Act 1988, discussed below – have had a significant impact on the rent-control and security of tenure issues, though the kind of harassment by landlords of tenants in order to get them out of the property, which made headlines in the 1960s when Rachman was exposed as using strong-arm methods against his tenants to remove them or to enforce increased rents, is now a criminal offence.

The detailed analysis of the statutory provisions in this area is outside the scope of this book,[62] but the law may be briefly outlined as follows. Leases may be of two kinds: fixed-term and periodic. Fixed-term leases are for specified periods of time (long leases are for twenty-one years or more, and are frequently for much longer periods), whereas with periodic leases (the most common arrangement between landlords and tenants) rent is payable on a periodic basis, usually each week or each month.

The following account refers to privately rented accommodation leased to tenants prior to 15 January 1989. As we will see, new legislation governs the position for leases created after that date.

For periodic leases, if a landlord wishes to evict a tenant, a *notice to quit*, issued by the landlord to the tenant, must be written. It must give at least four weeks' notice, and must inform tenants of their rights under the Rent Acts. Before any tenant can be required to leave the property, however, a county court possession order must be obtained by the landlord. With some exceptions, such as cases where the rent includes payment for board or attendances, or those where the landlord is resident in the same building, or has let the property for holiday purposes, or is a public body such as a local authority or housing association, all tenancies are *protected* by virtue of the Rent Act 1977, Part 1, as amended by the Housing Act 1980.

These statutory protections provide the private tenant with *security of tenure*. This means that, although the contractual agreement between landlord and tenant may be terminated by means of a notice to quit, the statutory protections take over, transforming the original contractual tenancy into a *statutory tenancy* with the same rent and conditions. A landlord may gain possession in such cases only by obtaining a court order (Rent Act 1977, s.98); such an order will be awarded either where there is suitable alternative accommodation available, or where the landlord has established that the tenancy falls into one or more categories provided by Schedule 15 of the Rent Act 1977. By virtue of this Schedule, a court *may* order possession if the tenant has broken an obligation of the tenancy, or is causing a nuisance, or has, by waste or neglect, accelerated the deterioration of the premises, or furniture therein, or has assigned or sub-let the whole of the premises without the landlord's permission, or is sub-letting at an excessive rent. Additionally, an order may be granted if the landlord, having previously occupied the premises, reasonably requires them again for himself or a member of his close family, providing that such possession will not throw the tenant into even greater hardship.

The Schedule also provides conditions which, if met, mean that the court *must* order possession. These conditions are, principally, that the landlord who previously occupied the premises now requires them again for himself or a close family member, or wishes to sell the property if the house is no longer suitable for his needs, provided that notice of such an intention was given to the tenant before the tenancy was created; that the landlord bought the premises to retire into and now wishes to move in or sell, provided, again, that appropriate notice was given; that the lease was for eight months or less of premises used for holidays during the holiday seasons, and notice was given to the tenant before the tenancy was created; that the lease was for twelve months or less of premises used for student accommodation, and notice was given to the tenant; that the tenancy was used for a minister of religion, an agricultural worker or a member of the armed forces, who was given notice before the tenancy was created.

Intended to realize the government's desire to stimulate the private rented housing sector, the Housing Act 1988, which was designed to facilitate increased returns on investment in this sector, governs the regulation of the private rented sector for new tenancies created after 15 January 1989.

This Act created three types of 'assured tenancy', 'periodic', involving regular payment of rent over an indefinite period, 'fixed-term', involving a tenancy created for a fixed period, and 'assured statutory periodic', which occurs when a fixed-term tenancy comes to an end. Rent increases desired by the landlord may be referred by the tenant to rent assessment committees, who will determine the appropriate market rent. The 'market rent' may differ from a 'fair rent' (discussed above) in that when assessing the former, factors such as not only the size and condition of the premises, but also the local availability of accommodation may be taken into account: this may well have the effect that the 'market' rent is higher than what might previously have been fixed as 'fair'.

A landlord may only terminate a periodic or assured statutory periodic tenancy by means of a court order, though an assured fixed-term tenancy may be terminated by the landlord's exercising his power contained in the agreement, in which case the tenancy becomes a statutory periodic tenancy.

Security of tenure is rather more limited under the 1988 Act than under previous statutory provisions, with some *additions* being made to the circumstances in which a court *must* order repossession. These circumstances are: where a building society, bank or other mortgagee requires possession of the property for sale if the mortgage was granted before the start of the tenancy; where the landlord intends to demolish, rebuild or carry out substantial work on the property; where the landlord requires possession from a succeeding tenant (though this does not include that tenant's spouse) within a year of the death of the assured periodic tenant; and where the tenant is three months in rent arrears at the time of both the giving of notice to quit, and the actual court hearing. The last of these circumstances represents a substantial reduction in security of tenure.

Additional situations in which the court has a *discretion* as to ordering repossession are where there has been persistent delay in payment of rent, or where the tenant has suitable alternative accommodation.

What seems to emerge is that, as governments wish to depress or stimulate various aspects of the provision of private rented accommodation, adjustments are made to the difficult balance between the rights of tenants (security of tenure, fair rents) and those of landlords (control over their property, returns on investment). At present, with the accent firmly on the policy of pursuing deregulation in this, as in other, sectors of the economy, the legal provisions provide somewhat reduced protection for the tenant in the interests of boosting this particular housing sector.

A further major change brought about by the Housing Act 1980 was the introduction of a new form of property-letting arrangement: the *shorthold tenure*. This, too, was an attempt to stimulate the dwindling private rented sector; the effect of the statutory provisions is to allow landlords to let property to tenants for a fixed term of between one and five years (amended by the 1988 Housing Act to a period of not less than six months). The tenant must be given specific notice that the tenancy is shorthold, and once the period of the tenancy has expired the landlord may regain possession through a court order or, by virtue of the Housing Act 1988, by giving two months' notice after the expiry of the fixed term.

This form of renting did not at first prove particularly popular among landlords, even though, from their point of view, it avoided the situation in which an undesirable tenant who could not be brought within Schedule 15 of the Rent Act 1977 remained in possession of the premises against the wishes of a landlord who could not remove that tenant. Since the Housing Act 1988, however, the indications are that the 'assured shorthold' tenancies, for which that Act makes provision, are becoming widely used because there is no security of tenure at all beyond the fixed period of the agreement.

Another major reason why the shorthold tenure provisions were not much used at first was the common use of an alternative mode of hiring out property: the *licence*.

In law, a licence is simply permission given by one person to another, which allows that other to enter upon land. The licence may be 'bare', as where a householder allows the next-door neighbour to make use of a back yard; or 'contractual', as where one pays to enter a cinema or theatre in order to watch the performance. The differences between the lease and the licence may be stated quite simply: a lease involves exclusive possession of the premises by the tenant, but a licence does not; a lease is a property interest which can bind subsequent owners of the premises (a landlord may sell the premises to another, but the 'sitting tenants' will retain their rights irrespective of that transaction), but a licence is usually held to be a purely *personal* right, held by the licensee and enforceable only against the individual landlord who granted the licence; and, perhaps most important of all, a licence does not attract Rent Act protection for the licensee, so anyone living in accommodation under a licence is not protected by those statutory provisions.

The contractual licence became popular with many landlords as a means of hiring out accommodation which avoided the protections given to tenants by the Rent Acts, especially after the decision in the case of *Somma* v. *Hazelehurst* in 1978,[63] where an unmarried couple each signed a separate (though identical) agreement with the owner of the premises. Each agreement stated that it was a licence, and included a term to the effect that the owner himself had the right to share the premises and to introduce one other licensee to share the use of the premises. It was held that neither of the couple had exclusive possession, nor did they share exclusive possession (because of the owner's stated right to share); the agreement was therefore held not to be a tenancy, and was outside Rent Act protection.

This use of licences was, however, fundamentally affected by the House of Lords' decision in *Street* v. *Mountford* in 1985.[64] This case concerned an agreement, entitled a 'licence agreement', granting occupancy of two rooms subject to termination by fourteen days' notice, and to certain conditions in the agreement. The occupant had signed a declaration to the effect that she understood that the agreement did not give her a tenancy protected by the Rent Acts. The occupant and her husband had exclusive possession, and this was conceded by the landlord. The question for the court was whether this agreement was indeed a licence, or whether the arrangement constituted, in law, a tenancy agreement. The court held that it was a tenancy, and stated that where residential accommodation had been granted for a term at a rent with exclusive possession, the grantor providing neither attendance nor services, the legal consequence was the creation of a tenancy, notwithstanding the statements in the agreement. On the question of *Somma*, Lord Templeman stated that in that case the agreement signed by the couple constituted the grant to them 'jointly of exclusive possession at a rent for a term . . . and the agreement therefore created a tenancy'[65], and he went on to say,

Although the Rent Acts must not be allowed to alter or influence the construction of an agreement, the court should, in my opinion, be astute to detect and frustrate sham devices and artificial transactions whose only object is to disguise the grant of a tenancy and to evade the Rent Acts. I would disapprove of the decision [in *Somma* v. *Hazlehurst*].[66]

Henceforth, said the court, the only question in such cases would be whether the occupier was a lodger or a tenant. The case would seem therefore to have put paid to the use of the contractual licence for residential accommodation, at least where the agreement specifically made it clear that the occupier was to enjoy exclusive possession. But what about the situation where the landlord inserted into the agreement a clause to the effect that the occupation was non-exclusive?

In *Antoniades* v. *Villers* and *A. G. Securities* v. *Vaughan* in 1988[67] the House of Lords seems finally to have resolved this remaining point. In the first of these cases, the two occupiers had moved into a small flat comprising one bedroom, a bed-sitting room, a kitchen and a bathroom. They had signed separate agreements, each containing non-exclusive possession clauses, though it was understood that they would be living together as husband and wife. The agreements purported to be licences, and the occupiers licensees; and there was an explicit statement to the effect that the intention of the parties was to create a licence which would not fall under Rent Act protection.

In the second case, four occupiers moved at different times into a four-bedroom flat with a sitting-room, bathroom and WC. They signed separate agreements with the owners, each for a six-month period, stating that there was no right to exclusive possession, and that the occupiers were licensees.

The House of Lords, in deciding what the true legal position in these cases was, stated that the basic question as to whether the agreement was a lease or a licence depends on the matter of exclusive possession, to be decided by reference to the intention of the parties to the agreement. In *Antoniades*, the court held that the nature of the accommodation was such that neither party could realistically have contemplated that the owner would use or share any part of the flat, or put anyone else in to share. It followed that in this case the true intention was the creation of a tenancy. But in *A. G. Securities*, the occupants entered into different agreements at different times and for different rents. Each agreement could be terminated without reference to those of the other three. Here, in the court's view, there was a common intention that the occupiers *should* be licensees, and certainly not joint tenants. If these decisions have finally resolved the vexed issue of the attempted use of licences by landlords to avoid Rent Act protection, then what might at first seem like a legal victory for tenants has to be seen against the new 'assured shorthold' provisions of the Housing Act 1988, discussed above, which may well serve landlords' interests even better than the short-lived use of the licence.

For many landlords, concerned only to let their property in order to obtain income from rents, the privately leased accommodation business has become singularly unattractive as a financial proposition. The high cost of the upkeep of the property (usually the contractual responsibility of the landlord and subject, in the case of tenancy agreements, to statutory provision, for example in the Housing Act 1961), and the impact of tax on rents received, have meant that many landlords today believe that they no longer have the control over their own property which they, as owners, feel they should have. Those who let property by means of leases no longer have the freedom to evict tenants whom they feel to be unsuitable (subject to the special conditions in the legislation) and the amount of rent they charge may well be challenged by the tenant by application to rent officers or tribunals. Consequently, many private landlords have looked to other areas of investment in which to utilize their capital for higher and less troublesome returns. Although private tenancies account for only about 15 per cent of the total residential accommodation in this country today, there remains a significant section of the population – migrant workers, students, the poor, minority ethnic groups – for whom home-ownership and council housing are unavailable or inappropriate, and it is this section which will find the decline in the private housing sector most worrying. With the demise of the licence, there are indications of the increased use of the 'assured shorthold' tenancy in its place, with its considerably reduced security of tenure.

It is unfortunately the case that the housing issue – in both private and public sectors – has long been a political football, being made the subject of the political ideologies of successive governments since the First World War when the council housing system began. In the 1990s the public housing sector continues to be squeezed through cuts in public spending, and the private sector remains on an ever-swinging pendulum which at times has swung in favour of landlords, at times in favour of tenants' protection. We have seen the attempt to revitalize private-sector housing, through the introduction of the shorthold lease in 1980, and continuing with the Housing Act 1988. Our brief discussion of land-use and its economic and political contexts shows that the type and degree of regulation will depend very much upon the dominant political and ideological complexion of any given period. At the present time it appears that, after a long period in which the law was used to attempt to control private land-use in the interests of the community, it is now often being used, especially in the housing context, to reinstate private property rights and to reinforce the ideology of private ownership.

Conclusion

In this chapter we have explored the relationships between law, property, and economic and political power. We have noted the main legal forms of property rights, and the various types and uses of property-objects. The basic contention at the end of our brief survey of these issues must be that property-ownership continues to be regarded as fundamental in our society, and that the law continues to be called upon to protect the interests of those who own and control that property. In some respects, such protection is unobjectionable, but in other respects, such as planning, property development and housing, the unfettered freedom of private property-owners to use their property as they wish has raised serious social problems which the state, through planning, pollution controls and rent legislation, has intervened to try to solve. At the end of the day, however, it is true to say that the marriage of welfare state legislation with the older body of property law represented in the Law of Property Act 1925 has reflected the social and political chasm between those who own and/or control property, and those who do not; between the private landlord and the tenant; between the property-developer and the homeless; between the polluter and the victims. The intervention, through planning legislation, of a body of professional planners has made the overall picture more complicated, but the structure and administration of planning policies and decisions also reflects, especially in certain fields, the predominance of the interests of the propertied classes. In a society where there is still a great gulf between rich and poor, it becomes all the more important to ensure that state measures through law should serve the interests of the latter, and not subjugate them to the power of the former.

6
Law and the settlement of disputes

Every social group contains within it the elements and conditions in which disputes will arise. Even the smallest social group will experience disputes between its members, and, as we would expect, the larger and more complex a social group becomes, the more varied and, perhaps, frequent will be the disputes which crop up within it. Hardly a day goes by in people's everyday lives without some problem occurring, some argument arising or some resentment or frustration being felt by one person or group over the activities of another. Family rows, arguments with friends, confrontations at work and so on are familiar to most people, as are the various solutions which we use to deal with those disputes.

The simplest disputes are dealt with by various informal, often quite good-natured, means. Within family units, there may be an invocation of an established family custom or rule, or the calling-in of a third party to arbitrate in the dispute. Rarely would family squabbles result in the initiation of any kind of formal proceedings to settle the matter. Similarly, the social and economic world outside such small units as friends or family rests upon various types of relationship between, for example, business enterprises, employers and employees, traders and consumers, and citizens and government agencies. When considering the frequency with which something goes wrong with the smooth running of these relationships, and a dispute arises, it is important to appreciate that the informal resolution of the problem, through concession or compromise, is by far the most usual way of settling the matter.

This mode of settling disputes through concession or compromise is especially important where the parties to the dispute are in some long-standing or permanent relationship with each other. In domestic situations, feuding neighbours will rarely resort to litigation to solve their disputes, partly because theirs is a continuing relationship, as is the relationship between employer and employee, or landlord and tenant. In the sphere of commercial agreements and business contracts, research by Macaulay and others[1] has suggested that people in business rarely invoke the law as a means of resolving business disputes over their contractual agreements, mainly because this is seen as having the effect of perpetuating the conflict and polarizing the disputants, instead of resolving the particular problem without damaging the continuing business relationships of the parties.

Often, a dispute will be settled by invoking some kind of rule.[2] The rule in question may be peculiar to a particular family;[3] or it may be established by people entering into a specific relationship, so that anticipated difficulties may be resolved without too much friction (as when those entering into business contracts insert into those contracts clauses which specify that, should a certain event occur, then by agreement certain results will follow – see below and chapter 11); or the rule may be a rule of *law*, which provides some form of solution to the particular type of dispute which has arisen. What is certain is that, just as the complexities and fluctuations of smooth-running social and economic relationships must inevitably raise problems which we call disputes, so the social structural arrangements within a social group will invariably contain *dispute-settling*, as well as *dispute-prevention*, mechanisms.

Although the vast majority of disputes are settled by informal means, there will, at least in the more complex and technologically developed societies, be various official, formal institutions and agencies whose purpose is the resolution of disputes. The clearest examples in our own society of such agencies are, of course, the courts of law and tribunals, one of whose most important functions is the authoritative settlement of disputes through the application of legal rules. These agencies will be considered later in this chapter.

The prevention and settlement of disputes in modern society

The twentieth century has seen a considerable growth in the potential for disputes between individuals, groups and state agencies. To begin with, the expansion of agencies created for the implementation of state interventionist policies in, for example, the field of welfare provision has created in turn the potential for disputes between individuals and social security officials, and between property-owners and planning authorities. Frequently, as we shall see, the legislation which has established the machinery for implementing such policies has also set up the institutional framework within which disputes in particular fields are to be resolved; and it is significant that in many such cases, the dispute-solving mechanisms adopted have not been ordinary courts of law, but rather specialized *tribunals*, which we will discuss in more detail later. In other areas, disputes which were once a purely private matter between the individuals concerned have been subject to regulation through new legal procedures and legal rules. In the sphere of industrial relations, the picture is complicated by the economic and political dimensions of increased trade union activity and strength. It is useful to begin this section by examining in more detail the developments which have taken place over the last eighty years or so in relation to industrial disputes.

Until the turn of the century, disputes at work were usually settled on an individual basis between employer and employee, and rarely to the latter's advantage. With the growth of trade unionism and the consequent increase in unions' bargaining-power, many individual problems over pay, conditions of work and so on are resolved by means of *collective bargaining* between managements and trade unions. This is not say, of course, that all trade unions have equal bargaining-power, nor that employees in all industries are able to turn to their unions to negotiate on their collective (or individual) behalf.[4] Some unions are larger and more powerful than others, while in some industries, especially those in which the labour force tends to be predominantly casual or part-time, there may be little union presence. In addition, employers may in some cases be unwilling to encourage, or even to recognize, trade unions in their particular business enterprise.

We noted in chapter 3 that trade union activity has always been, and remains, highly controversial in terms of its perceived relationship with industrial and economic stability, and both the major political parties have, during their periods in office, attempted in various ways to create a statutory framework for the regulation of industrial conflict. Union activity, especially the use of strikes as a means of settling collective industrial conflicts, was directly confronted by formal legal controls in the Conservative government's Industrial Relations Act 1971, the failure of which was followed in turn by the attempt in 1974 by the incoming Labour government to set up a less rigid procedure for settling disputes at work between unions and management, as part of an overall strategy for industrial harmony.[5] One aspect of this strategy was the introduction, in the Employment Protection Act 1975,[6] of the Advisory, Conciliation and Arbitration Service (ACAS), an administrative agency funded by, but operating independently of, government. We will say more about the work of ACAS presently. The Conservative government which took office in 1979 regarded union activity as being in need of further regulation and control, however, and during the 1980s a number of measures were introduced which significantly curtailed trade union activities with regard to, among other things, picketing, secondary industrial action and 'closed shop' disputes (see chapter 3).

With regard to such disputes at work between bodies of workers and their management, ACAS has an important role. One of the statutory functions of the service is to try, where possible, to effect a solution to the dispute by means of discussion and negotiation followed by an agreed settlement between the parties. In this way, the hope is that direct industrial action such as strikes may in many cases be avoided. The service has an important similar function, however, with regard to *individual* grievances and disputes between employer and employee. In the sphere of individual employment law, many such disputes may be brought before an Industrial Tribunal for formal settlement. Industrial Tribunals receive about 30,000 applications each year, mainly alleging unfair dismissal, although of these only about 25–30 per cent actually culminate in a tribunal hearing. The jurisdiction of these tribunals includes claims for unfair dismissal, claims arising from redundancy payments, allegations of sex or race discrimination at work, and disputes arising from matters involving health and safety at work. Before a claim is heard by an Industrial Tribunal, however, it is statutorily provided that the dispute must be referred to ACAS, once again in the hope of settling the matter through discussion and conciliation without recourse to the tribunal. Available figures suggest that, at least with regard to unfair dismissal cases (by far the largest single category of such disputes), up to two-thirds of the total number of claims are settled by means of intervention by a conciliation officer from ACAS.

From this brief discussion of individual and collective industrial disputes, we can see that state intervention through legal rules and frameworks may enter the arena of dispute-prevention and settlement in a number of ways. First, collective bargaining means that in many cases of potential dispute the parties effectively *prevent* disputes from disrupting their relationship by specifying, within collective bargaining agreements, agreed procedures and solutions should certain problems arise. Second, the law may provide basic criteria (such as definitions of 'trade dispute' or 'unfair dismissal') whereby a dispute is recognized as having particular features, or as setting in motion particular procedures for settlement. Third, the law may dictate the means whereby a dispute may be settled. This may take a *negative* form, as where governments may, through legal measures, attempt to curb certain industrial action such as strikes; or it may take a *positive* form, as where special agencies, such as ACAS or Industrial Tribunals, are created in order to resolve the dispute through discussion and conciliation and, if these fail, official resolution and the award of a remedy where appropriate.

If we look at the machinery of dispute-prevention and settlement in modern society more generally, we can see that there are many other areas in which one or more of these legal responses have been introduced. Sometimes, changes in the nature and structure of society and in dominant social attitudes have brought certain areas of dispute out into the open rather more clearly than previously, and new dispute-settlement agencies have been established to deal with these disputes and grievances. Several such agencies are worthy of particular note, in so far as they substantially supplement (and to a certain extent may supplant) traditional legal solutions and the provision of remedies through litigation. First, the Sex Discrimination Act 1975 prohibits the discrimination on the ground of sex in the fields of employment, housing, education and the provision of goods and services, and the body responsible for administering the provisions of this Act is the Equal Opportunities Commission – one example of what have come to be known as 'quasi-autonomous non-governmental organizations' ('quangos') set up to deal with specific areas. This commission has the power to investigate alleged discrimination, and can take steps to order such discrimination to cease. The Act does provide that court proceedings can ensue, but by and large the commission has powers to secure remedies for victims of sex discrimination without recourse to courts by issuing 'non-discrimination notices' to the respondent, requiring the cessation of the discriminatory practice. In addition, individuals complaining of discrimination can take complaints to the county court (or to the Industrial Tribunal, if the complaint concerns discrimination in employment).

Second, the Race Relations Act 1976 makes similar provision in the area of race discrimination. The Commission for Racial Equality can inquire into alleged racial discrimination in various fields, and here, too, individuals may take cases alleging discrimination to the county courts or, where appropriate, to an Industrial Tribunal.

Often, disputes and claims which *could* be the subject of court hearings are dealt with by some other, non-litigious, agency or procedure. One major device for dealing with disputes, and claims arising from disputes, is insurance, discussed more fully in chapter 9. It is theoretically possible to insure against *any* eventuality, but for most people, insurance usually covers such contingencies as burglary, property damage, injury at work and road accidents. Another example is the Criminal Injuries Compensation Board (CICB), set up in 1964 to award payments out of public funds to those injured as a result of crime. Although the victim of a crime would have a good claim in civil law against the offender, such actions have always been rare, and the majority of victims wishing to claim compensation do so by applying to the CICB. Each year, the board receives thirty-five to forty thousand applications for compensation, of which roughly half result in a monetary award, and this figure is steadily rising as crime itself increases. What kinds of crime may attract awards from the CICB? The revised wording of the scheme in 1969 uses the phrase 'crimes of violence', and the interpretation of this phrase by the board has caused problems. All traffic offences causing injury are excluded from the scheme, except where the vehicle is driven deliberately at the victim and is therefore being used as a weapon; and although the phrase clearly covers offences such as robbery, wounding and grievous bodily harm (as well as murder, in which case compensation is payable to the spouse of the deceased), it has also been held to cover cases where the injury was incidentally, or indirectly, attributable to what was in essence a non-violent crime, such as injury caused to someone's arm when a thief snatches a handbag or briefcase.

There have long been criticisms over various aspects of the board's work. To begin with, the scope of the board's jurisdiction has been criticized, not least because of ambiguities such as those noted above. Moreover, and as a result of the government's determination to reduce public expenditure, the board has been seriously affected by under-funding, both with regard to its staffing and other resources, and also with regard to its available budget for compensation. It was reported in 1992 that, because of rising crime and a continuing increase in the number of claims, the CICB would overshoot its budget by between a quarter and a third in the financial year 1992/3.[7] At the same time, it was reported that no additional funds would be made available by central government: the shortfall would have to be made good through cuts in other parts of the 'law and order' budget, including the police, leading one observer to note that 'the Government is caught in a vicious circle. Crime is up because of the recession, so there are more victims claiming compensation. Ministers' response to this is to cut the budgets of the very people who are supposed to prevent the crime which is causing all these financial difficulties.'[8]

By virtue of the Powers of Criminal Courts Act 1973, the victim of *any* crime may recover compensation, not from public funds, but through a court order made against the actual wrongdoer. This provision is much wider than the jurisdiction of the Criminal Injuries Compensation Board for, although the court is required by the Act to take into account the means of the convicted person when considering an order, the victim has more chance of recovering *some* compensation because the Act covers all crimes ranging from personal injury through to losses sustained as a result of false trade descriptions (see chapter 11).

To turn briefly to a means of resolving disputes of quite a different kind: we noted briefly in chapter 5 the Parliamentary Commissioner for Administration (PCA) and the Commissioners for Local Administration: the 'Ombudsmen'. The Parliamentary Commissioner (to whom complaints of central government maladministration may be referred through an MP) was created in 1967, and the Commissioners for Local Administration in 1974. At present there are three local commissioners for England (each responsible for one of the three areas into which England is divided for this purpose) and one for Wales, and complaints about local government maladministration are referred to the relevant commissioner through a local councillor.

'Maladministration' refers to the *manner* in which a decision is taken, and may include bias, incompetence, arbitrariness, failure to consider relevant facts, unfair discrimination or unjustifiable delay in reaching a decision. The Ombudsmen have no power to inquire into the *substance or merits* of a decision. There is, moreover, no power to investigate matters in respect of which the complainant has a right to take his or her case before a tribunal, before a court of law, or before a minister by way of appeal against the decision, unless the Commissioner is satisfied that in the particular circumstances of the case, it would be unreasonable to expect the complainant to pursue any of these avenues for resolution of the dispute. This proviso applies to both the Parliamentary Commissioner and the local commissioners. In 1989 the PCA received 677 complaints and during that year dealt with another 260 carried forward from 1988. The majority of these complaints related to decisions of the Department of Health and Social Security, and the Inland Revenue, though of the total number dealt with only 65 were upheld as revealing maladministration by the departments concerned. The local Ombudsmen receive rather more complaints – 9,033 in 1990–1 – though of these, once again, only a small number (254) were found to involve maladministration. One controversial feature of the British Ombudsmen system (unlike other countries operating similar systems) is the requirement that complaints must be filtered through MPs or local councillors: there is no direct right of access to any Ombudsman. In practice, however, the Parliamentary and local commissioners receive many complaints sent directly to them by aggrieved citizens. In the case of the PCA, since 1978 such direct communications have been sent to the complainant's MP requesting consent to investigation (which is usually given). Complaints sent directly to local commissioners are (since 1984) passed on to the local authority concerned, with a request that the latter seek a satisfactory settlement with the complainant or else refer the complaint back to the local commissioner for investigation. These recent changes in procedure are clearly an improvement on the practice of simply returning inappropriate complaints back to the aggrieved person, pointing out the correct procedure – a practice which inevitably resulted in many potentially sound complaints subsequently being dropped.

In all the cases discussed above, dispute-settlement through courts of law may be regarded, for a number of reasons, as inappropriate, and although in many (though not all) cases, courts constitute 'last resort' forums of dispute-settlement, court hearings comprise only a tiny proportion of resolutions of disputes. In addition to the examples already mentioned, two other major alternative methods of avoiding and resolving disputes must be noted: arbitration and dispute-avoidance in business or commercial contracts, and the use of tribunals.

Business disputes: avoidance and arbitration

We stated earlier that there is within the business and commercial world a general reluctance to call on lawyers and the courts for the solution of contractual disputes. Tillotson has noted that 'in the mid-nineteenth century contract litigation occupied a significant amount of the time of the civil courts . . . A century later, a survey of reported cases for 1957–66 revealed only fifty-six cases which were determined on the basis of points of contract-law.'[9] There are various reasons for this decline in the use of the courts as a means of dealing with business disputes. As we have noted, the stable continuation of business relationships between companies may be impaired by recourse to courts; additionally, litigation is extremely expensive, especially if the dispute involves complex contractual documents, or substantial amounts of time in the courtroom dealing with technical aspects of a business contract. Third, the basic common-law rules of contract (discussed in chapter 11) have been largely and increasingly superseded by specialized and technical statutory provisions requiring corresponding specialism in dispute-prevention and settlement devices and techniques.

Finally, business contracts almost always contain within them the agreed means of solving certain specified problems, should they arise. Suppose, for example, that X Ltd, a manufacturer of fitted kitchen furniture, agrees to supply Z Ltd, a discount furniture retail store, with a large quantity of kitchen units at an agreed price, the goods to be delivered by an agreed date. If X's workforce then takes industrial action, with consequent delays in production, or if X's source of raw materials is affected by, say, the sinking of a ship which is carrying a shipment of supplies for X, with the result in either case that X Ltd is unable to meet the contractually agreed delivery date, then how is this problem to be resolved? If Y Ltd sues X Ltd for breach of contract, difficult questions may arise as to whether the doctrine of frustration may apply (see chapter 11). An expensive and possibly protracted court action will be avoided, however, if the parties have inserted into their original contract a clause which states what shall happen if, for some specified reason, one of the parties is unable to fulfil the the contract through no fault of their own. Such a clause is called a *force-majeure* clause, and the kinds of incident which may be foreseen in such clauses might include strikes, the outbreak of war, fire, flood or any other occurrence which is outside the control of the parties and which may affect the performance of the contract. Should one of these incidents prevent or delay performance, then the agreed clause will specify what the consequences will be: the clause may provide that one or other party may terminate the contract (with agreed provisions as to which party shall bear any financial losses), or that the delivery date shall be extended for the duration of the adverse circumstances. This kind of clause is a very important means of dispute-prevention in business, for it provides the means of avoiding expensive, time-consuming and possibly detrimental litigation.

What happens, however, if the parties cannot agree on the applicability of a *force-majeure*, or some other, clause within the contract – for example, because of difficulties over the interpretation of the clause? Here again, recourse to the courts is unlikely. It is far more probable that the contract will contain provisions to the effect that in such an event the dispute is to be referred to *arbitration*. Arbitration is essentially intended to be an informal, private and speedy alternative to court hearings, and has the additional advantage of flexibility: the parties are free to stipulate the identity and, if appropriate, the qualifications and experience of the arbitrator; they can decide how many arbitrators – one, two or perhaps three – will be called upon to deal with the dispute (though in some instances, known as institutional arbitration, the proceedings are governed by rules and practices of a trade association to which the contracting parties may belong). The arbitrator is under a duty to act impartially and to observe any relevant rules of procedure (such as the obligation to ensure that each party is given the opportunity to put their side of the case). In general, an arbitration hearing is a private, less formal version of a court action, following much the same line of procedure.

Arbitrations can be invoked in a number of situations involving business contractual disputes – where there is a dispute of fact (such as whether, in our hypothetical example above, the industrial action by the workforce actually accounted for the failure to meet the contractual delivery date), where there is a dispute of law (such as whether the relevant contractual clause, properly interpreted, actually covers the eventuality of the sinking of the ship carrying raw materials), or, more frequently, where a dispute involves both fact and law (requiring both the finding of the facts and the application to them of the relevant law). Whichever kind of arbitration is required, and whoever acts in the capacity of arbitrator, however, the conduct and outcome of the arbitration proceedings are subject to the overriding control of the law.

It may at first seem odd that a dispute-settlement mechanism which is primarily regarded as informal, private and structured largely according to the contracting parties' own desires is none the less subject to an overriding legal control. There are, however, a number of reasons for the fact that, as one judge explained,

it is the policy of the law in this country that, in the conduct of arbitrations, arbitrators must in general apply a fixed and recognisable system of law, which primarily and normally would be the law of England, and that they cannot be allowed to apply some different criterion such as the view of the individual arbitrator or umpire[10] on abstract justice or equitable principles . . .[11]

First of all, no matter how detailed contractual specifications may be, there may well be gaps in the contractual provision which neither party anticipated, but which may prove significant. In such an event the general law of arbitration will fill such gaps. Second, there is a general principle within the law of contract that it is against public policy for any contractual term to oust or exclude the jurisdiction of the ordinary courts,[12] this being a well-established limitation on the otherwise much-vaunted and traditional judicial notion of 'freedom of contract'.[13]

Third, the legislation relating to arbitration in Britain contains specific provision concerning the courts' involvement in arbitration matters. The

Arbitration Act 1950 provided that, in order to ensure that an arbitration award was not based upon an error of law, either party to the arbitration could request that difficult points of law could be taken before the High Court by means of the 'case stated' procedure. The same Act provided that the court had the power to set aside an arbitration award if there was any error of fact, law or procedure revealed on the face of the award – although the court could not 'look behind' the award itself. Both of these provisions caused problems, however. There was a tendency for the 'case stated' procedure to be abused, with the sole intention by one party of delaying payment of sums awarded against them by the arbitration award. The appeal procedure caused additional delays and expense; and judicial review was made difficult by reason of many arbitrators' omitting their reasons from the awards, so that awards were made less likely to be set aside. Both the 'case stated' and the appeal procedures had the effect of transforming the arbitration procedure into a fully fledged court action, with the accompanying problems of delay and expense, and it was clearly the case that much financially lucrative arbitration work (including arbitrations on foreign disputes, which is arguably a 'valuable visible export')[14] was being lost.

To solve these and certain other problems, the Arbitration Act 1979 changed the law relating to judicial review. The 'case stated' procedure was abolished by this Act, and there is now a more limited right to refer a preliminary point of law to the court, either with the consent of the arbitrator, or with the consent of all the parties to the arbitration. As regards the appeal procedure, the jurisdiction of the court to set aside an award for errors on the face of the award has been abolished, and the 1979 Act provides that an appeal against an arbitration award requires either the consent of all parties, or the leave of the court, which will not be granted unless the question of law at issue could substantially affect the rights of one or more of the parties to the arbitration agreement. A final point to note is that the English insistence upon the surbordination of arbitration to ordinary English law is a rather more rigid rule than in many other legal systems. Perhaps recognizing this, and with due attention being given to the advantages of retaining arbitration business from overseas, the 1979 Act makes it possible in certain cases for the parties to an arbitration agreement to agree to exclude the possibility of an appeal to the court. Commentators seem to be agreed that the changes made by the 1979 Act are welcome and useful, and have 'already produced results in attracting international arbitration work back to London'.[15]

Apart from arbitration over disputes arising from contracts between businesses, there is often provision for aggrieved *consumers* to have their complaints against manufacturers or retailers dealt with by arbitration. Many businesses, through their trade associations, have introduced codes of practice approved by the Office of Fair Trading (OFT), which, among other things, often include conciliation and arbitration schemes for consumer complaints. Clearly, such schemes do not, and indeed cannot, exclude the right of a consumer to take legal action against a retailer or manufacturer, but in many cases the consumer may well find that such schemes provide satisfactory solutions to the problem without the need to incur expense and suffer the delays of court actions. Thus, for example, among the many codes of practice currently in operation with OFT approval is the ABTA Code of

Practice, drawn up by the Association of British Travel Agents. This deals, among other things, with the requirement under the code for brochures and booking forms to contain clear and comprehensive information, for arrangements for refunds on cancellation of bookings, and for a conciliation and arbitration scheme to deal with consumer complaints. Similar schemes are found in the Code of Practice for the Motor Industry and the code operated by the Radio, Electrical and Television Retailers' Association. The attempts at conciliation are intended not to operate by means of strict adherence to what the parties' rights would be in law, but to reach a satisfactory settlement (which may often be a compromise solution) without invoking strict legal rights. If conciliation fails, then the dispute can be referred to arbitration, which is carried out under the provisions of the Arbitration Acts. For many consumers, these schemes are a useful method of resolving problems, and of course from the traders' point of view they help maintain good relations with consumers.

These conciliation and arbitration schemes are quite separate from the 'small claims' procedure in the county court, introduced in 1973 as a means of dealing with consumers' claims against traders over transactions involving relatively small amounts of money. In such cases, a court action will usually be wholly inappropriate as a means of settling the dispute, and the 'small claims' procedure was designed as an appropriate alternative. Through the scheme, a consumer may bring a claim before a county court registrar for informal arbitration, if the amount in dispute is below £1000, without the formality of a full county court hearing. Although the numbers making use of the small claims procedure have steadily risen, the fact remains that the initiative for bringing the claim lies with the aggrieved party, and many ordinary people may be put off by the prospect of arguing their own case through the small claims procedure, even though an adviser with some expertise, such as a member of a Citizens' Advice Bureau, is allowed to help present such a case.

The above dispute-solving mechanisms are all part of the fabric of what has recently become known as 'alternative dispute-resolution' (ADR),[16] essentially referring to all methods of resolving disputes outside the courts of law, whose drawbacks have been mentioned above. There has been considerable political pressure, notably from the Lord Chancellor's Department, to reform both courtroom procedure and also the ways in which the legal profession carries out its work, with a view largely to cutting the huge cost to the Exchequer of legal aid (see chapter 13). One of the earliest alternatives to the use of courts – first created in the nineteenth century – was, and remains, the *tribunal*.

The growth of tribunals

Apart from the example of Industrial Tribunals mentioned earlier, there exists a vast and complicated undergrowth of various other tribunals, many of them created by means of legislation designed to implement welfare state policies and schemes during the twentieth century. It is with regard to the kind of work handled by these agencies that the increased potential for disputes in the public sector –

between groups, and between individuals, groups and state institutions – can best be appreciated.

The welfare state in Britain has provided various benefits for, as well as controls upon, the life of the ordinary citizen. Social security benefits, unemployment benefit, industrial injury compensation, unfair dismissal provisions, compulsory purchase, the resolution of problems between landlord and tenant – these areas, and many more, have either come into existence through welfare state philosophies and policies (such as state benefits for unemployment) or, as a result of those philosophies and policies, been taken out of the hands of private individuals and regulated by means of state interventionist policies (an outstanding example being the legislation affecting rents, and the relationship between landlords and tenants). All these areas are breeding-grounds for disputes and conflicts between the parties and agencies concerned. A worker may wish to challenge the grounds of a dismissal as being unfair; an employee injured at work may wish to claim compensation from the employer; a citizen claiming supplementary benefit may want to challenge the refusal of officials to allow the claim. If such disputes were taken before courts of law for resolution, there is no doubt that the court system would collapse under the weight of work; and in any case, the courts are, for many of these cases, inappropriate organs to deal with the dispute.

It would, for example, be somewhat out of place for a county court to have to hear a claim by a social security claimant where the claim may only amount to a few pounds per week, and where the usual delays affecting court cases would operate very harshly on the claimant, who might need a much more immediate decision.

To provide a system whereby these disputes may be dealt with without the trappings of the court of law, various governments have, through legislation, introduced a network of administrative tribunals designed to provide 'instant' justice cheaply, efficiently and with minimum delay and formality. These tribunals comprise not highly paid judges, but panels, with a chairperson who is (usually) legally qualified[17] and two other, non-legally-qualified, people who have expertise in the particular field over which the tribunal has jurisdiction. Thus, Social Security Tribunals decide appeals at the instance of an aggrieved claimant; Rent Tribunals deal with disputes between landlord and tenant; and Industrial Tribunals deal with claims from ex-employees that their dismissal was unfair, that their redundancy amounted to unfair dismissal, or that they were discriminated against on the grounds of race or sex. Apart from these examples, there are specialized tribunals dealing with problems of compulsory detention of mentally ill people in hospital (Mental Health Review Tribunals), appeals against decisions by the Home Secretary on matters concerning immigration (Immigration Appeal Tribunals), and appeals concerning pensions (Pensions Appeal Tribunals). Special tribunals also deal with complaints about services provided by various occupations and professions, such as the Solicitors' Disciplinary Tribunal and the Disciplinary Committee of the General Medical Council. In all, there are about sixty different types of tribunal, hearing about six times the number of disputes heard by courts of law.

Tribunals, like the welfare state apparatus of which they are a part, are creations of Acts of Parliament. Unfortunately, however, the pattern of their development has been piecemeal. A statue creating, for example, the social security system will also create the tribunals pertaining to social security appeals; and the Rent Tribunal is the creation of statutes providing for matters affecting landlords and tenants. The resulting diversity between tribunals was one of the problems discussed in the *Report of the Committee on Administrative Tribunals* (the Franks Committee) in 1957,[18] which was followed in 1958 by the Tribunals and Inquiries Act. The provisions of this and later enactments are now consolidated in the 1971 Act of the same name. While this diversity has led to a confusing network of tribunals dealing with different areas and incorporating different procedures,[19] it must be remembered that tribunals are *specialized* bodies, dealing with very limited areas. This specialization may be contrasted with courts of law, many of which, such as the county courts, must be 'jacks of all trades', having jurisdiction to hear many kinds of dispute involving various different fields of law. This specialization has inevitably meant the tailoring of particular tribunal procedures to the contingencies arising in the specific area of the tribunal's jurisdiction.

The Franks Committee said that tribunals should be characterized always by openness, fairness and impartiality, and made various recommendations towards this aim, most of which were implemented by the 1958 Act. There is now a Council on Tribunals, for example, which was recommended by the Franks Committee, and which has the task of keeping under review the constitution and working of tribunals; a second recommendation was that those who chaired tribunals should be legally qualified, and this is normally required by Acts which create tribunals. Further recommendations which were implemented were that representation should be possible before all tribunals, if necessary by a qualified lawyer; and that tribunals should, in general, give reasons for their decisions if asked to do so.

The issue of legal aid (that is, state subsidization of the cost of representation by lawyers) for persons appearing before tribunals who wish to be legally represented has been much discussed. Although legal aid is, generally speaking, still not available for tribunal representation, there is evidence to suggest that representation at tribunals can make a considerable difference to the outcome of the case,[20] and the Royal Commission on Legal Services, reporting in 1979, recognized that representation before tribunals, whether by a lawyer or other suitably qualified or experienced person, was a significant factor, noting that of the successful claimants before Supplementary Benefit Appeal Tribunals in 1976, no fewer than 72 per cent had been represented, as compared with 33 per cent of successful claimants who were unrepresented.[21] The Royal Commission on Legal Services recommended that where legal representation is needed, 'legal aid should be available unless legal representation is specifically prohibited by statute'.[22] The criteria to be applied would include not only those cases involving a significant point of law, complexity in terms of evidence, or the existence of the possibility of deprivation of a person's liberty or ability to follow an occupation, but also cases which involve an amount of money which 'although low, is significant in relation to the financial circumstances of the applicant';[23] cases where the special circumstances of the individual make representation desirable or where hardship might follow if it were withheld.[24] The Legal Aid Act 1979 provides that the Green Form Scheme, for legal advice and assistance falling short of court hearings, may extend to tribunal representation ('assistance by way of representation').[25]

Although it cannot be denied that, from the evidence referred to above, representation may make a considerable difference to the result of a tribunal hearing, there are arguments against involvement by lawyers in this area. There is a body of opinion which argues that an increase in the number of solicitors representing clients before tribunals would quickly lead to an increase in formality and legal technicality – problems which are endemic to a court of law and which the tribunal system is intended to minimize;[26] furthermore, as the Royal Commission on Legal Services acknowledged, there is at present widespread ignorance among the legal profession of those areas of law generally referred to as 'welfare law', which constitute the legal framework of rights and entitlements with which many tribunals of the welfare state are concerned. This could, of course, be remedied by the introduction of welfare law into lawyers' training and education courses, and this was indeed one recommendation of the Royal Commission.[27]

More fundamentally, many commentators (as well as the Franks Committee itself) have argued that there are important distinctions between courts of law – where representation by lawyers usually occurs – and tribunals. In particular, it is argued that many tribunals are in the main connected with particular departments of government concerned with welfare state legislation. This may well mean that considerations not of 'black-letter law', but of administrative *policy*, may be paramount or at least of equal status to the individual's grievance. As Street explains,

Ministers and top civil servant advisers have . . . frequently come to doubt whether the courts are the appropriate body to decide many of these cases. They see rightly that many of these disputes are not merely about private rights; the public good on the one hand and the interest of the particular citizen on the other must be weighed in the balance. They look at many decisions in the courts . . . and find them wanting in that they appear to disregard the social element in a problem.[28]

The reluctance by policy-makers to introduce into tribunals the formalistic and individualist approaches of the courtroom may well be one of the reasons why, except for a few tribunals (including the Employment Appeal Tribunal), legal aid has not been made available for representation by lawyers. It is certainly one of the reasons why so many enactments providing for tribunals omit to provide any appeal procedure from tribunals to a court of law; and the channels whereby a citizen aggrieved at a tribunal's decision may bring that decision before a court of law are at present severely restricted.

Generally speaking, even though in most cases there will be no possibility of an appeal to a court of law against a tribunal's decision, the courts do exercise, through the Queen's Bench Division of the High Court, a supervisory jurisdiction over the activities of tribunals, which may be invoked if a problem involving a point of law or a breach of procedural rules is alleged by an aggrieved claimant to have occurred at a tribunal hearing. This jurisdiction is discussed more fully in chapter 12, but here it may be noted briefly that the most important ways in which it can be invoked are, first, if the claimant alleges that the tribunal in question exceeded its statutory authority and acted *ultra vires*, or second, if it is alleged that a breach of the rules of natural justice occurred – that is to say, that the complaining party was given no opportunity to present his or her side of the case, or that the presiding chairperson was in some way biased or partial, or that there was a possibility of such bias, as regards the case and its outcome.[29]

Despite these distinctions which may be made between courts and tribunals, some have contended that the two forms of dispute-settlement forum are in reality very similar. Abel-Smith and Stevens, for example, argue that 'Courts are said to be administering rules of law while tribunals are thought to be administering both law and policy. We would maintain that no such clear line can or should be drawn . . . there is no fundamental difference between courts and tribunals. We would argue, therefore, that every effort should be made to merge the two'.[30] There is much in this view. The courts deal with policy, as well as with firm legal rules, as is discussed in chapter 7, and the general issue of the relative functions of courts and tribunals is one over which it is dangerous to generalize. Certainly, the courts have held in various cases that some tribunals, though ostensibly 'administrative', actually exercise *judicial* functions, in that they are concerned with questions of individuals' legal rights and relationships. It is in such cases that the rules of natural justice have been held to apply; they have been held *not* to apply in various cases where the decisions of tribunals have been held by courts to be purely *administrative* acts. Hartley and Griffith, after reviewing some of the difficulties into which this distinction has sometimes led the courts, consider that since the case in 1963 of *Ridge* v. *Baldwin*,[31]

case after case applied natural justice to new situations, until the point was reached where it was said in 1970 that the principles of natural justice would apply to all decisions affecting individual rights unless circumstances were such as to indicate the contrary. Since then the position seems to have stabilised to some extent and . . . it is . . . possible to discern limits to its scope. In particular, there has been a tendency to dilute the content of natural justice in the case of purely administrative decisions, and in such cases it has been said that all the law requires is that the decision-maker should act fairly.[32]

The English courts: the constitutional position

At the beginning of this chapter we noted that the vast majority of disputes which occur in modern society will be resolved satisfactorily without recourse to any formal dispute-settlement agency; we then considered the establishment of specialized agencies to deal with various types of dispute, either through advice and attempts at conciliation, or through other ADR forums such as tribunal hearings which are designed to provide solutions to certain disputes without the encumbrances and expense of courts of law.

It is not surprising to find, then, that although the court may be regarded as the clearest instance of official means of dispute-settlement in modern society, in fact only a tiny proportion of disputes are ever aired before the courts. The Royal Commission on Legal Services noted, for example, that in 1978 tribunals dealt with six times more disputes than the number of contested civil cases which came to trial in the High Court and county courts.[33] It will be readily appreciated that in civil cases there are many factors militating against court hearings. As we will see in chapter 13, litigation is expensive, even allowing for legal aid provision, and the case will usually be subject to delay; the resulting situation was outlined by the Royal Commission on Legal Services thus:

In 1978, of 143,577 actions commenced in the Queen's Bench Division . . . cases set down for hearing numbered 9,625, of which 1,793 came to trial. The investigations of the Royal Commission on Civil Liability and Compensation for Personal Injury published in March 1979 . . . showed that less than 2 per cent of cases in which an attempt was made to recover damages for personal injury reached the stage of a hearing in court.'[34]

We shall deal in more detail with personal injury claims in chapter 9; for the moment, it may simply be pointed out that the total number of cases coming before courts of law is extremely small when compared to the frequency with which disputes – many of which may involve legal aspects – occur and are settled without recourse to legal proceedings.

The court is, nevertheless, one of the most central institutions within the English legal system; the pronouncements of the higher courts, in particular, have great significance for, among other things, the substance of the law itself; dominant social and political attitudes and values are communicated through judicial utterances in the courts; and the courts of law are the ultimate arenas where disputes which cannot be settled in any other way may be taken. The courts are also a feature of the state, connected with, but in certain important ways independent of, other agencies of state and government. For these reasons, it is important to consider in more detail the present position of the courts of law within the legal system and within the social structure.

Constitutional lawyers used to regard as fundamental the doctrine of the 'separation of powers', whereby the courts, the legislature (Parliament) and the executive (government) are constitutionally separate, thus serving democratic ideals by ensuring that no one of these 'arms of the state' become all-powerful, through complex 'checks and balances' of each arm by the other two. Thus in theory the judges operate independently of party politics, and in a manner untainted by political bias. The doctrine may be challenged, however, on both constitutional and other grounds; the degree to which the judges may be seen as politically neutral will be discussed in chapter 14, but in the present context, consideration of the flaws in the doctrine of the separation of powers will serve to illustrate various features of the English courts.

The doctrine involves three propositions, each of which, it is argued, may be seen to be open to question. First, the doctrine requires that the same persons should not occupy positions in more than one of the three arms of the state – judiciary, legislature and executive. In practice, however, as is well known, members of the Cabinet (executive) are invariably members of one or other House of Parliament (legislature). Cabinet government as we know it in the United Kingdom could not possibly work without this convention, and this is one example of departure from the strict doctrine; as is the case of the Lord Chancellor, who is not only a Cabinet minister, but also a judge, is president of the House of Lords in both its legislative and judicial capacities, and is involved in the appointment of other judges. The mixture, in one appointment, of judicial, legislative and executive functions is striking.[35]

Second, the doctrine requires that each arm of the state exercises its functions independently of any control or interference from the others. Again, this requirement is not fulfilled. The House of Commons (part of the legislature) in theory controls the executive, but with a majority government the House can be effectively controlled, in fact, by the executive.[36] Either way, the requirement is breached, though their appears to be little or no attempt to influence the judicial function, at least regarding court hearings, today. (It seems that this was not always so. Paterson's research[37] clearly suggests that, as late as the nineteenth century, judicial appointments were intimately linked with candidates' party-political allegiances.) Formally, it is firmly established constitutionally that Parliament is the supreme law-making body in this country, so that the judges' task when confronted in court by a statutory rule is theoretically limited to the interpretation and application of that rule; they have no power to change it or declare it invalid (see chapter 7). This may be contrasted with the powers of the American Supreme Court to declare a statute invalid by reason of its being unconstitutional.

Third, the doctrine of the separation of powers requires that one organ of the state should not exercise the functions of either of the others. In practice, the distinction between functions may be seriously blurred. To take the outstanding illustration, an Act of Parliament may empower a minister of the government to make rules having legal effect; this is known as *delegated legislation*, and it is arguable that in some cases this device amounts to a minister having law-making power (as opposed to mere power to make regulations *in furtherance* of Parliamentary enactments). Important examples of delegated legislation are the powers given to ministers under the Health and Safety at Work Act 1974 and the Consumer Credit Act 1974; as we have seen, it is one of the functions of the courts to ensure, through their supervisory jurisdiction, that powers entrusted to ministers, tribunals or other executive or administrative agencies are not abused or exceeded.

Apart from the case of delegated legislative powers, which may be seen as a legislative function being exercised by a member of the executive, there is virtually no situation in which one arm of the state exercises the powers of either of the others, though we must note that the House of Lords does have both a legislative and a judicial capacity:[38] in practice, the judicial members of the House are judges, not politicians, whose role is to sit when the house operates in its judicial capacity. They rarely sit in legislative debates, and by the same token, the political members of the Lords do not participate in judicial hearings. There is, then, a separation of judicial and legislative functions in this particular institution.

Commenting on the separation of powers, Drewry neatly summarizes the position:

The point is that there are some aspects of 'separation of powers' which are eminently sensible. For example, it is probably a good idea to have a judiciary which is somewhat aloof from the rough and tumble of party politics. And words like 'legislative', 'executive' and 'judicial' are a useful shorthand way of describing a lot of things that go on in government, provided we remember that the boundaries between them are indistinct and that they are all functionally inter-related.[39]

The English court structure

English courts are arranged in a structure according to three sets of criteria. First, does the court deal with *civil* or *criminal* matters? This division is central to English law, though it is not easy to explain with any precision. Criminal-law rules cover offences such as murder, theft and assaults, offences against the consumer (food and drugs offences, false trade descriptions – see chapter 11), offences involving firearms and other weapons, crimes against public order and state security, and of course the many road traffic offences. These cases may be seen as disputes between the alleged offender and the state, representing the community at large.

Civil law comprises all legal rules which are not part of the criminal legal code, but the dividing line is difficult to draw. It is sometimes said that, while criminal proceedings are brought by the state, civil proceedings are brought by private individuals[40] against other individuals. Thus, a *plaintiff* sues a *defendant*. Criminal proceedings are often said to be public, and civil proceedings private, but this 'public–private' distinction is by no means watertight. Certainly, we speak of 'private law' remedies being available in civil actions for, say, breach of contact, and of criminal proceedings being brought on behalf of the public; but there are many occasions when *public* bodies may be party to civil actions, and *private* individuals may initiate criminal prosecutions. An example of the former would be an action between a local authority and a private company over a contract for the supply of goods; an example of the latter would be a prosecution of a shoplifter by the store concerned. Until recently, in England and Wales the prosecution of criminal offences was carried out by the police; the Prosecution of Offences Act 1985, however, created the Crown Prosecution Service, an agency independent of the police operating under the Director of Public Prosecutions (DPP), who has the function of designating regional areas, each with its own Chief Crown Prosecutor. The system replaces the previous practice whereby the police dealt with the process of prosecution, though the possibility of a privately initiated prosecution was specifically retained in the 1985 Act. In some cases the Attorney-General (a government official) alone has the authority to prosecute, and for certain other offences prosecution must be authorized by the DPP, who also has the power to take over the prosecution of serious offences.

A second distinguishing feature is often said to lie in the different *aims* of the two branches of the law. The traditional aims of the criminal law are the apprehension and disposition of wrongdoers, while the aims of civil law are usually stated to be those of restitution, or compensation.[41] The problems with this distinction appear when we consider that there are some cases in which civil awards may be intended by the court to be punitive. Such cases are rare, but may arise for example when a defendant may make a profit from wrongful conduct, over and above the amount of compensation which he or she must pay to the plaintiff. The publishers of a defamatory book, for example, may enjoy more profits than might otherwise accrue, simply because publicity surrounding the case might induce more people to buy the offending book. And there are instances in criminal law where compensation may be payable by a convicted person to the victim: the Powers of Criminal Courts Act 1973, for example, provides that compensation orders may be made by any criminal court against any person convicted of damaging other people's property or causing some other type of loss.

Despite these difficulties, there does remain, for practical purposes, a broad distinction between civil and criminal law along the lines of their respective aims and remedies, and this distinction is firmly embedded in the court structure. The civil courts, with one or two exceptions, deal exclusively with civil matters; the most important exception is probably the Queen's Bench Division of the High Court, which has some criminal jurisdiction by way of appeals from magistrates' courts and Crown courts through the 'case stated' procedure. Here, the appeal is made by either defendant or prosecution (the only instance where the latter can appeal from an acquittal) over a point of law raised by, say, the interpretation of a statute, where a decision of a higher court is required to clarify the matter.[42] On the criminal side, magistrates' courts do have some civil jurisdiction, mainly involving liquor, gaming and betting licences, and actions for certain debts, as well as some family-law matters, notably separation orders upon marriage breakdown and questions of custody and adoption of children.

The second criterion affecting the position of a given court in the overall structure is that concerning the *extent* of the court's jurisdiction. The county court, for instance, at the lowest rung of the civil court ladder, deals with actions in contract and tort involving sums of up to £25,000, and may also deal with cases involving sums between £25,000 and £50,000, depending on their financial substance, complexity or public importance. Proceedings involving mortgages, estates of deceased persons, and other equity matters where the amount involved does not exceed £30,000 are also heard by the county court. The High Court hears civil cases involving between £25,000 and £50,000 if the circumstances make it appropriate, and deals with all civil claims involving more than £50,000. The magistrates' court, dealing in the main with minor criminal offences, has a limited jurisdiction regarding sanctions for cases heard in that court. The Criminal Law Act 1977 and the Criminal Justice Act 1991 contain provisions for sentences for various crimes which may attract imprisonment or fines. Such provisions, it must be stressed, relate to the court's *summary* jurisdiction, and the vast majority of criminal cases, being of a relatively minor or trivial nature, are dealt with by these courts. For offences of a more serious nature, however, and in those cases where the accused elects to be tried *on indictment* (that is, with a jury), the case must go before the higher Crown court. We may note here that magistrates' courts also hold *preliminary examinations* in *all* criminal cases. This is a procedure to ascertain whether, on the face of the evidence, there is a case against the accused. If so, then the case will be dealt with either summarily or on indictment, depending on the offence and upon the circumstances.

Figure 1. THE CIVIL COURTS

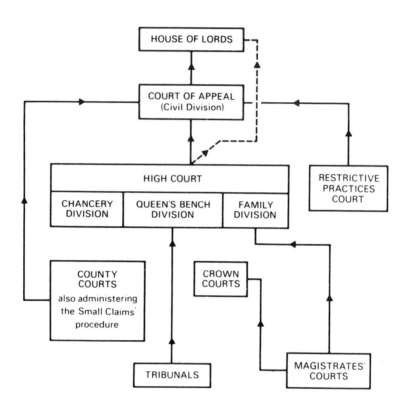

Channels of appeal from lower to higher courts. Appeals from tribunals are available only in rare cases, although the supervisory jurisdiction of the Queen's Bench Division may be invoked if a breach of natural justice, or an *ultra vires* decision, is alleged.

This is the 'leap-frogging' procedure introduced by the Administration of Justice Act 1969, whereby appeals may be made directly from High Court to House of Lords: (a) where both parties agree, and (b) where the trial judge grants leave, which he may do only if a point of law of public importance is involved concerning either the interpretation of a statute or a previous decision by which he considers himself bound. Final leave to appeal must also be granted by the House of Lords itself.

The third criterion affecting the position of a court in the hierarchy is the question of whether the court is one of *first instance* (where the original trial takes place) or whether it is a court of *appeal*. Magistrates' courts and county courts are both courts of first instance; and the Court of Appeal and the House of Lords are both appellate courts only. The courts which lie in between these levels of the structure may, depending on the case before them, be either of first instance or appellate jurisdiction. The three Divisions of the High Court – Chancery, Queen's

Figure 2. THE CRIMINAL COURTS

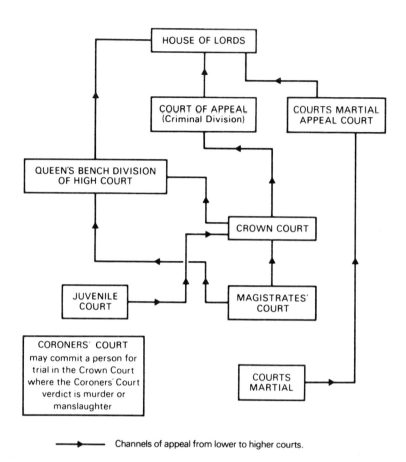

Channels of appeal from lower to higher courts.

Bench, and Family – are civil courts (excepting the criminal jurisdiction of the Queen's Bench as noted above) which deal, in the main, with first instance trials. In the Chancery Court, disputes over property, trusts, wills, revenue, bankruptcy and company matters are heard; in the Queen's Bench are heard contract and tort cases which cannot be dealt with in the county courts below; and the Family Division hears divorce cases and other matrimonial matters. But the Family Division may also hear appeals from magistrates' courts acting in their civil capacity over matrimonial and other family affairs; and the Queen's Bench may hear appeals by way of case stated and also, in the limited circumstances where they are permitted by statute, appeals from tribunal decisions.

The diagrams on pages 136 and above indicate the relative positions of, and channels of appeal between, the main courts of law in this country.[43]

The courts and society

The court structure is designed, through its appeal channels, to ensure that justice is done in all cases, although the suggestion has been made, perhaps not too seriously, that this appeal system could be somewhat modified:

The institution of one Court of Appeal may be considered a reasonable precaution; but two suggest panic. To take a fair parallel . . . our surprise would be great if, after the removal of our appendix by a distinguished surgeon, we were taken before three other distinguished surgeons, who order our appendix to be replaced: and our surprise would give place to stupefaction if we were then referred to a tribunal of seven distinguished surgeons, who directed that our appendix should be extracted again. Yet such operations . . . are an everyday experience in the practice of the law.[44]

Be this as it may, the system whereby the Court of Appeal and the House of Lords may hear appeals from lower courts tends to maintain, first, the idea that justice is being done, and second, the keeping of the judicial finger on the pulse of social and moral currents within society. The common law, which is law made by the judges through decided cases (discussed fully in chapter 7), has developed through the doctrine of *precedent*. This doctrine requires that, in theory, decisions of the higher courts are *binding* on all courts below them in the hierarchy. In practice, the strictness of the formal doctrine is diluted by the judges' use of a large number of interpretative techniques whereby the following of previous decisions (precedents) may be avoided.[45] To take a well-known example, in 1932 the House of Lords, in the case of *Donoghue* v. *Stevenson*,[46] decided that a manufacturer of goods owes a legal duty of care towards the ultimate consumer of those goods, assuming that there has been no reasonable opportunity for them to have been interfered with in the transition from factory to consumer.

The impact of this decision, thanks to the doctrine of binding precedent, has been that in cases since then a consumer who is injured or harmed in similar circumstances is able to recover compensation from the manufacturer, irrespective of the place in the court hierarchy where the case is heard, because that House of Lords decision in 1932 *bound* all lower courts to follow it. The case was examined by the courts over the ensuing years in later cases in such a way as to bring not only manufacturers but also repairers[47] and car-dealers,[48] not only bottles of ginger-beer but also various other articles, within its ambit.[49]

The doctrine of binding precedent is said to have the outstanding advantage of ensuring that the law is kept up to date, through authoritative pronouncements from the top of the judicial tree through the system of appeals, while at the same time maintaining stability within the law by requiring all other courts to follow higher courts' decisions. The extent to which these aims are achieved, and the extent to which the formal doctrine of precedent hides what may be, in fact, a considerable degree of judicial creativity in handling precedents, will be discussed in later chapters (in particular, chapters 7 and 14).

The dispensing of justice in dispute-solving, the maintenance of stability in the law through precedent, the keeping of the law at least minimally in touch with the needs of a changing society – these are the main and ostensible functions of the courts, as usually expounded by jurists and legal commentators. We might add another, less obvious, social function, however: that of *social control*. It is through the decisions of the higher appellate courts in particular that dominant ideological currents on morality, law and order, and other contemporary problem areas are propagated.[50] The received pronouncements constitute a kind of patchwork quilt of judicial decisions, each of which contains within its reasoning and premises some aspect of the judicial assumptions about social consensus and the importance of upholding such 'consensual values' in the dispensation of justice. We see these processes most clearly in the case of criminal law, where one fundamental function of the courts is the trial and disposition of those whom the law labels 'criminally deviant'.

According to some writers, the criminal justice system represents not simply the trial and disposition of the offender; it represents the systematic destruction of the accused's social identity. Garfinkel[51] wrote in 1956 of the court as a 'degradation ceremony', whereby 'the public identity of an actor is transformed into something looked on as lower in the local scheme of social types'.[52] In other words, the court process involves mechanisms and procedures which have the effect of revealing a convicted person as having all the *negative* characteristics of a 'criminal', a 'deviant', an outsider – characteristics which the accused is 'seen' to have had all along. The accused stands revealed 'as he or she really is', and is invested with the stigma of criminality which in turn brings all sorts of social consequences: 'We exercise varieties of discrimination, through which we effectively, if often unthinkingly, reduce his life chances. We construct a stigma theory, an ideology to explain his inferiority and account for the danger he represents, sometimes rationalising an animosity on other differences, such as those of social class.'[53] For we, the observers, remain 'normal' and within the boundaries of assumed consensual social standards of behaviour and values, while the convicted person is shown to be 'different' and apart from the rest of us.

A good example of these processes is the number of difficulties encountered by ex-prisoners on release, in finding social acceptance, accommodation and, most importantly, employment. Studies have shown[54] that not only ex-prisoners, but in fact *anyone* who has come into contact with the criminal justice system through investigation and arrest, even though *no* subsequent charge or conviction ensues, has extreme difficulty in being accepted for employment if the applicant's history is known to the potential employer. The Rehabilitation of Offenders Act 1974, which provides that when a person's conviction has been 'spent', that person should suffer no discrimination in applying for or securing employment and does not have to admit to a conviction before a prospective employer, may make some difference to the problems of ex-offenders in obtaining jobs, although this Act does not apply to certain occupations and clearly does not guarantee non-discrimination in cases where the conviction is known by a prospective employer.

The criminal justice system, then, as epitomized in courtroom procedure, is geared not simply to establishing a deviant trait, weakness or aberration in the person appearing before it; rather, the discovery of the criminally deviant act for which the accused is before the court is presented as indicative of a *total* deviant identity. As Garfinkel points out,[55] this process must, to be effective, be presented as carried out in the name of communally held social values against which the accused has offended; the judge must be seen to represent the community in upholding those values which are embodied in the law, and various writers have expanded on the ways in which this essentially *symbolic* representation is carried out.

Carlen, for example, has discussed the effect of the highly theatrical atmosphere of the magistrates' court.[56] The accused is physically removed from the rest of the proceedings and is therefore dislocated from the 'normal' people in the courtroom, with the exception of the magistrates whose physical position fulfils quite a different symbolic function: 'the magistrate sits raised up from the rest of the court. The defendant is also raised up to public view but the dock is set lower than the magisterial seat, whilst the rails surrounding it are symbolic of the defendant's captive state.'[57]

The trial proceeds by way of formalities, set procedures and ritualism, the whole ceremony being 'maintained partly to facilitate physical control of defendants and any others who may step out of place and partly to refurbish the historically sacred meanings attached to law'.[58]

Furthermore, the accused person is immediately stripped of all the characteristics of an autonomous, participating individual:

He is of interest only as a 'case'. The 'case', in turn, becomes the object of negotiation among the leading players in the courtroom. The defendant, although formally the focus of the bargaining is, in practice, excluded from participating. He is 'represented' and must wait patiently for the outcome of the deliberations of others. He is a man taken out of his world and transposed to the world of others.[59]

The position is significantly worse if the defendant is *not* represented by a lawyer, for in all probability the defendant will have little or no legal knowledge, and will frequently be unable to appreciate fully what is expected when he or she is asked to speak (see chapter 13).

It is significant that Garfinkel, in specifying the 'conditions of successful degradation ceremonies', is careful to note that the 'rules of the game' must be accepted by all the participants; the procedure and ceremony of the courtroom must be taken as 'given' by lawyers, judge, witnesses and defendant, and it is interesting that there have been occasions where failure by the defendants to accept the legitimacy of these 'ground rules' has resulted in what may be seen as *un*successful degradation ceremonies. In 1969, for example, seven young political radicals were tried in Chicago for 'conspiracy to cross state lines with the intention of organizing, promoting or encouraging a riot'. They had, in fact, planned in 1968 to arrange a protest demonstration at the Democratic Convention in Chicago, and it is important to remember that this was a period of political criticism and unrest among students, radicals and many others in Europe and in America.

The trial which followed is interesting not so much for the substantive offences charged, but rather for the way in which the defendants consistently and systematically refused to accept the very basis on which the trial was being conducted: there were frequent interruptions of counsel and judge by the defendants, usually to the effect that the latter were the victims not of a *legal* battle, but of political repression:[60]

the judge expressed a positive conception of his role as upholder of the orderly legal process, one who was attempting to be an impartial arbiter despite attacks by the defendants and the media . . . [the defendants] viewed the court in illegitimate terms, seeing it as the expression of a corrupt legal, political and social order which they desired to alter radically.[61]

The result was that the trial '*failed* as a degradation ceremony. If there was any appreciable change in status, it was the court which was degraded rather than the defendants. Because of the mass violation of ceremonial rules the court was unable to act in the tradition of efficiency and fairness which gives it definition.'[62] It is, moreover, interesting that this trial attracted considerable publicity, by no means all of which was uncritical of the ways in which the judge conducted the proceedings.

Although such cases are perhaps rare,[63] the conclusion we might draw from such occurrences is that, where there is refusal by defendants to accept the court's own definition of the situation, the court, in the person of the judge, is driven to unusual lengths to maintain some form of normal courtroom order, and to ensure that the forum is seen publicly to be acting impartially and within the strict constraints of legal rules as opposed to political ideologies. The clear discrepancies between the judges' and the defendants' perspectives on the trial itself in such cases serves to throw into sharp focus the hard edge of the social control function of the court, which in more normal circumstances is obscured by the ritual and ceremony of procedure and rules.

7
The making of legal rules

One of the most important functions of any legal system is the authoritative statement of the normative legal code – the legal rules – by which the society in question is to operate. As we have seen, legal rules are not necessarily the only normative codes which prescribe social behaviour (morals and etiquette are others), but legal rules are distinct in that they constitute the *official* code which has the backing of state powers of enforcement and sanctions. In this chapter we examine the principle sources in modern society whereby legal rules are created.

Parliamentary legislation: politics, pressures and public policy

According to the constitution, Parliament or, more correctly, the 'Queen in Parliament', is the sovereign lawmaker in Britain. This means that although the judges also make law, they must bow to the superior powers of the legislature, which may override judge-made 'common-law' rules by Acts of Parliament. In recent years Britain's membership of the European Community has brought dramatic consequences for this constitutional doctrine, as we will see in chapter 8. In this chapter, however, we will concentrate on the domestic law-making processes of the UK, and in this first section we consider the procedural aspects of legislation and discuss something of the background to and impact of legislative enactments.

Acts of Parliament proceed through the various stages of enactment as 'bills', of which there are several kinds. A public bill, dealing with matters affecting the public generally, may be introduced either by a minister – in which case it is termed a government bill – or by a private member of Parliament, when it is called a private member's bill. This should not be confused with a private bill, dealing with limited or sectional interests such as matters affecting a single local authority, which is promoted by the body concerned by *petition* to Parliament. Our main interest is with public bills and the procedural stages through which they must pass.

Government bills may originate in various ways. To begin with, the proposed legislation may derive from the manifesto on which the party in power based its general election campaign (such as the enactment in 1980 of the Housing Act which, among other things, implemented the Conservatives' manifesto commitment to give council-house tenants the right to buy their houses); or it may be introduced as a means of implementing government policy once elected to power (such as the British Telecommunications Act 1981, and the Gas Act 1986, which were the means of carrying out the continuing government policy of returning nationalized industries substantially to private control – in these instances, telephone and gas services). Legislation may be passed because of some national emergency or crisis which has occurred during the government's period in office. The Prevention of Terrorism (Temporary Provisions) Act 1974, passed after the spate of bomb attacks in Britain, was such a measure. On occasion, issues arise over which there may be public disquiet, or about which the government may feel the need for special investigation and, possibly, recommendations for new legislation.

Such issues might be investigated in several ways: a Parliamentary Select Committee, or a departmental (or inter-departmental) committee, may be established to look into the matter; or the government may set up a Royal Commission, whose terms of reference will specify the area and extent of its investigative brief. The findings of several Royal Commissions are discussed in this book, among them the Royal Commission on Legal Services (see chapter 13), established in 1976 as a result of considerable public criticism of lawyers, their work and their remuneration; and the Royal Commission on Civil Liability for Personal Injuries and Death (see chapter 9), established in 1973 to inquire into existing provisions for compensation in the areas of industrial injuries, motor accident injuries, injuries arising from defective products and congenitally handicapped children.

Royal Commissions report to Parliament, usually with recommendations for legislation which may or may not be taken up as part of the government's legislative programme. Indeed, it has been suggested that Royal Commissions may be established for a number of reasons, not all of them connected with any governmental desire to implement legislative change:

> . . . apart from examining a problem or issues which the government wants to tackle, but on which it is not committed to any particular policy, they may also be established, for example, to prepare the way for a policy to which the government is already committed, to forestall anticipated criticism or pressure, to pacify critics, to postpone the necessity for action, or to kill a proposal.[1]

Another source of legislation is the recommendations of the Law Commission, created in 1965 in order to review and make recommendations about any areas of the law which the commission feels to be in need of reform. Such reform might be achieved by means of repealing obsolete statutes, the codification of the law in specific areas, the reduction of the number of separate statutes in a given area, or the removal of anomalies within the law. Law Commission proposals, which are presented to Parliament, often have draft bills appended, although these are by no means always implemented.

It is from such sources as this that legislative measures are passed which do not necessarily create new law, but which are designed to amend or consolidate existing legal provision. The Tribunals and Inquiries Act 1971, the Representation of the People Act 1983, and the Trade Union and Labour Relations (Consolidation) Act 1992 are examples of such Acts. Finally, every government will introduce bills dealing with finance, such as the annual Finance Act which gives effect to the Budget proposals, and other bills which concern taxes and public expenditure.

Private members' bills may be the result of an MP being approached for support for a proposal put forward by particular interest-groups operating outside Parliament (see chapter 2), but a substantial number originate from the government, which may suggest to an MP that he or she propose a particular measure. The amount of parliamentary time allocated to private members' bills, however, is strictly limited. It has been noted that the amount of time permitted by successive governments in recent years for debate on private members' bills has been diminishing.[2] It has been suggested that 'private members' bills which are opposed do not pass unless they are given government time. This is because . . . time is restricted and any concerted opposition can talk a bill out.'[3] Another difficulty is that private members' bills do not, in general, enjoy the same facilities for discussion with civil service departments, drafting by the parliamentary draftsmen, or strong governmental support, as government bills, although a government may on occasion provide help and support for a private member's bill of which it approves. A government which does *not* wish to see such a bill enacted will use its powers to prevent the passage of the proposed legislation. In these circumstances it is not surprising that the majority of private members' bills fail: in the session 1985–6, out of a total of 112 private members' bills introduced, only 21 were eventually passed, compared with 50 government bills which were introduced in the same session, of which 48 were passed.

As far as government bills are concerned, there is invariably considerable consultation between ministers, the civil service departments concerned, and non-parliamentary organizations and interest-groups; 'where, as is often the case, the co-operation of the affected interests is highly desirable in order to make the bill most effective in practice, something very like a bargain may be struck and undertakings may be given on both sides'.[4] Such compromises are a remarkable (though not unique) feature of the English legislative system, and it is important to note that many of these discussions and consultations take place *before* the bill is introduced into Parliament: although we usually speak of Parliament as the law-making assembly, in practice most bills already have their initial shape and content clearly set out before their appearance in Parliament. Some critics question whether Parliament is not effectively by-passed in the modern law-making process.

If we consider briefly the various parliamentary stages of legislation, we see that the opportunities for change and amendment to proposed measures may be considerable. After a formal 'first reading' of a bill in the House where the proposal originates (this may be either the Commons or the Lords), there is a 'second reading', which is a full statement of the objectives of the bill. This is followed by a debate in which MPs – particularly, of course, opposition MPs – may table amendments to the bill. Frequently, the second reading stage is the point at which public attention becomes drawn to the proposal, through press coverage and, on occasion, vociferous campaigns for and against the measure by pressure-groups affected by the proposal. The bill then passes to the 'committee stage', where proposed amendments are discussed in detail: some will be incorporated, others will be rejected. For bills originating in the House of Commons, the committee which carries out these discussions – usually one of a number of Standing Committees – comprises MPs representing the different political parties roughly in proportion to the overall composition of the House. There will therefore be a government majority on the committee, though the attempt is made to ensure representation by minority parties. On rare occasions, such as when a bill proposes fundamental constitutional change, the committee comprises the full House. Another variation, if discussions on the proposed bill require detailed analysis, possibly with witnesses being called, is for the bill to go before a Select Committee. If the bill originates in the House of Lords, there is a less strict procedure, and the Lords have no Standing Committees.

When the committee reports back to the House, further amendments may be tabled. After this stage (and after any further proposed amendments have been dealt with) the bill is given its 'third reading'. The next step is for the bill to go through similar procedures in the other House, after which it is returned, with any proposals for amendments which may have been made in that other House, to the originating House. Finally, when this lengthy process is over, the bill receives the Royal Assent and becomes an Act of Parliament.

Of course, some amendments may be made for purely practical reasons, such as the need to simplify an otherwise over-complicated clause. But as often as not, amendments derive from our system of government which comprises not just one governing political grouping, having the power to realize whichever policies it pleases, but rather a number of political parties, whose presence in Parliament ensures, in theory and usually in practice, that no political party coming to power after an election may gain absolute control over the affairs of the nation. The basic task of the opposition, after all, is to *oppose* the policies of the government. This system is supposed to ensure the free discussion by all sides of all matters concerning government, including legislative proposals; it also results in the fact that much legislation is to some extent a political *compromise*: very few Acts emerge without some amendments being made on their way through the parliamentary process.

Once a measure has gained the Royal Assent (these days, merely a formality) and has become an Act, there may then be a considerable time before the Act is actually *implemented*: that is, brought into force. There may be inadequate resources available to fulfil the Act's provisions immediately; bodies affected by the Act many require time to adjust their procedures and practices so as to enable them to meet the Act's requirements; special machinery may have to be set up before the Act can be properly enforced; for such reasons as these, the implementation of statutes may be delayed, or the provisions of statutes implemented gradually, on a piecemeal basis. Piecemeal or delayed implementation is nowadays very common, and it is undeniable that it causes confusion to lawyers and lay people alike. To take just one example: the Consumer Credit Act of 1974 is an extremely complex and wide-ranging statute, regulating all aspects of consumer credit from hire-purchase to bank overdrafts. It contains nearly two hundred separate sections, uses new terms which require definition and familiarity among lawyers, brings together legal regulation of various transactions previously contained in a number of separate statutes – and took over ten years after its passage through Parliament before being fully implemented! Some measures towards improving this state of affairs were announced in 1982, when the government stated that where an Act contains neither a date of commencement (the preferred alternative) nor provision for a commencement order, then the Act should itself provide that it should come into force not less than two months after the Royal Assent.

As we noted in the last chapter, another important form of law is *delegated* (or *subordinate*) legislation. An Act of Parliament may authorize a specific body to enact rules having the force of law, in accordance with the power vested in that body by the parent statute. For example, local authorities may make by-laws 'for the good rule and government of the whole or part of the district or borough . . . and for the prevention and suppression of nuisances therein' by virtue of s.235 of the Local Government Act 1972. Another common example of delegated legislation is that of powers conferred on government departments to make regulations affecting a given issue: both the Social Security Acts of 1980 contain provisions, for example, which empower the Secretary of State to make orders and regulations concerning social security benefits; and the important regulations affecting the construction and use of motor vehicles are made under the authority of s.40 of the Road Traffic Act 1971, a measure consolidating earlier provisions which conferred similar powers on the Secretary of State responsible.

It must not be thought, however, that parent statutes give a blank cheque to subordinate legislators. There are various controls which, in theory at least, may be exerted over delegated legislation. The first is that Parliament itself must approve the initial parent statute which confers law-making powers on a particular body; the relevant sections in the parent Act may also provide that any delegated legislation made by virtue of that Act must be affirmatively resolved by Parliament. More usually, there is a requirement not that the regulation (usually a Statutory Instrument) must be affirmatively resolved, but simply that it must be 'laid before Parliament' for a certain period (usually forty days) during which MPs *may* raise questions on the measure, and possibly press for a resolution to annul it. In practice, however, such a response is infrequent: a government would rarely grant parliamentary time for such a debate. It might be thought that Parliamentary scrutiny of delegated legislation is not as rigorous as it might be, given that authority to create such legislation derives from Parliament itself.

The courts have the power to review delegated legislation in the event of its validity being challenged, and to declare it invalid if it is found to have been made *ultra vires* ('beyond the powers of') the authority being challenged. Delegated legislation may be *ultra vires* either because the authority has, literally, gone beyond the powers conferred on it by the parent Act, or because that authority has acted in a manner not in accordance with *procedures* laid down in the parent Act.

To say that no single political party can control the affairs of the nation, however, is not the same as saying that no single political or economic group, however loosely constituted, may gain such control in legislative or policy terms. We will see in chapter 14 how notions such as 'public policy' and the 'national interest' can obscure the social, political and economic divisions and interests in society. The same problem is inherent in the idea that legislation 'reflects public opinion', for public opinion is almost impossible to define or measure. The constitutional lawyer Dicey, writing at the turn of the century, stated that 'there exists at any given time a body of beliefs, convictions, sentiments, accepted principles, of firmly-rooted prejudices, which, taken together, make up the public opinion of a particular era . . . [which] has, in England, if we look at the matter broadly, determined, directly or indirectly, the course of legislation'.[5] He seems to have had some doubts, however, about the strength of his proposition, as is seen by his use of the qualifying phrases 'broadly' and 'directly or indirectly'. Dicey recognized the connections between legislation and powerful classes and interest-groups quite clearly, and must not be taken to have posited the existence of a blanket consensual 'public opinion' of the kind frequently referred to by judges and politicians. Dicey's answer to the problems raised by these facts is interesting:

Individuals . . . and still more frequently classes, do constantly support laws or institutions that they deem beneficial to themselves, but that certainly are in fact injurious to the rest of the world. But the explanation of this conduct will be found, in nine cases out of ten, to be that men come easily to believe that arrangements agreeable to themselves are beneficial to others. A man's interest gives a bias to his judgment far oftener than it corrupts his heart.[6]

There is, in other words, a tendency to presume that what is good for one group is good for all groups, and this is certainly the thrust of the ideological currents which dominate modern legislative and political activities and permeate all other groups in society through channels such as the media, political speeches and, of course, judicial pronouncements.

It must be acknowledged that, despite attempts by politicians and judges to justify policies on the grounds of 'public opinion', this notion is analytically elusive and, on any given issue, impossible to assess. For Parliament is much more than merely a debating-chamber for the discussion and implementation of policies supported by popular opinion. Often the parliamentary process itself represents only the most superficial element in the law-making process. Given the predominance of government bills, much legislative preparation, consultation and discussion occurs *outside* Parliament, within government departments, among members of the civil service, and between MPs, civil servants and interested outside groups. Some such groups – 'interest-groups' – exist for the purpose of permanently representing particular interests in all manner of ways, including making their views known on legislative proposals. Thus, there may be consultation with groups such as the Confederation of British Industry, the Trades Union Congress, the Law Society, the police and the British Medical Association, if the interests of the members of such groups stand to be affected by the proposals in question. Other groups – 'cause groups' or 'pressure-groups' – exist simply to campaign for a particular cause or issue, such as prison reform, divorce-law reform or nuclear disarmament. Whether, and at what stage, such groups will be consulted by government departments for their views on a particular matter is a complex question.

To begin with, we must take into account the dimension of *political power* in the consultative process. Some groups enjoy more power than others; if a proposal concerned the provision of council housing, it is probable that local authorities' views would be sought, but far less likely that local council tenants' federations would be consulted. If the proposal concerned changes in the prison system, it is unthinkable that the Prison Officers' Association would not be listened to, but most improbable that the views of a prisoners' rights organization would be heard. And even if interest-groups manage to present their arguments, it does not necessarily follow that their views will actually be taken into consideration: much will depend upon the political power and prestige, the general 'credibility', the level of organization and the degree of political skill possessed by particular groups.

Of course, as most commentators and researchers acknowledge, legislation is sometimes enacted which seems to be *dis*advantageous to powerful interest-groups and social classes. Examples are the measures designed to control and combat industrial pollution by the use of criminal sanctions, and the statutes which date back, in various forms, to the last century which impose stringent controls and requirements on those concerned in the management of factories to maintain standards of safety. How are such statutes to be explained?

Various answers may be given. First, if we consider the extent to which most such laws are actually *enforced* with any rigour, we often see that they are usually rather weak weapons against the proscribed activity. Often, enforcement is entrusted to a special agency, such as the Health and Safety Executive, which operates under special terms of reference and whose policies for enforcement frequently stop short of prosecution of offenders. Carson's study of the enforcement of the Factory Acts[7] suggests that prosecutions for violations were rare; instead, such violations were handled by warnings. The Equal Opportunities Commission, created by the Sex Discrimination Act 1975, has the responsibility for, among other things, investigating complaints of sex discrimination in employment and elsewhere, but has been criticized for being over-cautious in using its powers. Cranston reports[8] that of more than 21,000 infringements, over a six-month period, of the Trade Descriptions Act 1968 (enforced by local trading standards departments), only 1,003 were prosecuted – nearly 6,000 cases being dealt with by warnings and the rest being dealt with by means of advice given to the offending businesses. And Gunningham cites the statement by the Chief Inspector of the Alkali Inspectorate in 1967 that in forty-seven years the inspectorate had brought only three cases before a court.[9]

Second, it is not always the case that such legislation adversely affects powerful interests, despite appearances to the contrary. Carson's research into the origins of the factory legislation which was introduced during the nineteenth century reveals, in his view, how the powerful factory-owners who were close to the legislative process realized that legal controls might operate to their advantage by forcing competitors out of business.[10] It is possible to perceive the same kind of attitude today on the part of manufacturers and advertisers towards legislative controls which we call 'consumer protection'. Here, the ostensible objective of, say, legal controls on advertising (designed to secure minimum standards of truthfulness and decency) is to protect the consumer from irresponsible and misleading claims; but one latent function may very well be the maintenance of an acceptable and respectable public image of an industry which is shown publicly to be operating in the interests of truth, honesty and the consumer interest. The actual extent of stringent control may be questioned, especially in the light of the fact that the standards of advertising, and the inquiries into complaints about advertisements, are dealt with by the Advertising Standards Authority, which is itself composed of members of the advertising industry.[11]

The legislative process, then, is far from being one in which interests common to everyone are protected and promoted. We have repeatedly seen how values and interests differ immensely among various groups and classes in society, and that it is consequently impossible to identify any single 'public interest'. Rather,

The output of the legislature means rags or riches, servility or power, weakness or strength, to every interest group in the country. The institution which produces such extraordinary benefits or detriments cannot in its very nature be a merely impartial framework for struggle. Like every bureaucratic organization, it responds to the pressure of the powerful and the privileged.[12]

Of course, a significant proportion of the legislative output is, to a great extent, uncontentious in party-political terms, and much welfare state legislation, providing benefits and pensions, local authority services and other similar provisions, *does* operate to the benefit of the less powerful groups in society. None the less there are periods when such provision falls victim to the influential voices of the economically powerful groups and individuals wishing to see, for instance, cuts in public expenditure and the relocation of national resources towards private industry and enterprise. Overall, it is hard to avoid the conclusion, when considering the legislature, that the democratic ideal, in terms of government and law-making, is far from being a political and social reality.

Precedent and policy I: the common law

Judge-made law, as developed through the doctrine of binding precedent, or *stare decisis*, is one of the oldest and most fundamental features of the English legal system. The doctrine of precedent states that a decision made by a court in one case is *binding* on other courts in later cases involving similar facts. In this way, uniformity within the law is, in theory, to a large extent maintained, and one of the most basic demands of our conception of justice is met by the treating of like cases in like manner.

Allen,[13] in his review of the history of the doctrine, presents evidence that

English judges were making use of previously decided cases as guides as early as the thirteenth century. But it was not until the sixteenth century that the availability of reports of decided cases – and some of the earlier series of law reports were grossly unreliable and inadequate[14] – brought any certainty or consistency into the operation of what gradually became the doctrine of binding precedent.

Precedent is the basis of the common law: that body of law emerging from cases as they are decided by the judges. We have seen several examples of cases containing points of sufficient legal importance to constitute precedents – *Shaw* v. *DPP*[15] with its statement of the law relating to conspiracy to corrupt public morals, which was followed in *Knuller* v. *DPP* ten years later; *Donoghue* v. *Stevenson* in 1932,[16] containing Lord Atkin's statement of the 'neighbour principle' which was to become the foundation stone of the later cases involving negligence, and so on. What we are concerned with here is precedent in theory and in practice: how the *practical* operation of precedent compares with the *formal* rules of the doctrine.

To understand the doctrine of precedent we must recall the hierarchical structure of the English courts, and the appeal system.[17] At the lowest levels are the courts of first instance, then further up are the Divisional Courts, followed by the Court of Appeal; at the top of the structure is the ultimate court of appeal, the House of Lords. Cases reach the higher, appellate courts by reason of their being taken there on appeal by the party to the dispute who loses in the court below. The most authoritative decisions, then, are those of the higher courts – the Court of Appeal and the House of Lords – and it is these decisions which tend to constitute precedents, although it must be noted that High Court decisions can sometimes be regarded as authoritative.

Given this structure, the basic rules of the doctrine of precedent are fairly easily stated. First, all courts are bound to follow the previous decisions of courts which are *higher in the hierarchy* in cases which are similar to those previously decided cases. Thus, a decision of the Court of Appeal is binding on all courts below it, but is not binding on the House of Lords; a decision of the House of Lords is binding on all other courts; and, at the bottom of the structure, a decision of the county court is binding on no other court. Second, the binding nature of a precedent applies to all future cases which have like facts, and as we shall see presently, this feature of the doctrine may give rise to difficult problems of interpretation for the courts.

To what extent is one court's decision binding on itself? Beginning with the High Court: this court is technically not bound by its own decisions, though in practice High Court judges will usually follow previous High Court decisions unless there are good reasons not to do so. The Court of Appeal is, generally speaking, and subject to certain exceptions, bound by its own decisions. In *Young* v. *Bristol Aeroplane Co. Ltd* in 1944[18] the Court of Appeal explained the situations in which it might depart from its own previous decisions, these being: first, where the court is faced with two conflicting decisions of its own, it may choose which one to follow; second, the court is not bound to follow one of its own previous decisions which is inconsistent with a later House of Lords decision; and third, the court is not bound to follow a decision of its own which was given *per incuriam* – that is to say, a case which was decided without taking into account some statutory provision or precedent which would have affected the decision. Despite the attempts of Lord

Denning, while Master of the Rolls, to free the Court of Appeal from the constraints of the doctrine of precedent,[19] the House of Lords made it clear in no uncertain terms that, subject to the exceptional circumstances as stated in *Young*, the Court of Appeal remained bound by its previous decisions.[20]

With regard to the House of Lords: until 1966 this court considered itself bound by its own decisions (see chapter 14). This could mean that unless Parliament stepped in and changed the effect of a House of Lords decision by statute, such a decision, at least in theory, could never be modified, limited, extended or overruled, because there is no higher court to which such a decision might be taken on appeal. The essence of the doctrine of precedent is, again in theory, both certainty and flexibility: the possibility should always exist for judicial pronouncements to be modified or even removed, if the decision proves unjust, inadequate or outdated. Although there are contained within the doctrine of precedent mechanisms whereby earlier decisions *may* not be followed (see below), there could none the less be 'blockages', where a House of Lords decision bound all courts, including itself, thus preventing or at least seriously impeding the possibilities for change.

In 1966 the Lord Chancellor announced that henceforth the House of Lords would consider itself empowered to depart from its own previous decisions. The Practice Direction explaining this change[21] states that

Their Lordships . . . recognise that too rigid adherence to precedent may lead to injustice in a particular case and also unduly restrict the proper development of the law. They propose therefore to modify their present practice and, while treating former decisions of this House as normally binding, to depart from a previous decision when it appears right to do so.

In this connection they will bear in mind the danger of disturbing retrospectively the basis on which contracts, settlements of property and fiscal arrangements have been entered into and also the especial need for certainty as to the criminal law.

This was undoubtedly a sensible if overdue development, although it should be added that such departures are fairly infrequent;[22] it is arguable that the stability and continuity of the law would suffer if such departures 'appeared right' too often (see chapter 14). This limited slackening of the grip of the doctrine of precedent nevertheless, it is to be hoped, increases the court's ability to ensure that the principles enshrined in previous cases are not permitted to dictate injustice, and that legal principles and rules are kept in line with the demands of changing social and economic conditions.

But surely, it may be objected, no two cases are ever exactly alike? How 'alike' does a later case have to be before a court must follow a given precedent? The *practical* answer to these questions will be discussed in due course; but the *theory* of precedent rests upon the proposition that the similarity between any two cases derives not just from their specific facts, but rather from their respective 'law-and-fact' content. In law, every case has two aspects. First, there is the particular dispute itself – a fact-situation which the court must resolve with reference to relevant legal rules. For example, a consumer alleges injury suffered because of a faulty product; a motorist is prosecuted for driving while drunk; a husband brings an action against his wife for divorce. The second aspect is the precise legal issue which these facts raise: the circumstances provided in law whereby the consumer obtains a remedy, the legally prescribed conditions of liability under which the motorist may be convicted, or the legal grounds which must be shown before a divorce can be granted. It is to these issues that legal argument and the citation of precedents are directed. If the consumer's injury is caused by a defective bottle of shampoo, for instance, we do not have to search the Law Reports for previous cases in which a bottle of shampoo caused injury. It is enough that we discover a legal authority, through precedents, for the general legal proposition that a consumer may in appropriate circumstances recover compensation for injury caused by a defective product. The actual item which features in previous cases might be a car,[23] underwear,[24] or a bottle of ginger-beer;[25] what really matters is the legal principle involved, and not the specific facts of the previous case. This legal principle – the *ratio decidendi* – is the part of the decision which constitutes the binding precedent.

This seems a simple enough proposition, and it *would* be, if it were possible to state firmly and clearly what the *ratio* of a given case is. The fact is that different judges may interpret the judgments given in previous cases quite differently, and conclude that in their opinion the 'correct' reading of a case provides a *ratio* which may be wider or more restrictive (or compatible or incompatible with the case in hand) than the interpretation of their colleagues on the bench. There are some cases in which it is extremely difficult, if not impossible, to ascertain precisely the *ratio* of the case,[26] and to distinguish the *ratio* from the judges' statements which are not part of the points of legal principles (the *obiter dicta*) and which are not binding. As Twining and Miers point out, 'talk of *finding* the *ratio decidendi* of a case obscures the fact that the process of interpreting cases is not like a hunt for buried treasure, but typically involves an element of choice from a range of possibilities'.[27]

There is a strong connection between the facts of a case and the legal rules or principles which judges derive from those facts; and differences of fact between otherwise similar cases may have important consequences for the final decision in a new case. The doctrine of precedent allows for such situations by mechanisms whereby a judge may depart from a particular line of precedent, for the doctrine does not require that judges are mere slaves to the past. Indeed, one of the advantages claimed for the doctrine is that the judges have the freedom, or at least the discretion, to treat precedents with some flexibility.

The first such mechanism is inherent in the court structure itself: a court is free to *overrule* a decision of a court lower than itself, if it is of the opinion that the previous case was wrongly decided or has become out of date. Hence the Court of Appeal may overrule a decision of the High Court, and the House of Lords may overrule a decision of the Court of Appeal – and sometimes a previous decision of its own. Another device whereby precedents may be avoided (open to all courts irrespective of their place in the hierarchy) is known as *distinguishing on the facts*. This means that if a judge thinks that a precedent which otherwise covers the case in hand is nevertheless different in some *material* particular, then that precedent may be distinguished and not followed. Take, for example, the treatment of *Donoghue* v. *Stevenson*[28] in the later *Evans* v. *Triplex Safety Glass Ltd.*[29] In the latter case a car windscreen had shattered, due to some unexplained cause, and had injured the occupants of the car. The court refused to follow *Donoghue* v. *Stevenson* and hold the manufacturers of the windscreen liable in negligence because, unlike the faulty product in that previous case, the windscreen might have been interfered with, and the defect introduced, by any of a whole range of possible agencies other than the original manufacturer. This possibility of alternative cause was held to be a sufficiently material difference for the court to distinguish *Donoghue* (which nevertheless, of course, remained perfectly good law) and to conclude that the case before the court should be decided in favour of the respondent manufacturer.

Having explained the formal mechanisms of precedent, we must now consider how precedent works *in practice*.[30] Precedents constitute the common law; they contain the legal rules which the judges interpret as emerging from decided cases. Until a few years ago, many judges denied that they properly had any creative role at all, and even in recent times some judges have insisted on keeping judicial creativity within strict limits.[31] There were times in the past when the common law was explained by the judges as something which they merely 'declared'; the rules and principles themselves were held out to be always existing, albeit in unstated form, awaiting 'revelation' through the judges by means of some mystical process of reasoning. Law creation was thought to be exclusively the job of Parliament, not the judiciary. Thus Lord Esher could state in 1892: 'There is . . . no such thing as judge-made law, for the judges do not make the law, though they frequently have to apply existing law to circumstances as to which it has not previously been authoritatively laid down that such law is applicable.'[32]

Nowadays, the debate between adherents of this declaratory theory and those arguing, or accepting, that judges *do* make law is somewhat arid and fruitless, despite the arguments presented by Dworkin to the effect that judges always decide within existing limits of rule and principle and that there is always a 'right answer' if only it can be discerned.[33] Such views run against the tide of modern opinion, and indeed of judicial acknowledgements of their law-making activity. Most judges and commentators accept that judges create new law, and concentrate on the far more important issues regarding the *manner* and *extent to which* judges create legal rules, and the limitations which may operate on this creative judicial function.[34] We will explore these questions in much more detail in chapter 14, but at this stage several important aspects of judicial law-making must be noted. To begin with, modern judges acknowledge explicitly the role played by their conceptions of public policy in influencing their decision-making. Lord Denning in particular repeatedly pointed out[35] that the older, fictional ideas among judges and lawyers about the 'mere application of rules to facts' should give way to the immediate necessity of shaping the law to fit the needs of modern society. As Friedmann, in a thorough comparative review of the relationship between judge and doctrine in modern society, puts it: 'What would be fatal and illusory, would be any attempt to return to the nineteenth-century myth of a judiciary that simply interprets statutes or precedents, in accordance with legal logic, but need not concern itself with the deeper struggles and agonies of society.'[36] At the same time there may be good reasons, and indeed substantial social and political pressures, in reponse to which a particular judge fights shy of making policy decisions too explicit, or another judge insists on upholding some or other aspect of the fictions within the 'declaratory' theory of precedent. As Frank said some years ago,

> The reason for the judges' reluctance to admit their creativeness is not far to seek. The theory of our democratic government is that . . . the legislature expresses the popular will, legislation is the voice of the people . . . the courts would seem to be acting beyond their powers were they frankly to legislate. Fear of popular denunciation of illegal usurpation of power accordingly has led judges to obscure by words what they actually did, what they could not help doing.[37]

Sometimes, when faced with a case of novel implications which are not covered by precedents, judges justify and legitimize their decisions by an appeal to the 'public interest', discussed above and in chapter 14; but in cases of lesser import, we may find that the 'application' of precedents to cases is by no means as straightforward as it might be thought. There are many reasons why a judge may find himself in the position of what Twining and Miers have called 'the puzzled interpreter', a number of which are discussed by those authors,[38] but one important reason may be the presence of conflicting precedents. One of the peculiarities of the common law is that, in general, for every precedent cited by counsel in support of a client's case, the opposing side will have discovered, among the many thousands of reported cases, precedents of similar weight which will support the *other* party's case. It is often such clashes of precedent, giving rise to at least *arguable* propositions of law by counsel on both sides, which bring cases before the appeal courts in the first place, for if a case is directly and uncontentiously covered by a previous decision, there is little point in appealing. The issue then becomes – and it must be stressed that we are here discussing, in the main, the activities of the higher courts – *how* the presiding judges handle these arguments and the previous cases on which they are based.

Many judges would assert that the manner in which they select the relevant precedent is based upon logic: the idea that the law contains within it the solution to almost any fact-situation which may arise, which the judges must decide in line with what the law prescribes. There is some debate as to what is meant by the term 'legal logic'. One meaning is simply that the judges must decide 'rationally': this may just refer to the need to decide in a non-arbitrary manner, or it may refer to the use of certain principles of reasoning, such as that the judge *deduces* the solution to a case by applying a legal rule to the facts before him, or that he uses *inductive* reasoning (finding the facts in a case, then seeking out the relevant legal rule and 'fitting' it to that case).[39] Another meaning of 'legal logic' may take the law to be a 'closed system', whereby the 'correct' answer to any question may be derived from the legal rules (see chapter 1). These views miss one essential point. In referring to concepts like 'logic' the impression may often be given that the mode of reasoning used by judges is somehow scientific and demonstrable: that a conclusion follows 'logically' (that is, *inevitably*) from a given premise: given X, then Y logically must follow.

In law, however, this is not the case. The judge must make a *selective* decision as to which of two (or more) conflicting lines of precedent should apply to a case.

Campbell has written that 'legal logic' is not the logic of scientific demonstration, but 'it is the logic of rhetoric. In the court situation the lawyer, by use of the logic of argumentation, seeks to persuade his audience, the judge.'[40] Twining and Miers, after considering the various techniques with which lawyers and judges handle precedents, acknowledge that judges use a wide variety of reasons for their preference for one line of argument/precedent as against another, such as that a given rule is firmly established, or serves a useful function, and so on. They maintain that these stated reasons for choosing one solution as against any other constitute a set of constraints operating to control the exercise of discretion in deciding cases.[41]

The picture, then, unfolds: the judge, required by convention and a conception of justice to make decisions in line with previous cases which justify his conclusions objectively, must nevertheless make creative selections from the mass of precedents which may be cited. It is this essentially creative activity which is obscured by the 'declaratory theory', and by the use of the formal device of 'distinguishing on the facts', for, as we shall see in our illustrations shortly, the interpretation of facts by counsel and judges is as much a matter of contention as is the interpretation of the precedents themselves.

The different styles of individual judges may be attributable, then, to the extent to which their essentially creative role in handling precedents is acknowledged, and one useful analytical model whereby we may appreciate different modes of judicial behaviour is the distinction presented by an American writer, Karl Llewellyn. He suggested[42] that, over substantial periods of time, it is possible to discern patterns or styles of the judicial use of precedent. He distinguished between what he called the 'Grand' style of judging, where the judge bases his decision upon grounds of public policy, or with a view to the consequences of his decision, and takes a view of precedent which allows for creativity and flexibility; and the 'Formal' style of judging – the 'orthodox ideology'[43] – where 'the rules of law are to decide the cases; policy is for the legislature, not for the courts, and so is change even in pure common law'.[44]

While these 'styles of judging' will not be found in any pure or absolute form at any period, and should not be taken as literal and accurate descriptions of judicial practice in a given era,[45] this distinction does help us understand something of the differences in decision-making between different judges, and some of the problems which can crop up and recur within the body of case-law. We have seen something of the work of judges whom we might term 'Grand style': judges such as Lord Atkin and Lord Denning, who have been responsible for some of the landmark cases in English law, such as *Donoghue* v. *Stevenson* and many others. Even cases which have been heavily criticized, such as *Shaw* v. *DPP*, must be acknowledged as constituting firm statements by judges of new, or at least up-dated, common-law principles and rules. The impact of such cases need not be repeated here. But what examples may be given of 'Formal style' judging: that is, where the mode of judicial reasoning comprises adherence to the 'orthodox ideology' of precedent, an insistence on a strict application of legal and doctrinal rules, and a reluctance to admit the creative interpretative function of the judges?

A first illustration is the dissenting judgment of Lord Buckmaster in *Donoghue* v.

Stevenson itself.[46] His Lordship began by stating that

> the common law must be sought in law books by writers of authority and in judgments of the judges entrusted with its administration. The law books give no assistance, because the work of living authors, however deservedly eminent, cannot be used as authority, though the opinions they express may demand attention; and the ancient books do not assist. I turn, therefore to the decided cases to see if they can be construed so as to support the appellant's case.[47]

Having explained the doctrinal position, his Lordship then went on to examine a number of previous cases, and concluded that, on his reading of the precedents, none supported Mrs Donoghue's case, except for *George* v. *Skivington*,[48] which, Lord Buckmaster clearly suggested, ought not to be followed in the present case. Because he was, therefore, unable to tease out of the precedents any principle or rule which would tend towards making the ginger-beer manufacturer liable in negligence, his Lordship's conclusion was that the claim should fail.

In complete contrast, Lord Atkin's leading judgment in *Donoghue*, to which we have already referred,[49] contains passages which indicate that his Lordship was fully aware of the fact that he was advocating a dramatic extension to the common law:

> It is said that the Law of England and Scotland is that the poisoned consumer has no remedy against the negligent manufacturer. *If this were the result of the authorities,*[50] I should consider the result a grave defect in the law . . .[51]

> I do not think so ill of our jurisprudence as to suppose that its principles are so remote from the ordinary needs of civilized society and the ordinary claims it makes upon its members as to deny a legal remedy where there is so obviously a social wrong.[52]

The second example chosen here concerns a series of cases in the law of contract, all of which revolve around a similar basic fact situation: A has something to sell, and is approached by B, who is a con-man; B tells A that B is someone else, and A parts with the goods to B in exchange for B's worthless cheque. B then re-sells the goods to C, who buys innocently and with no knowledge of B's fraud. B makes off with C's money and A brings an action against C for the recovery of the goods.

The problem for the court is which of two innocent victims, A or C, should win, and keep the goods. The legal issue revolves around the nature of the original deal between A and B. This transaction cannot be a perfectly lawful contract, for it is tainted with B's fraud. Is that transaction, then, *void*, so that it has no legal validity whatsoever and the property in the goods cannot pass to B? Or is it *voidable*: that is, valid unless and until it is terminated (or 'avoided') by the injured party A, in which case, assuming that A does *not* terminate, the property in the goods passes from A to B, and B can then give a good title to those goods to C? If the first solution is taken, then A recovers the goods; if the second is adopted, then C retains the goods. This problem has resulted in some interesting manipulation of precedents.

In *Philips* v. *Brookes* in 1919,[53] a con-man walked into the plaintiff's jewellery shop and took away a valuable ring, leaving a cheque bearing the name 'Sir George Bullough'. The plaintiff had heard of Bullough, and accepted the cheque.

The con-man then pledged the ring as security for £350 from the defendant, and made off with the money. In this case, the court adopted the second solution outlined above, on the basis that a shopkeeper is happy to sell goods to anyone entering the shop, whatever the identity of that person may be. The contract between the plaintiff and the rogue was held to be voidable, and as the former had not terminated the transaction before the rogue had made the deal with the defendant, good legal title to the goods had passed to the defendant, who won the case.

On the basis of this case, one would have predicted that the court would make a similar decision in *Ingram* v. *Little* in 1961.[54] Here, the con-man called himself 'P. G. M. Hutchinson', a businessman, during negotiations with the plaintiffs, who were elderly ladies, over the sale of their car to him in exchange for a cheque. Eventually the cheque was accepted and the con-man took the car, which he then sold to the defendant who bought innocently and in good faith. But the Court of Appeal sought to distinguish *Phillips* v. *Brookes* on the basis that, since the ladies had taken the (rather inadequate) step of looking up 'P. G. M. Hutchinson' in the telephone directory and checking that such a person did reside at the address which the rogue had given them, this showed that they had intended to sell the car to Hutchinson, and only Hutchinson. Since the con-man was not Hutchinson, there could be no contract at all: the title to the car did not pass to the rogue or to the defendant, and so the plaintiffs here recovered their property.

These conflicting cases had to be dealt with in 1972 in the case of *Lewis* v. *Averay*[55] in the Court of Appeal. Again, the fact-situation is virtually identical. Here, the con-man claimed to be Richard Greene, the film-star of *Robin Hood*, and produced a studio pass as evidence of this. Both the pass and cheque which he presented in exchange for the plaintiff's car had been stolen, and the car was later traced to the defendant. Lord Denning, in the Court of Appeal (which, it will be recalled, is normally bound by its own decisions), noted that the two precedents were quite irreconcilable, and referred critically to the 'distinctions without a difference' created by the courts in the previous cases; in Lord Denning's view, such distinctions 'do no good to the law'. *Ingram* v. *Little* was said to be a case with which the court would not agree, and *Phillips* v. *Brookes* was followed. As Lord Denning said, it was regrettable that one of two innocent people had to suffer the loss, but the seller of the car must be taken to have contracted with the person before him, and it was up to him to assure himself of the credit-worthiness of that person. If he failed to do so adequately, then he must take the consequences. The 1972 decision, then, broke with the fine distinctions and formalism of the previous cases on the point, the court preferring to face the problem squarely and refusing to perpetuate a complicated debate based on precedents containing propositions of dubious helpfulness.

There are, of course, many hundreds of examples which could be cited to show how different judges have approached the problems raised by precedents. The issues, however, are clear: ought judges to hold themselves rigidly bound by previous cases, whatever the outcome? If they wish to reach a conclusion other than that apparently dictated by strict interpretation of the precedents, how are they to justify that conclusion? The 'Formal style' answer rests upon the tendency to tease out differences in the facts of cases, and make distinctions within the parameters of a legal principle, which may in the end only complicate and confuse the law. The 'Grand style' answer is based on the capacity to recognize the policy issues facing the courts in the disputes before them, and to reach decisions through a sound appreciation of the place within the common law of common sense, justice and a responsible creative role.

Equity and the common law

So far in this chapter, we have considered two sources of English law – parliamentary legislation and the common law. The latter is so called because of the gradual change, during the Middle Ages, from separate systems of local customary law in various regions to a uniform legal code *common* to the entire country. As we have seen, common law is case-law: that is to say, it is the body of legal rules and principles contained in the decisions of the judges (particularly those at the higher levels of the court hierarchy) in cases coming before them.

Under the old common law of five centuries ago, however, there were various problems for the litigant. A plaintiff had to ensure that the case was presented by means of the correct *writ* (the plaintiff's statement of claim) and that all particulars entered on the writ were correct, otherwise the case might be lost because of procedural defects. Apart from this, however, there could be other, more substantial, problems. For instance, the common-law courts only provided the remedy of *damages*, which in some cases was an inappropriate remedy – a plaintiff might wish to have the defendant prevented from continuing some activity, or to force him or her to carry out an obligation, for example, but such remedies were not available as a general rule in the common-law courts. Furthermore, the common law did not recognize simple breaches of contract as actionable. Breaches of contractual agreement could result in a remedy for the aggrieved plaintiff only if the action could be framed as a writ for debt or detinue (an action brought against someone wrongfully detaining the goods of another): the common-law courts had no conception of actions for breach of contractual promise *per se*. Third, common law did not deal adequately with the problems which stimulated the development of the *trust*. A trust is one means whereby property can be held by one person on behalf of another. A father, for example, who wishes to leave his property upon his death to his infant child may provide that the property shall be left in the hands of *trustees* who hold and administer that property for the benefit of the child, who will come into possession of the property on reaching the appropriate age. At common law, if such an arrangement occurred, then the property was deemed to be a gift to the trustees, and no beneficial rights of the child could be enforced in law.

Gradually, it became the practice for litigants who could not obtain satisfaction at common law to petition the Lord Chancellor, an official close to the sovereign and originally an ecclesiastic, for a remedy which could not be obtained in the common-law courts; as James puts it, 'The Chancellor could remedy these defects; he was one of the chief royal officials, and being closely associated with the king, he was bound by neither the rules nor the procedure of the common-law courts; nor was he likely to be over-awed by any man.'[56] By the sixteenth century, the practice whereby the Lord Chancellor came to administer 'real' justice where the common law failed had become established. The Court of Chancery, where these petitions were heard, gradually formulated a set of rules and principles known as 'equity', which supplemented the common law and proceeded side by side with it. Equitable relief includes the remedies of *specific performance*, having the effect of compelling defendants to carry out or perform specified activities, and the *injunction*, having the effect of preventing defendants from carrying out specified activities. The device of the trust came to be enforced in equity, not simply because of common-law defects, but because the Court of Chancery was concerned with providing justice according to the merits of a given case: for this reason, equitable remedies were, and still remain, discretionary remedies in the hands of the courts. Today, as a result of the Judicature Acts 1873–5, the rules and maxims of equity are administered and applied in the same courts as the common law, although the distinctions between these bodies of law are still very much alive. In particular, the discretionary nature of equitable remedies continues to place the judges in positions where their subjective views as to the substantial justice of a particular claim will make a considerable difference to the outcome, although the building-up of case-law and the operation of the doctrine of precedent have resulted in a situation where today the jurisdiction of equity (originally an inherently flexible tool for providing remedies where the common law gave none) has become stultified by procedural complexity and technicalities. It may be argued that the concern of equity to provide *substantial* justice has, over the years, given way to a preoccupation with the dictates of *formal* justice, the rigours of which it was originally set up to alleviate.

Precedent and policy II: statutory interpretation

A large proportion of the work of the judiciary in deciding cases consists of making decisions as to the interpretation of statutory law – does a particular statute cover the case before the court? – and here again, questions of precedent and policy arise. The doctrine of precedent also applies to statutory interpretation. For example, once the words 'mechanically propelled vehicle' in the Vehicles (Excise) Act 1949 have been interpreted to include 'cars', then that interpretation stands for future cases where the status of a car is in issue for the purposes of that Act.

The operation of the system of statutory interpretation is to a great extent fashioned by factors similar to those influencing the common law, discussed above, although the materials from which the judges must make their interpretative decision may be such that the range of possible interpretations is more limited. There may be dozens of precedents having a bearing on a case at common law, but perhaps only one or two conflicting statutory provisions to be considered by the court in a given case. The courts define their role in interpreting statutory provisions as (i) applying the statute to the facts before them, and (ii) giving effect to the intentions of Parliament, as expressed in that statute. There are then two basic issues: what were the intentions of Parliament in passing a particular statute? And do the facts in the present case before the court fall within the ambit of the provisions of the statute in question?

The courts have consistently refused to enter the world of party politics when dealing with the first question. They have denied themselves access to the one document which might throw considerable light on the intentions of Parliament – the reports of debates in *Hansard*[57] – in order, among other reasons, to avoid political 'contamination'; and have instead worked on the assumption that those intentions are expressly stated in the statute before them. Unfortunately, as anyone who has studied a road traffic or social security statute will know, such an assumption is far from justified. Modern statutes are extraordinarily complicated documents, often because of poor draftsmanship, and their construction and terminology may raise all kinds of problems. The courts have evolved for themselves various techniques of interpretation, apart from the limited assistance provided by the Interpretation Act 1978, and these common-law techniques may be simply stated. First, the 'Literal Rule' requires that words in statutes should be given their ordinary literal meaning; second, the 'Golden Rule' is designed to ensure that, in interpreting words literally, no absurdity or inconsistency results; and third, the 'Mischief Rule' is the principle whereby the courts may ask themselves what the 'mischief' was that the statute seeks to remedy. There is more form than substance to these 'rules', however, 'partly due to vagueness, but also because in many cases where one principle appears to support one interpretation, there is another principle, often of equal status, which can be invoked in favour of an interpretation which would lead to a different result'.[58]

In the vast majority of cases reaching the courts, there will be no ambiguity over the applicability or otherwise of a statutory provision to the case in hand. Such situations fall into the category of what Hart has termed 'core' meanings and applications. It is the minority of cases, reaching appeal courts, where a statute is vague or open to alternative interpretations, which cause problems for the courts. In such cases, using Hart's phrase, the statute and the fact-situation will be in that grey, blurred, 'penumbral' area where clear meanings do not exist. For, as Hart says,

fact situations do not await us neatly labelled, creased, and folded, nor is their legal classification written on them to be simply read off by the judge. Instead, in applying legal rules, someone must take the responsibility of deciding that words do or do not cover the case in hand with all the practical problems involved in this decision.[59]

It is at this point that the question as to the intention of Parliament may well merge with the question of the applicability of rules to facts, and with that of judicial attitudes to public policy. To begin with, the meanings and applications of a statute may well differ according to the objectives behind that statute. To take a hypothetical example: consider the meaning and scope of the word 'dwelling'. Clearly, this would include houses and flats; but would it include caravans or tents? If the statute in question used the term in connection with, say, assessment of a property for the purposes of local authority rates, then arguably, a tent, being moveable and temporary accommodation, would fall outside the scope of the term.

But if the statute prohibited the erection of a 'dwelling' at the side of a road, then it could be held that the putting up of a tent and staying in it might well contravene the statute.

It is clear, then, that there is a complex relationship between the meanings given to words, and the purposes of a given statute under consideration by a court. Far from being merely 'an exercise in grammar, based on the strict distinction between the legislative and the interpretative function',[60] statutory interpretation must be recognized as involving just as much a creative function, in many instances, as does the interpretation of previous cases – and, as hinted above, judicial attitudes to public policy may enter into the deliberations of the court. For example, we might note the clash between judicial ideology and the objectives of Parliament in the case of *Marcroft Waggons Ltd* v. *Smith*[61] in 1951, a case concerning the Rent Acts where

Lord Denning stated quite baldly that before the Rent Acts had come into operation, he would have considered the occupation of the woman in question to be by way of tenancy. As, however, this would mean that she would become fully protected he was quite prepared to view her occupation as being by way of licence which resulted, in that case, in the loss of any protection at all. His view was that the courts could reinterpret the common law in the light of legislation, even although the legislation would itself be based on the earlier interpretation of the common law itself.[62]

But such clashes serve to emphasize the fact that in statutory interpretation, as in the development of the common law, much depends upon the outlook, vision and ideologies of those entrusted with the development and administration of the law. Furthermore, clashes occur between the judges themselves as to the 'correct' way to deal with lacunae or areas of ambiguity within statutory provisions. Some judges, once again including Lord Denning, have argued for a *creative* role for judges, taking on for themselves the task of ascertaining the purpose of an Act and, to paraphrase Lord Denning, 'ironing out the creases' which may appear.[63] Others, including Viscount Simonds, who explicitly condemned Lord Denning's approach in a case in 1952, argue against such a creative role, preferring to leave all aspects of the legislative function to Parliament: 'if a gap is disclosed, the remedy lies in an amending Act'.[64] As Friedman has pointed out, there is a distinction between the 'literal' and the 'liberal' approaches to be found among judges,[65] and it may be that the impact of the European Community and the European Court on English judges and their practices will eventually bring about substantial changes in the judicial attitude to such matters as precedent and statutory interpretation. For one of the characteristics of EC law is the use of *general* statements of principle, rather than precise and detailed language. As Lord Denning pointed out in *H. P. Bulmer Ltd* v. *J. Bollinger S. A.*[66] in 1974, the English courts, when faced with the task of interpreting European legislation, must depart from the traditional methods of interpreting UK statutes, and 'must follow the European pattern', and 'divine the spirit of the Treaty and gain inspiration from it. If they find a gap, they must fill it as best they can. They must do what the framers of the instrument would have done if they had thought about it.'[67]

Whether the UK Parliament could consider it wise to follow the European practice of phrasing legislation in wide and general terms, leaving the judges to fill in any gaps and to develop the detailed application of such legislation, is an interesting question. Ought judges to take on such a clear legislative function? Would this not run counter to the constitutional idea of parliamentary sovereignty? To what extent might judges interpret such provisions restrictively and thus frustrate the intentions of Parliament? And through what controls – legal or political – might such judicial activity be monitored or checked? Moreover, the present methods of interpretation and development of the law by the judges – both in the common law and through the interpretation of statutes – have not always led to consistent or clear statements of law, as we shall see when we examine specific areas of law. Before moving on to examine the important areas of tort, criminal law, contract and administrative law, however, it is now necessary to build on our coverage of English legal institutions and law-making processes by considering the impact of the European Community on English law.

8
The European dimension
of English law

In 1972, under the Conservative government led by Edward Heath, the European Communities Act was passed, which made provision for Britain's membership of the European Economic Community, and in January 1973 Britain became an EEC member state. This simple statement conceals however, the substantial degree of political opposition, both inside and outside Parliament, to Britain's joining the EEC. Indeed, in 1975, shortly after the Labour government came to power, the country was subjected, for the first time, to a referendum on whether Britain should remain within the EEC. The result of the referendum – by a two-thirds majority and in line with then government policy – was that membership should continue.

Lack of conviction as to the wisdom of Britain's membership of the European Community (as the EEC came to be known) continues to the present time, with all the major political parties being seriously split on virtually every aspect of Britain's European membership, whether it be the simple fact of membership itself, or any other issue which is under debate. Through the late 1980s, the Thatcher government attempted to resist developments within the EC which would have, in the view of the prime minister, diminished the national identity and autonomy of Britain to a degree which she found unacceptable; in the early 1990s, we might single out for comment the controversy as to whether membership of the EC's Exchange Rate Mechanism (which was intended to keep European currencies stable) would benefit Britain's economy or not; and the debates which occurred in all EC member states over the Treaty on European Union (the Maastricht Treaty) signed in 1991, which, if adopted, would mean an increase in the powers of the European Parliament, commit member states to economic and monetary union, create a single European currency, and lead to a common defence policy for Europe. While the Maastricht Treaty was being debated – and in particular during the week in September 1992 prior to France holding its national referendum on the Treaty – we witnessed the spectacular failure of the British pound on the international money market: the British government desperately tried to bolster confidence in sterling by raising interest rates twice in one day to 15 per cent, only to find that lack of confidence in the pound was unaffected. Hours later, the government announced that interest rates would not, in fact, be raised to that level, but that for the time being Britain's membership of the EC's Exchange Rate Mechanism would be suspended.

It is against this political and economic background that European Community Law must be considered because, while the overriding aim of EC policies and measures is the establishment of greater economic and political unity between member states, there is markedly little unity among British politicians about many of the policies and measures – very many of them implemented through law – which are adopted.

The Treaty of Rome (1957) established the European Economic Community, and this, together with the Single European Act 1986, made provision, *inter alia*, for the harmonization of the legal codes of member states to the extent required for the proper functioning of the common market. Britain's membership of the EC necessitated both the adoption by Britain of measures required to achieve this harmonization, and the acceptance of the means whereby EC law is implemented in each member state. The effect of the European Communities Act 1972 is that the legal provisions contained in the Treaties have become part of the law of the United Kingdom, and there is also provision for the output of the European legislative bodies to be incorporated into English law. There are various kinds of EC legislation in addition to the Treaties themselves, the most important of which are the Regulation and the Directive.

Principal Institutions of the European Community

Before we discuss in more detail the forms which EC law-making may take, and the implications for domestic law in Britain, it is important to appreciate the principal institutions of the European Community. It is by means of these institutions that the political representatives of member states are able routinely to register the positions taken and views adopted by the governments of EC countries.

The Council, created by Article 147 of the EEC Treaty, comprises one representative of the government of each member state. The Council is essentially a co-ordinating body with regard to general EC economic policies. It should not be thought that Britain's representative on the Council is always the same person: exactly which government minister represents Britain's interests will depend on the issue under discussion – if it is transport policy, for example, then the British Minister for Transport will represent this country. The Council is presided over by the representatives of member States, each taking a six-month stint, and rotating in a strict cycle. This Council is distinguishable from the *European Council*, which refers to the meetings of the heads of government of all the member states – in fact, what we would normally understand by the term 'summit meetings'. These rather more high-powered meetings date back only as far as 1974, when the heads of government first agreed to meet regularly three times a year. The European Council, according to Lasok and Bridge,

(i) provides a forum for free and informal exchange of views between the Heads of Government; (ii) it can range over matters of Treaty competence, of political co-operation and of common concern to the member states; and (iii) it can generate an impetus for the progressive development of the Community.[1]

The institution of the European Council was formalized under the Single European Act 1986, and by virtue of Article 2 of that Act, it is now required to meet at least twice a year. Such developments as this highlight an important aspect of the European Community: although originally intended as an essentially *economic* union, the EC has increasingly aspired to wider – and certainly more controversial – goals, including the move to closer political and social ties between states, a common currency, and the attempt to maintain a unified EC profile in international political affairs.

Although the Council can initiate EC legislation, it is common for such initiatives to originate with the *Commission*. This body comprises seventeen Commissioners who, though citizens of member states, are chosen for their known independence. It is not their function simply to represent the interests of their own country; and member states must respect their independence and not try to influence them. A member state must have one Commissioner, but may not have more than two, and at present the larger states – France, the UK, Germany, Spain and Italy – have two Commissioners (in practice one from the party in government and one from the opposition parties) while the remaining states have one.

The Commissioners' period of office is four years, though this period is renewable. Although individual Commissioners may well undertake special responsibilities within the Commission (rather like ministers of the government), responsibility for the acts of the Commission is collective, not individual. The Commission is divided into twenty sections known as *Directorates General*, each one headed by a Director General who is responsible to the relevant Commissioner for the work of that section. The Commission has considerable administrative support – it is backed up by some 14,000 staff, including a large body of interpreters, and in addition each Commissioner has a private staff.

The functions of the Commission, in essence, are to initiate and co-ordinate EC policy and to act as the executive body of the Community. In the process of initiating and formulating policies, the Commission engages in consultation with interested parties from across the whole Community, including industry, trade unions and the civil service equivalents of each member state: it is clear that such consultation should ensure that the positions taken on any given matter by member states' governments are brought to the Commission's attention. The Commission's role includes the specification of detailed practical aspects of policy, and the final policy statements of the Commission go to the Council for deliberation.

The executive powers of the Commission include both the making and the enforcement of rules of European Community law, these powers deriving either from the general terms of the Treaty, or in some instances through specific delegation by the Council to the Commission of law-making powers with regard to specific areas, such as the common agricultural policy. The Single European Act 1986 has strengthened this law-making role as delegate of the Council. As to general law-making powers, Article 189 of the EC Treaty provides that

In order to carry out their task the Council and the Commission shall, in accordance with the provisions of this Treaty, make regulations, issue directives, take decisions, make recommendations or deliver opinions.

We will examine this provision in more detail below. With regard to the enforcement of EC rules, the Commission has a major role in investigating alleged breaches of Treaty obligations, and notifying the defaulting member state of the breach. In practice, it is usually the case that the member state concerned takes steps to remedy the problem well before the completion of an investigation. The Commission's enforcement powers extend to individuals (such as companies) who are in breach of, for example, EC competition law, and it has powers to bring legal action against such individuals which may result in substantial fines.

In addition to these important functions, the Commission also prepares the preliminary draft budget which then goes to the Council and duly becomes the draft budget, which in turn is placed before the European Parliament. The latter, as we will see, has considerable powers to require amendments or modifications to the draft budget, and ultimately has the power to reject it: the draft budget was in fact rejected by the European Parliament in 1979 and 1984. Finally, the commission is also the body which acts as negotiator in the process of making treaties.

At this point it will be clear that a considerable amount of output from the Commission must be referred for further deliberation and/or action to the Council. Given the fluctuating composition of the latter body, and its relatively infrequent meetings, there was established a body sitting, so to speak, between the Council and the Commission: this is a Committee of Permanent Representatives of the member states, normally known as COREPER (an acronym derived from the French term for this committee). COREPER is a permanent, full-time committee whose function is to sift and filter proposals coming from the Commission to the Council. Through this filtering process, only issues involving major problems or controversies actually come before the Council: the unproblematic and uncontentious proposals are effectively dealt with by COREPER.

Originally known as the European Assembly, an unelected body with few powers and certainly never meant to be a law-making body, the *European Parliament* (so called since the Single European Act 1986) has undergone significant change and is now (since 1979) composed of members democratically elected by the electorate of each member state. Over the years, however, the role and powers of the European Parliament have been considerably extended, and this is still an ongoing process (it will be recalled that the Maastricht Treaty of 1991 included provisions for strengthening the Parliament).

There are 518 Members of the European Parliament (MEPs) elected from the member states and each serving for five years. Germany, France, the UK and Italy each elect 81, Spain 60, the Netherlands 25, Belgium, Portugal and Greece 24, Denmark 16, Ireland 15 and Luxembourg 6. MEPs are not mandated by their home governments, but rather operate on a personally independent basis. Not surprisingly for a political body, however, MEPs do make political alliances, though these are political groupings which reflect European, as opposed to domestic, political stances. The essential function of the European Parliament is to act as a consultative body: this was the original role of the Assembly, and, although now enjoying somewhat wider powers, it remains its principal *raison d'être*. On some issues, the European Parliament must be consulted as part of the EC's specific procedural requirements, and it has been known for legal rules made by the Council to be annulled on the grounds that the latter failed to consult the European Parliament on the matter.[2]

If the European Parliament, having duly considered and discussed a proposal, rejects it, or wishes to propose amendments, then the Council will normally reconsider its proposal in light of the reasons for the rejection or proposed amendments. Clearly, the Council may accept and implement the amendments, but should it not wish to do so, or if it considers that the proposal should take effect despite rejection by the European Parliament, then it may pass its original proposal, provided that it does so unanimously and (in the case of a rejection) within three months (Single European Act 1986).

One of the most important powers of the European Parliament is that of political control over the Commission. It discusses the reports of the Commission; it may question individual Commissioners, who must answer either orally or by a written response; and it has power, ultimately, to dismiss the entire Commission by a vote of censure. This power, though threatened on occasion, has never been used. The European Parliament has no direct powers of control over the Council, although it has been held by the European Court that the European Parliament may bring an action against either the Council or the Commission if either of these bodies fails to act in circumstances where it should have done so.[3]

The *European Court of Justice*,[4] comprising thirteen judges (one from each member state and the President) has as its main task the responsibility of 'ensuring that in the interpretation and application of this Treaty the law is observed' (Article 164). Steiner concisely summarizes the role and functions of the Court thus:

It is the supreme authority on all matters of Community law, and in this capacity may be required to decide matters of constitutional law, administrative law, social law and economic law in matters brought directly before it or on application from national courts. In its practices and procedures it draws on Continental models; in developing the substantive law it draws on principles and traditions from all the member States.[5]

The judges are assisted by six advocates-general, chosen for their personal and guaranteed independence, whose primary function is to prepare analyses of cases coming before the Court and make recommendations to the Court on matters arising from those cases. The Court differs from English courts of law in a number of respects, not least being the fact that the European Court is not bound by a doctrine of precedent (see chapter 7), and that the general outlook taken by the Court is far more creative and proactive in its interpretations of the general provisions of the Treaties than that of its English counterparts.

The Single European Act 1986 created a new court – the Court of First Instance – which is intended to relieve the European Court of some of its very heavy workload, and which presently deals with a limited number of disputes, including those arising between the EC and its staff. There is provision for appeal from the Court of First Instance to the European Court, and, because there are very many such appeals, the creation of the Court of First Instance has had little effect on the case load of the European Court.

Article 177 (1) provides that

The Court of Justice shall have jurisdiction to give preliminary rulings concerning:
(a) the interpretation of this Treaty;
(b) the validity and interpretation of acts of the institutions of the Community;
(c) the interpretation of the statutes of bodies established by an act of the council, where those statutes so provide.

Article 177 also provides that, where such a question arises in any case before a court or tribunal[6] within any member state, that court or tribunal may refer the question to the European Court for a ruling. This jurisdiction is essentially one of preliminary rulings on matters of interpretation of European law (*not* the domestic law of member states). The European Court hears and decides disputes concerning matters of EC law arising from Article 177 references from domestic courts, and so has an important function regarding matters of interpretation of the Articles of the Treaty.

Now, given that European law takes precedence over the domestic law of the member states, it can happen that a legal rule of the EC is in direct conflict with a rule of domestic law. What is the consequence of this for English law, and the constitutional doctrine of the supremacy of Parliament? Can we still, in Britain, speak of the constitutional 'sovereignty' of our own Parliament, given the relationships between our own law and legislation and those of the European Community?

It will be recalled that, according to the constitution, the Westminster Parliament is the 'supreme law-making body' of the United Kingdom. All this has meant, historically, is that the courts had no power to override, or declare invalid, a properly enacted statute or its contents. The implication of EC membership is that, to a large extent, the Westminster Parliament may no longer be said to be the supreme law-making body in the United Kingdom (at least in so far as its legislative provision on matters affecting EC issues is concerned), for the EC legislature has superiority.

The point is well illustrated by considering the *Factortame* case in 1989–90.[7] The European Court had in 1964 stated, in the context of a case originating in Italy,[8] that

The transfer by the States from their domestic legal system to the Community legal system of the rights and obligations arising under the Treaty carries with it a permanent limitation of their sovereign rights . . .

The facts of *Factortame* were that, in 1988, the Westminster Parliament had passed a statute – the Merchant Shipping Act 1988 – which provided for the registration of British fishing vessels whose catches of fish would, after registration, count as part of the British fish quotas allowed by the European Community. The Act laid down that only British-owned ships managed and controlled from the United

Kingdom could be registered as British fishing vessels; 95 fishing ships, previously registered as British under a previous statute, but managed and controlled from Spain, were held to be excluded from registration.

The owners of the ships challenged the validity of the 1988 Act, arguing that it was contrary to Community law, which, of course, applied in the United Kingdom. The English Divisional Court, hearing the claim, sought a preliminary ruling under Article 177 from the European Court on the point of Community law involved in the case. Because it was expected that the European Court would take about two years to give a ruling on the point, and the owner of the boats concerned would clearly suffer hardship if they could not fish during that time, the Divisional Court in the meantime granted the owners an interim remedy, ordering that the relevant provisions of the Merchant Shipping Act 1988, and Regulations made under it, should be 'disapplied' and that the responsible minister should not enforce the provision of this Act pending the ruling from the European Court.

On appeal, both the Court of Appeal and the House of Lords held that the Divisional Court had no power under English law to make such an interim order – constitutionally, the courts have no power to override the provisions of a duly enacted statute – but the House of Lords was unsure as to whether any principle of European law gave English courts such a power.

In a separate action, the European Commission had brought proceedings in the European Court against the United Kingdom over the Merchant Shipping Act 1988, alleging that the UK had failed to observe its EC Treaty obligations by imposing the nationality requirement for registration. The European Court responded to this allegation by ruling that the United Kingdom must suspend the nationality requirements contained in the 1988 Act; the UK government duly complied with this decision.

The pincers finally closed on the UK government in the eventual ruling by the European Court in 1990,[9] in which the Court briefly stated that

Community law must be interpreted as meaning that a national court which, in a case before it concerning Community law, considers that the sole obstacle which precludes it from granting interim relief is a rule of national law must set aside that rule.

The House of Lords, on receipt of this ruling, went on to confirm the grant of interim relief to Factortame. And in *Kirklees Borough Council* v. *Wickes Building Supplies* in 1991,[10] in which Kirklees Council sought to prevent Wickes from continuing to open its stores for normal trading on Sundays, alleging that this was contrary to British Sunday trading law, the Court of Appeal acknowledged the implications of the *Factortame* decision, and required the plaintiff council to enter into an undertaking for the payment of compensation to the defendant company in the event of the British Sunday trading laws being found to be in contravention of Community law.

Despite the implications of these decisions for the sovereignty of the Westminster Parliament, and indeed the English courts, it must be remembered that the decision to join the European Community was a political one. This means that, strictly speaking, if political or economic policy so required, the UK could leave the Community, which would have the effect of restoring full legislative supremacy to the Westminster Parliament. During the period of membership, then, it may be true that the constitutional law-making supremacy of our own Parliament has been eroded, but there is no international agreement or provision which could affect Britain's right to decide to cease that membership, and then to proceed with political and economic policies in complete legal independence of the European Community. Having said this, there is an argument to the effect that Britain is now so firmly enmeshed in the policies and laws of the Community that pulling out is not a realistic possibility.

European Community law and the principle of direct effect

As we have said, the EC Treaties themselves are part of English law, and as Lord Denning stated in *H. P. Bulmer Ltd* v. *J. Bollinger S.A.* (1974),[11] 'any rights or obligations created by the Treaty are to be given legal effect in England without more ado'. Any rights or obligations *enjoyed by or imposed on any individual by the Treaties, therefore, are actionable in the English Courts*, and this is essentially the meaning of the terms 'direct effect' and 'direct applicability', as interpreted by the European Court. It is not always clear, however, exactly which provisions in the Treaties are in fact capable of being of direct effect:

Some provisions are regarded as binding on, and enforceable by, States alone; others are too vague to form the basis of rights or obligations for individuals; others are too incomplete and require further measures of implementation before they can be fully effective in law. Whether a particular provision is directly effective is a matter of construction, depending on its language and purpose as well as the terms on which the Treaty has been incorporated into domestic law.[12]

Apart from the substantive content of the Treaties, however, Article 189 of the EEC Treaty provides, as noted above, that the Council and the Commission may make rules and recommendations, and deliver opinions. Article 189 further provides that:

A regulation shall have general application. It shall be binding in its entirety and directly applicable in all member States.
   A directive shall be binding, as to the result to be achieved, upon each member State to which it is addressed, but shall leave to the national authorities the choice of form and methods.
   A decision shall be binding in its entirety upon those to whom it is addressed.
   Recommendations and opinions shall have no binding force.

Regulations, like the Treaties, are of direct effect and are directly applicable. Upon enactment, they immediately and automatically become binding law in all member states. *Directives*, which may or may not be of direct effect (see below), must usually be specifically implemented by the governments of member states. For example, the Directive concerning liability for defective products was enacted into English law by means of the Consumer Protection Act 1987, discussed in chapter 9.

Regulations and Directives are the most important of these various measures, since, as can be seen, these may well affect the domestic law of each member state either by – in the case of a Regulation – raising actual or potential conflict between the EC rule and a pre-existing domestic law or by – in the case of Directives – requiring the member state to enact the contents of the EC rule in new domestic legislation or by some other method which will have the effect of rendering the Directive part of domestic law.

In the process of deciding the many cases brought before it, the European Court has filled in some of the detail – left open by the general terms of the Treaty – as to the implications of the terms 'direct effect' and 'direct applicability' regarding the provisions of the Treaty and EC Regulations. It has been held that where a provision is of direct effect, then individual citizens of member states may initiate legal action against the government of that state. This is known as 'vertical' direct effect: the Treaty obligation is imposed on the member state, and affects the relations between the state and its citizens. Thus in the important *Van Gend en Loos* case in 1962,[13] the Court was asked, by means of an Article 177 reference, about the enforceability by individuals of a Treaty provision (Article 12) which prohibited member states from 'introducing between themselves any new customs duties on imports or exports'. The European Court ruled that, since the Treaty conferred rights and duties on individuals, in the sense that its provisions might well affect the relations between individuals and their national governments, then those rights and duties were enforceable at the suit of the individuals affected as long as certain conditions were satisfied. These conditions were stated in *Van Gend en Loos* to be first, that the provision in question must be clear and unconditional, and second, that the implementation of the provision is not dependent upon any subsequent action having to be taken by the member state.

'Horizontal' direct effect is the term used to refer to situations where EC law affects *interpersonal* relations, and where one individual may initiate an action under EC law against another *individual*. Thus in *Defrenne* v. *Sabena*,[14] Ms Defrenne sought compensation from Sabena Airlines, her employer, in relation to the unequal pay which she had received compared with the company's male workers. This, she argued, infringed the obligations on the employer contained in Article 119 of the Treaty, which provides that member states must ensure and maintain 'the application of the principle that men and women should receive equal pay for equal work'.

The question for the European Court was whether this provision of the Treaty was enforceable as between individuals. In its ruling, the Court stated that 'the fact that certain provisions of the Treaty are formally addressed to the Member States does not prevent rights from being conferred at the same time on any individual who has an interest in the performance of the duties laid down' and that therefore Ms Defrenne had the capacity in law to enforce those rights as against the defendant, since the defendant company had obligations towards her in respect of sex equality law enacted by the Belgian government in compliance with Article 119.

As stated above, EC Regulations are always of direct effect (Article 189). What about the status of EC Directives?

Article 189 provides that Directives are binding as to their aims and objectives, but leaves it open to member states as to exactly *how* the content of a Directive is to be incorporated into domestic law. At first sight, therefore, it would seem that Directives cannot by their nature be of direct effect: the European Court has held, however, that it is possible for a Directive to have direct effect.

The question arose in *Van Duyn* v. *Home Office* in 1974.[15] Article 48 of the Treaty is concerned to guarantee the right of free movement of workers between member states, subject to limitations on the grounds of public policy, public security or public health. A Council Directive of 1964 provided that member states only had a limited power to invoke the 'public policy' proviso to prevent workers from another member state from entering the country, and this Directive stated that such decisions must be based 'exclusively on the personal conduct of the individual concerned'.

Miss Van Duyn, a Dutch national, wished to come to the United Kingdom in order to work for the Church of Scientology . In previous instances the British government had decided that Scientology was not to be particularly encouraged, with the result that known members of the Church of Scientology were normally refused admission into the country.[16] Miss Van Duyn was duly refused entry, the government seeking to justify the exclusion on the grounds of the public policy proviso. She then brought proceedings against the British government, in the English courts, and the question arose as to whether Article 48 and the Directive in question had direct effect. Miss Van Duyn argued that Article 48 had direct effect; that she was therefore entitled to rely on its provisions before the English courts; and that the British government was not justified in refusing her entry, because since the public policy proviso (as defined in the Directive) was confined to matters of 'personal conduct', the simple fact of membership of the Church of Scientology had nothing to do with 'personal conduct'.

Ruling on the direct applicability of these provisions, the European Court held first, that Article 48 was of direct effect; and second, that the Directive in question was also directly effective. The Court stated that

If . . . regulations are directly applicable and, consequently, may by their very nature have direct effects, it does not follow from this that other categories of acts mentioned in [Article 189] can never have similar effects . . . In particular, where the Community authorities have, by directive, imposed on member States the obligation to pursue a particular course of conduct, the useful effect of such an act would be weakened if individuals were prevented from relying on it before their national courts and if the latter were prevented from taking it into consideration as an element of Community law . . .

On the particular facts of the present case, the European Court acknowledged that what counted as being justifiable 'grounds of public policy' would vary between member states, but made it clear that the conduct of the individual concerned need not actually be illegal within a given country in order to fall foul of the public policy proviso: it is enough if the conduct in question is generally regarded by the member state as socially harmful. Since *Van Duyn*, however, it has been held that the principle of *commonality between member states* of grounds of public policy should be developed.[17]

Since the *Van Duyn* decision, conflicting views have emerged as to whether Directives can be of direct effect. On the one hand, it is arguable that, since Article 189 makes a clear distinction between Regulations and Directives, leaving the latter up to member states to implement through domestic legal measures, only Regulations were intended to have direct effect. On the other hand, the obligations imposed by Directive are binding on member states and, as the European Court pointed out in *Van Duyn*, such a binding effect would be considerably weakened if individuals affected by a Directive could not pursue proceedings against member states which did not fulfil their obligations. And what of instances where Community obligations fell not on public bodies such as government departments, but upon private employers, such as obligations concerning equal pay? Can a Directive have direct effect on private organizations (that is, horizontal direct effect) as well as on governments?

Through a number of cases before the European Court during the 1980s – *Becker*,[18] *Marshall*,[19] *Van Colson*[20] and others – these issues were debated and various alternatives discussed. In *Marshall* v. *Southampton and South West Hampshire Area Health Authority*, the applicant had been dismissed by her employer, the Area Health Authority, when she was 62 years old. She argued that, since the retiring age for men was 65, this was sex discrimination contrary to Directive 76/207, which required equality of treatment between the sexes, but which had not been implemented in Britain even though the deadline for implementation had been passed. The question was whether Mrs Marshall could bring proceedings before an English court, based on the relevant Directive.

The European Court held that the different retirement age was indeed in breach of the Directive, but that because Article 189 specified that Directives were addressed to member states and not to individual employers, it followed that individuals could not base proceedings against the employer on the Directive in question.

The result, prior to 1990, was that where a Directive was held to have direct effect, an affected individual might bring proceedings against a member state (that is, there might be vertical direct effect) but not against another private individual or organization (that is, no horizontal direct effect). In 1990, however, the case of *Francovitch* v. *Italian Republic*[21] was heard by the European Court. Here, a number of employees of two Italian private companies brought proceedings against the Italian government. Some were owed wages by their employers when the company was declared insolvent, and Mr Francovitch was owed part of his salary by his employer. All the applicants had failed to obtain what was due to them, and they brought these proceedings against the government on the basis that the Italian government had failed to implement Directive 80/987, which stated that member states were required to take the necessary measures to ensure that workers received pay arrears if their employers became insolvent.

The European Court had already ruled that Italy was in breach of its Treaty obligations for having failed to implement this Directive, and now the group of workers sued the Italian government for *compensation*. The European Court held that member states were indeed liable to compensate individuals who suffered damage as a result of a failure to implement a Directive where three conditions were met. First, the Directive in question must confer rights on individuals; second, the content of those rights must be determinable by reference to the provisions of the Directive; and third, the damage suffered by the individuals concerned must be *caused* by the state's failure to implement a Directive, or even, it has been suggested, by an incorrect or inadequate implementation.

The effect of the *Francovitch* decision is somewhat to reduce the significance of the debate as to the direct effectiveness of Directives. The ruling places the responsibility for damage suffered on the state, and not on the private-sector employer. The type of issue which lay at the heart of cases such as *Marshall* above, it would seem, is no longer of great relevance: as has been suggested with reference to the facts of *Marshall*,

Francovitch . . . cuts right through the continuing debate on this issue by having the effect that private sector employees who were subjected to discriminatory retirement age between August 1978 (when the UK Government was required to correctly implement Equal Treatment Directive 76/207) and 7 February 1987 (when the prohibition on discriminatory retirement ages in the Sex Discrimination Act 1986 came into force) can sue the UK Government for compensation for the loss they suffered (by losing their jobs) as a result of the UK's failure to implement the Directive correctly.[22]

It remains to be seen what the further implications of *Francovitch* will be.

Finally in this section, the two other types of act – Decisions and Recommendations – may briefly be explained. Decisions, which may be addressed to member States or to individuals, are generally not directly applicable, although the European Court has held that, if the conditions for direct effect are satisfied, then a particular decision may be of direct effect. As Steiner points out, however, this matter

does not pose the same theoretical problems as Directives, since [Decisions] will only be invoked against the addressee of the Decision. If the obligation has been addressed to him and is 'binding in its entirety', there seems no reason why it should not be invoked against him.[23]

Recommendations are not binding and cannot be relied upon as the basis of proceedings before any courts.

European Community law: an overview

It is not possible in one chapter to examine in any detail the considerable body of substantive law of the European Community, contained in the various Treaties, Regulations and Directives, and all the domestic legislation through which Directives are implemented: for this, the reader should consult the specialist texts.[24] However, some idea of the nature and scope of EC policy can be gained by a brief overview of the main areas.

Originally, the European Economic Community, as it was first called, was solely concerned with economic, commercial and business matters, creating legislation designed to unify and remove barriers between the economic practices of the various member states, and business organizations operating within them. Article 8A of the EEC Treaty defined the internal European market as 'an area without internal frontiers in which the free movement of goods, persons, services and capital is ensured'. The principal means of achieving this aim is by means of the adoption of common systems of, for example, customs tariffs, across all member states, and of prohibitory legal rules designed to prevent inequality and discrimination. The *free movement of goods* is sought by means of removing barriers in the form of individual national customs duties on goods exported and imported, and no member state may discriminate against the goods or products of any other member state by means of the imposition of taxes on those goods in excess of any taxation imposed on any similar domestic version of the product.

It is provided in Article 36, however, that the provisions referred to above shall not preclude

prohibitions or restrictions on imports, exports or goods in transit justified on grounds of public morality, public policy or public security; the protection of health and life of humans, animals or plants; the protection of national treasures possessing artistic, historic or archaeological value; or the protection of industrial and commercial property. Such prohibitions or restrictions shall not, however, constitute a means of arbitrary discrimination or a disguised restriction on trade between member States.

Taking just one of these grounds as an example: in the case of *Conegate Ltd* v. *Customs and Excise Commissioners* in 1985[25] the ground of 'public morality' was considered. The facts were that the British customs seized a number of inflatable rubber dolls, described as 'love dolls', as well as other articles imported from Germany of the type which are sold in Britain in sex-shops. HM Customs was of the view that these articles were indecent and obscene, and that their importation was therefore illegal. The importers challenged this seizure, arguing that it was in breach of Article 30, which deals with measures which totally or partially restrain imports, exports or goods in transit. Additionally, the importers argued that such goods are not banned in the UK, and that therefore the seizure was discriminatory.

The public morality ground was, of course, considered in the arguments before the European Court. It had already been decided in a case in 1979[26] that the public morality ground in Article 36 could justify a ban on importing pornography: such a ban was not disguised protectionism for the UK's own market, since there was no lawful market in pornography in the UK. Could the same be said of the goods in the *Conegate* case?

The European Court held that there was nothing unlawful in the UK about making and marketing goods such as those seized, and the British government had done little to prevent such goods being sold. That being so, the applicants' argument succeeded, and the Court held that the seizure of the goods was not justified under Article 36. The various grounds stated in Article 36 have been held to justify, among other things, the import and export of gold collectors' coins (public policy), the imposition of restrictive requirements on importers of petroleum oils (public security), and the inspection on health grounds of imported apples as part of pest control procedures (health and life of humans).

The *free movement of persons* is the subject of Articles 48–50, providing for individual workers' right to enter, reside and work in any member state, subject to restrictions imposed by those states on the grounds of public policy, public security or public health (see the *Van Duyn* case, discussed above). 'Worker' is not defined in the EC provisions, but the term certainly excludes self-employed and professional persons, for whom provision is made through the provisions in Articles 52–8 on *freedom of establishment*; in order that professionally qualified people (such as lawyers and accountants) should be able to enjoy the same freedom as any other workers, it is necessary that the professional qualifications recognized in each member state carry equal validity and recognition in other states. This process is still taking place.

Articles 59–66 are concerned with *freedom to provide services*, and here again, the realization of a Community-wide freedom depends on the harmonization of national domestic laws in various respects. In Britain, statutes dealing with company law and financial services have been implemented partly to bring Britain's legal regulatory framework in these areas into line with those elsewhere in the Community. Finally, the *free movement of capital* is provided for by Articles 67–83 and 104–9.

In line with the free movement of people, Article 51 seeks to ensure that the social security systems of member states are co-ordinated in order to provide protection for workers from other member states.

As will quickly be appreciated, the establishment of a common market required that Community-wide competition policy be put into place (see chapter 3). Article 3 of the Treaty states that there must be 'the institution of a system ensuring that competition in the common market is not distorted', and the main general provisions setting out EC competition law are Articles 85 and 86.

Article 85 provides that

All agreements between undertakings, decisions by associations of undertakings and concerted practices which may affect trade between member States and which have as their object or effect the prevention, restriction or distortion of competition within the common market

are prohibited. Any such agreement is 'automatically void', although there is provision for certain agreements to be exempt. These are, in general terms, agreements which contribute to improving the production or distribution of goods or promoting technical or economic progress, while allowing consumers a fair share of the resulting benefit (Article 85(3)). 'Undertakings' include any persons or organizations, whether operating as sole traders, corporations (including local authorities) or partnerships (see chapter 3). There need be no formal agreement: the European Court held in a case in 1970 that a 'gentleman's agreement' can be sufficient. 'Concerted practices' means some co-ordinated co-operation between undertakings, the co-ordination being achieved through direct or indirect contact. Note that an agreement between two linked organizations, such as a parent company and its subsidiary, will not fall foul of Article 85. It must be shown that the action taken noticeably restricts competition within the Community: Article 85 does not prevent *all* agreements between businesses, but only those which affect competition to some significant degree (the *de minimis* principle).

Agreements which are caught by Article 85 would include agreements to fix prices or orchestrate price increases (for example, *Re Aniline Dyes Cartel*[27] and the consequent *Imperial Chemical Industries Ltd* v. *Commission*[28]), or to divide up the market artificially between organizations party to the agreement.

Article 86 concerns abuse of a dominant position, and deals with monopoly and near-monopoly trading. Specifically, it states that

any abuse by one or more undertakings of a dominant position within the common market or in a substantial part of it shall be prohibited as incompatible with the common market in so far as it may affect trade between member States.

It will be noted that this Article does not prohibit monopolies in themselves, but rather aims at 'dominant' undertakings involved in anti-competitive conduct. The rule will apply to more than one undertaking in the same market group which, when combined, create a dominant position (the 'enterprise entity' principle). The operation and effect of Article 86 can best be appreciated by means of a case-example.

It is an important part of the Commission's function to investigate suspected breaches of Community law, and to bring proceedings against suspected violators. United Brands Co., a world-wide concern trading in the cultivation, distribution and sale of bananas, had been found by the Commission to have abused its dominant position in the banana market within Europe. In *United Brands Co.* v. *Commission* in 1976,[29] the company sought to have that decision annulled.

The first task for the Court was to establish what the relevant market was. The approach to this is by means of the concept of 'product substitution', which refers to the extent to which consumers can buy, and producers supply, products similar to, or acceptable as substitutes for the product in question, (in this case, bananas). Having established this, the second question was whether United Brands Co. dominated the relevant market; the third, if so, whether the company had abused that dominant position in breach of Article 86. In confronting these questions, the Court had to investigate various aspects of the banana market within the European Community. As to the definition of the relevant market, could there be said to be a 'banana market' (as the Commission contended), or was the relevant market in fact better defined as a 'fresh fruit' market (as the company argued) in which bananas were sold alongside other fruit such as apples, oranges, peaches, strawberries and so on? If the court adopted the latter solution, then clearly the company's position in such a wider market would be substantially diminished. In the event, the Court decided in favour of the Commission's position: that there was indeed an identifiable 'banana market' quite distinct from the more general 'fresh fruit market'. The following extracts from the Court's decision indicate the reasoning which led to this conclusion:

The applicant submits . . . that bananas compete with other fresh fruit in the same shops, on the same shelves, at prices which can be compared, satisfying the same needs: consumption as a dessert or between meals . . .

The Commission maintains that there is a demand for bananas which is distinct from the demand for other fresh fruit especially as the banana is a very important part of the diet of certain sections of the community.

The specific qualities of the banana influence customer preference and induce him not to readily accept other fruits as a substitute.

For the banana to be regarded as forming a market which is sufficiently differentiated from other fruit markets it must be possible for it to be singled out by such special features distinguishing it from other fruits that it is only to a limited extent interchangeable with them and is only exposed to their competition in a way that is hardly perceptible.

The ripening of bananas takes place the whole year round . . .

Throughout the year production exceeds demand and can satisfy it at any time.

Owing to this particular feature the banana is a privileged fruit and its production and marketing can be adapted to the seasoning fluctuations of other fresh fruit which are known and can be computed.

There is no unavoidable seasonal substitution since the consumer can obtain this fruit all the year round.

The Court considered further economic aspects of the production of and trade in bananas and concluded,

The banana has certain characteristics, appearance, taste, softness, seedlessness, easy handling, a constant level of production which enable it to satisfy the constant needs of an important section of the population consisting of the very young, the old and the sick . . .

It follows from all these considerations that a very large number of consumers having a constant need for bananas are not noticeably or even appreciably enticed away from the consumption of this product by the arrival of other fresh fruit on the market . . .

Consequently the banana market is a market which is sufficiently distinct from the other fresh fruit markets.

The next question for the Court is whether United Brands Co. had a dominant position in the banana market. Noting that there was considerable variation between member states as to import, distribution and sales arrangements, the Court none the less held that six member states which the Commission had defined as the relevant market[30] 'form an area which is sufficiently homogeneous to be considered in its entirety'. The term 'dominant position' was defined by the Court as

a position of economic strength enjoyed by an undertaking which enables it to prevent effective competition being maintained on the relevant market by giving it the power to behave to an appreciable extent independently of its competitors, customers and ultimately of its consumers.

The Court considered the various features of the company's structure and systems of production, quality control (the company had perfected new banana-ripening methods in which it instructed the distributors/ripeners of the particular type of banana involved), transportation (the company was the only company of its kind capable of carrying two-thirds of its exports by means of its own fleet of ships), advertising, and so on; after taking into account the company's competitors and noting that 'an undertaking does not have to have eliminated all opportunity for competition in order to be in a dominant position', the Court observed that the company's market share was between 40 and 45 per cent (several times greater than its nearest rival) and concluded that, taking all these factors and more into account, 'The cumulative effect of all the advantages enjoyed by UBC thus ensures that it has a dominant position on the relevant market.'

Finally, the Court then had to consider the question as to whether United Brands Co. had abused its position. The Commission had found that the company had forbidden its distributors from reselling bananas while still green: this the Commission found to be an abuse, because it effectively stopped inter-state trade in green bananas. Further, the company routinely supplied fewer bananas than the market demanded, preventing distributors from penetrating new markets: this amounted to controlling the structure of the market. The company had also stopped supplying a Danish distributor, after finding that the distributor had promoted a rival brand of banana. And finally the Commission had argued that the company's selling prices, which differed according to the customer's member state and which were imposed at the port of entry, were unacceptable. Because these prices were fixed at the point of entry, the discrepancies could not be due to transportation costs.

The Court had little difficulty in holding that the company's prohibition on the resale of green bananas was an infringement of Article 86, as was the refusal to supply the Danish distributor. Of the latter, the Court had this to say:

Although it is true, as the applicant points out, that the fact that an undertaking is in a dominant position cannot disentitle it from protecting its own commercial interests if they are attacked, and that such an undertaking must be conceded the right to take such reasonable steps as it deems appropriate to protect its said interests, such behaviour cannot be countenanced if its actual purpose is to strengthen this dominant position and abuse it.

Even if the possibility of a counter-attack is acceptable that attack must still be proportionate to the threat taking into account the economic strength of the undertakings confronting each other . . .

Such a course of conduct amounts therefore to a serious interference with the independence of small and medium-sized firms in their commercial relations with the undertaking in a dominant position . . .

As to the fixing of differential prices at ports of entry, the Court held that this practice enabled the company 'to apply dissimilar conditions to equivalent transactions with other trading parties, thereby placing them at a competitive disadvantage', and that this was, once again, an abuse of its dominant position.

The *United Brands* case illustrates, among other things, the complexity of most cases brought before the European Court: it is not surprising that such cases take a considerable time to reach their conclusion.

In this chapter we have been able only to touch on the main provisions of European Community law, but it can be readily appreciated from our brief examination how far these various provisions affect the domestic legal system of the UK. In many respects, the original *economic* objectives of European union have long spread further into the realms of *other political* and *social* contexts. The controversial Treaty on European Union of 1991 (the Maastricht Treaty) included among its many objectives the establishment of a common currency, full economic and monetary union, a common defence policy, and a 'social chapter' concerning improved working conditions and relations between employers and employees. Britain, though a signatory to the Treaty, refused to accept the 'social chapter', and consequently is the only member state to which this part of the Treaty does not apply.

It seemed inevitable after the Danish people in their referendum had rejected the Maastricht Treaty, and the French had voted in its favour only by the narrowest of majorities, that the Treaty could not survive in its original form. In Britain, the government remains fiercely determined to avoid a federal Europe, with (in effect) a single government, economic policy and currency. Although it seems unlikely that the progress made so far towards European unity can be reversed, and likely that the future of the European Community will involve the continued pursuit of commonality of goals – economic, social and political – between member states, the political divisions between and within member states and their governments make the extent and speed of these developments extremely difficult, if not impossible, to predict. The British view is that the Community should not be a 'select club', but a Community embracing a wider Europe – possibly including east European countries – but falling well short of federalism.

9
Liability in English law: the law of tort

One of the most basic functions of law in any society is to specify the situations in which a person may be legally liable, that is, answerable to the law, for his or her acts or omissions. In English law, the major areas containing the fundamental principles of liability are crime, tort and contract, all of which, together with the important area of *public-law* regulation, have been briefly introduced in earlier chapters. In this chapter and the three following, the question to be discussed may be stated as follows: in what circumstances will the infringement of a legal obligation involve the imposition of legal liability, and hence some form of legal sanction, upon the violator?

The law of tort, or *civil wrongs*, incorporates as a basic general condition of liability, the proposition that a defendant is only liable if that person is in some way 'at fault'. As we saw in chapter 2, the proposition 'no liability without fault' is a general characteristic of English law: how, then, is this idea built into the law of tort?

Tort and capitalism

The high-water mark of the principle of 'no liability without fault' in English law was undoubtedly the nineteenth century. We have repeatedly noted how, in the twentieth century, the state has intervened to regulate more and more areas of social and economic life, but the nineteenth century – the period of economic individualism and *laisser-faire* – saw minimal state interference with the business and commercial life of the community. The best example of *laisser-faire* as reflected in the law is probably the law of contract, discussed fully in chapter 11. Contract law, as developed by the judges during the period, rested on the assumption that private individuals were best left to regulate and look after their own affairs and interests, the law only intervening where there had been some breach of legal obligation by a person who had voluntarily undertaken that obligation through a freely negotiated contract.[1]

With regard to the development of conditions of liability in tort, Fleming has pointed out that the nineteenth century saw an increase not only in traffic accidents, but also, and at the time perhaps more importantly, in accidents at work.

Both posed serious problems for the law of torts whose main preoccupation had hitherto been occasional assaults, defamation, boundary disputes, noxious neighbours, trespassing cattle and the like. Because Parliament was otherwise preoccupied, it fell to the courts to deal with the challenges of the new industrial society. By and large, their response was to try and contain the flood by raising the barriers to recovery.[2]

As far as industrial accidents were concerned, the area of tort which was usually invoked in the attempt to gain compensation was *negligence*, and in dealing with such claims, the courts worked on the same assumptions that underpinned the development of the law of contract: individuals entered into employment contracts voluntarily and freely, and therefore must be taken, in some cases, to have voluntarily taken on the risk of injury. Having done so, they were to be debarred from complaining about it later by the courts' application of the maxim *volenti non fit injuria*.[3] In other cases, the victims' own carelessness (or *contributory* negligence), which frequently contributed to their accidents, was held to prevent their recovering compensation;[4] while the development of the doctrine of *common employment*, whereby an employer could not be held liable to an employee for the wrongful acts of a fellow employee, effectively prevented many victims of industrial accidents from gaining compensation.[5] These responses, which rendered the law of tort rather less effective than it might have been in the provision of compensation for personal injury, were not merely the outcome of legalistic assumptions about the contract of employment; an equally important reason for these judicial responses was grounded in economic considerations. If these actions for compensation were to be allowed to succeed, who was to bear the cost, and on what principles?

It was felt to be in the better interest of an advancing economy to subordinate the security of individuals, who happened to become casualties of the new machine age, rather than fetter enterprise by loading it with cost of 'inevitable' accidents. Liability for faultless causation was feared to impede progress because it gave the individual no opportunity for avoiding liability by being careful and this confronted him with the unpalatable choice of either giving up his projected activity or shouldering the cost of any resulting injury.[6]

The law of tort as a means of allocating responsibility for harmful activity has attracted much attention from economists, who have produced analyses of tort law seeking to assess the efficiency of the law from the point of view of economic theory.[7] The 'economic approach to law' proceeds from the basic economic theory of supply and demand: in a perfectly competitive market within a capitalist system, if demand for a particular commodity exceeds supply, then the price of that commodity will rise, and if supply exceeds demand, the price will fall, until the point is reached where supply and demand are in equilibrium and customers obtain the goods they want at a price they are prepared to pay. Naturally, this model assumes that the price of the commodity reflects the cost of producing that commodity, and takes into account the cost of raw materials, resources used in production and so on. If the price does not reflect such factors then the price will be too low, and this means that there has been an inefficient use of resources.

Suppose, however, that X, the manufacturer of a particular commodity, produces a certain amount of pollution in the process of manufacture, and this pollution has a harmful effect on Y, who occupies land adjoining X's factory. In the absence of any legal rules regarding liability for the pollution, how would X and Y deal with the situation? According to Coase,[8] in a perfectly competitive market situation, the harm caused to Y would lead Y to negotiate with X for a reduction in the level of pollution. From X's point of view, the installation of equipment to prevent pollution would incur a cost, which in turn would have to be incorporated into the price of the product, which might lead to a fall in sales, and hence to a decrease in profit. Similarly, if X were to offer to compensate Y for the harm, then that compensation, too, would have to be taken into account in the price of the product, with identical results. But suppose Y were to pay X in exchange for a reduction in pollution by X? Here, if Y's payment exceeded the cost to X of reducing the level of pollution, then X would accept that payment and reduce the pollution, because X's profits would not be affected. X and Y would bargain along these lines until an agreement was reached whereby Y's payment to X corresponded with the cost to X of reducing – the point of equilibrium, and the point at which X would be said to be operating with the 'socially efficient' level of pollution (that is, an allocation of resources which is efficient from the point of view of all concerned).

Continuing Coase's analysis: suppose now that the law becomes involved, and requires X to compensate Y for the harm caused by the pollution. X must now consider the cost of compensating Y, as compared to the profit made by means of the pollution-causing production process. Coase argued that when *all* the profit had to be paid to Y as compensation, X would cease to increase the level of pollution and, once again, the 'socially efficient' level of harm would be produced. It should be noted that 'socially efficient' does *not* imply the complete cessation of pollution: that would be inefficient from X's point of view. From the 'Coase theorem', a number of conclusions follow. First, the analysis suggests that the intervention of law and the allocation of legal duties and rights to compensation would not affect the final outcome, because the parties would continue to bargain around the legal provisions until the 'social efficiency' level was reached. Second, the theorem assumes that the parties negotiate within a perfectly competitive market situation. This assumes in turn that there are no costs to the parties incurred within the process of negotiation itself ('transaction costs'). In practice there will be a number of costs attaching to the transaction, such as the cost of obtaining information, and perhaps the retention of lawyers to conduct the negotiations and so on. It is true to say that this analysis draws particular attention to the factor of transaction costs and acknowledges that the law may have a role to perform in regulating the allocation of such costs, but it is not clear which criteria might be used in the process of allocation.

Third, the analysis fails to take into account any values other than economic ones. For example, it might be the case that as a matter of general social policy it is preferable for the law to strive to eradicate all industrial pollution in the interests of the environment, rather than to permit a level of pollution which is decided by means of an economic efficiency criterion. Fourth, it often happens that those at risk from harm caused by others are in no position to bargain, either because they lack sufficient bargaining-power or because (as in the case of most road accidents) their relationship is not a permanent one, but is casual, fortuitous and fleeting. The 'Coase theorem' may be thought to underplay the role of the law in favour of 'market regulation' mechanisms, but surely the law in this area has a part to play in the allocation of liability: that is, in the allocation of resources to be used to compensate for or prevent harmful activities? Many would argue, for instance, that the law of tort fulfils, to some extent at any rate, a *deterrent* function: by imposing liability on those who might cause harm, such persons are encouraged to take steps to prevent that harm and so avoid liability.

Calabresi[9] has pursued this approach in the field of law relating to accidents, arguing that the 'principal function of accident law is to reduce the sum of the cost of accidents and the cost of avoiding accidents'.[10] The law of negligence, he argues, does this by imposing liability on the 'cheapest cost avoider'.[11] This view amounts to the proposition that the law here constitutes a deterrent to potential accident-causers by imposing liability on those who are in the best position to avoid the accidents. Thus,

If we can determine the costs of accidents and allocate them to the activities which cause them, the prices of activities will reflect their accident costs, and people in deciding whether or not to engage in particular activities will be influenced by the accident costs each activity involves. They will be influenced without having to think about it, for the accident costs will simply be a part of the price which will affect whether they buy one product or engage in one activity rather than another . . . if manufacturers of cars without seat belts were charged the accident costs which resulted from the absence of belts, no federal law would be needed requiring seat belts. A beltless car would save the cost of the belt, but bear the accident costs which resulted; a car with a belt would save on accident costs but bear the cost of putting in a belt. The decision as to whether belts were worth it would be made by buyers in the light of the price of each kind of car. The question whether safety sells would be given a market answer rather than the purely conjectural one to which we have become accustomed.[12]

For such a theory to work, as Atiyah has pointed out,[13] we must be able to identify the activities which cause the accidents, and the extent to which these activities are responsive to the price mechanisms. Atiyah argues that there are many forms of harm (such as diseases) which cannot be traced to particular activities; and some forms of harm which, though attributable to particular activities, are not reducible by means of general deterrence because the activity in question is not susceptible to price mechanisms. To use his example: smoking is known to be a cause of lung cancer, but continuous price increases on cigarettes through taxes do not appear to affect sales very much.

Furthermore, it may be very difficult, at the outset, to place costs on particular activities or the harm they create: in many cases, placing a price upon an activity or a harmful effect is highly artificial. And again, exactly who is to bear these costs? Taking Atiyah's example of road accidents:

. . . why should we treat motoring as an activity, rather than break it down into various sub-categories, such as driving for pleasure, driving to the pub, driving to work . . . and so forth. Secondly, many road accidents involve non-motorists, such as pedestrians, or cyclists. What, if anything, enables us to say that these accidents should be treated as part of the activity of motoring rather than walking or cycling? . . . In terms of 'cause' . . . vehicle manufacturers and designers and road makers are just as responsible as motorists for most road accidents. There is a good deal of evidence to suggest that the number and costs of road accidents could be reduced more effectively by concentrating on road improvements and on vehicle design, than by worrying about the motorist. How then can general deterrence work, unless we have some idea how to allocate the cost of road accidents between these various activities and causes?[14]

So far, theories such as those of Calabresi have received much critical appraisal, though little, at least in the United Kingdom, in the way of practical application. It may well be that the tort system does, in fact, incorporate within its framework and functions the objectives of general deterrence, at least in so far as is compatible with the principles of fault liability; but the law has not yet gone so far as to impose any generalized duties or liabilities upon enterprises which can often be shown, at least in part, to have contributed to accident causation. Some of the reasons for this, perhaps, can be found in the analysis of the relationship between tort law and capitalism presented by Abel.

Abel argues that there is a particular relationship between tort law and capitalism.[15] Though basing his discussion on American tort law, he suggests that his critique is equally applicable to other capitalist societies. His thesis is that, 'because capitalists have to maximize profit in a competitive market, they *must* sacrifice the health and safety of others – workers, consumers, those affected by environmental danger'.[16] Thus capitalism encourages injury, and tort law reflects this in various ways.

One effect of capitalism, argues Abel, is to reduce interpersonal relationships to those based on capitalist economics (the employment contract, whereby workers sell their labour for wages; the lawyer/client relationship, whereby the lawyer's services are bought and sold; and private health care systems – the norm in America, and increasingly encouraged in Britain despite the well-established national health service – whereby medical services, too, are subject to market forces operating on a privatized system). In addition, mass production and consumer consumption of goods thus produced creates an environment in which money and property are seen as the commodities having the highest value: 'hence money damages come to be seen as adequate compensation'.[17] Finally, says Abel, the logic of the use of money damages for injury is extended to compensation for pain, suffering, emotional distress, wrongful death and loss of consortium. Thus 'tort law under capitalism equates money with labour, possessions, care, emotional and physical integrity, and ultimately love'.[18]

Abel's argument, deriving from marxism, is summarized thus:

The lawyer . . . combines his expertise with the victim's injury (as the capitalist combines his capital with the worker's labour) to create a tort (a commodity) that has exchange value both in the state-created market (the court) and in the dependent markets it spawns (negotiated settlement). The lawyer (like the capitalist) exercises total control over this process; the victim (like the worker) has virtually no say over which torts are produced or how they are produced. When the transaction is complete, the victim receives the bare minimum necessary for survival (or less) and the lawyer takes the rest as a fee (the capitalist expropriation of surplus value) . . .[19]

It may be that Abel overstates his case here. To begin with, the English experience does not seem to bear out the idea of victims accepting only 'the bare minimum'. Atiyah has noted that in recent years 'the size of the largest awards has become very great . . . Awards of between £200,000 and £300,000 in the most serious cases are now quite common,'[20] and although he acknowledges that such increases are no more than might be expected if awards are to stay in line with inflation, it remains true that those receiving compensation through the tort system gain much more than those receiving compensation or benefit through any other system. Second, is it accurate to speak of the lawyer having 'total' control over the tort process? There is a great deal of control, but the victim/client initiates the proceedings, and is the one who decides, albeit on the lawyer's advice, whether to accept or refuse any out-of-court settlement which the defendant may offer. Third, we might question the extent to which the tort system and the legal procedures involved therein are unique to capitalism. Arguably the relationship between lawyers and clients which, as we will argue later (see chapter 13), is one based largely on power, is likely to be found in any society having a developed legal system relying on the provision of expert advice and representation, whatever its economic system.

Abel goes on to identify and discuss three general features of tort law under capitalism. First, there is the question of discrimination on the grounds of class, race and gender. Those less well off may for various reasons be less inclined to consult lawyers in the event of an actionable injury than the well-to-do (see chapter 13); different social classes and sections within them differentially face the risk of injury in the workplace and the home, and in terms of the risks inherent in goods and services which may be of poor quality but are all that can be afforded. Industrial injuries are more likely to be channelled into industrial injury compensation schemes than the tort system, the benefits being rather less than might be the case after a successful tort action,[21] and those injured at home are unlikely to have any redress from the tort system unless the injury fell within a known head of liability, such as injury caused by defective goods. There is inequality, too, between road-users of different social classes:

Imagine a car crash between A, who is unemployed and drives a worthless jalopy, and B, who owns a Rolls-Royce and earns a high income. If A is negligent and B non-negligent, A will have to pay for the damage to the Rolls and to B's earning capacity. But if B is negligent and A non-negligent, B will have to pay virtually nothing . . . If we make the hypothetical more realistic by giving both parties liability insurance the inequality remains: A's insurance premium will have to reflect the possibility of injury to B, and be higher than would be necessary to protect A and others like him, whereas B's premium will reflect the possibility of an injury to A, and be lower than would be necessary to protect a world of Bs. A thus pays part of the cost of protecting the privileges of B.[22]

On examination, these assertions cannot stand without some qualification. The first part of the argument may be true; but if we consider the second proposition concerning insurance premiums payable by A and B, the reality is that there are far more As than Bs, and so the insurance premiums payable by both parties will reflect the statistical likelihood of damage to Rolls-Royce cars as compared with cars of far less value, thus tending to *depress*, not inflate, A's premium. And let us not forget that B's insurance premium too must reflect the possibility of damage by B to *another* Rolls-Royce, as well as 'worthless jalopies'! We all know that, in fact, A will pay far less in insurance premium than will B: the reality of the situation is thus far less unequal than may first appear, although it must be conceded that the relative wealth of A and B will be such as to reduce the impact of the cost to B as compared to A.

Turning to a second concern – that of the production by capitalism of illness and injury – Abel considers that the pursuit of profit, and the accompanying drive to minimize expenditure in ways which will *not* return profit, mean that 'the capitalist . . . *must* be as unsafe as he can get away with being'.[23] To the extent that business entrepreneurs may be held liable for injury which is caused by their negligence, the financial compensation payable to the victim will in most cases be no deterrent against further negligence by the entrepreneur, because the amount paid out is recoverable in most cases by passing on the liability costs to the consumer in the form of higher prices for the goods or services which that entrepreneur provides. And businesses will tend to weigh the cost of safety against the cost of legal liability. It may be cheaper to pay out compensation in the event of injury caused by a faulty product than to incur expenditure in withdrawing or modifying that product and making it safe. Thus – using Abel's illustrations – the Ford Motor Corporation in America manufactured a car with a petrol tank it knew to be unsafe, and American Airlines flew a DC-10 plane which later crashed, despite their knowledge of a faulty component. As Abel argues,

The capitalist response to the threat of tort liability is to strive to externalize accident costs by concealing information . . ., threatening retaliation against those who seek compensation, and using the enormous resources of the enterprise . . . to coerce victims into accepting inadequate settlements, to overwhelm them in litigation, and to pass legislation that immunizes the enterprise from liability costs . . .[24]

The latter device is not far removed, of course, from the common-law responses to industrial injury claims in nineteenth-century England: to prevent their success by means of the doctrine of common employment, and the principles of contributory negligence and voluntary assumption of risk.

The third aspect of tort law and capitalism which Abel discusses is that of the reproduction of bourgeois ideology. Centrally, the insistence within tort law upon proof of a defendant's fault reinforces the element within bourgeois ideology of *individualism*. In fact, says Abel, tort law sustains individualism at the expense of social and economic reality: the fact that wrongs are caused 'by the confluence of multiple, ongoing, collective entities'.[25] Furthermore, tort law, by compensating property-owners for property damage, upholds the capitalist conception of private property and its place as a central social value: 'tort law proclaims the class structure of a capitalist society: you are what you own, what you earn, and what you do'.[26] And tort law, by providing money damages for non-pecuniary losses (such as pain and suffering), also translates human experiences into commodities having a cash value.

One recurring theme throughout Abel's critique is the way in which tort law functions on the premise that money compensation is appropriate for the victims of tortious acts or omissions. The main remedies available in tort will be discussed presently, along with some proposals for reform, but it is appropriate at this point to say something about the more important heads of tortious liability.

Liability in tort

Tort – the law of civil wrongs – encompasses a wide range of different heads of liability, each with its own conditions of liability. It includes liability for trespass (the intentional[27] invasion of personal or property rights); for statements which damage someone's reputation (libel and slander); for damage caused by animals or by fire; for loss resulting from false statements (deceit, negligent mis-statements);[28] and for loss or damage caused by dangerous premises. The tort of private nuisance is concerned with the *unreasonable interference* by one person with another's enjoyment of his or her land, and frequently involves not the intentional and unlawful act of a defendant so much as the unreasonable encroachment by a defendant upon a plaintiff's enjoyment of property caused by the former's *lawful* activity. For example, in *Sturges* v. *Bridgman* (1879)[29] the defendant operated a confectioner's business and the plaintiff alleged that the noise from the defendant's machinery interfered with his practice as a physician. The court held that such interference was indeed unreasonable and amounted to nuisance. It is true, however, that a defendant may commit this tort by means of an element of deliberate maliciousness, as where the neighbour of a music teacher, resenting the noise made in the course of music lessons, retaliated by making various cacophonous noises during the lessons simply to annoy the teacher (*Christie* v. *Davey*, 1893).[30]

Space does not permit a detailed discussion of all the heads of tortious liability, and the reader is referred to the various texts in this area.[31] Probably the single most important area of tort liability today, however, is that of *negligence*, concerned with liability for personal injury caused not intentionally, but through the defendant's negligent acts or omissions. The numerical predominance of claims arising from personal injury over those involving other, older areas of tortious liability was established in the nineteenth century, and this pattern remains today; the great majority of tort claims concern either accidents at work or injuries sustained in road accidents.[32] We shall see later that tort is one of a number or systems for providing compensation for injury. However, before considering the place of the tort system in the context of these other systems, it is important to appreciate the specific conditions of liability in negligence – as developed, in the main, by the courts – in order to understand the importance of this area of law in modern society.

The classic formulation of the law of negligence is that of Alderson B. in *Blyth* v. *Birmingham Waterworks Co.* in 1856: 'Negligence is the omission to do something which a reasonable man, guided upon those considerations which ordinarily regulate the conduct of human affairs, would do, or doing something which a prudent and reasonable man would not do.'[33] The negligent person, then, not only could but *should* have adopted an alternative course of action or inaction, from the one which was followed. The fact that a person followed a wrongful or 'unreasonable' course of conduct is, then, evidence of *fault* – of 'negligence'.

The requirement that fault should constitute the basic condition of liability in negligence, although well established many years previously, received its most lucid and well-known formulation in 1932 in the case of *Donoghue* v. *Stevenson* (see chapter 4). The case concerned the liability of a manufacturer to a consumer injured as a result of a defective product, and the relationship between the plaintiff and the defendant was explained by Lord Atkin in the House of Lords:

The rule that you are to love your neighbour becomes in law, you must not injure your neighbour; and the lawyer's question, who is my neighbour? receives a restricted reply. You must take reasonable care to avoid acts or omissions which you can reasonably foresee would be likely to injure your neighbour. Who, then, in law is my neighbour? The answer seems to be – persons who are so closely and directly affected by my act that I ought reasonably to have them in contemplation as being so affected when I am directing my mind to the acts or omissions which are called in question.[34]

His Lordship went on to formulate the general legal principles of liability for negligently manufactured products:

. . . a manufacturer of products, which he sells in such a form as to show that they left him with no reasonable possibility of intermediate examination, and with the knowledge that the absence of reasonable care in the preparation or putting up of the products will result in an injury to the consumer's life or property, owes a duty to the consumer to take reasonable care.[35]

Now, we noted previously that this principle has been modified through later cases, and that liability has been extended to cover various articles and to persons other than just manufacturers. Although, as we shall see later, manufacturers' liability for injuries caused by defective products is now regulated by statute, the general principle enunciated in *Donoghue* v. *Stevenson* has for many years governed claims for compensation for injuries suffered by consumers as a result of defectively made, serviced or repaired products, and has also formed the basis of the modern law of negligence generally.

The key words in the above quotations from Lord Atkin's judgment are 'duty', 'reasonable care' and 'reasonably foreseeable'; and these are the concepts which the judges have used to decide liability in later cases. For example, a negligent motor-cyclist who had caused a serious road accident was held to owe no duty to a plaintiff who suffered injuries as a result of seeing the aftermath of the accident because no risk of direct physical harm to her was 'reasonably forseeable' (*Bourhill* v. *Young*, 1943).[36] In another case, injuries were suffered by a blind person who fell into a hole in the street, dug by the defendants' workmen, around which there were, it was held, inadequate precautions for the protection of blind people. The defendants were held liable to the victim because a sufficient number of blind people walk on the streets to make it 'reasonably foreseeable' that such an injury would ensue if adequate precautions were not taken (*Haley* v. *London Electricity Board*, 1965).[37] In a third case, damage caused to the plaintiff's yacht by a number of borstal trainees who escaped from supervision owing to the alleged negligence of the borstal officers was held to be actionable because a duty of care was owed by the officers to the plaintiffs (*Home Office* v. *Dorset Yacht Co..* 1970).[38] As a final example: it has been held in a number of cases that if someone by their negligence creates a dangerous situation which harms, or threatens to harm, someone, then a duty is owed not only to that 'primary' victim, but also to someone who comes along to try to rescue that victim, as long as such an act by the rescuer is reasonably foreseeable. The duty to the rescuer is quite independent of the duty owed to the primary victim.[39]

In recent cases the courts have pointed out that the way in which the duty principle has been extended to new situations has generally been by examining the new case in the light of previous decisions – developing the law case-by-case and by analogy with the precedents. Given a particular set of facts and the established case-law, the courts would ask whether the defendant, given the foresight of a 'reasonable man', ought to have appreciated that by failing to take 'reasonable care', he or she might 'reasonably foreseeably' have caused injury to the plaintiff.

Signs of a more generalized approach first appeared in 1970, in the *Dorset Yacht* case, noted above, in which Lord Reid, discussing Lord Atkin's formulation of the duty principle, expressed the view that 'the time has come when we can and should say that [the Atkin test] should apply unless there is some justification or valid explanation for its exclusion'.[40] This view was taken further in the judgment of Lord Wilberforce in *Anns* v. *Merton London Borough Council* (1978)[41] as follows:

First one has to ask whether, as between the alleged wrongdoer and the person who has suffered damage, there is a sufficient relationship of proximity or neighbourhood such that, in the reasonable contemplation of the former, carelessness on his part may be likely to cause damage to the latter – in which case a prima facie duty of care arises. Secondly, if the first question is answered affirmatively, it is necessary to consider whether there are any considerations which ought to negative, or to reduce or limit the scope of the duty or the class of person to whom it is owed, or the damages to which a breach of it may give rise.[42]

This formulation, it will be noticed, treated as synonymous the concepts of 'proximity' and 'neighbourhood', both rooted in Lord Atkin's concept of 'reasonable foreseeability'. In essence, this general test would place a duty of care on all defendants where it was reasonably foreseeable that their carelessness might cause damage to the plaintiff, *unless* considerations such as those of public policy persuaded the court otherwise.

In a series of negligence cases during the 1980s, the *Anns* formulation came under increasing attack. In *Governors of the Peabody Donation Fund* v. *Sir Lindsay Parkinson and Co. Ltd* in 1984,[43] Lord Keith stated that the test as to whether a duty existed in any given case was dependent upon an analysis of the *specific* facts of the case, and that a material consideration would be whether it was 'just and reasonable'[44] to impose such a duty. This narrowing-down of the *Anns* test was reiterated by the House of Lords in 1987 in *Curran* v. *Northern Ireland Co-Ownership Housing Association Ltd*,[45] and in *Yuen Kun-yeu* v. *Attorney-General of Hong Kong*,[46] where Lord Keith suggested that

the two-stage test formulated by Lord Wilberforce for determining the existence of a duty of care in negligence has been elevated to a degree of importance greater than it merits, and greater perhaps than its author intended . . . Foreseeability of harm is a necessary ingredient of. . . a relationship [which may give rise to a duty of care] but it is not the only one. Otherwise there would be liability in negligence on the part of one who sees another about to walk over a cliff with his head in the air, and forbears to shout a warning.[47]

His Lordship stressed that everything depended upon all the circumstances of any particular case, and that in addition there may well be public policy considerations which may negative a duty of care: given a particular set of facts, *ought* the law to impose a duty upon the defendant?

We have already seen examples of the operation of public policy considerations. Lord Keith's hypothetical situation of the careless cliff-walker above can easily be accommodated by the principle of policy that in negligence there is in general (and subject to some exceptions) no duty to act positively for the benefit of others, no matter what the morality of the situation may require.

Other examples of cases clearly involving public policy would include *Donoghue* v. *Stevenson* itself; and in the *Dorset Yacht* case (considered above, chapter 4), the court had to consider the defendants' argument that the imposition of a duty of care upon borstal supervisors might impede the proper functioning of the borstal system (supervisors would be reluctant to take trainees outside the institutions as part of their training for fear of legal repercussions should any damage be done), and that this would clearly militate against the public interest in the efficient operation of the borstal system. Similarly, it has long been held that barristers may not be sued by their clients for alleged negligence in presenting a case in court; the modern justification for this is the policy reason that the public interest in the proper adminstration of justice requires that barristers enjoy a degree of legal immunity from such actions, otherwise the process of litigation might be impeded by fears of subsequent suits for negligence;[48] and the Court of Appeal in *Hill* v. *Chief Constable of West Yorkshire*[49] denied the possibility of a claim for compensation against the police by the mother of the last victim of the perpetrator of a series of murders. The court stated that the police owed no special duty of care to the victim to apprehend the offender, over and above their general public duty to enforce the law and suppress crime, and it is clear from the judgments in the case that this decision was largely the result of considerations of public policy. Clearly, it is well-established that such considerations may be taken into account by the courts in deciding whether a duty of care exists.

A further major blow to the Lord Wilberforce formulation was dealt by the House of Lords in *Caparo Industries plc* v. *Dickman* in 1990,[50] where Lord Bridge, discussing the major decisions where the test for the duty of care was considered, concluded that

> Since *Anns*'s case a series of decisions of the Privy Council and of your Lordships' House, notably in judgments and speeches delivered by Lord Keith, have emphasised the inability of any single general principle to provide a practical test which can be applied to every situation to determine whether a duty of care is owed and, if so, what is its scope . . . What emerges is that, in addition to the foreseeability of damage, necessary ingredients in any situation giving rise to a duty of care are that there should exist between the party owing the duty and the party to whom it is owed a relationship characterised by the law as one of 'proximity' or 'neighbourhood' and that the situation should be one in which the court considers it fair, just and reasonable that the law should impose a duty . . .[51]

It is most important, when considering this passage, to bear in mind that Lord Bridge was not here discussing the special problems of negligent misstatement causing financial loss – the issue with which the facts of *Caparo* were concerned – but rather the *general* test for the duty of care in negligence.

Anns was finally killed off in the summer of 1990 by the House of Lords in *Murphy* v. *Brentwood District Council*,[52] in which *Anns* was 'departed from' and the earlier decision in 1972 of the Court of Appeal in *Dutton* v. *Bognor Regis Urban District Council*[53] was held to have been wrongly decided. Lord Wilberforce's test for the duty of care has not survived. Since, however, none of the judgments in *Murphy* discuss in any detail the matter of the *general duty of care in negligence*,[54] it remains the case that the most recent formulation of the test for duty is that of Lord Bridge in *Caparo*, which we must, therefore, consider in more detail.

The Lord Bridge formulation may be recast in terms of three components which must be present before a duty of care will be owed. These are:

(i) the foreseeability of damage;
(ii) the relationship of 'proximity' between defendant and plaintiff; and
(iii) the proposition that it is fair, just and reasonable to impose a duty upon the defendant as regards the plaintiff in the circumstances of the case.

The first and third elements of this formulation give rise to no particular conceptual difficulty. Foreseeability of damage has, ever since *Donoghue* v. *Stevenson*, been accepted as an essential ingredient, and the 'fair, just and reasonable' element is another way of stating the established proposition that public policy plays an important part in the deliberations of the courts in deciding whether a duty should or should not be owed. In fact, the first and third elements of Lord Bridge's formulation are very similar indeed to Lord Wilberforce's formulation in *Anns*.

It is the second element – the 'proximity' relationship – which poses problems for a number of reasons. First of all, many cases involving physical harm[55] from *Donoghue* onwards have proceeded on the basis that 'proximity' is synonymous with 'reasonable foreseeability'. It is clear, however, that Lord Bridge regards the two concepts as having distinct meanings. This is consistent with the determined separating-out of the two concepts by the judges in England and elsewhere[56].

throughout the 1980s. But it begs the question as to how, precisely, 'proximity' is defined.

The judgments in *Caparo* offer little by way of help on this point. Lord Bridge himself acknowledges that 'the concepts of proximity and fairness embodied in these additional ingredients are not susceptible of any such precise definition as would be necessary to give them utility as practical tests'.[57] Of the other speeches, only that of Lord Oliver purports to throw light on the matter. He says:

the duty of care in tort depends not solely on the existence of the essential ingredient of the foreseeability of damage to the plaintiff but on its coincidence with a further ingredient to which has been attached the label 'proximity' and which was described by Lord Atkin . . . in *Donoghue* v. *Stevenson* . . . as 'such close and direct relations that the act complained of directly affects a person whom the person alleged to be bound to take care would know would be directly affected by his careless act.' It must be remembered, however, that Lord Atkin was using these words in the context of loss caused by physical damage where the existence of the nexus between the careless defendant and the injured plaintiff can rarely give rise to any difficulty.[58]

Close examination of the passage which Lord Oliver cites, however, reveals that Lord Atkin does not seem to have been making any such distinction between foreseeability and 'proximity'. The full passage from Lord Atkin's judgment reads as follows:

Who, then, in law is my neighbour? The answer seems to be – persons who are so closely and directly affected by my act that I ought reasonably to have them in contemplation as being so affected when I am directing my mind to the acts or omissions which are called in question. This appears to be the doctrine of *Heaven* v. *Pender*[59] as laid down by Lord Esher . . . when it is limited by the notion of proximity introduced by Lord Esher himself and A.L. Smith L.J. in *Le Lievre* v. *Gould*.[60] Lord Esher says: 'that case established that, under certain circumstances, one man may owe a duty to another, even though there is no contract between them. If one man is near to another, or is near to the property of another, a duty lies upon him not to do that which may cause a personal injury to that other, or may injure his property'. So A.L. Smith L.J.: 'The decision of *Heaven* v. *Pender* was founded upon the principle, that a duty to take due care did arise when the person or property of one was in such proximity to the person or property of another that, if due care was not taken, damage might be done by the one to the other'. I think that this sufficiently states the truth if proximity be not confined to mere physical proximity, but be used, as I think it was intended, to extend to such close and direct relations that the act complained of directly affects a person whom the person alleged to be bound to take care would know would be directly affected by his careless act. That this is the sense in which nearness of [*sic*] 'proximity' was intended by Lord Esher is obvious from his own illustration in *Heaven* v. *Pender* of the application of his doctrine to the sale of goods. 'This . . . includes the sale of goods, etc., supplied to be used . . . by a particular person . . . where it would be obvious to the person supplying, if he thought, that the goods would in all probability be used at once by such persons before a reasonable opportunity for discovering any defects which might exist . . .'[61]

The full passage reveals that Lord Atkin was concerned first, to differentiate the duty in tort from that of purely contractual obligation (a well-known feature of his judgment and a central issue in the legal arguments in the case) and second, to emphasize that 'proximity' was not confined to physical closeness. There is no indication in this passage that Lord Atkin intended that the term 'proximity' should refer to something other than reasonable foreseeability.[62]

There is no doubt that the use by Lord Bridge of the term 'proximity' in his formulation of the requirements for a duty in negligence has muddied these conceptual waters considerably. It is true enough that a number of passages appear in judgments in various recent cases which stress that the notions of 'foreseeability', 'proximity' and 'fair, just and reasonable' are merely pragmatic conceptual tools which are not susceptible of precise definition and which simply highlight the essentially flexible nature of the legal notion of 'duty' in tort generally. The following example is typical:

Indeed, it is difficult to resist a conclusion that what have been treated as three separate requirements are, at least in most cases, in fact merely facets of the same thing, for in some cases the degree of foreseeability is such that it is from that alone that the requisite proximity can be deduced, whilst in others the absence of that essential relationship can most rationally be attributed simply to the court's view that it would not be fair and reasonable to hold the defendant responsible.[63]

Indeed, it is strongly arguable that, in negligence cases involving physical harm where, *despite foreseeability*, no duty was held to exist, the reasons for this conclusion have almost invariably been 'public policy' considerations.

Certainly, it is hard to know when foreseeability will be sufficient to found a duty, and when something more ('proximity') will be required. It has been suggested that an element of circular reasoning has crept into the law in this area – 'there is a duty of care where there is proximity, and proximity means that the facts give rise to a duty of care'[64] – and the present situation has also been criticized on the grounds, *inter alia*, that

'proximity' is an excellent example of a normative concept masquerading as a factual one and causing nothing but confusion as a result . . . The point is not that questions about the normative relevance of 'proximity' could not sometimes, or even always, be satisfactorily answered in some way. The point is that, in practice, answers are never given, with the result that judgments based on 'proximity' seem at best off the point and at worst arbitrary.[65]

It seems, moreover, as we will see later, that the term 'proximity' may mean different things, depending on the particular context: the use of the term in cases involving psychological harm (the 'nervous shock' cases) seems to be quite different from its use in cases involving financial loss caused by negligent misrepresentation. It certainly seems that the Lord Bridge formulation is going to cause problems for the courts. In *B.* v. *Islington Health Authority* in 1991,[66] for instance, a case involving physical harm, Potts J. in the High Court alluded to the *Caparo* speeches by Lord Bridge and Lord Oliver, pointed out that the case (*not* the speeches!) was concerned with economic loss, and continued:

Thus I proceed on the basis that the nature of the duty of care in cases involving physical injury and consequential loss remains as it was before the decisions of the

House of Lords in *Caparo Industries plc* and *Murphy* v. *Brentwood District Council* . . . In *Donoghue* v. *Stevenson* . . . the foresight of a reasonable man was accepted as a general test as to whether a duty of care existed. In *Bourhill* v. *Young*[67] . . . Lord Macmillan said, at p. 104: 'The duty to take care is the duty to avoid doing or omitting to do anything the doing or omitting to do which may have as its reasonable and probable consequence injury to others, and the duty is owed to those to whom injury may reasonably and probably be anticipated if the duty is not observed.' This formulation of the duty is appropriate in the present case and I respectfully adopt it.[68]

It remains to be seen whether the judges, in later cases, will present us with a more precise indication of the meaning of 'proximity' in this context, or whether the term will turn out to be redundant, as adding little or nothing to the more familiar and well-established notions of 'reasonable foreseeability' and 'public policy'.

Such a development would signify, of course, a return to the Lord Wilberforce approach in *Anns*. Why were the courts during the 1980s and early 1990s so determined to replace this with a more cautious incremental approach?

An answer may be found if we look behind the doctrinal confusion. The willingness to expand the categories of negligence liability which characterized many of the judicial statements in cases during the 1970s[69] has given way during the 1980s and early 1990s to a clear judicial desire to keep negligence liability within narrower limits. Howarth[70] suggests that

The English law of negligence appears . . . to be confused and aimless for three main reasons. First, the judges seem to have no clear idea of what the law of negligence is for; secondly, they harbour vague fears about Americanisation; and thirdly, their conceptualisation of the law rests on an idea that, if not inherently flawed, at least invites confusion and misuse, namely the duty of care.[71]

There has, without doubt, been a resurgence of the fear of the opening of 'floodgates': it has frequently been argued by some judges that once one particular step is taken towards widening the availability of remedies in negligence, then the 'floodgates of litigation' will open. Such an argument was used, for example, in 1932 by Lord Buckmaster in his dissenting judgment in *Donoghue* v. *Stevenson*, and it is as well for the development of the law of negligence that it found little support in the majority opinion in that case. The floodgates did not, of course, open after 1932. They rarely do.

Even if we acknowledge, however, that the general test as stated by Lord Wilberforce in *Anns* was too wide, and that it is sensible for the courts now to impose limits on the scope of negligence, then we might none the less argue that the courts ought to create those boundaries in a straightforward, clear and logical manner, rather than by concealing their strategies of containment in a fog of highly complex conceptualization which serves only to confuse the law in this area.

Once it is established that a duty exists, a plaintiff must then prove that the defendant has been in breach of that duty – or, to put it another way, has acted in a manner in which a reasonable person, in the circumstances, would not act. Obviously, everything depends upon the circumstances of the case: the act or omission of the defendant must be judged in the light of available knowledge at the time (*Roe* v. *Minister of Health*, 1954);[72] the status of the defendant must be taken into account – if the defendant is a skilled person such as a surgeon, then 'the test is the standard of the ordinary skilled man exercising and professing to have that special skill';[73] and the reasonableness of the defendant's behaviour in the light of risk of injury must be taken into account – not only in terms of the *likelihood* of the injury occurring (for example, *Bolton* v. *Stone*, 1951),[74] but also in terms of the *seriousness of the injury*, should it materialize (for example, *Paris* v. *Stepney Borough Council*, 1951).[75] Whether it would have been practicable for the defendant to have taken further precautions against the injury might be a consideration (for example, *Latimer* v. *AEC*, 1953),[76] and in some cases the courts have weighed the risk to the plaintiff against the social or public importance of the defendant's activity – was the latter sufficiently important to justify taking the risk of harm to the plaintiff? (See, for example, *Watt* v. *Hertfordshire County Council*, 1954 .)[77]

At the end of the day, the court must decide whether the injury to the plaintiff was 'reasonably foreseeable', and whether or not the defendant acted with 'reasonable care'. These terms have frequently created problems for the courts in deciding issues of liability in negligence. The law, it has been said, requires that we 'guard against reasonable probabilities, not fantastic possibilities',[78] and there are many examples in the case-law of judges' attempts to maintain the dividing-line between possibility and reasonable probability.[79] This dividing-line is essential if fault is retained as a criterion for liability, for it is only the person who acts *un*reasonably who is held by the law to be culpably negligent.

The difficulties are well illustrated in the case of *Whitehouse* v. *Jordan* in 1981.[80] Here, a senior hospital registrar had been in charge of the delivery of a baby (the plaintiff) after a high-risk pregnancy. An attempt had been made by the registrar to carry out a forceps delivery; he had pulled the baby with the forceps several times and then, conscious of the risk to the mother's safety, proceeded to carry out a Caesarean section, which was done successfully. The plaintiff was born with severe brain damage, resulting, it was alleged, from the negligent pulling of the head with the forceps. This action was brought against the registrar, claiming compensation in respect of the damage which was caused, it was claimed, by the registrar's pulling too hard and too long with the forceps. There was considerable expert medical opinion to the effect that it was a matter of clinical judgment as to how to use forceps in such cases, and also evidence from one of the defendant's colleagues who had been present at the delivery that the defendant had not used the forceps violently or wrongly.

The plaintiff succeeded at first instance; on appeal by the defendant the Court of Appeal held that the registrar's conduct was an 'error of judgment' and not negligence. Indeed, in the opinion of Lord Russell in the House of Lords (on appeal by the plaintiff), the Court of Appeal seemed to consider that an error of judgment could *never* amount to negligence. In the event, the House of Lords found for the defendant, but made it plain that in the view of that court, an error of judgment *could* amount to actionable negligence if it constituted a lapse from the standard of skill and competence required in the making of clinical judgments. In other words, a doctor who, by the proper use of his or her professional skill and judgment, simply makes a mistake will not for that reason alone be guilty of negligence; a doctor whose mistake results from a failure to use proper skill and judgment, however, may well be held to have been negligent, because that would amount to a departure from the standards of the 'reasonable' doctor. It will be appreciated that, in many cases, such distinctions will be very difficult to draw, and it can be seen that one major hurdle for a plaintiff is to convince the court that the situation in which the injury occurred was one in which the defendant *ought to have* foreseen the likelihood of injury.

There has, moreover, long been controversy over the *extent* of the damage for which the negligent defendant is to compensate. In *Re Polemis* in 1921,[81] stevedores negligently dropped a plank into the hold of a ship. Unfortunately, the dropping of the plank somehow caused a spark which ignited inflammable benzine vapour which had leaked from tins in the hold. Fire resulted, and the ship was destroyed. The dropping of the plank was found to have been negligent; but there was a finding of fact that the *fire* was not a reasonably foreseeable consequence of that negligent act. In the event, the defendants (the employers of the stevedores) were held liable for *all* the damage, including the damage by fire. The case may be taken to have decided that once there was a negligent act having some *foreseeable* consequences (such as, in this case, physical damage caused by the falling plank), then the defendants are liable for *all* the damage which actually ensues, both foreseeable and *un*foreseeable.

In 1961 the Privy Council decided the case of the *Wagon Mound (No. 1)*,[82] another case concerning a ship. Here, the defendants had negligently allowed fuel oil to leak from their ship on to the waters of a harbour. The oil caught fire, in an unforeseeable manner, and the plaintiffs' wharf was extensively damaged by the fire. In this case the court held that the defendants were liable *only for the foreseeable damage*, and not for the (unforeseeable) fire damage. This case has been accepted as representing the law on this point, although later cases have complicated the issue somewhat by the introduction of distinctions between *kinds* of damage. The implications of such distinctions have been stated as follows:

It is not necessary that the precise concatenation of circumstances should be envisaged. If the consequence was one which was within the general range which any reasonable person might foresee (and was not of an entirely different kind which no one would anticipate) then it is within the rule that a person who has been guilty of negligence is liable for the consequences.[83]

In *Bradford* v. *Robinson Rentals Ltd* in 1967,[84] for example, the plaintiff, who was employed by the defendants, was driving an unheated van in the course of his job; the weather was extremely cold, and the plaintiff suffered severe frostbite as a result. The court held that he was entitled to recover compensation, despite the fact that frostbite was thought to be unlikely and hence unforeseeable; the defendants were held liable because frostbite was part of the general *kind of harm* which might be expected to result from exposure to extreme cold.[85]

The decision as to whether or not damage is within a 'general range' of foreseeable consequences in any given case may, however, give rise to difficulty. Consider the case of *Tremain* v. *Pike* in 1969[86] – a case which both illustrates the difficulties in this specific area, and also highlights some aspects of the doctrine of binding precedent (see chapter 7). The plaintiff worked on the defendants' farm, where the rat population had been allowed to become too large. The plaintiff had come into contact with rats and had contracted a rare[87] disease called leptospirosis, caused by contact with rats' urine. Because of this, the plaintiff sued the defendant, alleging that he had been negligent in failing to keep the number of rats on the farm under proper control, and that as a result the plaintiff had suffered injury.

The problem was whether or not the disease fell into a category of injuries which a reasonable person could foresee might result from a failure to control the number of rats on a farm. This is an issue which is clearly not susceptible of any precise delineation, but in the opinion of the judge, Payne J., the various precedents were distinguishable from the present case. He referred to *Bradford* v. *Robinson Rentals Ltd* in his judgment, quoting Rees J. in that case as referring to 'cold injuries'[88] and noting that Rees J. had, in the earlier case, resolved in the plaintiff's favour the question of whether frostbite was 'the type and kind of injury which was reasonably foreseeable'.[89] Payne J., however, went on to dismiss *Bradford*'s applicability to the case as being concerned only with *degrees* of harm caused by cold.[90] The judge then held that leptospirosis was not simply a matter of *degree* of harm caused by rats, but was injury of a completely different *kind* from that which might have been foreseen – notably rat bites, and poisoning resulting from contamination of food by rats. The plaintiff therefore failed in his claim.

Various questions might be raised about the learned judge's mode of reasoning in this case, and his use of the precedent of *Bradford* v. *Robinson Rentals Ltd*. First of all, Rees J., in *Bradford*'s case, very clearly and explicitly referred to frostbite in terms of its 'type and kind' and *not* simply in terms of *degrees* of cold injury, as Payne J. seems to infer. Second, in an area where the precision sought by Payne J. is so elusive, would it not have been better to acknowledge a category of harm called 'rat injuries', just as Rees J. had referred in *Bradford* to 'cold injuries'? The decision did not go to appeal, and we are left with a rather odd conclusion. If the case is to be taken as authority, farmworkers should note that the success of any claim they might make for injuries caused by rats might well depend upon which end of the rat they make contact with! Had the case gone to the Court of Appeal, the result might well have been different, for as Winfield suggests, 'the case is out of line with the general trend of decisions since *The Wagon Mound*'.[91]

Though the principle of 'reasonable foreseeability' may be seen to be linked to the idea of 'fault liability' and thus firmly embedded in the law of negligence, it is clear that no hard and fast test exists whereby a court can simply conclude that there was or was not a duty of care, that there was or was not negligence, or that the damage was or was not foreseeable. The necessary flexibility of approach can be appreciated from the cases discussed above, as can the important role played by judicial conceptions of public policy. Some recent decisions, however, make it necessary for us now to consider what might be termed 'sub-sets' of the tort of negligence, each with problems and principles additional to the basic require-ments of 'duty', 'breach' and 'damage'. These sub-sets are (i) liability for acts or omissions causing purely economic loss; (ii) liability for statements causing economic loss; and (iii) liability for psychological, or psychiatric, harm.

Negligent acts or omissions causing economic loss

The common-law development of the tort of negligence has proceeded on the basis that, if a plaintiff is to succeed and recover compensation from a defendant, not only must proof of fault be established, but also physical injury or material loss to the plaintiff's person or property. Once this injury or loss is shown, then it is well established that the plaintiff can recover damages in respect of any financial losses which are consequent on that physical or material loss. In actions for personal injury, then, there may be awards of compensation in respect of pain and suffering and loss of amenity, as well as an amount for the injury itself. These will be discussed in more detail presently. But apart from these physical losses, the plaintiff may recover medical expenses and any other financial loss which is attributable to that injury, such as loss of earnings or earning capacity suffered as a result of the injury.

But it has long been held by the courts that financial losses suffered through someone's negligence are *not* recoverable if there has been no *physical* damage or injury. This was settled in 1875 in *Cattle* v. *Stockton Waterworks Co.*,[92] and has been reaffirmed on many occasions since then. In *Spartan Steel and Alloys Ltd* v. *Martin and Co. (Contractors) Ltd* in 1973,[93] the defendants negligently damaged an electricity cable, cutting off power to the plaintiffs' factory. At the time, there was work in progress in the plaintiffs' furnace, and the material then in the furnace depreciated in value. Apart from claiming in respect of this damage, the plaintiffs claimed for further losses of profit on materials which they were unable to produce because of the power cut. They recovered compensation in respect of the material which was actually in the furnace, but were unable to recover in respect of the further losses of profit. The court gave various reasons for this decision, Lawton L. J. relying on the authority of *Cattle*'s case, and Lord Denning providing various policy reasons for holding that purely economic loss was not recoverable. He felt one important consideration was the possibility that, if this claim were allowed, many others would follow: 'Some might be genuine, but many might be inflated, or even false. A machine might not have been in use anyway, but it would be easy to put it down to the cut in supply. It would be well-nigh impossible to check the claims.'[94]

In *Junior Books Ltd* v. *Veitchi Co. Ltd*[95] in 1982 the position was reconsidered by the House of Lords. The defendant flooring specialists had been specifically nominated by the plaintiffs' architects as sub-contractors to lay the floor in the plaintiffs' new factory, which was being built by the main building contractors. There was no contract between the plaintiff and the defendants, but the plaintiffs alleged that they had placed reliance on the defendants, as specialists, to ensure that the floor was properly laid. About two years after the floor had been laid, cracks began to appear in it, and had continued to appear in it ever since. The plaintiffs alleged that the defendants had been negligent in laying the floor and claimed £206,000 as being the cost of replacing it, together with a number of costs incidental to the replacement work. These included the cost of storage of books and removal of machinery during the work, loss of profits due to disturbance of business, wages of employees and overheads.

Although there was, in this case, no danger of physical damage either to persons or to property, the House of Lords unanimously agreed that there *could* be liability for these losses, on the basis that the relationship between plaintiff and defendant was sufficiently close (in terms of the reliance by the plaintiffs on the defendants as flooring specialists) to justify the imposition of a duty of care upon the defendants towards the plaintiffs.

Orthodoxy was, however, reaffirmed by the Court of Appeal in *Muirhead* v. *Industrial Tank Specialities Ltd*[96] in 1985. Here, the plaintiff, a wholesale fish merchant, contracted with ITS to install a tank in which to store live lobsters. To keep the lobsters alive, sea-water had to be pumped continuously through the tank to oxygenate the water. The pumps for this operation were supplied by ITT, the second defendants, and powered by electric motors made by a French company and supplied through their English subsidiary, Leroy Somer Electrical Motors Ltd, the third defendants.

The electric motors continually cut out, and the plaintiff frequently had to call out electrical engineers to re-start them, incurring costs in so doing; if the motors failed during the night, this would not be discovered for some time, and this was particularly problematic since, if the re-circulation and oxygenation stopped, the lobsters would die within ninety minutes. On one occasion, indeed, the whole stock of lobsters died, and the plaintiff incurred more costs in salvaging and refrigerating the dead lobsters.

Eventually, it was established that the cause of the problem was the inability of the motors to handle the full voltage range of the UK supply. The plaintiff claimed compensation in respect of various losses incurred, these being the cost of the pumps; the costs incurred as a result of electrical engineers having to attend to the defective equipment; loss of interest on capital; loss of the lobsters; and loss of profits on intended sales of lobsters, the latter sum being estimated at £127,375. One of the main problems was whether, and to what extent, the manufacturers of the motors were liable in negligence to the plaintiff.

The Court of Appeal considered that *Junior Books* was distinguishable from the present case. The 'very close relationship'[97] which existed between the parties in *Junior Books* – said by Lord Roskill in that case to be 'as close as it could be short of actual privity of contract'[98] – did not exist between the parties in the present case. The plaintiff could, then, recover compensation for his material losses, but not for the loss of profits ultimately arising from the faulty motors.

It is clear from *Muirhead* and subsequent cases[99] that there is still in general no liability in negligence for acts or omissions causing purely economic loss. This will apparently be so even though there may be close relationships – along *Junior Books* lines – between plaintiff and defendant. In *Greater Nottingham Co-Operative Society* v. *Cementation Piling and Foundations Ltd*[100] the owner of a building sued the defendant sub-contractor over delay in completing work on the building. There was here an actual contract between the parties which had required the defendants to take reasonable care. This relationship, though closer even than that in *Junior Books*, was held by the Court of Appeal not to give rise to a duty of care in tort regarding the financial losses of the plaintiffs: the parties ought to have sorted their respective obligations and liabilities out by means of their contract, and in the absence of such contractual stipulations, it was not open to the plaintiff to allege liability in tort.

Such attempts to use tort actions to disturb or subvert contractual obligations have been condemned in a number of cases.[101]

The picture has been considerably complicated through a series of cases in the 1980s involving defective buildings, the latest of which is *Murphy* v. *Brentwood District Council* in 1990.[102] The basic scenario of these cases is as follows. A builder constructs a building in such a way that it is defective. During the building operation, however, the local authority becomes involved through one of its employees, such as a building inspector or surveyor, carrying out an inspection of the architects' plans and/or the actual site in pursuance of its statutory powers to do so. The operation is passed by the inspector as being sound. Some years later, when the fundamental defects in the building – which may be foundations dug insufficiently deep,[103] an inappropriate drainage system[104] or some other deep-seated defect in the structure – have caused visible problems, such as cracking walls and floors, the owner and/or occupier of the building sues the local authority (the builder being typically no longer available to sue) in respect of the allegedly negligent inspection which ought to have revealed the original defect in the construction process.

The first problem is the nature of damage suffered in these cases. The courts have insisted – in most of[105] the cases referred to in the last paragraph – that the plaintiffs' losses were *economic*, and not *physical*. Why? The answer may be found by comparing the typical facts of these 'defective building' cases with those of *Donoghue* v. *Stevenson*. In the latter case, the defendant negligently created a dangerously defective product which subsequently caused physical harm to the plaintiff. In the 'buildings' cases, even if the defendants did cause a dangerously defective building to be constructed, that building had not, at the time of the action, gone on to cause physical harm to anyone:

If a dangerous defect in a chattel is discovered before it causes any personal injury or damage to property, because the danger is now known . . . the defect becomes merely a defect in quality. The chattel is either capable of repair at economic cost or it is worthless and must be scrapped. In either case the loss sustained by the owner . . . is purely economic.

I believe that these principles are equally applicable to buildings. If a builder erects a structure containing a latent defect which renders it dangerous to persons or property, he will be liable in tort for injury to persons or damage to property resulting from that dangerous defect. But if the defect becomes apparent before any injury or damage has been caused, the loss sustained by the building owner is purely economic. If the defect can be repaired at economic cost, that is the measure of the loss. If the building cannot be repaired, it may have to be abandoned as unfit for occupation and therefore valueless. These economic losses are recoverable if they flow from breach of a relevant contractual duty, but, . . . in the absence of a special relationship of proximity they are not recoverable in tort.[106]

On this point, then, the 'defective buildings' cases can be brought into line with the orthodox position on economic loss.[107]

A broader issue is the degree of legal protection now afforded to home-owners who are the victims of the original builders' negligence. *Dutton* v. *Bognor Regis*[108] and *Anns* v. *Merton*[109] provided the occupier with a potential remedy against the local authority whose employee had been negligent. *Murphy* denies them such a remedy:

It must, of course, be kept in mind that the decision (in *Anns*) has stood for some 13 years. On the other hand, it is not a decision of the type that is to a significant extent taken into account by citizens or indeed local authorities in ordering their affairs. No doubt its existence results in local authorities having to pay increased insurance premiums, but to be relieved of that necessity would be to their advantage . . . To overrule it is unlikely to result in significantly increased insurance premiums for householders . . . The decision is capable of being regarded as affording a measure of justice, but as against that the impossibility of finding any coherent and logically based doctrine behind it is calculated to put the law of negligence into a state of confusion defying rational analysis . . .

. . . I would hold that *Anns* was wrongly decided as regards the scope of any private law duty of care resting upon local authorities in relation to their function of taking steps to secure compliance with building byelaws or regulations and should be departed from . . .[110]

Murphy has been criticized for, *inter alia*, this aspect of the decision. It has been argued that local authorities ought to shoulder this type of liability precisely because they are in the best position to check that the foundations, drains and so on are sufficient or adequate before those features of the building are covered over and lie hidden, slowly wrecking the building above, for ten or fifteen years. Liability might be an additional spur to ensure that inspections are properly carried out, especially, it has been suggested, if the construction industry is prone to save money by cutting corners on non-obvious aspects of the building work. There are, in other words, important policy aspects of the *Dutton/Anns/Murphy* scenario which the court in *Murphy* did not, it might be thought, adequately address.

Negligent statements causing economic loss

The principle that purely economic loss is irrecoverable in negligence was modified significantly in 1964 in the important case of *Hedley Byrne and Co. Ltd* v. *Heller and Partners Ltd*,[111] which we discussed in chapter 4. In that case Lord Devlin drew attention to the artificiality of the distinction between physical and economic, as opposed to purely economic, loss. The effect of *Hedley Byrne* was to make possible the recovery of compensation for financial loss sustained through reliance by the plaintiff upon statements made negligently by the defendant, but only where there exists a 'special relationship' between the parties. *Hedley Byrne*-type liability is, it must be stressed, confined to liability for negligently made *statements*, and is best regarded as an exception to the general 'economic loss' rule. The phrase 'special relationship' has in recent cases in this area been recast in terms of a 'relationship of proximity': it must be carefully noted that, although 'proximity' has been discussed already in a more general context, the term is used in this section with reference only to the law relating to negligent misstatement.

The term 'special relationship' which must exist between plaintiff and defendant before there can be liability was not defined with any degree of precision in *Hedley Byrne* itself. In this context, it is certain that reasonable foreseeability alone will not suffice to found a duty of care; Lord Reid spoke of

those relationships where it is plain that the party seeking information or advice was trusting the other to exercise such a degree of care as the circumstances required, where it was reasonable for him to do that, and where the other gave the information or advice when he knew or ought to have known that the inquirer was relying on him.[112]

Lord Morris of Borth-y-Gest said that

if, in a sphere in which a person is so placed that others could reasonably rely on his judgment or skill or on his ability to make careful inquiry, a person takes it on himself to give information or advice to, or allows his information or advice to be passed on to, another person who, as he knows or should know, will place reliance on it, then a duty of care will arise.[113]

Lord Devlin pointed out that, had there been payment to the bank in exchange for the information, then the solution in law would have been clear: there would have been liability for breach of contract if the information provided was wrong. Payment would also constitute 'very good evidence that [the advice] is being relied on and that the informer or adviser knows that it is'.[114] But in the absence of payment

it will be necessary to exercise greater care in distinguishing between social and professional relationships and between those which are of a contractual character and those which are not . . . I do not think it possible to formulate with exactitude all the conditions under which the law will in a specific case imply a voluntary undertaking, any more than it is possible to formulate those in which the law will imply a contract. But in so far as your lordships describe the circumstances in which an implication will ordinarily be drawn, I am prepared to adopt any one of your lordships' statements as showing the general rule . . .[115]

It was asserted by Lord Oliver in the later case of *Caparo Industries plc* v. *Dickman*[116] that it can be concluded from the judgments in *Hedley Byrne* that

the necessary relationship between the maker of a statement or giver of advice ('the adviser') and the recipient who acts in reliance upon it ('the advisee') may typically be held to exist where (1) the advice is required for a purpose, whether particularly specific or generally described, which is made known, either actually or inferentially, to the adviser at the time when the advice is given; (2) the adviser knows, either actually or inferentially, that his advice will be communicated to the advisee, either specifically or as a member of an ascertainable class, in order that it should be used by the advisee for that purpose; (3) it is known either actually or inferentially, that the advice so communicated is likely to be acted upon by the advisee for that purpose without independent inquiry; and (4) it is so acted upon by the advisee to his detriment. That is not, of course, to suggest that these conditions are either conclusive or exclusive, but merely that the actual decision in the case does not warrant any broader propositions.[117]

It will quickly be appreciated, however, that an immense – perhaps infinite – number of communications between people may satisfy these conditions. Because of this, and the courts' abiding concern to avoid a situation where there may be liability 'in an indeterminate amount for an indefinite time and to an indeterminate class',[118] judges in later cases have been at pains to keep the generality of the basic *Hedley Byrne* proposition within limits.

In *Mutual Life and Citizens' Assurance Co. Ltd* v. *Evatt*, a Privy Council decision in 1971,[119] the plaintiff, a policy-holder in the defendant company, asked for advice from the defendants about the financial soundness of another company with which the defendants were closely associated. Relying on the information provided, the plaintiff invested money in the other company. Because the information was incorrect, the plaintiff lost his money. The court held by a majority that the plaintiff had failed to establish that a duty of care existed on the facts, because he had alleged neither that the defendants were in the business of supplying such information or advice, nor that they claimed any special qualification, skill or competence to do so. If such a requirement were necessary, this would have the effect of limiting the duty of care to professional advisers such as accountants. The minority opinion in the case – which has been preferred in later cases to that of the majority – was however of the view that

when an enquirer consults a businessman in the course of his business and makes it plain to him that he is seeking considered advice and intends to act upon it in a particular way, any reasonable businessman would realise that, if he chooses to give advice without any warning or qualification, he is putting himself under a moral obligation to take care . . . [it is] within the principles established by the *Hedley Byrne* case to regard his action in giving such advice as creating a special relationship between him and the enquirer and to translate his moral obligation into a legal obligation to take such care as is reasonable in the whole circumstances.[120]

It is plain that the duty will not arise where the information is given in a purely social or informal context, such as off-the-cuff statements at a party. But the real difficulty lies in establishing exactly what requirements must be satisfied, on any given set of facts, in order for the court to deduce that the maker of the statement owed a duty of care to the recepient. The cases – especially those decided in the last five years or so – do not generate a coherent body of legal principle.

Throughout the judgments in recent cases, we can discern the influence of public policy considerations, and in particular a determination to keep within limits the types of situation which might give rise to liability. Consider the important decision of the House of Lords in *Caparo Industries plc* v. *Dickman*.[121]

The defendants were auditors who had audited the accounts of a company in which the plaintiff company owned shares. The plaintiffs made a successful take-over bid for the company, only to find that the target company's assets were substantially less than the accounts had indicated. They brought this action against the auditors, alleging negligent misstatement causing financial loss to the plaintiffs. The central question of law raised by the case was whether auditors owed a duty, in the preparation of the audited accounts, to shareholders who might rely on those accounts for the purpose of buying shares in the company. In the House of Lords, it was held that no such duty was owed by auditors to either actual or potential shareholders. The statutory purpose of the auditor's task was to *protect* existing shareholders as a body, and to facilitate their effective and informed control of the company; it was not to provide information which might enable individual shareholders to purchase more shares and make a profit. Clearly, the refusal to open up liability to 'an indeterminate class' can be seen at work here.

Judgments in *Caparo* refer to the requirements not only that the statement must be relied on, and of course that the recipient of the statement must suffer financial loss as a result, but also that defendants must have knowledge that their statement would both be communicated to, and be relied on by, the plaintiffs. It is not clear whether this must be *actual* knowledge[122] or whether knowledge may be *inferred* from the circumstances.[123] The former requirement would be highly restrictive, and there are certainly cases which support the latter proposition.[124] The trouble is that even after *Caparo*, we cannot isolate the requirements for liability for negligent misstatement with anything approaching precision. In the post-*Caparo* decision in *James McNaughton Paper Group Ltd* v. *Hicks Anderson & Co.*,[125] Neill L. J. in the Court of Appeal referred to a number of factors which might be relevant in establishing whether a duty of care existed. Accepting Lord Oliver's statement of conclusions from *Hedley Byrne*, cited above, his Lordship went on to note as relevant:

(1) the purpose for which the statement is made . . . (2) the purpose for which the statement was communicated . . . (3) the relationship between the adviser, the advisee and any relevant third party . . . (4) the size of any class to which the advisee belongs . . . (5) the state of knowledge of the adviser . . . (6) reliance by the advisee . . .[126]

Several more considerations might be linked to this list of factors. For example, how far might it be said that the relationship between adviser and advisee is 'akin to contract'?[127] Did the advisee's reliance on the statement actually cause the loss?[128]

As the law now stands, it is not possible to provide a definitive statement as to when a duty might arise in this area of law. It is difficult not to have sympathy with the courts' desire to keep this developing area within bounds, but at the same time it is very difficult to see how accurate legal advice may be given to those who have suffered perhaps substantial losses in circumstances involving negligent statements by others, and who, not unreasonably, look to the law to provide clear guidance as to whether they may obtain a legal remedy.

Negligent acts or omissions causing psychiatric illness

Subject to what has been said regarding the current judicial thinking on the duty of care, the basic principles governing liability for *physical* damage or loss resulting from someone's negligence are fairly well-established. There is, similarly, little difficulty where a plaintiff suffers psychiatric illness consequent upon physical harm. But what of the case where someone suffers no physical harm at all, but claims that as a result of a defendant's negligent act or omission, he or she has suffered some form of psychiatric illness: what the courts for many years referred to as 'nervous shock'?

To begin with, it has long been the case that 'nervous shock' must be distinguished from 'ordinary' distress or grief. The latter is not recoverable in negligence:

The driver of a car . . . even though careless is entitled to assume that the ordinary frequenter of the streets has sufficient fortitude to endure such incidents as may from time to time be expected to occur in them . . . and is not to be considered negligent towards one who does not possess the customary phlegm[129]

although exactly what the difference comprises has never been clear. Apart from this, the history of liability for 'nervous shock' is characterized by two features. First, we must recognize that, until relatively recently, the nature and causes of psychiatric harm were little enough understood by the medical profession, let alone the judiciary; and second, it is true to say that judicial reluctance to open the doors to recovery for such harm was, and remains, due to a degree of suspiciousness on the part of the judges as to the authenticity of such claims. How could it be established, for example, that a plaintiff *was* suffering from a clinically diagnosable psychiatric condition, as opposed to 'normal' distress or grief? How might fraudulent claims be avoided? Even if such a condition *were* to be established, how could it be shown to have been *caused* by a defendant's negligence?

Thus in 1888, in *Victoria Railway Commissioners* v. *Coultas*,[130] a level-crossing attendant negligently allowed a pregnant woman to cross the railway line in her carriage in front of an oncoming train. She suffered nervous shock and a miscarriage. The Privy Council refused her claim on the basis that such damage was simply too remote a consequence. By 1901, however, in *Dulieu* v. *White*,[131] a more positive approach began to develop, though still reflecting caution by the courts. Here, a pregnant barmaid suffered nervous shock when a negligently driven van crashed into the pub where she was working behind the bar. It was held that this harm was recoverable, as long as the shock was sustained by reason of the plaintiff's reasonable fear for her own personal safety.

In *Hambrook* v. *Stokes Bros* in 1925,[132] a mother saw a lorry out of control, careering down a hill from around a bend round which her three children had just gone on their way to school. She suffered severe nervous shock through fear that her children had been injured. Once again, compensation was allowed, the Court of Appeal being of the view that the qualification in *Dulieu* was too narrow. This decision established first, that a plaintiff need no longer be in fear of physical injury to herself; second, that a claim might succeed where the harm was suffered *after* the disaster had occurred (as opposed to being about to occur); and third, that there was a qualification on the right to recovery, this being that the plaintiff's shock had to result from what she had seen with her own unaided senses, and not as a result of what someone else had told her.

The House of Lords in *Bourhill* v. *Young* in 1943[133] denied liability to a woman who suffered both physical and psychiatric damage. She had been alighting from a stationary tram when, on the other side of the tram, a motor-cyclist negligently collided with a car. The plaintiff had heard the crash (in which the cyclist was killed) and a little later on witnessed the scene and saw blood on the road. It was as a result of these experiences, she alleged, that she had suffered the damage complained of. The exact *ratio* of the case is not clear, though it was noted that the plaintiff did not witness the crash itself with her own eyes and ears, and was never in any physical danger herself from the crash (being protected, as it were, by the tram), and that therefore she was, as far as the motor-cyclist was concerned, an unforeseeable plaintiff.

Boardman v. *Sanderson*,[134] decided in 1964, was more in line with *Hambrook*: the defendant had negligently reversed his car over the foot of the plaintiff's young son. The plaintiff was within earshot and heard the boy's screams, though did not actually witness the accident himself. Again, the plaintiff recovered compensation.[135]

It will no doubt have been noticed that, in most of the cases where recovery was allowed, there was a close family tie between plaintiff and – so to speak – the 'primary victim' of the incidents in question. There was no such relationship in *Bourhill* v. *Young*, but there are cases in which plaintiffs have recovered despite the lack of close ties. In *Chadwick* v. *British Railways Board* in 1967, for example,[136] the plaintiff became ill after helping in the rescue of passengers in a terrible railway accident. The court held that the circumstances of the injuries to the passengers and of the accident in general were such that it was reasonably foreseeable that those witnessing its results would suffer psychiatric harm. And in *Wigg* v. *British Railways Board* in 1986,[137] it was held that it was reasonably foreseeable that a train-driver who stopped the train and got down to help a passenger who had fallen in front of the train, owing to the negligence of the guard in giving the starting-signal, but who had in fact died, might suffer nervous shock. These cases are, however, explicable by virtue of the fact that in both cases the plaintiffs were classed as 'rescuers'. As pointed out above, a defendant who, by his or her negligence, creates a dangerous situation which threatens 'primary' victims, also owes a duty towards those who might reasonably foreseeably come along to try to rescue those victims, and who themselves succumb to the danger.[138]

In *McLoughlin* v. *O'Brian* in 1983,[139] a mother received news, while at home, that her family had just been involved in a road accident in which their car had been in collision with a lorry. The crash had been caused by the defendant lorry-driver. Mrs McLoughlin was taken to the hospital, where she was informed that one of her children had been killed and that her husband and other children had been seriously injured. She saw the injured members of her family in the state in which they had been brought to hospital and before they had received any medical treatment: these circumstances were described by Lord Wilberforce as 'distressing in the extreme and . . . capable of producing an effect going well beyond that of grief and sorrow'.[140] The mother subsequently suffered severe shock, organic depression and a change of personality, in respect of which she brought this action against the lorry-driver.

In the House of Lords, two views emerged from the judgments. In the opinion of Lord Bridge, liability here should depend, quite simply, on the test of whether the injuries were reasonably foreseeable, although he added the qualification that the illness would have to amount to more than the degree of shock which a person of reasonable fortitude might suffer. He specifically rejected the 'floodgates' argument as being greatly exaggerated.

Lord Wilberforce, however, stated what has become known in these 'nervous shock' cases as the 'aftermath' principle. On his view, recovery was allowed, but only where the shock came through sight or hearing of the event or its 'immediate aftermath'; on the facts, arrival at the hospital some two hours after the crash was held to be within the 'immediate aftermath'. Furthermore, in his Lordship's view, there must be a close relationship between the plaintiff and the 'primary victim' (subject to the qualification regarding 'rescuers', noted above):

As regards the class of persons [who may recover], the possible range is between the closest of family ties, of parent and child, or husband and wife, and the ordinary bystander. Existing law recognises the claims of the first; it denies that of the second, either on the basis that such persons must be assumed to be possessed of fortitude sufficient to enable them to endure the calamities of modern life or that defendants cannot be expected to compensate the world at large . . . The closer the tie (not merely in relationship, but in care) the greater the claim for compensation. The claim, in any case, has to be judged in the light of the other factors, such as proximity to the scene in time and place, and the nature of the accident.[141]

From the judgments of *McLoughlin*, it is not easy to state any clear *ratio*; the Lord Bridge test based on reasonable foreseeability was adopted in two cases in 1991 – *Hevicane* v. *Ruane*[142] (where the court's reasoning seems to be quite at odds with the authorities) and *Ravenscroft* v. *Rederiaktiebolaget Transatlantic*.[143] In neither case were the conditions for the 'aftermath' principle satisfied, and yet plaintiffs in both cases succeeded, at least at first instance.

In the autumn of 1991, however, came the House of Lords decision in the litigation arising from the Hillsborough Football Stadium tragedy in Sheffield in April 1989, reported as *Alcock and others* v. *Chief Constable of South Yorkshire Police*.[144] It is necessary to outline the facts in some detail.

On the day of a semi-final FA Cup football match between Liverpool and Nottingham Forest, to be played at Sheffield Wednesday's Hillsborough Stadium, the South Yorkshire police allowed a large crowd of intending spectators into the ground, and into an area reserved for Liverpool supporters which was already full. In the resulting crush, 95 people were killed and over 400 injured. The match was to have been televised live, and scenes of the disaster were broadcast during the course of the disaster. It was acknowledged that the television broadcasts were carried out in line with television broadcasting guidelines: none of the television pictures depicted the suffering or dying of any recognizable individuals. The defendant admitted liability in respect of those killed and injured in the disaster. The plaintiffs in this action all claimed compensation for the psychiatric illness they suffered as a result of either seeing the television broadcasts or actually being present in other parts of the stadium, and knowing that their relatives or friends might be killed or injured in the crush. The defendant denied liability to these plaintiffs on the ground that he owed them no duty of care.

In fact, of the original sixteen plaintiffs in the litigation, only ten appealed to the House of Lords. Nine of these plaintiffs had lost relatives; the tenth had lost her fiancé. All but two of them had witnessed either television or radio broadcasts of the tragedy; the others had been at the stadium, though not in the affected part of the ground: they had witnessed the tragedy at first hand. One of these two plaintiffs had learned of his two brothers' deaths by telephone next morning; the other plaintiff, who lost his brother-in-law, identified the latter's body in the temporary mortuary at the football ground at around midnight the same night.

The plaintiffs were unsuccessful for a number of reasons. Lord Keith, considering the three elements said to be inherent in any claim of this kind – 'the class of persons whose claims should be recognised; the proximity of such persons to the accident; and the means by which the shock is caused'[145] – felt that with regard to the first factor, reasonable foreseeability should be the guide: he 'would not seek to limit the class by reference to particular relationships such as husband and wife or parent and child', because the key issue was 'close ties of love and affection' rather than specific relationships; even an unrelated bystander might not be excluded from the range of reasonably foreseeable victims of shock 'if the circumstances of a catastrophe occurring very close to him were particularly horrific'.[146] As to the element of 'proximity', he stressed the need for the plaintiff to be close to the accident 'in time and space', either through actual presence or through coming upon the 'immediate aftermath'. And Lord Keith reiterated the requirement that the means whereby the shock is caused should be by sight or hearing of the event or its immediate aftermath, and not by receiving the news through a third party.

On this basis, Lord Keith rejected the claims of the plaintiffs who were present at the stadium on the grounds that neither had shown evidence of particularly close ties of love or affection with the deceased. On the same basis he rejected the claims of those not at the stadium, with the exceptions of those who had lost a son and the woman who had lost her fiancé. However, these three plaintiffs had witnessed the event on television; in Lord Keith's opinion,

the viewing of these scenes cannot be equiparated with the viewer being within 'sight or hearing of the event or its immediate aftermath' . . . nor can the senses reasonably be regarded as giving rise to shock, in the sense of a sudden assault on the nervous system. They were capable of giving rise to anxiety for the safety of relatives known or believed to be present in the area . . . and undoubtedly did so, but that is very different from seeing the fate of the relative or his condition shortly after the event. The viewing of the television scenes did not create the necessary degree of proximity.[147]

Lord Ackner pointed out that the plaintiffs in this case were effectively seeking to extend the principles governing liability for shock beyond previous case-law and stressed that in this area of law there was a real need for some limitation upon the extent of admissible claims. He too would not confine the class of potential plaintiffs to those within specific named relationships, but stressed the essential requirement for 'close ties of love and affection'. As to 'proximity to the accident', his Lordship felt that in the case of the plaintiff who had identified his brother-in-law at the makeshift mortuary at the stadium the same night, the fact that some eight hours had elapsed since the event which had caused the death meant that this could not possibly be described as part of the 'immediate aftermath'.

The other plaintiff who had been at the football ground, and who had lost two brothers, was dealt with fairly briefly and his claim dismissed, on the apparent ground that his claim had not been presented 'upon the basis that there was such a close and intimate relationship between them as gave rise to that very special bond of affection which would make his shock-induced psychiatric illness reasonably foreseeable by the chief constable', and that, as there was therefore 'no evidence to establish the necessary proximity which would make his claim reasonably foreseeable',[148] his claim was not valid.

As regards the plaintiffs who had witnessed the event on television, Lord Ackner agreed that this could not be equated with 'sight or hearing of the event or its immediate aftermath'.

In the course of his judgment, Lord Oliver, too, stressed the need to establish the requisite degree of 'proximity' between plaintiff, primary victim and the accident itself. Largely echoing the speeches of Lords Keith and Ackner, his Lordship spoke of the need to establish that there was, as between primary victim and plaintiff, an 'affectionate relationship'.[149] Once again, receipt of the information by means of television was dismissed as not providing the necessary 'degree of immediacy',[150] and Lord Oliver pointed out that all of the plaintiffs except for the two who were present at the stadium received news of the deaths 'second hand and many hours later'.[151] In the case of the two plaintiffs who were at the ground,

their perception of the actual consequences of the disaster to those to whom they were related was again gradual. In my judgment, the necessary proximity was lacking in their cases too . . . but . . . there is also lacking the necessary element of reasonable foreseeability.[152]

Interestingly, Lord Oliver referred at several points to the lack of logic – in his view inevitable – in this area of law, and concluded that the policy considerations inherent in the 'nervous shock' decisions could be better stated by means of legislative enactment.

The other two judgments, by Lord Jauncey and Lord Lowry, add little to the reasons already outlined for rejecting the plaintiffs' appeals.

The current state of the law, as contained in the *Alcock* case, has been criticized as profoundly unsatisfactory. In terms of the issues which future plaintiffs must address, and on which they must satisfy a court, the following are among the problems which the case raises:

1. For exactly how long, in terms of hours, does an 'immediate aftermath' last? Two hours in *McLoughlin* was held to be admissible; eight hours in *Alcock* was held to be too long. Where is the cut-off point?

2. If the relationship between the plaintiff and the primary victim is not to be specified, but must none the less be one involving 'close ties of love and affection', what exactly must a plaintiff establish? We may assume that such ties will easily be demonstrated in the case of spouses or as between parents and children; but how may the evidentiary burden be discharged in cases involving less obviously close relationships?

3. Although perception of the event by means of television was rejected as insufficiently proximate by all the judges in *Alcock*, Lord Ackner somewhat confusingly suggested that there might well be cases where such perception would be 'the equivalent of the actual sight or hearing of the event or its immediate aftermath'. He cited the example of Nolan L.J. in the Court of Appeal as

an example of a situation where it was reasonable to anticipate that the television cameras, whilst filming and transmitting pictures of a special event of children travelling in a balloon, in which there was media interest, particularly amongst the parents, showed the balloon suddenly bursting into flames ... Many other such situations could be imagined where the impact of the simultaneous television pictures would be as great, if not greater, than the actual sight of the accident.[153]

Why, logically, should there be any distinction between such a hypothetical case and that which actually occurred? And might it not be argued that the perception of a live television broadcast could in fact be a greater stimulus to shock than physical presence at the event? The awareness of *not* being present, and the inability to do anything to help or save the victims, might well be *more* of a trigger inducing psychiatric illness.

It is clear that the courts are determined to confine the boundaries of liability in this area of law by means of the 'aftermath' doctrine: several judges in *Alcock* explicitly doubted whether the *Hevicane* and *Ravenscroft* decisions were correct,[154] and made it clear that liability cannot simply depend on foreseeability. The area is replete with difficulties of 'drawing the line' which can only perpetuate uncertainty in the law; and, finally, recent cases do little to indicate judicial awareness of modern psychiatric knowledge of shock, or post-traumatic stress disorder.

To summarize our discussion of these difficult areas of law: although the law relating to liability for negligence causing physical harm may remain relatively straightforward, this certainly cannot be said of recent developments relating to economic loss (whether caused by acts, omissions or statements) or psychiatric illness. The decisions of the late 1980s and early 1990s have as a common theme the judicial desire to keep within limits the number and types of situations in which negligence liability may arise, and this is clearly sensible, as long as the law remains clear as to where those limits lie. The trouble is that the resulting case-law is, as we have seen, difficult, highly technical and on occasions inconsistent. Fine distinctions abound, and it is hard to resist the conclusion that in the recent use of the term 'proximity' the courts have fashioned for themselves a formidable weapon whose very vagueness and imprecision provide them with a means of reaching conclusions in new cases which owe more to judicial determination to pursue the policy of keeping negligence liability within limits, than to the case-by-case 'reasoning by analogy' approach which the higher courts claim to have resurrected.

It is clear that our phrase 'conditions of liability' must be explained not simply in terms of the application of clear rules of law, to be applied to cases as they occur. Rather, it must be explained in terms of broad principles resting upon the foundation of fault liability; and subject to the interpretation and creativity of the judges, and the part played by judicial conceptions of what is 'reasonable and just', 'the best policy' or 'the just solution'. Hopefully, cases decided in the near future will, however, reduce some of the complexities discussed in this section to something approaching a clearer set of legal principles.

Liability for defective products

Although the modern law of negligence may be said to have grown from the celebrated dicta of Lord Atkin in *Donoghue* v. *Stevenson* in 1932, the law of negligence as it relates to a manufacturer's liability has been criticized on a number of grounds. The Thalidomide tragedy, for example (see chapter 4), was a situation where, had the issue been fully argued before the courts, it is by no means clear that the makers of the drug would have been held liable under the common law of negligence. Did the manufacturers owe a duty of care to the unborn children? And even if they did, had they been in breach of that duty? If it were established that they had researched and tested the drug according to the then accepted standards for testing within the pharmaceutical industry, then presumably they might be said to have acted 'reasonably', and not been negligent.

Again, the somewhat arbitrary distinction between the legal rights of a *buyer* of defective goods, and those of the consumer who was not the buyer, seemed to many to be of dubious justification in the modern world. A buyer of defective goods – whether suffering injury or not from those goods – has a remedy against the seller for *breach of contract* (see chapter 11). For such a breach, the seller is *strictly* liable: the buyer has a remedy against the seller without having to prove negligence. If the consumer is not the buyer, however, then the doctrine of privity of contract prevents that person from suing for breach of contract, because only parties to a contract can bring an action arising from that contract. Could the non-purchaser sue the manufacturers in tort? The answer must be: only if that person could establish, first, that he or she had suffered injury or loss as a result of the defective goods, and second, that the manufacturer had been guilty of a breach of the duty to take reasonable care: that is to say, had been negligent.

Establishing negligent manufacture is often difficult enough, but the problem is compounded by the fact that many defective goods causing injury are not manufactured in Britain, but are made overseas and imported for sale. Given the clear problem posed by attempting to sue a manufacturer in, say, Hong Kong, the only alternative then would be to attempt to fix liability upon a British defendant – the importer, distributor or seller – and once again, this could only be done (in the absence of a contract) by establishing that such a person or organization owed a duty of care and had been negligent.

For some years, therefore, there was mounting pressure by consumer organizations and others for reform of the law which would provide a remedy for consumers injured by defective goods (whether or not they had bought the goods) and which would not depend upon proof of negligence, or *fault*. The Law Commission proposed in 1977[155] that producers' liability in tort for injury or death caused by defective products should be strict, and these proposals were echoed, in general, by the Royal Commission on Civil Liability and Compensation for Personal Injury (the Pearson Commission), which reported in 1978.[156] More important was the EC Directive on product liability, adopted by the Council of the European Communities in 1985. It will be recalled that member states must implement EC Directives within three years, and in Britain the relevant enactment is Part 1 of the Consumer Protection Act 1987.

The Act imposes strict liability for personal injury or property damage upon the 'producer' of 'defective goods' (the latter specifically including electricity, gas and water, but not unprocessed agricultural produce). The producer may be the manufacturer *or* the importer of the goods, or anyone who puts their name or mark on the goods: this means that a supermarket chain which packages and sells goods carrying its own label, even though not the manufacturer of those goods, will be strictly liable should those goods prove defective and cause injury or damage. In certain circumstances the ordinary retailer of the goods may count as 'producer' for the purposes of this Act: if the injured person requests from the seller the name of the producer, and this information is not given within a reasonable time, then the seller becomes liable as 'producer'. The injured consumer need not be the purchaser of the goods: the person who receives the defective product as a gift is protected in exactly the same way as the consumer who buys the product.

It is still necessary to establish that the damage or injury was *caused* by the defective article, and that the article was indeed defective. A product is defective, as provided by s.3 of the Act, when its safety is not such as persons generally are entitled to expect. 'Safety' includes safety in the context of risk of damage to property as well as risk of death or personal injury. Factors which can be taken into account when determining this are the manner in which, and the purposes for which, the product has been marketed, its presentation, the use of any mark in relation to the product, and any instructions or warnings included with the product; what might reasonably be expected to be done with or in relation to the product (i.e. the use to which it might be put); and the time when the product was supplied by its producer – though the existence of a defect may not be inferred simply because the product has since been superseded by a better product, for example a 'Mark II' model. It seems clear from the wording of this part of the Act that the common-law concept of 'reasonableness' is likely still to have relevance in establishing whether an article was indeed defective. There would be few problems in establishing the defectiveness of, say, an electrical appliance which was faulty and which electrocuted the user when switched on; but suppose that a person obtains an electric hot-air paint-stripper, and uses it to dry his hair, suffering burns as a result. If the manufacturer did not include in the packaging a warning against such a use, would that make the article 'defective'? Or would such a warning be thought unnecessary because 'persons generally' (the reasonable person?) would appreciate that such a use would be highly dangerous? Such questions must presumably await decision by the courts.

One of the more controversial aspects of the Act is the inclusion, among other defences,[157] of the 'state of the art', or 'development risk' defence. This defence, which the EC Directive made optional for member states to enact, provides, as enacted by the United Kingdom,[158] that the producer shall not be liable if 'the state of scientific and technical knowledge at the relevant time[159] was not such that a producer of products of the same description as the products in question might be expected to have discovered the defect if it had existed in his products while they were under his control' (s.4(1)(e)). It is thought that this will enable many manufacturers to escape liability. Consider once again the Thalidomide case. As suggested above, it may well be that the manufacturers could have escaped liability in negligence by establishing that all reasonable care was taken in testing and manufacturing the drug, in accordance with the then established knowledge and practices of the pharmaceutical industry. Would not the manufacturers similarly escape liability under the Consumer Protection Act by invoking this defence?[160]

There is an absolute ban on actions brought under Part 1 of the Act after ten years of the supply of the product; and actions must be brought not later than three years after the date of the existence of the cause of the action, or of the consumer's knowledge of the damage, whichever is the later: this latter time-period, as mentioned above, applies by virtue of the Limitation Act 1980 to actions for personal injury in any case. This Act applies the limitation period to actions for property damage brought under the 1987 Act.

It is still too early to say what impact the product liability legislation will have upon the law of negligence, or for that matter what relevance the common law of negligence will have in assisting courts in the interpretation of the 1987 Act. It has been suggested that 'in a scheme of strict liability there may be temptation to lean more in favour of the user than under the law of negligence, but it is likely that principles of law long accepted by the latter will continue to be the basis for decision-making'.[161]

In appropriate cases, plaintiffs injured by defective products will almost certainly be more ready to bring legal actions than were plaintiffs when the area of manufacturers' liability was exclusively within the domain of the tort system. At the same time, the greater likelihood that a strict liability regime will result in more decisions against manufacturers may well urge potential defendants to settle disputes out of court – not least through insuring against such losses – and this might be one reason why litigation in this area has yet to reach the higher courts in the UK. Some of the other reasons why potential plaintiffs might view an action based in negligence with some trepidation are implicit in the above discussion; we may add, however, that from the point of view of a prospective plaintiff considering bringing an action in tort, there may well be a considerable degree of unpredictability as to the outcome of a dispute involving personal injury, or financial or property damage. We must remember at all times that the tort system requires that negligence is established before liability ensues. Given what may be substantial uncertainty about this, many injured plaintiffs may well look elsewhere for compensation. The major alternative sources of financial benefit which have developed alongside the tort system are *insurance* and the *social security* system. The first of these has had particular importance in the law of tort because of the development of the doctrine of vicarious liability.

Vicarious liability and the role of insurance

In *Bayley* v. *Manchester, Sheffield and Lincolnshire Railway*[162] the wrongdoer was a railway porter, employed by the defendant company, and the plaintiff was a passenger intending to travel on a train bound for Macclesfield, his destination. The porter, however, mistakenly believing that the train was going elsewhere, seized the plaintiff and pulled him off the train, causing him injury. The plaintiff could, of course, have brought an action directly against the over-zealous porter, but instead sued the railway company for the wrongful act of their employee in the course of his job, and the company was held liable for that wrongful act.

The doctrine which allowed the plaintiff to do this is that of vicarious liability, which is of great importance in modern tort law. It is the principle, applicable only in certain circumstances, of holding one person liable for the wrongs of another. In the above example, the railway company (a legal 'person') was held liable for the tortious act of its employee, the porter.

Seen from the standpoint of the master, this appears as an example of strict liability. He is held responsible for a wrong which he has not himself committed, but is imputed to him. But seen from the standpoint of the relationship between the injured party and the wrongdoer, vicarious liability means a transfer of the primary responsibility from the immediate tortfeasor to a third party: the employer.[163]

For the doctrine of vicarious liability to apply, the plaintiff must prove, in addition to establishing the specific conditions of liability attaching to the tort which the wrongdoer has allegedly committed, that the wrongdoer was *employed* by the defendant,[164] and that the injury occurred in the course of the wrongdoer's employment.

On the face of it, this may seem rather odd. Surely, it might be argued, this runs against the fundamental idea of 'no liability without fault', which is supposedly the very basis of tortious liability? Might it not be seen as unjust to hold a person liable in this way?

To answer these questions: 'justice' is a particularly difficult and elusive concept, and its meaning and scope are wholly dependent upon definitions and contexts. Vicarious liability only seems 'unjust' as long as we continue to base our general conditions of tortious liability on fault. Once it is appreciated that the idea of vicarious liability is founded upon notions quite distinct from that of fault, it is possible to explain and justify the doctrine in various ways. Atiyah has analysed a number of justifications for the doctrine, and, finding most of them wanting, concludes that 'the most rational justification that can be offered for vicarious liability today'[165] is that of *loss distribution*, an idea closely connected with that of insurance.

In the great majority of cases an employer who has to pay damages for the torts of his servants does not in fact have to meet these liabilities out of his own pocket. The cost of the liabilities is distributed over a large section of the community, and spread over some period of time. This occurs partly because of the practice of insurance, and partly because most employers are anyhow not individuals but corporations. Where the employer insures against his legal liabilities he will charge the cost of insurance to the goods or services which he produces. In general this cost will be passed on by the employer in the form of higher prices to the consumer.[166]

It has recently been suggested that the traditional confinement of the doctrine of vicarious liability to those cases where the defendant was the employer of the wrongdoer is in need of modification, if the principle of loss distribution is not to be undermined. McKendrick has pointed out[167] that there has been a large increase in the number of self-employed workers in Britain in recent years, rising from about 1,950,000 in 1979 to around 3,345,000 in 1990. This increase is explicable in large part by

the desire of employers to evade the scope of employment protection legislation and by the tax advantages offered to self-employed workers. Many of these self-employed workers are in no better position than employees to pay compensation to an injured party and they are unlikely to be carrying appropriate insurance cover.[168]

In addition, there are a large number of part-time, temporary and casual workers who are not regarded in law as being employed under a contract of employment.[169] McKendrick argues that, even though not technically in an employment contract in the eyes of the law, the employer is still, in these cases, usually in the best position to bear the burden of compensation, through insurance and the ability to pass on the costs through the pricing of products. The law therefore ought to recognize this, and extend the conditions under which vicarious liability will apply to these situations which fall short of comprising strict employer/ employee relationships as conventionally understood.

The role of insurance must not be underestimated. As we saw in chapter 6, very few disputes having a legal element actually come before courts of law, and most claims for compensation for personal injury (if they are not dealt with through the separate system of social security benefit, the industrial injuries compensation scheme, or some other alternative system) are handled by means of insurance. Even if a case comes before a court, the bodies which stand to win or lose are actually the insurance companies, for both motorists and employers are required by law[170] to insure against the risk of legal liability for accidents caused through negligence.

It must be understood that frequently the insured person is insured *against legal liability*, and so if the defendant is *not* liable according to the conditions contained in the law, the insurance company will not have to compensate the injured person. As Hadden explains the situation,

The driving force behind [the] tendency to see the law as a means of conscious and explicit risk allocation is the urge to insure. Any sizeable commercial undertaking regards its legal liability . . . in the event of an accident . . . as an additional running cost to be met by an annual premium on a wide range of policies. Many individuals also insure against their common law liability. The drivers and owners of motor vehicles are required to do so by statute.[171]

The statutory obligation upon drivers and employers to insure underlines the fact that loss distribution is a principle of *social policy*. Compensation through insurance payments is made to the aggrieved person, not by one individual but, ultimately and in small doses, by a sizeable section of the community. Such a philosophy is far removed from the *laisser-faire* individualism which underpinned the establishment of individual fault as a primary condition of liability in tort a century ago, and which is now increasingly giving way to other, competing notions regarding compensation for injury. The main point of focus has become the injured person, rather than the blameworthy defendant. The development of insurance, which has taken place, so to speak, alongside but outside the scope of the law of tort, is one important factor leading many critics of the tort system to cast doubt on the adequacy of that system as a means of providing compensation in modern society. In recent years, the connection, explained above, between insurance and tortious liability has given rise to new and potentially serious problems, especially in the United States. There, the introduction of strict liability imposed on manufacturers for defective products has encouraged litigation which, coupled with the massive awards of compensation by American courts, has created a crisis within the insurance industry, and among the corporate and individual clients of that industry. Since liability insurance is intended to reflect the risk of liability, many corporations (and, indeed, individuals such as, in particular, medical practitioners) have been faced with enormous increases in annual insurance premiums, reflecting the insurance companies' apprehension regarding legal liability and huge awards of damages. In England in 1987 the two largest medical insurance companies announced rises of around 80 per cent in medical practitioners' annual insurance premiums, said to be due to larger numbers of claims and high compensation awards. In some cases, it is reported, the cost of insurance premiums has become so high as to force some commercial enterprises to close down, and to persuade individuals such as dentists and doctors to carry out only the most minimal and 'safe' treatments upon their patients, for fear of subsequent actions for negligence should something go wrong. It remains to be seen how this crisis will be resolved, especially if it is true that, as has been suggested, 'there is now a greater public awareness of the possibilities of litigation'.[172]

Apart from the development of insurance, welfare state legislation has, over the years, provided a fairly comprehensive scheme for the provision of benefits for certain accidents and illnesses. This exists completely separately from the tort system. First, legislation has provided that an employee who is injured at work in circumstances 'arising out of and in the course of his employment' may claim compensation from the Department of Social Security. There is no need for the claimant to establish any negligence: the simple fact of injury at work is sufficient for entitlement to benefit. This state-run 'no-fault' scheme runs side by side with the tort system, so that an injured employee may have a claim against the employer in negligence or some other claim in tort, as well as a claim for benefit under the state scheme. Second, the social security system, created and modified by means of a long series of statutes, provides various benefits and allowances for non-industrial sickness and disability. There is a major difference between pursuing claims from the DSS and taking legal action through the tort system, however, apart from the distinction concerning fault: the state payments are considerably less than the lump-sum compensation payment which a successful claim in tort may bring, though the certainty of a successful claim from the DSS is far greater than the risky business of establishing a claim in negligence in a court of law.

In recent years, criticism has mounted of the tort system as a primary means of providing compensation for the victims of injury. Compelling arguments for reform have been presented, pointing out that the tort system is cumbersome, expensive and slow, and full of technicalities and pitfalls which have the result that many injured people are unable to obtain compensation for their injuries.[173] The Thalidomide tragedy in the 1970s was largely responsible for triggering a major review of the English systems for compensation for personal injuries by means of a Royal Commission set up in 1973 under the chairmanship of Lord Pearson. The Commission reported in 1978,[174] and its report covered three major areas, in addition to the recommendations on strict product liability discussed above. These areas were compensation for industrial injuries, for motor accident injuries and for handicapped children. Regarding injuries at work, the Commission felt that the existing system of state-controlled benefit paid through the social security system was basically sound, and recommended no major changes in that system. It recommended modifying the system of compensating severely handicapped children, however, proposing that a special benefit should be payable to parents and guardians of such children, as an addition to the child benefit provisions already in force, and payable through the (then) Department of Health and Social Security.

The Commission's most novel proposal related to injuries sustained in road accidents. Noting that an estimated 407,600 such accidents result in death or injury every year, and that compensation for the victims was available only by means of the slow and expensive tort system, the Commission recommended a new, state-run compensation system, based on the 'no-fault' principle. The scheme would have been funded by means of a levy upon the price of petrol, and victims of motor accidents would have been entitled to compensation, payable at the same rates as for industrial injuries. These recommendations, however, met with a lukewarm reception;[175] the proposals were not acted upon by the then government and it now seems highly unlikely that they will be implemented.

To a certain extent, the introduction of strict liability for injuries caused by defective products by means of the Consumer Protection Act 1987, discussed above, may go some way towards improving the situation, but many problems remain. A survey carried out in the mid-1970s by the Oxford Centre for Socio-Legal Studies[176] revealed that only about 12 per cent of accident victims receive compensation through the tort system. Most victims in the sample never even considered claiming compensation, and of those who did, many did not pursue claims because of ignorance about the law and the legal profession, problems raised by the need to produce evidence of fault, delays in the legal process, and the substantial costs involved in litigation. In 1988 the Report of the Review Body on Civil Justice[177] found that High Court cases could often take up to five or six years from the original incident to the courtroom conclusion, and county court cases, involving disputed sums of less than £3,000, could take three years or more. In a successful High Court action, the legal costs could swallow up half or even more of the damages awarded, while in the county court, it was found that legal costs could even exceed the sums awarded as damages.

Of course, on an analysis such as that of Abel, discussed above, nothing short of radical socio-economic change in society would adequately meet many of the shortfalls of the processes both of accident causation and of injury compensation. Many have, none the less, been concerned to propose reforms of the English tort system, and have looked approvingly at systems for personal injury compensation elsewhere. In particular, the system which has been introduced in New Zealand has attracted considerable attention. In 1967 proposals were put forward in that country by a Royal Commission on Compensation for Personal Injury (the Woodhouse Commission),[178] and these proposals were implemented in 1974. The effect of the New Zealand system is that liability in tort for personal injuries has been abolished, and in its place there is a comprehensive system whereby all persons injured in accidents at work, on the road or as a result of criminal attack, or who suffer occupational diseases, receive compensation from the state, as of right and without having to prove fault. The state funds are provided by means of employers' contributions, contributions from self-employed people, levies payable in respect of motor vehicles, and general taxation. Although the New Zealand scheme has its limitations, many critics of the English system have urged that some such state-administered, no-fault, comprehensive system for compensation be introduced in this country to replace the existing 'plethora of systems' whereby claims for accident compensation may be made.

It is clear that there has been at least a partial shift in official attitudes to personal injuries caused by accidents.[179] The focus, once upon the necessity of proving fault on the part of the defendant, is now upon the injured victim and the social desirability of providing compensation for that injury, whether it arises from an accident at work, on the road, or through some tragic misfortune such as the side-effects of drugs. The extensive system of social security benefits, provided by the state, is clear evidence that policy-makers recognize the high risk of accidents in modern life. If industrial injury and sickness benefit are available through state-run schemes, then surely the time has come for the state to take on the responsibility for providing benefits to other victims of accidents, especially road accidents and cases of severe handicap. Many critics would argue that such reforms are long overdue. Already the vast majority of victims of accidents who recover compensation do so through social security rather than through the tort system. The Pearson Report itself pointed out that, whereas the tort system provided, each year, about 6.5 per cent of persons injured (about 215,000 out of 3 million) with around £202 million, the social security system provided over 1½ million people with a total of £421 million.[180] It seems certain that changed attitudes towards compensation for personal injury, coupled with the major development of insurance (both private and 'social'), must carry the implication that the retention of fault as a condition of liability in this part of the law is outdated and grossly inadequate for the task of providing compensation for many cases of personal injury.

Remedies in the law of tort

Although the tendency, over the centuries, has been the absorption of older self-help remedies into the law, there are situations today in which the law itself provides self-help remedies without the aggrieved person having to sue. Although the old forms of retaliation and satisfaction for wrongs, such as feuds and duelling, have long been outlawed in the interests of preserving public order, there are still cases where 'such force as is reasonable in the circumstances' may be used by any person in the course of preventing a crime. This provision, now contained in s.3 of the Criminal Law Act 1967, replaces the old common-law rules about self-defence. There is no doubt, however, that the law places limits on the amount of force which may legitimately be used in self-defence; it may not be out of proportion to the force used or threatened by the attacker. Again, in the law of tort, a trespasser on someone's land who refuses to leave on request may be ejected, using only reasonably necessary force; and the law of private nuisance provides that a sufferer from a nuisance may take steps to abate that nuisance. The best-known instance of this is perhaps the right of an occupier of land to cut off branches of a neighbour's trees which overhang that land (although the cut foliage belongs to the neighbour). As Winfield has said, however, 'self-help is apt to be a perilous remedy, for the person exercising it is probably the worst judge of exactly how much he is entitled to do without exceeding his rights'.[181]

Today, it is far more likely in cases of private nuisance (see above) that the aggrieved person will make an initial complaint to the local authority, for various statutes have provided that where waste disposal, atmospheric pollution, noise or unhealthy premises amount to a nuisance, the local authority will have either a power or a duty to take steps to regulate the activity in question or require that it ceases altogether. Where a local authority has no such power to intervene, or is unwilling to do so, the plaintiff must ask a court to grant an *injunction*. Originally available only in equity, the injunction is now (like all equitable remedies) available in all courts, and its effect is that the defendant is ordered by the court to cease the activity complained of. Although perhaps most often thought of as a remedy for private nuisance, the injunction is available for all torts except false imprisonment and negligence, and is given at the court's discretion. Though clearly useful and appropriate in many cases in tort, it is none the less true that the most frequently sought remedy in tort is not the injunction, but the award of *damages*.

Damages – financial compensation for loss suffered – is, historically, the only remedy which the old common law offered, and so the development of the rules governing awards of damages is to a great extent the result of judicial deliberation in cases coming before them.[182] In many cases, an award of damages, if adequately assessed, may be a wholly appropriate remedy, particularly where the loss sustained is of a material nature. In the law of contract, damages for loss through a breach of contract will usually be relatively easy to assess, especially if the parties have inserted into their contract a 'liquidated damages' clause, which is an agreed estimate of the financial liability of each party in the event of a breach. In tort, however, the damages claimed by a plaintiff are 'unliquidated damages', or sums of money awarded at the court's discretion which are not predetermined.

To award financial compensation in cases of *personal injury*, however, is quite a different matter. It is highly artificial in the sense that money cannot actually compensate for the loss of a leg, an eye or a life. To be fair, the judges have long recognized this problem;[183] none the less, they have the task of estimating a fair and just figure to compensate, as far as money can compensate, for a plaintiff's injuries. There is the distinction between 'general' and 'special' damages alleged by the plaintiff; the former being non-quantifiable damage such as the injury itself, the latter being quantifiable damage such as loss of earnings, which must be specified by the plaintiff in the statement of claim. There are various heads of damage, moreover, within each category. Non-pecuniary damage, in cases of personal injury, will include, where relevant, separate sums of money in respect of pain and suffering,[184] loss of amenity (awarded where a plaintiff, because of the injury, is no longer able to enjoy particular activities), and of course the injury itself.[185] Pecuniary loss, apart from loss of earnings, includes medical expenses (both past and future) and other incidental financial losses.

Some types of damages are intended not to compensate, but to meet other objectives. Damages may be *nominal*, in cases where no specific harm or injury is alleged apart from the bare breach of the plaintiff's legal right. Nominal damages must be distinguished from *contemptuous* damages, awarded where the court, though deciding in favour of the plaintiff, has formed so low an opinion of the plaintiff's case that, traditionally, the award comprises the smallest coin of the realm – and the plaintiff may well not be awarded costs. (This means that the plaintiff's legal costs are met by the plaintiff, and not the defendant.)[186] *Exemplary* damages occur when an award is increased by reason of the defendant's malicious or otherwise reprehensible motives or conduct.[187] These distinctions and categories do not greatly affect the substantive legal rules and principles within the law of tort, but they do affect procedure and formality, and may well have consequences for the kind and amount of damages a plaintiff will eventually claim, as can be seen from the cases referred to above.

Such considerations may well make it difficult for legal advisers to predict the outcome of a case with any accuracy, and such uncertainties are enhanced by the problems attendant on the artificiality of putting a monetary figure upon physical injuries. In practice, the judges work to a fairly uniform scale of awards for particular injuries,[188] but in some respects the predictability factor is not easily calculable. This may be important, for an injured plaintiff may well have to decide whether to take the claim before the court – where there may potentially be a very high award of damages – or before, say, an Industrial Injuries Tribunal, where the success of the claim may be more certain, but the amount of compensation less than might be the case in a court hearing. Or the plaintiff may have to weigh up the advantages of accepting an out-of-court offer of a settlement from the defendant or the defendant's insurers, as against the possibilities of obtaining more money, if the claim is successful, in a court action.

Some heads of damages are notoriously less certain then others. Prior to 1982, the award of damages for 'loss of expectation of life' involved an extremely speculative judgment by the courts as to the amount which was appropriate for this loss.[189] Section 1 of the Adminstration of Justice Act 1982, however, abolished the head of loss of expectation of life, thus removing at least one of the uncertainties in the law. The same Act also went some way towards dealing with another difficulty in this area. Before the 1982 Act, the rule was that damages were awarded as a lump sum, given once and for all to the injured plaintiff. This meant that the plaintiff's medical advisers had to make a very careful assessment of the chances of any worsening of the plaintiff's condition in years to come, for should an injury prove, in the course of time, to be more serious or more complicated than was originally thought, there was no possibility of bringing a further action for more money. The Administration of Justice Act 1982 confronted this problem by providing, in s.6, that where the condition of a plaintiff may seriously deteriorate, or where the plaintiff may as a result of the tortious act or omission develop a serious disease in the future, rules may be made so that the court may assess damages provisionally, on the assumption that such deterioration or disease will *not* occur. Further damages may then be awarded at some future date if the deterioration or disease in fact occurs.

In all the circumstances, it is not surprising that the common-law rules governing the award of damages have been criticized. Possible reforms might include the removal of compensation for personal injury from the arena of tort law altogether, and the substitution of a state-run system of insurance to replace the existing role of tort. Of course, such reforms cannot solve the problems identified by Abel, for whom the only solution to the inequalities of the tort system within a capitalist economy that cultivates accidents and injuries is a socialist alternative, which ensures 'that those at risk regain control over the threat of injury and illness'[190] and that the *risk* of injury is spread more equally. But as Abel acknowledges, such a transformation cannot be made without changing not only the law but society itself. The difficulties of such a project are, perhaps fortunately, well outside the scope of the present discussion, but it remains true that the tort system and its capacity (and willingness) to provide compensation is just as much a reflection of social and economic developments as is any other institution or procedure of law.

Liability in English law: crime and the criminal justice system

We have seen, at various points in this book, the ways in which certain activities and values come to be incorporated into law; such incorporation may be positive, as where the law is used to protect specific interests and values, or negative, as where the law, especially the criminal law, is used to proscribe certain activities because they offend certain dominant values (such as the sanctity of private property, or the values attaching to particular moral beliefs), or because they are seen as an affront to the very foundations of social existence (such activities would include murder, rape and other violent behaviour). Definitions of 'deviant behaviour', then, are not something 'pre-social' – that is, eternal, permanent and deriving from periods prior to social life as we know it; rather, they are dependent upon particular social structural arrangements at given periods of history. Whatever the origins of particular legal rules proscribing 'unacceptable' behaviour may be, those legal rules do have certain things in common, one of the most important of which is that they invariably provide for some form of legal *sanction* to be visited upon the offender upon conviction by a court.

A second feature is that, through the operation of ideological currents as reflected in the mass media, judicial pronouncements and political policies (as enunciated in and implemented by legislation), the criminal offender who has infringed or flaunted dominant moral and ideological norms (we are not here speaking of the speeding motorist or car-parking offender) comes to be seen publicly as a *marginal* individual, acting in a way which is antagonistic or threatening to the lives, property or values of everyone else. We will discuss this in more detail later, but the corollary of this phenomenon is that the role of the legal personnel who administer the criminal justice system (police, magistrates, judges, prison and probation officers and so on) is seen to be the apprehension, conviction, condemnation and disposal of these deviants *on behalf of* the rest of the social group – the 'public'.

This presentation of the criminal deviant as marginal, anti-social and reprehensible is achieved partly by the ritualism, ceremony and awe-inspiring atmosphere and procedures of the courtroom, and partly by the condemnatory attitudes which have traditionally been a hallmark of the judges presiding in criminal courts: 'I think it highly desirable that criminals should be hated, that the punishments inflicted upon them should be so contrived as to give expression to that hatred, and to justify it so far as the provision of means of expressing and gratifying a healthy and natural sentiment can justify and encourage it.'[1] Those words were written in 1883, but we find similar expressions in more recent statements by certain members of the judiciary: 'It is a mistake to consider the objects of punishment as being deterrent or reformative or preventive and nothing else . . . The ultimate justification of any punishment is not that it is a deterrent, but that it is the emphatic denunciation by the community of a crime.'[2]

Well away from the sphere of judicial utterances, we find that within certain schools of thought in social science, similar kinds of notion, stripped of the emotive impact of judicial pronouncements, have been presented. One of the best-known expositions of the relationship between criminal law and popular morality is that of Durkheim, who argued, first, that 'The totality of beliefs and sentiment common to average citizens of the same society forms a determinate system which has its own life: one may call it the *collective* or *common conscience*',[3] and second, that 'an act is criminal when it offends strong and defined states of the collective conscience'.[4]

In previous chapters, we have criticized strongly the idea that social values can be characterized in our own society as *consensual*, but certain facts nevertheless stand out. First, such a view is firmly held within the legal system itself, especially by the judges;[5] second, it is undeniable that our everyday ideological and common-sense attitudes and experiences tell us that most of us *do* adhere to a certain core of ideas about such activities as violent behaviour and theft, no matter how subtly these ideas may have been inculcated through our learning processes and through the various other institutions, such as the media, which are concerned with the presentation of dominant ideological currents. Third, there is within social science a line of thought and reasoning among some writers (notably Talcott Parsons)[6] which posits ideas about crime and the criminal legal code resting upon these notions of consensus. Some of the consequences and doubts about such assumptions, especially when held by those involved in the administration of the criminal justice system, are discussed later in this chapter, but to begin with it is necessary to examine some of the fundamental principles and conditions of liability in criminal law.

Liability in criminal law

The element of fault, which we have already discussed in the context of tort law, has similar prominence in criminal law as regards the general conditions of liability, except in specific circumstances. Consideration of the distinction between criminal law and tort may reveal why fault continues to be defined by legislators and judges as of fundamental importance to the criminal justice system.

Tort claims, and other civil proceedings, are instituted by individuals or bodies in order to obtain compensation from, or some other private remedy against, other individuals or bodies. Criminal proceedings are generally (though not invariably: see chapter 6) brought under *public* authority – nominally the Crown – against the wrongdoer. The legal sanctions differ too: the objectives of the criminal justice system may be punishment, deterrence, rehabilitation, or a mixture of all three, and these are sought to be achieved in a significant number of cases by deprivation of liberty, through confinement in prison or some other institution such as the detention centre. Criminal sanctions, therefore, are generally to be regarded as more severe than civil sanctions, in that they adversely affect a person's liberty, reputation and opportunities: for example, in relation to employment and other activities (see chapter 6). Because of this – and because, indeed, one aim of the system may be seen as the deliberate stigmatization of the offender as reprehensible – lawyers have in general steadfastly maintained the principle that only the blameworthy or morally guilty person should be subjected to those sanctions.

The general conditions of liability in criminal law reflect this principle by requiring that the prosecution in a criminal trial establish, beyond reasonable doubt,[7] not only that the accused brought about the prohibited situation, but also that this was done in a manner which shows the accused's guilt or blameworthiness. These two aspects of liability are present, as we shall see, in most, though not all, criminal offences as defined in the law. They may be seen as distinct elements, both of which must be established before a criminal conviction can follow. The all-important expression is the Latin maxim *actus not facit reum nisi mens sit rea*, roughly translated as 'the act is not blameworthy unless the mind is guilty'. To recap: the distinction is made in criminal law between the criminal *act*[8] and the element of *guilty mind* in the commission of a crime, and in general both must be present for there to be criminal liability.

The first element, known as the *actus reus*, refers to the observable 'doing' or 'bringing about' of the prohibited consequence. In murder, for example, it is the bringing about of someone's death; in theft, the appropriation of someone's property; in criminal damage, the destruction or damaging of someone's property; and so on. If, then, X is charged with criminal damage after having thrown a stone through P's window, or with the theft of P's car, it must be established by the prosecution that these acts – the *actus reus* in each case – were in fact done by the accused. The commission of these acts must be shown to have been *voluntary*, and for this reason, someone committing a prohibited act while in a state of unconsciousness, such as a trance, or a lapse of consciousness brought about by a physical illness,[9] will normally be excused because the act is not the outcome of the accused's rational will. Such a person is said to be in a state of 'non-insane automatism', or 'acting like a robot'.

For example, in *R.* v. *Bailey* in 1983,[10] the accused was a diabetic and received insulin treatment. After his girl-friend had left him and begun an association with another man, the accused went to see the man. During that meeting, the accused said he felt unwell, and drank some sugar and water, but ate nothing. A few minutes later, he struck the other man on the head with an iron bar, causing severe injuries. Charged with the offence of causing greivous bodily harm contrary to s. 18 of the Offences Against the Person Act 1861, the accused in his defence claimed that he had acted in a state of automatism, caused by hypoglycaemia following his failure to take food after drinking the sugar and water. Following his conviction at the Crown Court, the accused appealed, and the Court of Appeal held that, in these circumstances, the defence of automatism could be appropriately pleaded. It is important to stress that the defence of automatism is concerned with those cases where the accused can be said to have acted *involuntarily*: in *R. v. Broome and Perkins*[11] in 1987, the defendant drove his car several miles, in a hypoglycaemic state, and was convicted of the offence of driving without due care and attention – though he may not have been aware of what he was doing, his condition was not, in the view of the court, one of automatism because he clearly had *some* command of the controls of the car.

The defence of automatism must be distinguished from the general defence of insanity, discussed presently. Moreover, the state of automatism may be induced by causes other than medical ones: a car-driver may be attacked by a swarm of bees, or struck by a stone from the road, and in such cases, it has been suggested,[12] the driver cannot sensibly be said to be acting voluntarily.

It must not be thought that the *actus reus* is invariably a positive *act*. Everything depends upon the definition of the offence. It may be constituted by an *omission*, such as a failure to take out insurance on a car contrary to the road traffic legislation. In *R. v. Stone and Dobinson*[13] it was held that a couple were liable for the death of the sister of one of them, who lived with them and who had become infirm and unable to care for herself. Her death was due to neglect by the couple, and the Court of Appeal held that as the couple had undertaken the duty of looking after her, the neglect of that duty which led to her death could constitute the offence of manslaughter.

Again, the *actus reus* may compromise a *state of affairs*, such as being in possession of prohibited ('controlled') drugs.[14] In some cases, the definition of an offence, and its interpretation, may lead to peculiar results. In the odd case of *Winzar v. Chief Constable of Kent*[15] the accused was convicted of the offence of being found drunk in the highway. He had been on the premises of a hospital, and, having been discovered to be drunk, had been told to leave. The police were called, and they removed him into their police car parked on the highway outside the hospital. It was this act by the police which constituted the commission of the offence by the accused, who had carried out no voluntary act whatsoever!

The second vital element in the vast majority of criminal offences refers to the *mental state* of the accused at the time of the offence, and this is known as *mens rea*. This is sometimes called the 'guilty mind', 'evil intent', 'guilty knowledge' or just the 'mental element'. The latter is, arguably, preferable, as it is perfectly possible for an accused to satisfy this condition of liability without having acted in an 'evil' way. A person might act out of pity, sympathy or compassion, but still be guilty of an offence: the motive of the accused is, in general, irrelevant to the question of liability. Someone administering a lethal overdose of drugs to a dying relative in severe pain, in order to save that person from further suffering, is committing murder; some may think the motive laudable, but in law there has been an intentional taking of another's life. Motive is, however, certainly admissible, and indeed often cogent, evidence at the trial as tending to show guilt.

The test of *mens rea* has traditionally been thought of as *subjective*: the rules of criminal liability involve an enquiry into the state of mind of the *accused* (although, as we shall see presently, the generality of this statement now must be qualified, at least with regard to recklessness). This subjective test may be contrasted with the *objective* test applied in the law of negligence, discussed in chapter 9, which asks the question: did the defendant's conduct measure up to that of a hypothetical 'reasonable' person? Though previous authority suggested otherwise,[16] the Criminal Justice Act 1967 provides, in s.8, that a court or jury

(a) shall not be bound . . . to infer that [an accused] intended or foresaw a result of his actions by reason only if its being a natural and probable consequence of those actions; but

(b) shall decide whether he did intend or foresee that result by reference to all the evidence drawing such inferences from the evidence as appear proper in the circumstances.

It is important to appreciate that, again in contrast to civil cases which are almost always tried by a single judge, criminal cases are tried either by magistrates, who are not trained lawyers, or in serious cases in the Crown court, by a judge with a jury. The presiding judge must explain to the jury the relevant law in the case, and because of the difficulties which this task can involve, quite a few criminal convictions are appealed on the basis of alleged misdirections by judges to juries.

Liability depends upon the *actus reus* and the *mens rea*: how may the latter be defined? Recent decisions, particularly those concerning recklessness, discussed in more detail below, have made it extremely difficult to present a general definition of the term. The 'state of mind' to which the term *mens rea* refers will differ from offence to offence. Generally speaking, the clearest state of mind is an *intention* by the accused to bring about the prohibited consequence (*actus reus*), though sometimes the definition of the offence makes it clear that only a *specific intention* to bring about the *actus reus* will suffice; for many offences, the requirement as to *mens rea* will be satisfied by showing that the person brought about the *actus reus* either *intentionally* or *recklessly*. The latter term may for the moment be defined as 'the taking of an unjustified risk', though this statement, as we will see presently, needs further elaboration.

At common law, a person who brought about prohibited consequences through his or her *negligence* – which is clearly a somewhat less blameworthy mental state than intention or recklessness – was not normally held to have satisfied the requirement for *mens rea*, but today we must qualify this in two respects. First, a number of statutory offences may be committed through negligence (notably careless and dangerous driving); and second, recent cases concerned with the definition of recklessness, discussed presently, indicate that there are situations where negligent conduct will count as recklessness for the purpose of satisfying the *mens rea* requirement. Finally, we might note that harm might be caused by someone through *blameless inadvertence*.[17] Criminal liability will not normally attach to someone in such circumstances, although as we shall see presently, it is possible for a person to be criminally liable even though his or her state of mind is wholly blameless, if the offence concerned is one which does not require proof of *mens rea* at all – an offence of *strict liability*.

A few words must be said at this stage about the meaning and scope of the terms introduced above, along with several other expressions, such as 'wilfully' and 'maliciously', in the statutory definition of various offences.

'Intention'

Although this is a common and everyday word, its meaning in the context of criminal liability has given rise to difficult problems. Perhaps the clearest and most basic example of intention is where the accused commits the offence with the specific *purpose* of doing so. For example: D loads a gun and fires it directly at P, with the specific purpose of killing P. Here, the accused's intention is obvious, and the test of *mens rea* will clearly be satisfied. But suppose that D places a bomb on an aircraft, timed to explode when the plane is in mid-air, with the purpose of claiming insurance money in respect of the destroyed cargo: it is virtually inevitable that the explosion will kill the crew, but can D be said to have *intended* their deaths? D's *purpose* is not to kill, but to profit financially. We would none the less be surprised if D were to escape liability on this basis, but can D's action here be termed 'intentional'? Most of us would agree that in this example the virtual certainty of death would lead us to assert that D must have 'intended' this result, and would be guilty of murder,[18] the *mens rea* of which requires, at least, an intention to kill or cause grievous (that is, really serious) bodily harm.

Consider next the facts of *Hyam* v. *Director of Public Prosecutions*.[19] Here, the accused set fire to a house with the purpose of frightening a woman into leaving the area. The woman's children were killed in the fire. Did the accused *intend* the deaths of the children? The trial judge directed the jury that, if they were satisfied that 'when the accused set fire to the house she knew that it was highly probable that this would cause death or serious bodily harm then the prosecution will have established the necessary intent'. This direction would imply that knowledge that a consequence was highly probable amounts, in law, to an intention to bring it about. On appeal, the House of Lords considered carefully the direction to the jury. The House affirmed the conviction, but offered somewhat differing views as to the meaning of 'intention' relating to the law of murder.

The difficulty is whether *foresight of probable consequences* can amount to *intention*. And, to compound the issue, if it is accepted that such can be the case, then *how* probable must those consequences be? Would a 51 per cent chance be sufficient probability? Or only probability amounting to 'virtual certainty'? The use by judges of phrases such as 'highly probable' and 'highly likely' do nothing to clarify the issue. The House of Lords in *Hyam* appeared to accept that foresight of 'highly probable' consequences could amount to intention in the crime of murder, but the position was certainly not clear.

The opportunity to clarify the matter arose in *R.* v. *Moloney* in 1985.[20] The accused was charged with murder, having fired a shotgun at close range at his stepfather after a drunken and heated discussion about their skill with guns. The defence was that there had been no intent to injure or kill, and that the accused had not realized that the gun was pointing at his stepfather. In the leading judgment in the House of Lords, Lord Bridge of Harwich acknowledged that the law on this point was confusing, and pointed out that the crime of murder is one of 'specific intent': that is to say, a crime which requires proof of intent, either direct or 'oblique' (as in blowing up the aircraft). Offences of 'specific intent' stand in contrast to those of 'basic intent', where either intention *or* recklessness will suffice.

Lord Bridge pointed out that, in general, judges should, when directing juries as to the law concerning crimes of specific intent, avoid 'any elaboration or paraphrase of what is meant by intent, and leave it to the jury's good sense to decide whether the accused acted with the necessary intent',[21] explaining that it would only be in rare cases that additional direction was needed which referred to foresight of consequences. He went on to lay down 'guidelines'[22] on this point for courts' future reference. In essence, these guidelines emphasize that the significance of the accused's foresight of consequences is a matter of evidence on the basis of which a jury draws its inference, and Lord Bridge continued:

In the rare cases in which it is necessary to direct a jury by reference to foresight of consequences, I do not believe it is necessary for the judge to do more than invite the jury to consider two questions. First, was death or really serious injury in a murder case (or whatever relevant consequences must be proved to have been intended in any other case) a natural consequence of the defendant's voluntary act? Secondly, did the defendant foresee that consequence as being a natural consequence of his act? The jury should then be told that if they answer yes to both questions it is a proper inference for them to draw that he intended that consequence.[23]

The matter was further considered by the House of Lords in 1986 in *R. v. Hancock and Shankland*.[24] The facts of the case, which arose during the miners' strike of 1984, were that the defendants, who were two striking miners, had pushed two blocks of concrete off a bridge spanning a motorway. On the motorway below, a taxi was carrying another miner to work. In front of, and behind, the taxi were police vehicles forming a convoy. One of the concrete blocks hit the taxi, and the driver was killed. The defendants claimed that they had no intention of killing or injuring anyone, since they thought that the blocks would fall on to the middle motorway lane, and that the taxi was being driven in the nearside lane. The trial judge directed the jury in terms of the guidelines in *Moloney*, and the accused were convicted. On appeal, the Court of Appeal stated that the term 'natural consequence' in Lord Bridge's guidelines in *Moloney* was potentially misleading, in that the term should have been elaborated by the trial judge to indicate that it meant 'highly likely' (an elaboration which was indeed given in *Moloney* by Lord Bridge, but in another passage in his judgment) and not just 'something which followed in an unbroken causal chain from the initial event, whether it was highly likely or not'.[25] The Court of Appeal allowed the appeal.

In the House of Lords, Lord Scarman, in his leading judgment, had sympathy with this view. His Lordship, who stated that cases in which additional explanation was needed as to foresight of consequences were unlikely to be so rare as was suggested by the House in *Moloney*, reiterated the view expressed in that case that the 'foresight of consequences' factor is 'no more than evidence of the existence of intent',[26] and stressed that the probability of a consequence of an act is an important matter for the jury to consider. Although Lord Scarman recognized that Lord Bridge had emphasized the importance of probability, but admitted that reference to this element was missing in the paragraph containing the 'guidelines', he went on to explain his own doubts about the value of elaborate guidelines, given that 'juries are not chosen for their understanding of a logical and phased process leading by question and answer to a conclusion but are expected to exercise practical common sense'.[27] Certainly, when foresight of consequences is an important part of prosecution evidence, juries should be told of the importance of the probability factor: in view of the absence of such an explanation in the trial judge's direction in the present case, the Crown's appeal should be dismissed.

Although the cases since *Hyam* have, through the judgments of the House of Lords, attempted to clarify, and indeed simplify, the law on this difficult point, it is hard to avoid the impression that, as Clarkson and Keating have argued, 'the concept "intention" can be expanded or restricted to meet the demands of justice in any particular case',[28] and that the final word on the subject has yet to be given. However, the suggestions as to directions to juries on this difficult point given by the Lord Chief Justice in the Court of Appeal in *R*. v. *Nedrick* in 1986[29] might be thought to be rather clearer than the cases discussed above. In that case (which involved facts very similar to those in *Hyam*), Lord Lane C.J. stated that, in the rare cases where the probability factor is in issue,

When determining whether the defendant had the necessary intent, it may . . . be helpful for a jury to ask themselves two questions. (1) How probable was the consequence which resulted from the defendant's voluntary act? (2) Did he foresee that consequence?

If he did not appreciate that death or serious harm was likely to result from his act, he cannot have intended to bring it about. If he did, but thought that the risk . . . was only slight, then it may be easy for the jury to conclude that he did not intend to bring about that result. On the other hand, if the jury are satisfied that at the material time the defendant recognised that death or serious harm would be virtually certain (barring some unforeseen intervention) to result from his voluntary act, then that is a fact from which they may find it easy to infer that he intended to kill or do serious bodily harm, even though he may not have had any desire to achieve that result.[30]

The complexities of the debate on 'intention' and 'foresight of consequences' also have implications for the law relating to the definition of 'recklessness', as will be seen presently; for the moment, however, it should be noted that the modern approach to *mens rea* incorporates within the concept of 'intention' the terms 'maliciously', 'knowingly' and 'wilfully'. The word 'maliciously' has repeatedly been held simply to import a requirement for *mens rea* in the sense of 'basic intent': that is, intention or recklessness. In some statutory definitions, the term 'knowingly' appears; the word has been variously interpreted, but would seem to require that *mens rea* as to the elements of the *actus reus* of the particular crime must be proved. The word 'wilfully' is capable of two interpretations. Some cases have interpreted it simply as reiterating the need to prove the voluntariness of the accused's conduct, while others have read the term as importing a requirement of full *mens rea*. Recent decisions seem to support the first interpretation of the term.

'Recklessness'

It will be recalled that, for crimes of basic intent, the requirement of *mens rea* will be satisfied on proof that the accused acted intentionally or recklessly. Like 'intention', however, the term 'recklessness' has been subjected to judicial deliberation in recent years, with less than satisfactory results. Prior to 1981, it was settled law that a person was reckless if he or she foresaw that harm might be done as a consequence of an act, but none the less went on to take that risk. The leading case, decided in 1957, was that of *R.* v. *Cunningham*.[31] The facts were that the accused, in order to steal the contents of a gas meter in an unoccupied house, tore the meter from the wall, leaving gas leaking from the pipe. The gas seeped into the house next door, and was inhaled by a person living there. The accused was charged with, and convicted of, maliciously administering a noxious thing so as to endanger life, contrary to s.23 of the Offences Against the Person Act 1861. On appeal, the Court of Criminal Appeal held that the trial judge had misdirected the jury by telling them that 'malicious' simply meant 'wicked'. In the opinion of the court, 'malicious' in a statutory definition of a crime imported a requirement either for specific intention (discussed above), or wilful taking of a known risk – recklessness – that the harmful consequence might ensue. In other words, *Cunningham* decided, or at least was taken to have decided, that 'recklessness' for the purposes of *mens rea* in criminal law necessitated a knowledge by the accused of the risk that was being taken, and that the risk was unjustifiable.

In 1981, however, the case of *R.* v. *Caldwell*[32] was heard by the House of Lords. The facts were that the accused, who bore a grudge against the proprietor of a hotel, decided while drunk to get his own back. He broke into the hotel, and started a fire inside. The fire was quickly put out. The accused was charged with arson under the provisions of the Criminal Damage Act 1971. Section 1(1) of that Act provides that 'a person who without lawful excuse destroys or damages any property belonging to another intending to destroy or damage any such property or being reckless as to whether any such property would be destroyed or damaged shall be guilty of an offence'. Lord Diplock, in the House of Lords, discussed the meaning of recklessness within this subsection, and stated that

a person charged . . . under s.1(1) of the 1971 Act is 'reckless as to whether any property would be destroyed or damaged' if (1) he does an act which in fact creates an obvious risk that property will be destroyed or damaged and (2) when he does the act he either *has not given any thought to the possibility of there being any such risk* or has recognised that there was some risk involved and has none the less gone on to do it.[33]

This passage, to which italics have been added, clearly indicated a departure from the older test of recklessness as enunciated in *Cunningham*: under the test in *Caldwell*, the accused need not be shown to have *known* of the unjustifiable risk being taken, and the *Caldwell* criterion is thus considerably wider in scope. This test has, however, been applied to the offences of reckless driving (*R.* v. *Lawrence*)[34] and other statutory offences where recklessness is an element of the *mens rea* required. An important exception is the offence of rape: in *R.* v. *Satnam* in 1984[35] the Court of Appeal held that *Caldwell* recklessness did not apply. Although the court in *Caldwell* did not overrule *Cunningham*, and in theory therefore the latter test still applies for crimes which must be committed 'maliciously' (*Caldwell* applying to those crimes whose statutory definition includes the word 'recklessly'), it seems clear that the *Caldwell* approach is preferred by the judges. In *R.* v. *Seymour* in

1983,[36] the House of Lords held that the *Caldwell* test of recklessness applied to the common law offence of 'motor manslaughter' – a significant extension of the *Caldwell* approach, which had until then been applied only to statutory offences – and it was stated in that case that the *Caldwell* definition should apply for all offences 'unless Parliament has otherwise ordained'.[37]

However, as Card points out,

With the exception of the common law offence of involuntary manslaughter, *Caldwell*-type recklessness has not been applied to 'reckless' or 'recklessly' in any offence other than a statutory offence in whose statutory definition one of these terms appears[38]

and the continuing applicability of the *Cunningham* test for some offences was shown when the *Cunningham* test was approved in *R. v. Spratt* in 1991,[39] a case concerned with the common-law offences of assault and battery; and in *R. v. Savage* and *R. v. Parmenter*, heard together in 1991,[40] which were both concerned with offences against the person, the House of Lords stated that *Cunningham*-type recklessness applied.

An interesting question which may be raised in those instances where *Caldwell* recklessness is held to apply relates to the situation where the accused *has* given some thought to the matter, and has decided that there is, in fact, no risk. If the risk in the event materializes, can such a person be brought within the ambit of *Caldwell* recklessness? Smith and Hogan think not:

a person who has formed the view that there is no danger is not reckless in the *Caldwell/ Lawrence* sense. He is not aware of the risk; and he has not failed to give thought to whether there is a risk or not.[41]

The complexity of the issue deepens if we now ask: what about where the accused *has given thought* to whether there is any risk, had decided that there *is*, in fact, some risk, and has gone on to attempt to *minimize or eliminate it*. It seems that if the accused believes that the risk has been eliminated, then, should it in fact materialize, he or she will not fall within the *Caldwell* test. In *R. v. Crossman* in 1986,[42] a lorry driver believed that the load on his lorry was 'as safe as houses', despite being advised otherwise by the loaders. The load fell off the lorry and killed a pedestrian. His conduct was held not to have been reckless, since he believed that there was no risk.

Where there *is* a risk, however, even though it may be small, the position would appear to be different. In *Chief Constable of Avon and Somerset v. Shimmen* in 1986,[43] the accused was a martial arts expert. He was demonstrating his skill while walking with friends along the street, and made as if to kick near a shop window. He misjudged his kick, and broke the window. He claimed to have thought about the risk of breaking the window, but had minimized the risk as much as possible by aiming his kick to miss the window by about two inches. On these facts, it is plain that he knew that there was still *some* risk; he had gone on to take it, and thus fell within the *Caldwell* criterion. Note that in both these cases, the accused had considered whether there was a risk, and both had been wrong in their conclusion. In terms of moral blameworthiness, it is not easy to reconcile these decisions.

Apart from this, the *Caldwell* test of recklessness raises serious questions about the relationship between recklessness and negligence. The law usually drew the line of criminal liability between recklessness and negligence (the reckless person being liable, the negligent person not being liable). An inadvertent risk-taker, however negligent the inadvertence might be, was not liable under the *Cunningham* test; but the *Caldwell* test would clearly appear to imply the criminal liability of one who was unaware of the (obvious) risk, but *ought* to have known about it – that is, a person who was negligent. As things stand, the law on this point is unsatisfactory and ambiguous, and is clearly in urgent need of fundamental clarification. Many commentators are of the view that the *Caldwell* approach is wrong, not least because it undermines the traditional *subjective* enquiry into the accused's state of mind, and replaces this in certain instances with an *objective* test as to the blameworthiness of the accused. But the other side of the argument must be considered: is it not plausible for us to say, 'you created this risk which would have been obvious to any reasonable person: the fact that you did not give it any thought makes you culpable, even though not as culpable as you would have been if you *had* thought about it and none the less went on to take it'? If such an argument has validity, then the lesser degree of culpability may be reflected, of course, in the sentence of the court.

The Law Commission has proposed, in Clause 18 of its draft Criminal Code of England and Wales,[44] that recklessness be redefined statutorily in terms of the pre-*Caldwell* formulation. The relevant part of the clause would provide that a person acts 'recklessly' with respect to:

(i) a circumstance when he is aware of a risk that it exists or will exist;
(ii) a result when he is aware of a risk that it will occur,
and it is, in the circumstances known to him, unreasonable to take the risk.

There is clearly a strong argument for Parliament to clarify the recklessness criterion by means of legislation, though this does not at present seem likely.

Strict liability

We have seen from the preceding discussion how important individual words and phrases within statutory definitions may be. The crucial importance of ascertaining the meaning and scope of such words becomes clearer still when we consider the impact of *strict liability* offences, which require discussion in a little detail.

So far in this chapter, the criminal offences discussed have been offences which, like the bulk of offences in English law, require proof of both *actus reus* and *mens rea*. They reveal the importance which lawyers have always attached both to the voluntariness of the action and to the mental state of the accused at the time of an alleged offence. There are, however, many offences, usually created by statute, which do *not* require proof of the mental element. Such offences are called 'strict liability' offences, and an accused charged with such an offence is liable to conviction on proof of *actus reus* alone.

We are faced here with the problem of reconciling a deeply embedded principle of 'no liability without fault' with a body of legal rules which appear to render liable a person who may not have been 'at fault', in that there may be a conviction for a strict liability offence despite the absence of intention or recklessness on the part of the accused. As with the development of the doctrine of vicarious liability in tort, this apparent paradox in the law is explicable only by examining the changing content and functions of criminal law in modern society. Traditional views as to the function of the criminal law, as expressed, in particular, by members of the judiciary, have tended to focus upon the social necessity of protecting the public from such harmful acts as violence and unauthorized interference with, or appropriation of, private property. More generally, the criminal law is seen as protecting the community at large from acts which are held to be injurious, for example, to state security. These views have, in general, rested upon ideas connecting 'crime' and 'wickedness'. Lord Denning, for example, has written that for centuries, 'in order that an act should be punishable it must be morally blameworthy. It must be a sin.'[45] And Hart has suggested that a crime is 'conduct which, if duly shown to have taken place, will incur a formal and solemn pronouncement of the moral condemnation of the community'.[46]

However, many developments in social and economic life, such as industrialization and the growth of the welfare state, have necessitated changed attitudes to the role of criminal law and its functions in modern society. As Friedmann puts it, 'a whole new area of criminal law has developed out of the steadily increasing responsibilities of the modern state for the maintenance of certain crucial standards demanded by the proper functioning of a modern industrialised and urbanised society'.[47] The role of the criminal law here, runs the argument, is not to mete out criminal sanctions for 'moral wrongdoing', but rather to use criminal law deliberately as an instrument of social policy to maintain certain standards of, for example, safety in factories and on the roads,[48] purity and hygiene in the preparation of foodstuffs and other edible goods,[49] and honesty and fair dealing in matters such as the provision of professional services and commercial transactions with the consuming public.[50] Almost invariably, offences connected with these activities are ones of strict liability. Friedmann argues that strict liability has been introduced in these areas as a matter of 'a balance of social interests':[51] it is more important that such offences should be strictly punished than that conviction should be contingent upon discovery of individual moral 'guilt'.

The point is that these offences may be said to comprise a special category within criminal law. They are not so much concerned (as is the conventional criminal offence) with punishing an offender for previous blameworthy conduct, as with the establishment of standards which must be continuously observed in certain kinds of social and economic activity. They have been called 'regulatory' offences or even 'administrative' offences. It has even been suggested that these 'public welfare' offences should be dealt with by specialized administrative courts rather than ordinary courts of criminal jurisdiction, in order to stress the distinctive quality and objectives of the type of offence.[52]

The difficulty is that the dividing line between 'traditional' crimes and strict liability or 'regulatory' crimes is not easy to draw. An offence is one of 'strict liability' when (i) no indication exists in the wording of the offence that *mens rea* is required, and (ii) the courts actually interpret that wording as excluding a requirement for *mens rea*. Not only do the two conditions for strict liability not always coincide; it is also the case that judicial interpretations of statutory offences as ones of strict liability have carried the phenomenon into areas of social activity having little to do with public welfare or the maintenance of safety or hygiene standards. Jacobs has argued[53] that the influence of individual judges in the development of strict liability has been considerable, and that it is possible to discern fluctuations in the degree to which the judiciary as a whole has been prepared to interpret offences as implying strict liability, thereby eroding or undermining the conventional view of criminal liability as necessarily involving proof of fault. The judges are certainly influenced not only by the wording of the statutes themselves – the principal indicator as to whether *mens rea* is to be inferred or not – but also by their view of the seriousness of the offence in question, and the amount of social danger associated with that offence. This has meant, for example, that legislation concerning prohibited drugs has been interpreted by the judges as involving offences of strict liability,[54] as once was the offence of bigamy,[55] neither of which would seem to constitute 'public welfare' offences as designated by Friedmann.

Such judicial developments have not gone unquestioned by critics and commentators. Apart from a general feeling amongst lawyers and others that liability should continue to depend upon proof of fault as a matter of justice, Glanville Williams has argued[56] that, just as Parliament omits, when creating new offences, to make specific reference to the age of criminal responsibility or the defence of insanity because they belong to the 'general part' of the criminal law, and so hold good (despite the absence of specific expression) for all offences unless explicitly excluded, so 'the law of *mens rea* belongs to the general part of the criminal law, and it is not reasonable to expect Parliament every time it creates a new crime to enact it or even to make reference to it'.[57]

In *Gammon (Hong Kong) Ltd* v. *Attorney-General of Hong Kong* in 1985,[58] Lord Scarman stated that

(1) there is a presumption of law that mens rea is required before a person can be held guilty of a criminal offence; (2) the presumption is particularly strong where the offence is 'truly criminal' in character; (3) the presumption applies to statutory offences, and can be displaced only if this is clearly or by necessary implication the effect of the statute; (4) the only situation in which the presumption can be displaced is where the statute is concerned with an issue of social concern; public safety is such an issue; (5) even where a statute is concerned with such an issue, the presumption of mens rea stands unless it can also be shown that the creation of strict liability will be effective to promote the objects of the statute by encouraging greater vigilance to prevent the commission of the prohibited act.[59]

It has been suggested that the judges in recent years have been less prepared than previously to interpret statutory offences as involving strict liability; support for such a view derives, for example, from the words of Lord Diplock in *Sweet* v. *Parsley*, a case involving prohibited drugs,[60] where he stated that the implication of *mens rea* 'stems from the principle that it is contrary to a rational and civilised criminal code . . . to penalise one who has performed his duty as a citizen to ascertain what acts are prohibited by law ... and has taken all proper care to inform himself of any facts which would make his conduct unlawful'.[61]

As a matter of a 'balance of social values' it may be thought acceptable that certain 'public welfare' offences are interpreted as implying strict liability; especially when, as frequently happens, the accused is not an ordinary individual but a company or corporation for whom the sanction will – on the rare occasions on which they are prosecuted – almost invariably be a fine (as in the case of breaches of factory legislation or pollution control legislation).[62] Many consider it far less acceptable for the criminal law to embark upon a course of development whereby in other circumstances an individual is rendered criminally liable, and possibly subject to sanctions of extreme gravity,[63] without the necessity of establishing some form of *mens rea*. At present, criminal liability continues, for the most part, to insist upon *mens rea* as a condition of liability, subject to the exceptions noted, and though (as we shall see later in a somewhat different context) some have argued for the complete abolition of the *mens rea* requirement, it is surely pertinent to ask whether departures from the conventional general conditions of liability for *any* criminal offence should be left to the sometimes idiosyncratic and invariably fluctuating tides of judicial interpretative thought.

Defences

It follows from the foregoing discussion that – leaving aside strict liability offences – if the defence can show that the accused in a criminal trial did not commit the *actus reus*, or did not have the requisite *mens rea*, then there must be an acquittal, because 'the act is not blameworthy unless the mind is guilty'. For example, the harm or damage may have been caused purely accidentally, with no intention or recklessness on the part of the accused; or the accused may have been labouring under a mistake as to the facts alleged. A man charged with theft, for instance, who took another's property in the genuine, though mistaken, belief that it was his own, will not be guilty of a criminal offence. The mistake as to fact must be such as to render innocent the accused's actions had the facts been as he believed them to be: a man charged with unlawful possession of heroin (a controlled drug) cannot argue his innocence on the basis that he was under the mistaken impression that the substance in his possession was cocaine, for cocaine is also a controlled drug! A mistake as to *law* is no defence. Everyone is presumed to know the law (as long as this has been published so that it *can* be known), and ignorance of the law is no defence. If this were otherwise, it is argued, everyone charged with criminal offences could escape liability by pleading ignorance of the law.

In some special circumstances, it may be established that the accused was *incapable* of forming criminal intent sufficient, in law, for a conviction. There is a presumption, for example, that children below the age of criminal responsibility are incapable, because of immaturity, of distinguishing between right and wrong, and are therefore not capable of forming *mens rea*. The age of criminal responsibility has been changed over the years, the trend being to raise the age; at present, the age of responsibility is ten, although children between ten and fourteen may be found guilty of an offence only if sufficient evidence is forthcoming that the child could, in fact, distinguish between right and wrong.

Normally a man has no defence if the offence is committed while he is drunk or under the influence of drugs: an exception to this may be a case where the offence charged requires proof of *specific intent* (see above) and the intoxication prevented the accused from forming the necessary intent. For crimes of basic intent, the House of Lords in *DPP* v. *Majewski*[64] held that the consumption of alcohol did not prevent the accused from acting voluntarily, and so having the necessary basic *mens rea*. There are, once again, clear policy reasons for limiting the extent to which intoxication may constitute a defence in criminal law.

More difficult are those cases where the accused pleads lack of responsibility for actions by reason of some mental illness or disability. In law, 'insanity' constitutes a defence to any charge, and the rules as to insanity in law remain as laid down by the judges in *M'Naghten's Case* in 1843.[65] Under these rules, every person is presumed sane unless the contrary is proved, and it is a defence to show that, at the time of the commission of the offence charged, the accused had 'such a defect of reason resulting from a disease of the mind as not to know the nature and quality of his action; or if he did know it, that he did not know he was doing wrong'.

Modern psychiatric diagnosis has long overtaken this antiquated approach to mental illness, and the formula has caused problems for judges and expert psychiatric witnesses alike. The basic difficulty is what constitutes a 'disease of the mind'. This is not a phrase used by psychiatrists, and there are conflicting judicial decisions about the conditions which may or may not fall into the category. Does a physical illness having repercussions on the brain, and hence upon consciousness, constitute a disease of the mind (*R.* v. *Charlson*)?[66] Does minor mental illness, such as depression, constitute a disease of the mind within the *M'Naghten* test? In *R.* v. *Clarke* in 1972[67] the answer was that such a depressive state which involved fits of absent-mindedness and confusion was not a disease of the mind. In *R.* v. *Sullivan* in 1984[68] the accused had attacked someone while suffering from an epileptic seizure during which he had temporarily lost consciousness. The House of Lords held that this fell within the M'Naghten Rules as being a 'disease of the mind', in that there was impairment, however temporary, of the accused's faculties of reason, memory and understanding. Lord Diplock did, however, express his reluctance at using the term 'insanity' to describe such a physical and mental state as that of the accused, suggesting that it lay within the powers of Parliament to change the terminology involved in such cases.

Many have criticized the present law on this matter: fundamentally, the judges are not well qualified to analyse issues involving mental illness, and indeed psychiatry itself has been criticized for its alleged inability to provide sound and precise definitions of mental illnesses.[69] Nevertheless, the judges have insisted upon retaining the out-dated M'Naghten test for the purposes of liability in criminal law, although legislation in recent years (notably the Mental Health Act 1983) has gone some way towards alleviating the problems by providing measures specifically designed for the treatment, if necessary in secure conditions, of offenders found to be suffering from mentally abnormal conditions such as psychopathy and psychosis. It must also be borne in mind that, until the suspension of the death penalty in England in 1965, a successful defence of insanity was often the only means of avoiding execution for murder: since the abolition of capital punishment, murder has carried a mandatory sentence of life imprisonment, which may if necessary be served in an institution for the criminally mentally ill. Perhaps because of this, since 1965 there has been a fall in the numbers pleading insanity in cases of murder.

Additionally, the Homicide Act 1957 provides another defence linked, like insanity, to abnormality of mind, though this defence is available only for charges of murder. This is the defence of 'diminished responsibility', which, if shown, has the effect of reducing the charge of murder to the lesser charge of manslaughter. Manslaughter may be voluntary or involuntary: the former occurs when a person intentionally kills another under provocation (which must be sufficient to make a reasonable person lose his or her self-control – a question for the jury to decide), or by reason of diminished responsibility. Involuntary manslaughter comprises other homicides carried out without 'malice aforethought'.[70]

To establish the defence of diminished responsibility, the defence must prove that, at the time of the offence, the accused was 'suffering from such abnormality of mind (whether arising from a condition of arrested or retarded development of mind, or any inherent causes, or induced by disease or injury) as substantially impaired his mental responsibility'.[71] The practical effect of a successful plea of diminished responsibility is to avoid the mandatory sentence of life imprisonment attracted by a conviction for murder, and to allow the sentencing judge to pass a sentence appropriate to the circumstances and gravity of the offence (see below).

Finally in this section, it is necessary to refer briefly to the question as to whether criminal law recognizes as defences *necessity* and *duress*. Duress may be defined as a situation in which the accused is forced by another – perhaps at gunpoint or because of threats to his life – to commit an offence. Necessity covers the situation where someone is not under threat from another person, but where failure to commit the offence would result in some disastrous consequence for the perpetrator. Although some have suggested that there is little difference between a threat posed by a *person* and one posed by a *circumstance*,[72] the law none the less has always made such a distinction. Necessity has never been recognized as a general defence,[73] although duress has been accepted as available as a defence to any criminal charge with the exception, until 1987, of that of murder as a principal – that is, as the actual killer. If it is accepted as a general proposition that the distinction between duress and necessity is 'a distinction without a difference, since . . . duress is only that species of the genus of necessity which is caused by wrongful threats',[74] then the law is clearly illogical. As to the non-availability of the defence of duress where the accused is charged with murder as a principal, this was the result of the House of Lords decision in 1975 in *Director of Public Prosecutions for Northern Ireland* v. *Lynch*,[75] where the court held that the defence of duress *was* available where the charge was murder as a *secondary* party: in that case, the accused was threatened with being shot if he refused to drive another offender to a place where the latter intended to kill a police officer. The House of Lords in 1987, however, in *R.* v. *Howe*[76] decided that *Lynch* was wrongly decided, and should be overruled.[77] In the leading judgment of Lord Hailsham, there are passages which make it clear that the decision is at least partly the result of considerations not of precedent but of public policy,[78] and the effect of this decision is to deny the defence of duress on any charge of murder, whether as a principal or as a secondary party, or attempted murder.[79]

Of course, the courts recognize that different degrees of culpability (even in homicide)[80] may exist, and that trial courts may take lesser degrees of culpability into account when deciding the appropriate sentence to impose on the convicted offender. It is to a consideration of the post-conviction process – sentencing – that we now turn.

The criminal justice system

The judges' main concern in sentencing convicted offenders is (and always has been) stated to be 'the protection of the public' and the reflection in their sentencing policies of what they take to be the social condemnation of offence and offender concerned. The element of strong moral condemnation must not be underemphasized for, as we have seen, it occupies a central place in legal ideology: the very basis of criminal liability involves the requirement that in the majority of criminal offences there must be proof of the 'guilty mind', or *mens rea*, before conviction can ensue. This is the means whereby the moral responsibility of the offender and the voluntariness of his or her acts are written into the conditions of liability within the criminal law, and the requirement of moral blame is deeply rooted in our ideas about what constitutes a criminal offender. This is one of the main reasons why there has, at various times, been reluctance on the part of judges and other lawyers to admit principles of liability based on 'strict liability' or 'liability without fault'.

Given this background, the main general objectives of sentencing in our legal system have usually been presented as falling into three categories: *retribution, deterrence* and *rehabilitation*.

Retribution is straightforward punishment inflicted on the offender in response to the offence. It is the type of legal sanction which Durkheim called 'repressive' (see chapter 1) and is perhaps the oldest type of sanction, having its Old Testament justification in the phrase 'an eye for an eye'. Examples of retributive sentences might include the Great Train Robbery case in 1965,[81] which attracted sentences of thirty years for the participants; and the judicial comments in the 'Angry Brigade' trial and the IRA bomb trials in the 1970s reveal that retributive principles were at least partly at work in the assessment of the sentences in these cases.[82]

Until recently, it was generally accepted that the sentencing policy of the courts tended to be not retribution, but deterrence. Deterrence is a double-edged principle. It should, of course, deter offenders themselves from committing further crimes, but also, and very importantly, it has been seen by the judges as serving to inhibit the rest of the community from indulging in criminal behaviour. The message is, simply, 'if you do this, this is what you can expect'. The deterrent principle has for some years been widely used, though whether or not the policy works in these ways is somewhat debatable.

To begin with, in order to be effective, a deterrent sentence must be publicized among the community, and although most crimes, serious and petty, are covered in national and local media, how many of us have any idea of the sentence we might expect if we were caught, for example, shoplifting or stealing from cars? Probably very few people have any accurate knowledge of the kinds of sentence such activities might attract, and it is only the sensational and unusual cases which attract much publicity. Apart from this, however, doubts have been raised about the efficacy of deterrence in sentencing policies upon potential offenders within the community at large. To take the most prominent example, that of capital punishment for murder: this is believed by many to be the 'ultimate deterrent', but available evidence does not support the proposition that the death penalty is any more effective a deterrent than long periods of imprisonment;[83] and, proportionately, there is no evidence that the suspension of the death penalty in 1965 has resulted in an appreciable increase in the murder rate in Britain, as many at the time of suspension feared it would. And the government White Paper *Crime, Justice and Protecting the Public* (1990) thought that it was 'unrealistic to construct sentencing arrangements on the assumption that most offenders will . . . base their conduct on rational calculation'.[84]

The third principle which may underlie criminal sanctions is that of rehabilitation. Now, while the principles underlying the aims of retribution and deterrence are to some extent compatible, the aim of rehabilitation involves considerations which are quite different, and must be regarded as an objective quite distinct from the first two. Essentially, the rehabilitative sentence is tied not to the *offence* and its gravity, but to the *offender* and his or her 'needs': the sentencing judge must make a choice in any given case as to whether to pass a sentence linked to the offence (retributive or deterrent) or an *individualized* rehabilitative sentence, designed to reform or 'treat' the offender for an identified 'problem'.

Which of these principles is most prominent today? According to Ashworth, the general aim of sentencing is 'probably a modified version of . . . *modern retributivism*: punishment of those who break the criminal law is justified so as to restore the balance which the offence disturbed'.[85] Recent legislation would certainly seem to support this assertion, and it is appropriate at this point to discuss the recent reforms contained in the Criminal Justice Act 1991 in order to understand in a little more detail the operation of sentencing.

The government White Paper *Crime, Justice and Protecting the Public* in 1990 formed the basis for a far-reaching series of reforms contained in the Criminal Justice Act 1991, which, apart from those special cases provided for by the mental health and children's legislation, is now the basis for most sentencing decisions in this country.

The Act is underpinned by clear policy elements. The intention is to attempt to keep offenders out of prison, unless a custodial sentence is warranted by the seriousness of the offence. Section 1 provides that a custodial sentence – that is, imprisonment or, in the case of offenders under 21, detention in an institution for young offenders – may not be passed unless the court is of the opinion that

the offence, or the combination of the offence and one other offence associated with it,[86] was so serious that only such a sentence can be justified for the offence; or where the offence is a violent or sexual offence, that only such a sentence would be appropriate to protect the public from serious harm from him.

The effect of this section is that custody is only justified when no other form of sentence *can* be justified. The emphasis is clearly on the seriousness of the offence when the court is contemplating this issue, and the stress on the offence, rather than the offender, is also seen in s.2, which provides that where a custodial sentence is passed, the appropriate term shall depend on the seriousness of the offence; and where the offence is of a violent or sexual nature, the court may sentence the offender to a longer term if the court considers it necessary for the protection of the public from 'serious harm' from that offender. Where a custodial sentence is to be passed, the court must normally consider pre-sentence reports on the offence and the offender from probation officers or social workers.

Where a sentence of imprisonment is passed, the Act provides for early release in various circumstances. A short prison sentence of less than one year will result in *unconditional* early release after six months; for a sentence of between one and four years, early release will normally be after half the sentence is served, though release in these cases is *on licence*, and conditions may be attached: if the released offender commits an imprisonable offence before the date at which the full sentence expires, he or she may be recalled to prison. For prisoners sentenced to four years or more, early release on licence will take place after serving two-thirds of the sentence, though release may occur earlier if recommended by the Parole Board and accepted by the Secretary of State. Those serving life imprisonment sentences may be released on licence by the Secretary of State. Offenders released on licence are under the supervision of the probation service, and the intention to increase the numbers so released, coupled with the provision mentioned above regarding reports on offenders, caused considerable concern within the social work and probation professions because of the additional work having to be carried out by these underfunded organizations.

A second policy underlying the 1991 Act is the promotion of non-custodial sentences, and in particular *community orders* – probation, community service,[87] attendance centre, supervision and curfew orders, together with the combination order, which combines probation with a requirement to carry out a specified number of hours of unpaid work. Section 9 provides that conditions may be attached to a probation order, such as a residence requirement or a requirement to submit to treatment for alcohol or drug dependency. In this part of the Act we see once again the objective of keeping offenders, as far as possible, out of prison, though again, the imposition of a community sentence must be justified by the seriousness of the offence.

With regard to the remaining possible sentences open to a court, the Act makes provision for fines to be linked to the offender's income; for non-serious offences a court may still impose conditional and absolute discharges.[88]

How is a court to assess the seriousness of the offence, and arrive at the most appropriate type and severity of sentence? The fundamental principle of *proportion* remains: the sentence must be proportionate to the gravity of the offence, and the

Court of Appeal will reduce (and in some cases increase)[89] a sentence which it feels is out of proportion. A court may not assess the seriousness of an offence by reference to a person's previous convictions (s.29(1)), although it may consider 'aggravating factors of an offence disclosed by the circumstances of other offences committed by the offender' (s.29(2)). It is not easy to reconcile these two subsections, and just before the Act came into force, the Lord Chief Justice, Lord Taylor, said that 'one of the things we will certainly have to look at in the Court of Appeal is how various, rather loosely-worded phrases in the new Act are going to be interpreted'.[90] It is likely, too, that existing guidelines as to sentencing practice laid down by – in particular – the Court of Appeal in previous decisions will continue to be taken into account.

The statutory definitions of criminal offences provide some guidance for the court by stating a *maximum* amount of fine or length of imprisonment which a judge may give out for that offence.[91] Below this maximum, the judge has a considerable amount of discretion as to precisely where on the scale of gravity of sentencing measures the offender is placed. There are statutory guidelines and policy directives, however, and there are, in addition, restrictions in the form of statutory provisions. Section 1 of the Criminal Justice Act 1982, as amended by the 1991 Act, for example, provides that no court may pass a sentence of imprisonment on a person under twenty-one.

Within these constraints, however, the sentencing judge has a considerable amount of discretion. The maximum sentence will be reserved for the most serious manifestations of a particular offence; 'average' examples will attract somewhat lesser sentences; and cases thought to be less serious than the 'average' will attract lesser sentences.

In the case of an offence whose seriousness may range from the very trivial to the most grave, such as theft, the range of sentences at the disposal of the court may start from non-custodial measures (such as fines or conditional discharges) at the bottom of the scale, to substantial periods of imprisonment where large amounts of money are involved. It must be remembered, however, that much depends upon the precise offence with which the accused is charged by the police. Many statutes contain a whole series of substantive offences, each with its own stated maximum sentence, and detailing specific offences involving the presence or absence of aggravating factors. The Theft Act 1968, for instance, not only contains the 'master definition' of theft in s.1, but also provides for a number of offences, all related to theft in the sense that they involve the unlawful appropriation of others' property, but differing in the additional factors which they involve: 'robbery' (s.8) is, basically, theft *plus* the element of force or violence, while 'blackmail' (s.21) concerns unwarranted demands for money or property belonging to another 'with menaces'.[92]

The precise position of the sentence upon the scale for a given offence will be the result of 'fine tuning' by the judge: this is to say that after having considered the seriousness of the offence, and after having decided on the appropriate type of sentence, the judge will consider factors presented in mitigation by the accused or his or her counsel, such as the accused's background, age, domestic or emotional circumstances. Reports concerning the offender, prepared by probation officers or social workers, together with any psychiatric or other medical evidence, if appropriate, will be taken into account; and although there is no obligation on the judge to act upon any recommendations made by any of these experts, the judge will usually incorporate such reports into the final decision as to sentence.

The Criminal Justice Act 1991, while marking a general move in the direction of retributive sentencing linked to the offence, none the less still reflects an acceptance that in many instances it is appropriate to work towards an offender's rehabilitation. We noted above, for example, that a condition may be attached to a probation order which requires the offender to undergo treatment for alcohol or drug dependency; and the courts have long recognized that, even for some offenders with a long criminal record, there may be a 'psychological moment' at which a probation order may be effective in dissuading the offender from further criminal behaviour. Apart from the practical considerations of sentencing, however, there are fundamental theoretical and philosophical differences between rehabilitation and other objectives of sentencing which reflect the uncertainties surrounding such questions as why people commit offences, and what are the most appropriate responses by the criminal justice system.

The essence of rehabilitation is that the offender is subjected not to straight-forward punitive measures, but instead to measures intended to reform, treat or cure the 'criminal deviance'. We are not simply referring here to the mentally abnormal offender, diagnosed as suffering from some medically defined mental condition. The rehabilitation view, at its strongest, is that *all* offenders commit crime for some identifiable reason, or some *cause*. It is also important to realize that although some measures are specifically designed for an offender diagnosed as having some medically treatable problem, such as Hospital Orders under the Mental Health Act 1983, it is by no means unknown for a court to pass an indeterminate sentence of imprisonment (that is, a 'life' sentence) designed to allow for the offender's release at some future unspecified date. Release is dependent upon the 'improvement' of the offender's condition, where the offender is not found to fall within the ambit of the Mental Health Act and where the offence indicates none the less that the offender is dangerous to the public. Many have argued that the aim of rehabilitation should be adopted as a general objective on practical and humanitarian grounds, but – leaving aside the current position as reflected in the 1991 legislation – there are considerable practical and theoretical problems with this policy.

The essence of rehabilitation is the assumption that the offender committed the criminal act as a result of some 'cause' which can in some way be countered or treated. If treatment is thus prescribed by the court, it follows that there must be something to treat: this may be diagnosed as a response to social or emotional pressures, or some psychological or psychiatric condition, or even some external causal factor such as the influence of environmental pressures upon the offender's behaviour.

The fundamental problems which such a view raises for the criminal law can be fairly simply stated. Criminal liability in our legal system depends upon the offender's guilt. Guilt, as we saw earlier, is measured in law by means of the doctrine of *mens rea* – did the accused intentionally or recklessly commit the prohibited act? This is turn raises the assumption that, had the offender chosen to do so, he or she *could* have avoided doing the prohibited act; it is the very fact that the accused chose to commit it that makes that person criminally liable. Criminal liability, then, rests upon the assumption that our behaviour is the outcome of our *freedom of will*: we act as we do because we choose to, not because of any compelling or determining factors which dictate our behaviour for us. This 'free will' model of human behaviour is the bedrock of our legal system, and especially the criminal justice system.

Now, if the commission of the offence is said to be the result of *causal factors* such as psychological or environmental pressures, then it cannot be said that the offender *chose* to do the prohibited act. We have no direct control over such pressures, and therefore such behaviour cannot be said to be the result of 'free will'. The rehabilitative ideal, then, is built upon a conception of human behaviour which we may call 'causal' or 'deterministic' as opposed to 'free will', and the contradiction between the legal model and the rehabilitative, deterministic model is clearly seen at the level of the trial. At the conviction stage, the proceedings rest upon the idea of voluntaristic free choice by the accused, but at the sentencing stage, after conviction, the assumption changes if a rehabilitative measure is being considered by the court. Instead of 'freedom of choice', the underlying assumption becomes one of determinism: the view that behaviour is *not* the outcome of free will and free choice, but is caused by factors over which the accused has little or no control. As various writers have pointed out,[93] the main thrust of the social sciences, including psychology and psychiatric theories about crime – which, as Cohen and Clarke stress,[94] have had most effect upon the criminal justice system – is deterministic:

The greater the detail in which circumstances are investigated and the greater the weight that is consequently given to the offender's environment, perhaps going back over many years, the more does the offence appear to be the natural and 'inevitable' outcome of the chain of circumstances so uncovered, and hence the less the apparent responsibility of the offender.[95]

In the courtroom, deterministic influences may appear in the use of psychiatric, probation and social enquiry reports : indeed, some probation officers in particular expressed worries over the Criminal Justice Act 1991, which requires reports to concentrate on the offence; this necessitates a major change in probation practice because, in the past, reports have largely focused on offenders, their backgrounds and their individual problems. At higher, policy-making levels, deterministic influences may become reflected in policies and legislative provisions through the involvement of social scientists concerned with crime – especially criminologists with expertise in psychiatry – in institutions such as the Home Office Research Unit.[96]

The reaction by many lawyers, steeped in the traditional ideas about criminal responsibility and liability, is often one of suspicion and disquiet at the influence in the criminal courtroom, and the penal system generally, of these 'non-lawyers'. Not only is there suspicion about the basis and accuracy of some criminological theory, so much of which has been criticized on empirical or theoretical grounds,[97] but also there is a worry among many lawyers about the degree of discretion placed in the hands of psychiatrists, social workers and others involved in the rehabilitation processes. The lawyer's concern is with the problems of justice and fairness, which are so basic to legal ideology, and as Bean puts it, 'discretionary powers [of the experts] may be essential to rehabilitation, but if used widely they are antithetical to notions of fairness. Rehabilitation deals with personality facets which by their very nature are oblique and not always open to objective assessments.'[98]

The dichotomy between punishment and rehabilitation is, then, far wider and deeper than a concern with merely practical issues. Reflected within it are strong ideological currents and commitments by the experts on both sides of the debate, with paternalism, rehabilitation and discretion on the one side, and a concern for 'due process of law', justice and 'free will' on the other. While the Criminal Justice Act 1991 may represent victory for the 'justice model', history suggests that this Act is unlikely to be the last word on sentencing policy and practice, and we can expect the debates in this area to continue.

Perhaps the root problem is that we know very little indeed about criminal behaviour, and there are many divergent theories and assumptions about crime and the penal system. It is true that very few of the measures introduced by Parliament for dealing with criminal offenders seem to have any lasting effect on the propensities of many offenders. One of the great difficulties with research into crime is the multiplicity of factors which may or may not explain why person X never offends at all, person Y never offends again after receiving a small fine for shoplifting, and person Z appears before the courts time and time again, despite a series of ever-increasing periods in prison. Why do we know so little about criminal behaviour?

Criminology and the criminal justice system

In examining and assessing the study of criminal behaviour – criminology – it is hard to avoid the feeling that not only the answers, but also many of the questions, produced by this area of study are extremely misleading. To understand the complexities in the area, it is essential to grasp the underlying assumptions and the ideological implications on which criminological study has often been based, and to understand the multidisciplinary nature of this area of study.[99] Psychiatrists, psychologists, sociologists, lawyers and even biologists have at one time or another presented theories purporting to 'explain' criminal behaviour, and usually the objective – apparent or latent – underlying much of this body of theory has been an overriding concern with the eradication of crime and how best to achieve it: what has been called the 'correctional' perspective.[100] In this respect, of course, the aim of criminology coincides with the stated aims of lawmakers, law-enforcers and judges.

But in other respects, social science and law diverge. The determinist criminologist, searching for 'causes of crime', cannot accept what the law takes for granted: that an offender need not have acted in the unlawful way, that he or she could have chosen to act otherwise. And if the determinist criminologist is correct, there is neither point nor justification in punishment, which becomes irrelevant. The only consideration is to change, through treatment and/or rehabilitation, those causal factors which 'propel' the offender towards criminal behaviour.

But what are these 'causal factors' which are supposed to precipitate delinquency? The fact is that despite the impressive quantity of research undertaken over the years, and the vast amounts of money and labour utilized to produce it, criminology has so far failed to identify any such 'causes' with any precision or consistency. Psychologists and psychiatrists have claimed to have found the 'causes' in mental illness, personality defects or inadequate socialization;[101] biologists have claimed to have discovered that some crimes are triggered by genetic abnormality;[102] and sociologists have argued that the causes of crime are environmental (slum conditions, economic deprivation, peer-group influence and so on) rather than emanating from 'inside the offender's head'.[103] No convincing confirmation of any of these ideas, many of which (though not all) have been attempts to find '*the*' cause of crime, has yet been established.[104]

Why is criminology in this state, and along what lines might we proceed if we are to come closer to understanding criminal behaviour? Interestingly, it is not criminology which has recently provided new ideas about crime and criminal behaviour, but a body of theory and empirical data which arose from a reaction *against* the assumptions of determinist criminology: the sociology of deviance. Matza provides a useful analytical framework with which to appreciate the problems of study. He has argued that three specific charges may be laid against conventional criminology.[105]

First, says Matza, criminology has concentrated upon the offender rather than the nature of the criminal *law* which symbolizes the division between offender and law-abiding citizen; second, criminology has been based upon a quest for a 'scientific' basis, and for 'laws' about human behaviour; and third, criminology has insisted upon stressing that the offender, having committed an offence, is somehow 'abnormal', or 'different' from the rest of the community.[106]

In recent years, some sociologists have argued that these assumptions are unfounded. Deterministic ideas about human behaviour have been challenged, as have the assumptions about 'scientific method' in the study of criminal behaviour. Human behaviour, argue the critics, is simply not subject to scientific 'laws' in the same way as are, say, gravity or electricity. People *do* make choices; and moreover, the apparent motivation for an action may not necessarily be the real motivation, for people act out of stubbornness, maliciousness and greed while *explaining* their deeds in terms of more acceptable motivations. Arguably there *is* conscious planning of behaviour, and this element of consciousness or *voluntarism* must be taken into account when studying criminal deviance. Thus, Taylor has argued that

we must make certain that the deviant is allowed a say in his own causal story. He does have a special authority over the reasons which led him to behave in a particular way, and to ignore this is indicative of a type of arrogance which has made criminologists at times look more like puppet masters than social scientists.[107]

One example of this is the definition by some criminologists, and of course by many observers and judges, of juvenile violence as 'senseless' or 'irrational'. Some have questioned this definition, arguing that although such violence and aggression may *seem* meaningless in terms of the values and experiences of the observer, it may well have meaning, sense and purpose to the perpetrator. It may represent, for instance, a felt need to assert masculinity or prove toughness among a peer-group,[108] or it may be a manifestation of what have been called 'subterranean values':[109] that is, a correspondence between such 'meaningless acts' and the social values of the dominant adult middle-class groups in society. Thus, within 'delinquent' attitudes may be seen a search for thrills and excitement, a disdain for work and a degree of aggressiveness which have their parallels in middle-class society, with its quest for adventure through leisure pursuits, its lack of attachment to hard work and fondness for the 'soft job', and the general social acceptance of, and even taste for, violence as seen in the apparently insatiable public appetite for aggression in films and television. On this analysis, the aggressive juvenile may appear somewhat less irrational and certainly less alien than the image presented by conventional analyses.

Sociologists of deviance, then, have argued that the deviant person must be recognized not only as having control over his or her own behaviour, but also as having the capacity to invest that behaviour with social meaning, which may not always be apparent to researcher, judge or social worker.

What of the criticism of criminology that it is misleading to regard convicted or apprehended offenders as 'different' from law-abiding people? It has been argued that the distinction between deviant and non-deviant may in many cases be due only to the fact that the person defined by a court as 'deviant' happens to have been caught. How many people regarded as 'normal' and 'law-abiding' have in fact committed offences at one time or another *without* being caught? The use of 'self-report studies' has revealed that most, if not all, of us commit offences at some point in our lives,[110] and one writer comments:

One is not surprised to find that 'self-reporting' studies in which individuals are asked to give (in complete confidence) details of their criminal activities, reveal that many of us have committed an offence serious enough to warrant a jail sentence. What is lacking is some sort of study of the criminal activities and general social awareness of those criminologists who affect surprise at such widespread criminality.[111]

Moreover, some studies reveal similarities between certain behaviour defined as 'against the law' and behaviour which, though not illegal, often has the same type of consequences: 'It is not only labelled vandals who break other people's property, not only professional con-men who con others into believing or parting with something, not only blackmailers who exploit a position of strength . . . [We] need to be alerted to similarities between deviant and normal transactions.'[112] Illustrations might include the practices of debt-collection agencies which, literally, may frighten people into parting with money they may or may not owe;[113] misleading advertisements which persuade people to part with money on the strength of ambiguous and exaggerated claims for their products; and motorists who damage others' property through their inattention to the road. None of these is usually officially labelled 'criminal', but in all these cases the money is none the less lost, the property no less damaged.

Finally, some writers have looked at the crucial factor of 'getting caught', and have opened up enquiries into differences in law-enforcement practices. Not only does it seem that social class, age and racial characteristics may well affect one's chances of attracting police attention and becoming processed through the legal system,[114] but also there is a large amount of what Sutherland[115] called 'white-collar crime' which, even if discovered, often does not result in prosecution and conviction. Sutherland's definition of white-collar crime comprised crimes committed by business corporations, such as tax evasion and monopolistic practices,[116] but other writers have included offences such as the use of office and factory equipment for personal purposes, the taking of articles from the workplace and unauthorized use of employers' telephones and so on. Sutherland and others have argued that this is just as much 'crime' as theft or robbery, but is not usually treated as such for various reasons, such as the high respectability of the perpetrators, the ambiguity or even acceptability with which the community seems to regard such acts, the absence of 'criminal stigma' attaching to both offence and offender, and the degree of differentiation in law-enforcement and prosecution practices.[117]

One conclusion we might draw from the above discussion is that we need to think more carefully about what we understand as 'crime'; Box has argued that the criminal law and its enforcement represents an ideological mystification of the real relations and techniques of social control. By giving prominence to crimes such as murder, rape and robbery, these techniques 'render invisible the vast amount of avoidable harm, injury and deprivation imposed upon the ordinary population by the state, transnational and other corporations'.[118] Box cites the examples of bribing government officials, fraudulent advertising and causing illness or death of workers through wilfully failing to observe safety precautions, and points out that these

deaths, injuries and economic losses caused by corporate acts are not the antics of one or two evil, or mentally disturbed, or relatively deprived senior employees. Rather they represent the rational choices of high-ranking employees, acting in the corporation's interests, to *intend* directly to violate the criminal law or governmental regulations, or to be *indifferent* to the outcome of their action or inaction, even though it might result in human lives obliterated, bodies mangled, or life-savings lost.[119]

Perhaps the lawyer, judge, probation officer or social worker, faced with the practical problems of dealing with individual offenders, dismisses too lightly the problems which these studies and analyses raise. While none of the measures currently available to the courts in sentencing offenders seem particularly successful in either deterring potential offenders or reducing the chances of further crimes by convicted offenders, it is also true that the newer criminological/sociological work on criminal deviance has, as Cohen has put it, shown an 'inability to mount a serious alternative to dominant conservative crime-control policies'.[120] Those policies, says Cohen, are just as firmly entrenched as ever. So, too (more amazingly), are the illusions of conventional, positivist criminology . . . [which] retains its credibility as a science, despite the fact that in terms of its success in explaining, identifying or treating criminals, it should long ago have been relegated to the status of alchemy, astrology or phrenology.[121]

Cohen's comments are indicative of a general realization during the 1980s onwards that by considering the kinds of factor noted above – and especially those analyses which tend to present the offender as some kind of 'victim'[122] – we may be blinded to the social reality of crime, and to its impact upon individuals and the community. The development of agencies such as Rape Crisis Centres and women's refuges, and studies of the *actual* victims of crime – notably the British Crime Surveys in 1982, 1984 and 1988[123] and the Islington Crime Survey in 1986[124] – have reinforced the idea that 'official' statements about crime and criminal offenders cannot simply be dismissed as misleading. The studies have shown that many vulnerable sections of the community – women, ethnic minority groups and the elderly – have a fear of crime which is based on a perfectly rational appreciation of their vulnerability and of the harsh reality of criminal behaviour and its consequences. The heightened awareness in recent years of sexual violence against women, and the physical and sexual abuse of children (not new phenomena, but ones which for many years lay hidden from the public eye) has brought home to many professional and lay people the need to take the necessary steps to protect the victims of violence and abuse: for some professionals working within child-care services, the necessity in many cases for physical removal of the offender from the community has forced them to rethink their previous beliefs that offenders are best treated within the community.

All these factors are an indication of an acceptance among many sociologists and others of the need to 'take crime seriously', and to incorporate the problem within the political agenda. Taylor has argued[125] that crime and its control has long been a central issue in Conservative Party ideology, but that the Labour Party has presented no alternative policies, largely because in the post-war years the social democrats of the left 'insisted that the problems [of rising crime] were temporary, being a product of certain obvious features of wartime conditions and also being open to the ameliorative effects of the programme of social reconstruction that had just been initiated in 1945'.[126] The result of this has been, according to Taylor, that the conservatives have managed to monopolize state policy on crime, law and order. The thrust of Taylor's argument is that the political left should take up this issue and recognize the reality of crime in modern Britain – increased violence in inner-city areas, the increase in the incidence of sexual offences, the burglary rate, and so on.

For whatever the arguments presented by commentators and reformers, it must be remembered that crime, its treatment and control involve important *political* dimensions. The Conservative governments of the 1980s and early 1990s placed 'law and order' high on the agenda and introduced various measures as responses to these problems, such as the Criminal Justice Act 1982, the Police and Criminal Evidence Act 1984 and the Criminal Justice Act 1991.

There is no denying the social, economic and political importance of crime in modern society. In the current uncertainty as to how best to understand and confront the problem, it remains vital, as many of the commentators emphasize, to continue to stress and explore further the connections between crime and the structural conditions of society: what significance has social class, age, sex or ethnic background? What impact does mass unemployment – particularly among the young – have on criminal behaviour? To what extent is the increase in rape and in other sexual offences linked to sexist conventions and practices (the availability of pornography, the persistent oppression of, and violence towards, women in employment, in the media, as parents and so on) within society generally? What of 'street crime' (attacks and robberies on the street)? Is there – as some self-professed 'socialist' commentators would argue – a problem of 'black crime' in the inner cities? Or is this a reflection of racism on the part of the police and within society generally? What about corporate crime and its consequences?

The issues are stark and they demand serious and urgent analysis: given the impact of crime on people's daily lives, it seems worthwhile to ask whether, even if the attempted analysis of criminal behaviour by researchers has so far proved fruitless, it is wise to place faith in politicians whose attitude to poverty, inner-city deprivation, unemployment and homelessness is regarded by many as – to put it mildly – indifferent; or whether to accept as reality the outpourings of a mass media whose standards of integrity and even truthfulness are regarded by many as among the lowest in the world. Understanding crime, and building a rational criminal justice system geared to respond to and deal with the problems generated by crime, depends now more than ever before upon our ability not only to recognize the reality of the problem at the level of individual behaviour and of the experiences of crime by its victims, but also to attempt – as objectively as possible – to locate and analyse it within its social, economic and especially *political* contexts in modern society.

11
The development and role of the contract

The contract is the legal cornerstone of all transactions in business and consumer life. It is the legal device which facilitates *exchange* of goods or services between individuals and groups (such as businesses) in our society, and may be defined as a legally binding agreement between two parties whereby each party undertakes specific obligations or enjoys specific rights, conferred by virtue of that agreement. The expression 'breach of contract' refers to the fact that the agreement is legally binding: if one party fails to honour his or her part of the bargain, then the other can sue, and obtain a remedy through the courts for that breach.

Of course, not every agreement is a legally binding contract. Purely social or domestic agreements, mere requests by one party for information, a series of negotiations between two parties and collective agreements between trade unions and employers have all been held by the judges not to constitute contracts,[1] and the judges have also refused to regard lotteries or football pools transactions as legally enforceable contractual relationships.[2] Regarding social and domestic arrangements, the courts have asserted that the parties to the agreements did not intend to enter into a legal relationship, and this 'intention to create legal relations' is often said to be one of the legal conditions for the formation of a contract. However, as one leading textbook on the law of contract states, 'in commercial agreements it will be presumed that the parties intended to create legal relations and make a contract'.[3] Whether such a presumption is realistic under modern business conditions will be discussed presently, but for the moment it is important to deal with one or two common misconceptions about the legal notion of the contract.

First, it is often supposed that only a *written* agreement can constitute a contract in law. Nothing could be further from the truth. Every time we buy a newspaper, a postage stamp or a packet of washing powder, we make a legally binding contract, which has just as much legal significance as a complex written contract such as an agreement to buy a house or a car, or a hire purchase transaction. Second, it is often believed that a contract is concluded whenever we enter a shop and ask for a specific item. 'The shopkeeper is offering to sell goods,' runs the argument, 'and the customer walks in and accepts that offer.' This fallacy is often heard when an aggrieved customer has been told that the goods in a shop window, for example, arc wrongly priced, and the customer cannot understand why he or she cannot insist on being sold the goods at that (wrongly) marked price.

The reason why no contract exists in this situation lies in the rules of contract themselves. The judges, who have been responsible for developing this part of the law, have distinguished between a genuine *offer* (an essential part of every contract) and an *invitation to treat*.

They have stated on a number of occasions that the acts of placing goods in a shop window, and advertising goods in newspapers, are *not* offers but invitations from the trader to the customer to make the trader an offer to *buy* the goods. Thus, in the leading case of *Pharmaceutical Society of Great Britain* v. *Boots Cash Chemists Ltd* in 1952,[4] the defendants operated a self-service store where, as is usual, customers collected the goods they intended to purchase, and took them to the cash-desk. At the defendants' cash-desk was a registered pharmacist. The Pharmacy and Poisons Act 1933 made it unlawful to sell any specified poison unless 'the sale is effected under the supervision of a registered pharmacist'. The issue for the court was the point at which the 'sale' took place: if it took place when customers put articles from the self-service shelves into their baskets, then there was no supervision by a pharmacist, but if the sale took place at the cash-desk, then there was such supervision. The Court of Appeal decided that the sale took place at the cash-desk, and not before; the presence of the goods on open shelves was in the court's opinion only an invitation to treat, and the customer, by presenting the goods at the cash-desk, was making an offer to buy them.

For this reason, the trader can, perfectly legally at common law, refuse to serve any customer on any grounds. In the realm of consumer contracts, statutory intervention has introduced some restrictions on this right. An example of this is the Trade Descriptions Act 1968, which forbids false or misleading descriptions being attached to goods in, for example, advertisements. Generally, however, the right to refuse service remains.[5] Such a rule clearly operates for the trader's protection, and it has been suggested, by way of justification for the rule, that shopkeepers should be able to favour their regular customers, especially in times of shortages. Against this, however, it might be argued that the principle of 'first come, first served' would be fairer: if shopkeepers present themselves as being in the business of selling goods, they should be held bound to sell items they stock at the prices marked. Atiyah has pointed out[6] that the courts have never discussed questions such as this, though Smith and Street argue that

It would be wrong if a shopkeeper was obliged to sell goods to a man he hated, or a barber to cut the hair of a filthy person merely in because his window display or price list was an offer. Secondly, there would be no opportunity to rectify mistakes and where an article had, by mistake, a ridiculously low price tag, then acceptance would create a very uneconomic situation for sellers, and in supermarkets and department stores could lead to wholesale fraud where unscrupulous buyers switched prices.[7]

This is all very well, but what if an unscrupulous shopkeeper switches prices, or claims untruthfully that an article has been wrongly priced? The real answer, it seems, is that the common law has always been more ready to protect the interests of businesses than those of the ordinary consumer; as we shall see, it has taken a whole series of statutes to create a legal environment of adequate protection for the consumer. Such biases in the law can only be clearly understood by examining the relationship between the law of contract and the economic and political context in which the law was developed.

The contract is, in essence, an exchange of promises. Sometimes the agreement refers to a promise to be fulfilled by one party in the future (an *executory* contract), though more often in everyday contracts the exchange is instantaneous and the contract completed straightaway (as in the case of ordinary purchases in shops): these are called *executed* contracts. The willingness of judges to award remedies for a broken contractual promise dates back to the fifteenth and sixteenth centuries, when a legal action called *assumpsit* was developed to enable a plaintiff suffering loss or damage through the defendant's breach of promise to recover compensation. This writ of *assumpsit* is the basis for the modern law of contract, developed by the judges in the eighteenth and, more particularly, nineteenth centuries. It is only relatively recently that Parliament has intervened in the basic common-law area of contract.

Economically, the last century saw the rapid expansion of trade and industry, bringing increased numbers of commercial disputes, often involving novel complexities. The courts of law were frequently looked to for the solution of such commercial and business disputes. The rules of contract law were not confined to dispute-solving, however; to a large extent, clear rules about commercial agreements meant that people in business could *plan* their activity and enterprises by reference to consistent and certain rules of law. They could calculate and predict the best ways of dealing, of buying and selling, in the knowledge that the rules they adhered to were also binding on those with whom they had business relations. The law of contract, then, was developed in response to the changing needs of business, and this continues to be so in modern society.

So far we have been looking mostly at the development of contract law by way of common law. Generally, in no area of law, especially when developed by the judges, is there a very high degree of clarity or consistency, and the law of contract is no exception. Though some would argue that this allows flexibility, Parliament has stepped into the area of contract law, as it has in many other areas. An early example in the nineteenth century was the Sale of Goods Act 1893 (now re-enacted, with amendments, as the Sale of Goods Act 1979), which was introduced in response to problems arising in the common law of contract. Borrie and Diamond explain that there was 'considerable criticism, notably by businessmen, of the cumbersome and technical shape of the law – of the many volumes of law reports, of varying quality and poorly indexed, in which the law was contained'.[8] The Sale of Goods Act 1893 was designed to codify existing common-law rules, though despite this origin as a codified body of law for the guidance and protection of those in business, it has frequently been used to provide remedies for the consumer, as we shall see later.

The law of contract, then, developed through the cases, was designed as a framework for the solution of disputes and the efficient planning and running of business enterprises. The classical model of the contract as developed by the judges enabled them to disentangle and make sense of agreements which might well have involved long negotiations, complex documentation and ambiguous statements of rights and obligations. The legal model of the contract is characterized by the notion of an agreement between two parties, whose constituent elements (which must always be present if the contract is to be legally recognized as such) are an *offer*, an *acceptance* of that offer, an *intention to create legal relations* (discussed above) and *consideration*.

The phenomena of offer and acceptance are readily understood if we are speaking of agreements, but as we have seen, offers must be distinguished from invitations to treat, and from stages in negotiations where an apparent offer might be interpreted by the court as a mere request for information[9] or as merely one stage in a continuing series of negotiations. It is, for example, established[10] that in cases concerning the sale of land, where the typical transaction is complex and protracted, the courts will not readily hold that a firm offer exists in the absence of very clear evidence to the contrary. Acceptance in the law of contract is best understood by examining, first, what constitutes acceptance of an offer, and second, what constitutes effective communication of that acceptance – for the acceptance of the offer *must* be communicated to the offeror.

Acceptance may be explicitly made by written or oral statements, and such acceptance poses no particular problem. However, acceptance of an offer may be inferred by a party's conduct. In the leading case on this point, *Brogden* v. *Metropolitan Railway Co.* in 1877,[11] Brogden had supplied the railway company with coal for some years without there being any formal agreement between them. They decided to put their business relationship on a formal basis, and the company sent a draft form of agreement to Brogden. He added the name of a person who was to act as arbitrator in the event of a dispute, signed the form and returned it marked 'approved'. Nothing more was done in the matter by either party, though both carried on their business with each other thereafter in accordance with the terms of the draft agreement. When a dispute arose between the parties, Brogden denied that any contract existed between them. The problem here was that raised by a general rule in contract, which stipulates that an acceptance must exactly fit the offer. If the draft agreement sent to Brogden was an offer, then by adding in the name of the arbitrator Brogden had added a new term to that draft, and so by returning it was probably making a new offer to the company, which it was up to the latter to accept, reject or modify. As the company did nothing more about the matter, however, and certainly did not do anything which could be said to constitute explicit acceptance of Brogden's offer, was there at any time an acceptance? The House of Lords held that the acceptance of the offer was constituted by the subsequent conduct of the parties in carrying out their business arrangements in a manner which showed that they both approved the terms of the draft agreement, and that the contract came into existence either when the company ordered its first load of coal from Brogden on these terms, or when Brogden supplied it.

The facts of *Brogden*'s case also illustrate another problem concerning offer and acceptance. As we have said, an acceptance, to be effective in law, must exactly fit the offer rather like two pieces of a jigsaw puzzle which fit each other exactly. If an apparent acceptance did not thus fit the offer, then that apparent acceptance was regarded by the courts as a *counter-offer* whose legal effect was to destroy the original offer. If we take the following statements:

1   'I will sell you my car for £500.'
2   'That's too much. Will you take £400?'
3   'No.'
4   'Very well, then, make it £500.'

and examine them, it looks at first sight as though there is, eventually, a contract. But in law, statement 1 is an offer, which is refused in statement 2. The second statement also contains an offer, however, and this is the *counter-offer* which destroys the original one. In statement 3, that counter-offer is rejected. What, then, is the status of statement 4? It *looks* like an acceptance of the offer in statement 1, but as that offer has been destroyed, it cannot constitute an acceptance of anything! Following the logic of the law of contract, the status of statement 4 is that of *yet another offer*, which may or may not be accepted by the seller of the car. There is no contract in existence in this example.[12]

Moving to the matter of communication of the acceptance: it would be illogical to hold people bound by transactions they know nothing about, and so, although an offer may be made to the whole world,[13] anyone accepting that offer must make that acceptance known to the offeror. It may be that the offeror specifies a particular way in which the acceptance is to be communicated, in which case the acceptor must respond in the manner specified. In many cases, acceptance of an offer will be immediate, by means of spoken words, but most business contracts are made by letter or other posted documents. If acceptance is made by sending a letter by post, the legal rule is that the acceptance is complete as soon as the letter is posted; [14] the same applies to telegrams, but not to telex communication, where the acceptance is complete only when actually received by the offeror.[15] *Mere* silence can never constitute acceptance,[16] though the everyday situation in which we pass a supermarket cashier, paying for our goods and carrying them away without a word being said, is a good example of the cashier's acceptance of our offer to buy the goods (remembering the rule about invitations to treat!) by conduct.

What happens if the offeror has a change of mind and wishes to withdraw the offer? The courts have developed, through the cases, a series of rules covering this situation. First, an offer may be stated to be open for a specified time: it may stipulate, for example, that it is to be open for three days. After that time, if no acceptance is forthcoming, the offer will lapse. If there is no specific period stated, then the offer will normally remain open for a reasonable time. This is, of course, a sensible rule, for if it were otherwise, an offer could theoretically be open for years on end – long after the unwanted car, for instance, had rusted away.

Second, the offeror may wish to take positive steps to indicate the revocation of the offer, in which case the withdrawal of the offer must be communicated to the person to whom it has been made; the revocation must be carried out before the offer has been accepted. In *Byrne* v. *Van Tienhoven* in 1880,[17] an interesting situation arose where the plaintiffs telegraphed their acceptance of the defendants' offer when they received it; unknown to the plaintiffs, however, the defendants had previously posted a letter withdrawing their offer. The court here held that there was a binding contract, because the defendants' withdrawal was not received until after the acceptance had been made – a stricter rule, it will be noted, than the 'postal rule' for acceptance.

The doctrine of *consideration* has long been shrouded in mystique by lawyers and judges, and generations of students have been perplexed by the tortuous language of definitions of the term, such as that in *Currie* v. *Misa* (1875).[18] In this case, 'consideration' was stated to be 'some right, interest, profit or benefit accruing to one party, or some forbearance, detriment, loss or responsibility given, suffered or undertaken by the other'. In essence, consideration encapsulates the idea of the contract as a two-way arrangement, each party giving and receiving something of value, whether of a monetary nature or not. It is this exchange of 'something of value' which constitutes consideration, and the term may thus be thought of as the price paid for goods and services received: such an approach is 'easier to understand, it corresponds more happily to the normal exchange of promises and it emphasises the commercial character of the English contract'.[19]

Usually, the consideration will comprise money or cheques given in exchange for valuable goods or services, but the courts will regard as good consideration anything which they perceive as having value to the parties. Thus, in *Chappell and Co. Ltd* v. *Nestlé Co. Ltd* in 1960,[20] the defendant company offered records of a tune called 'Rockin' Shoes' for the sum of 1s 6d (7½ pence) plus three wrappers from their chocolate bars. The main purpose of this 'special offer' was, of course, to advertise their chocolate, and the wrappers were discarded by the defendants on receipt. The plaintiffs owned the copyright in the tune, and were thus entitled to a royalty payment of 6¼ per cent of the retail price of each record sold. The defendants in fact offered the plaintiffs 6¼ per cent of the sum of 1s 6d, but this was refused, the plaintiffs arguing that the chocolate bar wrappers were also part of the price. The House of Lords accepted this argument, holding that the wrappers were indeed part of the consideration, irrespective of the fact that the defendants threw them away: 'a contracting party can stipulate for what consideration he chooses. A peppercorn does not cease to be good consideration if it is established that the promisee does not like pepper and will throw away the corn'.[21] The rule as usually stated is that 'consideration must be sufficient, but need not be adequate'. What this rather obscure term means is that as long as the courts recognize the consideration as having *some* value to the parties, they will not concern themselves as to whether that consideration in fact reflects the true economic worth of the subject-matter of the bargain. The judges have always insisted that their role is to uphold agreements made voluntarily, and not to enquire into the economic soundness or sense of those agreements. This is why, if A promises to sell B a brand new Rolls-Royce for the sum of one pound, A will be legally bound by that promise, for money is always good consideration, irrespective of whether the amount actually represents the market value of the car.

Through the cases, the judges have evolved a series of rules concerning consideration and its sufficiency in law, and the main rules can now be briefly set out.

Past consideration is insufficient consideration

If my neighbour, while I am away on holiday, decides to do me a good turn by mowing my lawn, and upon my return I gratefully promise to pay her five pounds for what she has done, then she cannot sue me for the money if I fail to pay. This is because, although she may have *hoped* for payment, she did the work without actually discussing payment with me; legally, consideration must be made with an existing bargain in mind. In this example, the 'consideration' is said to be *past*, and is insufficient in law.

Past consideration must, however, be contrasted with *executed* and *executory* consideration, both of which are perfectly valid in law. Executory consideration is given when the parties make an agreement, the completion of which is to be at some point in the future. For instance, X offers to sell his car to Y for £1,200, and Y accepts, promising to pay the money within a week. Here, there is an exchange of promises, both parties agreeing that the exchange will be made at some future point. The consideration here is the promise to pay – it is executory consideration, and is valid in law. The usual example of executed consideration is that of a reward offered for the return of a lost dog. If A offers £5 to anyone who will find and return her lost dog, and B returns the dog to her, B's act is both the acceptance of A's offer and also the requested consideration, and so B can claim payment of the reward.

Can performance of an existing duty be sufficient consideration?

Suppose that A's alleged consideration, in respect of an agreement with B, is in fact something which A is already under an obligation to do. Is this valid consideration? In general, the consideration must contribute to the agreement in some way, and the cases dealing with this point can best be approached from this point of view. It is generally settled that a duty imposed by the general law cannot be good consideration though if a party does *more than* that legal duty, then this may be valid consideration. In *Glasbrook Brothers* v. *Glamorgan County Council* in 1925,[22] a colliery company, threatened by a strike which it was thought might involve violence, approached the police for protection of the mine. The police took the view that a mobile body of officers would be sufficient to protect the mine, but the colliery management wanted a police guard stationed at the mine. The police authorities agreed to provide such a guard for the sum of £2,200. The colliery company refused to pay this sum and, when sued for it, argued that, as the police had done no more than they were legally obliged to do, there was no consideration. The House of Lords held that, while the police were certainly under a public duty to provide protection as far as was necessary, they had in this case done more, by complying with the company's request, than they were legally obliged to do, and had therefore given valid consideration.

The point was illustrated more recently in *Harris* v. *Sheffield United Football Club Ltd*,[23] where the dispute concerned a claim against the football club for payment for the substantial police presence at football matches. The club argued that the police were doing no more than their existing public duty in providing protection and enforcing law and order at football grounds, and that the police were therefore not entitled to payment for this. The court held that the provision of police at the football club during matches went beyond what the club was entitled to have provided in pursuance of their public duties; that the police were under no public duty to protect against the 'mere apprehension' of possible crime; and that therefore the club was obliged to pay for this 'special provision'.

Similarly, in *Ward* v. *Byham* in 1956,[24] an unmarried man and woman entered into an agreement whereby the woman undertook to look after their child in exchange for a payment of £1 a week from the man, on conditions stipulated by the latter that the child would be 'well looked after and happy' and would be 'allowed to decide for herself' whether or not she wished to live with the mother. When the mother married another man, the weekly payments ceased, and she sued for breach of contract. Although it was clear that by virtue of the National Assistance Act 1948 there was an existing legal duty on the mother of an illegitimate child to maintain that child, the Court of Appeal held that the mother had undertaken to do more than her legal duty by agreeing to 'look after the child well' and to allow the child to decide with whom she wanted to live.

Apart from an existing legal duty, however, there are cases where an existing *contractual* duty has been alleged to be good consideration. It has until recently been taken as settled law that if the plaintiff only does what is already required by an existing contract with the defendant, this cannot suffice as consideration for a new agreement. Thus in *Stilk* v. *Myrick* in 1809,[25] the plaintiff was a seaman. In the course of a voyage on which he had worked, two sailors had deserted the ship, and the captain had promised the rest of the crew extra money if they would work the ship short-handed. On failing to receive the extra wages, the plaintiff sued for them. The court held that his claim failed, because he and the rest of the crew were already bound by their original contract to deal with normal emergencies of the voyage, and were doing no more than their existing contractual duty in working the ship back home. The court acknowledged, however, that if they had exceeded their duty, it would have been different.[26]

However, through its decision in *Williams* v. *Roffey Bros and Nicholls (Contractors) Ltd* in 1990,[27] the Court of Appeal has – to say the least – modified this basic proposition. The defendants, who were building contractors, contracted to refurbish a block of 27 flats. They sub-contracted the carpentry work to the plaintiff, the agreed price being £20,000, and the plaintiff was to receive interim payments at reasonable intervals as the carpentry work progressed. After receiving a total of £16,200, the plaintiff ran into financial difficulties, partly because he had not properly supervised his workers, but partly because the carpentry work had been underpriced from the outset. The defendants, who would have been liable under a penalty clause in the main contract if the work was not finished on time, were aware of the plaintiff's circumstances, and they agreed to pay the plaintiff an extra £10,300 to ensure that the carpentry work continued and was duly completed on time. The plaintiff then carried on the work, and duly received one further payment of £1,500. The plaintiff then stopped work on the remaining flats and brought an action against the defendants claiming £10,847.

The case appeared to be – in the words of one of the judges in the Court of

Appeal[28] – 'a classic *Stilk* v. *Myrick* case', in that the new agreement was unsupported by fresh consideration: the plaintiff was to receive extra money for carrying out his existing contractual obligation, while the promisor (the defendant) received no new or additional benefit. Counsel for the defendants conceded that, in practical terms, the defendants obtained the benefits of (i) seeking to ensure that the plaintiff continued work, (ii) avoiding the penalty for delay, and (iii) avoiding the trouble and expense of engaging someone else to complete the carpentry work. However, it was argued for the defendants, these *practical* advantages did not amount to 'additional benefits' in law, since the plaintiff was only promising to do what he was already contracted to do.

However, both Glidewell L.J. and Purchas L.J. denied that the present situation was covered by *Stilk* v. *Myrick*: both referred to the modern concept of economic duress, whereby one party obtains a benefit from the other by taking unfair advantage of the other's difficulties, and suggested that *Stilk* and similar cases might be explained better as examples of economic duress rather than cases turning on the issue of consideration. In the words of Purchas L.J., cases like *Stilk*

involved circumstances of a very special nature, namely the extraordinary conditions existing at the turn of the eighteenth century under which seamen had to serve their contracts of employment on the high seas. There were strong public policy grounds at that time to protect the master and owners of a ship from being held to ransom by disaffected crews. Thus, the decision that the promise to pay extra wages . . . was not supported by consideration is readily understandable.[29]

Glidewell L.J., after discussing the modern notion of economic duress summarized the law as follows:

(i) if A has entered into a contract with B to do work for, or supply goods or services to, B in return for payment by B and (ii) at some stage before A has completed his obligations under the contract B has reason to doubt whether A will, or will be able to, complete his side of the bargain and (iii) B thereupon promises A an additional payment in return for A's promise to perform his contractual obligations on time and (iv) as a result of giving his promise B obtains in practice a benefit, or obviates a disbenefit, and (v) B's promise is not given as a result of economic duress or fraud on the part of A, then (vi) the benefit to B is capable of being consideration for B's promise, so that the promise will be legally binding.[30]

There was no suggestion that economic duress played any part in the facts of the present case, and, that being so, the court had no difficulty in holding that the second agreement was binding in law.

The case is open to comment on a number of grounds, not least that of the reasoning process of the court. It has been suggested that the court may have been 'guided less by technical questions of consideration than by questions of fairness, reasonableness and commercial utility'[31] and that this case, along with other recent cases in contract law, reflects a judicial change of approach which is moving away from analyses based on the technical rules of consideration, towards an approach which fully recognizes, and acts on, the hard commercial reality which motivates parties such as those in *Williams* v. *Roffey Bros*. It remains to be seen how far the courts will extend the reasoning behind the decision in *Williams*; does it matter whether the plaintiff or the defendant initiates the 're-negotiation'? Or whether the modification is positive (that is, promising more money for the same work) or negative (the same money for less work)? As always, we must await future decisions.

A related situation is that in which A pays, or promises to pay, part of a debt already owed by A to B, in return for which B promises to release A from the balance of the debt. The general rule is that B is not bound by that promise, and can sue A for the balance, because A has provided no fresh consideration for the new bargain. Although it has been suggested that this rule should, logically, be modified in the light of *Williams* v. *Roffey*,[32] it has been well-established since *Pinnel*'s case in 1602,[33] and is usually called 'the rule in *Pinnel*'s case'. In order for A to be discharged from the remainder of the debt, it follows that A must provide consideration *other than* mere part-payment of the existing debt. There are a number of ways in which such valid consideration may be provided. A may agree, for example, to pay the smaller sum, at B's request, before the date at which the debt is due, or at a different place; or the part-payment may be accompanied by some other item, given by way of an additional gift, again at B's request. Another situation where the rule in *Pinnel*'s case will not apply is where the amount of the debt to B is in doubt, or is disputed – for here there is the possibility that the part-payment offered by A is in fact more than the full amount actually owed.

It used to be the case that, if the part-payment was made by A by means of a negotiable instrument, such as a cheque, then this was sufficient consideration to discharge the whole debt. The Court of Appeal held in *D. and C. Builders Ltd* v. *Rees* in 1966[34] that 'no sensible distinction can be taken between payment of a lesser sum by cash and payment of it by cheque . . . When honoured, it is actual payment. It is then just the same as cash. If a creditor is not bound when he received a payment by cash, he should not be bound when he received payment by cheque.'[35] Finally at common law, if the part-payment is made by a third party, C, to B, then any action by B against A for the balance will fail.

In equity, there has developed yet another situation in which the rule in *Pinnel*'s case may not apply, and this is known as the doctrine of *promissory estoppel*. In *Hughes* v. *Metropolitan Railway Co.* in 1877,[36] it was said by Lord Cairns that

It is the first principle upon which all Courts of Equity proceed, that if parties who have entered into definite and distinct terms involving certain legal results . . . afterwards by their own acts or with their own consent enter upon a course of negotiations which has the effect of leading one of the parties to suppose that the strict rights arising under the contract will not be enforced or will be kept in suspense or held in abeyance, the person who otherwise might have enforced those rights will not be allowed to enforce them where it would be inequitable, having regard to the dealings which have thus taken place between the parties.[37]

This reasoning was applied in the important case in 1947 of *Central London Property Trust Ltd* v. *High Trees House Ltd*,[38] where the facts were as follows: in 1939, the plaintiffs leased a block of flats to the defendants at an agreed annual rent. In 1940, the plaintiffs agreed to reduce the rent by half because the onset of war had caused many of the flats to become empty, and there was no express time-limit set for the duration of this rent reduction. The defendants paid the reduced rent from 1940 until 1945, by which time the flats were again occupied. The plaintiffs then claimed the *full* rent, both for the immediate future and also for the period 1940–5. Now, applying the rule in *Pinnel*'s case strictly, the plaintiffs would have been entitled to the full amount, for just as we have seen in other cases, the defendants had provided no new consideration for the second agreement in 1940. But Denning J., as he then was, held that the 1940 agreement was intended as a temporary arrangement, and that from 1945 the originally agreed rent should be payable, though the plaintiffs were *not* entitled to claim full back-rent because of the 1940 agreement. The absence of fresh consideration, he thought, did not matter, for the defendants were not seeking to enforce any contract. Applying the doctrine as expounded by Lord Cairns in *Hughes*' case, the court held that the plaintiffs had here made an agreement which led the defendants to rely upon it to the extent of receiving reduced rent from their tenants; the defendants were thus led to suppose that their duties under the original rental agreement were, at least, in abeyance, and it would therefore be inequitable (unfair) to allow the plaintiffs to go back on their agreement of 1940.

The doctrine of promissory estoppel is thus a further exception to the rule in *Pinnel*'s case, though there is judicial and academic agreement that the scope of the doctrine is at present unclear. It seems that the defendant must have acted in reliance upon the promise in order for the doctrine to operate, and that the doctrine can be invoked only as a defence to, and not as the basis for,[39] a claim. Apart from this, there are various aspects of the doctrine which are as yet unsettled, and in the light of *Williams* v. *Roffey* and other cases in which the courts have shown a preparedness to decide issues in the light of economic and commercial reality rather than through appeals to strict legal doctrine, it may be that the whole range of cases dealing with these difficult and technical aspects of consideration may soon be reviewed by the courts.

Consideration must move from the promisee

What this rule really stipulates is that the consideration must be provided by the parties to the agreement themselves, and not by some third party. In the law of contract generally, the doctrine of 'privity of contract' operates to exclude any claim by a person based on a contract to which that person is not a party; in other words, only the parties to a contract can sue on that contract. Thus, if A and B agree that each shall pay £100 to X, and B fails to pay his share, then X cannot sue B for the money, because X, though the beneficiary of the agreement, is not a party to that agreement, and provides no consideration.[40]

Having briefly outlined the legal requirements for a binding contract, we can see that the legal model of the contract, comprising offer, acceptance, consideration and intention to create legal relations, is in essence a conceptual model. Applying the legal idea of the contract to real-life transactions and disputes is thus rather like placing an outline drawing over an original picture, to see how far one corresponds with the other. In this way, the judges have deciphered the intricacies of business transactions, and recast them in terms of what are in essence fairly simple rules of law. Was there a clear offer made by one party to the other? Was that offer accepted by the other party? Was there consideration? Did the parties intend to create a legal relationship between themselves? If the judges can identify these elements, then there is a contract, breach of which will lead to a remedy for the aggrieved party.

From our discussion so far, it may be appreciated that much of the law of contract is based on judicial responses to the practical needs of business and commerce, and this may be said of the courts' recognition that there are some situations where the ordinary rules of contract should not apply. If one party makes a serious mistake, for example, so that she is not in fact getting what she thought she was getting, the contract may be made void by the court in the absence of true agreement as to the subject-matter of the contract. Again, certain categories of person, notably the mentally ill, children and those who enter into contracts while too drunk to appreciate their actions, are recognized as not having full appreciation of the obligations they may be taking on, and so contracts made by such persons may be set aside. In the case of minors, contracts for 'necessaries' (food, clothing, accommodation and employment) will be enforceable against a minor, while other contracts will not. Again, sometimes a contract cannot be fulfilled, not because one party is in breach of the contract, but because of some event outside the control or anticipation of the parties. If I contract to hire a concert-hall for an evening, and the hall burns down through no fault of the owner before the night of the performance, there is nothing left to contract about. Here, the law regards the contract as *frustrated*, and the Law Reform (Frustrated Contracts) Act 1943 provides for the court to try to put the parties back in the same financial position they were in before the contract was made.[41]

It must be acknowledged, however, that there are some aspects of the law of contract which have been criticized. One criticism concerns the fundamental notion of the contract as an *agreement*. In its everyday meaning, the term 'agreement' usually connotes the idea of people putting their heads together and willingly and intentionally coming to an explicit arrangement. In law, however, the approach taken to the phenomenon of agreement is said to be an *objective* one: this means that the judges do not enquire into the innermost thoughts and intentions of the parties, but look rather at the outward appearance of a transaction. If a disinterested onlooker would infer from the parties' words and/or deeds that an agreement exists, then such an agreement *does*, in law, exist, even though this might not have been the subjective intent of one or both of the parties at the time. We will see more of the problems resulting from this approach, especially in the context of consumer contracts, presently.

Another criticism which some commentators (and indeed judges) have levelled at the law of contract is that the conceptual model of the legally binding contract can often be far removed from real-life situations. Atiyah suggests that in some cases 'it may be very difficult, if not impossible, to find a real offer and acceptance or to decide who is the offeror and who the offeree. Such cases show that to insist on the presence of a genuine offer and acceptance in every case is likely to land one in sheer fiction'.[42] According to another critic:

The legal obligation is strictly limited to the promises. These promises are discovered in *the* unvarying method by which human beings contract with each other, namely by means of 'offers' embodying 'promises' directed by 'offerors' to particular 'offerees' who 'accept' by manifesting assent . . . Case variations were hung on the construct like ornaments on a Christmas tree, glittering but essentially useless.[43]

And the view of one member of the House of Lords is that 'English law, having committed itself to a rather technical and schematic doctrine of contract, in application takes a practical approach, often at the cost of forcing the facts to fit uneasily into the marked slots of offer, acceptance, and consideration.'[44]

How much force is there in the view that the legal contractual model is over-rigid and often unrealistic? Undoubtedly, there are many cases where a good deal of judicial ingenuity has been put into the task of establishing the existence of a contract from a set of given facts; and there are areas within the law (such as the scope of promissory estoppel – see above) which are unclear. There are cases, too, where the courts' conclusions that, on given facts, binding contracts exist, seem to us rather odd: an example is *Thompson* v. *L.M.S. Railway*, decided in 1930,[45] which we will examine presently. But as most modern commentators point out,[46] the ideas of offer, acceptance and consideration are not applied in a wholly inflexible manner, and the rules of contract, it has been suggested, 'from their admittedly rigid and out-dated "base-line" . . . shade off towards a more realistic middle ground more in keeping with the merely approximate certainty of business life'.[47] It might also be suggested that the apparent artificiality and rigidity of the rules of contract owe at least as much to the unrealistic assumptions on which they are based as to the judges' attempts to wrap those rules around real commercial situations.

We have already identified the prevailing social and economic philosophy of the nineteenth century as *laisser-faire* individualism, where the affairs of business, employment, trade and manufacture were thought best left to the individuals concerned, with a minimum of state intervention through government police or Parliamentary legislation. The legal counterparts of *laisser-faire* philosophies underlying the law of contract during the period are the twin assumptions of *freedom* and *equality* of contract. In a developing and consolidating capitalist economy, private enterprise and free competition is crucial, and the attitude of judges and legislators was that it was up to the individuals concerned to strike the best bargains they could negotiate. It was certainly not up to the courts or Parliament to repair bad bargains.

The assumptions of freedom and equality of contract, then, are explicable in terms of the economic philosophies of the day: people were assumed to be free to make whatever bargains they wished on the best terms they could get, and everyone was assumed to enjoy equal positions of bargaining-power. As we saw in chapter 1 in the context of employment contracts, by no means everyone in society *did* have such freedom and equality of bargaining-power. Because the judges never accepted a role as rectifiers of bad bargains, all kinds of possibilities for oppressive contractual terms, dictated by the more powerful of the contracting parties, were opened up. The only thing the judges would look at was the *form* which the agreement took – was it a contract? As long as the agreements before them satisfied the legal tests explained above, the details as to price, interest rates or other matters pertaining to the *content* of the contract did not concern them.

Contract and the consumer: the exclusion clause problem

As far as the ordinary customer, forced by everyday necessity into contracts with traders and companies of all kinds, was concerned, there was no recognition of unequal bargaining-power, nor any conception of consumer protection through Parliamentary legislation. Indeed, 'the idea that the state on behalf of the community should intervene to dictate or alter terms of contracts in the public interest is, on the whole, alien to the classical theory of common-law contract'.[48]

Now, the law of contract differs from other areas of law such as criminal or tort law, in that the obligations imposed through a contract are *self-imposed* obligations, supposedly entered into freely by the parties. Crime and tort do not contain any idea of self-imposed obligation, but rather comprise obligations imposed upon everyone by the state. Because of this feature of contract, and because of the determination of the judges to uphold the principles of contractual freedom, it was, in theory and in practice, possible to write virtually any term into a contract, even to the extent of providing for the *exempting of one party from any legal liability* if certain breaches should take place. Most of us have seen examples of these *exclusion clauses* in hotels ('The management accepts no responsibility for loss or damage to guests' property howsoever caused') and in contracts for the hire of machinery ('No liability is accepted in respect of any damage caused to the hirer or his property by this machine'). On bus or train tickets there usually appear such words as 'Issued subject to the terms and conditions of the Blankshire Transport Authority'. If we were to examine those terms and conditions, we would find numerous clauses exempting the authority or company from liability for loss caused by, for example, delayed or cancelled buses or trains, or loss of or damage to passengers' property over a certain financial limit. The effect of such clauses is clear: if we attempt to sue for loss caused by, say, a cancelled train leading to a missed appointment, we would find ourselves unable to recover compensation because the company has explicitly exempted itself from such legal liability.

The courts' attitude to such clauses in contracts has been somewhat ambiguous. In line with the assumptions underlying the law of contract, the judges have on the whole accepted that such clauses are perfectly legal and enforceable (the reasoning being that, assuming freedom of contract, consumers disliking such clauses could always take their business elsewhere). At the same time, however, they recognized, through cases coming before them, the possibilities for oppressive and exploitative treatment of consumers by traders in stronger bargaining positions, so that they adopted a strict manner of interpreting such clauses, with ambiguities being resolved in the consumer's favour.

There are, nevertheless, many examples of cases where the judges have interpreted exclusion clauses in such a way as to produce what might be thought unfair, and sometimes fantastic, results. In *Thompson* v. *London, Midland and Scottish Railway Co.* (1930), [49] for example, Mrs Thompson bought an excursion railway ticket. On the ticket were printed the words 'for conditions see back', and on the back of the ticket were the words 'Issued subject to the conditions and regulations in the company's timetables and notices and excursion and other bills'. On such notices were words to the effect that excursion tickets were issued subject to the conditions in the timetables, which could be purchased at the station for 6d (2½ pence). Had Mrs Thompson read these conditions, she would have found, among other 'small print' clauses, the condition: 'Excursion tickets . . . are issued subject to . . . the conditions that neither the holders nor any other person shall have any right of action against the company . . . in respect of . . . injury . . . loss, damage or delay, however caused.' On her return from the excursion, Mrs Thompson fell when getting off the train, because of the negligence of an employee of the railway company, and was injured. She claimed compensation for her injury, but the Court of Appeal dismissed her claim on the ground that she had *agreed* to the clause in the timetable, and had therefore lost her right to sue. 'She had not read the ticket or the timetable, but she had "agreed" to the condition by accepting the ticket which drew her attention to it, devious though the treasure-hunt was.'[50] The case is all the more surprising when we consider that, as a matter of fact, Mrs Thompson could not have appreciated the exclusion clause even if she had found it because *she could not read!* (It is now provided, by virtue of the Unfair Contract Terms Act 1977, that any exclusion clause which purports to 'exclude or restrict' liability for 'death or personal injury resulting from negligence' is of no legal effect.)

But in *Thompson*'s case, how could the court maintain, in the circumstances, that the plaintiff had 'agreed' to the condition? The answer is, as we have already seen, that the courts, though desirous of giving effect to the wishes of the contracting parties, look to the objective, outward appearances of the transaction. In the court's view, Mrs Thompson had indicated her agreement by accepting the ticket, and the only relevant additional consideration was whether the railway company had taken reasonable steps to bring the clause to passengers' attention – it would clearly be absurd and unjust to hold a person bound by contractual terms, the existence of which the party had no chance whatsoever of knowing. In the above case, the court held that the company *had*, by the various pointers on tickets and notices, taken reasonable steps to bring its conditions to travellers' attention.

These days, it is true, the courts have tended to take a somewhat more realistic view. In *Thornton* v. *Shoe Lane Parking Ltd* in 1971,[51] the plaintiff went to park his car in the defendants' car-park. Outside the car-park, a sign listed the parking charges, and stated that cars were parked there 'at owners' risk'. As the plaintiff drove to the entrance, the automatic barrier rose, a ticket was ejected from a machine and a light turned from red to green. The plaintiff took the ticket and drove into the car-park. Upon the ticket was printed, among other things, a statement to the effect that the ticket was issued subject to conditions displayed on the car-park premises. These conditions were in fact displayed at various places, but were not visible to drivers as they entered the car-park. Indeed, drivers would have had to walk around the car-park in order to locate the displays. One of these conditions purported to exclude the defendants' liability for damage to cars and also for injury to customers. On returning to pick up his car, the plaintiff was injured in an accident. The defendants subsequently sought to rely on the condition exempting them from liability. In the Court of Appeal, Lord Denning had no doubt that in this case, given the all-embracing nature of the exclusion clause, there was insufficient notice given by the defendants to the plaintiff. Indeed, in his Lordship's opinion, 'in order to give sufficient notice' of so wide a clause, 'it would need to be printed in red ink with a red hand pointing to it, or something equally startling'.[52] Megaw L.J. pointed out that the first attempt to bring the conditions to the plaintiff's attention was at a time when

as a matter of hard reality it would have been practically impossible for him to withdraw from his intended entry on the premises ... It does not take much imagination to picture the indignation of the defendants if their potential customers, having taken their tickets and observed the reference therein to contractual conditions ... were one after the other to get out of their cars, leaving the cars blocking the entrances to the garage, in order to search for, find and peruse the notices![53]

The plaintiff's claim succeeded.

The common-law approach is illustrated further by the rule that if a person *signs* a document, then that person is bound by the clauses contained therein, whether he or she has read them or not.[54] The judges, in line with their general views on contractual equality and freedom of choice, have taken the attitude that if someone signs a document without reading it, then he has only himself to blame for the consequences. The common-law position has been changed by the Unfair Contract Terms Act 1977, which provides that in consumer contracts for the sale and supply of goods, all exclusion clauses are of no legal effect (see below). A 'consumer sale' is one where (i) the goods are sold in the course of a business, (ii) the goods are not bought in the course of a business, and (iii) the goods are of a type normally bought for private use or consumption. If any of these conditions are not met, the transaction is regarded as a 'non-consumer sale', and exclusion clauses in such transactions will be valid only if the court holds that they are 'fair and reasonable'.[55]

The problems raised by these common-law rules for ordinary consumers were clear. First, if consumers wished to travel by rail, to have laundry cleaned by a cleaning company, to buy goods on hire-purchase, to buy a second-hand car or to have a television repaired, they were at the mercy of the traders concerned and their contractual exclusion clauses. As far as the reality of contractual freedom and equality were concerned, the only real choice was to take it or leave it. The consumer was in no position to negotiate with, for instance, a railway clerk or car-dealer over terms. The imbalance of bargaining-power between traders and consumers was a basic fact of commercial life.

The situation for the consumer was worsened by the development of *standard-form contracts*: 'Their terms are set out in printed forms which are used for all contracts of the same kind, and are only varied so far as the circumstances of each contract require. Such terms are often settled by a trade association for use by its members for contracting with each other or with members of the outside public.'[56]

Such contracts may save time, but they may also put the consumer at a disadvantage. There are a huge number of trade associations, ranging from the Association of British Launderers and Cleaners and the British Carpet Manufacturers Association, to the Motor Agents Association and the National Association of Shoe Repair Factories, and it is highly probable that the consumer will be faced with exactly the same terms, *whichever* laundry, car or carpet retailer or shoe repairer is approached. If the supplier is in a monopoly position, as is British Rail, for example, the bargaining position of the consumer is even weaker: once again we see the consumer's real 'freedom of choice' – 'take it or leave it'.

While it is true that the judges have proved incapable, through their conservatism and the inflexibility of their common-law techniques, of providing adequate protection for the consumer, their concern for justice has led them, in cases of clear oppression or exploitation, to adopt interpretative techniques and doctrines of law enabling them to avoid giving effect to the grosser forms of exclusion clause. The narrowness with which judges have interpreted such clauses, for example, has meant that in many cases traders were prevented from hiding behind ambiguous escape clauses,[57] especially where the problem concerned *implied* terms – that is, *implied by law* into a contract without any *express* agreement by the parties. The Sale of Goods Act, as originally enacted in 1893, provided for the inclusion into every contract for the sale of goods of certain implied terms regarding the *fitness of the goods sold for their purpose* (provided that the purpose was made known to the trader) and the *merchantable quality* of those goods, and the Act proved a useful weapon on the side of the consumer, despite the provision in the Act that these terms could be expressly excluded.[58] Hair dye which made the user's hair fall out would be unfit for its purpose; a new car with a bad scratch would not be of merchantable quality (even though 'fit for its purpose' inasmuch as it was mechanically sound). Compensation would be recoverable in both cases for breach of the implied terms, unless an exclusion clause provided to the contrary.

At common law, the judges' invention of the doctrine of 'fundamental breach' of contract, involving the presumption that the trader could not sensibly be taken to have intended to exclude liability for breach of the fundamental promise in the contract,[59] also proved valuable in the continuing struggle against the imbalance of bargaining-power. But despite such developments, the problem of contractual 'freedom' has remained: 'Though in various ways the courts have been willing and able to do battle on behalf of the consumer against the supplier of goods and services, they have made it more difficult for themselves to wage this battle effectively by their reluctance to overthrow the fiction of contract.'[60]

State intervention: the solution to the consumer problem?

This enormous gap between the theory of contractual freedom and equality, and the reality of modern consumer transactions, has been bridged only relatively recently by state intervention through consumer protection legislation and, to an extent, by an increased sense of 'consumer awareness' by many trading concerns.

By the mid-twentieth century, concern over the relative lack of protection afforded to the consumer at common law resulted in the emergence of vociferous consumer protection lobbies. There are various reasons for the emergence of such lobbies at this time. Generally, there had been an economic boom during the 1950s, and the widespread availability of mass-produced expensive consumer goods such as cars, televisions and other domestic items brought the ordinary consumer into contact with hire-purchase, standard-form contracts, and transactions involving 'small print' clauses on an unprecedented scale. Furthermore, 'coupled with this came a variety of new foods, firstly in cans and bottles, but later frozen or fast dried, and of other goods such as detergents and fabrics. The introduction of such items itself brought about greater demands and advertising began to make considerable impact on the population.'[61] There were specific areas of concern, such as high-pressure sales techniques imported largely from America, product safety and reliability, and misleading descriptions of goods and services. A notorious example of the latter was the use of 'small print' exclusion clauses in holiday brochures and booking forms which prevented disappointed holiday-makers from obtaining effective legal redress even when the services were not provided.

There were, of course, a number of statutory and common-law provisions which even before these developments did constitute protection and/or redress for the consumer in certain cases. Various statutes and regulations governed weights and measures, and standards of hygiene and purity in the sale of food and drugs. The Sale of Goods Act and the important Hire Purchase Act of 1938 provided important, if limited, protection for the consumer; and at common law, the landmark decision of the House of Lords in *Donoghue* v. *Stevenson* in 1932 had paved the way for a series of cases brought in negligence (see chapter 9), where compensation could be recovered by a plaintiff who had suffered loss or damage as a result of negligence on the part of a manufacturer, repairer or supplier of faulty goods.[62] An action in negligence could not be brought, however, unless there had been loss or injury, and so this action was ruled out in cases where goods had proved faulty but no damage had ensued. In the case of goods which were intrinsically dangerous, such as guns, it was settled as early as 1837 in *Langridge* v. *Levy*[63] that the seller could be liable for injuries resulting from defects in those articles.

Apart from these fairly limited cases, however, the private-law framework of contract, involving exclusion clauses and standard-form contracts, prevailed, even though it was increasingly clear that these provisions were inadequate and frequently unfair in their operation in a new affluent consumer society. The impact, then, of campaigning bodies such as the Consumers' Association (publishers of *Which?* magazine) in Britain, and individuals like Ralph Nader in the United States, is a good indicator of the extent to which matters hitherto left to private law were becoming an important and urgent *public* concern. The major political parties soon pledged their support for measures designed to protect the consumer, and indeed the steady stream of 'consumer protection' statutes, mostly passed since the early 1960s, has been the outcome of various governments' legislative programmes.

When considering legislation designed to protect the consumer, it is important to bear in mind that, although the majority of statutes affect the contractual relationship between consumers and traders, some legislation, such as the Trade Descriptions Act 1968 and the Food Safety Act 1992, imposes *criminal liability* on retailers and manufacturers (see chapter 10), while other statutory provisions, such as those concerning the liability of producers for injury caused by defective products contained in the Consumer Protection Act 1987 (see chapter 9), affect the pre-existing position in the law of *tort*. In what ways has Parliament provided protections and remedies for the consumer through modern legislation?

Consumer protection legislation: some examples

Hire-purchase and consumer credit

'A county court judge is credited with the remark that hire purchase consists in being persuaded by a man you don't know to sign an agreement you don't read to buy furniture you don't want with money you haven't got.'[64] More precisely, under a hire-purchase agreement, the consumer enters into a contract whereby the goods are *hired* from the trader by the customer, who then pays a series of instalments which are technically payments for this hire. On payment of the final instalment, the customer exercises his or her *option to purchase* the goods, and only then becomes the legal owner.

Hire-purchase agreements are distinct from other similar types of consumer credit transaction, of which the most noteworthy are credit sale agreements (where the buyer becomes the owner of the goods immediately, though still paying for them by instalments) and conditional sale agreements (where the goods are paid for by instalments, the buyer not becoming the owner until a specified condition, usually the payment of the last instalment, is fulfilled). It must also be noted that although, in many such transactions, the credit agreement will be between the customer and the dealer, a very common variation on this theme is for the credit contract to be made between the customer and a *finance company*: on choosing the goods, the customer here enters into a hire-purchase contract with the finance company, and the dealer sells the goods directly to that company for cash. The finance company then becomes the legal owner, and all obligations arising under the hire-purchase contract are between the finance company and the customer. We shall see later that the customer's legal rights against the dealer, in the event of the goods proving to be defective, are unaffected; but for the moment, let us continue to concentrate on the nature of the credit agreement itself, and to address the question of why these agreements have caused so much trouble to many consumers.

The attraction of hire-purchase in a consumer society is that it enables the consumer to enjoy the goods immediately, while paying for them over a period of time, and is thus for many people a means of acquiring expensive goods which they could not otherwise afford. The arrangement was not, however, without its drawbacks for the consumer. To begin with, the use by some companies of door-to-door sales-people, trained in high-pressure sales techniques

techniques of subtle and not-so-subtle persuasion, led to situations like that quoted above; often, the customer was pressured into signing a contractual document, frequently without reading its small print clauses (which would probably be incomprehensible to all but a trained lawyer anyway) and without realizing that substantial legal obligations were being taken on. It was all very well for MacKinnon L.J., faced with a typical hire-purchase contract, to remark in 1938 that 'if anybody is so foolish as to enter into an agreement such as this, I do not know that his case can be considered harsh', but this attitude ignores the realities of modern sales and advertising techniques. By and large, there was no reason at common law why a trader could not impose, through a hire-purchase contract, onerous and oppressive terms on the customer while protecting his own interests through exclusion clauses. An example was the notorious 'snatch-back' or repossession clause found in many such contracts, whereby the trader could, on default by the customer in paying an instalment on time, take the goods immediately, despite the fact that the customer may have defaulted on the twenty-third of twenty-four payments, all previous instalments having been paid punctually. Here, the customer was left with nothing, and the trader could sell or re-hire the goods to someone else.

To attempt to overcome these problems, at least in so far as they have arisen from hire-purchase agreements, a number of statutes have been enacted. The most noteworthy of these, the Hire Purchase Act 1965, brought together and consolidated previous legislation in this area, and provided important protection for the hire-purchase customer. The 1965 Act has, however, now been superseded by the more wide-ranging Consumer Credit Act 1974, which was largely based on the recommendations of the Crowther Committee on Consumer Credit, whose report was published in 1971.[65] This report recognized that, in practice, there is little difference between hire-purchase, credit sale and conditional sale transactions, and so the Consumer Credit Act regulates *all* 'consumer credit agreements' as defined in s.8 of the Act. Such an agreement is one where an *individual* (that is, not a corporate body such as a company) enters into an agreement with *any other person* (that is, a dealer, finance company or any other agency dealing in credit), which involves the latter providing the former with credit not exceeding £15,000. Note that the Act fixes the maximum amount of *credit* involved in a consumer credit agreement, and not the maximum price of *goods*; so that, for example, if a person wishes to buy, on credit, a car costing £16,000, and enters into an agreement which specifies that a credit charge of £1,500 is payable in addition to the cash price of the car, then if the customer puts down £3,000 as a cash deposit, the transaction will be covered by the Act, although the total price of the car is in fact £17,500.

The main protections afforded by the Consumer Credit Act to the consumer entering into a hire-purchase or other consumer credit transaction are as follows. First, the Act follows the provisions of the Hire Purchase Act 1965 in ending the practice of 'snatching back' the goods, though naturally the 1974 provision extends beyond hire-purchase to cover all consumer credit deals. Essentially, once one-third of the total price has been paid by the customer, the creditor cannot repossess the goods in the event of the customer's default, except through a county court order – and this will be given only after the customer has been allowed more time to pay up (s.90). Second, the problem of the doorstep sales technique is tackled by ss.67–73, the effect of which is that if the customer enters into a consumer credit agreement anywhere other than on trade premises (for example, in his or own home, as opposed to a shop or showroom), then the customer is given a 'cooling off' period of five days after the final agreement is signed in which to cancel the agreement without incurring any liability whatsoever. Once the agreement is thus cancelled (by means of a written notice to the creditor/dealer), the customer is entitled to the return of any money paid, and the creditor is similarly entitled to the return of the goods.

Naturally, the protections provided by the Act are not all one-sided: the creditor-dealer, it is recognized, may in some circumstances stand to lose on the transaction, and this is especially true if the customer simply terminates the contract at some point. The agreement may be terminated by the customer at any time during the period of the agreement, in which case the goods taken back by the creditor will, of course, have become second-hand and will probably have depreciated somewhat in value. To try to recompense the creditor in such circumstances, the Consumer Credit Act (re-enacted and widening the provisions of the 1965 Act) provides in s.99 that, on termination by the customer, all payments due up to the point of termination are payable; and if these sums amount to less than *half* of the total price of the goods, then the customer must pay additional sums so that 50 per cent of the total price is paid (s.100). This section also provides that this rule is variable by the agreement itself specifying a smaller sum; or if the court considers that a smaller sum would adequately compensate the creditor, that court may order that such a smaller sum be paid.

Further, the problem of technical small print coupled with consumer ignorance is tackled by the 1974 Act (again, following the provisions of earlier legislation). Sections 60–4 of the Act provide, among other things, that the Secretary of State may, by regulations, specify the form and content of documents embodying regulated agreements 'with a view to ensuring that the debtor or hirer is made aware of' (s.60) the rights and duties arising under the agreement and the protections and remedies available under the Act. Documents whereby such agreements are executed must contain all pertinent terms, readily legible, and must be signed by both parties to the agreement (s.61). Copies of the agreement must be given to the customer (ss.62–3); and, by s.64, in the case of a cancellable agreement (see above) the prescribed form must contain notice as to the right to cancel.

The Consumer Credit Act sets out to regulate not only such consumer credit transactions as hire-purchase, but also virtually all other situations in which credit facilities are made available to the consumer. There are many other ways, apart from hire-purchase, of obtaining credit, such as personal accounts schemes operated by individual stores; credit cards such as Access and Barclaycard; bank loans, and overdraft facilities. Invariably, just as with hire-purchase, the consumer using such schemes will pay more, in the form of interest charged by the scheme's operators. Although most credit schemes (and certainly all of the well-known ones) are highly scrupulous in their dealings with the public, there are other less prominent and more suspect operators of credit deals. The Consumer

Credit Act imposes stringent requirements on all traders and others who offer goods or services on credit. The objective behind the Act is 'truth in lending', and all those in the 'credit industry' are required to obtain a licence from the Director General of Fair Trading (who may take away that licence for malpractice: see Part III of the Act). In addition, the Act provides for such matters as the disclosure to customers of true rates of interest (s.20); prohibitions on canvassing for trade by credit brokers and debt counsellors off their trade premises (ss.48–9), sending to minors any circular inviting them to gain credit (s.50), or giving unsolicited credit cards (s.51); and the general control of all credit transactions such as bank overdrafts, budget accounts, credit cards and so on.

The Consumer Credit Act is an important and wide-ranging measure, in many ways reflecting the socio-economic realities of modern consumer credit deals. It cannot, however, prevent the many cases of hardship experienced by people who, having entered into credit deals, find themselves, by reason of redundancy or other unanticipated change in circumstances, unable to make the payments which the credit agreements require. Moreover, the Act is extremely complex, which raises a further major problem: despite the various statutory provisions containing protections and remedies for aggrieved consumers, their efficiency depends ultimately upon consumer awareness of the rights and remedies involved. We shall say more about this problem presently.

Exclusion clauses in contracts for goods and services

The common-law position regarding exclusion clauses in consumer contracts for goods and services has been significantly changed by a number of statutes. The original Sale of Goods Act 1893 contained provision, as we saw above, for the inclusion in any contract for sale of goods, of a series of *implied terms* as to fitness for purpose and merchantable quality. Additionally, the Act provided that if the sale was by description (for example, the sale of a car advertised as being a 1990 Ford, or a store selling a table marked 'pine') then there was an implied condition that the goods would in fact correspond to that description; and a similiar implied condition that goods sold on the basis of a sample would correspond to that sample.

Two important points must be made about the 1893 Act. First, these implied conditions (breach of which entitled the aggrieved buyer to repudiate the contract) could be explicitly excluded by the seller; and second, the Act applied to the sale of *goods*, and not the supply of *services*. Thus, if a court held that a contract was for services, and not for the sale of goods, then the consumer was unprotected by any of the implied terms. The provisions as to implied terms in the 1893 Act have been re-enacted in the Sale of Goods Act 1979, but this Act must be read in the light of the important provisions of the Supply of Goods (Implied Terms) Act 1973, and the Unfair Contract Terms Act 1977. As to the supply of services: the Supply of Goods and Services Act 1982 provides that in contracts for services, there are implied terms[66] that the supplier will use reasonable care and skill in carrying out the service, and that the service will be carried out within a reasonable time and at a reasonable price. Further, where the contract also involves the transfer of property to the customer (as where a garage repairs a car's brakes, and in doing so fits new brake linings) then the implied terms as to fitness for purpose, merchantable quality, title, description and sample, contained in the Sale of Goods Act 1979, apply.

The overall effect of the Supply of Goods (Implied Terms) Act 1973 and the Unfair Contract Terms Act 1977 is that in consumer contracts (defined above), *none* of the above implied terms in contracts for goods or services can be excluded. In addition, the 1977 Act provides that no exclusion clause may restrict or exclude liability for death or personal injury arising from negligence, and that any clause excluding liability for other loss arising from negligence may only be valid if, in the opinion of the court, it is reasonable in the circumstances. Furthermore, any insertion by a trader into a consumer contract of any term which purports to exclude liability for breach of the implied terms, is now a criminal offence by virtue of subordinate legislation under the authority of the Fair Trading Act 1973.[67] Finally, there is in the 1977 Act a wide power enabling courts to declare invalid any clause in standard-form contracts, where a trader attempts to exclude liability for a breach of contract, or where a trader tries to provide a different service from that specified in the original contract, thus preventing traders from substituting one service or article for that originally contracted for. The extent to which the courts will use this power effectively remains to be seen as and when cases are brought before the courts.

There is no doubt that these statutes, taken together, constitute an important reform of the law regarding exclusion clauses in consumer contracts, although it may still be the case that the general ignorance of what remains a very complex area of law results in the Acts being of limited use as a means of protecting the consumer. It is known, for instance, that shop assistants may misrepresent customers' rights when faced with customer complaints; a customer bringing faulty goods back to the shop may be told that the fault must be dealt with through direct communication with the manufacturer, or that the fault is simply 'not the shop's responsibility'. This is, of course, incorrect: the effect of the legislation has been to place the responsibility for defective goods firmly and squarely on the shoulders of the *retailer*. Even where a retailer admits responsibility, the customer may be told that he or she must accept a credit note, rather than a cash refund. This, obviously, is in the trader's interest, as a credit note may be redeemed at that shop only, and no other. In fact, the customer can insist upon a cash refund; but here again, consumers' ignorance of their legal rights may serve to neutralize any real benefits conferred upon them by legislation. To take an extreme case: suppose a contractual document such as an order form or guarantee *does* contain clauses purporting to exclude liability for implied terms. Is it realistic to expect the average consumer to appreciate that the clause is invalid by virtue of the Unfair Contract Terms Act? Arguably, the mysteries of consumer protection legislation are largely outside the ordinary person's experience, and it would be naive to believe that consumers are, in general, aware of the rights and protections conferred upon them by what, after all, are technical and complex legislative enactments.

Misrepresentation

A misrepresentation is, in law, a false statement of fact (as opposed to a statement of opinion, belief or law) made by one contracting party which induces the other party to enter into the contract. A misrepresentation is, then, 'pre-contractual': it takes place before the contract is entered into. It may well be that the contents of the statement do not subsequently become incorporated into the terms of the contract, and so the victim will not be able to sue for breach of the contract itself. The Misrepresentation Act 1967 provides remedies for the person who falls victim to such false statements of fact, whether made fraudulently, negligently or innocently. A statement in a holiday brochure that a hotel is 'two minutes from the sea', or a business offered for sale and stated by the seller to be 'worth £15,000 a year', will amount to misrepresentations if they are false, and if the other party is induced by them to make the contract. In cases where misrepresentation is established, the aggrieved party will have private-law remedies of compensation and/or the right to terminate (or 'rescind') the contract, depending on the circumstances of the case and the kind of misrepresentation involved.

Criminal liability

As noted already, various statutes govern such matters as weights and measures, and purity in the preparation and sale of food and drugs. This legislation is administered by local authority departments, and breach of any of the regulations by any trader, or any person involved in the preparation of food and drugs, may result in a criminal prosecution.

Apart from these provisions, the Trade Descriptions Act 1968 makes it a criminal offence to apply a false trade description to any goods or services. A trader who holds out for sale a refrigerator, for example, bearing the sign 'reconditioned', will be guilty of an offence if the article is not, in fact, reconditioned; as will a car-dealer who says that a second-hand car has only covered 30,000 miles when in fact it has been run for 130,000. Note also that the powers of Criminal Courts Act 1973[68] provides that those convicted of offences under the 1968 Act (among others) may be ordered to pay compensation to any person who has suffered loss as a result of a false trade description, or as a result of a food and drugs offence.

Is the consumer now adequately protected through legislation?

Various points may be made about the current legal provision for consumer protection. First, it must be remembered that none of the consumer protection measures, whether substantive statutes or regulations made under empowering statutes, makes any changes in the fundamental common-law notion of the contract. The contract remains the 'bridge' between trader and customer; what has happened is that some of the common-law assumptions about contractual agreements, notably equality of bargaining-power and freedom of contract, have been seen to be misconceived, with the result that the most oppressive manifestations of the traditional judicial approach to contract – mainly exclusion clauses which unfairly protect one party at the expense of the other – have been modified or forbidden.

The net result for the consumer, therefore, is that although the opportunities for legal redress have been considerably extended, the precise forms of legal action through which remedies may be obtained have remained the same as they were a hundred years ago. The private-law action appropriate for most consumer grievances is still breach of contract, whether the breach is of an express contractual term, or one of the terms implied by statute.

This must lead us to consider problems such as consumers' ignorance of their legal rights, and the difficulties they face in seeking redress. The aggrieved person must first be aware that he or she *has* a possible remedy in law: legal advice in consumer matters may not be easily obtained, especially when we consider that a full county court action may be out of the question, although of course it may well be that an action through the 'small claims' procedure (see chapter 6) will be appropriate in many cases.

Connected with this is a second major problem. Because consumer protection legislation has been grafted on to the foundation-stone of contract, the technicalities in this area of law are considerable. Even now, a contractual document such as a hire-purchase contract or an insurance proposal form, though containing terms which are perfectly lawful, will invariably contain phrases and expressions which have technical legal meaning, and which most consumers will not easily understand. It is not a simple matter for a person with no legal training to appreciate distinctions between express and implied terms, or to grasp the different legal consequences which various kinds of misrepresentation may have. For many consumers, taking action in a dispute may be seen as being more trouble than the goods are worth. However much consumer rights may be publicized, through the media and information published by the Office of Fair Trading or Citizens' Advice Bureaux, the complexities involved in ascertaining the parties' rights in a contractual dispute may deter all but the most dogged consumer from pursuing what may be a good legal case through to its conclusion.

But what other means of redress are available to an aggrieved consumer? Probably the only effective alternative to some form of legal action is the voluntary provision by many trade associations of codes of practice, which are encouraged and approved by the Office of Fair Trading.[69] Such codes, introduced by organizations including the Association of British Travel Agents, the Association of Manufacturers of Domestic Electrical Appliances, the Motor Agents Association and the Association of British Launderers and Cleaners, usually make provision for clear statements by their members of prices and descriptions of goods and services, spare parts to be kept in stock, complaints to be dealt with promptly, and a conciliation and arbitration procedure if the dispute cannot be settled amicably.

Such codes of practice are examples of 'business self-regulation', the businesses involved wishing to foster good consumer relations (most of us would return to a shop which handled our complaint efficiently and fairly) and to show what

Cranston has called 'good corporate citizenship'.[70] Such schemes are not without their critics. Like the Advertising Standards Authority, these codes and standards are operated by the industries themselves, and it may be argued that they are hardly likely to be wholly impartial when their own interests are at stake. Moreover, not every trading concern belongs to a trade association, and these will not be subject to that association's code; it may well be that it is precisely this type of business whose practices are most suspect. Consideration of such arguments leads Cranston to conclude that 'businesses support self-regulation and are prepared to allocate resources to it if it forestalls legal control and reaps goodwill. Should it threaten to impinge on profits, however, many will ignore it'.[71] Be this as it may, it is probably true to say that many consumers have benefited from such codes of practice in cases in which they would almost certainly not have taken the problem to a legal agency for solution. The practical problems facing consumers with disputes which have slipped through the preventative net of consumer protection legislation must lead us back to the statement by the Molony Committee on Consumer Protection in 1962:[72] 'The consumer's first safeguard must always be an alert and questioning attitude.' Despite the reforms of the law through statutory provision, this seems still to be the best advice.

Contract and business: the positive role of the contract

If contracts between traders and consumers have been beset by problems such as the imbalance of bargaining-power, such difficulties rarely hinder contractual relations between businesses. It is worth re-emphasizing that the law of contract was developed as a response to the needs of business in an expanding capitalist economy, not only as a means of dispute-solving, but also, and very importantly, as a positive aid to rational business planning. The rights and duties taken on by contracting parties need to be clear, if promises are to be effectively fulfilled and disputes avoided. In theory, the law of contract fulfils an important business function by providing exactly this clarity, even though in practice neither consumers nor people in business go about their daily lives with a keen conscious awareness of contract law.

Essentially, the legal framework of the contract, with its attendant ramifications of exclusion clauses, limitation clauses and doctrines of frustration and fundamental breach, may be seen as providing the business community with the means whereby rational, calculated risks and transactions might be carried out in the relatively secure knowledge that rights and obligations could, in the final analysis, be enforced through law. This is an important issue for our understanding of contract law in the modern business world, for it is frequently only as a last resort that lawyers and courts are used to compel contractual performance by one party through litigation by the other. Macaulay, in the United States,[73] and Beale and Dugdale in England,[74] have carried out surveys among people in business which suggest that business contracts are *not* entered into with legal remedies in mind. As Beale and Dugdale put it, 'such factors as low-risk mutually accepted norms and duties, and various extra-contractual devices may operate to reduce the use of contract law ... there is not much scope for using contractual remedies'. Furthermore, both studies found that 'lawyers and legal remedies also tend to be avoided as being inflexible; lawyers are thought not to understand the needs of commerce and those firms who had consulted solicitors were not all satisfied. A similar reluctance to use the law was evident on the planning side'.[75]

The picture emerging from these studies is that business relations between contracting parties rest much more firmly on mutual goodwill and the need for co-operation in both present and possible future transactions, and the prospect of bringing actions to obtain legal remedies is thought by many to be highly damaging to these vital factors. It appears that in this context, as with industrial relations, the law is regarded as being too formal and inflexible to serve the needs of the parties efficiently and constructively.

This is not to suggest that no problems arise within business contracts; certainly, there *is* litigation, frequently over international transactions, and there are signs that litigation in the area of contract is in fact increasing.[76] Such litigation will, however, only take place when negotiation between the parties and perhaps an attempt to resolve the problem through arbitration (see chapter 6) have failed. Tillotson[77] provides us with a number of examples of complex business contracts – almost invariably standard-form contracts – and notes that the use by contracting parties of such standard-form contracts may cause problems sometimes referred to as the 'battle of the forms'. Here, both parties, intending to do business with each other, use their own standard-form documents in communications and negotiations. The contents of these forms may well differ in material particulars. In such cases it can be very difficult, if not impossible, to identify a contractual agreement as defined by the judicial model of contract, for, as will be recalled, any response to an offer which differs from the terms laid out in that offer cannot, according to the rules of contract, constitute an acceptance of that offer, but must be a counter-offer. In the event of such problems being brought before the courts, the outcome seems somewhat 'hit or miss'.[78] The court may find that, despite the fact that the situation does not 'fit' the contractual model, an enforceable agreement none the less exists;[79] on the other hand, the court may hold that no contract exists, but that the plaintiffs may be entitled to payment by the defendants for any losses incurred.[80] At present, where contracting businesses each use their own standard-form documents, each insisting that the transaction is to be based on its terms, the law has no clear answer to the question as to which set of terms prevails, except by the use of highly pragmatic analyses of the facts of each case. It might justifiably be asked whether this area is one where the legal rules of contract need to be changed so as to enable the courts to deal more clearly and consistently with this type of problem, thus diminishing the gap between legal doctrine and the reality of business transactions, and eliminating as far as possible the need for the courts to distort the classical model of the contract to make it 'fit' modern business practices.

The surveys referred to above make it clear that, in many commercial situations, businesses do not in fact rationally plan their transactions (or consider possible problematic consequences thereof). In the modern commercial world, it is common for the law of contract, theoretically – and in the eyes of the courts – so central to business transactions, to be marginalized, or not even thought of at all. Where more formal contractual arrangements are made (for example, where the transaction involves large amounts of money) then more use may well be made of contract-law mechanisms. For example, consider the extent to which businesses may try to incorporate into their contracts agreed consequences in the event of anticipated contingencies. There will be provision within the contract (notwithstanding the possibility of inconsistencies in the forms used by each party) regarding prices and price increases, delivery dates, provision for arbitration and *force majeure* clauses, which attempt to deal in advance, so to speak, with events which may happen and are completely outside the will and control of the parties (such as war, floods, earthquakes or even strikes), and which may seriously affect the performance of the contract.

In summary, it is true to say that, in business contracts, the old legal rules about offer and acceptance, and the established forms of legal remedy for breaches of contract, are today nowhere near as important as the influence on business of modern commercial practices and economic pressures; and if the reader has formed the impression that consumer contracts and business contracts are worlds apart, then that is not far from the truth. The fact is that their respective problems are not, *essentially*, legal problems at all: one has a dispute over goods and services with a supplier or manufacturer – a practical, everyday problem – and the other has a 'business relations' difficulty. While both types of dispute clearly have legal implications – and indeed the law may offer, at least in theory, specific remedies – it is nevertheless true that, whether due to sometimes unintelligible technicality, inaccessibility of adequate legal solutions, suspicion of the law's formality and inflexibility, or a fear that litigation may damage good business relationships, consumers and people in business have in common a reluctance to resort to the legal system for solutions – the very legal system whose judges created, back in the last century, the contractual device which underlies such disputes. Today, the classical notion of the contract is, for everyday purposes, frequently an inadequate and even outmoded means of analysing and resolving what may be important and expensive disputes.

The very notion of 'freely negotiated agreements' is, moreover, becoming increasingly eroded both by state intervention (through statutory rules and regulations) and by factors such as international agreements and EC legislation. State and inter-state intervention is, in one form or another, replacing 'free agreement' as the cornerstone of financial transactions of all kinds. Whether the law, as it affects the ordinary consumer or business concern, will duly progress to take account of these social and economic changes remain to be seen; but at present when we consider that, as Friedmann puts it, 'the evolution of the law of contract in response to fundamental social changes has overwhelmingly occurred outside the court room',[81] we must conclude that, especially with regard to the common law, legal recognition of and adaptation to twentieth-century changes in economic and commercial life are long overdue.

12
Law and government

Among the topics and themes discussed so far has been the increase in state intervention in almost all sectors of social and economic life over the past hundred years or so: the growth of the welfare state, with the accompanying expansion of machinery for dispute-prevention and solution through administrative tribunals and other bodies; the vast increase in legal controls over many activities which, in earlier times, were left to the private arrangements of the individuals and groups concerned; and the changing nature of the state itself, which has moved from a relatively non-interventionist stance to much more positive and direct regulation and control. In the context of the post-1979 Conservative governments the ostensible aim of central government has been to deregulate, and to return nationalized and public-sector industries and services to the private sector; but, paradoxically, in so far as this has been achieved, it has been achieved largely by placing considerable directive power in the hands of central government. The expansion of government activity has necessitated, of course, an increase in administrators and administrative agencies charged with the various tasks involved in the implementation of state policies and programmes. Much of the organization of state activity is structured along the lines of bureaucracy, which may, as Weber maintained, be a more efficient form of organization than any other,[1] but which at the same time constitutes a source of irritation for many who define themselves as being on the receiving-end of organizations whose tasks are hindered by excessive red tape.

For many people, the expansion of state intervention has engendered a deep mistrust of state agencies, at both central and local levels; many fear that the degree of decision-making power which Parliament has vested in these agencies is excessive, and that its use constitutes, potentially or actually, an unwarranted intrusion into the affairs of private individuals and groups. It is not the purpose of this chapter to provide detailed descriptions of the various organs of government (such as the civil service, the structure of local authorities or the working of Parliament), but rather to explore some important aspects of the relationships between modern government and the law.

It is important to remind ourselves that legal controls are by no means the only way of regulating the actions of an administrative agency. There may well be complex frameworks of *economic* and/or *political* controls operating at both central and local government levels. One obvious mode of political control is through the ballot box at local and national elections; and there are many rather less obvious and more subtle ways in which political pressure may be put upon one agency by the actions of another. A mixture of political and economic controls can be seen in the following example. Although the deployment of resources within a police force is, by virtue of the provisions of the Police Act 1964, a matter for the discretion of the Chief Constable of that force, it is still the case that a police force is partly dependent for financial resources upon the police committee of the county council.[2] It may sometimes be that the council may influence the activities of its police force indirectly, by means of economic pressures made possible by this partial control of resources.[3]

In some cases of dispute between public bodies, we may find that the problem is dealt with by means of a mix of political and legal devices. Consider the matter of local authorities' independence of central government. It is often thought that locally elected authorities such as district and county councils enjoy a high degree of autonomy of central government, to the extent that, apart from the many and varied duties imposed upon them by statute to provide local services and facilities,[4] the policies of local councils can be formulated and implemented without intrusive interference or control by central government. Such autonomy has, however, always been limited; and in recent years government legislation has further diluted local autonomy in a number of ways.

To begin with, a local authority's income is only partly derived from local sources. For many years local income came from rates levied on domestic and commercial property, plus other forms of revenue such as rents from council houses. In 1990 the local rating system for domestic properties was abolished and replaced by the community charge (the 'poll tax'), a flat-rate charge payable by every adult person. This highly unpopular tax proved short-lived, and has been replaced by the 'council tax', a charge based once again on the value of property. Finance raised locally, however, only accounts for a small proportion of a local authority's income – the poll tax only brought in about a quarter of the income needed by local government – and the remainder comes from central government in the form of a substantial grant.

This financial connection may be a source of friction between local and central government, and is an increasingly important means of control by the latter over the former. This may be particularly marked if the local authority and central government are controlled by opposing political parties. The Conservative governments of the 1980s, for example, deeply committed to the reduction of public expenditure, looked critically at those local authorities which they regarded as profligate spenders,[5] and (through the Rates Act 1984 and Local Government Finance Act 1988) introduced the device of 'capping', whereby those local authorities might be penalized for exceeding centrally determined annual budgets. Further, the Local Government Act 1985 abolished the Greater London Council and the six metropolitan councils – all, prior to abolition, Labour-controlled. The White Paper which preceded this legislation[6] argued a case based on a need to increase efficiency at local government level, though it noted also that the search by these authorities for a wider role in local government might 'lead them to promote policies which conflict with national policies which are the responsibility of central government'. Many saw in this White Paper, and in the Act of 1985 which followed, a direct attack by central government upon elected local bodies which happened to disagree profoundly with central government policies. There had in recent years been several instances of such disagreements. There was, for example, the reluctance of some (Labour-controlled) authorities to implement the provisions of the Housing Act 1980, which put into effect the government's policy of giving council house tenants the right to buy their homes (see chapter 5). Some authorities at first signalled their refusal to carry out these provisions, and even when it became clear that to do so would be unlawful, some councils none-the-less adopted a policy of deliberately 'going slow' in the implementation of the statutory right to buy.

Some commentators have perceived a more general shift in the relationship between central and local government, in the direction of greater concentration of power in the hands of the former at the expense of local democracy,[7] though Hartley and Griffith comment that this kind of argument

is too often conducted in highly emotional tones and it is suggested by some that democracy and responsiveness to the needs of men and women are attainable only at the grassroots level and, by others, that Whitehall knows best. The approach should surely be to decide which questions are most efficiently decided at which level. And here 'efficiently' should mean providing the best service to those who need it.[8]

This comment begs several important questions. Does the 'best service' mean the cheapest, or at any rate the most 'economic'?[9] Or should the *quality* of service be paramount, irrespective of the cost? How is 'need' to be defined? Who is to decide? And who is to bear that cost? The paramount aim of central government in these matters is often stated to be 'value for money', though the term is meaningless without explanation as to what is meant by 'value'. Local authority expenditure is currently very tightly controlled by means of the Audit Commission for Local Authorities, created by the Local Government Finance Act 1982. The Act required the auditor to satisfy herself that a local authority has ensured 'economy, efficiency and effectiveness' in its use of resources, and the elasticity of these terms has facilitated significant control over local authorities. The Audit Commission itself, though ostensibly rigorously independent of central government, may be thought none the less to have critical linkages: its members are appointed by the Secretary of State for Local Government, who may also direct the Commission as to how it carries out its functions.[10]

Many would argue that these are not matters for lawyers at all, but are rather matters of *policy*, to be decided by administrators who are entrusted with the task by Parliament. Indeed, as we saw in chapter 6, the doctrine of the separation of powers, though not rigidly adhered to in England, requires at the very least that the judiciary should adjudicate on questions of *law*, and should not delve into matters which are the rightful constitutional province of the executive or the legislature. The dividing-line between law and policy is, however, by no means always easy to draw, as we shall see.

Remedies in administrative law

Expanding briefly on one or two of the instances mentioned above: the term 'welfare state' often conjures up images of various state benefits (old-age pensions, social security, supplementary benefits and unemployment benefit); it refers to such institutions as the education system, social services, the legal aid system (see chapter 13), the health service, and many of the various functions of local government. As we have seen, interventionist policies, and legislation which implements these policies, often does intrude upon 'private affairs'. Statutory power, for example, is given to local authorities to purchase privately owned buildings or land compulsorily, for purposes such as clearance or redevelopment programmes – though the authority must compensate the owner for doing so, and must also ensure that the proper procedures laid down in the relevant statutes are complied with. Similarly, planning legislation provides that people must obtain planning permission before altering the structure or use of any land or buildings. If a householder builds, say, a garage without complying with these requirements, then it may mean that the garage has to be taken down again. Here again, the authority must act within its legal powers, and must not step beyond those powers or act in an unreasonable manner. If a public authority can be shown to have acted in one of these ways, then the aggrieved citizen may have a remedy in law.

Consider, for example, the case of *Cooper* v. *Wandsworth Board of Works* in 1863.[11] Here, a statute provided that before any building was commenced, seven days' notice had to be given to the local Board of Works in order that the board could inspect the land and give any necessary directions for drainage. The Act also provided that, in the event of such notice not being given before building commenced, the board could lawfully demolish the building. The plaintiff had begun to build a house, and the work was well in hand when the Board of Works, claiming that the required notice had not been given, pulled down the house without giving the plaintiff any notice of its intention to do so, nor any opportunity to explain why notice had not been received. The plaintiff sued the board for trespass, arguing that although the statute clearly gave the board the power to demolish the building, the board should have given the plaintiff the opportunity to present his side of the story: in other words, he claimed that he should have been given a fair hearing before the demolition was carried out.

The court decided in the plaintiff's favour, stating that 'although there are no positive words in [the] statute requiring that the party shall be heard, yet the justice of the common law will supply the omission of the legislature'. This case raises a number of important issues which we shall explore later, but at this point it is important to note the dual role of the law in the field of government and administration. On the one hand, the law *facilitates*, through statutory provision, the carrying out of administrative functions; on the other hand, it provides in many cases (though not all) for *controls* on administration. Hence, aggrieved citizens suffering excesses or breaches of statutory powers by administrative agencies may be entitled to some form of legal remedy against the agency concerned.

Cooper's case is a good illustration of the principles of what we might call the 'ordinary liability' of public bodies. Such liability can be contrasted with other forms of liability which can attach to such bodies; the distinction has been explained by Wade thus:

There is the family of ordinary private law remedies such as damages, injunction, and declaration; and there is a special family of public law remedies, principally certiorari, prohibition and mandamus, collectively known as the prerogative remedies. Within each family the various remedies could be sought separately or together or in the alternative. But each family had its own distinct procedure. Damages, injunctions and declarations were sought in an ordinary action, as in private law; but prerogative remedies had to be sought by a procedure of their own, which could not be combined with an ordinary action . . . This difficulty was removed in 1977 by the provision of a comprehensive procedure, 'application for judicial review', under which remedies in both families became interchangeable.[12]

In *Cooper*'s case, the plaintiff brought his action on the basis of trespass, a part of the law of tort, and was awarded damages – a member of the 'family' of ordinary private-law remedies. The Board of Works was held liable, just as if the board had been a private individual. This, of course, is because the board was a *corporate body*: that is, a body treated in law as if it were a person, as in the case of the limited company. Within the field of administration and government, many agencies and departments enjoy corporate status. Thus, local authorities, many government departments and central government itself (as the *Crown*) are corporate bodies, as are such varied agencies as health authorities, the British Railways Board, the Civil Aviation Authority, the National Coal Board, the British Broadcasting Corporation and many more. The status of such bodies, and their relationship with government departments involved with their functions, is established by the statutes (or, as in the case of the BBC, the Royal Charters) which bring them into existence. Their liability for wrongful acts, however, depends upon a variety of factors, such as the precise extent of their powers or duties as laid down in the relevant statutes, or the kind of wrongful act which is complained of.

It is crucial, for example, especially when considering private-law remedies of the kind sought in *Cooper*'s case, to identify the appropriate defendant. In *Stanbury* v. *Exeter Corporation* in 1905,[13] the plaintiff brought an action for negligence against a local authority, which was the employer of an inspector of animals. The Diseases of Animals Act 1894 imposed a duty on local authorities to appoint inspectors, and regulations made by the relevant government minister under the Act imposed certain duties on them. In this case, the inspector had seized sheep believed to be infected, at a market, and it was of this action that the plaintiff complained. The action failed, however: the court pointed out that the inspector's duty was imposed directly upon him by ministerial regulation, and *not upon the local authority which employed him*. The authority could thus not be held vicariously liable (see chapter 9) for the alleged wrongful act of the inspector, for in these circumstances it was the inspector, and not the local authority, who should properly have been the defendant.

It is convenient to mention briefly here the liability in private law of the *Crown* (the legal form of central government administration) in general. The main provisions are contained in the Crown Proceedings Act 1947, which puts the

Crown in the same position as any other public authority with regard to its liability in tort and contract. Liability will therefore attach to any breach of contract by the government to which it is a party; and to any tortious act, except in so far as an otherwise tortious act might be expressly authorized by statute. This means that if a statute provides that a government department is empowered to do an act which inevitably results in, for example, discomfort to other private individuals, then what would otherwise be actionable private nuisance is rendered lawful by virtue of that statutory authority. (For example, statutory authority may be given to run a railway which will probably cause discomfort to those living near the railway line.)

Two other important private-law remedies should be noted. These are the equitable remedies of the injunction and the declaration. The injunction is an order requiring a defendant to abstain from doing something (or, in the case of a mandatory injunction, to *do* something);[14] a declaration is simply a statement by the court as to the legal position in a given situation. The latter remedy has been criticized as lacking enforceability, though Garner has pointed out that 'administrative agencies are not to be expected to ignore an adverse declaration of a High Court judge'.[15]

Often, specific remedies are provided by statute, as, for example, where special tribunal machinery is created, or where planning legislation provides for public inquiries in the event of objections to proposed actions. It is in matters such as these that allegations may arise that an agency or minister concerned has failed to observe the procedures laid down by statute; or has acted *ultra vires*, that is, exceeding or abusing the statutory powers; or has committed a breach of natural justice. In such cases, it may be possible to invoke the special public-law remedies known as the 'prerogative remedies' of *certiorari*, prohibition and *mandamus*. The first two were explained by Lord Atkin thus:

Both writs are of great antiquity, forming part of the process by which the King's Courts restrained courts of inferior jurisdiction from exceeding their powers. Prohibition restrains the tribunal[16] from proceeding further in excess of jurisdiction; *certiorari* requires the record or the order of the court to be sent up to the King's Bench Division, to have its legality inquired into, and, if necessary, to have the order quashed . . . But the operation of the writs has extended to control the proceedings of bodies which do not claim to be, and would not be recognised as, courts of justice. Whenever any body of persons having legal authority to determine questions affecting the rights of subjects, and having the duty to act judicially, act in excess of their legal authority they are subject to the controlling jurisdiction of the King's Bench Division exercised in these writs.[17]

Mandamus has the effect of commanding a person or agency to perform a public duty imposed on it by law. The circumstances in which these writs may be granted will be discussed in more detail presently, but there are one or two general points which can conveniently be explained here.

First, a change in 1977 in the procedural rules governing the availability of remedies in administrative law reduced, to some extent, the procedural problems involved in obtaining these remedies.[18] The application procedure has been simplified, though problems remain. The applicant must have 'a sufficient interest in the matter to which the application relates'.[19] The 'sufficient interest' (or *locus standi*) provision may mean that 'if a busybody (or public-spirited citizen, according to taste) applies to the court for a remedy, he may be told that the affair is none of his business and that he has no *locus standi* to bring the proceedings'.[20]

Historically, the precise *locus standi* requirements varied, depending on which prerogative remedy was being sought, the requirements for *mandamus* being rather stricter than for *certiorari* or prohibition.[21] *Locus standi* in cases involving the latter two remedies will be satisfied by the applicant's showing that he has a 'genuine grievance because something has been done or may be done which affects him';[22] but what of applications for *mandamus*, especially since the streamlining of the procedure and the use of the term 'sufficient interest' with regard to all the remedies? In *Inland Revenue Commissioners* v. *National Federation of Self-Employed and Small Businesses Ltd*,[23] a case in which *mandamus* was being sought, the House of Lords discussed the matter of *locus standi* in the light of the newer phrase 'sufficient interest', and it is clear from this case that the strict test insisted upon in earlier cases no longer applies.[24] An applicant need no longer have a specific legal *right* in the matter; and while there are no precise or exact requirements stated in the *IRC* case, Lord Wilberforce explained that

There may be simple cases in which it can be seen at the earliest stage that the person applying for judicial review has no interest at all, or no sufficient interest to support the application: then it would be quite correct at the threshold to refuse him leave to apply . . . But in other cases this will not be so. In these it will be necessary to consider the powers and duties in law of those against whom the relief is asked, the position of the applicant in relation to those powers or duties, and to the breach of those said to have been committed. In other words, the question of sufficient interest can not, in such cases, be considered in the abstract, or as an isolated point: it must be taken together with the legal and factual context.[25]

There are, in addition, time-limits relating to applications for these remedies. The changed Rules of the Supreme Court provide that in the case of 'undue delay', or in the case of an application for *certiorari* a delay of more than three months, the court may refuse relief if it is of the opinion that the award of a remedy would cause substantial hardship, would substantially prejudice the right of any person, or would be detrimental to good administration. These provisions relate not only to the prerogative remedies, but also to cases involving administrative action where private-law remedies such as declarations, injunctions or damages are sought.

An applicant should also note that the prerogative orders, like the equitable remedies of injunction and declaration, are *discretionary*: even if the challenge to the administrative agency is held to be good, the remedy *may* not be granted if an alternative remedy is available, or if the court thinks that the applicant's own conduct has been unreasonable. For example, in *ex parte Fry*[26] a fireman was ordered to clean another officer's uniform. Rather than carrying out the act, and complaining about it afterwards, he refused to clean the uniform on the ground that the order was not lawful. He was subsequently brought before his commanding officer, who cautioned him by way of punishment. The fireman applied for *certiorari* in the attempt to quash this disciplinary sanction. His application was refused. In the Court of Appeal, Singleton L.J. spoke of his refusal to obey the order as 'extraordinarily foolish conduct' and continued: 'in these days it behoves everyone to act reasonably. If every fireman or every policeman is to take it upon himself to disobey an order of this kind and to say "I do not think it is lawful", it will become almost impossible to carry on any public service.'[27]

Given these considerations, and the almost infinite variety of statutory bodies exercising a vast array of discretionary powers as well as statutory duties, a number of questions arise. What should be the appropriate role of the law *vis-à-vis* administration? On what grounds may the judges intervene in administrative decision-making? In what kind of case is judicial review applied for? How appropriate are the present remedies, and the procedures for obtaining them, in modern society?

The role of law in the administrative process

We described above the dual role played by the law in relation to the administrative process. Regarding its function as a *facilitating* mechanism: all this means is that we invariably find that administrative agencies (such as tribunals) and procedures (such as those affecting the granting or refusal of planning permission) are established by means of legal machinery: statutes or statutory instruments.[28] It is with regard to the *controlling* function of the law that debates and controversies arise.

Some writers, notably the constitutional lawyer Dicey writing towards the end of the last century,[29] consider that the role of the law is to guarantee and protect individual freedom against an increasingly powerful and interventionist state. Dicey contrasted the English position, as he saw it, with that of France, and was deeply critical of the French system of administrative law (the *droit administratif*), which he regarded as a 'body of special rights, privileges or prerogatives as against private citizens'.[30] Rather than create a system of law quite separate from private law, Dicey insisted, it was essential that the administration should remain subject to the 'ordinary law', administered by the 'ordinary courts'. This was an essential means of controlling administrative power, of preserving and protecting the rights of the citizen, and of opposing what he regarded as the move towards collectivism: state intervention on behalf of the community at the expense of individual interests and liberties. Dicey's exposition of the relationship between law and administration was, of course, closely related to his ideological commitment to individualism and his dislike of collectivist state action.

In fact, not only did Dicey misrepresent the French administrative law system,[31] but he also failed to take into account the extent to which various specialized administrative agencies and procedures, all subject to 'non-ordinary' legal rules, had developed in England by the end of the nineteenth century.[32] Despite this, Dicey's work has been very influential,[33] not least because of his insistence on the importance of the *rule of law*: the idea that everyone, including government ministers and other adminstrative agencies and public bodies, must act according to the law and within the powers vested in them by statutory authority. Furthermore, Dicey's exposition of the rule of law embraces the important proposition that the ordinary courts have inherent jurisdiction to scrutinize administrative actions and declare upon their validity or otherwise, and thus operate as defenders of individual interests and liberties. These principles are still seen by many as crucially significant: 'the rule of law remains . . . a vital necessity to fair and proper government. The enormous growth in the powers of government makes it all the more necessary to preserve it.'[34] Many writers and judges, following Dicey, thus look critically on many statutes which confer extensive discretionary powers on administrative bodies or government ministers, or which purport to exclude administrative action from judicial scrutiny in the courts.

In their analysis of regulatory agencies,[35] Baldwin and McCrudden explain that regulatory agencies, which are increasingly used to carry out important government functions, do not fit easily into the existing constitutional framework because

they expend considerable resources in deciding disputes between parties and in interpreting a particular body of law, yet differ from courts and tribunals. They enforce the law as well as interpret it. They employ a substantial number of specialist staff. They exercise continuing influence over a specific industry, trade or social practice. They constitute an identifiable species, yet are of the broader genus variously referred to as quangos, fringe bodies, non-departmental public bodies or public corporations.[36]

Examples of regulatory agencies discussed by Baldwin and McCrudden include the Gaming Board, the Health and Safety Executive, the Civil Aviation Authority, the Commission for Racial Equality, the Advisory, Conciliation and Arbitration Service, the Monopolies and Mergers Commission, and the Office of Fair Trading. Agencies such as these are created for a number of reasons: they are specialized bodies; they are seen to be distanced in important ways from central government itself; they are, by virtue of their expertise and organization, efficient in the performance of their functions; and they may be 'said to play an important role as insulators between government and the public'.[37]

Despite their expertise and efficiency, however, regulatory agencies often attract the criticisms that they tend to favour certain interest-groups as against others, and that they are insufficiently accountable for their decisions and actions. In terms of *political* accountability (that is, to ministers) there may well be problems arising from both the relative invisibility of discreet ministerial direction, and the reluctance of ministers to intervene 'so as to avoid potential political flak in a difficult area'.[38]

In terms of *legal* accountability, clearly regulatory agencies must remain within the terms of their functions as provided by the statutes which set them up; Baldwin and McCrudden discuss the strengths and weaknesses of the jurisdiction of the courts to review agencies' actions and decisions in order to ascertain whether the body concerned has overstepped those powers. One problem here is that the courts intervene only when aggrieved parties take the initiative in challenging an agency's decision, and even in these (relatively rare) instances, any intervention by the courts is on the ground that something has gone wrong in the individual case, rather than on the basis of a continuous monitoring of the agency's work.

This comment typifies what Harlow and Rawlings[39] call 'red light' theories of administrative law: such theories perceive the role of administrative law (as developed and implemented through the courts) as an important means of controlling government and administration, and of setting limits to the exercise of administrative power. Such positions may be contrasted with those of 'green light' theorists, who regard the use of administrative power for the benefit of the community as wholly appropriate. On this view, the law should be used to provide the means whereby administrative activity can more effectively and efficiently be carried out, and this may include the provision of compensation for those whose private interests are adversely affected by administrative action.[40] The lawyer's task, according to 'green light' theorists, is to advise on methods of rational and effective administration; the courts, however, are looked on as frequently being an obstacle to effective administration because of their excessive formalism and adherence to rigid rules.

On the question of controlling abuse of administrative power, 'green light' theorists tend towards the view that *internal political* controls, through specialized administrative agencies and procedures, are preferable to the types of control which the judges try to impose. Griffith (a 'green light' theorist) has this to say:

> The whole history of administrative tribunals shows the need for specialist bodies in certain areas of administration and adjudication. Certainly, if such bodies deal with questions which they were not set up to deal with, and . . . so act outside their jurisdiction, they should be reviewable by the courts. Otherwise they should not be interfered with by the judges who are more likely than not to introduce inconsistency and injustice into complex areas of administration.[41]

Griffith is sceptical of the ways in which the judges in England approach the issue of review of administrative action, holding not only that they are for the most part ill-equipped with regard to expertise in most areas of administration, but also that they cannot help but make political decisions, disguised as matters of law, because of their social and professional background. We shall consider this proposition in more detail presently.[42] Whether it is wise to place a great deal of faith in the capacity of political institutions (particularly those involving the democratic process) to impose effective curbs on excessive administrative zeal or abuse of power is debatable. We have seen how powerful interest-groups can influence the legislative process, and interest-groups exist, too, within the administration – notably the civil service.[43] Might there not be a danger that administrative policies emanate from misplaced ideas of community or national interest which are really sectional interests in disguise?

Harlow and Rawlings, in a comprehensive discussion of law and the administrative process, stress the awesome complexity of modern administration. They point out that the modern trend is indeed towards the kinds of control envisaged by 'green light' theorists, and explain that independent, quasi-independent and regulatory agencies have increasingly been introduced to supervise administrative action in many spheres. Examples are the Council on

Tribunals, established in 1958 after the report of the Committee on Administrative Tribunals and Enquiries (the Franks Committee);[44] the Supplementary Benefit Commission, dealing with claims for supplementary benefit (in which area there is considerable scope for discretion by the administrators concerned); and the Parliamentary Commissioner for Administration (the Ombudsman), appointed to investigate cases of maladministration in government departments and other public bodies specified in the statute creating the office.[45] In such cases, Parliament, through legislation, has entrusted certain functions to specialized agencies, not the ordinary courts, although the latter have insisted on their jurisdiction to review the decisions of such agencies in certain circumstances.

As Harlow and Rawlings point out, the twin questions which recur, especially where there are issues involving some form of adjudication, are first, whether Parliament or some legal forum should decide this issue; and second, if the latter, whether matters of adjudication on questions of law should be dealt with by the courts or by tribunals. These interrelated questions have often lain behind judicial pronouncements as to the legality of administrative action; and if in considering the instances discussed in this chapter the impression is gained that at times administrators and judges have been at loggerheads, with the former striving to minimize judicial intervention and the latter struggling to retain a degree of control over administrative action, then that impression is not far from the truth. The judiciary is firmly committed to the 'red light' approach, and has consistently and jealously guarded what it regards as the legitimate jurisdiction of the 'ordinary courts' over administrative action. The judges have purported to ensure that tribunals, public bodies and government ministers remain true to principles of legality, and do not exceed or abuse powers entrusted to them by Parliament. Unfortunately, because administrative law in England has developed in such a sporadic and piecemeal fashion with very few clear and consistent principles, such 'principles of legality' are not easy to ascertain. Indeed, some argue that the judges have taken advantage of this lack of precision, together with the discretionary nature of public-law remedies, to pick and choose the issues in which they are prepared to intervene. We shall return to this matter presently.

The grounds for judicial intervention in administrative activity

The main doctrinal foundation on which judicial review of administrative action is based is that of *ultra vires*. To understand this doctrine, however, we must clarify the various types of function which an agency may perform, for the readiness of the courts to intervene depends (or so it appears from the cases) on what *kind* of decision is being challenged.

Given the great variety of administrative powers and procedures, is it possible to develop a coherent classification of functions? The Committee on Ministers' Powers thought so, in its report of 1932.[46] The committee distinguished between 'judicial' and 'administrative' functions on the basis that the former 'disposes of the whole matter by a finding upon the facts in dispute and an application of the law . . . to the facts so found', while the latter involves 'administrative action, the character of which is determined by the minister's free choice'. Thus, 'administrative' is characterized by policy considerations and discretionary choice, and not the application of legal rules. A third function, 'quasi-judicial', was explained as referring to a decision involving the finding of facts, and applying administrative policy thereto.

How helpful are these distinctions? Wade considers that some such analysis helps clarity of thought, but warns that 'the courts are addicted to distinctions which are more superficial and more confusing . . . and which by no means always help clarity of thought. Nor is it very profitable to take concepts out of their particular contexts and analyse them in the abstract.'[47] Griffith, discussing this aspect of the committee's report, is less charitable, perceiving judicial forces at work behind the scenes:

You will recall that the quasi-judicial decision was distinguished from the judicial by the fact that the Minister who made the . . . quasi-judicial decision acted according to policy whereas the judge in his judicial functions did, of course, nothing of the kind. In a purely administrative decision, there was no obligation to consider and weigh submissions and argument, to collate evidence or to solve issues. Everything was at the discretion of the administrator.

This nonsense, screaming its absurdities to heaven, was received with respectful, even smug, acceptance by His Majesty's judges. Respectful because they agreed with it. Smug because they were largely responsible for it. What pleased the courts was the almost infinitely extensible or contractable nature of these concepts. Previously the opportunity for the courts to intervene had been measured by a piece of string to which they could add bits or from which they could cut bits but only with some difficulty. Now they were presented with . . . a piece of elastic. If they wished to intervene the administrative became the judicial or the quasi-judicial. If they wished not to intervene they put on their music-hall turn which begins with the words 'Parliament has entrusted the Minister . . . with the power to take these decisions. Far be it from us to presume to replace the discretion of the Minister . . . with our own'.[48]

Examination of the extremely complex case-law in this area seems to support Griffith's somewhat acerbic remarks, especially those cases which have come before the courts in recent years. Let us consider briefly judicial activity through the cases. It is extremely difficult to classify the case-law into watertight compartments, but three general areas will be examined: judicial responses to attempts to oust their jurisdiction, disputes raising the question of *ultra vires*, and cases in which the judges have considered the applicability or otherwise of the principles of natural justice.

Can the courts' jurisdiction be excluded?

Statutory provisions may attempt to prevent the courts from intervening in administrative action in a number of ways. It may be, for example, that a statute provides that a decision of an administrative agency 'shall be final', or even 'shall not be questioned in any legal proceedings whatsoever'. What effect have such phrases had on the courts' capacity to question such decisions?

It has been held on a number of occasions[49] that such terms as this are to be interpreted to mean that there is no appeal from the decision, in the sense that there can be no re-hearing of the case, nor consideration of the facts or the merits of the case before any court; but that the possibility of judicial intervention still exists for the purposes of reviewing the *legality* of the decision: did the deciding agency act *ultra vires?* Was there some other jurisdictional defect affecting the legality of the decision? As Lord Denning said in one case, 'Parliament only gives the impress of finality to the decisions of the tribunal on condition that they are reached in accordance with the law',[50] and the courts have consistently reserved to themselves the jurisdiction to enquire into that condition.

In *Anisminic Ltd* v. *Foreign Compensation Commission* in 1969,[51] a case regarded by many commentators as representing a high-water mark of judicial intervention, the issue concerned the payment of compensation by Egypt to companies and individuals who had suffered damage to their property during the Suez crisis of 1956. The compensation was to be distributed by the Foreign Compensation Commission in accordance with the statutory provision that 'the determination by the Commission of any application made to them under this Act shall not be called into question in any court of law' (Foreign Compensation Act 1950, s.4(4)). One of the principles informing the work of the commission was that only British owners of property were to receive compensation. Because Anisminic Ltd, though originally a British company, had been sold to an Egyptian concern, the commission excluded that company from receiving compensation. On application by the company to challenge this decision, the House of Lords held that the commission, by enquiring into the successors in title of the company, had exceeded their jurisdiction, that their decision was null and void on the ground that it was *ultra vires*, and that the clause purporting to exclude the court did not protect the commission from judicial intervention on this ground.

What is interesting about the *Anisminic* case is that the court interpreted the decision of the Foreign Compensation Commission to be an error as to its jurisdiction. As a matter of fact, the compensation fund had been established in 1959, and the relevent statutory instrument containing the commission's terms of reference clearly stated that applicants and their successors in title should be British nationals at that date. Anisminic Ltd had, however, ceased to be in British hands *before* 1959; it would seem that it was, therefore, excluded from compensation. Could not the commission have reached this decision while remaining within its jurisdiction? The House of Lords thought not, and the effect of such a conclusion would have been to exclude judicial intervention (because the commission's decision would not then have been *ultra vires*) by reason of the ouster clause. Is this an example of the courts' interpreting facts in particular ways *because they wish to intervene?* Wade is of the opinion that 'there is no situation in which these clauses can have any effect. The policy of the courts thus becomes one of total disobedience to Parliament.'[52]

A less dramatic method of restricting judicial review is for a statute to enact that an administrative decision may be challenged as long as the challenge is brought within a specified period, but may not be challenged after that period has expired. In *Smith* v. *East Elloe Rural District Council*[53] the allegation was that a local authority had acted wrongfully in taking land by means of a compulsory purchase order, the making of which had been procedurally defective. The Acquisition of Land (Authorization Procedure) Act 1946 provided, *inter alia*, that compulsory purchase orders could be challenged on certain grounds within six weeks, after which such an order could 'not be questioned in any legal proceedings whatsoever'. The House of Lords held that this statutory provision served to exclude the jurisdiction of the court after the six-week period had expired, and the action was not permitted to proceed. From an administrative point of view, it seems sensible that a specific period is provided, after which challenge is ruled out, for 'in cases involving public works, such as roads or hospitals, it is desirable that construction should not be too long delayed . . . it is even more desirable that persons should be prevented from bringing review proceedings after a substantial amount of work has been completed'.[54] The *East Elloe* case has been followed more recently in *R. v. Secretary of State for the Environment ex parte Ostler* in 1976,[55] where an individual sought unsuccessfully to challenge compulsory purchase orders for a road scheme; the complainant had not brought his application within the six-week period because he had not realized that his property would be affected.

Ultra vires: unlimited judicial intervention?

As we have seen, the basic ground for judicial intervention in administrative activity is that the agency in question has exceeded or abused its powers. The *ultra vires* doctrine is extremely wide in its ambit, covering both *substantive ultra vires* (where the body has abused or exceeded its powers) and *procedural ultra vires* (where a specified procedure has not been complied with, such as a requirement to observe the rules of natural justice, considered in the next section). Once again, much depends on the way in which judges interpret both the administrative action and the statutory provisions which authorize that action. One crucial distinction which must be made when considering the authority of an administrative agency is that between statutory *duties* and discretionary *powers* entrusted to an administrative body. If the agency is under a duty to do something, the non-performance of that duty will be actionable. If, however, the agency is simply empowered to do something, then this implies discretionary choice in the matter. However,

discretionary powers are normally accompanied by express or implied duties. For instance, a licensing authority may have a discretion to attach such conditions as it thinks fit when granting a licence; but it shall be under a legal duty to exercise a genuine discretion in each individual case, and not fetter its choice by adopting rigid rules; and the conditions imposed must not be irrelevant to the purposes for which the power was conferred upon it.[56]

Thus, for instance, in *R. v. London County Council ex parte Corrie* in 1918,[57] the secretary of a branch of the National League of the Blind applied for permission from the LCC to sell pamphlets, in aid of blind people, in public parks. The LCC wrote to her, stating that the council's policy was not to issue permits for such purposes, and that it was 'not possible to make exception to this rule even in a most deserving case'. The secretary argued that the council, by implementing a blanket policy of refusal of permits in all cases, was fettering its discretion to give or refuse consent to particular applications; that it was under a duty to consider her application on its merits; and that only after doing so could it exercise its discretion to give or refuse consent. The court agreed with this argument.

But does this mean that if a statutory provision entrusts an agency with discretionary powers, the courts cannot intervene in the exercise of those powers as long as no accompanying duty is breached? What, for example, do the courts make of statutory terms such as 'if it appears to the Minister that . . .' or 'if the Minister is satisfied that . . .'? To what lengths ought a minister to go in his enquiries? How must a minister satisfy himself as to a particular state of affairs? If a statute provides, for instance, for objections to a proposal to be heard, does it provide that a minister *must* hear objections, or simply that he *may* do so? And if he does hear them, is he obliged to take those objections into account? Often such questions as this are not easily answered, and are certainly very rarely addressed specifically in the statutes themselves. As has been suggested above, the courts do not readily accept that administrators should have unfettered discretion. Consider, for example, the important case of *Padfield* v. *Minister of Agriculture* in 1968.[58]

Here, the Agricultural Marketing Act 1958 provided that complaints about marketing schemes established under the Act could be heard by a committee of investigation 'if the Minister in any case so directs'. The plaintiff complained about prices paid to farmers such as himself in southern England by the Milk Marketing Board. The minister refused to refer the complaint to the committee of investigation, claiming that he had an absolute discretion in deciding whether or not to refer such complaints. He argued that the complaint should have been handled by the Milk Marketing Board rather than the committee, and that if the latter had dealt with the complaint, he would have been expected to give effect to the committee's recommendations. The House of Lords held that these reasons were not good reasons in law, and that, although the minister had considerable discretion in the matter, he was not entitled to act in such a way as to frustrate the intentions of the statute.

In so far as any general principles are discernible in the law as to when courts may or may not hold administrative action to be *ultra vires*, the leading case usually cited is *Associated Provincial Picture Houses Ltd* v. *Wednesbury Corporation* in 1948.[59] In this case, Lord Greene in the Court of Appeal explained that

It is true that discretion must be exercised reasonably. Now what does that mean? Lawyers familiar with the phraseology used in relation to exercise of statutory discretions often use the word 'unreasonable' in a rather comprehensive sense. It has frequently been used and is frequently used as a general description of the things that must not be done. For instance, a person entrusted with a discretion must . . . direct himself properly in law. He must call his own attention to the matters which he is bound to consider. He must exclude from his consideration matters which are irrelevant to what he has to consider. If he does not obey those rules, he may truly be said, and often is said, to be acting 'unreasonably'. Similarly, there may be something so absurd that no sensible person could ever dream that it lay within the powers of the authority. [Consider] the example of the red-haired teacher, dismissed because she had red hair. This is unreasonable in one sense. In another it is taking into consideration extraneous matters. It is so unreasonable that it might almost be described as being done in bad faith; and, in fact, all these things run into one another.[60]

Although the '*Wednesbury* principle' has been referred to by the courts in many later cases, it hardly provides a clear legal test for deciding whether an administrative agency has or has not acted unreasonably in particular circumstances. In *Secretary of State for Education and Science* v. *Tameside Metropolitan Borough Council* in 1976,[61] a case concerning the implementation of the then Labour government's policy of introducing comprehensive education, a Conservative-controlled borough council informed the Secretary of State that it did not intend to reorganize the grammar schools in its area along comprehensive lines. Plans had, in fact, been drawn up for the reorganization of the schools by the preceding Labour-controlled administration in the borough, and the Secretary of State directed the council that it must implement those plans. The statutory provision entitling the minister to give such a direction was contained in s.68 of the Education Act 1944, which stated that 'if the Secretary of State is satisfied . . . that any local education authority . . . have acted or are proposing to act unreasonably . . . he may . . . give such directions . . . as appear to him to be expedient'. The House of Lords upheld the decision of the council. The court's interpretation of the statutory provision was that 'unreasonably' meant behaving in a manner in which no reasonable authority would behave; it did not mean behaving in a manner with which the minister simply disagreed, and the facts revealed no evidence on which the Secretary of State could have come to the conclusion that the authority was acting 'unreasonably' in the above sense of the word. Interestingly, in *Council of Civil Service Unions* v. *Minister for the Civil Service* in 1985,[62] the word 'irrational' seems to have been substituted for 'unreasonable' in Lord Diplock's explanation of the grounds for judicial intervention:

One can conveniently classify under three heads the grounds on which administrative action is subject to control by judicial review. The first ground I would call 'illegality', the second 'irrationality' and the third 'procedural impropriety' . . . By 'illegality' as a ground for judicial review I mean that the decision-maker must understand correctly the law that regulates his decision-making power and must give effect to it . . . By 'irrationality' I mean . . . a decision which is so outrageous in its defiance of logic or of accepted moral standards that no sensible person who had applied his mind to the question to be decided could have arrived at it.[63]

It is clear from such cases that an apparently unlimited discretionary power will not preclude the courts from finding grounds for intervention, nor from declaring, where they think it appropriate, that the exercise of such discretion might be *ultra vires*.

It will be recalled that in *Padfield*'s case, the court referred to the 'intention of the statute'. On this difficult question of judicial intervention in the use of statutory powers, the judges frequently exercise themselves in deciding whether or not ministerial or other administrative action runs counter to or with the spirit of relevant statutory provision.[64] The difficulty here, however, is that, as we have seen,[65] statutory interpretation is not a precise science, and must frequently be a matter of subjective opinion by the judges.

As the *Wednesbury* principle makes clear, another justification for overturning the exercise of administrators' discretionary powers is that the agency in question has taken into account irrelevant considerations,[66] or has acted with improper motives or through misplaced or excessive philanthropy. In *Bromley London Borough Council* v. *Greater London Council* in 1982,[67] the GLC, following its election promise to cut London Transport fares, had sought to levy a supplementary rate upon the London boroughs in order to finance the reduction. Bromley LBC challenged the validity of this supplementary rate, and both the Court of Appeal and the House of Lords held that the GLC had exceeded its powers. Not only did the GLC have a statutory duty to encourage the 'economic' operation of London Transport[68] and not deliberately (and avoidably) run the system at a considerable loss, but also, said the House of Lords, the GLC in taking these steps was in breach of its 'fiduciary duty' towards ratepayers to maintain a fair balance between the provision of services and the cost to those ratepayers. It is interesting that, in the Court of Appeal, the GLC was expressly criticized for interpreting an election promise as a firm mandate – something which, in the *Tameside* case, the local authority was applauded for doing.

There are many other situations in which the courts have invoked the doctrine of *ultra vires*: where local authority by-laws have been held to be unreasonable,[69] for example, or where a person possessing a statutory power has been held to have wrongly delegated that power to another.[70] The cases mentioned here show how wide the applicability of the *ultra vires* doctrine is, especially in the hands of judges who, it seems, will try to find grounds for intervention if they desire to step in. It is certainly hard to state precisely any set of principles which consistently inform judicial decisions in this area, and some of the grounds for intervention (such as 'unreasonableness') are intrinsically flexible and imprecise. It may be, too, that the extent of judicial intervention depends upon the overall complexion of the judiciary at any particular period.[71] Sometimes, the judges have been somewhat reluctant to interfere with ministerial discretion,[72] and at others, they seem prepared to go so far as to take 'it upon themselves to tell Ministers that they acted wrongly not because they had taken decisions which were *ultra vires* in substance or in procedure but because they had taken policy decisions on grounds of which the courts disapproved'.[73]

The inconsistency and flexibility of *ultra vires* would seem to suggest that a major obstacle to any systematic development of consistent principles is not so much the presence of the 'red light' as the fact that the judges keep moving it.

Natural justice: 'administrative' or 'judicial' – does it matter?

Similar patterns of judicial activity can be seen in considering the applicability or otherwise of the principles of natural justice. This term has no mysterious or magical meaning: it simply refers to a duty to act fairly, and this duty is usually defined as comprising two aspects. The first, the *audi alteram partem* principle, is that a body having a duty to observe natural justice shall give each party the opportunity to be heard; the second principle, *nemo judex in causa sua*, means that 'no-one shall be judge in his own cause', or in other words, that the decision must not be biased.

In his explanation of *certiorari* and prohibition, Lord Atkin referred to 'any body of persons having legal authority to determine questions affecting the rights of subjects, and having the duty to act judicially'. 'Acting judicially', it will be recalled, has long been regarded as different from 'acting administratively', and in the law relating to natural justice much has depended on this distinction. We have seen some criticisms of this, and there is a strong argument that this distinction between 'judicial' and 'adminstrative' is fallacious. Even so, the distinction is one to which the courts have over the years subscribed; and, at least until *Ridge* v. *Baldwin* in 1964,[74] they held that the duty to observe natural justice existed only where the agency in question was acting *judicially*, and not where the decision was purely *administrative*. Let us consider some of the more important cases.

We have already encountered, in *Cooper* v. *Wandsworth Board of Works* in 1863,[75] circumstances where the courts in the last century were prepared to hold that a public body had acted wrongly in carrying out an action affecting the property of another without giving that other a chance to put his case. If, however, we look more closely at the nature of the power which was vested in the Board of Works, it is plainly administrative: the board was not engaged in any form of *adjudication* of Cooper's legal rights, but rather had an administrative discretion to take certain action (to pull down the house) if a specific condition was satisfied (failure to give due notice before starting to build). The court none the less interpreted the board's decision as being 'judicial', Byles J. stating categorically that 'they had acted judicially, because they had to determine the offence, and they had to apportion the punishment as well as the remedy'.

For many years thereafter, the courts' approach to the question as to whether natural justice applied was to consider the nature of the function performed by the adminstrative body: was it judicial or administrative? Even when it was held that the agency was performing a judicial function, however, the matter still remained as to *how* the principles of natural justice should be observed. In *Local Government Board* v. *Arlidge* in 1915,[76] for example, a local authority had made a closing order in respect of Arlidge's house, which the authority thought was unfit for habitation. Arlidge appealed against this decision to the Local Government Board; a public inquiry was duly held before a housing inspector, and the latter sent his report back to the board, who then confirmed the closing order. Arlidge sought to quash this decision on the grounds, *inter alia*, that he had not been given an oral hearing by the board, and had not been allowed to see the inspector's report. The House of Lords rejected his complaint, being of the opinion that, *although the board was acting judicially*, it was not appropriate to expect that it should operate like a court of law, but that as long as it acted fairly it could legitimately follow its own procedures.

In *Errington* v. *Minister of Health* in 1935,[77] a case concerning a slum clearance order, council officials and civil servants had private discussions after a public inquiry had been held, and visited the houses affected by the order without informing the owner. The court here held that the order was made in breach of natural justice, and quashed the clearance order, stating that although the minister's final decision was an administrative one, the public inquiry procedure was judicial or quasi-judicial, and natural justice should have been observed. But in 1948, in *Franklin* v. *Minister of Town and Country Planning*,[78] the minister had made a draft order designating Stevenage as the first 'new town' under the New Towns Act 1946. A public inquiry was held after objections were made to this proposal. Before this, the minister had made public statements that Stevenage was to be a new town, and had answered objectors at a meeting by saying, 'It is no good your jeering – it is going to be done.' After the inquiry, the minister confirmed the order. Rejecting the challenge to the legality of the minister's action on the grounds of bias, the House of Lords held that the minister's actions throughout were 'purely administrative', and that therefore there was no obligation to observe natural justice.

It is difficult to reconcile decisions like these, but it was not until 1964 that a different approach began to be adopted. In that year, in *Ridge* v. *Baldwin*,[79] a chief constable who had been acquitted of criminal charges was dismissed by the Watch Committee. Although there was no statutory duty to do so, the House of Lords held that he should have been given a hearing before the dismissal, and that the dismissal was therefore void. After this case, the courts began to decide that natural justice might apply even though the functions called in question might be administrative ones. In *Re H.K. (An Infant)* in 1967,[80] the court held that natural justice applied to an immigration officer's decision as to whether an immigrant was entitled to enter the country, even though the decision was stated to be neither judicial nor quasi-judicial. The Lord Chief Justice said that there was a requirement to act 'fairly', and this line has been followed in later cases.

Hartley and Griffith suggest that the approach based on the nature of the decision has given way since *Ridge* v. *Baldwin* to one based on the *interests* affected by the administrative decision in question, and that 'the more seriously [an individual's] interests are affected the more likely it is that natural justice will apply'.[81] Such interests include freedom of movement, liberty, property, reputation, occupation and the possession of a particular office or status – though the public interest, too, may well have to be balanced against individual ones. Even if natural justice is held to apply in a particular case, however, the question may still remain as to *how* the principles have to be observed; the court may decide, depending on its view of the case, that a procedure akin to a court hearing may be necessary, or that there is simply a duty to 'act fairly'. It is hard to tease out of the case-law any coherent guidelines by which we can safely predict which way a court will decide. Once again, it seems that much hangs on whether the courts wish to intervene. Whether they do or not, they have at their disposal, in the case-law, a veritable wardrobe from which they can select reasons with which to clothe their decisions with a cloak of legal principle.

Conclusion

Who applies for judicial review, and in what kind of cases? Recent surveys by Sunkin[82] have provided interesting data on the use made of the judicial review procedure in recent years. Taking and analysing the judicial review caseload for the period 1981 to 1986, Sunkin found that the total number of cases had significantly increased, from 356 applications in 1981 to 877 in 1985; by 1987 the number of applications had risen to 1,267, and by 1989, to 1,309. The total figures conceal variations between years in the types of problem involved: the 71 cases in 1987 concerning homeless persons, for example, had increased to 177 in 1989, while the 1987 figure of 697 cases involving immigration had dropped to 419 in 1989. These variations are, suggests Sunkin, partly explained by 'surges of litigation' in particular areas – for example, the number of Tamil refugees seeking asylum in Britain generated an increase from around 20 applications per year which sought to challenge refusal of asylum, to over 290 in 1987. And the number of cases involving homelessness, having fallen from 66 in 1985 to 32 in 1986,[83] rose steeply to 177 in 1989, no doubt because of the housing crisis.

By far the greatest number of applications were made by individuals (though many of these might be brought on behalf of groups). Applications brought by companies, local authorities and others were far fewer, though there was a marked increase in applications for judicial review initiated by local authorities during the period, many of which were against central government; and during 1987–89 there was an increase in applications instituted by companies: 'there is also some evidence that the range of issues litigated by the company applicants broadened, implying that judicial review was being used across a broader spectrum of commercial contexts'.[84]

As to the agencies whose decisions were being challenged, central government departments (and in particular the Home Office) comprised the largest category, followed by local authorities, courts and tribunals, and other agencies such as professional bodies, the BBC, the British Railways Board and the Criminal Injuries Compensation Board. Despite the overall increase in applications, and the diversity of both applicants and respondents, however, Sunkin's analysis shows that the vast majority of challenges to central government involved immigration, and those affecting local government concerned questions of housing and rates. In other areas, such as planning, environment and public health, tax cases, and cases involving disciplinary proceedings (for example, against lawyers and professionals within the health service), the figures are very variable and over the years 1987–9 show no particular trend.

Despite the potential scope of judicial review in controlling administrative agencies, therefore, Sunkin's conclusion in 1987 was that

During the past five or six years, judicial review has provided a facility primarily used by applicants in a very limited range of subject areas against a correspondingly narrow band of public agencies.[85]

Sunkin reiterates this in his 1989 report, and, no doubt in the light of the overall increase in those applying for judicial review, asserts that

There is undoubtedly tremendous potential for a further expansion in the quantity of judicial review litigation, but whether this occurs will depend on factors such as the availability of legal aid and the existence of alternative means of redress.[86]

Sunkin's 1987 study suggested that the courts are not particularly effective in imposing limits on administrative action through the procedure of judicial review, and this adds weight to the arguments of 'green light' theorists who, as we have seen, question the role of the judges in this area for other reasons. Baldwin and McCrudden point out, however, that judicial review today has functions other than the grievance-remedial one, or for that matter the idea that, by keeping regulatory agencies within their statutory confines, the courts are in effect ensuring that the intention of Parliament is being carried out: 'Increasingly ... a supplementary justification is claimed by the judges and attributed by commentators to the judges ... This emphasises that the judges are also concerned with setting standards of good and fair administration.'[87] Unfortunately, Baldwin and McCrudden explain, this standard-setting activity is beset by unpredictability as to how courts will react in any particular cases, or even as to the factors they will regard as relevant; inconsistency between decisions; and a tendency to approach judicial review in terms of the values associated with ordinary civil litigation, which, it may be argued, focuses on too narrow a range of issues, and is too individualized, to come to grips with the complex decision-making activities of large regulatory agencies.

Despite these problems, however, most would acknowledge that some safeguards are needed to protect the citizen or groups against excessive administrative zeal. How might this be done?

Arthurs[88] sees an alternative method of controlling administrative misconduct while retaining a role for the judges. He argues that 'administrative law' should be promoted, not in terms of its inheritance from Dicey, but rather in terms of the creation of a system of administration whose functions are defined through law but whose control is vested – again by the use of legislative provision – in bodies which are politically accountable, and whose quality is enhanced so that 'the original quality of decisions'[89] may be improved. 'Such measures would include clearer statements of legislative purpose, better defined and more open procedures to ensure participation, more careful training of administrative decision-makers, systems of internal appeal, and external, but largely nonjudicial, accountability.'[90] The role of the judges would thus be considerably reduced, though Arthurs sees a minimal role for them in an *ultra vires* jurisdiction, to ensure that administrators remain within their powers, and a role in the protection of 'constitutional values'. Baldwin and McCrudden suggest, among other things, that the process of judicial review should be widened out to encourage and allow the courts the opportunity of getting to grips with the multi-faceted work of regulatory agencies, rather than focusing upon narrow aspects of law; they raise the question, too, whether in addition there is a case for a new office – that of a 'director of civil proceedings' – which a number of commentators have suggested, and whose functions would include the bringing of proceedings, the monitoring of applications, and the task of ensuring that relevant arguments are put before the courts. In sum, they argue that 'a more articulate, a more structured, and a more consistent approach to judicial review is necessary'.[91]

McAuslan[92] has argued, however, that current developments in administrative law are fundamentally out of step with the aims and objectives of modern administration. He uses the notion of 'collective consumption', by which he means 'those consumption processes whose organisation and management cannot be other than collective given the nature and size of the problems'.[93] Examples include education and health services, environmental, housing and transport facilities, and land-use and planning. The point about such services is that they are, and must be, 'organised, planned and managed on a collective public basis – by central and local governments or by quangos – as they are consumed collectively'.[94]

McAuslan points out that the development of administrative agencies to make decisions and carry out policies in these, and many other, areas has involved different types of problems – problems which have not been addressed by the courts in their skirmishes with administration. What, he asks, have any of the 'judicial intervention' cases

> contributed to the management of a council housing waiting list, or the treatment of patients in the National Health Service, or clients in Supplementary Benefit offices, or members of minority groups by the police, or consumers of public utilities . . . ? It is precisely because the answer is 'nothing' that the period that witnessed a great growth in the process of collective consumption saw also . . . the equally rapid growth of . . . collective grievance-handling agencies, that is agencies whose costs are borne on public funds; access to which is either free of all procedural restrictions or subject to minimal ones; and whose *modus operandi* is a collective investigation of a grievance followed, usually, by a process of negotiation or cajoling to try to provide a remedy or solution to the aggrieved party.[95]

McAuslan argues that tensions within the administrative framework, caused by reductions in public expenditure and consequent struggles over resources, become resolved into legal disputes. In essence, however, such disputes are often *political* problems, concerning resource allocation and different approaches to policy. The courts' response to such cases – examples cited are *Bromley London Borough Council* v. *Greater London Council*, the *Tameside* case, discussed above, and *Norwich City Council* v. *Secretary of State for the Environment*,[96] where the minister intervened to speed up the sale of council houses under the Housing Act 1980 (see chapter 5) in response to a 'go slow' policy by the local council, and was held to have been justified in so doing – is to *individualize* and thus *privatize* what are essentially collective, *public* questions. Analysing these cases, McAuslan, like Griffith, considers that the judges perform a political role, albeit disguised in legalistic terms; and that that role is essentially concerned with protection of the individual against the collective, the private against the public.

Another call for radical reform in this area came in 1992 from the Lord Justice of Appeal, Sir Harry Woolf.[97] Noting Sunkin's findings, Woolf is of the opinion that the present structure of judicial review cannot cope with the caseload, and that there is reason to believe that this caseload will increase still further.[98] What could be done about this? First, Woolf points out that of the total number of applications for review each year, between half and two-thirds are in fact turned down by the court: there is, then, a part to be played by legal advisers in filtering out unmeritorious applications. Second, the workload might be allocated between more judges and more courts, rather than requiring all applications for review to go before the Queen's Bench Division of the High Court. In particular, he suggests that those cases which have no wider import than the interests of the individual affected might be dealt with by county court judges (subject to a right of appeal on a point of law to the Court of Appeal), while cases having implications for a greater section of the public could continue to be heard before the High Court. In the former category Woolf would place urgent cases, such as those concerned with homelessness or immigration.

In the longer term, and again with homelessness and immigration cases in mind, Lord Woolf considers use could be made of the tribunal device (see chapter 6) so that

The way forward over a period of time should thus involve creating a unified system of tribunals for resolving administrative disputes, with the High Court and Court of Appeal required to resolve only difficult problems of law and points of principle and policy of high importance to the development of administrative law.[99]

The arguments put forward in favour of these proposals are convincing, and the proposals themselves for the most part attractive, at least in so far as they would serve to contain and process the rising number of applications for review more quickly and effectively. It is hard to disagree, in the final analysis, with McAuslan's comment that 'the time is ripe for a relook, a rethink and rewrite on the evolution of our modern system of administrative law and its relationship to the state, policy-making and resource allocation within the state including policy-making by the judges'.[100]

13
The legal profession

The law is one of the most powerful carriers of dominant social definitions of acceptable and unacceptable conduct. It is perhaps the most significant social institution for the settlement of disputes, and it contains within its rules and procedures the means whereby infringements of the law, from the trivial to the most serious, can be dealt with. Lawyers form an important group of the various personnel involved in these procedures, and it is important to understand the kinds of service which lawyers provide, as well as the occupational, social and educational background of this body of experts whose work is so closely tied up with the maintenance of social norms embodied in the law and the legal system.

Lawyers, it is often said, are a response to a social need. Disputes crop up in all corners of society, among every social class, and such disputes and problems can involve anything from marriage breakdown to criminal charges, contested wills to commercial transactions. The trouble is that in many cases the solution to the dispute is not something which can be determined like a mathematical equation. Most cases involve questions of social values, the most fundamental of which is probably 'justice', and judgments about those cases are based upon evaluation rather than issues of hard fact. Law embodies dominant social norms and values, and lawyers are engaged in their everyday work in maintaining those values through their function of implementing the law.

Much of that everyday work, however, attracts criticism, often on the grounds that there is a substantial discrepancy between the way in which lawyers perceive their work in the provision of legal services, and the inadequacy of the profession's responses to the community's legal problems. Examples are the statutory protection enjoyed until recently[1] by solicitors in their monopoly of conveyancing (the expensive legal procedures involved in the transfer of real property);[2] the failure to respond to the problems created for the individual by state intervention in the provision of welfare and employment protection; and the general failure by many lawyers, to put it simply, to 'get through to the community'. In recent years, the legal profession has drawn heavy fire, too, from the government, largely on the basis that the ways in which lawyers have traditionally carried out their work are 'restrictive practices'; that the profession should address itself to ensuring that the public gets 'value for money'; and that consequently much of the organization and working practices of the profession are in need of reform. We shall discuss these changes presently.

Set up in 1976, largely as a result of public disquiet about the legal profession and its work (such as the high cost of conveyancing), the Royal Commission on Legal Services (the Benson Commission), from whose report[3] much of the data about lawyers in this chapter are drawn, reported in 1979. The report did little to reassure the critics, although it certainly did much to reassure the legal profession. Virtually nothing was contained in its recommendations by way of changes in the organization of either of the two branches of the profession – solicitors and barristers – and most of the positive proposals made were directed towards increasing lawyers' work (and hence their income) and maintaining their highly privileged and protected status. In the course of this chapter, we will examine various aspects of lawyers and their work, and many of the issues dealt with by the Benson Commission will be discussed. On a more general level, however, it is important to examine some aspects of the structural position of lawyers in our society, and to understand the legal profession in relation to the particular social structure in which it operates.

Lawyers have traditionally held themselves out as 'professionals', which, sociologically, carries the implication that, as professionals, lawyers occupy key positions within society. They are respected by the lay person as having possession of specialized knowledge, and the supposed, or claimed, ability to solve the client's problems. Some sociological analyses of professions suggest that professional people are identifiable by reason of their possession of certain traits, or characteristics: (i) command of a systematic body of theoretical and specialized knowledge; (ii) professional authority; (iii) the approval and support of the community; (iv) a rigorous code of ethics regulating their activities; and (v) a professional 'culture'.[4] A somewhat similar set of characteristics was listed in the Benson Report, and it has been commented that this approach

ensured that, among other things, self-regulation would continue and that the 'altruistic' nature of the lawyer/client relationship would preclude the introduction of the market. The client would continue to be grateful to the lawyer for a service based on trust, confidentiality, and independence rather than upon competition and economic choice. The term 'money' was not to be discussed with or by the client, as the crucial terms were 'service' and 'justice' – and on justice no price can be placed.[5]

It is obvious that professionals such as lawyers or doctors claim to have command of specialized, expert knowledge.[6] The difficulty lies in deciding exactly what kind of knowledge it is. Professionals usually claim that their training and skills enable them to diagnose and identify problems, and to solve those problems by the application of objective, scientific knowledge. Some would argue, however, that professionals (especially doctors and lawyers) rarely, if ever, *merely* bring to bear objective scientific knowledge, but rather that they are frequently involved in making value-judgments about clients and their problems. A number of critics, for example, have suggested that 'mental illness' is often not so much a clinically diagnosable condition, susceptible to treatment through applying factual scientific medical skills, as a condition which is *socially* defined, arising from a patient's failure to conform to dominant social norms, which then puts the patient out of step with both social and medical expectations.[7] Similarly, the medical treatment of many aspects of women's health is seen by critics as a reflection of *attitudes* towards women and health care, rather than a matter of purely scientific objectivity.[8] This is not to suggest that all medical skill is fundamentally a matter of value-judgment and personal opinion: there can be little room for alternative explanations and diagnoses when a medical practitioner is faced with a broken leg, and clinical expertise is called upon to provide the appropriate treatment for the problem thus identified. The point is that there may be *some* – perhaps many – areas of physical and mental illness where medicine is less dependent on rational scientific knowledge than the profession would publicly concede.

The lawyer's claim is to a body of knowledge which, though rational, is even more rarely based upon scientific principles. Law is, as we have said, a normative discipline, involving judgments about fact-situations which necessarily involve interpretation, definition and values. A client may enter a solicitor's office, for example, and request that the solicitor undertake divorce proceedings on that client's behalf. A broken marriage, however, is not like a broken leg: it may not be easy, to begin with, to ascertain that the marriage *has* broken down. Even when that 'diagnosis' is chosen, the appropriate 'treatment' may be selected from a range of possible ways of dealing with that problem, from persuading the client that conciliation may be more apt than a divorce, to accepting the client's plea that proceedings for ending the marriage through legal formalities be initiated. Whichever solution is offered by the solicitor will be the outcome not of hard-and-fast clinical rules, but rather of the lawyer's 'professional judgment' about what the client wants or needs.

It is the body of professional knowledge, and the claim to be able to use it to deal with clients' disputes and problems, that maintains and enhances the lawyer's professional authority. Lawyers present themselves to clients, and indeed to the community, as having the *authoritative voice* on all legal matters, and this arguably structures to a great extent the relationship between lawyer and client. Some have argued that the professional–client relationship is one based on *power*; the professional has what the client wants or needs; he or she defines the manner in which the service is to be given and, equally importantly, defines the very *nature* of the client's problem. Typically, the client cannot argue that the professional's opinion or advice is wrong, inaccurate or inappropriate, for it is usually acknowledged by the client that the professional knows best what is in the client's interests.

Abel, drawing upon sociological analyses of professions, has produced a substantial analysis of the legal profession in the United Kingdom, and the ways in which it has attempted to respond to both criticism and structural changes in the market for legal services. He notes that

Producers of a service who succeed in constructing a marketable commodity only become an occupation. In order to become a profession they must seek social closure. This project has two dimensions: market control and collective social mobility . . . All occupations are compelled by the market to compete . . .[9]

The professional project is directed not only toward controlling the market but also toward enhancing professional status ... the lengthy training professionals must complete perhaps may better be understood not as the acquisition of technical skills but as a sacrifice necessary to justify future privilege: only this can make sense of the relative poverty endured by students, their prolonged celibacy, the tedium of study, the indignities of apprenticeship, the anxiety inflicted by examinations and the lengthy postponement of adulthood.[10]

Abel discusses, among other issues, the questions of 'how lawyers constructed their professional commodity (legal services) and sought to assert control over their market and to enhance their collective status',[11] and he shows how in recent years the legal profession has increasingly come under pressure from various quarters, with the result that it can no longer maintain its position of independence, exclusivity and high status so easily.

What has happened is that the legal profession can no longer justify itself simply by reference to the 'professionalism' which in the past served to legitimate its position in the community. The government line since 1979 has been to confront all occupational groups perceived as operating restrictive practices, occupying a monopolistic or near-monopolistic position in the marketplace, or failing to provide services which offer value for the client's money: the legal profession has been acutely affected by these policies. Among the alleged 'restrictive practices' within the legal profession, identified by – in particular – the three Green Papers published in 1989 which contained the Lord Chancellor's plans for reform,[12] were the right to argue the client's case in court (the 'right of audience'), conveyancing, and various other rules and conventions concerning barristers. One effect of the pressures for change has been to undermine seriously the profession's privileged position as a 'professional' group, and to force lawyers to enter and operate within the open competitive marketplace. And apart from these concerns, there was continuing worry within government over the spiralling cost to the public purse of the provision of legal services – especially the cost of legal aid – bringing further confrontation between lawyers and the government (usually in the person of the Lord Chancellor).

Even before these assaults by the government, which we will examine in more detail presently, the legal profession has in recent years been undergoing profound change for other reasons. The profession's *control* of the supply of lawyers and legal services has decreased: whereas once the legal profession closely controlled its own intake by means of apprenticeship and instruction by the profession itself, the huge expansion of law courses in higher education has led to the current situation where entry into the profession is at present almost exclusively by graduates with law degrees.[13] This, coupled with a period of growth within the profession during the 1980s, has resulted in a large increase in the numbers of practising lawyers, especially solicitors, whose ranks have risen twelve times as fast as they did in the first half of this century. This expansion has been accompanied, however, by a tendency for the legal profession to lose certain types of work – for example, through people choosing to represent themselves in courts and tribunals, through 'do-it-yourself' divorce procedures, or through other professional groups such as accountants making inroads into tax law – which was once among the lawyer's exclusive specialisms.[14] It is not surprising that the Benson Commission recommended measures which would offset this tendency – measures such as, in particular, the continuation of the divided profession (whereby solicitors remain the protected intermediaries between clients and barristers), the retention of the conveyancing monopoly (which in the past accounted for about half of solicitors' income), and the maintenance of solicitors' rights of audience.

The legal profession, through the Commission, made much of the ideal of equality – that all are entitled to receive the same quality of legal services, irrespective of their personal circumstances – to support the recommendation for a vast increase in state subsidization through legal aid; and also argued the increased need, in the face of welfare state intervention in so many aspects of people's lives, to protect people from unjust interference or denial of rights by state authorities. This was one reason for the Benson Commission's proposal to extend legal aid to tribunal hearings (see chapter 6).

Of course, one abiding concern of the legal profession, and an important plank in its edifice of legitimation, has been its *independence*, both of state or other institutions and in terms of its self-image as disinterested and objective in its dealings with clients and with the law. Indeed, the claim to independence has been an important aspect of the legal profession's maintenance of its monopoly of legal services. The trouble is that if the state is called upon for substantial financial public subsidization through legal aid, then the state, on behalf of the community, can stake its own claim to a say in the way in which the profession is run. The Benson Commission tried to head off this possibility by raising the flag of independence: 'Legal services are required more and more by private individuals who are in dispute with authority in one of its many forms and to protect the interests of clients in such cases, the independence of the legal profession is of paramount importance'[15] and by expressing the fervent hope that 'the profession should have a period of orderly development free, so far as possible, from external interventions'.[16]

As hinted above, however, such a period of peace and quiet was not to be. But before examining recent developments in more detail, it is important to gain a general overview of the organization and work of the legal profession.

The divided profession and its work

The legal profession is divided into two branches, solicitors and barristers.[17] Each have their own controlling bodies – the Law Society and the Bar Council respectively – and an intending lawyer must decide, at a relatively early stage in legal training, whether to practise as a solicitor or a barrister, because apart from the initial period of legal education (usually a law degree course) the two branches are mutually exclusive in terms of personnel and training, although rather less so in terms of their work. The controlling bodies exercise strict codes of professional ethics and standards of practice: this is one of the ways in which the exclusivity of the profession, and its claim to produce high standards of work, are maintained. Both bodies act as disciplinary agencies to deal with any alleged breach of these codes, and for serious breaches a member of either branch of the legal profession may be 'struck off'.

This exclusivity is further promoted by the impact of training and socialization. All lawyers undergo extensive periods of education, both through formal academic learning and through practical training in legal work. In the case of solicitors, this practical training takes the form of a two-year period, after obtaining a law degree, as an 'articled clerk' (a kind of apprentice solicitor attached to a firm of practitioners). For intending barristers, the period of training is rather more complicated and less financially secure, but possibly more intensive because of the immersion of the novice in the traditions and practices of the Bar. Apart from undertaking various examinations in law, the prospective barrister must also join one of the four Inns of Court, where the life of the barrister is learned. The various rules and institutions of the Bar (such as the apparently odd rule that the intending barrister must eat dinners at the Inn at least twelve times a year) serve to socialize the novice into the established ways of that branch of the profession, where customs, traditions and etiquette play so great a part. Barristers' professional, and often much of their social, life involves an exclusive and somewhat socially isolated experience, where the company in which they move comprises, very often, other barristers and judges who are members of the same Inn.

For many people, the image of the typical lawyer and his or her work is that presented in the formal setting of the courtroom. Here, it is traditionally the barrister, in wig and gown, who presents the case and expresses the arguments on the client's behalf; the solicitor's task is to deal directly with the client, to ensure that the barrister chosen is properly and fully instructed, to collect and collate all relevant evidence (such as witnesses' statements, letters, photographs and so on) and to ensure that all relevant persons are present in court on the day of the trial.

This image of lawyers and their work is, however, somewhat misleading: the traditional division of functions in the courtroom is gradually being broken down. Although only barristers have full 'rights of audience' (that is, the right to address the judges' bench directly on the client's behalf) in all courts, solicitors have full rights of audience, too, in magistrates' and county courts, and in some Crown courts.

The issue of rights of audience has assumed highly controversial proportions in recent years. The Courts and Legal Services Act 1990 provides that solicitors (and for that matter anyone else) may apply for additional rights of audience. This provision followed the Lord Chancellor's proposals in the White Paper *Legal Services: A Framework for the Future*,[18] and is designed to enhance both the quality of advocacy, and the freedom of choice as to who should be able to act as an advocate. Applications for additional rights of audience are considered by the Lord Chancellor's Advisory Committee on Education and Conduct, and the views of that Committee are then taken into account by the deciding forum, comprising the Lord Chancellor and four senior judges. The Act provides that the criteria by which such applications must be judged are (i) appropriate qualifications by the applicant; (ii) whether the applicant belongs to a professional body which exercises effective control over its members; (iii) whether that professional body's rules prevent applicants from unfairly discriminating as between clients; and (iv) whether those rules are 'appropriate in the interests of the proper and efficient administration of justice' (s.17)3)).

As soon as the 1990 Act was passed, the Law Society submitted its application for additional rights for solicitors, which would extend their rights of audience to all Crown court cases where no jury was used (for instance, guilty plea cases and committals for sentence), and further applications for additional rights were submitted by the Government Legal Service and the Director of Public Prosecutions (for the Crown Prosecution Service). All these applications were opposed by the Bar, for obvious reasons. The latter two applications were rejected; though the Law Society's application was not found acceptable in its original form, the Advisory Committee felt that solicitors could enjoy additional rights subject to their undertaking training in the skills of advocacy. There is no doubt that the debates as to the appropriate allocation of rights of audience as between barristers, solicitors and – in particular – the Crown Prosecution Service – is set to continue.

Moreover, while the traditional practice has always been to recruit judges, at all levels except magistrates (who are not legally qualified), from the ranks of barristers, the Royal Commission on Assizes and Quarter Sessions (the Beeching Commission) recommended in its report in 1969 that Circuit Judges[19] should be appointed from the ranks of both branches of the profession. The Courts Act 1971 (which implemented the Beeching Commission's proposals in so far as they were accepted) provided that Recorders[20] may be appointed from solicitors and barristers of ten years' standing, and that Circuit Judges may be appointed from barristers of ten years' standing, or may be Recorders who have held that post for at least five years. Thus, 'solicitor-Recorders' of five years' standing may be appointed as Circuit Judges.

A second important qualification to the 'courtroom image' of the legal profession is that nearly all of the profession's work is done *outside* the courtroom. Both solicitors and barristers are often retained for the giving of advice. Such advice may be on taxation or company matters, matrimonial or property affairs, civil or criminal disputes and so on. It must not be supposed that solicitors are ignorant of the law; it is only in certain cases that the advice of a barrister is sought. Indeed, one of the arguments often put forward for retaining the division of the legal profession is that it enables barristers to become highly expert on specialized and technical areas of law which the more down-to-earth and practical nature of solicitors' work is thought not to allow. It may, however, fairly be said that the two branches engage in the same sort of work – that of advice and consultancy – and, for solicitors in particular, such work is usually far more rewarding financially than court work.

Conveyancing, together with other property matters, has traditionally accounted for about half of solicitors' work, though this proportion has fallen quite substantially in recent years.[21] Conveyancing involves a series of fairly complicated stages, including the completion of forms, negotiations between the buyers and sellers of real property, and the drawing-up and exchange of contracts between them for the transfer of that property. Although in theory anyone can undertake their own conveyancing (riddled with pitfalls though it is), there are legal restrictions as to who can undertake this work for payment. The solicitors' monopoly of conveyancing came under attack as part of the government's proposals for reform in the 1980s, and the Administration of Justice Act 1985 removes that monopoly by providing for the establishment of a new occupational group of 'licensed conveyancers'. The Building Societies Act 1986 provides that conveyancing services could be carried out by building societies and other organizations apart from private solicitors' firms, though this development may have little impact on the profession's ultimate control of this type of work, since only solicitors or licensed conveyancers employed by building societies may actually carry it out. Building societies may not carry out conveyancing for their own borrowers, the justification being that there may well be a conflict of interest between the roles of the building society as lender of money and as independent legal adviser. Although the Lord Chancellor's Green Paper on conveyancing had proposed that financial institutions should compete with private solicitors for this type of work, there did not seem to be a great deal of interest shown by those institutions.

Another major area of solicitors' work involves *matrimonial disputes*, which may raise issues such as separation or divorce proceedings, the attendant problems concerning children and the disposal between the parties of family property. Since the widening of the grounds for divorce, introduced in the Divorce Reform Act 1969 (now the Matrimonial Causes Act 1973), divorce itself is for many people largely a legal formality, with undefended divorce petitions as the norm. Usually, only if there are difficulties concerning the fate of the children of the marriage, or questions as to the matrimonial property, or if the divorce petition is defended by one spouse, will there be a full court hearing.

Connected with domestic and family matters is *probate* work, which involves the sorting-out of wills and the estates of deceased persons. Sometimes, such a case can involve court proceedings, as for example where a will is contested, but such court cases are relatively infrequent. For the solicitor, however, this type of work, dealt with, so to speak, from the office, constitutes a sizeable proportion of the total workload.

Much of the remainder of the solicitor's business is taken up with company and taxation matters, advising as to business contracts or partnerships – such work usually being non-contentious, involving no disputants – and providing assistance and advice on contentious matters. Usually, this involves negotiation between the two sides to the dispute but falls short (except in criminal cases) of court proceedings. We must remember that court proceedings are, in the vast majority of dispute situations, an expensive last resort, and the solicitor will usually make every effort to settle the matter without recourse to the courtroom; we must also remember that, just as the majority of disputes are settled outside the courtroom, so an even larger proportion of disputes occurring in society are never aired inside the solicitor's office at all. Many problems which a lawyer would regard as 'legal' are resolved in one way or another without the use of lawyers.

When studying the considerable spread of types of work undertaken by lawyers, it is important to bear in mind, first, that a considerable number of lawyers – at the time of the Benson Commission report about 3,000 barristers and 5,000 solicitors[22] – are employed not in private practice, but in industry, trade and commerce[23] in both public and private sectors, and in national and local government. In 1990 there were more than 6,500 barristers and about 54,700 solicitors either engaged in private practice or with practising certificates. Second, it is by no means inevitable that clients bringing their problems to solicitors' offices will always deal directly with qualified solicitors. Much of the day-to-day work in a solicitor's office may be carried out by articled clerks, working towards their final examinations after which they will become qualified, or else by *legal executives*,[24] who work in solicitors' offices and who, though not qualified solicitors, carry out a good deal of work in their capacities as legally trained assistants. Although legal executives are trained through the courses and examinations of the Institute of Legal Executives, there is no reason why a Fellow of the Institute should not continue with legal education with a view to becoming qualified as a solicitor.

Given the wide range of problems which are brought to solicitors' offices by clients, it will of course sometimes be necessary for the solicitor to engage the services of a barrister, either because litigation is envisaged, or in order to take specialized advice. This will mean that the fee-paying client must retain, and duly pay for, the services of two lawyers instead of one; and this is one very important argument which is often put forward in favour of unifying the two branches of the profession. The proposals for a fused legal profession were considered by the Benson Commission.[25] It was argued before the Commission that the divided profession can lead to situations where cases are delayed, or where problems are dealt with inefficiently; some argued that clients' confidence in the legal services provided might be reduced by seeing the case passed over to a barrister whom they have never met, after having developed trust and confidence in the solicitor to whom they brought the case; and last but not least, it was argued that a fused profession would greatly reduce clients' costs because only one expert who deals with the case from beginning to end would have to be paid, rather than two or perhaps more.

The Royal Commission considered these arguments, and discussed also those for retaining the divided profession in its present form. The latter can be summarized as follows. First, it is said that a barrister should be kept free from direct access by clients in order to ensure that his or her specialized skills are efficiently used, and that he or she is able, as a result of a certain distancing from clients, to provide completely objective advice on their problems. Second, it is argued that fusion would lead to a decline in the quality of advocacy, and hence to a decline in the quality of the administration of justice itself, by effectively 'diluting the specialist knowledge and standards of the Bar'.[26] Noting an increased need for specialism in legal services, and the need for effective advocacy of a high standard, the Commission rejected the proposals for fusion and recommended that the divided profession continue in its present form. The report states that the problems of inefficiency could arise under *any* mode of organization of the profession; that the problems of delay are due to a variety of causes, and are not attributable simply to the division of the profession; that although costs might be reduced by fusion in small cases, costs might well be greater in long and complex cases (although the basis on which the Commission reached this conclusion is not clear); and that a two-branch profession is more likely to ensure high standards, especially with regard to advocacy.

The government in its response to the Benson Report accepted the recommendations on fusion, though in practical terms the increase in solicitors' rights of audience, discussed above, may be thought to blur seriously the dividing-line between solicitors and barristers. In such ways effective fusion may ultimately come about – more by circumstance (and continuous pressure for greater rights of audience from solicitors) than by design.

The social composition of the legal profession

Like all professional groups, as commentators agree, the legal profession is essentially middle-class in outlook and, usually, in origin.[27] Plowden, discussing the comparison between doctors and lawyers, points out that

what distinguishes law from medicine is its necessary and intimate connection with social structure. As long as British social structure is such as the traditional ruling class can still command some deference, the law, to be sure of respect, must partake of the style of that class. Until the thought of a High Court judge pronouncing a life sentence in a Birmingham accent no longer seems incongruous, High Court judges must speak with the tones of Oxbridge, and so must ambitious barristers, and so must solicitors who do not wish to be thought inferior to barristers.[28]

The middle- and upper-class background of lawyers is even more marked among barristers than among solicitors, though there are those who would argue that the class distinctions are gradually being broken down between the branches of the profession. Table 1, reproduced from the Benson Commission report,[29] shows clearly the predominance of professional and managerial backgrounds, as indicated by fathers' occupations. While the figures relating to 'University graduates studying for Bar exams/training to become solicitors' do not show any marked differentiation, it is noteworthy that by the time prospective entrants to the Bar are admitted (at least in the case of two of the Inns – Gray's and Middle Temple), the preponderance of professional or managerial backgrounds has increased quite strikingly. In so far as educational background is an indicator of social class, a survey carried out by the Law Society's Research and Policy Planning Unit in 1989 of a sample of about 1,000 solicitors[30] showed that over one-third had attended fee-paying independent (or public) schools; 11 per cent had attended direct-grant grammar schools; 34 per cent had been to state grammar schools; and only 14 per cent had attended secondary modern or comprehensive schools. The report on the survey states that the proportion of solicitors who have attended independent or public school has in fact been declining over the years.

The peculiarities of recruitment into the legal profession, coupled with its unique position within the social structure, tend to favour the middle- and upper-middle-class aspirant lawyer. The sheer cost of legal education, particularly postgraduate training, is, for many potential recruits, probably prohibitive, and these expenses must be found during the period of training during which novices are not allowed to take on cases for themselves and earn their own fees. It was

TABLE 1 Occupation of the fathers of
certain classes of young people

	Fathers' occupation		
	Professional or managerial	Manual	Intermediate or other occupation
All young people:	%	%	%
aged 16–19[1]	21	66	13
aged 16–19 in full-time education[1]	32	50	18
aged 20–24 in full-time education[1]	50	30	20
University entrants:[2]			
studying professional subjects	58	15	27
studying law	54	16	30
University graduates:[2]			
studying for Bar exams	59	11	30
training to become solicitors[3]	56	15	29
Admissions to Bar:[4]			
Middle Temple	76	14	10
Gray's Inn[5]	77	8	16

Notes:

[1] Data from the General Household Survey (1974 and 1975). Parental occupation is classified according to the Registrar General's socio-economic grouping.

[2] Data from the Universities Statistical Record (1976 and 1977). Parental occupation is classified according to the Registrar General's Classification of Occupations, 1966.

[3] Graduates stating they were entering articles or studying for the Law Society's examinations.

[4] Data supplied by the Inns and classified as far as possible according to the Registrar General's socio-economic groupings. Data from the Middle Temple relates to the first half of 1977, and from Gray's Inn to 1977 and 1978.

[5] The information given relates to 70 per cent of admissions. In the remaining 30 per cent of cases either the father was deceased or insufficient information was available about his occupation.

Source: Royal Commission Report on Legal Services, 1979, Table 2.1.

announced in 1990 that the Bar was to introduce a scheme to pay pupils during their pupillage year, and in fact some barristers' chambers paid pupils somewhat better than the scheme proposed.[31] But even after qualification, a high income is not immediately guaranteed, partly because barristers must build up their reputation before cases begin to arrive regularly, and partly because fees earned for the first few cases may well take months to be paid. The Benson Commission's figures on lawyers' earnings for the year 1976–7 are illuminating in that they show the considerable differentials between high and lower earners within the two branches of the profession: clearly, the actual figures would now have to be adjusted upwards. According to the Benson Report, the *average* net fees of all barristers before tax were £8,715, but the *median* net fees were £6,643.[32] This differential reflects the small number of high earners, and the commission report states that the median net fees for this period for junior barristers (that is, all barristers who are not Queen's Counsel) with three years or less in practice were £2,648. It is the 10 per cent or so of QCs who generally manage to build up highly successful and remunerative practices, and this, of course, takes a considerable period of time.

For an intending solicitor, the two years spent as an articled clerk are usually fairly lean financially, as articled clerks are by no means well paid. The Benson Commission report found that the median figure for articled clerks' salaries in November 1976 was £1,635. Many clerks supplement this with income from other sources.[33] Such considerations suggest that an intending lawyer, whichever branch of the profession he or she chooses, would do well to come from a background which is financially secure, and preferably have some form of independent income with which to supplement the leaner times of training and early experience. Not surprisingly, surveys have shown[34] that many lawyers *do* come from middle- and upper-middle-class backgrounds: for example, studies of judges, who are traditionally recruited from the ranks of barristers, clearly show a predominance of public school and Oxford or Cambridge university educational backgrounds.[35]

Not only is the legal profession predominantly middle- and upper-middle class: it is also a profession dominated by *white male* practitioners. The significantly lower proportion of black and other ethnic minority lawyers to white, and the lower numbers of women in the profession (especially the Bar) has attracted considerable criticism over the years. With regard to solicitors, it was only in 1985 that a Race Relations Committee was established by the Law Society to monitor entry by members of black and other ethnic minority communities; it was found in 1986 that only 1 per cent of solicitors came from such backgrounds, although by 1991 the number enrolling with the Law Society was around 14 per cent of the total. There is evidence of discrimination against black students upon graduation, and of difficulties due to ethnic background in the working environment even when jobs can be obtained.[36] The picture with respect to barristers is no better. Although the Bar has long attracted – and indeed encouraged – students from overseas, the expectation was that, once qualified, they would return to practice in their home countries. Writing in 1988, Abel reported that

in the last ten years, . . . a small but significant racial minority has emerged in the Bar as the black population of Britain has grown, and legal aid has helped them secure representation . . .

Although the Senate . . . has acknowledged the existence of racial discrimination, it rejected affirmative action as a solution. It did amend the Code of Conduct in 1984 to prohibit discrimination . . . and in autumn 1986 it issued guidelines on applications for pupillages and tenancies and on distribution of work in chambers, prohibiting racial discrimination; but it may be equally noteworthy that barristers' clerks objected to these limitations on their discretion and the Senate chose not to make them practice rules in order that they might remain hortatory but unenforceable.[37]

There is little doubt that the Bar's record on this issue is unimpressive. There remains evidence that black barristers experience discrimination and racism both in obtaining places in chambers and in obtaining work. In order to do something to remedy the situation, the Bar, and later the Law Society, announced recently a 5 per cent target for the employment of black barristers and solicitors entering practice: whether this will make any dramatic difference remains to be seen.

The number of women practising lawyers is rather higher for both branches of the profession, but even here, there is no reason to believe that equality has been achieved. Despite a lamentable history within the solicitors' branch[38] that included a ban on women until 1919 (a change forced on the profession by legislation passed in that year), the proportion of women registering for articles in 1985–6 was 46.5 per cent of the total. But this does not mean that there is equality in terms of career progression: Law Society figures for 1991 show that

only twelve per cent of partners in solicitors' firms were women. Looked at another way, of all the women who practise, only 28 per cent are partners. The equivalent figure for men is 62 per cent.[39]

The history of the Bar is similar to that of the Law Society. Abel, reviewing the various surveys carried out over the past thirty years or so, identifies a number of barriers operating to discriminate against women at the Bar:[40] discrimination in obtaining pupillages and tenancies; scholarships awarded by the Inns of Court, which are available only to men; the exclusion of women from meetings; the refusal of banks to grant overdraft facilities to women barristers starting out in their careers; the obstacles posed by the profession's 'unconscious acceptance of the traditional division of labour in childbearing',[41] which forced many women to leave the profession for family reasons; and so on. The Benson Commission found that overall, women barristers earn substantially less than their male counterparts. There are very few female heads of chambers, and women comprise only 2 per cent of QCs. Abel rightly remarks that

there seems to be little basis for the extraordinary complacency about sexism recently expressed by the Bar: 'the Senate believes that (discrimination against women) is a thing of the past. That is not to say that sex discrimination is nowhere to be found, only that it has ceased to be a serious problem'.[42]

In 1992 there were no women Law Lords; one out of 27 Appeal Court judges, and two out of 83 High Court judges, were women. Two out of a total of 447 circuit judges were non-white.[43]

The social class, gender and ethnic homogeneity of lawyers contrasts dramatically with many of their clients; and the social and legal implications of such differences have given rise to considerable concern in recent years.

Lawyers and the public

Even if we are all agreed that the central value to be promoted by the legal profession is justice, it is unlikely that there will be anything like consensus on the contours of that concept . . . The problem is aggravated because different conceptions of justice are associated with subgroups, socio-economic strata and cultural or ethnic enclaves . . . the danger is always that a legal profession will become captive to a class or group and promote its interests exclusively.[44]

Traditionally, the clientele of lawyers has almost exclusively been middle class. People in business, individuals with enough money or property to need lawyers to protect it, those rich enough to afford expensive litigation – these have been the backbone of the solicitor's clientele. Since lawyers' services so often concerned property of one kind or another, those without property – the poor, the working class – had little cause to have resort to legal services. Many lawyers mistakenly deduced from this, however, that the poor did not have *any* legal problems, and so little or no attempt was made by the profession to overcome the difficulties experienced by those without property regarding access by legal services.

But what are these difficuties? It was once thought that too many solicitors' offices were located in parts of towns and cities which were predominantly business, rather than residential or shopping, areas, though research has shown that this is true only of London.[45] The Benson Commission noted the *uneven distribution* of solicitors: in 1971 there was one solicitor's office per 2,000 people in Guildford and Bournemouth, but only one per 16,500 in Tower Hamlets, one per 37,000 in Bootle, and one per 66,000 in Huyton.[46] Additionally, solicitors' offices open during office hours, and for many working people a visit to a solicitor means taking time off work. This is clearly another reason for reluctance to make such visits. Few working-class people will be personally acquainted on a social basis with solicitors, and so the idea of going to see a lawyer might for many people be a worrying venture into the unknown.

Added to this physical distance is a *social* distance between solicitors and many ordinary people:

The legal profession presents to many a deterrent image. There is the fear of looking foolish in the surroundings of a professional man's office; there is a wide chasm in symbols of communication, dress, language and behaviour. The clinical austerity of the average solicitor's office gives no indication of its intention to serve the ordinary man's needs.[47]

A further problem is that before someone takes a case to a solicitor, he or she has to be aware that the problem may be a *legal* one. It is tempting to characterize certain kinds of problem as *essentially* 'legal', and to conclude that one answer to this problem of 'consumer awareness' might be better publicity by the legal profession. Indeed, the Benson Commission recommended that solicitors should be allowed to advertise their services to the public,[48] and since 1984 individual firms may advertise. Such changes, however, fail to take account of a point mentioned earlier: that a problem *may* be defined as 'legal', but it may also be defined and dealt with in other ways. As Morris puts it,

For a client with a problem it seems likely that the way it is defined may well be a function of the organisation or agency to which it is initially referred, rather than any intrinsic property of the particular problem . . . Thus a person with a notice to quit may well approach an agency with a request for accommodation – in other words a housing rather than a legal problem.[49]

More dramatically, research carried out in the United States[50] entailed a group of lawyers being asked to identify the *legal* incidents in a group of *social work* cases. Adding together all the legal incidents recognized (and defined as such) by the lawyers, there were found to be 'legal incidents' in almost all cases. As Alcock has remarked, 'If nothing else this research demonstrated that legal problems could always be found if one looked hard enough.'[51]

The point is that, in many cases, to have a problem defined as 'legal', and some form of legal solution provided or proceedings started on one's behalf, might be positively disadvantageous for a client. All kinds of problem, notably disputes with landlords over rent or attempted eviction, wrangles with local authority agencies or services, employment disputes and problems with social security officials, involve *continuing relationships* between the client and the 'opposition'. To institute legal proceedings may well prejudice the future relationships involved, especially taking into account the fact that in many such cases the client will be in a relatively weak position compared with the other party.

In the light of all these factors, it is not altogether surprising that the Benson Commission discovered clear social-class patterns among a large sample of respondents who used lawyers' services in 1977 (Table 2), although the social-class differentiation is less marked for legal problems which do not concern property.

Suppose that a person of limited means *does* manage to overcome the social and psychological hurdles, and confronts a solicitor with a problem. To what extent

TABLE 2 Use of lawyers' services in 1977 by socio-economic group of household head

Socio-economic group of household head	Sample	Used lawyers' services on some personal matter in 1977	Was main or sole contact with lawyer on some personal matter in 1977
		%	%
	(15,441)	(15)	(12)
Professional	779	25	18
Employers/managers	2,199	21	16
Intermediate and junior non-manual	2,703	19	15
Skilled manual and own-account workers	5,510	13	9
Semi-skilled manual	2,171	11	9
Unskilled manual	801	10	8

Source: Royal Commission Report on Legal Services, 1979, Table 8.8.

does the cost factor (surely the single most important consideration for most people) inhibit access to legal services, and to what extent has state provision of subsidized legal services, through legal advice and legal aid, solved the problem of the cost barrier?

Legal aid and advice

Everyone knows that legal services are not cheap. Solicitors' fees for non-contentious matters are high, and if a case goes to court, there may well be barristers' and court fees to pay as well as the solicitor's own charges. A survey by Zander of 664 personal injury cases during 1973–4 in London, Birmingham, Liverpool and Manchester 'showed average costs of contested cases at £1,027, for cases that settled at the door of the court at £1,323, and for those that settled without a hearing at £464'.[52] It has been suggested that these figures would probably have to be more than doubled to reflect current costs.[53] The Civil Justice Review, initiated in 1985 by Lord Hailsham, the then Lord Chancellor, whose report appeared in 1988,[54] found that plaintiffs' costs in London in 1984 were, on average, £6,830, and outside London £1,540; and it was estimated that when both sides' costs were taken into account, costs in the High Court were between 50 and 75 per cent of damages awarded, but in the county court these could be as high as 125 per cent of damages.

If a case is complex, or is taken on appeal to a higher court, then of course costs escalate dramatically. For many people – and not necessarily the poorest sections of the community – such costs would render legal solutions out of the question were there no state-subsidized system of financial *legal aid*. Such a system has been in operation in this country since 1951, when the scheme provided by the Legal Aid and Advice Act 1949 was implemented. There had been financial assistance available before that time, through the 'Poor Person's Procedure' for High Court actions, and through other limited schemes, but the 1949 Act was the first extensive and systematic attempt to provide a generally available, state-subsidized legal aid system. Financial legal aid, available for civil and criminal court cases, has been supplemented by provision for *legal advice and assistance*, whereby solicitors may undertake work falling short of court appearances[55] (the Green Form Scheme). Both schemes (which are quite separate) are now provided for in the Legal Aid Act 1988. Apart from the schemes operated by practising solicitors, the Sex Discrimination Act 1975 and the Race Relations Act 1976 set up the Equal Opportunities Commission and the Commission for Racial Equality respectively, and both these bodies may give legal assistance, including representation, to complainants bringing discrimination cases to courts and tribunals.

The legal aid scheme is based on the idea that the legal profession should provide state-subsidized legal services for individuals with legal problems who qualify for such aid under whichever regulations and conditions are in force. At present, if a person takes a problem, such as a dispute over a defective new car, to a solicitor, the first enquiry should be about eligibility for legal advice under the

.Green Form Scheme. Under this scheme a solicitor may undertake ordinary legal work (except court work) up to a limit, initially, of three hours' work for matrimonial cases and two hours for other types of problem. With the consent of the local Legal Aid Area Committee, this limit may be extended. In an ordinary dispute there is little point in rushing to the court if the matter can be settled by means of negotiations between the parties, and it *may* be that the whole dispute can be concluded in this way by means of the Green Form Scheme. Since 1977, undefended divorce cases have not been eligible for legal aid, but the Green Form Scheme is available. It is worth noting, too, that the work which a solicitor may undertake includes assistance with certain hearings to which the client may be a party (known as Assistance by way of Representation, or ABWOR), and this may extend to tribunal representation. At present this form of assistance is available for matrimonial cases heard by magistrates' courts, Mental Health Review Tribunal hearings, representation of clients in respect of whom there is a police application under the Police and Criminal Evidence Act 1984 for extended detention in custody, and care proceedings where the parents are to be represented. In the year 1991–2, the Green Form and ABWOR were used by over one million people.[56]

Eligibility for help under the scheme depends upon the client's *disposable income and capital*: that is, income and capital after certain deductions have been made for rent, taxes and other necessary outgoings. Depending on the figures thus arrived at, the client may have to make a contribution towards the total cost (the more the income and capital, the greater the contribution). The figures pertaining to income and capital limits for eligibility are revised from time to time; in 1992 figures were announced whereby, if disposable income does not exceed £75 per week and capital does not exceed £1,000, the client makes no contribution. If income exceeds £145 per week, the client is not eligible under the scheme and must pay for the advice and assistance received. For weekly disposable incomes falling between these figures, the balance between the client's contribution and the value of the work done is paid for from state funds. The cost of the scheme in 1991–2 was £100 million.

If a client's problem involves court work – as might happen, for example, if the car-dealer in the above example refused to repair or replace the defective car – or if a client is facing criminal charges, then the question will arise as to the client's eligibility for *legal aid* for representation in court. There are differences between civil and criminal legal aid procedures which should be noted.

Civil legal aid, technically available for nearly all civil court hearings (except defamation and, as noted above, undefended divorce cases) is administered by the Legal Aid Board, created by the Legal Aid Act 1988, which is independent of both government and the legal profession. A client applying for civil legal aid must satisfy two sets of criteria: a means test, and the question of the merits of the action to which the client proposes to be a party. The financial means test once again involves consideration of disposable income and capital; contributions may be payable if the client's income warrants it. The financial limits have been raised over the years to take account of inflation and rising income levels, and the figures introduced in April 1992 were: income below £3,060 per year and capital below £3,000 – no contribution; income above £6,800 per year (£7,500 for personal injury cases) or capital above £6,750 (£8,560 for personal injury cases) – not eligible. Those falling between these limits will make a contribution on a sliding scale depending on their income and capital.

The 'merits' test is much less straightforward. The Legal Aid Board which considers the application must be satisfied that the applicant 'has reasonable grounds for taking, defending or being a party to the proceedings' (Legal Aid Act 1988, s.15(2)), and the application will be refused if the board considers that it would be unreasonable to grant representation. In practice, the test is interpreted as being whether a reasonable solicitor would advise the client, if the latter had sufficient money of his or her own, to continue with the case, though the Legal Aid Board has stated that, in cases affecting a person's status, reputation or dignity, legal aid might be appropriately granted even though there was little financial benefit in pursuing the action.

Despite the periodic increases in these figures, the limits still exclude a large proportion of the community whose financial standing is such that they are outside the means test limit, but not so great as to enable them readily to undertake civil litigation without considerable personal financial strain. The civil legal aid system has so far not extended to sufficient people, and fundamental revision of the financial eligibility criteria would go a long way towards remedying this situation. The government, however, as we shall see presently, is far more concerned about the current cost to the Exchequer of legal aid than about extending its applicability.

Regarding *criminal* legal aid, there is a means test similar to that for civil legal aid, administered this time by the clerk of the court where the case is being heard. The major difference between civil and criminal legal aid, however, is with regard to the 'merits' test. The application must show that legal aid is in the interests of justice (Legal Aid Act 1988, s.21(2)), and section 22(2) of the Act provides that the factors to be taken into account in determining whether representation should be granted in the interests of justice are:

(a) the offence is such that if proved it is likely that the court would impose a sentence which would deprive the accused of his liberty or lead to loss of his livelihood or serious damage to his reputation;

(b) the determination of the case may involve consideration of a substantial question of law;

(c) the accused may be unable to understand the proceedings or to state his own case because of his inadequate knowledge of English, mental illness or other mental or physical disability;

(d) the nature of the defence is such as to involve the tracing and interviewing of witnesses or expert cross-examination of a witness for the prosecution;

(e) it is in the interests of someone other than the accused that the accused be represented.

In practice, the vast majority of people tried in the Crown courts receive legal aid, though there is much more variability between magistrates' courts as to whether legal aid is granted to defendants appearing before them.[57] The fact that there is now a national 'duty solicitor' scheme (whereby a rota of solicitors attending magistrates' courts ensures that a lawyer is always on hand to give help and advice to those appearing before the magistrates) may well have made some difference to the proportion who are represented.

The cost of legal aid

We have noted at several points in this chapter the ways in which the government's attack on what it saw as the 'restrictive practices' of the legal profession has resulted in change. This sustained and determined onslaught, designed to make the profession more competitive and to open up more avenues of choice for the client, has been matched in its intensity, and in the degree of hostility generated towards the government (and the Lord Chancellor in particular), only by the continuing struggle between government and profession over the cost to the public purse of the legal aid scheme.

There is no doubt that the number of clients applying for both civil and criminal legal aid has rocketed over the last seven or eight years, with a correspondingly large increase in the cost of financing the system.[58] Lord Hailsham (who served as Lord Chancellor for many years) described the legal aid system as 'the largest and most rapidly rising social service of them all'.[59] The reasons for this vast increase in the demand for legal services have been stated to be the problems consequent on unemployment (mortgage difficulties, problems with debts) and the rise in crime, though the advent of the duty solicitor scheme for criminal cases must have contributed to the cost of criminal legal aid, irrespective of any rise in the number of those accused of criminal offences. The legal aid scheme cost around £700 million in 1991–2, and is estimated to hit the £1,000 million mark in the next year or so.

It is perhaps not too surprising, given the government's commitment to reducing public expenditure generally, that the cost of subsidizing legal services should be critically examined with a view to cutting that cost. In 1986 it was announced by the government that there would be a cut in dependants' allowances for legal aid calculations, with the result that clients' contributions would be increased. This announcement was heavily criticized both inside and outside Parliament, not least on the grounds that the change would hit most heavily those with a number of children, who could least afford to pay the enhanced contributions, and all for a saving of only £7.5 million.

At about the same time as this announcement, the government set up its 'Efficiency Scrutiny' of the legal aid scheme, with a wide brief to 'consider the determinants of expenditure on the legal aid scheme by looking at its operation and administration in practice and to make recommendations'. The recommendations made by the inquiry would, if implemented, have meant the abolition of the Green Form Scheme and its replacement by a simple requirement that initial advice to clients in all except criminal cases should be obtained from other advice agencies; the removal of a considerable amount of advocacy from the ranks of barristers – in particular, county court actions and Crown court trials not involving juries – with a corresponding widening of solicitors' rights of audience in these courts; and several other changes which would have had the effect of cutting the costs of legal aid and advice. It was likely that the burden of providing the initial advice would have fallen upon Citizens' Advice Bureaux, whose National Association, despite the likelihood of an increase of £16 million in its budget to handle the work, eventually opposed the proposals.

Predictably, the Law Society's reactions to the recommendations of the government's Efficiency Scrutiny were to welcome the proposals to increase solicitors' rights of audience, but to oppose strongly the plan to remove the Green Form Scheme. As Hansen put it, 'on a conservative estimate solicitors stood to lose more than £25 million worth of work'.[60] Certainly, there was a fear on the part of solicitors that, should the Green Form Scheme go, the result would probably be to render some inner-city solicitors' practices uneconomic, and this would mean, in the end, a reduction in available legal services in the very areas where the need was greatest.

The government's response to the Efficiency Scrutiny was the Legal Aid Act 1988, containing many of the proposed changes. These included the controverisal removal of the administration of legal aid from the Law Society to the new Legal Aid Board, with a membership appointed by the Lord Chancellor. The Efficiency Scrutiny to abolish the Green Form Scheme was not, however, taken up, doubtless in the light of the storm of protests.

In the years following the Legal Aid Act 1988, the battle over the cost of legal aid raged. The view of the Law Society was that the legal aid system as presently organized and financed is, despite its cost, in crisis through lack of adequate government funding – the financial eligibility limits have not been changed in line with rises in earnings:

Between January 1980 and January 1988, average earnings rose by 107 per cent but the legal aid limits increased by only 37 per cent. In April, 1986, Lord Hailsham became the first Lord Chancellor to actively reduce eligibility: dependants' allowances were cut from 50 per cent to 25 per cent above supplementary rates. This had the greatest effect on families with children.[61]

The net effect of the failure to adjust the eligibility figures is not that the poorer sections of the community are disenfranchised from legal aid: in fact, the poor continue to be eligible for legal aid. The problem is the middle-income stratum of society, too wealthy to qualify for legal aid, but assuredly not sufficiently rich to be able to pay for lawyers' services out of their own pockets. Both the Lord Chancellor's own review of legal aid[62] and independent surveys[63] have shown a decline in the numbers who are financially eligible.

Between 1986 and the present time, the Lord Chancellor, in the attempt to control the huge cost of the legal aid scheme, and the legal profession, in the attempt both to protect and expand the scheme and to protect their own interests and those of their clients, have been locked in battle over the future of legal aid. The developments are so rapid that little would be gained here by detailing the numerous proposals so far put forward in the debate.[64] What is certain is that, to date, the battles initiated by the government have been, in the main, won by the government. The Courts and Legal Services Act 1990 reflected the government's policies regarding 'restrictive practices', and in particular the objectives of encouraging more competition in the provision of legal services.[65] This Act made changes with respect to conveyancing and litigation, and put in place new arrangements for the handling of complaints against solicitors and others who provide legal services. In particular, it created the Legal Services Ombudsman, who has substantial powers to investigate complaints.[66] Although in practice the 1990 Act may not radically affect the existing organization of the profession, it none the less represents a significant move in the direction of more government intervention in the ways in which legal services are provided. It would be surprising if the government, through the initiatives devised by the Lord Chancellor, were not in the end successful in making substantial changes to the legal aid scheme with a view to cutting its cost.

The 'unmet need' for legal services

It will be plain from the discussion above that the legal profession holds itself out as providing essential services for the community. Apart from the arguments which assert that the profession is motivated predominantly by self-interest, other criticisms may be levelled at the profession, directed in the main to the matter of how effective it actually *is* in delivering legal services to the community as a whole.

The deliberations of the Benson Commission on the issues of legal aid, and on the possibilities of solicitors' using advertising to inform the public about their services, reflect the general concern which has been felt over the years by some lawyers and other groups about the degree to which legal services are available to 'ordinary people'. It is true to say that more concern has been shown about this question by younger lawyers and 'fringe' groups than by the established professional bodies, especially the Law Society. The Legal Action Group, for example, was set up in 1971 by a group of lawyers dissatisfied with existing provision of services in the less well-off sections of the community. This group is concerned not with the traditional lawyers' problems of property and business, but with the growing number of problems created by the plethora of welfare state legislation which is now termed 'welfare law' – social security, tribunal hearings, housing legislation, consumer affairs and employment problems.

Out of a general feeling among many individual lawyers that the poorer sections of the community are not obtaining the legal advice and help which they may need, various developments have taken place. Law centres have been established in many cities, aiming to provide legal services, including representation, for the whole community in a particular locality.[67] Usually the centres are set up in busy shopping areas, so that legal services may be available to ordinary people in the local High Street. The staff operating in such centres invariably includes qualified solicitors, and finance, always a serious problem in such cases, is derived from various sources such as charities and local authorities. The scarcity of resources in recent years has led to serious difficulties for all centres, which in some cases have led to closure. It was reported in March 1991 that the latest casualty [is] Tottenham Law Centre in the borough of Haringey. Four other London law centres have been told they must close; several have been told they must merge and many others have had their funds cut back: Hillingdon for example has lost 84 per cent of its funding from the local authority and Hammersmith and Fulham may lose 52 per cent.[68]

One of the difficulties here, apart from the sheer scarcity of resources, is that local authority departments may well be the source of people's problems (especially housing departments) and, in a period of cuts in overall public spending, the reduction of grants to law centres may not only save money but also remove what might be something of a thorn in the side of the local council.

Law centres, in addition to providing free legal advice and assistance for individual clients, frequently provide assistance for local groups and campaigns. This type of work has attracted criticism, not least from the Benson Commission in 1978. Such criticism from the professional establishment is quite consistent with the law's general refusal to recognize and accommodate *group* or *class* interests within its procedures. As White says, the legal system, and especially the legal aid system, operates on the principle whereby problems and conflicts are *individualized*, thus 'preventing the use of litigation and the legal system as means to advance groups' interests'.[69]

It seems inappropriate to exclude the provision of assistance for groups who may find themselves, collectively, in conflict with, for example, local authority departments or officials of the Department of Social Security; for these are the very types of conflict, usually involving some kind of legal procedural framework or rules, which tend to occur within local communities. The importance of the provision of these types of legal service should be recognized, especially those which currently operate independently of the formal organization of the Law Society. After all, as the Legal Action Group has argued, it was 'the involvement of law centres in local issues that contributed much to their popularity and their effectiveness in securing benefits for the community. It has caused controversy, but instead of analysing the issues and reaching a conclusion, the [Royal] Commission simply condemns this kind of work.'[70]

In some areas, legal advice centres have been set up, with similar aims to law centres but limiting their work to the provision of advice only. These centres are usually staffed by solicitors who volunteer to work at the centres on a rota basis, and who otherwise work full-time in their usual offices. This can raise certain problems, not least the fact that relatively few practising solicitors have detailed knowledge of those areas of law which are the concern of the ordinary person. It is only recently that 'welfare law' courses have been introduced on to law degree courses in educational institutions, where the emphasis has traditionally been on teaching those legal subjects which will be the mainstay of the practising lawyer's work (contracts, trusts, conveyancing and so on: see chapter 15); there is a very real ignorance among many practitioners about housing law, social security law and other similar areas.

Apart from law centres and legal advice centres, Citizens' Advice Bureaux have rapidly expanded in number. There are about 900 bureaux, handling over three million cases, of which it is estimated that legal advice was needed in about one-third.[71] The CAB organization has an efficient and encyclopaedic information system, which may be used for the purpose of giving advice by any CAB office. Of course, a CAB adviser who is not a lawyer may well define a client's problem as essentially 'non-legal', and a client with an accommodation or a family problem may be referred to local authority departments for help rather than advised to take any formal *legal* action. And in the realm of criminal law, we noted above the development of 'duty solicitor' schemes, now provided for in the Legal Aid Act 1988.

Conclusion

We have in the legal profession a prestigious and influential group of practitioners, supposedly there to ensure that the law's promises of justice for everyone are satisfied, but whose social class composition distinguishes them from the majority of the community they claim to serve. Their most lucrative work continues to be the handling of the problems of the rich rather than the trials of the poor;[72] the way in which the profession is being reorganized is having the result that, while some large City of London firms thrive, others are having to reduce their size, and the smaller provincial solicitors' firms are under threat:

The expertise of the large City firms, the fact that they are mostly engaged in uncontentious business and that most of their High Court litigation is in chambers, where they do not need a barrister, reduce their interest in fusion of the profession and the rights of appearance in higher courts for solicitors. Their partnerships are sufficiently attractive to tempt young talent to leave the Bar, and the libraries and information retrieval systems which these firms can afford take care of the rest . . . The time is certainly up for the one-person general practice, and even two or three-member partnerships are vulnerable. The strain which the complexity of law and clients' demands puts on these small firms is reflected in their high proportion of negligence claims and the frequency with which the Law Society has to step in to compensate clients for fraud or malpractice.[73]

The existing scheme for state provision of financial help for the less well-off is inadequate and will probably get worse, bringing problems for clients and solicitors' firms alike. Moreover, as things are turning out, government policies will bring about rather different results over the next few years than the ones anticipated by the Benson Commission. Commentators seem to be agreed that the old image of the solicitor as a 'professional person' is giving way to commercial reality; the modern lawyer must be concerned with profitability and remaining competitive in an uncertain market. Before expressing unreserved regret at these general developments, however, we might wish to question the appropriateness of solicitors' definitions of clients' problems as essentially 'legal' in any case.

However radical agencies such as law centres may be thought by the more conservative lawyers, and however welcome and useful the developments and agencies represented by groups like the Legal Action Group have been in the short term, they do not remove any of the basic problems concerning the legal profession and its relationship with the community. Lawyers are not, in the nature of things, radical, because of their training, professional socialization, history and social status, and because the lawyer by definition works with an inherently conservative force: the law itself. The work of the legal profession is structured by the law, and so, to an increasing extent, is the profession itself.

If the community needs lawyers, then changes in the structure, work, outlook and remuneration of the legal profession will not change the fact that lawyers, like every other occupational group, seek the work which is most rewarding financially. The government, in its determination to instigate radical change in the profession, is inspired not, despite the rhetoric, by the desire to provide better legal services to those sections of the community who need them, but by the determination to cut public expenditure and promote competition. Little else is changing: the affairs of business, the transfer of real property and the problems of the wealthy continue to provide the lawyer with work and high income, whereas the problems of the poor – dealing with landlords, settling local authority and social security problems, representing defendants in court or at tribunals – are not the kind of work which brings in large amounts of money. The agencies which for some years effectively provided legal advice and representation for the poor – especially law centres – are just as much victims of the cuts in public spending as those who have become disentitled to legal aid.

But in the final analysis, the attraction to the legal profession of business and 'property' types of work is understandable, given the concentration by the *legal system* in general on the management and protection of property. It is primarily the law, therefore, not the lawyers themselves, which highlights the problems of the middle and upper-middle classes at the expense of the poor, and it is at least arguable that, were social and economic inequality in our society to be attacked through changes in the legal, political and economic structure, then consequent changes in the attitudes, work and organization of the legal profession would not be far behind.

14
The judges

Although we often speak of 'the judges' as though they were a homogeneous group within the court and judicial structure, there is in fact a whole variety of judges, operating in different courts and at different levels in the court hierarchy[1] (quite apart from those legally qualified persons who chair tribunals, discussed in chapter 6). At the top of the hierarchy of courts of law are members of the House of Lords and the Court of Appeal, appointed from the ranks of Court of Appeal judges and High Court judges respectively; lower down, the judges of the High Court are appointed from among senior and eminent barristers; and at county court level, Circuit Judges and Recorders are appointed from the ranks of the legal profession (theoretically including solicitors, but at present still mainly drawn from barristers).

The exception to this general pattern of judicial recruitment from among practising barristers is, of course, found in the magistrates' courts, where the bench only exceptionally comprises trained lawyers; usually, laymen and women are appointed as Justices of the Peace on the basis of their experience and general standing in the local community. Although they receive some training in the law, magistrates are to a large extent dependent for legal knowledge upon their clerks, who are legally qualified and whose task it is to advise the court on matters of law in cases heard before them. In certain urban areas, however, *stipendiary magistrates*, who are full-time paid magistrates, are appointed from among barristers and solicitors.

The popular image of the judge is of someone removed socially and, in an important sense, physically from the day-to-day activities and preoccupations of society, though this clearly is hardly accurate in the case of magistrates. The role of the judge in court has been compared to that of an umpire, taking relatively little part in the trial itself, but presiding over the proceedings, seeing fair play between the disputants, ensuring that no misleading or prejudicial evidence is presented, and controlling the trial with the aim of arriving at a decision based upon the facts as elicited through legal argument and examination of witnesses and other evidence by either side. Where there is a jury trial (today, usually only in the Crown court) the task of the judge is, additionally, to summarize the evidence on both sides of the case for the jury's benefit, making sure that the jurors are acquainted with the relevant law to apply to the facts, and sending them away to reach a decision based on a full appreciation of the points at issue in the case.

In criminal cases, the presiding judge or magistrate must also pass sentence upon conviction of the accused, and this function has done much to capture the popular imagination. Before the suspension of capital punishment in 1965, and certainly during the days of the eighteenth century when there were over two hundred capital offences on the statute-book, the judge had, literally, the powers of life and death over those convicted of such offences:

> In the court room the judges' every action was governed by the importance of spectacle . . . scarlet robes lined with ermine and full-bottomed wigs in the seventeenth-century style, which evoked . . . awe from ordinary men. The powers of light and darkness were summoned into the court with the black cap which was donned to pronounce sentence of death, and the spotless white gloves worn at the end of a 'maiden assize' when no prisoners were to be left for execution.[2]

According to Glanville Williams, the English legal system has produced 'judges of intelligence, alertness, patience, toleration and firmness . . . A very large number have been men of outstanding ability and attainments, who have throughout their judgeships been held in the very highest esteem.'[3] And more recently Pannick states that 'because judges are men, not machines, we must expect judicial frailties and not judge them too harshly',[4] but concludes that 'English judges have every reason to be proud of the quality of their performance'.[5]

Are these rather complacent opinions justified? In this chapter we take up various questions concerning the judges, their functions, their backgrounds and their mode of appointment; in particular, we will examine the charge that in twentieth-century society, where there is continuous change in social values, economic patterns, political institutions and class differences, the judiciary has shown itself to be a highly conservative force, unable or unwilling to bring itself (and the legal system which it administers) up to date and into line with modern social conditions.

The social background of the judiciary

If, as was suggested in chapter 13, the members of the legal profession (especially barristers) tend to come from social and educational backgrounds which are predominantly middle and upper-middle class, then it may fairly be said that members of the higher levels of the judiciary represent a distillation of those social-class currents within the legal system.

To begin with, senior judges are appointed exclusively from the ranks of experienced and established barristers, whose social background still tends to be at the higher levels of the social-class structure. We should not, therefore, be surprised to discover that studies have consistently shown that judges tend to have extremely homogeneous backgrounds and educational patterns. Griffith[6] cites a number of surveys which show a marked pattern of public school education, followed by Oxford or Cambridge university. The most recent study cited found that of the 34 Law Lords and Lords Justices of Appeal, 29 had attended public schools and Oxford or Cambridge university.[7] Regarding the social background of the higher judiciary, Blom-Cooper and Drewry, in their study of the House of Lords,[8] found that out of 49 of the 63 Law Lords holding office between 1876 and 1972, 34 had fathers who were lawyers or members of other professions.

The uniform social and educational pattern which such studies consistently reveal raises certain questions about the general social and political outlook of the judicary as a whole. There are many instances of judicial utterances which some might consider to cast doubt upon the extent to which some judges are fully acquainted with modern social reality outside their own social class, sex and age-group. Examples include the judge who asked, in a case in 1985, 'Who is Bruce Springsteen?' and the statement by the judge in a rape trial in 1982 that the victim, who had innocently hitched a lift in the accused's car, had been 'guilty of a great deal of contributory negligence'.[9]

In more general 'party-political' terms, the social-class distribution of the judges is exactly that sector which we normally associate with support for the Conservative Party – in its pre-Thatcherite form – which generally represents the interests of the higher levels of the social-class structure (for example, by protecting business interests, maintaining the institutions of private propery and private enterprise, concerning itself with issues such as the preservation of law and public order in the face of arguments for legal, political and social change, but preserving a paternalistic concern for the less privileged). Blom-Cooper and Drewry state that

the uniformly middle-class backgrounds of the judges, coupled with a long spell of legal training (in itself, a powerful instrument of socialisation) does much to shift the ideological complexion of the judiciary well to the right of centre, whatever the extent of overt party political affiliation in individual judges.[10]

Indeed, in support of the last point, there is some evidence suggesting that 'overt party political affiliation' on the part of individual Law Lords is of itself no indicator of the way in which such a judge is likely to decide a case.[11] Lee has analysed the various surveys which examine critically judges' education and social origins, and suggests that little should be read into the mere fact alone that many of them come from upper-middle class, Conservative-oriented backgrounds: he argues that the thesis presented by Griffith and others – that their background invariably inclines towards Conservative views and hence decisions – seems

to assume, mistakenly, that judges have homogeneous views. It does seem to assume, mistakenly, that they always decide for the Conservative government. It does seem to assume, mistakenly, that the interests of the State, its moral welfare, the preservation of law and order and the protection of property rights are all dangerous values to be associated solely with the Conservatives. It does seem to assume, mistakenly, that cases involve one class against another.[12]

Lee is at pains to shatter what he regards as 'simplistic, naive and misguided'[13] allegations of class bias within the judiciary, and argues that

the legitimate complaints of the Left about occasional judicial decisions will never be taken seriously so long as they are submerged in a welter of rhetoric about the background of the judges. At no point is the connection between background and decisions explained. At no point are alternative explanations canvassed. It is foolhardy to dismiss all judicial decisions because of the judiciary's background.[14]

Though there is much force in this argument in so far as it warns against a crude generalization which links judicial background with political views which find expression in judicial decisions, it remains true that from time to time judicial utterances are reported in the national press which must raise serious doubts among some members of the community about the lack of bias within the judiciary. Griffith, whose approach is particularly criticized by Lee, cites several worrying examples of overt racist and sexist comments by individual judges, usually resulting in condemnation by either the Lord Chancellor or other members of the judiciary. The danger is that unacceptable statements by individual judges may well undermine public confidence in the judiciary as a whole, and despite Lee's warning, such a possibility must be taken seriously.

With regard to magistrates, the official policy is to avoid any political influence and to seek to appoint people 'drawn from many walks of life' in order to make sure that 'the bench . . . is broadly balanced'.[15] Though few would argue with this aim, it seems that the reality is that the magistracy is not as 'broadly balanced' in political terms as it might be. Government figures published in 1992 revealed that there is a strong preponderance of Conservative-voters among magistrates:

The Government gave information on political affiliations of magistrates in 10 areas at the time of appointment . . . A clear pattern emerges. In the two Oldham constituencies, for instance, Labour polled about 52 per cent of the vote at the general election but only 27 per cent of magistrates support Labour. Tories with 32 per cent of the vote, make up 36 per cent of the Bench. The same is true of Bristol, where Labour won 40 per cent of votes, slightly higher than the Tories. Yet 142 Bristol magistrates say they are Tory, and 85 Labour.[16]

Clearly, more needs to be done with the respect to the selection and appointment of magistrates to ensure that the 'broad balance' is better achieved.

Judges, politics and the process of decision-making

As Griffith says, 'the most remarkable fact about the appointment of judges is that it is wholly in the hands of politicians'.[17] At the lower levels of judicial appointment (magistrates up to High Court judges), appointments are made by, or on the advice of, the Lord Chancellor, who is both a member of the Cabinet and a judge in the House of Lords; and in the case of judges of the Court of Appeal and House of Lords, appointments are made, technically, by the Prime Minister on the advice of the Lord Chancellor.

The practice of recruiting judges from the ranks of practising barristers has met with considerable criticism. Some have argued that alternative methods of recruiting and training judges would have the effect of broadening judges' outlooks, and of widening somewhat the social spectrum of judges' social and educational backgrounds. Lord Scarman, an ex-Law Lord, has stated that 'it is just not good enough to rely on what the Lord Chancellor, the Lord Chief Justice or the Master of the Rolls tell someone privately . . . it is all too haphazard; an old-boy network when we have grown out of school'. He suggests a more formalized training system for judges – possibly a Judicial Studies Board – which would make it possible for solicitors, as well as barristers, to become judges.[18] Pannick has argued similarly that a Judicial Appointments Committee, comprising solicitors, barristers, academic lawyers, judges and perhaps some lay members, should be set up to advise on the appointment of judges, and that more formal training for new judges should be instituted:

We need judges who are not appointed by the unassisted efforts of the Lord Chancellor and solely from the ranks of middle-aged barristers. We need judges who are trained for the job, whose conduct can be freely criticized and is subject to investigation by a Judicial Performance Commission; judges who abandon wigs, gowns and unnecessary linguistic legalisms . . .[19]

There once was a time when judicial appointment was commonly based upon candidates' party-political service, loyalty or experience, or upon their political affiliations or known views. Paterson, drawing on the material in Heuston's *Lives of the Lord Chancellors, 1885–1940*, found that it was possible to identify such appointments;[20] and it is also possible to identify, through decided cases, the effects of such a system of judicial appointments. To take one well-documented example, in the trio of cases at the turn of the century involving trade union activities – *Allen* v. *Flood* (1898),[21] *Quinn* v. *Leathem* (1901)[22] and the *Taff Vale Railway* case (1901);[23] Lord Halsbury, then Lord Chancellor, and a judge with extremely conservative and anti-union views, attempted in all three cases to 'pack' the bench with colleagues having similar attitudes to his own. He was successful in doing so in all but the first. The net result of these decisions (taken together with the known anti-union attitudes of both judges and politicians over the preceding two hundred years)[24] was such that trade unionists were left in no doubt that the judges (and by implication the law itself) were anything but their allies. We shall look at other examples of political attitudes of the judges later, but for the moment we should note that, as Lord Hailsham, himself a House of Lords judge until his recent retirement, an active and prominent member of the Conservative Party and a man with considerable experience of life as Lord Chancellor, has said, 'activity in politics is not, and never has been, a bar to appointment to the bench'.[25]

Stevens, in analysing the development since 1800 of the House of Lords as a judicial body,[26] has documented carefully the progress of that institution from being essentially *political*, where final appeals were heard not by professional judges, but by peers of the realm, to being an institution whose judicial function came to be carried out by professional lawyers. These developments occurred quite late in the history of the House of Lords, from the Reform Act 1832; through the intervention by Peel in the case involving conspiracy charges against the Irish political activist Daniel O'Connell in 1844, when the Lord President of the Privy Seal advised lay peers against intervening in the matter under consideration by the Law Lords;[27] up to the restructuring of the court system in the 1870s and the constitutional crisis of 1910 and 1911. The origin of the House of Lords as an essentially political body, then, with its judicial function only gradually becoming distinct from its political function, serves to sharpen the distinction between the former's central concern with *law*, and the latter's concern with *policy*.

To say this, however, is merely to acknowledge a particular historical development, which has culminated in the firmly established convention that lay peers take no part in the judicial activities of the House (these being the concern of the Law Lords, the professional judges elevated to the House by reason of their experience as judges). This historical perspective serves to highlight the link between the judiciary and other political institutions: the judiciary, at all levels of the court structure, is a part of the overall political structure of society, albeit a part which enjoys the reputation for independence of any executive governmental function, as we saw in chapter 6. But this *constitutional* position of independence, as we shall see presently, does not necessarily mean that political considerations play no part in the process of judicial decision-making.

The delicate balance between being seen to be independent of politics, and at the same time a part of the political structure, has been discussed in various ways and with various emphases by many commentators. Hay[28] notes the behind-the-scenes 'stage-managing' of local assizes during the eighteenth century, in which local gentry and visiting judges shared a common concern that the populace should remain faithful to law, state and the established political order, hence posing no threat to the existing social and political arrangements. The death penalty, the formal and symbolic trappings of the courtroom, the presence of an enormous number of capital offences on the statute-book, all combined to make this essentially *political* task of maintaining the status quo relatively easy, as well as obscuring the instrumental political concerns of the rulers of the period behind the appeal to the neutrality and supremacy of the law. Another historical study, by Glassey,[29] has traced the relationship between appointments to the magistracy and political affiliation and patronage between 1675 and 1720, showing the clear connections between such appointments and long-established families of high social status during the period.

Some have discussed the issue of public confidence in the independence of the judiciary. For example, Campbell[30] examined the Scottish judiciary with a view to dealing with the extent to which there may be said to be a 'crisis of legitimacy': to what extent has there been a decrease in public *belief* in the independence and impartiality of the judiciary? 'The national press no longer takes for granted the excellence and impartiality of our judges; rather there are inquiries into their social and educational backgrounds and the importance of their political affiliations.'[31]

After comparing the modes of judicial appointment of various countries, and discussing in particular the questions of who makes the appointment, what qualifications a candidate for judicial office must have, and whether there is adequate training and promotion of judges, Campbell offers various criticisms of the Scottish system of judicial appointment. He emphasizes that his concern is not so much with the question of whether abuse of the system actually takes place, but rather with the extent to which public confidence in the judges is fostered or discouraged. His conclusion is that 'if the point at issue is *credibility* and *ostentatious impartiality* the Scottish system must be adjudged a failure'.[32]

In recent years the English judiciary, too, has been 'battered and bruised'[33] by a series of cases in which there was a clear and most serious miscarriage of justice. First we saw the release from prison of the Guildford Four and the Maguire Seven, and later the Birmingham Six, all of whom had been convicted of terrorist activity including the bombing of public houses in Guildford and Birmingham. It eventually transpired that all of the defendants in these cases had served long periods of imprisonment for crimes they did not commit, though all of the cases had previously been re-examined and duly rejected by the Court of Appeal. Not surprisingly, among the questions asked in the media at the time was simply: why had the court not recognized earlier the weaknesses in the Crown's case against these defendants (and in particular the police and scientific forensic evidence in some cases)? The Birmingham Six case is interesting for, among other things, Lord Denning's previous refusal to grant legal aid to the defendants in 1975 to allow them to bring an action against the West Midlands police:

If the six men win it will mean that the police were guilty of perjury, that they were guilty of violence and threats, that the confessions were involuntary and were improperly admitted in evidence and that the convictions were erroneous. That would mean the Home Secretary would either have to recommend they be pardoned or he would have to remit the case to the Court of Appeal. This is such an appalling vista that every sensible person in the land would say: 'It cannot be right that these actions should go any further'.[34]

In other words, it seemed to his Lordship more important that public confidence in the criminal justice system should not be undermined, than that six innocent men should be freed.

There was general agreement that this series of events did little to bolster public confidence in the higher judiciary,[35] and there are more cases of people in prison in respect of whose convictions there may be serious doubt. In the wake of the release of the Birmingham Six came the announcement of the establishment of a Royal Commission on Criminal Justice (chaired by Lord Runciman), whose terms of reference include issues arising after trial. It is to be hoped that the Commission's report will include recommendations which will be effective in preventing future miscarriages of justice and, if it does so, that such recommendations will not meet the same fate as so many other Royal Commission proposals in recent years.

In a more general context, and drawing on many cases from various areas of social activity as illustrations, Griffith has catalogued and discussed the extent to which the role of the judiciary (in particular the judges of the higher courts) can be seen to overlap into the sphere of *political* decision-making.[36] In particular, Griffith discusses the broad areas of industrial relations, personal rights and freedoms, property rights and squatters, judicial control of ministerial discretion, the uses of conspiracy, and cases involving students and trade union members. He argues that 'judges are a part of the machinery of authority within the State and as such cannot avoid the making of political decisions';[37] and that the senior judges in particular have, by reason of their legal education and their working life as practising barristers, 'acquired a strikingly homogeneous collection of attitudes, beliefs, and principles, which to them represents the public interests'.[38] For Griffith, the idea of an impartial and neutral judiciary, especially in cases involving a political element, is mythical:

judges in the United Kingdom cannot be politically neutral because they are placed in positions where they are required to make political choices which are sometimes presented to them, and often presented by them, as determinations of where the public interest lies; . . . that interpretation of what is in the public interest and therefore politically desirable is determined by the kind of people they are and the position they hold in our society; . . . this position is part of established authority and so is necessarily conservative and illiberal.[39]

Griffith's book met with considerable criticism, particularly, as one might expect, from members and ex-members of the judiciary. Lord Devlin, once a judge in the House of Lords, responded to some of Griffith's assertions and arguments.[40] To a large extent, Devlin's reply may be summarized as a resounding 'so what?' To begin with, he explains, there is no denying the homogeneity of political and other outlooks on the part of the judges, but then the same is true of most other institutions in our society, or at least, those of them which 'like the law are not of a nature to attract the crusading or rebellious spirit'.[41]

Further, argues Devlin, the question posed by Griffith, which is, 'do the judges allow their devotion to law and order to distort their application of the law when they apply it to those who do not think as they do?' is beset by the difficulty of lack of unanimity among the senior judges, whom Griffith, according to Devlin, seeks to present as 'a small group of senior judges who are policy makers':[42] 'The law lords are sometimes divided: more frequently they quarrel with the Court of Appeal.'[43] And the constraints imposed by the length of Griffith's book do not, argues Devlin, allow any rigorous analysis of the cases under discussion. Devlin accepts that Griffith's perspective may be seen as the view from the left, and explains that criticisms of the judiciary might also be made by those taking a different ideological stance: 'Professor Griffith cites cases on the use of police powers which he finds to be "alarming"; someone right of centre could probably produce a list of cases which would alarm him by their tenderness towards crime.'[44] In short, Devlin is inclined to the view that too much is made by Griffith of the 'politics of the judiciary', for 'their politics are hardly more significant than those of the army, the navy and the airforce; they are as predictable as those of any institution where maturity is in command'.[45]

It is hard to resist the comment that the politics of the armed forces may well be significant; there are countless examples of military coups and dictatorships in various parts of the world throughout recent history, and in contemporary Britain we need only look as far as the role and strategies of the armed forces in Northern Ireland. And Devlin's criticisms do not detract from the general thesis presented by Griffith that the political inclinations of the judiciary can, and sometimes do, influence the outcome of cases coming before them. Devlin may well be correct when he points out that the tendency of the judiciary and of the law itself is to constitute a force for stability, law and order, and we should therefore not be too surprised when the judges, charged with the administration of the law, seek to maintain that stability, sometimes in the face of determined and militant forces for change.

Judicial insistence on the maintenance of 'law and order' may well, however, be inconsistent on occasion with other currents in society, where rapid change has long been the norm in many areas of social life. No longer a relatively stable, predominantly agricultural economy, present-day society with its almost daily advances in technology, its seemingly permanent economic crises and its multiplicity of moral and political divergences, exhibits instability in virtually every aspect of social and political activity. Given the truism that, in the twentieth century, the law in one way or another touches more and more people in an ever-increasing range of activities, it is hardly surprising to find tensions within some parts of the legal system between forces for change and forces for conservatism; such tension must be at its clearest when issues involving policy or politics come before the courts.

To say that there is a danger (which Devlin would have denied) that general political affiliations and attitudes may affect judicial decision-making is not to suggest any kind of 'judicial conspiracy', nor that the antics of Lord Halsbury in the trade union cases of 1898–1902 would be repeated in English courts today. The point is rather that any manifestation of political or ideological stance is a matter for neither surprise nor denial. Judges play a creative role in the legal system, not only by virtue of their development of the common law, but also in the manner in which they perceive and interpret 'facts' in cases before them. Cases directly or indirectly involving political considerations (public order, industrial relations, state security, issues of morality or race relations, to mention but a few examples) and cases involving quite new issues which are without precedent *do* crop up from time to time. It would thus be quite unrealistic for us to expect judges, given their backgrounds and professional experience, to analyse and interpret the facts of cases in a manner divorced from their personal perceptions and preconceptions of the social and political world. What is interesting is not that political nuances enter judicial pronouncements *per se*, but rather the complex ways in which the reasoning in such decisions is presented. In short, to what extent do the judges operate in a context of unbridled freedom to decide cases as they choose, and to what extent are there institutional constraints which tend to limit the lengths to which they may go?

We may make several general comments at this point, before discussing specific aspects of the problem. To being with, an important constraining factor is the necessity, noted by Weber,[46] Frank[47] and others, for judicial decisions to be presented not as the outcome of subjective, arbitrary or capricious reasoning by the judge, but as the result of the application of *objective* criteria. This is the difference between the statement 'in my opinion, you are guilty' and the statement 'according to the law, you are guilty'. The former statement we would regard as somewhat suspect, as being unfair or biased. The issue of public credibility and confidence in the judiciary is once again relevant here: we would not place much faith in a legal system which allowed judges to decide cases according to their whim or their personal views about the parties to a dispute. We expect judges to decide cases in accordance with existing law, without personal views or prejudices colouring their judgment.

Despite such expectations, however, some writers have argued, from differing standpoints, that there are strong elements of subjectivity in judicial decision-making. Some American legal writers have denied that judicial decision-making is simply a matter of 'rules determining decisions', but maintain that judges often decide cases according to intuition, or 'hunch',[48] and proceed to justify ('rationalize') their decisions by dressing them up in the cloak of legal rules. Others adopt a rather more complex approach, stressing the subtle relationships between legal rules and judicial creativity. Another argument centres on the debates about the 'rule of law', one interpretation of which[49] is that in our society we live under 'the government of laws, and not of men'. This means that 'governments and all who exercise power as part of established authority are themselves bound by the existing body of laws'.[50] Some writers, notably Thompson, have argued that there have been many occasions in history where judges have used this proposition to mask decisions which in reality reflect the 'rule of a class'.[51] Against such an argument, it might be said that it is precisely *because* those in authority, including judges, are subject to existing legal rules that judges can act only within a framework of constraints which those rules impose upon them.

The necessity of deciding cases by means of objective criteria brings us to consider a second and extremely important constraining factor operating upon judicial reasoning and decision-making. This factor is the existence of that set of criteria whereby the judge reaches a decision: the legal rules and principles themselves. There are various schools of thought as to the extent to which judges are constrained by the law itself, and much will depend, in general terms, upon the nature of the legal system under consideration. In England, there once was a time – during the nineteenth century in particular – when the 'declaratory theory' of judging prevailed.

This theory holds that judges have no creative, or law-making, functions, and little or no discretion in handling rules; their task is the declaration and application of existing rules to cases coming before them. Even the common law, which is the outcome of judicial law-making (see chapter 7), was held to be the result of the judges' merely declaring what the law *is*, and not the result of law-making activity. Few today would hold to this theory in such a form, although Dworkin, in particular, has argued[52] that judicial discretion in handling rules does not exist in the sense that most modern writers would believe.

Dworkin has presented the idea of law as 'integrity', meaning that

law's constraints benefit society not just by providing predictability or procedural fairness, or in some other instrumental way, but by securing a kind of equality among citizens that makes their community more genuine and improves its moral justification for exercising the political power it does ... [Integrity] argues that rights and responsibilities flow from past decisions and so count as legal, not just when they are implicit in these decisions but also when they follow from the principles of personal and political morality the explicit decisions presuppose by way of justification.[53]

Integrity thus seems to constitute some kind of ideal, in the light of which a judge, in determining the solution to a case, constructs his or her decision by interpreting the relevant law. It is linked to the notion of coherence both in terms of the content of laws and the ways in which those laws are interpreted.[54] And, ultimately, integrity, so Dworkin argues, enables the judge to ascertain the 'right' answer as between two conflicting rules or principles. Thus, Dworkin's hypothetical judge, when faced with having to decide between two conflicting principles, makes a choice between the two, and declares that he

settle[s] on this choice because I believe that though the impulse behind each of the two principles is attractive, the second is more powerful in these circumstances. This requires me to declare a certain number of past judicial decisions mistakes and to overrule these if my jurisdiction permits. But the number of decisions I must count as mistakes is neither so great nor of such fundamental importance, viewed from the perspective of legal practice as a whole, that disregarding them leaves me no solid foundation for the more general interpretation I have just described.[55]

Integrity is thus about continuity and coherence in law and adjudication; Dworkin argues that it enables the judge to arrive at a 'right' answer where there is no clear solution. Space does not permit anything more than this all-too-brief statement of Dworkin's arguments, let alone a detailed discussion of them; it must be said, however, that in terms of legal theory, those arguments seem to add little to the existing body of legal writings on and about law, in so far as they posit an ideal to which legal officials such as judges 'ought' to subscribe (see above, chapter 2), and in terms of judicial discretion in decision-making it must be said that the 'right answer' thesis runs against the tide of modern academic and even, today, judicial opinion[56] as to the extent to which judges are constrained by the framework of legal rules and principles.

It is interesting to compare Dworkin's picture with other approachs. We have already noted the older 'declaratory theory' of judging, which holds that what judges do is not to create but merely to *declare* the law; and it is noteworthy that the sociologist Max Weber, writing in the early twentieth century, presented a classification of various *kinds* of law and legal system,[57] one of which – the 'logical formal rational' type of law[58] – comprised a set of legal precepts from which the legal answer to every case might be found. Such a legal system in such a 'pure' form has, however, never existed, even within European legal systems (especially the German system) whose highly codified legal rules approximated most closely to this particular theoretical model.

Regarding the English system with its common-law traditions, Weber acknowledged that there were aspects which approximated more to other types of law in his classification. In particular, he perceived elements of 'substantive rationality' within a common-law system, which means that decisions in particular cases may be guided by *criteria other than those of the law itself*, such as an appeal to ethics, religion or political ideology. This type of law, then, is by no means a 'seamless web' which always provides the 'right answer', but is rather a complex framework of legal *and non-legal* rules, standards and principles, any or all of which may operate either to constrain or to free a judge in making a decision in a given case.

The extent to which legal rules and principles constrain judicial choice in decision-making remains, therefore, a matter for some debate. We may agree with Lord Radcliffe who stated that 'there never was a more sterile controversy than that upon the question whether a judge makes law. Of course he does. How can he help it?'[59] But the real issues surely are precisely how, and to what extent, rules and principles serve to limit that discretion and law-making activity.

In confronting these issues, a number of factors must be considered. First, what clues may be found within the judgments of the courts themselves? Second, how do the judges actually perceive and define their role, and what light do those perceptions and definitions throw on the matter of judicial creativity?

Regarding the first of these factors, a study of the speeches of the law lords over a twelve-month period by Murphy and Rawlings[60] examines the ways in which the judges' speeches are 'glued together'[61] and what the authors call the 'strategic deployment of discursive techniques'[62] used by the judges in dealing with the cases before them. Noting some critics' characterization of some House of Lords decisions as 'superficial', these authors argue, with reference to a number of cases decided during the period of the study, that there may be detected within law lords' speeches a considerable degree of assertiveness – often unsupported by any sustained or developed line of reasoning drawn from detailed discussions of previous cases or legal principles. This is not true of all the cases analysed, however, for in certain cases 'we find lengthy discussions of case law or of historical background, and sometimes extensive "overview" discussions conducted in the manner of a treatise writer. In other words, the law lords have some criteria of selection which determine when an elaborate discussion is required.'[63] The specific charge of superficiality, the authors explain, is hard to analyse, partly because it depends largely on what critics themselves consider to be significant or insignificant issues, or superficial or thorough discussions. What must be differentiated, however, are superficiality and *particularization*; the latter refers to a prominent technique used by the judges on occasion, whereby the issues in a case may be reduced to, say, defining the meaning of a particular word in a statutory provision, on which matter the case is deemed to rest. Particularization may, in some cases, result from the convention that law lords' judgments only deal with matters raised before the court by counsel, and it may be that on occasion a particular matter is elevated to pivotal status by counsel in the course of argument.[64] The effect of particularization, it is argued, is to reduce the issues in a case to 'manageable proportions, a process which thereby generates a fairly common necessity of evading or suppressing "difficulties". Particularization is not reducible to a "superficial" treatment of conventional legal material.'[65]

Another technique used by the judges – predominantly, according to Murphy and Rawlings, when faced with a problem of statutory interpretation – is to explore the implications and possible consequences of deciding in accordance with the 'literal' as opposed to the 'ordinary' or 'common-sense' meaning of a term. It is argued, however, that when a given interpretation is adopted, there is little by way of sustained and careful enunciation of the reasons for that choice of interpretation. In yet other instances, the judges purport to seek the purpose of legislation, or claim to fill 'gaps' in statutes by means of judicial modification, or present complex statements as merely asserting the obvious – again with little explicit reasoning to support the conclusions arrived at. Where there is no 'statutory text' to interpret, examples are given which suggest that judges will explicitly consider matters of 'policy' (that is, factors outside the existing legal rule framework itself); though, here again, the authors claim that with regard to at least one of the cases discussed, 'there is no indication in any of the speeches of how [the relevant] matters are to be worked through thoroughly in the writing of a judgment. Rather, assertion suffices.'[66]

When evaluating this kind of study, it is important to remember that it is conducted at a particular level of analysis concerned only with the text of the judgments, and does not in itself address the central question of the structural position of the higher judiciary. Neither does it deal, as the authors acknowledge, with the social implications of the cases discussed, in terms of the *effects* of the decisions; nor with the extent to which judges' decision-making – or even their 'assertions' – were the outcome of the political predilection of particular judges. Although the study illuminates what are often cited as lacunae or weaknesses of reasoning within the law lords' judgments, these political dimensions are not discussed, despite the authors' ultimate recognition that 'we are led to questions of power and how power circulates within a society'.[67]

This political dimension is arguably of great significance, especially when we note that the cases under review concerned, among other matters, the legal position of trade unions,[68] the role of the Advisory, Conciliation and Arbitration Service,[69] the law relating to immigration,[70] the status of a tax avoidance scheme,[71] the law relating to contempt of court[72] and the question of the extent to which a government department can withhold documents from inspection by a court in the 'public interest'.[73] All of these are issues on which writers such as Griffith would presumably argue that the political position of the judges was vitally important in analysing the judgments. In assessing the methodology of this study, then, one question we might wish to consider is the nature of the relationship between the position of the judges and the way in which judgments are constructed. Arguably, one does not automatically illuminate the other; and each is in itself inadequate in explaining the connections between what judges *are* and what they *do*, and between what they *do* and what they *say they do*. Such connections are particularly important when the judges choose to adopt a creative role in individual 'hard' cases – cases, that is, where existing rules do not apparently cover the facts before the court – or in some other kinds of cases identified by Paterson, discussed below.

Paterson's study concerns the work of the judges in the House of Lords[74] with a view to discovering the law lords' own perceptions of their role and their work. Rather than concentrating upon the judges' structural position in society, Paterson's methodology was that of role analysis: the examination of 'the conduct that is expected of [the judge] in the particular social position which he occupies'.[75] His findings are based on observation of cases, interviews with law lords, barristers and others working closely with these most senior judges, and the analysis of (mainly) common-law cases heard by the House of Lords between 1957 and 1973. We learn that the law lords are to a large extent both actors and their own audience, in that their judgments seem to be influenced only by their fellow law lords. This finding is qualified to the extent that certain conventions tend to constrain this apparent independence – such as the convention, mentioned above, that a judgment should discuss only matters raised by counsel during the case, or raised and considered by the courts below. Although this convention is strongly adhered to, it is acknowledged that the judges can and do structure the course of counsel's argument by means of interventions and questions.

Paterson acknowledges a point made by other observers, which is that much will depend upon individual judges' personalities; the senior, presiding judge in particular can influence or control the course of argument, and some judges are more prepared than others to intervene. Judges' personalities will also affect the final outcome of the case. Whether or not a judge is prepared to dissent from the majority; whether a judge possesses particular persuasive powers, or even obstinacy, leading him or her to try to direct or force the conclusions of colleagues; or whether judges feel they must defer to the opinions of colleagues whose experience or intellect they respect: all are factors which illustrate the *individualistic* aspect of what is commonly thought of as a *group* decision-making process.

Paterson examines the work of the law lords from the point of view of the perceived objectives of judicial decision-making, especially in terms of what he calls

the tension between the drive for stability and certainty in the common law, which requires that disputes be adjudicated in accordance with previously announced norms and the drive for adjudication on the basis of individuated justice, which in certain cases will require that previously announced norms will be radically altered or departed from.[76]

That the law lords acknowledge this tension between justice and certainty emerges clearly from the many quotations from judges. The problem is especially acute in those 'hard' cases where there is no binding or strongly persuasive precedent, where precedents or principles may conflict, where the *ratio* of an ostensibly relevant precedent is unclear, or where the court is being asked to distinguish or overrule a binding or strongly persuasive precedent.[77]

Continuing to use role analysis, Paterson analyses the various types of judicial response to these problems, by identifying various potentially conflicting expectations of a judge which are raised in reaching a decision. The main expectations are that the judge should justify the decision by reasoned argument, that he or she ought not to legislate (that being the role of Parliament), that the decision should be consistent with existing law, and that the decision should achieve a just and fair result. These expectations may conflict: for instance, where the judge is being asked to overrule a precedent (thus creating new law) in order to reach what he or she feels is a just decision. The responses which judges may make when faced with such conflict are, argues Paterson, threefold. First, the judge may react *positively*, by redefining the judicial role so that the conflict is reduced, or by meeting with colleagues to discuss the problem. Second, the response may be *adaptive*, involving either the ranking or the weighing of the competing expectations, or (perhaps more significantly) evading the issue by means of 'dissimulation' – essentially, obscuring the existence of the conflict: 'The law lords imply that compliance with each of the expectations involves no breach of the others, when in truth they actually violate one or more consequent on a ranking according to the criteria [used for such ranking] or according to the comparative ease with which the expectations' violation can be concealed.'[78] The third response may be *withdrawal*: that is, a judge's acknowledgement that a given result may not be to his or her personal liking, but that the judge's role obliges him or her to arrive at that result none the less.

Applying these approaches more generally, Paterson emphasizes the extent to which the general character of the House of Lords over particular periods may change, largely because of the dominance of presiding law lords with entrenched views on the role of that court. Thus, the period 1957–62 was characterized by an adherence to precedent rather than an expansion or rationalization of the law – this reflecting the views of the then senior law lord, Viscount Simonds. From 1962 until 1966, there was a more activist 'judicial law-making' approach, albeit under the cloak of 'dissimulation', which Paterson perceives as characteristic of the dominant member of the court during this period, Lord Reid. In 1966 the House of Lords made its announcement that it would no longer regard itself as necessarily bound by its own decisions, declaring itself free to depart from those decisions 'when it appears right to do so',[79] and in the years following this Practice Direction, Paterson explains, Lord Reid remained the dominant force in enunciating the principles and limitations affecting any proposed break with a previous House of Lords decision. Essentially, these principles, as presented over a period of time and in a number of cases by Lord Reid, were that the freedom to overrule previous Lords' decisions should be used sparingly; that a case ought not to be overruled if to do so would upset people's expectations of the law, render the consequences of the overruling unforeseeable, engage the judges in piecemeal reform in an area of law which ought to be comprehensively reformed, or involve a change in the way in which statutes or other documents had been interpreted; and that a case ought to be overruled if it caused uncertainty in the law or was not considered to be just or in keeping with the contemporary social conditions or conceptions of public policy.

These principles, moreover, had to be related, according to Lord Reid, to the area of law in question. Areas such as property, contract, family and criminal law, where certainty was of vital importance, were not ones in which the freedom to overrule would be used as readily as the areas of tort and public and administrative law, where judicial development of the law has been regarded by the judges as legitimate and appropriate.

Paterson thus explores the relationship between judicial freedom of choice and the constraints (real or apparent) which limit or restrict that choice. He concludes that the law lords *do* have considerable discretion in reaching decisions, but that there are real constraints which may curb excessive activism: institutional forces, the perceived need to decide according to law, and the restraint shown by judges themselves, which can shift over periods of years. The overall picture presented is thus at odds not only with that of adherents of the 'declaratory theory' of judging, but also with that of Griffith, in so far as he has argued that there is a lack of 'any clear and consistent relationship between the general pronouncement of judges on [the] matter of creativity and the way they conduct themselves in court'.[80] Paterson counters this view by pointing out that 'we have seen that the perceptions elicited from the law lords in interviews, from their publications and speeches, of these norms and guidelines (i.e. their perceptions of their role) were highly consistent, both *inter se*, and with their performance in actual cases'.[81] This conclusion would certainly seem to be supported by Paterson's analysis of the twenty-nine cases heard by the Lords between 1966 and 1980 in which the court was asked to depart from one of its own precedents. Although some caution must be exercised when evaluating the judges' responses to interview questions, in that law lords are hardly likely to admit to any political predilections in deciding cases (and indeed the interviewer is hardly likely to antagonize the subject by asking such questions), Paterson's research provides a useful and interesting insight into the apparent working of the higher judicial minds.

The difficulty involved in making generalized statements remains, however, as is shown by Paterson, and by others such as Devlin[82] and Stevens.[83] Perhaps all that can be said is that the framework of rules, principles and practices operates as a set of constraining influences on judicial decision-making, but that these influences will act upon judges to differing degrees, depending on factors such as the nature or novelty of the case in hand, the attitude of particular judges to the questions of judicial discretion and creativity, the court where the case is heard[84] and so on. Assuming that such a constraining framework *does* affect, to a greater or lesser degree, judicial handling and interpretation of cases coming before them, the next question is that of the manner in which that discretion is, so to speak, wrapped up and delivered in the form of judicial pronouncements. We have already considered some aspects of this problem as it has been addressed by Murphy and Rawlings,[85] but one important task remaining is to consider some of the criteria used by the judges to justify those 'hard' case decisions which are not clearly dictated by existing rules or precedents; these cases include those areas identified by Griffith and Devlin where the political outlook of the judges may tend to sway their decisions.

We have, in previous chapters, seen examples from the areas of criminal law, administrative law, tort and contract in which judicial conceptions of public policy have played a part in determining the outcome of novel cases. The terms 'public policy' and the 'national interest' are two frequently used bases for such decisions, especially where, as we have suggested, the existing framework of law provides no clear answer. In many such cases, most people would probably find the result of this reasoning and justification process quite unobjectionable, as, for example, in the case of *Donoghue* v. *Stevenson* in 1932[86] where no clear rule existed to decide the liability of a manufacturer whose alleged negligence resulted in injury to the consumer of his product (see chapter 9). In more recent cases, such as *Hill* v. *Chief Constable of West Yorkshire* (1989)[87] and *Emeh* v. *Kensington and Chelsea Area Health Authority* (1985)[88] in tort, and *Williams* v. *Roffey Brothers* (1990)[89] in contract, judicial conceptions of *public policy* have increasingly been openly admitted by judges as constituting one of the bases on which they reach a particular decision, even though in some cases a particular approach to public policy has failed to attract general judicial approval or acceptance.[90]

Allied to judicial acknowledgment of the importance of policy issues is the technique, frequently employed by judges engaged in statutory interpretation, of appealing to 'reason' or 'common sense'. Murphy and Rawlings provide several examples of this technique: an example is *Bromley London Borough Council* v. *Greater London Council* in 1982 – the 'Fares Fair' case.[91] Here, the Labour majority on the GLC attempted to implement its election manifesto promise to reduce fares on London Transport buses and underground trains by imposing a supplementary rate upon the London boroughs, by means of which the fare reduction might be financed. Bromley Council challenged this action on the ground that it was not within the GLC's statutory powers, and applied to the court for an order quashing the supplementary rate.

The case is interesting for several reasons: the public controversy which greeted the Lords' decision in favour of Bromley; the explicit condemnation of the GLC's actions by some of the judges in both the Court of Appeal[92] and the House of Lords;[93] the five judgments of the House of Lords which, though eventually reaching the same conclusions, seem to follow quite different paths to get there;[94] and the way in which all of the judges in the Court of Appeal and the House of Lords made much of the significance of the word 'economic' as it appeared in the relevant legislation, the Transport (London) Act 1969. Section 1 of this Act provided that the GLC had[95] a duty to develop policies to 'promote the provision of integrated, efficient and economic transport facilities and services for Greater London'. All the judges agreed that the word 'economic' must be interpreted in such a way as to give it its 'ordinary business' meaning of being 'cost-effective', despite the fact that, as various observers have pointed out,[96] the provision of public transport by a local authority is a highly complex operation, having due regard to social as well as the financial aspects; it cannot sensibly be reduced to a relatively simple, particularized[97] question of the meaning of ambiguous statutory terminology.

The judges are often to be found engaged in *presuming*: in declaring what Parliament 'must be taken' to have intended. In this, as in other matters, the higher courts tend to justify decisions by means of *assumptions*; and in many areas where the 'public interest' is involved in judicial deliberations, we find that decisions ultimately rest upon the assumption that our society is characterized by a strong uniformity of political, economic and moral values, and by standards of behaviour in which every 'reasonable' person is presumed to concur. It is instructive to consider the deeper assumptions underlying these ideas: first, that there really exists such a uniformity of values; and second, that the judges have the capacity, and indeed a duty, to ensure that such values are protected and maintained through the law. There are many manifestations of this pattern of judicial activism: we will consider some example-areas.

First, the judges have always regarded *national security* as being of paramount importance, even to the extent of displacing individual claims of right. Several instances may be noted. In *Duncan* v. *Cammell Laird* in 1942[98] the defendants had built the submarine *Thetis* which sank during tests with the loss of ninety-nine men.

The plaintiffs were the legal representatives of the victims, suing for compensation for the men's deaths. Their case depended upon bringing evidence of the plans and other documents relating to the design of the submarine, but the Admiralty objected to the disclosure of such documents in court because it might prejudice national security. In the House of Lords, this objection was upheld, despite the crucial nature of this evidence for the plaintiffs' case. The readiness of the courts to accept the word of ministers of government that certain evidence should not be adduced in court attracted considerable criticism, though it was not until *Conway* v. *Rimmer* in 1967[99] that the House of Lords took back for itself the power, in appropriate cases, to decide whether or not ministerial objection to disclosure was in fact sufficient to displace the interests of the individual party to the dispute.

Similar considerations motivated the judges in *Attorney General* v. *Jonathan Cape Ltd* and *Attorney General* v. *Times Newspapers Ltd* in 1975,[100] when the courts held that publication of Cabinet discussions, even though they took place some years previously, might be restrained 'when this is clearly in the public interest'; and in *Home Office* v. *Harman* in 1981,[101] a case in which a solicitor acting for a convicted prisoner in an action against the Home Office showed certain Home Office documents to a journalist, who duly wrote an article criticizing the Home Office. The documents had been made public during the court action, but the solicitor was held to have acted in contempt of court in revealing their contents to the journalist. In the Court of Appeal, Lord Denning said that he perceived 'no public interest whatever in having these highly confidential documents made public. Quite the other way. It was in the public interest that these documents should be kept confidential . . . I regard the use made by the journalist in this case of these documents to be highly detrimental to the good ordering of our society.'[102]

We may note also the débâcle concerning the book *Spycatcher*, written by an ex-security officer. The government pursued legal actions in various parts of the world in order to restrain publication of this book, and although the attempt to suppress it failed in Australia and elsewhere, the English courts had little difficulty in accepting the government's contention that the book was prejudicial to the national interest, and ordering that, specifically, publication of extracts from the book by newspapers in the United Kingdom would be unlawful – despite the fact that the book itself was readily available in a number of bookshops, having been imported from other countries where publication was not prevented![103]

A second example-area concerns morality. The judges have consistently regarded themselves as arbiters of moral standards, defending their ideas of a somewhat conservative and, some would say, out-dated morality in the name of what Lord Devlin referred to in 1959 as the 'public morality', which the law could and should be used to protect and maintain. He argued that 'there are certain standards of behaviour or moral principles which society requires to be observed; and the breach of them is an offence not merely against the person who is injured but against society as a whole'.[104] We saw some examples of the judges' belief in their role as protectors of the 'public morality' in chapter 2; yet the judicial protection of moral standards extends beyond the range of criminal law. Such concerns are the basis of much judicial comment and decisions in family law, and in the law of contract we find cases such as that of *Pearce* v. *Brooks* in 1866,[105] where the judges refused to accept the legality of an agreement between the plaintiffs and the defendant whereby the former had hired out a carriage to the latter, to be used for the purposes of prostitution.[106] In *Glynn* v. *Keele University* in 1971,[107] a student who was excluded from residence on the campus for nude sunbathing failed in his attempt to challenge this disciplinary action. Although the court accepted that, in denying him a chance to put his side of the case, the university official had acted in breach of natural justice (see chapter 12), the court none the less felt that the offence was such as to 'merit a severe penalty according to any standards current even today'. And in 1972, in *Ward* v. *Bradford Corporation*,[108] the Court of Appeal denied a remedy to a student teacher who had broken the rules of her hall of residence by permitting her boy-friend to remain in her room overnight for a period of about two months. She had been expelled by the college and, despite irregularities in the manner in which the disciplinary procedure had been carried out, Lord Denning stated firmly his belief that her behaviour was not suitable for a trainee teacher: 'she would never make a teacher. No parent would knowingly entrust their child to her care'.[109]

In such matters of morality, the tension between judicial conservatism and an increased social tolerance of moral behaviour which is not to everyone's taste is manifest. It is worth asking the question whether, in today's climate in which sexual and other moral matters are relatively freely discussed and practices once regarded as beyond the pale are fairly openly indulged in, the attitude of the judges may in some cases be too far removed from the 'real social world', so to speak, to protect the interests of all involved. Having said this, however, one oustanding case in which the judges showed themselves well aware of modern public attitudes towards sexual morality was *R* v. *R* in 1991[110] – the case which overturned the common-law rule that a husband could not be criminally liable for committing rape upon his wife. In the Court of Appeal, Lord Lane stated that the old common-law rule had become 'anachronistic and offensive and we consider that it is our duty having reached that conclusion to act upon it' – a view with which the House of Lords unanimously agreed. There can be no doubt that this decision was both welcome and long overdue.

Other notable areas where the courts have referred, in the various cases before them, to the 'public interest', or equivalent terms, include the law of property, where the judges have consistently upheld the protection of traditional rights to private property as against, for example, private tenants (through restrictive interpretation of rent legislation) and squatters; the law relating to conspiracy, where, until the Criminal Law Act 1977 clarified and somewhat restricted the range of the offence, the judges had been quite prepared to uphold convictions for the offence even though the activity allegedly planned by the conspirators had not been carried out;[111] and the law relating to public order and industrial disputes.[112]

The problems underlying these assumptions and views on the part of the judiciary revolve around the difficulty of identifying exactly what constitutes the 'public interest' in a given area – even if such a monolithic entity exists at all. By what criteria do the judges, who wield considerable power in such cases, discover which particular body of attitudes or standards in our society constitutes *the* public interest? Perhaps Lord Devlin, once again, expressed the view of most judges:

English law has evolved and regularly uses a standard which does not depend on the counting of heads. It is that of the reasonable man . . . It is the viewpoint of the man in the street . . . He might also be called the right-minded man. For my purpose I should like to call him the man in the jury-box, for the moral judgment of society must be something about which any twelve men or women drawn at random might after discussion be expected to be unanimous.[113]

But how likely *is* such consensus? Society is by no means homogeneous: it is composed of many groups and individuals differing in terms of sex, age, ethnic and cultural background, social class and political power. Would it be possible to obtain a unanimous judgment from any group of randomly selected people on the issues of industrial relations, prostitution or any of the other areas where the assumptions held by the judges, particularly in the appellate courts, have come to the fore? Surely *any* interest-group might convincingly register a belief that *their* policies, beliefs or attitudes were an accurate reflection of a 'public morality' or a 'public interest'? Unless we are, literally, to embark upon a national referendum on all such matters, there would seem to be no clear way of ascertaining what the majority of people believe to be right or acceptable behaviour, with any degree of accuracy.

Furthermore, Lord Devlin and other judges using similar terminology commit a serious analytical error in using phrases such as 'society believes this' or 'society has decided that'. Such loose phrases obscure the fact of pluralistic interests and differential access to policy-making channels within the social structure. What is, therefore, presented as being in the 'public interest' may in fact serve limited, sectional interests. As Coulson and Riddell put it,

to say that a decision is in the national interest usually means to identify the interests of one group of the population as the National Interest, while conveniently forgetting the interests of those members of the nation who are not benefited by the decision. By the appeal to nationalism, sectional decisions may appear more palatable to people they *don't* benefit.[114]

Conclusion

On the one hand we have, especially at the pinnacle of the court structure, a body of judges whose social class and educational background are likely to persuade them towards a conservative, perhaps even reactionary outlook on the social world, and a belief that there are traditional and widely held social values which they, as judges, have to uphold; and on the other, we have the rest of society, comprising groups and individuals with strikingly heterogeneous beliefs, attitudes and principles. How far can the judiciary in its present form contribute to the solution of the many social problems affecting the rest of the community? Few would deny the importance of a judiciary which commands the confidence and respect of those subject to its pronouncements, but the *caveat* must always be put, that the members of that body must be prepared to take on the responsibilities of ensuring that the law keeps in step with the changing needs of society. Whether the judges, as presently constituted, can ever modify their attitudes and actions to further these broad social aims may be doubted. It has been suggested that 'it seems improbable that courts will ever be able to accomplish, save by minuscule changes moving with glacial slowness, the sort of revolutionary shifts in power which would be necessary to change the system entirely'.[115]

It is no answer for the judges to argue that such changes in society and in law are the business of Parliament, not the judiciary, for, as we have seen, there is abundant evidence that judges are (and always have been) prepared to engage in deciding issues which have clear and controversial political import. Some have tried – not always successfully – to reform the law in an explicit manner; others, by taking refuge behind ambiguous statutory terminology or appeals to nebulous concepts such as the public interest, have cloaked judicial discretion and activism with the guise of 'mere applications of the law'.

Some of the criticisms of the judiciary might be answered through reforms such as those suggested by Pannick[116] in a book which, though often critical, offers little by way of development of a systematic theoretical discussion of the relationship between judges and the social and political structure: the admission of professional lawyers other than barristers into the judicial hierarchy (see chapter 13), or the recruitment into the legal profession of a wider cross-section of the population. Perhaps the judicial profession should be one which, as in some other countries, is open to graduates of law who receive appropriate training from the outset and who may be promoted through various levels of the court structure depending on ability and experience. Such reforms, however, may be thought to be inevitably limited, for there remains the fact that judges are, by definition, part and parcel of state authority, and that their task is the administration of a powerful force which tends to resist change: the law itself. The problems which critics of the judiciary raise are not merely *legal* problems: they go to the very heart of the political structure of society, and any reforms which may make far-reaching changes will inevitably arise through pressure brought to bear on legal *and* political institutions in modern society.

15
Conclusion: law, the individual and the state

Throughout this book, certain themes and problems have recurred. One of these themes is the need for change in many of the legal, economic and political structures of our society. Some of these changes – particularly, short-run reforms – may appropriately come about through specific and detailed recommendations of bodies such as Royal Commissions or, perhaps more importantly, the Law Commission. Some changes may occur through pressure-group activity or, in more limited ways, through judicial law-making. Other changes, however, especially the more far-reaching ones, will occur only through prolonged and sustained questioning and criticism of the legal system, and the social and political context within which that system operates. In this chapter we discuss some of the problems involved in the matter of legal and social change; various questions will be raised and a number of criticisms presented, in order to provoke further discussion of some important debates.

It may at first seem strange to insist on such a firm connection between law, and economic and political issues. Traditional legal education in Britain – and, to be sure, elsewhere[1] – has for many years been founded on the premise that the study of law is the study of legal rules. But as Jackson, among many others, has pointed out,

Once one gets away from the rules of law and into the realm of the effects on people there are vast territories to explore. The lawyer's reply has been that these are not 'legal questions' at all. It is so much more comfortable to build a snug nest, lined with the pure theory of law, than it is to see what is happening as a result of the law and its administration.[2]

We might go further and argue that the branches of law which comprise mainstream legal education in Britain – traditionally, contract, tort and property – must be supplemented, not only by materials relating to the socio-economic and political contexts in which these rules and principles operate, but also by the study of other areas of legal regulation such as planning, social security, housing legislation and consumer protection. The positive move in recent years towards incorporating the learning of legal skills – including advocacy and negotiation – within law courses should prove immensely beneficial, for areas of substantive law such as those noted above involve specialized and technical legal rules and procedures, requiring as much proficiency in lawyering skills as in basic knowledge of the rules.

Even the Benson Commission, reporting on the provision of legal services,[3] whose report was not exactly a blueprint for radical change, recognized the importance of including 'welfare law' in legal education. But if we scrutinize these areas of law more closely, we find that in many cases it is not legal rules that generate, or dictate, the outcome of particular disputes or problems, so much as considerations of policy, taken into account by decision-makers in whose hands Parliament has vested substantial degrees of discretion. For example, areas such as planning law, social security, housing and child-care law are only partly regulated by legal rules: often, those rules only comprise the *framework* provided by statute, within which a variety of *discretionary, administrative* decisions are made by a variety of administrative agencies – usually by means of extensive powers vested in those bodies by statute. When we go further and ask *how* these decisions – many of them affecting the lives of private individuals – are made, we invariably find that questions of politics, in the guise of 'policy considerations', frequently dictate the outcome of the decision-making processes.[4]

The provisions of what we refer to for convenience' sake as the 'welfare state', moreover, leave little room for complacency. It may be true that, since 1945, the expansion of the welfare state has brought improved standards of living for many sections of the community. But we have noted difficulties with the operation of, for example, rent legislation, both in terms of its effect on the private housing market and in terms of the restrictive interpretation put upon rent legislation by the judges, especially by allowing for several years the widespread evasion of Rent Act regulation by the use of licences.[5] We may doubt the extent to which consumer protection legislation has produced *effective* remedies for the ordinary consumer;[6] and we may have reservations about the adequacy of planning controls and their implementation.[7] Furthermore, we may have misgivings about the machinery of the welfare state designed to deal with disputes between the citizen and administrative agencies; as we have seen, many such disputes have quite deliberately been taken out of the courts (the traditional institutions for the solution of legal disputes and the provision of remedies) and placed in the hands of tribunals. These may be cheap and speedy methods of solving disputes; but at the same time they have raised problems over the complexity of the substantive legislation itself, the procedures (if any) for appeals, the provision of legal aid, and the adequacy of the courts (through administrative law) in terms of the development of clear and consistent principles for the regulation of administrative activity.[8]

Perhaps most importantly, the limitations of welfare state legislation must be realized: the social security system may have provided for support in circumstances of unemployment and poverty, for example, but state interventionist policies – implemented through law – have not solved the underlying causes of economic inequality, poverty and unemployment, poor housing, inequality of opportunity because of age, sex, ethnic background or social class, or any of the other factors which are so divisive of modern society. What is more, the administration of the welfare state ultimately takes its place in the scale of priorities of any government at any particular period; and at the present time welfare state finance (that is, 'public spending') has been seriously and adversely affected by the policies of governments which, in their quest for a 'sound economy' through investment and profitability, and their ideological goal of returning as many industries and services as possible to the private sector, have curtailed spending in the public sector to a crippling extent at both central and local levels. Critics have pointed to the impoverishment of the health service, the undermining of social security benefits, cuts in education provision, and of course the introduction of measures designed to save money in the provision of legal aid and advice. Some have gone so far as to suggest that the welfare state is being systematically dismantled in favour of a political and ideological milieu in which, to put it crudely, individual citizens are forced back on to their own initiatives rather than continuing to be dependent on the 'nanny state'. Critics also point out that the high levels of unemployment and poverty in Britain today are in fact the direct result of government spending cuts and sustained high interest rates through the 1980s and into the 1990s. It would seem that government today takes as its first priority not the well-being of the whole community, but a continued subservience to powerful national and international financial interests.

Even a cursory examination such as the above shows how inextricably law and politics are interwoven. We have so far referred only to the general concept of the 'welfare state' to illustrate this, but before discussing these issues and their implications for social and legal change in greater depth through other examples, it is useful to outline several other general propositions which have an important bearing on questions of law and society.

First, though frequently called upon to address itself to resolving social and economic problems of various kinds, the law is a clumsy and cumbersome instrument in many respects, with regard both to the implementation of general policies and to the attainment of justice in individual cases. The common law, for example, as administered and developed by the judges, has failed to adapt itself easily (if at all) from the economic assumptions of the last century to the state-interventionist social and political context of the twentieth century; we have seen examples of this in contract law, in the law of tort, and with regard to judicial attitudes to administrative agencies and their powers. Why is the common law so slow to adapt? One reason, of course, is the conservatism of the judiciary, many instances of which have been discussed in various contexts already. Additionally, however, the common law lacks the institutional machinery for rapid adaptation to new situations. This is partly because 'the kind of case that may offer scope for judicial zeal for reform may not arise at the appropriate time: litigants and appellants cannot be relied upon to produce precedent fodder when it is needed',[9] and partly because of the grip of statutory provisions and – much more important – the vast body of precedents which bind the courts and thus impose constraints upon the judges' reforming capacities.

Even where appropriate cases do fall before the courts, the judges do not always recognize the need for change (consider, for example, the reluctance to abandon the concepts of 'equality and freedom of contract' – fictitious even in the last century – in the realm of consumer contracts); even where the need is perceived, the law develops in a piecemeal and often inconsistent manner. Because the law of negligence, for example, has developed in this way, an attempt by a plaintiff to recover compensation for personal injuries may (unless the case falls, in the court's opinion, squarely within the ambit of precedent) be more a game of chance than a rational means of providing remedies for injuries arising from accidents in industry and on the roads. In the former case, an injured party may be better advised to recover compensation through the industrial injuries scheme than to play for higher stakes in a court of law with the enhanced risk of losing.

In negligence, as in other areas of law, the judges' solution to many of the issues before them has been found in the idea of 'reasonableness': is the alleged nuisance an 'unreasonable interference'? Did a local authority behave 'reasonably' in exercising its statutory powers? The concept is found in statutes too: for example, is an exclusion clause in a business contract 'reasonable' in terms of the provisions of the Unfair Contract Terms Act 1977? The criterion of reasonableness is notoriously vague, and a plethora of precedents is of little help in enabling a plaintiff or defendant (or rather, their legal advisers) to assess the likelihood of success or failure in court. True, the judges have recognized from time to time the elasticity of the notion: 'what to one judge may seem far-fetched may to another seem both natural and probable'.[10] But it seems that the conceptual maze of the common law in these and in other areas, despite the exhortations of Lord Denning to consider policy and 'the reason of the thing',[11] cannot arrive at a satisfactorily clear and exhaustive set of rules and principles which reflect the urgent necessity for a remedy where injury or harm has been sustained.

The common-law tradition, then, with its idiosyncratic modes of thought and reasoning, and its capacity for change muzzled by the past in the shape of precedent and out-dated judicial attitudes, seems increasingly awkward and umsympathetic in the modern world. Even if we agree that the judges *could* bring about change, and that the common law *could* catch up with the continually fluctuating demands placed upon the legal system by developments within society, such change can only occur with the willing co-operation of those steeped in common-law tradition and doctrine: the judiciary and the legal profession. And there is an unfortunate reluctance (not least because of the vested economic interests of the profession)[12] to press for, or even to accept the need for, change. It is only when the legal profession is under threat – by attacks on their traditional areas of work, by the growth in independent advice agencies, and now by the government, whose determination to cut public spending must result in a reduction of solicitors' income from the legal aid fund – that lawyers' self-interest suddenly makes them aware of areas of work (criminal trials, welfare law, tribunal representation) in which they were hitherto largely uninterested, but with regard to which they now hold themselves out as indispensable.

Parliamentary legislation, too, has inherent limitations in its capacity to address pressing social and economic problems. Though increasingly used as the means of implementing social and economic programmes throughout the twentieth century, there are many respects in which statutory provisions may fall short of both expectations and parliamentary intentions. This may be because of restrictive interpretation by the courts; it may be because of drafting difficulties; it may be because the legislation was introduced half-heartedly in the first place, and fails to embody the provisions for which affected groups and individuals had hoped. Women, and black and other ethnic minority groups, have expressed disappointment at the perceived lack of impact of sex and race discrimination legislation, for example. No doubt it is true that the statutes contained omissions, but we must not expect massive change from the law alone, as Cotterrell reminds us:

The failure to see law as merely one aspect of a complex social whole affected by many social forces, and to see law as shaped by these forces probably to a far greater extent than it can shape them, leads to inevitable disillusionment when the legal instrument fails to achieve what the legal reformer intended.[13]

A second major problem confronting reformers or campaigners for legal and political change is that law has the characteristic of containing within its precepts *authoritative*, even *final*, definitions of problem-areas and, as a consequence, their solutions. Once embedded in legal form, a given controversy or problem is not easily redefined in other ways. Rock has written that

the main significance of law . . . is that it is imperialistic. It is buttressed by state agencies which enjoy a 'monopoly of the legitimate use of physical force'. The edicts of a legal system are intended to cover the whole network of minor moral worlds irrespective of their acquiescence. Although other major moral codes attempt to achieve such a domination, law is the sole sytem which is vigorously enforced in a coercive fashion.[14]

And 'enforcement' refers not only to law-enforcement by the police, but also to devices such as court orders in civil cases (injunctions; the award of damages) and in administrative law disputes (the prerogative remedies), as well as the law relating to contempt of court.[15] Essentially, once an issue is the subject of legislation, it can become *frozen* with regard to its definition, its ambit and the assumptions upon which it is based. Might one result of this be that attempts to negotiate alternative explanations of the issue, to restate its scope and implications and to expose the weaknesses of the underlying assumptions, tend to founder upon the unyielding structure of the legal and political system?

This is not to say that laws, once enacted, cannot be altered: such a proposition is clearly false. When we begin to examine the conditions under which those laws *may* be altered, however, we are invariably faced once more with the crucial dimension of political power, and its differential possession and use by different sections and groups within society. Given the enormous range of currently controversial social and political issues in which the law, the individual and the state are involved, it is useful to try to analyse some of the processes at work in the legal and political structure, whereby the output of both legislature (through statutes) and, it must be noted, government *in the absence of legislation*[16] might be influenced.

Defining the issue: imposition or negotiation?

The legal system and the legal order are reflections of the total social order, and this in turn is a manifestation of political forces and formations. These forces and formations comprise not only stated policies, as announced and implemented by government and other political institutions, but also the forces of ideology: the world-views, the currents of moral, political and economic thought, and the 'master definitions of reality' which are disseminated and inculcated through political discourse, educational curricula, the mass media and, of course, the law. Ideological constructs by which we understand the world, however, are neither fixed nor unique: ideological currents change, often in response to economic change.

To take one example, the idea during the 1950s that Commonwealth immigration was of benefit to the country because of a labour shortage during a period of economic boom has given way, during the 1980s and 1990s, to the notion that immigration must be strictly curbed, again in the national interest. This notion is informed partly by prejudice and racist attitudes but, equally importantly, by the fact that continued immigration would serve little economic purpose during a period of recession and unemployment. The consequent 'slamming of the door' through successive statutes restricting immigration (notably the Immigration Act 1971 and the British Nationality Act 1981) reflects these changes. At the same time, however, the ideology of liberalism that has informed race relations legislation (currently the Race Relations Act 1976), which outlaws discrimination on the grounds of colour, race or ethnic or national origins or nationality and citizenship, stands in marked contrast to racist and restrictive immigration policies.[17]

This example highlights another facet of ideology: although it is often said, particularly by marxist commentators, that the state and the ruling class control and disseminate a 'dominant ideology',[18] it must not be supposed that the state and its agencies operate within one fixed set of ideological constructs. Nor should the term 'dominant ideology' obscure the fact that there are invariably *alternative* explanations of, and attitudes to, social phenomena. Often, ideological clashes are played out on party-political platforms, inside and outside Parliament (as, for example, in debates on the limits of legitimate activity by trade unions, the question of nationalization of industries such as coal, steel, gas and transport, and debates about reforms of the education system). There are other arenas, too, both public and private, in which ideological confrontations, within courts of law and behind the closed doors of government departments or state agencies, what Gramsci explained[19] as the 'hegemonic struggle' for dominance between opposing ideological views is played out; and implicit within this proposition is the recognition that such struggle takes place *between* as well as within state agencies.

As a result, we often find that individual statutes, because they have their own unique history and are based upon particular ideological assumptions, may contradict the stated objectives of other enactments in similar areas. The comparison between immigration control and race relations legislation is an illustration, as is the comparison between the aims and assumptions upon which the Sex Discrimination Act 1975 and the social security and supplementary benefit regulations are based. The 1975 Act purports to extend and guarantee equal opportunities for women, especially in the workplace, and thus may be said to be predicated on an ideal of women's economic independence. Contrast this with the 'co-habitation rule' within the supplementary benefit regulations, whereby an unmarried woman who is regarded as living with a man outside marriage is barred from claiming supplementary benefit in her own right, because she is presumed to be financially supported by any man with whom she lives. How far is this consistent with the ideal of promoting women's economic independence?

It will be appreciated from the discussion so far that, apart from the inherent limitations of law in securing legal and social justice and equality in society, *some* limited progress towards these ends may be made through struggle within the political and legislative process. Possibilities exist for alternative explanations of social problems, and hence solutions thereto, to be argued for – both inside and outside Parliament. Hence, 'law must be regarded as an *arena of struggle*, a field in which different class and political positions engage, with consequences that are not deductible from any general theory of law'.[20] At the same time, any framework within which such debates may take place must recognize the varying degrees of preparedness of the state to take different positions into account. It would seem that there are matters over which there is little or no possibility for negotiation. Few of us, collectively or individually, can engage on an official level with state departments or agencies over matters involving national security, the investigation of crime, defence or the maintenance of public order. On such issues, the state retains its monopoly of both definition and coercive enforcement. They are matters over which governments and other state agencies are simply not prepared to negotiate. The definitions of, and solutions to, problems posed by such issues may thus be said to be almost invariably *imposed* by the state: the solutions, moreover, are almost invariably in the form of criminal-law rules carrying penal or, in the Durkheimian sense of the word, *repressive* sanctions.

Thus we can understand the relative ease with which jury-vetting in 'sensitive' trials may occur;[21] with which public concern over telephone-tapping and other intrusions into private lives are met with bland reassurances;[22] and with which the powerful police lobby, having emerged as an increasingly overt political pressure-group in recent years,[23] had little difficulty in persuading the government to give priority to measures designed to provide them with new and wide-ranging powers of investigation in the form of the Police and Criminal Evidence Act 1984.

To expand briefly[24] on the latter example: the Police and Criminal Evidence Act 1984 was introduced as a response to the stated need of the police for wider powers with which to investigate crime and apprehend offenders. The Act extends the powers of police officers to stop and search people and vehicles (without arrest) if the officer has reasonable grounds for believing that stolen goods or prohibited articles (offensive weapons or items for use in connection with theft, burglary or other property offences) are present. The Act extends the powers of the police regarding the entry and search of premises. It governs the law of arrest, interrogation and general treatment of suspects and persons arrested; detention for questioning; and the practice and procedures governing complaints against the police.

The Act was, and remains, highly controversial: it took two years to be passed, and there were several hundred amendments made to the original bill. Critics inside and outside Parliament expressed grave concern over what they regarded as the serious erosion of civil liberties and the imbalance between police powers and the protection of individual rights. Among the many interesting aspects of the long process of enactment of this measure, however, was the fact that, while the protests of civil libertarians fell on deaf ears, the complaints from professional groups such as lawyers, doctors, priests and journalists over the applicability of the proposed new powers to seize documents and other items which were held in confidence resulted in major changes to the legislation, whereby special procedures were introduced to protect such material: might this be an example of the differential impact on the law-making process by groups with differential degrees of political power?

There are other areas, too, where it may be said that the state, through law and other processes, imposes definitions upon society, though the objectives behind such interventions may not properly be termed 'repressive'. The importance of presenting certain areas of social and economic life as 'given', and thus not open to redefinition, often lies in the ideological and/or functional significance of the institution in question. Thus, for example, family-law rules rest almost without exception upon a particular set of ideological assumptions about the 'normal' family. The 'normal' family in turn constitutes a crucially important unit within society, serving the functions of reproduction, socialization of children and maintenance of the labour-force (through the provision of shelter and subsistence). Economically, too, the family is a basic 'consumer unit': it constitutes perhaps the most significant market (as is clear from television advertisements aimed at the family) for the goods and services on whose continued consumption the national economy depends.

Similarly, the rules of contract, tort, property and administrative law all rest upon assumptions or acknowledgments of their social and economic functions, discussed at various points in this book. To the extent that the sanctions accompanying these areas of law are not primarily designed to be penal, but are *compensatory* in nature, we may conclude that the purposes served by such areas of regulation are not repressive, but *integrative*: they help to maintain existing social relations, to remedy dislocations in those relationships caused by disputes and to 'oil the wheels' of social interaction.

There are, however, limits to the extent that dominant ideological definitions – of problem-areas in particular – can be successfully imposed by state agencies. At specific moments, and with reference to particular issues, the definition of problems may be *negotiated* with and through the state. For example, persistent campaigning by liberal reformers has had the result of achieving reforms, albeit limited ones,[25] in the areas of women's rights, race relations, sexual morality and welfare rights. Might it then be argued that these reforms, however piecemeal and partial they may be, nevertheless constitute evidence that in these areas, too, orthodox and traditional ideologies *can* be challenged, and that official definitions and assumptions *can* be negotiated? Certainly, in the field of individual rights, it is vital to analyse and consider carefully and precisely the issues at stake, and to recognize that inequality may manifest itself in a number of ways. We have, at various points in this book, drawn attention to the dimensions of social class and of differential possession of political power, and it has been argued that much of our law is the result of the social and economic divisions within society. It would be crude in the extreme to assert that there is simply 'one law for the rich and one for the poor', but the fact remains that much of our law – especially where property and its protection are concerned – is the outcome of social and economic forces closely connected with wealth and political power.

Conclusion

If there is bias within the legal and political structure, or a reluctance to take into account the experiences of inequality of many sections of the community, these faults do not always take the form of the overt repressiveness of, say, the legal treatment of the trade union movement in its early days. More often than not, they take on far more subtle guises: restrictive interpretation of statutory provisions by the courts; the presentation of highly complex phenomena such as crime in terms of simplistic 'law and order' politics through the utterances of politicians and the mass media; the disingenuous invitations of politicians to campaigning groups to air their grievances in settings designed more for just 'letting off steam' than for working towards real solutions.

On the other hand, calls for change may come from sources other than pressure-groups or campaigning individuals. Lord Scarman, addressing himself to the issue of individual rights (particularly as embodied in the Universal Declaration of Human Rights adopted in 1948 by the General Assembly of the United Nations, and the European Convention of Human Rights and Fundamental Freedoms formulated in 1950 by the Council of Europe), notes that the United Kingdom, along with many other European states, has ratified and adopted the latter convention, and suggests that 'it may be that since the passing of the European Communities Act 1972 the Convention already has or will, without further enactment by the British Parliament, become part of English law'.[26] Though recognizing the limitations of a person's right to take a complaint alleging a breach of the convention by a member state to the European Court, Scarman welcomes these developments; he discusses the absence of any entrenched Bill of Rights within the (unwritten) British constitution, and laments the professed inability of the English courts to challenge any enactment of Parliament, however oppressive it may be. He stresses the urgent need for an entrenched Bill of Rights, which could not easily be overridden or repealed by successive governments, and which would form the national basis for the honouring of international agreements:

Do you think that the deeply disturbing practices of interrogation to which resort was had in Northern Ireland would have occurred, had British law possessed at the time a fully developed code of fundamental human rights? . . . put at its mildest, the present situation of the United Kingdom at the Bar of European justice and in the eyes of international legal opinion is embarrassing.[27]

While acknowledging that such statements as the Universal Declaration of Human Rights are essentially 'natural law' statements,[28] and therefore comprise statements of faith rather than concrete principles of law; and while acknowledging also the persistent problem of all international law – that of adequate enforcement against states who infringe it – it is becoming increasingly important to take the matter of individual rights seriously, and to recognize it for the political issue it is.

Many people and organizations (such as the National Council for Civil Liberties, and those such as the Charter 88 Campaign who argue for an entrenched Bill of Rights) have long argued that the civil liberties supposedly enjoyed in Britain have diminished, continue to diminish, and ought increasingly to be protected. Too easily and too often we witness examples of the growing tendency to vest more and more power in state agencies – apart from the question of police powers, concern is often expressed about powers to collect and store information about private citizens on capacious and interlinked computer files, and powers to withhold such information from individuals affected, in the 'national interest',[29] Some commentators perceived that Britain in the 1980s showed a distinct swing to the political right, towards a more rigid, intolerant and authoritarian society in which a premium is placed on security and order at the expense of individual legal and political liberty.[30]

If such fears are well-founded, it is all the more important that the mystifying functions of ideology, perpetuated by official agencies, are exposed for what they are. If individual and collective freedoms and genuine equality between sections of the community are to be pressed for and protected, then the law has an important part to play. Its use as an ideological weapon must be exposed, but its force as a limitation upon power must be recognized and strengthened. Thompson has argued that 'the rhetoric and the rules of a society are something a great deal more than sham. In the same moment they may modify, in profound ways, the behaviour of the powerful, and mystify the powerless. They may disguise the true realities of power, but, at the same time, they may curb that power and check its intrusions.'[31] While, therefore, it is useful and necessary to expose the social, legal and political inequalities which are masked behind the political and legal rhetoric of rights, justice and equality, many would go on to argue that it is also essential to recognize that 'the rule of law itself, the imposing of effective inhibitions upon power and the defence of the citizen from power's all-intrusive claims, seems . . . to be an unqualified human good'.[32]

It is vital that our understanding of law is not reduced to a definition of law as *merely* a reflection of inequality within the overall social order; and that our conceptions of justice and equality are not confined to cynical acknowledgments that these terms may be and often have been defined in ways which bolster the dominant ideology of the powerful, and thus maintain their social and economic interests. The analysis of law and the legal system, and their role in society, should rather include the task of exposing those instances where the use of the law *is* merely ideology, merely rhetoric; the identification of those issues where individual and collective rights can be extended and protected by means of challenging orthodoxy and negotiating advances; and the continuing struggle to establish social, political and legal institutions through which equality may be better attained and individuals and groups better protected. Given the existing legal and political structure, such analysis and criticism is the positive and proper function of all who stand to be affected by law in modern society.

NOTES

Chapter 1: Law and society

1 W. Twining and D. Miers, *How to Do Things with Rules* (3rd edn, 1991, Weidenfeld and Nicolson), p. 131.
2 See chapter 11.
3 There are various exceptions to this general statement, of which the best known are perhaps the offence of perjury (lying in the witness box), the making of a false statement in order to induce someone to buy something, which may fall foul of the Trade Descriptions Act 1968 (creating criminal offences for false or misleading trade descriptions, discussed in chapter 11), the law relating to misrepresentation, or lying on an official document (such as an income tax return or claim for social security benefit) which may lead to prosecution.
4 For a useful discussion of some important contributions in this area, see B. Roshier and H. Teff, *Law and Society in England* (1980, Tavistock), chapter 2; R. Cotterrell, *The Sociology of Law: An Introduction* (2nd edn, 1992, Butterworths).
5 K. Llewellyn, 'The Normative, the Legal, and the Law-Jobs: The Problem of Juristic Method' (1940) *Yale Law Journal*; and see also Llewellyn and Hoebel, *The Cheyenne Way* (1941, University of Oklahoma Press).
6 R. Summers, 'The Technique Element in Law' (1971) 59 *Calif. Law Rev.*
7 H. L. A. Hart, *The Concept of Law* (1961, Oxford University Press), p. 26.
8 R. M. Dworkin, *Taking Rights Seriously* (1977, Duckworth), chapter 2.
9 Ibid, p. 26.
10 See ibid, pp. 23–4.
11 H. L. A. Hart, *The Concept of Law*, op. cit.
12 Max Weber, *Law in Economy and Society*, ed. M. Rheinstein (1969, Harvard University Press), especially chapter 12.
13 Students might follow up discussion of these concepts in any textbook on sociology. For a selection of titles, see 'Suggestions for Further Reading'.
14 E. Durkheim, *The Division of Labour in Society* (1964, Free Press, New York; Macmillan, London).
15 See in particular T. Parsons, 'Law and Social Control' in W. M. Evan (ed.), *Law and Sociology* (1962, Free Press, New York).
16 E. A. Hoebel, *The Law of Primitive Man* (1954, Harvard University Press).
17 E. Schur, *Law and Society* (1968, Random House), pp. 79–80.

18 See chapter 11.

19 W. Chambliss and R. Seidman, *Law, Order and Power* (2nd edn, 1982, Addison-Wesley), p. 38.

20 See, especially, F. Tönnies, *Community and Association* (1887).

21 Chambliss and Seidman, op. cit., p. 40.

22 Ibid.

23 S. Macaulay, 'Non-Contractual Relations in Business' in V. Aubert (ed.), *Sociology of Law* (1972, Penguin). See below, chapter 11.

24 For an excellent discussion on this, see E. J. Hobsbawm, *Industry and Empire* (1969, Penguin).

25 See chapter 5.

26 K. W. Wedderburn, *The Worker and the Law* (3rd edn, 1986, Penguin), p. 76; and see generally H. Pelling, *A History of British Trade Unionism* (1973, Penguin); B. Perrins, *Trade Union Law* (1985, Butterworths); A. Harding, *A Social History of English Law* (1966, Penguin); E. P. Thompson, *The Making of the English Working Class* (1975, Penguin).

27 See in particular, Thompson, op. cit.

28 For example Wedderburn, op. cit.; P. Davies and M. Freedland, *Labour Law: Text and Materials* (2nd edn, 1984, Weidenfeld and Nicholson).

29 The omission of the feminine adjective is deliberate: the position of women in nineteenth-century society was such that they were thought not to have any affairs to regulate; the struggle of equality for women has continued throughout the twentieth century. Today, we have a legislative beginning in the forms of the Equal Pay Act 1971 and the Sex Discrimination Act 1975, but apart from legal enactments, the social and economic struggle for women's rights continues.

30 (1880) 6 Q. B. D. 530.

31 (1946) 115 L. J. P. C. 41.

32 *Bank voor Handel en Scheepvaart N. V.* v. *Slatford* [1953] 1 Q. B. 248 at p. 295.

33 See *Ready Mixed Concrete Ltd* v. *Minister of Pensions and National Insurance* [1968] 1 All E. R. 433; and the discussion in I. T. Smith and J. C. Wood, *Industrial Law* (4 edn, 1989, Butterworths).

34 P. J. Harris and J. D. Buckle, 'Philosophies of Law and the Law Teacher' (1976) *The Law Teacher*, p. 6.

35 D. Lockwood, 'Some Remarks on "The Social System" ' (1956) *British Journal of Sociology*, vol. 7.

36 R. White, in P. Morris, R. White and P. Lewis, *Social Needs and Legal Action* (1973, Martin Robertson), p. 15.

37 Ibid, p. 17.

38 K. Marx, 'The German Ideology' in T. Bottomore and M. Rubel (eds), *Karl Marx: Selected Writings in Sociology and Social Philosophy* (1961, Pelican), p. 228.

39 L. Althusser, 'Ideology and Ideological State Apparatuses' in B. R. Cosin (ed.), *Education: Structure and Society* (1972, Penguin/Open University).

40 Bottomore and Rubel, op. cit., p. 93.

41 A. Gramsci, *Prison Notebooks* (1971, Lawrence and Wishart).

42 Op. cit.

43 See in particular, R. Miliband, *The State in Captalist Society* (1973, Quartet Books); N. Poulantzas, *State, Power, Socialism* (1978, New Left Books); L. Althusser, *For Marx* (1977, New Left Books); Gramsci, op. cit.

Chapter 2: Law and morality

1 Above, chapter 1.
2 Lloyd, *Introduction to Jurisprudence* (5th edn by Lord Lloyd of Hampstead and M. D. A. Freeman, 1985, Stevens), p. 109.
3 Lon L. Fuller, *The Morality of Law* (1964, Yale University Press).
4 Ibid, p. 39.
5 This exception being that of requirement 2.
6 Lloyd, op. cit., p. 132.
7 John Finnis, *Natural Law and Natural Rights* (1980, Oxford University Press), p. 274.
8 Ibid.
9 Ibid. p. 59.
10 To the objection, 'why not more? Or less?', Finnis asserts that 'other objectives and forms of good will be found, on analysis, to be ways or combinations of ways of pursuing (not always sensibly) and realizing (not always successfully) one of the seven basic forms of good, or some combination of them' (p. 90).
11 Ibid. p. 89.
12 Lloyd, op. cit., p. 142.
13 Lord Devlin, *The Enforcement of Morals* (1959, Oxford University Press), p. 4.
14 Ibid. p. 10.
15 See *Rance v. Mid-Downs Health Authority*, reported in the *Independent*, 6 March 1990. It was held in this case that, had an abortion been carried out on a 27-week-old foetus, it would have been unlawful, since the judge was satisfied on the evidence that the baby had been capable of being born alive, in that the child could breathe and exist independently of its mother, if only for a short time, at that date. See now Human Fertilisation and Embryology Act 1990, s. 37.
16 *Gillick v. West Norfolk and Wisbech Area Health Authority and Department of Health and Social Security* [1986] A. C. 112.
17 The Court of Appeal's decision in the case of 'J' is reported in the *Guardian*, 11 July 1992. For a general account of law and medicine, see M. Brazier, *Medicine, Patients and the Law* (1992 edn, Penguin).
18 Prof. Ian Kennedy, reported in the *Guardian*, 11 July 1992.
19 We find considerable variation in the particular structure of the family in different societies at different periods; for example, the Israeli *kibbutz*, and polygamous forms of marriage giving rise to extensive and complex family structures.
20 And even in Soviet Russia, contrary to popular Western beliefs, the Constitution provided for the private ownership of certain amounts and types of property.
21 J. Hall, *Theft, Law and Society* (1952, Bobbs Marill).
22 D. Hay, 'Property, Authority and the Criminal Law' in D. Hay *et. al.*, *Albion's Fatal Tree* (1977, Peregrine), p. 21.
23 Ibid.
24 H. Becker, *Outsiders* (1963, Free Press of Glencoe), p. 9.
25 E. Schur, *Crimes Without Victims* (1965, Prentice Hall). For a more extended debate on this issue, see also E. Schur and H. Bedau, *Victimless Crimes* (1974, Prentice Hall).
26 'Adult' in this context means 'person aged 21 or over'. This was unaffected by the reduction in 1969 of the age of majority from 21 to 18 (Family Law Reform Act 1969, s. 1).
27 S. Hall, 'Reformism and the Legislation of Consent', in National Deviancy

Conference (ed.), *Permissiveness and Control* (1980, Macmillan), p. 9.

28 1957, Cmnd. 247, HMSO, para. 13.

29 Ibid., para. 257.

30 Devlin, op. cit., pp. 13–14.

31 H. L. A. Hart, *Law, Liberty and Morality* (1962, Oxford University Press).

32 J. S. Mill, *On Liberty* (Everyman edition, 1962, Fontana), p. 135.

33 [1962] A. C. 220.

34 Ibid, p. 267. See also *DPP* v. *Withers* [1974] 3 All E. R. 984.

35 Ibid., p. 268.

36 [1973] A. C. 435.

37 Ibid., p. 457. See *DPP* v. *Withers*, op. cit.

38 [1992] 2 All E. R. 552.

39 One defendant had been charged and convicted of taking, and second defendant of possessing, indecent photographs of children – a much more worrying matter than that of the private activities of consenting adults. These defendants had pleaded guilty to the various charges, and now appealed against their sentence, not their convictions.

40 [1992] 2 All E. R. 552 at p. 558.

41 [1934] All ER Rep. 207.

42 [1934] All ER Rep. 207 at p. 212 *per* Swift J.

43 *A–G's Reference (No. 6 of 1980)* [1981] 2 All E. R. 1057.

44 [1981] 2 All E. R. 1057 at p. 1059.

45 [1992] 2 All E. R. 552 at p. 559.

46 Reported in the *Independent*, 5 February 1992.

47 Ibid.

48 [1981] 4 E. H. H. R. 149.

49 N. Padfield, 'Consent and the Public Interest', *New Law Journal* 27 March 1992, p. 432.

50 *R.* v. *Lemon* [1979] 1 All E. R. 898.

51 See the *Guardian*, 18 April 1973, reproduced in L. Blom-Cooper and G. Drewry, *Law and Morality* (1976, Duckworth), pp. 234–5. For a more recent statement along the same lines (albeit nearly 20 years later), see Mrs Whitehouse's letter to the *Independent*, 9 July 1992.

52 See generally Blom-Cooper and Drewry, op. cit., chapter 7.

53 See, for example, A. Dworkin, *Pornography* (1981, Women's Press).

54 [1991] 1 All E. R. 306.

55 [1991] 1 All E. R. 306 at p. 318.

56 See, for example, the debate as to whether Scientology should be recognized as a religious organization: see G. Robertson, *Freedom, the Individual and the Law* (6th edn, 1991, Penguin), pp. 383–6.

57 See Robertson, ibid., chapter 5; and G. Robertson, *Obscenity* (1979, Weidenfeld and Nicolson), especially chapter 3; Blom-Cooper and Drewry, op. cit.

58 See Robertson, *Freedom, the Individual and the Law*, op., cit.; and G. Robertson, *Obscenity*, op. cit., where several examples of judicial attempts to clarify the meaning of the term, with varying degrees of success, are given. See also relevant chapters on the law of obscenity in standard texts on criminal law: see 'Suggestions for Further Reading'.

59 Post Office Act 1953, s. 11.

60 *Knuller* v. *D. P. P.* [1973] A. C. 435, *per* Lord Reid at p. 458.

61 Departmental Committee on Obscenity and Film Censorship, Report (1979, Cmnd. 7772, HMSO).

62 *New Law Journal*, 16 March 1984, p. 245.

63 Ibid., pp. 245–6.

64 Robertson, *Obscenity*, op. cit., p. 14.

65 Section 2 of the 1911 Act was widely criticized as being far too wide in its ambit, prohibiting the disclosure of much that was not, in fact, necessarily secret in the interests of national security. The section was replaced by the Official Secrets Act 1989, which specifies that a criminal offence may be committed through the unauthorized disclosure of information, relating to a number of categories of 'official information', which include security and intelligence, defence, international relations, information obtained in confidence from other states, and special investigations under statutory warrant.

66 *R.* v. *Secretary of State for the Home Department ex parte Brind* [1990] 2 W. L. R. 787.

67 The Murder (Abolition of Death Penalty) Act 1965 was extended indefinitely by parliamentary resolution in December 1969.

68 Children and Young Persons Act 1969. See also the White Paper which preceded this Act, *Children in Trouble* (1968, Cmnd. 3601 HMSO), for a full statement of the philosophies underlying the Act.

69 See Blom-Cooper and Drewry, op. cit., pp. 195–201; also R. Leng, 'Mercy Killing and the CLRC', *New Law Journal*, 28 January 1982.

70 *Report of the Advisory Committee on Drug Dependence* (Wootton Report) (1968, HMSO).

71 B. Wootton, *Crime and Penal Policy* (1978, Allen and Unwin), p. 144; and see Blom-Cooper and Drewry, op. cit., chapter 2.

72 See A. Morris, H. Giller, *et al.*, *Justice for Children* (1980, Macmillan); D. Thorpe *et. al.*, *Out of Care* (1980, Allen and Unwin).

73 For an excellent discussion on these issues, see A. Morris and S. Nott, *Working Women and the Law: Equality and Discrimination in Theory and Practice* (1991, Routledge and Kegan Paul); M. Barrett and M. McIntosh, *The Anti-Social Family* (1983, Verso).

74 See Law Commission, *Reform of the Grounds of Divorce: The Field of Choice* (1967, Cmnd. 3123, HMSO); Church of England, *Putting Asunder: A Divorce Law for Contemporary Society* (1966, Church of England).

75 See in particular S. Hall, op. cit.; I. Taylor, *Law and Order* (1981, Macmillan); A. Hunt, 'The Politics of Law and Justice' in *Politics and Power*, vol. 4 (1981, Routledge and Kegan Paul), especially pp. 4–6.

76 B. Pym, 'The Making of a Successful Pressure Group' (1973) *British Journal of Sociology*, vol. 24, no. 4.

77 Ibid., p. 451.

78 H. Becker, op. cit., p. 149.

79 J. Gusfield, *Symbolic Crusade* (1963, University of Illinois Press).

80 T. Duster, *The Legislation of Morality* (1970, Free Press, New York).

81 H. Becker, op. cit., pp. 135–46.

82 I. Paulus, *The Search for Pure Food: A Sociology of Legislation in Britain* (1974, Martin Robertson).

83 N. Gunningham, *Pollution, Social Interest and the Law* (1974, Martin Robertson).

84 However, some other European countries, and some American states, have

relaxed somewhat the laws concerning possession of small amounts of cannabis.
85 Duster, op. cit., p. 6.
86 J. Young, *The Drugtakers: The Social Meaning of Drug Use* (1971, Paladin). See also P. Worsley (ed.), *The New Introducing Sociology* (1987, Penguin), ch. 11.
87 Ibid., p. 50.
88 Ibid., p. 51.
89 'Reformism and the Legislation of Consent', op. cit. See also, in the same volume, V. Greenwood and J. Young, 'Ghettos of Freedom'.
90 Hall, p 3
91 Ibid., p. 4.
92 Ibid., p. 16.
93 Ibid., pp. 17–18.
94 Ibid., p. 33.
95 Ibid., p. 38.

Chapter 3: Law and the regulation of economic activity

1 See D. Held, 'Central Perspectives on the Modern State' in D. Held *et al.* (eds), *States and Societies* (1983, Martin Robertson), and extracts in Part One of that volume.
2 See J. T. Winkler, 'Law, State and Economy: The Industry Act 1975 in Context' (1975) *British Journal of Law and Society* 103; D. Held *et al*, op. cit., Part 4.
3 A. V. Dicey, *The Law of the Constitution* (first published 1885); (10th edn, 1959, Macmillan).
4 See L. Althusser, 'Ideology and Ideological State Apparatuses' in *Lenin and Philosophy and Other Essays* (1971, New Left Books).
5 For other perspectives on the state, see R. Miliband, *The State in Capitalist Society* (1973, Quartet Books); N. Poulantzas, *Political Power and Social Classes* (1973, New Left Books); R. Quinney, *Critique of Legal Order*, (1974, Little, Brown); J. Holloway and S. Picciotto, *State and Capital* (1978, Edward Arnold); D. Held *et al*, op. cit.
6 See the reports during November 1983 of the refusal by the then Secretary of State for Defence, Michael Heseltine, to give any assurances that demonstrators in the vicinity of military bases might not be shot if, in the opinion of the security forces, such action was appropriate.
7 E. K. Hunt and H. J. Sherman, *Economics: An Introduction to Traditional and Radical Views* (3rd edn, 1978, Harper and Row), p. 80.
8 E. Hobsbawm, *Industry and Empire* (1969, Penguin), pp. 47–8.
9 T. Hadden, *Company Law and Capitalism* (2nd edn, 1977, Weidenfeld and Nicholson), p. 3, and see chapter 1 generally.
10 Individual directors can, of course, be *personally* liable for such offences as fraud. In such cases, the complete range of sentences is available upon conviction.
11 [1961] A. C. 12.
12 The decision follows the earlier case of *Salomon* v. *Salomon* [1897] A. C. 22.
13 (1875) L. R. 7 H. L. 653.
14 [1966] 2 All E. R. 674.
15 In the law of agency, an agent is one who brings about a contract with one person on behalf of another. Thus if an estate agent sells a house on behalf of the seller A to the purchaser B, then the contract is between A and B. A is said to be the agent's

principal. Note that the relationship between the agent and the principal, usually said to be a 'consensual' one, may well be contractual.

16 See chapter 8.

17 See any standard text on company law: for example, Smith and Keenan's *Company Law for Students* (9th edn, 1990, by D. Keenan, Pitman); J. Farrar *et al.*, *Company Law* (3rd edn, 1992, Butterworths).

18 In an insurance contract, the first two parties are the insurance company and the insured person. The 'third party' is then the person who is not a party to the contract, but to whom insurance money may be payable in the event of liability on the part of the insured person to that third party where such liability is insured against.

19 Road Traffic Act 1972, s. 143(1).

20 W. Friedman, *Law in a Changing Society* (1972, Penguin), p. 321.

21 In the United States, usually thought of the epitome of free-market competition, we find, paradoxically, a far more extensive system of state regulation of business and industry than in the United Kingdom. This regulation is largely carried out by a myriad specialist Federal agencies, the best-known of which is probably the Federal Trade Commission; among the many legislative provisions regulating the American business world is the 'anti-trust' legislation, the equivalent of European competition law, which is designed to combat, among other things, monopolization of sections of business and industry through mergers, take-overs and restrictive practices which, history has shown, might well result through the unrestricted freedom of large and powerful business enterprises to dominate the market, and thus *reduce* competition, by such means.

22 See R. M. Martin, 'Pluralism and the New Corporatism' (1983) *Political Studies*.

23 Winkler, op. cit., p. 106.

24 *Independent*, 17 June 1992. And see further G. Borrie, 'The Regulation of Public and Private Power' (1989) *Public Law* 552.

25 (1977) Cmnd. 6706.

26 See the extracts and discussion in P. Davies and M. Freedland, *Labour Law: Text and Materials* (2nd edn, 1984, Weidenfeld and Nicolson).

27 Such a dispute lay at the root of, for example, *Express Newspapers Ltd* v. *McShane* [1980] 2 W. L. R. 80, and *Duport Steel and Others* v. *Sirs and Others* [1980] 1 All E. R. 529.

28 N. Millward, M. Stevens, D. Smart and W. Hawes, *Workplace Industrial Relations in Transition* (1992, Dartmouth Publishing).

29 *Independent*, 24 September 1992.

30 G. Bannock, *The Juggernauts* (1973, Penguin), p. 33.

31 J. Tillotson, *Contract Law in Perspective* (2nd edn, 1985, Butterworths), p. 185.

32 See below, chapter 14.

Chapter 4: Some Important Legal Concepts

1 J. Salmond, *Jurisprudence* (12th edn, ed. P. J Fitzgerald, 1966, Sweet and Maxwell), p. 125.

2 On this see, for example, C. Hill (ed.), *Rights and Wrongs* (1969, Penguin), especially the editor's introductory chapter; J. W. Bridge, D. Lasok, *et al.* (eds), *Fundamental Rights* (1973, Sweet and Maxwell); D. Lasok, A. J. E. Jaffey, *et al.* (eds), *Fundamental*

Duties (1980, Pergamon); H. Davies and D. Holdencroft, *Jurisprudence: Texts and Commentary* (1991, Butterworths), ch. 8.

3 For a detailed commentary and discussion on the various approaches to the analysis of rights and duties, see Davies and Holdencroft, op. cit.

4 Op. cit.

5 Ibid, p. 217.

6 H. L. A. Hart, 'Definition and Theory in Jurisprudence' (1954) 70 *Law Quarterly Review* 37.

7 D. Lloyd, *The Idea of Law* (1991, Penguin), pp. 312–14.

8 Op. cit., p. 220.

9 'Fundamental Legal Conceptions' (1913); see especially Davies and Holdencroft, op. cit., ch. 8.

10 Glanville Williams, 'The Concept of Legal Liberty' in *Essays in Legal Philosophy* (ed. R. Summers).

11 See R. W. M. Dias, *Jurisprudence* (5th edn, 1985, Butterworths).

12 See Lloyd, *Introduction to Jurisprudence* (5th edn. by Lord Lloyd and M. D. A. Freeman, 1985, Stevens), pp. 443–5.

13 H. L. A. Hart, 'Definition and Theory in Jurisprudence', op. cit.

14 See also H. L. A. Hart, *The Concept of Law* (1961, Oxford University Press) and 'Positivism and the Separation of Law and Morals' (1958) 71 *Harvard Law Review* (also in R. M. Dworkin, *The Philosophy of Law* (1977, Oxford University Press), pp. 17–37. For a thorough critical discussion of Hart's work, see N. MacCormick, *H. L. A. Hart* (1981, Edward Arnold).

15 Glanville Williams, 'Language and the Law' (1945) 61 *Law Quarterly Review*, pp. 71, 179, 293, 384.

16 *Introduction to Jurisprudence*, op. cit., especially pp. xi–xiii.

17 'Definition and Theory in Jurisprudence', op. cit., p. 49.

18 'Positivism and the Separation of Law and Morals', op. cit.

19 Ibid.; in Dworkin, op. cit., p. 22.

20 [1932] A. C. 562.

21 For cases of similar novel import, see for example *Rylands* v. *Fletcher* (1868) L. R. 3 H. L. 330; *Nagle* v. *Fielden* [1966] 2 Q. B. 633. See also *Home Office* v. *Dorset Yacht Co. Ltd* and *Hedley Byrne & Co. Ltd* v. *Heller and Partners Ltd*, discussed below.

22 Except for the established cause of action where a plaintiff was a party to a contract (in which case the action was in contract, not in tort), and cases in tort which involved articles which were either inherently dangerous (such as guns or poisons) or had a defect which was known to the manufacturer. See the dissenting judgment of Lord Buckmaster in *Donoghue* v. *Stevenson*, op. cit.

23 *Donoghue* v. *Stevenson* [1932] A. C. 562 at p. 582.

24 See chapter 7.

25 [1970] 2 All E. R. 294.

26 The duty of care has been held to apply to repairers, to car-dealers, to surgeons and many others. See chapter 9.

27 [1970] 2 All E. R. 294 at p. 323.

28 Ibid., pp. 297–8.

29 See chapter 9.

30 [1964] A. C. 465.

30a See *Airedale National Health Service Trust* v. *Bland* (*Independent*, 5 February 1993) where the House of Lords stated that it was lawful for doctors to remove the life support treatment of one of the victims of the Hillsborough football stadium disaster; Anthony Bland had been in a persistent vegetative state for over three years with no possible hope of recovery. All the judges acknowledged the difficulties posed by the legal, moral and ethical aspects of the case.

31 See P. S. Atiyah, *Accidents, Compensation and the Law* (4th edn by P. Cane, 1987, Weidenfeld and Nicolson); see also The Sunday Times, *The Thalidomide Children and the Law* (1973, Deutsch).

32 [1971] p. 110.

33 [1983] Q. B. 1053.

34 *Rees* v. *United Kingdom* (Judgment of 17 October 1986). See for a discussion of this topic G. J. Naldi, 'No Hope for Transsexuals?', *New Law Journal*, 6 February 1987.

35 K. W. Wedderburn, *The Worker and the Law* (3rd edn, 1986, Penguin); see also H. Pelling, *A History of British Trade Unionism* (1963, Penguin).

Chapter 5: Law and property

1 J. Westergaard and H. Resler, *Class in a Capitalist Society* (1976, Pelican), p. 109.

2 R. Best, 'Laying the Land Use Myths', *New Society*, 2 April 1970.

3 See the table in D. Massey and A. Catalano, *Capital and Land* (1978, Edward Arnold), p. 59.

4 See K. Marx and F. Engels, *The German Ideology* in Marx and Engels, *Collected Works*, vol. 5 (1976, Lawrence and Wishart), especially pp. 89–92.

5 E. Durkheim, *The Division of Labour in Society* (1964, Free Press, New York), p. 384.

6 See the extract by Durkheim in V. Aubert (ed.), *Sociology of Law* (1972, Penguin).

7 K. Renner, *The Institutions of Private Law and their Social Functions* (1949, reprinted 1976, Routledge and Kegan Paul), p. 117; and see extract in V. Aubert, op. cit., p. 39.

8 Renner, op. cit., p. 107; Aubert, op. cit., p. 35.

9 Renner, op. cit., p. 120; Aubert, op. cit., p. 43.

10 W. Friedmann, *Law in a Changing Society* (1972, Penguin), p. 101.

11 Ibid. And see R. Dahrendorf, *Class and Class Conflict in Industrial Society* (1959, Routledge and Kegan Paul), chapter 2. See also A. Sampson, *The Changing Anatomy of Britain* (1982, Hodder and Stoughton), chapters 21 and 22.

12 Westergaard and Resler, op. cit., p. 154.

13 Ibid., pp. 150–71.

14 A. Gouldner, *The Coming Crisis of Western Sociology* (1971, Heinemann), p. 63.

15 Ibid., p. 71.

16 D. Lloyd, *The Idea of Law* (1991 reprint, Penguin), p. 323. See also S. Coval *et al.*, 'The Foundations of Property and Property Law' (1986) 45 C. L. J. 457.

17 [1969] 2 A. C. 256.

18 [1969] 2 A. C. 256, *per* Lord Pearce at p. 305.

19 Section 28 of the Misuse of Drugs Act 1971 has now provided a defence to a charge of unlawful possession of prohibited drugs, provided that the accused can establish that s/he did not know or suspect, nor had any reason to suspect, that s/he was in possession of a controlled drug.

20 See also the cases of *R.* v. *Searle and Randolph* [1972] Crim. L. R. 779; and *R.* v. *McNamara* (1987) 87 Cr. App. Rep. 246, CA.

21 There are other, infrequently invoked, legal rules pertaining to these issues. One is

the law relating to gifts: the donor of an alleged gift cannot change his or her mind and take it back from the recipient, as long as there was initially a clear intention on the part of the donor to make the gift, and as long as there was *delivery* of the gift to the recipient by the donor (or an agent acting on behalf of the donor), or through some symbolic means, such as handing over a key to a safe containing the substance of the gift.

22 Bills of Exchange Act 1882, s. 73.

23 See, for coverage of this topic, C. Hamblin and F. B. Wright, *Introduction to Commercial Law* (3rd edn, 1988, Sweet and Maxwell); I. Davies, *Textbook on Commercial Law* (1992, Blackstone); R M. Goode, *Commercial Law* (1982 Penguin); or any other up-to-date standard text in this area.

24 See *CBS Songs Ltd* v. *Amstrad Consumer Electronics plc* [1988] 2 W. L. R. 1191.

25 Wrongful use of computers may involve criminal liability. Apart from the possibility of offences under the Theft Act 1968, the Computer Misuse Act 1990 creates three new offences: unauthorized access to computer material, unauthorized access with intent to commit or facilitate commission of a further offence, and unauthorized modification of computer material. On this see Wasik, 'The Computer Misuse Act 1990' [1990] *Criminal Law Review* 767.

26 *Intellectual Property and Innovation* (1986) Cmnd. 9712, HMSO.

27 See D. Wilson (ed.), *The Secrets File: The Case for Freedom of Information in Britain Today* (1984, Heinemann); N. S. Marsh (ed.), *Public Access to Government-Held Information* (1987, Stevens).

28 For a detailed account of the Data Protection Act 1984, see N. Savage and C. Edwards, *A Guide to the Data Protection Act* (2nd edn, 1985, Blackstone).

29 A. W. B. Simpson, *An Introduction to the History of the Land Law* (1973, Oxford University Press), p. 4.

30 G. C. Cheshire and E. Burn, *Modern Law of Real Property* (14th edn by E. H. Burn, 1988, Butterworths), p. 28.

31 See Simpson, op. cit., chapter 1.

32 Cheshire, op. cit., p. 7.

33 For example, Cheshire, op. cit.; Sir R. Megarry and H. W. R. Wade, *Real Property* (5th edn, 1984, Sweet and Maxwell); D. Hayton, *Cases and Commentary on the Law of Trusts* (9th edn, 1991, Sweet and Maxwell); Sir R. Megarry and M. P. Thompson, *Manual of the Law of Real Property* (7th edn, 1992, Sweet and Maxwell); E. H. Burn, *Maudlsey and Burn's Land Law: Cases and Materials* (6th edn, 1992 Butterworths); J-A. MacKenzie and M. Phillips, *A Practical Approach to Land Law* (3rd edn, 1991, Blackstone) or any of the other standard texts in this area.

34 See major texts on planning law, such as A. Telling, *Planning Law and Procedure* (8th edn, 1990, Butterworths); D. Heap, *An Outline of Planning Law* (10th edn, 1991, Sweet and Maxwell); V. Moore, *A Practical Approach to Planning Law* (3rd edn, 1992, Blackstone).

35 S. Ball and S. Bell, *Environmental Law* (1991, Blackstone), p. 161.

36 Ibid., p. 165.

37 An example of such an investigation is given in P. McAuslan, *Land, Law and Planning* (1975, Weidenfeld and Nicolson), pp. 591–9.

38 See chapter 12.

39 P. Ambrose and B. Colenutt, *The Property Machine* (1975, Penguin).

40 Cited in M. Harwood, *Cases and Materials on English Land Law* (1978, Professional Books), p. 82.

41 P. Ambrose, *Whatever Happened to Planning?* (1986, Methuen), pp. 72–3.

42 Ibid., p. 258.

43 McAuslan, op. cit., p. 12.

44 P. McAuslan, 'The Ideologies of Planning Law' (1979) 2 *Urban Law and Policy*, p. 3.

45 Ambrose, 1986, op. cit.

46 Ambrose and Colenutt, op. cit., p. 63.

47 Ambrose, op. cit., p. 259.

48 Ambrose and Colenutt, op. cit., p. 19.

49 Standard texts on environmental law include S. Ball and S. Bell, *Environmental Law*, op. cit; D. Hughes, *Environmental Law* (2nd edn, 1992, Butterworths); see also L. Krämer, *EEC Treaty and Environmental Protection* (1990, Sweet and Maxwell).

50 D. Hughes, *Environmental Law* (2nd edn, 1992, Butterworths), p. 319.

51 See S. Payne, 'No Smoke without Precautions', *New Law Journal*, 16 August 1991.

52 S. Ball and S. Bell, *Environmental Law*, op. cit., p. 245.

53 Housing and Construction Statistics.

54 *Key Data 1991/92* (1991, HMSO).

55 Ibid.

56 See D. Hoath, *The Law Relating to Public Housing* (1989, Sweet and Maxwell); D. Hughes, *Public Sector Housing Law* (2nd edn, 1987, Butterworths).

57 For discussion of the detailed legal provisions, see up-to-date texts on housing such as M. Partington and J. Hill, *Housing Law: Cases, Materials and Commentary* (1991, Sweet and Maxwell); A. Arden, *Manual of Housing Law* (4th edn, 1989, Sweet and Maxwell); and see the annotations to the Housing Acts in *Current Law Statutes* (Sweet and Maxwell/Stevens).

58 See *Norwich City Council* v. *Secretary of State for the Environment* [1982] 1 All E. R. 737.

59 For a recent discussion on the stance of the Labour Party on housing issues, see Jane Darke (ed.), *The Roof Over Your Head: A Housing Programme for Labour* (1992, Spokesman Press).

60 *The Economist*, 19 May 1979; R. Forrest and A. Murie, *Selling the Welfare State: The Privatisation of Public Housing* (1988, Routledge and Kegan Paul).

61 For discussions on this issue, see D. White, 'The Council House Buyers', *New Society*, 19 November 1982; articles in *Critical Social Policy* (1981, vol. 1, no. 2; and 1982, vol. 1, no. 3; R. Forrest and A. Murie, op. cit.

62 For more detailed coverage of the law relating to the private rented sector, see in particular J. Fox-Andrews and D. W. Williams, *Assured Tenancies* (1989, Estates Gazette) on the Housing Act 1988; and see A. Arden, *Manual of Housing Law*, op. cit; C. J. Wright, *Housing Improvement and Repair* (1986, Sweet and Maxwell).

63 [1978] 2 All E. R. 1011.

64 [1985] 2 W. L. R. 877.

65 Ibid., at p. 890.

66 Ibid.

67 [1988] 3 W. L. R. 1205.

Chapter 6: Law and the settlement of disputes

1 S. Macaulay, 'Non-Contractual Relations in Business' (1962) *Amer. Soc. Rev.* See below, chapter 11.

2 On rules in general, see chapter 1. On dispute-settlement in general, see S. Roberts, *Order and Dispute* (1979, Penguin).

3 See W. Twining and D. Miers, *How to Do Things with Rules* (3rd edn, 1991, Weidenfeld and Nicolson), chapter 1.

4 See M. Salamon, *Industrial Relations Theory and Practice* (1987, Prentice Hall); on individual employment law, see G. Pitt, *Employment Law* (1992, Sweet and Maxwell); S. Anderman, *Labour Law* (1992, Butterworths).

5 See Salamon, op. cit.

6 Now the Employment Protection (Consolidation) Act 1978, as amended by the Employment Acts 1980 and 1982.

7 *Independent*, 28 August 1992.

8 Harry Fletcher, of the National Association of Probation Officers, quoted in the *Independent*, ibid.

9 J. P. Tillotson, *Contract Law in Perspective* (2nd edn, 1985, Butterworth), p. 213.

10 An umpire may be brought in to adjudicate if, where there is an arbitration panel of two, there is disagreement between the arbitrators.

11 *Orion Compania Espanola de Seguros* v. *Belford Maatschappij voor Algemene Verzekgringeen* [1962] 2 Lloyd's Rep. 257, *per* Megaw J. at p. 264.

12 See, for example, *Baker* v. *Jones* [1954] 2 All E. R. 553; and for a case on this point involving an arbitration agreement, see *Scott* v. *Avery* (1856) 5 HL Cas 811.

13 See chapter 11.

14 Tillotson, op. cit., p. 219.

15 R. M. Goode, *Commercial Law* (1982, Penguin), p. 980. See also Mustill and Boyd, *The Law and Practice of Commercial Arbitration in England* (2nd edn, 1989, Butterworths).

16 See generally A. Bevan, *Alternative Dispute Resolution* (1992, Sweet and Maxwell); K. Mackie, *Handbook on Dispute Resolution; ADR in Action* (1991, Routledge); S. Roberts, 'Mediation in the Lawyers' Embrace' (1992) 55 *Modern Law Review* 258; and for insight into the political context of the ADR debates, see Lord Mackay of Clashfern, 'Access to Justice – The Price' (1991) *The Law Teacher*, vol. 25, no. 2.

17 The Franks Committee thought that chairpersons of appeal tribunals should be legally qualified, and chairpersons of other kinds of tribunal preferably so qualified. Although these recommendations were not incorporated into the Tribunals and Enquiries Act, it is generally the case that statutes creating tribunals require the chairperson of an appeal tribunal to be a lawyer.

18 Cmd. 218, (1957, HMSO).

19 For examples of different kinds of tribunal, see M. Zander, *Cases and Materials on the English Legal System* (6th edn, 1992, Weidenfeld and Nicolson), pp. 45–54; and the *Royal Commission on Legal Services Report* (1979, Cmnd. 7648, HMSO), chapters 2 and 15.

20 See Zander, op. cit., pp. 531–4; J. Baldwin, 'The Adjudication of Claims', *New Law Journal*, 5 and 12 June 1992.

21 *Royal Commission on Legal Services Report*, op. cit., pp. 168–9.

22 Op. cit., p. 172.

23 Ibid., p. 174.

24 Ibid.

25 See chapter 13.

26 J. Farmer, op. cit.

27 Recommendation 39.5.

28 H. Street, *Justice in the Welfare State* (1975, Stevens), p. 5.

29 See chapter 12.

30 B. Abel-Smith and R. Stevens, *In Search of Justice*, extract in M. Zander, op. cit., pp. 46–53.

31 [1963] 2 all E. R. 66.

32 Hartley and Griffith, op. cit., p. 336.

33 Op. cit., p. 167.

34 Op. cit., p. 14.

35 See J. A. G. Griffith's analysis of the activity of one recent Lord Chancellor, Lord Hailsham, in *The Politics of the Judiciary* (4th edn, 1991, Fontana), pp. 244–6; and see S. Lee's assessment of Lord Hailsham in *Judging Judges* (1988, Faber and Faber), chapter 19.

36 In practice, a minority government may be overturned by the House of Commons. An example of this occurred in 1979 with the successful vote of 'no confidence' brought against the Labour government, resulting in a general election.

37 A. Paterson, 'Judges: A Political Élite?' (1974) *British Journal of Law and Society*, vol. 1, no. 2.

38 The House of Lords is, constitutionally, one of the two Houses of Parliament: legislatively, the law-creating body is 'The Queen in Parliament' – that is, the sovereign, the House of Lords and the House of Commons.

39 G. Drewry, *Law, Justice and Politics* (2nd edn, 1981, Longman), p. 4.

40 Including public bodies such as local authorities, and other incorporated bodies such as companies.

41 Above, chapter 1

42 On this see R. M. Jackson's *The Machinery of Justice in England* (8th edn, by Jackson and Spencer, 1989, Cambridge University Press); P. Smith and S. Bailey, *The Modern English Legal System* (2nd edn, 1991, Sweet and Maxwell).

43 The reader is referred for more detailed descriptions to more specialized literature: see R. M. Jackson, op. cit; M. Zander, op. cit; P. Smith and S. Bailey, op. cit.

44 A. P. Herbert, *Wigs at Work* (1966, Penguin), pp. 92–3.

45 See Twining and Miers, op. cit., especially chapter 8.

46 [1932] A. C. 562. See chapter 9.

47 For example, *Haseldine* v. *Daw* [1942] 2 K. B. 343.

48 *Andrews* v. *Hopkinson* [1957] 1 Q. B. 229.

49 Cases have involved such items as hair dye, tombstones and underwear: see chapter 9.

50 See for example the discussions of the judges in *Roberts* v. *Hopwood* [1925] A. C. 578; *Bromley London Borough Council* v. *Greater London Council* [1983] 1 A. C. 768; *Ward* v. *Bradford Corporation* (1971) 70 L. G. R. 27 (see chapter 14); and other cases referred to in chapters 3 and 14.

51 H. Garfinkel, 'Conditions of Successful Degradation Ceremonies' (1956) *American Journal of Sociology*, p. 420. Abridged version in C. Campbell and P. Wiles (eds), *Law and Society* (1979, Martin Robertson), p. 189.

52 Garfinkel, op. cit., p. 420; Campbell and Wiles, op. cit., p. 189.

53 E. Goffman, *Stigma* (1968, Pelican), p. 15.

54 See for example R. Schwartz and J. Skolnick, 'Two Studies of Legal Stigma' (1962) *Social Problems*, vol. 10, p. 133; R. Boshier and D. Johnson, 'Does Conviction Affect Employment Opportunities?' (1974) *British Journal of Criminology*, vol. 14.

55 Op. cit.

56 P. Carlen, *Magistrates' Justice* (1976, Martin Robertson).

57 Ibid., p. 21.

58 Ibid., p. 25. See also D. Hay, 'Property, Authority and the Criminal Law' in D. Hay

et al., *Albion's Fatal Tree* (1977, Peregrine); E. P. Thompson, *Whigs and Hunters* (1977, Peregrine); Z. Bankowski and G. Mungham, *Images of Law* (1976, Routledge and Kegan Paul), chapter 4.

59 Bankowski and Mungham, op. cit., p. 88.

60 See *Contempt* (1970, Swallow Press, Chicago); T. Hayden, *Trial* (1970, Jonathan Cape).

61 R. J. Antonio, 'The Processual Dimension of Degradation Ceremonies: The Chicago Conspiracy Trial: Success or Failure?' (1972) *British Journal of Sociology*.

62 Ibid., pp. 295–6.

63 Other examples would, however, include the refusal of defendants in criminal trials arising from bombing incidents by the IRA to acknowledge the legitimacy of English courts in trying them in the 1970s.

Chapter 7: The making of legal rules

1 D. Miers and A. Page, *Legislation* (2nd edn, 1990, Sweet and Maxwell), p. 25.

2 D. Marsh, P. Gowin and M. Read, 'Private Members Bills and Moral Panic: The Case of the Video Recordings Bill 1984' (1986) *Parliamentary Affairs*, vol. 39, p. 179.

3 D. Marsh, M. Read and B. Myers, 'Don't Panic: The Obscene Publications (Protection of Children, etc.) Amendment Bill 1985' (1987) *Parlimentary Affairs*, vol. 40, p. 73. See also A. Mitchell MP, 'A Home Buyer's Bill: How not to pass a Private Member's Bill' (1986) *Parliamentary Affairs*, vol. 39, p. 1.

4 T. C. Hartley and J. A. G. Griffith, *Government and Law* (2nd edn, 1981, Weidenfeld and Nicolson), p. 211.

5 A. V. Dicey, *Law and Public Opinion in England* (1905, Macmillan); extract in V. Aubert (ed.), *Sociology of Law* (1969, Penguin), p. 74.

6 Ibid.

7 W. G. Carson, 'Some Sociological Aspects of Strict Liability and the Enforcement of Factory Legislation' (1970) *Modern Law Review* 396.

8 R. Cranston, *Regulating Business: Law and Consumer Agencies* (1979, Macmillan). And see I. Ramsay, *Consumer Protection: Text and Materials* (1989, Weidenfeld and Nicolson), especially pp. 192–202.

9 N. Gunningham, *Pollution, Social Interest and the Law*, (1974, Martin Robertson). See also W. Chambliss and R. Seidman, *Law, Order and Power* (2nd edn, 1982, Addison-Wesley).

10 W. G. Carson, 'Symbolic and Instrumental Dimensions of Early Factory Legislation' in R. Hood (ed.), *Crime, Criminology and Public Policy* (1974, Heinemann); see also extract in C. Campbell and P. Wiles (eds), *Law and Society* (1979, Martin Robertson).

11 See the discussion in I. Ramsay, op. cit., chapter 9.

12 W. Chambliss and R. Seidman, *Law, Order and Power* (1st edn, 1971, Addison-Wesley), p. 73.

13 C. K. Allen, *Law in the Making* (7th edn, 1964, Oxford University Press), chapter 3. Also R. Cross and J. Harris, *Precedent in English Law* (4th edn, 1991, Oxford University Press); L. Goldstein (ed.), *Precedent in Law* (1991, Oxford University Press).

14 See examples given in Allen, op. cit.; and see Glanville Williams, *Learning the Law* (11th edn, 1982, Stevens), pp. 34–40.

15 [1962] A. C. 220. See chapter 2.
16 [1932] A. C. 562. See chapters 4 and 9.
17 See chapter 6.
18 [1944] 2 All E. R. 293.
19 See *Gallie* v. *Lee* [1969] 2 Ch. 17; *Barrington* v. *Lee* [1972] 1 Q. B. 326.
20 See in particular *Davis* v. *Johnson* [1979] A. C. 264. This case is discussed in M. Zander, *The Law-Making Process* (3rd edn, 1989, Weidenfeld and Nicolson), pp. 133–7 and pp. 195–204; and in W. Twining and D. Miers, *How to Do Things with Rules* (3rd edn, 1991, Weidenfeld and Nicolson), pp. 88–115 and chs 8 and 10.
21 (1966) 1 W. L. R. 1234. See A. Paterson. *The Law Lords* (1982, Macmillan/SSRC); M. Zander, *The Law-Making Process*, op. cit., pp. 180–87.
22 See Paterson, op. cit.
23 *Andrews* v. *Hopkinson* [1957] 1 Q. B. 229.
24 *Grant* v. *Australian Knitting Mills* [1936] A. C. 85.
25 *Donoghue* v. *Stevenson* [1932] A. C. 562.
26 Some recent examples of difficult cases are *R.* v. *Caldwell* [1982] A. C. 341 concerning recklessness in criminal law (see chapter 10); and perhaps *Bromley London Borough Council* v. *GLC* [1982] 2 W. L. R. 62, which concerned the legality of the GLC's levying a supplementary rate on the London boroughs in order to subsidize its policy of reducing London Transport fares (see chapter 12).
27 W. Twining and D. Miers, op. cit., p. 313.
28 Op cit.
29 [1936] 1 All E. R. 283.
30 See Twining and Miers, op. cit., chapter 8.
31 See for example Lord Devlin, *The Judge* (1979, Oxford University Press), chapter 1.
32 Cited in Allen, op. cit., p. 308.
33 See R. Dworkin, *Taking Rights Seriously* (1978, Duckworths).
34 Devlin, op. cit. And see chapter 14.
35 See especially *Spartan Steel and Alloys Ltd* v. *Martin and Co. (Contractors) Ltd* [1973] 1 Q. B. 27.
36 W. Friedmann, *Law in a Changing Society* (1972, Penguin), p. 74.
37 J. Frank, 'Words and Music: Some Remarks on Statutory Interpretation' (1947) *Columbia Law Review*, vol. 47, p. 1267.
38 Twining and Miers, op. cit., especially chapters 4 and 6.
39 Allen, op. cit., pp. 161–3.
40 C. Campbell, 'Legal Thought and Juristic Values' (1974) *British Journal of law and Society*, vol. 1, p. 18; see also J. Shklar, *Legalism* (1964 Harvard University Press), chapter 1; and Twining and Miers, op. cit., chapter 7.
41 Twining and Miers, op. cit., chapter 8.
42 K. Llewellyn, *The Common Law Tradition: Deciding Appeals* (1960, Little, Brown).
43 Ibid., p. 38.
44 Ibid. See also A. Paterson, *The Law Lords* (1982, Macmillan/SSRC), chapter 6, especially p. 130.
45 Paterson, op. cit. See also Lord Lloyd, *Introduction to Jurisprudence* (5th edn by Lord Lloyd of Hampstead and M. D. A. Freeman, 1985, Stevens), pp. 689–91; W. Twining, *Karl Llewellyn and the Realist Movement* (1973, Weidenfeld and Nicolson); R. Stevens, *Law and Politics* (1979, Weidenfeld and Nicolson), p. 78.
46 [1932] A. C. 562 at pp. 566–78.

47 Ibid. at p. 567.

48 (1869) L. R. 5 Ex. 1.

49 See above, chapter 4.

50 Italics added.

51 *Donoghue* v. *Stevenson*, op. cit., at. p. 582.

52 Ibid. at p. 583.

53 [1919] 2 K. B. 243.

54 [1961] 1 Q. B. 31.

55 [1972] 1 Q. B. 198.

56 P. James, *Introduction to English Law* (12th edn, 1989, Butterworths), p. 29–30.

57 See the criticisms of this practice by D. Pannick, in 'The Law Lords and the Needs of Contemporary Society' (1982) *Political Quarterly*, vol. 53, no. 3. See also Twining and Miers, op. cit., and Zander, op. cit.

58 Twining and Miers, op. cit., p. 365.

59 H. L. A. Hart, 'Positivism and the Separation of Law and Morals' (1958) 71 *Harvard Law Review* 593, p. 607.

60 Friedmann, op. cit., p. 56.

61 [1951] 2 K. B. 496.

62 A. Arden, *Housing: Security and Rent Control* (1978, Sweet and Maxwell), p. 20. See also J. A. G. Griffith, *The Politics of the Judiciary* (4th edn, 1991, Fontana), Part Two, for examples of similar cat-and-mouse exercises between the judges and Parliament.

63 See the judgment of Lord Denning in *Seaford Court Estates Ltd* v. *Asher* [1949] 2 K. B. 481.

64 In *Magor & St. Mellons RDC* v. *Newport Corporation* [1952] A. C. 189.

65 Friedmann, op. cit., pp. 56–61.

66 [1974] 1 Ch. 401.

67 Ibid., at p. 425. See also V. Sacks and C. Harlow, 'Interpretation European Style' (1977) 40 *Mod. Law Rev.*, p. 578; Zander, op. cit., pp. 384–9.

Chapter 8: The European dimension of English law

1 D. Lasok and J. W. Bridge, *Law and Institutions of the European Communities* (4th edn, 1987, Butterworths), p. 212.

2 See *Roquette Frères SA* v. *Council* (case 138/79) and *Maizena GmbH* v. *Council* (Case 139/79).

3 See the *Roquette Frères* case above, and *European Parliament* v. *Council* (Case 13/83) [1986] 1 C. M. L. R. 138; *Parliament* v. *Council (Chernobyl)* (Case C70/88 [1990] E. C. R. 2041.

4 The European Court of Justice must not be confused with the separate European Court of Human Rights, created under the European Convention on Human Rights. This court, located in Strasbourg, deals with alleged violations of the convention by European states against individuals.

5 J. Steiner, *Textbook on EEC Law* (3rd edn, 1992, Blackstone), p. 18.

6 Defined as any body exercising a judicial function: that is to say, having a jurisdiction concerning the rights and duties of individuals.

7 *R.* v. *Secretary of State for Transport, ex parte Factortame Ltd* [1989] 2 All E. R. 692; [1990] 3 W. L. R. 852. *Commission* v. *United Kingdom* (Case 246/89) [1989] E. C. R. 3125.

8 *Costa* v. *ENEL* (Case 6/64) [1964] C. M. L. R. 4255.

9 *R.* v. *Secretary of State for Transport, ex parte Factortame Ltd* (C213/89) above.

10 [1991] 4 All E. R. 240.

11 *Bulmer* v. *Bollinger SA* [1974] 3 W. L. R. 202.

12 Steiner, op. cit., p. 24.

13 *Van Gend en Loos* v. *Nederlandse Administratie der Belastingen* (Case 26/62), [1963] C. M. L. R. 105.

14 Case 43/75, [1976] 2 C. M. L. R. 98.

15 Case 41/74, [1975] 1 C. M. L. R. 1.

16 See *Schmidt* v. *Secretary of State for Home Affairs* [1969] 2 Ch. 149.

17 Later cases – in particular *R.* v. *Bouchereau* in 1977 (Case 30/77) and *Adoui and Cornuaille* v. *Belgian State* in 1982 (Cases 115 and 116/81) – have adopted a rather more restrictive approach to this issue. In the former case, involving the proposed deportation by the British government of a French national who had been convicted of unlawful possession of drugs, the court stated that the use of the public policy proviso

> presupposes . . . the existence, in addition to the perturbation of the social order which any infringement of the law involves, of a genuine and sufficiently serious threat to the requirements of public policy affecting one of the fundamental interests of society.

and in the latter case, concerning the refusal of the Belgian government to admit two French women on the grounds that they were allegedly prostitutes, the court said that

> a Member State may not (by means of the public policy proviso) expel a national of another Member State from its territory or refuse access to its territory by reason of conduct which, when attributable to the former State's own nationals, does not give rise to repressive measures or other genuine and effective measures intended to combat such conduct.

18 *Becker* v. *Finanzamt Münster-Innenstadt* (Case 8/81), [1982] 1 C. M. L. R. 499.

19 *Marshall* v. *Southampton AHA* (Case 152/84), [1986] 1 C. M. L. R. 688.

20 *Von Colson and Kamann* v. *Land Nordrhein-Westfalen* (Case 14/83), [1986] 2 C. M. L. R. 430.

21 [1992] I. R. L. R. 84.

22 [1992] I. R. L. R. p. 53.

23 Steiner, op. cit. p. 38.

24 See, in particular, J. Steiner, op. cit.; D. Lasok and J. W. Bridge, *Law and Institutions of the European Communities* (5th edn, 1991, Butterworths); T. C. Hartley. *The Foundations of European Community Law* (2nd edn, 1988, Oxford University Press).

25 Case 121/85; [1987] Q. B. 254; [1986] 2 All E. R. 688.

26 *R.* v. *Henn and Darby* (Case 34/79); [1980] 1 C. M. L. R. 246; [1981] A. C. 850.

27 [1969] C. M. L. R. D23.

28 [1972] C. M. L. R. 557.

29 Case 27/76; [1978] 1 C. M. L. R. 429.

30 Because of special factors concerning the market for bananas in these countries, Britain, France and Italy were excluded from the Commission's view of the relevant geographical market.

Chapter 9: Liability in English law: the law of tort

1 See P. S. Atiyah, *The Rise and Fall of Freedom of Contract* (1979, Oxford University Press); and see below, chapter 11.

2 J. G. Fleming, 'The Pearson Report: Its "Strategy" ' (1979) *Modern Law Review*, p. 250.

3 See for example *Thomas* v. *Quartermaine* (1887) 18 Q. B. D. 685; and *Membury* v. *Great Western Railway Company* (1889) 14 App. Cas. 179.

4 Under the old law, the loss lay where it fell: the establishment of the plaintiff's contributory negligence was a bar to recovering any compensation. Today, the position is as provided by the Law Reform (Contributory Negligence) Act 1945, whereby a negligent plaintiff is not precluded from recovery, although damages will be reduced in proportion to the extent to which the plaintiff is held to be to blame for the accident. For examples, see *Froom* v. *Butcher* [1976] Q. B. 167 (passenger's failure to wear car seat-belt held to be contributory negligence); *Sayers* v. *Harlow Urban District Council* [1958] 1 W. L. R. 623 (plaintiff, trapped in a public lavatory by a faulty door lock, attempted to climb out; held contributorily negligent not for attempting to escape, but for the manner in which she attempted it).

5 See *Priestley* v. *Fowler* (1837) 3 M and W 1; also *Hutchinson* v. *York, Newcastle and Berwick Rail Co.* (1850) 3 Exch. 343.

6 J. G. Fleming, *The Law of Torts* (7th edn, 1988, Law Book Co. of Australia), p. 7.

7 See P. Burrows and C. G. Veljanovski (eds), *The Economic Approach to Law* (1981, Butterworths), especially the introductory essay by the authors; Atiyah's *Accidents, Compensation and the Law* (4th edn by P. Cane, 1987, Weidenfeld and Nicolson), pp. 506–42.

8 R. Coase, 'The Problem of Social Cost' (1960) 3 *Journal of Law and Economics*.

9 G. Calabresi, *The Costs of Accidents: A Legal and Economic Analysis* (1970, Yale University Press).

10 Ibid., p. 24.

11 Defined by Calabresi as the party who is in the best position to make the cost–benefit analysis between accident and accident avoidance, and to act on that decision once it is made.

12 Calabresi, in Keeton, O'Connell and McCord (eds), *Crisis in Car Insurance* (1968, University of Illinois Press), pp. 243–4; cited in Atiyah, op. cit., pp. 509–10.

13 Atiyah, op. cit., chapter 24.

14 Ibid., p. 512.

15 R. L. Abel, 'Torts', in D. Kairys (ed.), *The Politics of Law: A Progressive Critique* (1982, Pantheon Books).

16 Ibid., p. 188.

17 Ibid., p. 187.

18 Ibid.

19 Ibid., p. 188.

20 Atiyah, op. cit., p. 191.

21 Ibid., pp. 341–3.

22 Abel, op. cit., p. 190. Also noteworthy is the fact that legal aid is not available for actions brought for defamation: it might be said that only those who can afford legal services have the privilege of protecting their reputation through the law.

23 Ibid., p. 190.
24 Ibid., p. 192. The Ford *Pinto* case is reported as *Grimshaw* v. *Ford Motor Co.* (1981) 174 Cal. Rptr. 348. For a discussion of more recent multiple disasters where negligence on the part of corporations has been alleged, see C. Pugh and M. Day, 'Toxic Torts', *New Law Journal*, 15 and 22 November 1991.
25 Ibid., p. 194.
26 Ibid., p. 195.
27 In *Fowler* v. *Lanning* [1959] 1 Q. B. 426 it was suggested that trespass to the person may be committed negligently. On the basis of dicta in the later cases of *Letang* v. *Cooper* [1964] 2 All E. R. 929 (*per* Lord Denning) and *Wilson* v. *Pringle* [1986] 2 All E. R. 440, however, the better view seems to be that unintentional (i.e. negligently inflicted) injury would attract liability in negligence, leaving trespass exclusively concerned with *intentional* harm.
28 *Hedley Byrne and Co. Ltd* v. *Heller and Partners Ltd* [1964] A. C. 465; negligent misstatement is discussed more fully below.
29 (1879) 11 Ch. D. 852. For more recent cases, see for example *Halsey* v. *Esso Petroleum Co.* [1961] 1 W. L. R. 683; *Bridlington Relay Ltd* v. *Yorkshire Electricity Board* [1965] 2 W. L. R. 349.
30 [1893] 1 Ch. 316. See also *Hollywood Silver Fox Farm* v. *Emmett* [1936] 2 K. B. 468.
31 See for example *Winfield and Jolowicz on Tort* (13th edn, by W. V. H. Rogers 1989, Sweet and Maxwell; *Street and Brazier on Torts* (8th edn, 1988, Butterworths); M. Jones, *Textbook on Torts* (3rd edn, 1991, Blackstone); C. Baker, *Tort* (5th edn, 1991, Sweet and Maxwell).
32 See the *Report of the Royal Commission on Civil Liability and Compensation for Personal Injury* (the Pearson Report) (Cmnd. 7054, 1978, HMSO); and Atiyah, op. cit.
33 (1856) 11 Exch. 781 at p. 784.
34 [1932] A. C. 562 at p. 580.
35 Ibid., at p. 599.
36 [1943] A. C. 92.
37 [1965] A. C. 778.
38 [1970] A. C. 1004. See chapter 4.
39 See *Haynes* v. *Harwood* [1935] 1 K. B. 146; *Baker* v. *T. E. Hopkins & Son Ltd* [1959] 3 All E. R. 225; *Videan* v. *British Transport Commission* [1963] 2 Q. B. 650.
40 [1970] A. C. 1004 at p. 1027.
41 [1978] A. C. 728.
42 [1978] A. C. 728 at pp. 751–2.
43 [1984] 3 W. L. R. 953.
44 [1984] 3 W. L. R. at p. 960.
45 [1987] 2 All E. R. 13.
46 [1987] 2 E. R. 705.
47 [1987] 2 All E. R. at p. 710.
48 *Rondel* v. *Worsley* [1969] 1 A. C. 191; *Saif Ali* v. *Sydney Mitchell and Co.* [1980] A. C. 198.
49 [1987] 1 All E. R. 1173.
50 [1990] 1 All E. R. 568.
51 [1990] 1 All E. R. 568 at pp. 573–4.
52 [1990] 3 W. L. R. 414.
53 [1972] 1 Q. B. 372.
54 The extended discussions on duty in the case pertain to the special considerations

arising from the specific facts of the case.

55 As opposed to economic loss or psychological harm: see below.

56 Two Australian cases are worthy of mention here. In *Jaensch* v. *Coffey* (1984) A. L. R. 417, a case concerning liability for psychiatric harm, there is in the judgment of Deane J. an interesting but tortuous argument in support of the alleged distinction between foreseeability and proximity in Lord Atkin's speech in *Donoghue*; and in the course of his judgment in *Sutherland Shire Council* v. *Heyman* (1985) 60 A. L. R. 1, Brennan J. said that 'it is preferable, in my view, that the law should develop novel categories of negligence incrementally and by analogy with established categories, rather than by a massive extension of a prima facie duty of care restrained only by indefinable considerations which ought to negative, or to reduce or limit the scope of the duty or the class of person to whom it is owed' – a statement which clearly calls for a return to the case-by-case approach, and which it seems to have become *de rigeur* for the English judiciary to cite with approval.

57 [1990] 1 All E. R. 568 at p. 574.

58 [1990] 1 All E. R. 568 at pp. 584–5.

59 (1883) 11 Q. B. D. 503.

60 [1893] 1 Q. B. 491.

61 [1932] A. C. 562 at pp. 580–1.

62 Though see *Jaensch* v. *Coffey*, op. cit.

63 *Caparo* v. *Dickman*, op. cit., *per* Lord Oliver, at p. 585.

64 R. Martin, 'Professional Negligence and Morgan Crucible' (1991) 7 *Professional Negligence* 37 at p. 38.

65 D. Howarth, 'Negligence after *Murphy*: Time to Re-Think' (1991) 50 Camb. L. R. 58 at p. 71.

66 [1991] 2 W. L. R. 501.

67 [1943] A. C. 92.

68 [1991] 2 W. L. R. 501 at p. 507.

69 See for example *Home Office* v. *Dorset Yacht Co*, op. cit.; *Dutton* v. *Bognor Regis U. D. C.* op. cit.; *Anns* v. *Merton L. B. C.*, op. cit.

70 Op. cit.

71 Ibid., p. 91.

72 [1954] 2 Q. B. 66. The court held that there was no liability for the failure by an anaesthetist to see a hair-line crack in a glass container during an operation carried out in 1947: the medical profession had not been made aware of the risk of such invisible cracks until it was brought to their attention in 1951.

73 *Bolam* v. *Friern Hospital Management Committee* [1957] 2 All E. R. 118 at p. 121 *per* McNair, J.

74 [1951] A. C. 850. The court had to consider the likelihood of cricket-balls being hit out of the defendants' ground and hitting people in the road outside; this was considered too remote to require the defendants to have taken additional precautions, e.g. by building a higher perimeter fence around the ground. Compare *Miller* v. *Jackson* [1977] Q. B. 966.

75 [1951] A. C. 367. The court considered here the seriousness of eye injury to a one-eyed plaintiff as compared to a normal-sighted person; the seriousness of such an injury was held to be such as to have required the defendants to have provided goggles.

76 [1953] A. C. 643. The defendant factory-owners were held to have acted

reasonably in cleaning up after a flood; despite the clean-up, the plaintiff fell on the slippery floor and was injured. The defendants need not, as the plaintiff claimed, have closed down the factory: the risk of injury did not require so great a precaution.

77 [1954] 1 W. L. R. 835. Here, a heavy jack was being carried on a vehicle to free a trapped woman; the jack fell on to and injured the plaintiff fireman. The court held that the attempt by the fire service to save life was of sufficient importance as to justify the taking of the risk of injury to the plaintiff. See also *Daborn* v. *Bath Tramways Motor Co. Ltd* [1946] 1 All E. R. 333.

78 *Fardon* v. *Harcourt-Rivington* (1932) 146 L. T. 391, at p. 392.

79 See for example *Bolton* v. *Stone*, above.

80 [1981] 1 All E. R. 267.

81 [1921] 3 K. B. 560.

82 [1961] A. C. 388.

83 *Stewart* v. *West African Terminals Ltd* [1964] 2 Lloyd's Rep. 371, at p. 375.

84 [1967] 1 W. L. R. 337.

85 See also *Hughes* v. *Lord Advocate* [1963] A. C. 837; *Muirhead* v. *Industrial Tank Specialities Ltd* [1986] 1 Q. B. 507 at pp. 531–3.

86 [1969] 1 W. L. R. 1556.

87 In 1990, in reply to a parliamentary question, the Secretary of State for Employment reported that in the period 1985–9 there were 299 cases of leptospirosis in England and Wales, of which 180 were known to have been ocupationally related; 139 of these were connected with agricultural and abattoir workers. In the same period there were 15 reported deaths from the disease. Apart from these 'at risk' occupations, it is now usual for enthusiasts of some water-sports, notably canoeing, to be issued with leaflets explaining and warning about the disease.

88 Ibid., at p. 1562.

89 Ibid.

90 Ibid. at p. 1563.

91 *Winfield and Jolowicz on Tort* (13th edn by W. V. H. Rogers, 1989, Sweet and Maxwell), p. 144. As an interesting postscript to the discussion of this case: in 1988 a building worker who contracted leptospirosis during the construction of a canal bridge through contact with rats' urine sued his employer for damages, claiming that the defendant should have taken steps to kill the rats which were known to be present on the site, and should have warned the workers to take precautions. The plaintiff was successful in his claim and was awared £125,000 compensation. See the *Guardian*, 2 November 1988.

92 (1875) L. R. 10 Q. B. 453.

93 [1973] Q. B. 27.

94 Ibid. at p. 38. This is, of course, the 'flood-gates' argument once again. The fallaciousness of the argument in the present context, it might be thought, lies not so much in the fact that more cases might be brought before the court – for any new development in the law must bring new claims – as in the fact that such claims are somehow thought difficult, or 'impossible to check'. Why should scrutiny of claims brought in respect of economic loss be any more difficult than claims brought in respect of personal injury? One view might be that, as such loss is far more amenable to evaluation than is, say, the worth of a broken leg or the loss of an eye,

the task of the court would in some ways be easier; problems of evidence and proof of facts would surely be no more difficult, and claims no more dishonest or frivolous, than is already the case with personal injury, or for that matter any other, litigation.

95 [1982] 3 All E. R. 201.

96 [1986] 1 Q. B. 507.

97 Ibid. at p. 528.

98 [1982] 3 All E. R. 201 at p. 214.

99 For example *Simaan General Contracting Co.* v. *Pilkington Glass Ltd (No. 2)* [1988] 1 All E. R. 791.

100 [1988] 2 All E. R. 971.

101 See *Simaan General Contracting Co.* v. *Pilkington Glass Ltd* above; *Pacific Associates Inc.* v. *Baxter* [1989] 2 All E. R. 159.

102 [1990] 3 W. L. R. 414.

103 As in *Anns* v. *Merton L.B.C.* [1978] A. C. 728, and *Investors in Industry Commercial Properties Ltd* v. *South Bedfordshire District Council* [1986] 1 All E. R. 787.

104 As in *Peabody Donation Fund* v. *Sir Lindsay Parkinson & Co. Ltd* [1984] 3 All E. R. 529.

105 Except for *Anns*, where the loss was held – wrongly, according to *Murphy* – to be physical.

106 *Murphy* v. *Brentwood* [1990] 3 W. L. R. 414 at pp. 435–6 *per* Lord Bridge.

107 The reasoning begs questions, however. If, while digging in my garden, I negligently throw a spadeful of rocks over my garden wall, and these damage my neighbour's car parked in his driveway, what is the loss suffered by my neighbour? Surely the answer must be the cost of repairing the car. I cannot deny that I have caused physical damage, or that I would be liable to recompense my neighbour were he to sue me in negligence. But that is not the point. It remains true that his *actual loss* is purely economic!

108 [1972] 1 Q. B. 373. In *Dutton*, Lord Denning said (at pp. 397–8): 'It was [the council inspector's] job to examine the foundations to see if they would take the load of the house. He failed to do it properly . . . The council should answer for his failure. They were entrusted by Parliament with the task of seeing that houses were properly built. They received public funds for the purpose. Their very object was to protect purchasers and occupiers of houses. Yet they failed to protect them. Their shoulders are broad enough to bear the loss.'

109 [1978] A. C. 728.

110 [1990] 3 W. L. R. 414 at pp. 432–3 *per* Lord Keith.

111 [1964] A. C. 465.

112 [1964] A. C. 465 at p. 486.

113 [1964] A. C. 465 at p. 503.

114 [1964] A. C. 465 at p. 529.

115 [1964] A. C. 465 at pp. 529–30.

116 [1990] 1 All E. R. 568.

117 [1990] 1 All E. R. 568 at p. 589.

118 Cardozo C. J. in the American case *Ultramares Corp.* v. *Touche* 255 N. Y. Rep. 170 (1931).

119 [1971] 1 All E. R. 150.

120 [1971] 1 All E. R. 150 at p. 163 *per* Lords Reid and Morris.

121 *Supra.*

122 See the judgment of Lord Bridge: [1990] 1 All E. R. 568 at p. 576; and see *JEB Fasteners Ltd* v. *Marks Bloom & Co* [1981] 3 All E. R. 289.

123 See the judgment of Lord Oliver, quoted above. See also M. Jones, *Textbook on Torts* (3rd edn, Blackstone), pp. 67–71.

124 See, for example, *Smith* v. *Eric S. Bush* and *Harris* v. *Wyre Forest District Council* [1989] 2 W. L. R. 790.

125 [1991] 2 W. L. R. 641.

126 [1991] 2 W. L. R. 641 at pp. 651–2. This list was described as 'helpful' in *Morgan Crucible Co. plc* v. *Hill Samuel Bank Ltd* [1991] 1 All E. R. 148.

127 See the *Bush* and *Harris* cases, above, n. 124.

128 See the *JEB Fasteners* case, above, n. 122.

129 [1943] A. C. 92 *per* Lord Porter at p. 117.

130 (1888) 13 App. Cas. 222.

131 [1901] 2 K. B. 669.

132 [1925] 1 K. B. 141.

133 [1943] A. C. 92.

134 [1964] 1 W. L. R. 1317.

135 See also *Hinz* v. *Berry* [1970] 1 All E. R. 1074.

136 [1967] 2 All E. R. 945.

137 (1986) 136 N. L. J. 446.

138 See note 39 above.

139 [1983] A. C. 410.

140 [1983] A. C. 410 at p. 417.

141 [1983] A. C. 410 at p. 422.

142 [1991] 3 All E. R. 65.

143 [1991] 3 All E. R. 73.

144 [1991] 4 All E. R. 907.

145 [1991] 4 All E. R. 907 at p. 912.

146 [1991] 4 All E. R. 907 at p. 914.

147 [1991] 4 All E. R. 907 at p. 915.

148 [1991] 4 All E. R. 907 at p. 921.

149 [1991] 4 All E. R. 907 at p. 930.

150 [1991] 4 All E. R. 907 at p. 931.

151 Ibid.

152 [1991] 4 All E. R. 907 at pp. 931–2.

153 [1991] 4 All E. R. 907 at p. 921.

154 The defendants' appeal in *Ravenscroft* is reported briefly as a Note, at [1992] 2 All E. R. 47: in essence, their appeal was allowed by the Court of Appeal in light of the views expressed by the House of Lords in the *Alcock* decision.

155 Law Com. No. 82, *Liability for Defective Products*, 1977.

156 Op. cit.

157 Other defences are (i) that the defect did not exist at the time of supply (the 'relevant time'), (ii) that in the case of a defective component contained in a product, the defect was solely attributable to the design of the other product of which it formed part; (iii) that the defect is solely attributable to compliance with a legal obligation, (iv) that the defendant neither supplied the goods in the course of a business nor produced them for profit, or (v) that the producer did not supply the goods to anyone.

158 See C. Newdick, 'The Future of Negligence in Product Liability' (1987) 103 *L. Q. R.* 288, p. 309.

159 The 'relevant time' is the time when the product was put into circulation.

160 Interestingly, the German version of the Act specifically provides that pharmaceutical manufacturers may not avail themselves of the 'development risk' defence.

161 See Newdick, op. cit.

162 (1873) LR 8 CP 148.

163 W. Friedmann, *Law in a Changing Society* (2nd edn, 1972, Penguin), p. 168.

164 The doctrine only applies if the wrongdoer and defendant are in a relationship of employment: it does not apply if the wrongdoer is an independent contractor. On this distinction, see chapter 1.

165 P. S. Atiyah, *Vicarious Liability in the Law of Torts* (1967, Butterworths), p. 13.

166 Ibid., pp. 22–3.

167 E. McKendrick, 'Vicarious Liability and Independent Contractors – A Re-examination' (1990) 53 *Mod. Law Rev.* 770.

168 Ibid., p. 771.

169 See for example *O'Kelly* v. *Trusthouse Forte plc* [1983] I. C. R. 728.

170 The current statutes are the Road Traffic Act 1972 and the Employers' Liability (Compulsory Insurance) Act 1969.

171 T. Hadden, 'Contract, Tort and Crime: The Forms of Legal Thought' (1971) *L. Q. R.*, pp. 253–4.

172 Dr P. Ford, secretary of the Medical Protection Society, reported in the *Guardian*, 25 August 1987.

173 See for example T. G. Ison, *The Forensic Lottery* (1967, Staples Press); The Sunday Times, *The Thalidomide Children and the Law* (1973, Deutsch); P. S. Atiyah, *Accidents, Compensation and the Law* (4th edn by P. Cane, 1987, Weidenfeld and Nicolson).

174 *Report of the Royal Commission on Civil Liability and Compensation for Personal Injury* (the Pearson Report) (Cmnd. 7054, 1978, HMSO).

175 See J. F. Fleming, 'The Pearson Report: Its "Strategy" ' (1979) *Mod. Law Rev.*, p. 250; N. S. Marsh, 'The Pearson Report on Civil Liability for Death and Personal Injury' (1979) *L. Q. R.*, p. 513; D. K. Allen *et al.*, *Accident Compensation after Pearson* (1979, Sweet and Maxwell).

176 D. Harris *et al.*, *Compensation and Support for Illness and Injury* (Clarendon Press, 1984).

177 Cm. 394 (1988, HMSO).

178 *Report of the Royal Commission of Inquiry into Compensation for Personal Injury in New Zealand* (1969, NZ Government Printer).

179 See, for example, the judgment of Lawton L.J. in *Whitehouse* v. *Jordan* op. cit.

180 Fleming, op. cit., p. 251.

181 *Winfield and Jolowicz on Tort* (13th edn by W. V. H. Rogers, 1989, Sweet and Maxwell), p. 635.

182 Some statutory provision has affected the common law in this area, notably the Fatal Accidents Act 1976 (consolidating previous enactments), which provides that in the event of the death of a person by reason of another's tort, the deceased's dependants may bring an action against the wrongdoer if the deceased would have had a right of action had s/he lived; and the Administration of Justice Act 1982, considered below. See *Winfield and Jolowicz on Tort*, op. cit., chapters 24 and 27.

183 See the cases cited in *Winfield and Jolowicz on Tort*, op. cit, pp. 628–30.

184 No damages are recoverable under this head if the plantiff is unable to experience pain or suffering (for example, because of unconsciousness).

185 On this, see J. Munkman, *Damages for Personal Injury and Death* (8th edn, 1989, Butterworths). Up-to-date information as to current amounts awarded for various injuries may be found from time to time in the *New Law Journal* and in *Current Law*.

186 See *Dering* v. *Uris* [1964] 2 Q. B. 669.

187 See *Rookes* v. *Barnard* [1964] A. C. 1129 and *Cassell and Co. Ltd* v. *Broome* [1972] A. C. 1027.

188 See Munkman, op. cit.

189 See *Benham* v. *Gambling* [1941] A. C. 157; *Gammell* v. *Wilson* [1980] 3 W. L. R. 891; *Yorkshire Electricity Board* v. *Naylor* [1968] A. C. 529.

190 Abel, op. cit., p. 208.

Chapter 10: Liability in English law: crime and the criminal justice system

1 J. Stephen, *A History of the Criminal Law of England* (1883).

2 Lord Denning, in *Report of the Royal Commission on Capital Punishment* (1953, Cmd. 8932, HMSO), p. 18.

3 E. Durkheim, *The Division of Labour in Society* (1964, Free Press, New York; Macmillan, London), p. 79.

4 Ibid., p. 80.

5 See chapter 13.

6 See for example T. Parsons, *The Social System* (1951, Routledge and Kegan Paul).

7 This is the standard of proof which must be attained by the prosecution in a criminal case. The term has been defined and explained by judges to juries in various ways, some of which have met with disapproval from the appellate courts. In 1952 the Court of Criminal Appeal thought that juries should be told that to convict, they should be 'satisfied so that they can feel sure' of the guilt of the accused. Today, the term is usually explained to juries in terms of 'being sure' of guilt. The standard of proof is rather less in civil cases: plaintiffs must establish their case 'on a balance of probabilities', so that it is more likely than not that the plaintiff's version is the true one. See R. Cross, *Evidence* (6th edn, 1985, Butterworths), chapter 4.

8 The term *actus reus* may also include omissions to act, and states of affairs. See below.

9 *R* v. *Charlson* [1955] 1 All E. R. 859.

10 [1983] 2 All E. R. 503.

11 (1987) 85 Cr. App. Rep. 321.

12 *Hill* v. *Baxter* [1958] 1 Q. B. 277 *per* Pearson J., at p. 286.

13 [1977] 2 All E. R. 341.

14 Misuse of Drugs Act 1971, s. 5.

15 (1983) *The Times*, 28 March. See also *R* v. *Larsonneur* (1933) 24 Cr. App. Rep. 74.

16 *Director of Public Prosecutions* v. *Smith* [1961] A. C. 290.

17 See J. C. Smith and B. Hogan, *Criminal Law* (7th edn, 1992, Butterworths) p. 70.

18 So thought Lord Hailsham in *Hyam* v. *DPP* [1975] A. C. 55.

19 [1975] A. C. 55; [1974] 2 All E. R. 41.

20 [1985] 1 A. C. 905.

21 Ibid. at p. 926.

22 Ibid.

23 Ibid. at p. 929.

24 [1986] 1 A. C. 455.

25 Ibid. at p. 460.

26 Ibid at p. 471.

27 Ibid at p. 473.

28 C. M. V. Clarkson and H. M. Keating, *Criminal Law· Text and Materials* (2nd edn, 1990, Sweet and Maxwell), p. 161.

29 [1986] 1 W. L. R. 1025.

30 Ibid., at p. 1028.

31 [1957] 2 Q. B. 396; [1957] 2 All E. R. 412.

32 [1982] A. C. 341; [1981] 1 All E. R. 961.

33 [1981] 1 All E. R. 961 at p. 967.

34 [1981] 1 All E. R. 974.

35 [1984] 78 Cr. App. R. 149.

36 [1983] 2 All E. R. 1058.

37 [1983] 2 All E. R. 1058 at p. 1064.

38 Card, Cross and Jones, *Criminal Law* (12th edn by R. Card, 1992, Butterworths), pp. 73–4.

39 [1991] 2 All E. R. 210 CA. This case was overruled on the substantive point of law involved, in *R* v. *Parminter* and *R.* v. *Savage*, below.

40 [1991] 4 All E. R. 698.

41 Smith and Hogan, op. cit., p. 65.

42 [1986] Crim. L. R. 406. See, however, *R.* v. *Reid* [1992] 1 W. L. R. 793, where dicta by Lord Goff, at p. 813, and Lord Browne-Wilkinson, at p. 819, suggest that a situation such as that in *Crossman* might now lead to a conviction, if the actual risk would be 'obvious and serious' to a 'reasonable person'.

43 [1986] Crim. L. R. 800.

44 Law Commission: *A Criminal Code for England and Wales* (1989; Law Com No. 177).

45 Lord Denning, *The Changing Law* (1953, Stevens), p. 112.

46 H. L. A. Hart 'The Aims of the Criminal Law' (1958) 23 *Law and Contemporary Problems*, p. 405.

47 W. Friedmann, *Law in a Changing Society* (2nd edn, 1972, Penguin), p. 202.

48 See Health and Safety at Work Act 1974.

49 See Food Safety Act 1990.

50 See Trade Descriptions Act 1968.

51 Friedmann, op. cit., p. 203.

52 Ibid., p. 206.

53 F. G. Jacobs, *Criminal Responsibility* (1971, Weidenfeld and Nicolson), chapter 4.

54 *Yeandel* v. *Fisher* [1966] 1 Q. B. 446; *Warner* v. *Metropolitan Police Commissioner* [1969] 2 A. C. 256.

55 *R.* v. *Wheat and Stocks* [1921] 2 K. B. 119, a case based on a particular interpretation of *R.* v. *Tolson* (1889) 23 Q. B. D. 168. *R.* v. *Gould* [1968] 1 All E. R. 849 has made it clear that the offence is *not* one of strict liability.

56 Glanville Williams, *Criminal Law* (2nd edn, 1961, Stevens).

57 Ibid., pp. 259–60.

58 [1984] 2 All E. R. 503.

59 [1984] 2 All E. R. 503 at p. 508.

60 [1969] 1 All E. R. 347, HL.

61 [1969] 1 All E. R. 347 at p. 362.

62 See S. Box, *Power, Crime and Mystification* (1983, Tavistock), chapter 2.

63 Offences under controlled drugs legislation carry possible sentences of imprisonment, as do various road traffic offences such as causing death by dangerous driving, held in *R. v. Ball and Loughlin* (1966) 50 Cr. App. Rep. 266 to be an offence of strict liability.

64 [1976] 2 All E. R. 142; 2 W. L. R. 623.

65 (1843) 10 C & Fin. 200.

66 [1955] 1 All E. R. 859.

67 [1972] 1 All E. R. 219.

68 [1984] 1 A. C. 156.

69 See for example the work of R. D. Laing and the 'Anti-Psychiatry' school.

70 For a detailed discussion, see Smith and Hogan, op. cit.; Card, Cross and Jones, op. cit.

71 Homicide Act 1957, s. 2.

72 See especially the comments by Lord Hailsham in *R. v. Howe* [1987] 1 A. C. 417 at p. 429.

73 See the well-known case of *R. v. Dudley and Stevens* (1884) 14 Q. B. D. 273. For a superb discussion of this case and its background, see A. Simpson, *Cannibalism and the Common Law* (1984, Penguin).

74 *R. v. Howe*, op. cit., at p. 429.

75 [1975] A. C. 653.

76 [1987] 1 A. C. 417.

77 As to the House of Lords' ability to reverse its own previous decisions, see chapter 7.

78 See for example Lord Hailsham's judgment at pp. 433–5.

79 *R. v. Gotts* [1992] 1 All E. R. 832, HL.

80 See the discussion referred to at note 78 above.

81 *R. v. Wilson and others* [1965] 1 Q. B. 402.

82 Other examples might include the trial of the Kray twins, that of Sutcliffe (the 'Yorkshire Ripper') and of course the exemplary sentences given out to young people convicted of 'mugging' offences in the early 1970s, on which see S. Hall, C. Critcher, *et al.*, *Policing the Crisis* (1978, Macmillan).

83 See especially the discussion by N. Walker, *Sentencing in a Rational Society* (1972, Penguin), chapter 4.

84 Cm. 965, para. 2.8.

85 A. Ashworth, *Sentencing and Penal Policy* (1983, Weidenfeld and Nicolson), pp. 16–18.

86 The Act provides that the court may consider the seriousness of the offence together with one other 'associated offence', which is another offence for which the accused has been convicted, or for which the accused is now being sentenced, or which the accused has asked to be taken into consideration. In practice, a person may be charged with a number of offences, or ask for a number of offences to be taken into consideration: it is likely that the most serious of these other offences will be the 'associated offence'. The theory behind this provision seems to be that, in

difficult or marginal cases, consideration of one other offence may tip the balance, in terms of seriousness, between a custodial and a non-custodial sentence.

87 Introduced by the Powers of Criminal Courts Act 1973, as amended by s. 68 of the Criminal Justice Act 1982, this is an order which may be made in respect of a person aged sixteen or over, convicted of an offence which might be punishable with imprisonment. The CSO requires the person to perform unpaid work 'for the community' for a specified number of hours.

88 An 'absolute discharge' means that the offender goes free, a technical conviction having been recorded; a 'conditional discharge' is also a discharge from court, but conditions are attached, the most common one being that the offender must not commit any further offence for a specified period or else he or she will be liable to be dealt with in a sentence reflecting the new offence *and also* the one for which the conditional discharge was given. See Criminal Justice Act 1991, Schedule 1.

89 In some cases a case may be referred to the Court of Appeal by the Attorney-General if a sentence is regarded as too lenient. In such cases, the Court of Appeal may increase the sentence: Criminal Justice Act 1988, s. 36.

90 *Independent*, 30 September 1992.

91 Note that there is a mandatory sentence of life imprisonment on conviction for murder.

92 See generally J. C. Smith, *Theft* (6th edn, 1989, Butterworths).

93 See for example P. Bean, *Rehabilitation and Deviance* (1976, Routledge and Kegan Paul); M. Clarke, 'The Impact of Social Science on Conceptions of Responsibility' (1975) *British Journal of Law and Society*, vol. 2, no. 1; S. Cohen, 'Criminology and the Sociology of Deviance in Britain' in P. Rock and M. McIntosh (eds), *Deviance and Social Control* (1974, Tavistock).

94 Op. cit.

95 Clarke, op. cit., p. 32.

96 Cohen, op. cit.; Bean, op. cit. See also A. E. Bottoms, 'Reflections on the Criminological Enterprise' (1987) 46 *Camb. Law Jo.* 240.

97 See, especially, the critical surveys of criminological research in I. Taylor, P. Walton and J. Young, *The New Criminology* (1973, Routledge and Kegan Paul); see also J. Young, 'Thinking Seriously About Crime: Some Models of Criminology', in M. Fitzgerald, G. McLennan and J. Pawson (eds), *Crime and Society* (1981, Routledge and Kegan Paul, in association with Open University Press); D. Downes and P. Rock, *Understanding Deviance* (1982, Oxford University Press); S. Cohen, *Visions of Social Control* (1985, Polity Press); D. Garland, *Punishment and Modern Society* (1990, Oxford University Press); M. Cavidino and J. Dignan, *The Penal System* (1992, Sage).

98 Bean, op. cit., p. 145.

99 For an excellent recent survey, see K. S. Williams, *Criminology* (1991, Blackstone).

100 D. Matza, *Becoming Deviant* (1969, Prentice Hall).

101 H. J. Eysenck, *Crime and Personality* (1970, Paladin); C. R. Hollin, *Psychology and Crime* (1989, Routledge and Kegan Paul).

102 See the theories of C. Lombroso in *L'Uomo Delinquente* (1876, 5th edn, Bocca, Turin); S. Mednick, T. Moffitt and S. Stack, *The Causes of Crime: New Biological*

Approaches (1987, Cambridge University Press); the debate as to genetic abnormalities regarding chromosomal structure is discussed by T. Sarbin and J. Miller, 'Demonism Revisited: The XYY Chromosomal Anomaly' (1970) *Issues in Criminology*, p. 195.

103 For examples see W. Bonger, *Criminality and Economic Conditions* (1969, Indiana Free Press); D. Matza, *Delinquency and Drift* (1964, Wiley); D. Sutherland and D. Cressey, *Principles of Criminology* (1966, Lippincott); A. Turk, *Criminality and the Legal Order* (1969, Rand McNally); S. Box, *Recession, Crime and Punishment* (1987, Macmillan); R. Davidson, *Crime and Environment* (1981, Croom Helm).

104 See N. Walker, 'Lost Causes in Criminology' in R. Hood (ed.), *Crime, Criminology and Public Policy* (1974, Heinemann).

105 D. Matza, (1964), op. cit.

106 On this, see the discussion of the work of Garfinkel, Carlen, etc. in chapter 6, above.

107 L. Taylor, *Deviance and Society* (1973, Nelson), pp. 189–90.

108 See for example W. Miller, 'Lower-Class Culture as a Generating Milieu of Gang Delinquency' (1958) *Journal of Social Issues*; J. B. Mays, *Crime and its Treatment* (2nd edn, 1975, Longman).

109 D. Matza and G. Sykes, 'Juvenile Delinquency and Subterranean Values' (1961) *Amer. Socio. Review*, p. 712.

110 See for example J. F. Short and F. I. Nye, 'The Extent of Unrecorded Juvenile Delinquency' (1958) *Journal of Criminal Law, Criminology, and Police Science*, p. 256; S. Box, *Deviance, Reality and Society* (2nd edn, 1982, Holt, Rinehart and Winston).

111 L. Taylor, op. cit., pp. 11–12.

112 S. Cohen, Introduction to *Images of Deviance* (1971, Penguin), p. 20.

113 See P. Rock, *Making People Pay* (1973, Routledge and Kegan Paul).

114 See for example I. Piliavin and S. Briar, 'Police Encounters with Juveniles' (1964) *Amer. Jo. Soc.* 70; C. Werthman and I. Piliavin, 'Gang Members and the Police' in D. Bordua (ed.), *The Police: Six Sociological Essays* (1967, Wiley); J. Skolnick, *Justice Without Trial* (1966, Wiley); M. Cain, *Society and the Policeman's Role* (1973, Routledge and Kegan Paul); S. Damer, 'Wine Alley: The Sociology of a Dreadful Enclosure' (1974) 22 *Sociological Review*, p. 221.

115 D. Sutherland, 'Is White Collar Crime "Crime"?' (1945) *Amer. Soc. Review*.

116 See F. Pearce, *Crimes of the Powerful* (1976, Pluto Press).

117 See V. Aubert, 'White Collar Crime and Social Structure' (1952) *Amer. Socio. Review*; Pearce, op. cit.; S. Box, *Power, Crime and Mystification* (1983, Tavistock); P. Tappan, 'Who is the Criminal?' (1947) *Amer. Socio. Review*; M. Levi, *Regulating Fraud*, (1987, Tavistock).

118 S. Box, *Power, Crime and Mystification* (1983, Tavistock), p. 14.

119 Ibid., p. 25.

120 S. Cohen, 'How Can We Balance Justice, Guilt and Tolerance?', *New Society*, 1 March, 1979, pp. 475–6.

121 Ibid.

122 A. Phipps, 'Radical Criminology and Criminal Victimisation: Proposals for the Development of Theory and Intervention' in R. Matthews and J. Young (eds), *Confronting Crime* (1986, Sage).

123 M. Hough and P. Mayhew, *The British Crime Survey: First Report* (1983, Home Office Research Study 76, HMSO); M. Hough and P. Mayhew, *Taking Account of*

Crime: Findings from the Second British Crime Survey (1985, Home Office Research Study 85, HMSO); P. Mayhew, D. Elliott and L. Dowds, *The British Crime Survey: Third Report* (1989, Home Office Research Study 111, HMSO).

124 T. Jones, M. McLean and J. Young, *The Islington Crime Survey: Crime Victimisation and Policing in Inner City London* (1986, Gower). See also M. Maguire and J. Pointing (eds), *Victims of Crime: A New Deal* (1988, Open University).

125 I. Taylor, *Law and Order: Arguments for Socialism* (1981, Macmillan).

126 Ibid., p. 46.

Chapter 11: The development and role of the contract

1 See, for example, *Balfour* v. *Balfour* [1919] 2 K. B. 571 (agreement between husband and wife); *Ford Motor Company Ltd* v. *Amalgamated Union of Engineering and Foundry Workers* [1969] 2 All E. R. 481 (agreement between management and union). The latter case now has statutory backing in s. 18 of the Trade Union and Labour Relations Act 1974.

2 *Jones* v. *Vernon's Pools Ltd* [1938] 2 All E. R. 626 (pools agreement held binding 'in honour only').

3 Cheshire, Fifoot and Furmston, *Law of Contract* (12th edn by M. P. Furmston, Butterworths, 1991), p. 116.

4 [1952] 2 All E. R. 456.

5 This right is now subject to certain statutory restrictions, notably the Race Relations Act 1976, and the Sex Discrimination Act 1975, which provide, among other things, that customers may not be refused service on grounds of race or sex.

6 P. S. Atiyah, *Introduction to the Law of Contract* (4th edn, 1989, Oxford University Press), chapter 3.

7 G. Smith and A. J. Street, *The Consumer Adviser* (1978, Institute of Trading Standards), p. 63.

8 G. Borrie and A. L. Diamond, *The Consumer, Society and the Law* (4th edn, 1981, Penguin), p. 23.

9 See, for example, *Harvey* v. *Facey* [1893] A. C. 552.

10 *Harvey* v. *Facey*, op. cit.; *Clifton* v. *Palumbo* [1944] 2 All E. R. 497. But compare *Bigg* v. *Boyd Gibbins Ltd* [1971] 2 All E. R. 183.

11 (1877) 2 App. Cas. 666.

12 *Hyde* v. *Wrench* (1840) 3 Beav. 334.

13 *Carlill* v. *Carbolic Smoke Ball Co.* (1892) 2 Q. B. 484.

14 *Adams* v. *Lindsell* (1818) 1 B. and Ald. 681.

15 *Entores Ltd* v. *Miles Far East Corporation* [1955] 2 All E. R. 493.

16 *Felthouse* v. *Bindley* (1862) 11 C. B. N. S. 869.

17 (1880) 5 C. P. D. 344.

18 (1875) L. R. 10 Exch. 153.

19 Cheshire, Fifoot and Furmston, op. cit., p. 73.

20 [1960] A. C. 87.

21 Ibid at p. 114 *per* Lord Somervell.

22 [1925] A. C. 87.

23 *The Times*, 4 April 1986.

24 [1956] 2 All E. R. 318.

25 (1809) 2 Camp. 317.

26 See *Hartley* v. *Ponsonby* (1857) 7 E. & B. 872.

27 [1990] 1 All E. R. 512.

28 [1990] 1 All E. R. 512 at p. 527 *per* Purchas L.J.

29 [1990] 1 All E. R. 512 at p. 526.

30 [1990] 1 All E. R. 512 at pp. 521–2.

31 J. Adams and R. Brownsword, 'Contract, Consideration and the Critical Path', (1990) 53 *Modern Law Review* 536, p. 537.

32 Ibid., especially pp. 540–1.

33 (1602) 5 Co. Rep. 117a.

34 [1966] 2 Q. B. 617.

35 Ibid at p. 623 *per* Lord Denning.

36 (1877) 2 App. Cas. 439, HL.

37 Ibid., at p. 448.

38 [1947] K. B. 130.

39 Though see Lord Scarman's comments in *Crabb* v. *Arun District Council* [1976] Ch. 179.

40 *Tweddle* v. *Atkinson* (1861) 1 B. and S. 393.

41 *Taylor* v. *Caldwell* (1863) 3 B. and S. 826; *Krell* v. *Henry* [1903] 2 K. B. 740; *Chandler* v. *Webster* [1904] 1 K. B. 493; the *Fibrosa* case [1943] A. C. 32.

42 Op. cit., p. 43. See also H. Collins, *The Law of Contract* (1986, Weidenfeld and Nicolson).

43 Money, quoted in J. P. Tillotson, *Contract Law in Perspective* (2nd edn, 1985, Butterworths), p. 52.

44 Lord Wilberforce, in *New Zealand Shipping Co. Ltd* v. *A. M. Satterthwaite and Co. Ltd* [1975] A. C. 154 at p. 167.

45 [1930] 1 K. B. 41.

46 Cheshire, Fifoot and Furmston, op. cit; Tillotson, op. cit.; Atiyah, op. cit.

47 Tillotson, op. cit., p. 52.

48 W. Friedmann, *Law in a Changing Society* (2nd edn, 1972, Penguin), p. 123.

49 [1930] 1 K. B. 41.

50 Borrie and Diamond, op. cit., p. 40.

51 [1971] 1 All E. R. 686.

52 Ibid., at p. 690.

53 Ibid., at p. 693.

54 This is usually known as the 'Rule in *L'Estrange* v. *Graucob*', the case normally cited as authority for this proposition ([1934] 2 K. B. 394), though in fact there is earlier authority to the same effect.

55 Unfair Contract Terms Act 1977.

56 G. H. Treitel, *Law of Contract* (7th edn, 1987, Stevens), p. 166.

57 See, for example, *Andrews* v. *Singer* [1934] 1 K. B. 17; *Houghton* v. *Trafalgar Insurance* [1954] 1 Q. B. 247; *Hollier* v. *Rambler Motors (AMC) Ltd* [1972] 1 All E. R. 399. Generally, see Borrie and Diamond, op. cit.

58 *Andrews* v. *Singer*, op. cit.

59 For example, *Karsales (Harrow) Ltd* v. *Wallis* [1956] 1 W. L. R. 936; *Farnworth Finance Facilities Ltd* v. *Attryde* [1970] 2 All E. R. 774. But despite dicta in *Karsales* to the effect that a fundamental breach operates as a rule of law, so that its effect was to nullify the contract, later cases suggest a different view. In particular, in *Suisse Atlantique Société d'Armement Maritime S.A.* v. *N.V. Rotterdamsche Kolen Centrale* [1967] 1 A. C. 361

and in *Harbutt's 'Plasticine' Ltd* v. *Wayne Tank and Pump Co. Ltd* [1970] 1 Q. B. 447, the approach taken was that the doctrine of fundamental breach was a rule of construction, not of law. This meant that an aggrieved party could elect, despite the breach, to continue with the contract and simply sue for damages, *or* to terminate the contract altogether. The present position must be gleaned from both the decision in *Photo Production Ltd* v. *Securicor Transport Ltd* [1980] 1 All E. R. 556 and the Unfair Contract Terms Act 1977, the effect of these being that the aggrieved party who has suffered the other party's fundamental breach retains the right either to terminate or continue the contract, though the exclusion clause itself may be invalidated because it does not pass the test of reasonableness provided for in the 1977 Act.

60 Borrie and Diamond, op. cit., p. 43.

61 Smith and Street, op. cit., pp. 10–11.

62 An action in negligence also avoids the problems caused by the doctrine of privity of contract (discussed above). See *Donoghue* v. *Stevenson* [1932] A. C. 562.

63 (1837) 2 M. & W. 519.

64 Borrie and Diamond, op. cit., p. 160.

65 Cmnd. 4596 (1971, HMSO).

66 Note that, unlike the corresponding provisions in the Sale of Goods Act, the Supply of Goods and Services Act 1982 speaks of implied *terms*, and not *conditions*. A contractual term may be either a condition or a warranty, the former being a *basic* obligation, the latter being a *subsidiary* obligation. Breach of a condition entitles the aggrieved party to sue for damages, and also to terminate the contract, while breach of a warranty entitles the aggrieved party to sue for damages only. Whether a given contractual term is a condition or a warranty is, in the absence of statutory guidance, a matter of interpretation for the courts, and so the effect of this use of words in the 1982 Act is that the remedy available to an aggrieved party will depend upon the seriousness and circumstances of the breach.

67 Consumer Transaction (Restrictions on Statements) Order, 1976 S. I. No. 1813, as amended by 1978 S. I. No. 127.

68 As amended in 1977.

69 Provision for such approval is contained in the Fair Trading Act 1973. For interesting discussions on the OFT, see in particular R. Baldwin and C. McCrudden, *Regulation and Public Law* (1987, Weidenfeld and Nicolson), chapter 9; and I. Ramsay, *Consumer Protection* (1989, Weidenfeld and Nicolson), chapter 7.

70 R. Cranston, *Consumers and the Law* (2nd edn, 1984, Weidenfeld and Nicolson), p. 32.

71 Ibid., p. 62.

72 *Final Report of the Committee on Consumer Protection* (1962, Cmnd. 1781, HMSO).

73 S. Macaulay, 'Non-Contractual Relations in Business' (1963) *American Sociological Review* 28.

74 H. Beale and T. Dugdale, 'Contracts between Businessmen: Planning and the Use of Contractual Remedies' (1975) *British Journal of Law and Society*, vol. 2, no. 1, p. 45.

75 Ibid., p. 59.

76 See P. Vincent-Jones, 'The Litigation Explosion', *New Law Journal*, 16 November 1990, p. 1602.

77 Tillotson, op. cit. See also Atiyah, op. cit., and Collins, op. cit.

78 Tillotson, op. cit., p. 68.

79 See *Butler Machine Tool Co. Ltd* v. *Ex-Cell-O Corporation* [1979] 1 All E. R. 965.

80 This is called a *quantum meruit* payment. For a recent example see *British Steel Corporation* v. *Cleveland Bridge and Engineering Co. Ltd* [1984] 1 All E. R. 504.

81 Friedmann, op. cit., p. 124.

Chapter 12: Law and government

1 See chapter 1.

2 Under the provisions of the Local Government Act 1985, those police forces which were, prior to the Act, regulated by committees of the metropolitan districts (abolished under the Act) are now under the regulation of Police Authorities, whose members are drawn from district councillors and magistrates.

3 See *R.* v. *Secretary of State for the Home Department, ex parte Northumbria Police Authority* [1989] Q. B. 26; [1988] 2 W. L. R. 290.

4 Various statutes impose a variety of duties upon local authority bodies to carry out their functions. See, for further detail, C. Cross and S. Bailey, *Cross on Local Government Law* (8th edn, 1991, Sweet and Maxwell), or any other standard text on local government law.

5 For example, the South Yorkshire County Council, which for many years had maintained a policy of cheap public transport, drew considerable fire. The enormous subsidy from the rates needed to maintain such a policy (which had the result that the average fare within South Yorkshire towns was around seven pence) was defended by the council on the ground that public transport was an essential facility for the community, and therefore *should* be heavily subsidized, though this argument met with little sympathy from political opponents both locally and nationally.

6 *Streamlining the Cities* (1983, Cmnd. 9063, HMSO).

7 The arguments are discussed in A. Cochrane, 'The Attack on Local Government: What it is and What it isn't' (1985 *Critical Social Policy*, Issue 12). See R. Baldwin and C. McCrudden, *Regulation and Public Law* (1987, Weidenfeld and Nicolson); C. Turpin, *British Government and the Constitution* (2nd edn, 1990, Weidenfeld and Nicolson); S. Leach and G. Stoker, 'The Transformation of Central–Local Government Relationships', in C. Graham and T. Prosser (eds), *Waiving the Rules: The Constitution under Thatcherism* (1988, Open University Press); M. Grant, 'Central–Local Relations: The Balance of Power', in J. Jowell and D. Oliver (eds), *The Changing Constitution* (2nd edn, 1989 Oxford University Press).

8 T. C. Hartley and J. A. G. Griffith, *Government and Law* (2nd edn 1981, Weidenfeld and Nicolson), p. 104.

9 See *Prescott* v. *Birmingham Corporation* [1955] Ch. 210 and *Bromley London Borough Council* v. *Greater London Council* [1982] 2 W. L. R. 62, for judicial interpretation of this word in the context of statutes providing for public transport schemes. See also chapter 14.

10 On this see, in particular, M. Radford, 'Auditing for Change: Local Government and the Audit Commission' (1991) 54 *Modern Law Review* 912.

11 (1863) 14 C. B. (N. S.) 180.

12 H. W. R. Wade, *Administrative Law* (6th edn, 1988, Oxford University Press), pp. 583–4.

13 [1905] 2 K. B. 838.

14 This remedy is rarely used, because the prerogative remedy of *mandamus* serves the same function.

15 J. F. Garner and B. L. Jones, *Administrative Law* (7th edn, 1989, Butterworths), p. 226.

16 'Tribunal' is used here in the wide, general sense, meaning any panel having jurisdiction to decide cases, including courts.

17 In *R.* v. *Electricity Commissioners* [1924] 1 K. B. 171 at p. 204.

18 Rules of the Supreme Court, Order 53, as amended by Rules of the Supreme Court (Amendment No. 4) Ord. 1980 S. I. 1980 No. 2000); and Supreme Court Act 1981, s. 31. It must not be forgotten, however, that there remain in these procedures 'protections against claims' against public authorities which 'it [is] not in the public interest for courts of justice to entertain', such claims including 'groundless, unmeritorious or tardy attacks on the validity of decisions made by public authorities in the field of public law': *O'Reilly* v. *Mackman* [1982] 3 All E. R. 1125 *per* Lord Diplock at pp. 1130–1. This case established that applicants cannot evade these safeguards by using private-law procedures where the public-law element in the application should lead to an application for judicial review.

19 Ibid.

20 Hartley and Griffith, op. cit., p. 369.

21 See especially *R.* v. *Lewisham Union Guardians* [1897] 1 Q. B. 498.

22 *R.* v. *Liverpool Corporation, ex p. Liverpool Taxi Fleet Operators Association* [1972] 2 Q. B. 299 *per* Lord Denning MR at p. 309.

23 [1982] A. C. 617.

24 See also *R.* v. *Metropolitan Police Commissioner, ex p. Blackburn* [1968] 1 All E. R. 763; and *R.* v. *Secretary of State for the Environment, ex parte Rose Theatre Trust Co.* [1990] 1 All E. R. 754.

25 [1982] A. C. 617 at p. 630. See also *R.* v. *H. M. Treasury, ex parte Smedley* [1985] 2 W. L. R. 576.

26 [1954] 2 All E. R. 118.

27 [1954] 2 All E. R. 118 at p. 121.

28 See above, chapter 7.

29 A. V. Dicey, *The Law of the Constitution* (first published 1885); (10th edn, reprinted 1985, Macmillan).

30 Ibid., p. 336.

31 For informative and concise discussions on the French system of administrative law, see for example Wade, op. cit., pp. 14–15; S. A. de Smith and R. Brazier, *Constitutional and Administrative Law* (6th edn by R. Brazier, 1989, Penguin), pp. 533–5.

32 See Baldwin and McCrudden, op. cit., chapter 2.

33 See the critique of Dicey's writings on the rule of law by H. W. Arthurs, 'Rethinking Administrative Law: A Slightly Dicey Business' (1979) *Osgoode Hall Law Journal*, vol. 17, no. 1.

34 Wade, op. cit., pp. 25–6.

35 *Regulation and Public Law*, op. cit.

36 Ibid., p. 1.

37 Ibid., p. 6.

38 Ibid., p. 37.

39 C. Harlow and R. Rawlings, *Law and Administration* (1984, Weidenfeld and Nicolson).

40 Ibid., chapters 1 and 2.
41 J. A. G. Griffith, 'Constitutional and Administrative Law' in P. Archer and A. Martin (eds), *More Law Reform Now* (1983, Barry Rose).
42 And see chapter 14.
43 For useful material on the civil service, see Hartley and Griffith, op. cit., chapter 5; B. Sedgemore, *The Secret Constitution: An Analysis of the Political Establishment* (1980, Hodder and Stoughton); L. Chapman, *Your Disobedient Servant* (1979, Penguin); A. May and K. Rowan, *Inside Information: British Government and the Media* (1982, Constable); De Smith and Brazier, op. cit., pp. 192–204.
44 Above, chapter 6.
45 The Parliamentary Commissioner Act 1967.
46 Cmd. 4060 (1932, HMSO).
47 Wade, op. cit., p. 46.
48 J. A. G. Griffith, *Administrative Law and the Judges* (1978, Haldane Society), p. 10.
49 For example, *R. v. Medical Appeal Tribunal, ex p. Gilmore* [1957] 1 Q. B. 574.
50 [1957] 1 Q. B. 574 at p. 585.
51 [1969] 2 A. C. 147.
52 Wade, op. cit., p. 727.
53 [1956] A. C. 736.
54 Hartley and Griffith, op. cit., pp. 367–8.
55 [1977] Q. B. 122.
56 De Smith and Brazier, op. cit., p. 539.
57 [1918] 1 K. B. 68. And see, for example *R. v. Torquay Licensing Justices, ex p. Brockman* [1951] 2 K. B. 784; though compare *British Oxygen Co. v. Board of Trade* [1971] A. C. 610, where the House of Lords accepted that an authority may validly work with reference to a general rule or policy so long as it is 'always willing to listen to anyone with something new to say' (at p. 625). And in *R. v. Secretary of State for the Environment, ex p. Brent London Borough Council* [1982] 2 W. L. R. 693, the minister had, after consultation with local authorities, obtained statutory power to reduce the rate support grant (see above) to authorities which in his opinion were excessive spenders. After the Act was passed, the minister would not hear any further representations from local authorities, and decided on reducing the grant in respect of several local authorities. The Divisional Court held that he had wrongfully fettered his discretion by refusing to 'listen to any objector who shows that he may have something new to say' (ibid. at p. 733.)
58 [1968] A. C. 997. But see *Nakkuda Ali v. Jayaratne* [1951] A. C. 66; and see also *Congreve v. Home Office* [1976] Q. B. 629; *Secretary of State for Education and Science v. Tameside M.B.C.* [1977] A. C. 1014.
59 [1948] 1 K. B. 223.
60 At p. 229. For a recent example of the problems concerning an authority's taking into account irrelevant considerations, see R. v. *Inner London Education Authority, ex parte Westminister City Council* [1986] 1 W. L. R. 28, where the ILEA proposed to enter into a contract with an advertising agency whereby the latter would conduct a campaign, at a cost of £651,000, to inform the public about intended expenditure cuts imposed by central government, and to encourage public opposition to those cuts. Westminster Council challenged this expenditure of ratepayers' money as being outside the powers of the ILEA. The latter sought to rely on its statutory powers to publish 'information on matters relating to local government' as

justifying this expenditure. The court held that, while seeking to inform the public was a relevant consideration in approving the budget for the campaign, the desire to encourage the public to adopt the ILEA policy of opposing government cuts was an irrelevant consideration: since, in the view of the court, the irrelevant consideration was the dominant consideration, the decision by ILEA was held to be invalid.

61 [1976] 3 All E. R. 665. And see *Laker Airways Ltd* v. *Department of Trade* [1977] Q. B. 643. For discussions see J. Jowell and A. Lester, 'Beyond *Wednesbury*; Substantive Principles of Administrative Law' (1987) *Public Law*, p. 368.

62 [1984] 3 All E. R. 935.

63 Ibid. at p. 950. In the *GCHQ* case, Lord Diplock went on to consider whether there might be a further ground for striking down administrative action: that of 'proportionality'. This concept has its origins in European law, and means that administrative authorities must use appropriate means to achieve a particular objective, and must not go beyond what is necessary to achieve that objective. Thus in *Commission* v. *United Kingdom* [1982] 3 C. M. L. R. 497, the European Court held that the United Kingdom government had acted disproportionately, in the above sense, in restricting the importation of poultry products in order to prevent a particular disease: as the ban affected countries where the disease had not been detected for a number of years, the action was out of proportion to the objective.

In the English case of *R.* v. *Barnsley M.B.C., ex parte Hook* [1976] 1 W. L. R. 1052, the Court of Appeal held that the revocation of a market-stall holder's licence on the grounds that the holder had urinated in the street was disproportionate to the offence, which it described as an 'isolated and trivial incident'. But in the more recent case of *R.* v. *Secretary of State for the Home Department, ex parte Brind* [1990] 2 W. L. R. 787, the same court took a different view of the concept. The case concerned the Home Secretary's prohibition on broadcasts of direct statements by representatives of illegal organizations in Northern Ireland; the legality of this action was challenged by a number of journalists, on the ground, *inter alia*, that the Home Secretary's prohibition was out of proportion to the stated aims of preventing offence being caused to viewers and listeners, and ensuring that terrorist organizations were starved of publicity. The court declined to accept the 'proportion' argument as a separate ground, preferring to treat the situation within the general test of 'unreasonableness'.

64 See for instance *Congreve* v. *Home Office* [1976] Q. B. 629.

65 See above, chapter 7.

66 For example, *R.* v. *Birmingham Licensing Planning Committee, ex p. Kennedy* [1972] 2 Q. B. 140.

67 [1982] 2 W. L. R. 62. And see *Prescott* v. *Birmingham Corporation* [1955] Ch. 210; *Roberts* v. *Hopwood* [1925] A. C. 578.

68 See note 9 above.

69 *Powell* v. *May* [1946] K. B. 330; the *Tameside* case, above.

70 Though the courts accept that a minister's powers can properly be delegated to his or her departmental officials.

71 See chapter 14.

72 For example, various cases decided during wartime suggest judicial reluctance to interfere with administrative action of certain types, probably on the basis that such intervention is inappropriate during emergency conditions. The best known

such case is probably *Liversidge* v. *Anderson* [1942] A. C. 206.

73 Griffith, *Administrative Law and the Judges*, op. cit., p. 16, discussing the *Padfield* and *Tameside* cases.

74 [1964] A. C. 40.

75 Above, note 9.

76 [1915] A. C. 120. And see *Board of Education* v. *Rice* [1911] A. C. 179.

77 [1935] 1 K. B. 249.

78 [1948] A. C. 87.

79 Op. cit.

80 [1967] 2 Q. B. 617.

81 Hartley and Griffith, op. cit., p. 334. See *R.* v. *Hull Prison Board of Visitors* [1978] Q. B. 678.

82 M. Sunkin, 'What is Happening to Applications for Judicial Review?' (1987) *Modern Law Review* 432; 'The Judicial Review Case-Load, 1987–1989' (1991) *Public Law* 490.

83 The reason for this fall, suggests Sunkin, was a reaction to comments made in *Puhlhofer* v. *Hillingdon Council* [1986] A. C. 484 to the effect that too many litigants were making use of judicial review in the attempt to challenge decisions of local authority housing departments.

84 Sunkin, 1991, op. cit., p. 498.

85 Sunkin, 1987, op. cit., p. 465.

86 Ibid., p. 499.

87 Baldwin and McCrudden, op. cit., p. 70.

88 Op. cit.; above, note 33.

89 Ibid., p. 44.

90 Ibid.

91 Baldwin and McCrudden, op. cit., p. 77.

92 P. McAuslan, 'Administrative Law, Collective Consumption and Judicial Policy' (1983) *Modern Law Review* vol. 46, no. 1.

93 Ibid., p. 2.

94 Ibid.

95 Ibid., pp. 5–6.

96 [1982] 1 All E. R. 737.

97 Rt. Hon. Sir Harry Woolf, 'Judicial Review: A Possible Programme for Reform' (1992) *Public Law* 221.

98 This is, in Lord Woolf's opinion, because of the judicial review cases generated by recent legislation, notably the Children Act 1990 and the Environmental Protection Act 1990.

99 Op. cit., p. 230.

100 Op. cit., p. 20. And see Jowell and Lester, op. cit; Lord Scarman, 'The Development of Administrative Law: Obstacles and Opportunities' (1990) *Public Law* 490.

Chapter 13: The legal profession

1 The Administration of Justice Act 1985 creates a new 'profession' of licensed conveyancers: see below.

2 See G. Chambers and S. Harwood-Richardson, *Solicitors in England and Wales: Practice, Organisaton and Perceptions* (1991, Law Society).

3 *Report of the Royal Commission on Legal Services* (The Benson Report) (1979, Cmnd. 7648, HMSO).

4 See, for example, E. Greenwood, 'Attributes of a Profession', *Social Work*, July 1957.

5 P. Thomas, 'Thatcher's Will' (1992) *Journal of Law and Society: Special Issue – Tomorrow's Lawyers* (ed. P. Thomas), p. 4.

6 See R. Dingwall and P. Lewis (eds), *The Sociology of the Professions: Lawyers, Doctors, and Others* (1983, Macmillan).

7 See, for example, I. Kennedy, *The Unmasking of Medicine* (1983, Granada).

8 See, for example, the articles on women's health care in B. Hutter and G. Williams, *Controlling Women* (1981, Croom Helm).

9 R. Abel, *The Legal Profession in England and Wales* (1988, Blackwell), p. 10.

10 Ibid., p. 17.

11 Ibid., p. 31.

12 These were 'The Work and Organisation of the Legal Profession' (1989, Cm. 570); 'Contingency Fees' (1989, Cm. 571); and 'Conveyancing by Authorized Practitioners' (1989, Cm. 572).

13 See Abel, op. cit., Part IV; M. Partington, 'Legal Education in the 1990s', (1992) *Journal of Law and Society*, op. cit.

14 See Abel, op. cit., chapter 12, esp. pp. 177–89.

15 Benson Commission Report, op. cit., p. 52.

16 Report, op. cit., recommendation 3.2.

17 See generally Abel, op. cit., parts II and III.

18 'Legal Services: A Framework for the Future' (1989, Cm. 740, HMSO).

19 The Circuit Judges are full-time judges who preside over Crown courts and county courts; 'circuit' refers to the fact that for administrative purposes the country is divided into regions or circuits, each of which has not only judges, but also barristers, who work within that circuit.

20 Recorders fulfil the same function as Circuit Judges, but operate on a part-time basis.

21 See M. Zander, *Cases and Materials on the English Legal System* (6th edn, 1992, Weidenfeld and Nicolson), p. 687.

22 Benson Commission Report, op. cit.; Surveys, p. 46.

23 See K. Mackie, *Lawyers in Business and the Law Business* (1989, Macmillan).

24 On legal executives, see Abel, op. cit., pp. 207–10; R. Smith, 'Lawyers Whose Time has Come', *New Law Journal*, 11 October 1991.

25 Op. cit., chapter 17.

26 Ibid., p. 199.

27 Abel, chapters 4 and 11.

28 W. Plowden, 'Tomorrow's Lawyers' in M. Zander (ed.), *What's Wrong with the Law?* (1970, BBC), p. 124.

29 Op. cit., Surveys, p. 59.

30 G. Chambers, 'Solicitors in Private Practice: A Survey of Education, Career and Social Background', *New Law Journal*, 12 and 19 June 1992.

31 See Zander, op. cit., pp. 639–41.

32 Benson Commission Report, op. cit.: Surveys, para. 18. 78–9.

33 Ibid., Surveys, Section 16.

34 Abel, op. cit.; and see P. McDonald, ' "The Class of '81" – A Glance at the Social Class Composition of Recruits to the Legal Profession' (1983) *Journal of Law and Society*, vol. 9, no. 2.

35 See J. A. G. Griffith, *The Politics of the Judiciary* (4th edn, 1991, Fontana), chapter 1.

36 D. Harvie, 'Minorities in a Recession', *New Law Journal*, 29 May 1992.

37 Abel, op. cit., p. 78.

38 Ibid., pp. 172–6.

39 Harvie, op. cit.

40 Abel, op. cit., pp. 79–85.

41 Ibid., p. 82.

42 Ibid., p. 85. A report published by the Bar Council in 1992 entitled *Without Prejudice?* revealed significant evidence of inequality of treatment between men and women at the Bar, examples of which include greater difficulty for women in finding pupillage and many discriminatory practices against women barristers: see *The Independent*, 25 November 1992.

43 Harvie, op. cit. For overall figures relating to the male/female split among barristers and judges at all levels as at November 1992, see *The Independent*, 25 November 1992.

44 M. D. A. Freeman, *The Legal Structure* (1974, Longman), pp. 116–17. See also Abel, op. cit.; M. Galanter, 'Why the "Haves" Come Out Ahead: Speculations on the Limits of Legal Change' (1974) *Law and Society Review*, vol. 9, p. 226; and M. Galanter, 'Mega-Law and Mega-Lawyering in the Contemporary United States', in R. Dingwall and P. Lewis, op. cit.

45 See Zander, op. cit. pp. 646–7.

46 Benson Commission Report, op. cit., p. 46.

47 Freeman, op. cit., p. 166.

48 See *Law Society's Gazette*, 28 January 1987.

49 P. Morris, 'A Sociological Approach to Research in Legal Services' in P. Morris, R. White, P. Lewis, *Social Needs and Legal Action* (1973, Martin Robertson), p. 52.

50 Fogelson and Freeman, 'Social Casework and Legal Knowledge' in S. Wheeler (ed.), *Controlling Delinquents* (1968, Wiley).

51 P. C. Alcock, 'Legal Aid: Whose Problem?' (1976) *British Journal of Law and Society*, vol. 3, no. 2, p. 154.

52 Zander, op. cit., p. 490.

53 P. S. Atiyah, *Accidents, Compensation and the Law* (4th edn by P. Cane, 1987, Weidenfeld and Nicolson), p. 267.

54 *Report of the Review Body on Civil Justice* (1988, Cm. 394, HMSO).

55 In 1980 the Legal Advice Regulations brought representation by solicitors in *civil* proceedings in magistrates' courts under the Green Form Scheme.

56 See J. Baldwin, 'The Green Form: Use or Abuse?', *New Law Journal*, 2 September 1988.

57 H. Levenson, series of articles in *Legal Action Group Bulletin* (1981).

58 A. Gray and P. Fenn, 'The Rising Cost of Legally Aided Criminal Cases', *New Law Journal*, 29 November 1991; C. Glasser, 'Legal Aid – Decline and Fall', *Law Society's Gazette*, 19 March 1986; Lord Mackay of Clashfern, 'Access to Justice: The Price' (1991) 25 *The Law Teacher* 96; Zander, op. cit., pp. 511–15; Abel, op. cit., pp. 116–19, 226–34.

59 *New Law Journal*, 4 April 1986.

60 *New Law Journal*, 7 November 1986.
61 O. Hansen, 'A Future for Legal Aid?' (1992) *Journal of Law and Society*, op. cit., p. 89.
62 *Eligibility for Civil Legal Aid: A Consultation Paper* (1991).
63 See surveys noted by Zander, op. cit., p. 513.
64 For excellent accounts of the developments up to mid-1992, see especially Zander, op. cit.; and also R. White, *The Administration of Justice* (2nd edn, 1991, Blackwell). Coverage of the legal aid controversy in the quality daily press tends to be good; and news and commentary in the *New Law Journal* is usually interesting and reliable.
65 On this Act see M. Partington, 'Change or no-change? Reflections on the Courts and Legal Services Act 1990' (1991) 54 *Modern Law Review* 702.
66 Zander, op. cit., p. 688; 'Ombudsman Starts Work', *New Law Journal*, 11 January 1991; R. Smith, 'A Place of Last Resort', *New Law Journal*, 1 November 1991.
67 See R. Campbell, 'The Inner Cities: Law Centres and Legal Services' (1992) *Journal of Law and Society*, op. cit.
68 *New Law Journal*, 15 March 1991.
69 R. White, 'Lawyers and the Enforcement of Rights', in Morris, White and Lewis, op. cit., p. 19. See also G. Bates, 'A Case for the Introduction of Class Actions in English Law', *New Law Journal*, 3 July 1980.
70 *Legal Action Group Bulletin*, November 1979, p. 253.
71 Benson Report, op. cit., p. 12. It was reported in the *New Law Journal*, 30 May 1985, that CABx referred some 370,000 clients per year to solicitors.
72 See Benson Report, op. cit.: Surveys, Section 16.
73 A. H. Hermann, 'Scholarship and reorganisation of the profession', *Financial Times*, 4 December 1987.

Chapter 14: The Judges

1 Above, chapter 6.
2 D. Hay, 'Property, Authority and the Criminal Law' in D. Hay *et al*, *Albion's Fatal Tree* (1977, Peregrine), p. 27.
3 Glanville Williams, *Proof of Guilt* (1963, Stevens), p. 22.
4 D. Pannick, *Judges* (1987, Oxford University Press), p. 18.
5 Ibid., p. 205.
6 J. A. G. Griffith, *The Politics of the Judiciary* (4th edn, 1991, Fontana), pp. 30–8.
7 *Labour Research*, January 1987.
8 L. Blom-Cooper and G. Drewry, *Final Appeal: A Study of the House of Lords in its Judicial Capacity* (1972, Clarendon Press).
9 These and other examples are cited by Pannick: op. cit., chapter 2.
10 Op. cit., p. 169.
11 D. Robertson, 'Judicial Ideology in the House of Lords: A Jurimetric Analysis' (1982) *British Journal of Political Science*, vol. 12.
12 S. Lee, *Judging Judges* (1988, Faber and Faber), p. 34.
13 Ibid., p. 36.
14 Ibid., p. 38.
15 Lord Chancellor's Department booklet, 1988.
16 *Independent*, 5 July 1992.
17 Op. cit., p. 20.
18 *The Times*, 8 October 1987.

19 Op. cit., p. 205.

20 A. Paterson, 'The Judges: A Political Élite?' (1974) *British Journal of Law and Society*, vol. 1, no. 2.

21 [1898] A. C. 1.

22 [1901] A. C. 495.

23 *Taff Vale Railway Co.* v. *Amalgamated Soc. of Railway Servants* [1901] A. C. 426.

24 See chapter 1.

25 Cited in Paterson (1974), op. cit., p. 125. On this, see also P. F. Smith and S. H. Bailey, *The Modern English Legal System* (2nd edn, 1991, Sweet and Maxwell); Pannick, op. cit., chapter 3.

26 R. Stevens, *Law and Politics: The House of Lords as a Judicial Body 1800–1976* (1979, Weidenfeld and Nicolson).

27 Ibid., pp. 32–4.

28 Op. cit.

29 L. K. J. Glassey, *Politics and the Appointment of Justices of the Peace 1675–1720* (1979, Oxford University Press). And see A. H. Manchester, *Modern Legal History* (1980, Butterworths), chapter 9.

30 C. Campbell, 'Judicial Selection and Judicial Impartiality' (1973) *Juridical Review*. And for a more general discussion see Pannick, op. cit., chapter 3.

31 Ibid., pp. 254–5. An analysis of the situation concerning judicial appointment and public credibility in the judges in the troubled province of Northern Ireland is given in K. Boyle, T. Hadden and P. Hillyard, *Law and State: The Case of Northern Ireland* (1975, Martin Robertson).

32 Campbell, op. cit., p. 279.

33 M. Tregilgas-Davey, 'Miscarriages of Justice within the English Legal System', *New Law Journal*, 17 May 1991.

34 Quoted in Griffith, op. cit., pp. 289–90.

35 Or in the police, for that matter. The West Midlands Serious Crime Squad had to be disbanded due to corruption, and investigations into the activities of this group of officers continued for some months afterwards.

36 Griffith, op. cit.

37 Ibid., p. 272.

38 Ibid., p. 275.

39 Ibid., p. 319.

40 P. Devlin, 'Judges, Government and Politics' (1978) 41 *Modern Law Review* 501. See also Lee, op. cit.

41 Ibid., p. 506.

42 Ibid., p. 508.

43 Ibid., p. 506.

44 Ibid., p. 507.

45 Ibid., p. 510.

46 M. Weber, *Law in Economy and Society* (1979 edn, Harvard University Press), chapter 3.

47 J. Frank, *Courts on Trial* (first published 1949); (1973 edn, Princeton University Press).

48 Hutcheson, 'The Judgement Intuitive: The Function of the "Hunch" in Judicial Decisions' (1928) 14 *Cornell Law Quarterley* 274.

49 The phrase has been subjected to a number of definitions. For a discussion of the

constitutional definition, see H. W. R. Wade, *Administrative Law* (6th edn, 1988, Oxford University Press), chapter 2; C. Turpin, *British Government and the Constitution: Text, Cases and Materials* (2nd edn, 1990, Weidenfeld and Nicolson), chapter 1; S. A. de Smith, *Constitutional and Administrative Law* (6th edn. by R. Brazier, 1990, Penguin), chapter 2. See above, chapter 12.

50 Griffith, op. cit., p. 321.

51 E. P. Thompson, *Whigs and Hunters* (1977, Peregrine), p. 259.

52 R. Dworkin, *Taking Rights Seriously* (1977, Duckworth); *Law's Empire* (1986, Fontana).

53 *Law's Empire* pp. 95–6.

54 Ibid., chapter 6.

55 Ibid., pp. 271–2.

56 See Lord Devlin, 'The Judge as Lawmaker' in P. Devlin, *The Judge* (1979, Oxford University Press); Lord Reid, 'The Judge as Lawmaker' (1972) 12 *Journal of the Society of Public Teachers of Law* 22; and for discussion of these judges see Stevens, op. cit., chapter 13, and A. Paterson, *The Law Lords* (1982, Macmillan/SSRC).

57 Weber, op. cit.

58 See Weber, op. cit., especially the Introduction by M. Rheinstein, pp. L–LI.

59 Quoted in Stevens, op. cit., p. 447.

60 W. T. Murphy and R. W. Rawlings, 'After the *Ancien Regime*: The Writing of Judgments in the House of Lords 1979/1980' (1981) 44 *Modern Law Review* and (1982) 45 *Modern Law Review*.

61 (1981) M. L. R., p. 617.

62 Ibid.

63 Ibid., p. 621.

64 For example, see the discussion on *Bromley L.B.C.* v. *Greater London Council*, below and see chapter 12. In this case, much was stated to depend on the interpretation of a single word – 'economic' – used in the statute under consideration.

65 (1981) M. L. R., p. 622.

66 (1982) M. L. R., p. 41.

67 Ibid., p. 61.

68 *Express Newspapers Ltd* v. *McShane* [1982] 2 W. L. R. 89; *Duport Steels Ltd* v. *Sirs* [1980] 1 W. L. R. 142.

69 *United Kingdom Association of Professional Engineers* v. *ACAS* [1980] 2 W. L. R. 254; *Engineers' and Managers' Association* v. *ACAS* [1980] 1 W. L. R. 302.

70 *Zamir* v. *Secretary of State for the Home Department* [1980] 3 W. L. R. 249.

71 *Inland Revenue Commissioners* v. *Plummer* [1979] 3 W. L. R. 689; another case concerning tax liability heard during the relevant period, and discussed by Murphy and Rawlings was *Vestey* v. *Inland Revenue Commissioners* [1979] 3 W. L. R. 915.

72 *Attorney-General* v. *British Broadcasting Corporation* [1980] 3 W. L. R. 109.

73 *Burmah Oil Co. Ltd* v. *Governor and Company of the Bank of England* [1979] 3 W. L. R. 722. See below for further discussion of this point.

74 A. Paterson, *The Law Lords*, op. cit.

75 Ibid., p. 3.

76 Ibid., p. 123.

77 See above, chapter 7.

78 Op. cit. p. 130. But see Griffith's review, (1982) *Journal of Law and Society*, Winter,

p. 298, where it is suggested that 'dissimulation' is 'a synonym for dishonesty'.

79 [1966] 1 W. L. R. 1234. See chapter 7.

80 Griffith, op. cit., pp. 260–1.

81 Paterson, op. cit., p. 188.

82 Op. cit.

83 Op. cit.

84 The case of Lord Denning is illustrative here, though by no means typical of the judges as a whole. In 1957 he was appointed to the House of Lords, but he returned to the Court of Appeal in 1962. Believing that the Court of Appeal has more significance as an appellate court than the House of Lords, it is there (no doubt in the knowledge that his decisions might be reviewed in the Lords itself) that some of Lord Denning's most controversial and 'creative' judgments have been delivered.

85 Op. cit.

86 [1932] A. C. 562.

87 [1989] A. C. 53, HL. See also the unsuccessful attempt to sue the Metropolitan police in negligence reported in the *Independent*, 8 October 1992: the Court of Appeal stated that, following *Hill*, the police should be immune from actions for negligence over matters of crime investigation and detection.

88 [1985] Q. B. 1012, CA.

89 [1990] 1 All E. R. 512.

90 Again, Lord Denning has provided a number of examples. Frequently challenging orthodox legal doctrine in cases where he felt it to be inappropriate in modern society, Denning's decisions in the Court of Appeal have often been overturned in the House of Lords. See, for example, the progress of *Gallie* v. *Lee* [1971] A. C. 1004; *Morgans* v. *Launchbury* [1974] A. C. 127; and *Duport Steel Ltd* v. *Sirs* [1980] 1 W. L. R. 142. Lord Denning was also one of a very small number of judges who unsuccessfully argued that, in the law of contract, unfair or oppressive exclusion clauses ought to be struck down as 'unreasonable'. Such a view found little support among other judges, though Parliament has now intervened in this area: Unfair Contract Terms Act 1977. See chapter 11.

91 [1982] 1 All E. R. 126 (CA); [1982] 1 All E. R. 153 (HL).

92 Notably Watkins L. J. ('a hasty, ill-considered, unlawful and arbitrary use of power'), at p. 149.

93 '. . . a thriftless use of moneys obtained by the GLC', *per* Lord Diplock, at p. 166.

94 G. Cunningham, MP, remarked of the Lords decision, in a parliamentary debate, 'Each of the five judgments rambles over the territory in what can only be called a head-scratching way, making it impossible for the consumer of the judgment to know at the end what the law is held to be, except negatively, and then only negatively on a few points. When one puts the five judgments together, the effect is chaos.' Quoted by J. A. G. Griffith, 'The Law Lords and the GLC', *Marxism Today*, February 1982. See also D. Pannick, 'The Law Lords and the Needs of Contemporary Society' (1982) *Political Quarterly*, p. 318.

95 The Greater London Council, along with the other metropolitan councils, was abolished in 1985. See chapter 12.

96 For example, Pannick, op. cit.

97 See also *R.* v. *London Transport Executive, ex p. GLC* [1983] QB 484.

98 [1942] A. C. 624.

99 [1968] A. C. 910.

100 [1975] 3 All E. R. 484.
101 [1981] 2 W. L. R. 310.
102 Ibid.
103 *Attorney-General* v. *Guardian Newspapers and others* [1987] 1 All E. R. 1248.
104 Lord Devlin, *The Enforcement of Morals* (1959, Oxford University Press), p. 7. See above, chapter 2.
105 (1866) L. R. 1 Ex. 213.
106 See also the discussion of the court in *Coral Leisure Group* v. *Barnett* [1981] I. C. R. 503.
107 [1971] 1 W. L. R. 487.
108 [1970] 70 L. G. R. 27.
109 Ibid.
110 [1991] 4 All E. R. 481. See V. Laird, 'Reflections on *R.* v. *R.*' (1992) 55 *Modern Law Review* 386.
111 Sometimes it is hard to see how the prosecution could establish that the substantive harm *could* be done. In *Shaw* v. *D. P. P.* (the *Ladies' Directory* case, discussed in chapter 2), for example, by what means could it be shown that publication of the Directory *had* 'corrupted public morals'?
112 See the cases analysed by Griffith, op. cit., chapter 3.
113 Devlin, op. cit., p. 15. In the light of the jury-vetting procedures which have been used in recent years, one may seriously wonder just how 'random' the selection for jury service may have become.
114 M. Coulson and C. Riddell, *Approaching Sociology* (2nd edn, 1980, Routledge and Kegan Paul), p. 14. See also Griffith, op. cit., chapter 9.
115 W. Chambliss and R. Seidman, *Law, Order and Power* (2nd edn, 1982, Addison-Wesley), p. 249.
116 D. Pannick, *Judges*, op. cit.

Chapter 15: Conclusion: law, the individual and the state

1 See for example the *Report of the Consulative Group on Research and Education in Law* (1983, Research Council of Canada) for an account of the not dissimilar pattern of Canadian legal education.
2 R. M. Jackson, *The Machinery of Justice in England* (7th edn, 1977, Cambridge University Press), p. 586. See also W. Twining, 'Is Your Text Book Really Necessary?' '(1970) *Jo. Society of Public Teachers of Law*, vol. 11. For an explanation of the manner in which law is usually taught, see A. Bradney *et al.*, *How to Study Law* (2nd edn, 1991, Sweet and Maxwell); P. H. Kenny, *Studying Law* (2nd edn, 1991, Butterworths).
3 *Royal Commission on Legal Services* (Benson Commission), *Report*, (1979, Cmnd. 7648, HMSO). See chapter 13.
4 See R. Baldwin and C. McCrudden, *Regulation and Public Law* (1987, Weidenfeld and Nicolson).
5 See above, chapters 5 and 7.
6 See above, chapter 11.
7 See above, chapters 5 and 12.
8 See T. Mullen, 'Representation at Tribunals' (1990) 53 *Modern Law Review* 230.

9 Jackson, *The Machinery of Justice in England* (8th edn, 1989, Cambridge University Press), p. 494.

10 Lord Macmillan in *Glasgow Corporation* v. *Muir* [1943] A. C. 448 at p. 457.

11 Lord Denning in *Dutton* v. *Bognor Regis UDC* [1972] 1 Q. B. 373 at p. 397. For the subsequent history of this case, see chapter 9.

12 See above, chapter 13.

13 R. Cotterrell, *The Sociology of Law: An Introduction* (2nd edn, 1992, Butterworths), p. 65.

14 P. Rock, *Deviant Behaviour* (1973, Hutchinson), pp. 131–2.

15 See G. Robertson, *Freedom, the Individual and the Law* (6th edn, 1989, Penguin), pp. 284–93.

16 One example of this is the decision to introduce new plastic cards for each person, bearing his or her national insurance number. The reason for this was stated to be that plastic cards were more durable than the old cardboard version. What worried many people, however, was the fact that across the back of the new cards is a magnetic strip, on which could be stored personal information, of an undisclosed kind, about the card-holder. Such a potentially far-reaching development might have been thought to have required full parliamentary debate, and possibly legislation. No such debate took place, however, and the new cards were introduced without legislative approval. Apart from this somewhat dramatic example, government regulations, emanating from individual departments, in the form of delegated legislation, frequently by-pass the parliamentary process (see chapter 7) and it seems increasingly to be the case that government legislation reserves to ministers considerable powers to issue directives or other orders: see for example the powers of the Home Secretary to issue Codes of Practice under the Police and Criminal Evidence Act 1984; the powers enjoyed by the Minister of Education under the Education Reform Act 1988; the powers given to the Lord Chancellor by virtue of the Legal Aid Act 1988 and the Courts and Legal Services Act 1990.

17 See M. Barker, *The New Racism* (1981, Junction Books), especially chapters 1–3.

18 Cf. K. Marx and F. Engels, *The German Ideology* (1974, Students' Edition, Lawrence and Wishart), at p. 64: 'The ideas of the ruling class are in every epoch the ruling ideas, i.e. the class which is the ruling *material* force of society, is at the same time its ruling *intellectual* force ... The ruling ideas are nothing more than the ideal expression of the dominant material relationships, the dominant material relationships grasped as ideas; hence of the relationships which make the one class the ruling one, therefore, the ideas of its dominance.'

19 A. Gramsci, *Prison Notebooks* (1971, Lawrence and Wishart).

20 A. Hunt, 'The Politics of Law and Justice' in Politics and Power Editorial Board, *Law, Justice and Politics* (1981, Routledge and Kegan Paul), p. 4.

21 See G. Robertson, op. cit., pp. 299–303; P. Hain, *Political Trials in Britain* (1984, Penguin) chapter 6.

22 In 1980 the government, in response to public disquiet about the extent to which telephone-tapping by the police and security services took place, published a White Paper, *The Interception of Communications in Great Britain*, whch revealed that the Home Secretary had given the police warrants to tap phones in only 467 cases in 1979. This report omitted figures relating to taps made by the Ministry of Defence. However it was revealed in the *New Statesman*, just before the White Paper, that a new government establishment in London could handle 1,500 telephone

interceptions *at once*. See Robertson, op. cit., pp. 120–8, for a full discussion of the current practices (as far as they are known) and the various safeguards against abuse.

23 For materials on the police generally, see R. Reiner, *The Politics of the Police* (1985, Wheatsheaf Books); P. Scraton, *The State of the Police* (1985, Pluto Press); J. Morgan, *The Police Function and the Investigation of Crime* (1990, Avebury).

24 The Police and Criminal Evidence Act 1984 is a long and extremely complex statute; the reader is referred, for full details of the Act, to M. Zander, *The Police and Criminal Evidence Act 1984* (2nd edn, 1990, Sweet and Maxwell); F. Hargreaves and H. Levenson, *A Practitioner's Guide to the Police and Criminal Evidence Act 1984* (1984, Legal Action Group).

25 The legislation in these and other areas is characterized by a liberalism which, arguably, does little to further the causes of any of the affected groups, especially women and ethnic groups. As stated above, the social, economic and political determinants of a problem cannot be changed by a stroke or two of the legislative pen. Legislation cannot by itself perform miraculous changes in attitudes, prejudices, social structural arrangements or economically determined inequality. Equality of opportunity for women is not simply a matter of 'making them more like men', any more than equality for ethnic groups is promoted by legislation which implicitly tries to make 'black people more like white'. Instead, there is a need to appreciate the deeply embedded cultural and social patterns of discrimination against women, and to enable and encourage all members of a multi-ethnic society to realize and appreciate their different cultural backgrounds and histories. It would be naïve in the extreme to believe that women's rights legislation and anti-discrimination legislation can remove the ingrained prejudices and practices of a society which has treated women as second-class citizens for so long, and which has such a long history of exploitation of Asian and Caribbean countries and their peoples. In time, the educative nature of law, though limited, may induce changes of a wider-ranging nature, and obviously such developments are to be hoped for, though if law has an educative role, it is not aided by comments from politicians which pander to the very prejudices which Parliament has attempted to eliminate. Margaret Thatcher's comment in 1979 that Britain was being 'swamped' by immigrants with alien cultures (see M. Barker, op. cit., p. 1) was hardly helpful, and may be thought, especially given the virtual cessation of immigration to Britain as compared to the 1950s and 1960s, to be downright irresponsible.

26 Sir Leslie Scarman, *English Law: The New Dimension* (1974, Stevens), pp. 12–13.

27 Ibid., pp. 18–19.

28 See chapter 3.

29 See R. N. Cohen, *Whose File is it Anyway?* (1982, NCCL); R. Delbridge and M. Smith, *Consuming Secrets* (1982, Burnet Books); J. Michael, op. cit. In 1984 the Data Protection Act was passed, providing for controls on and regulation of data-users and protection for the data-subject: predictably, however, computerized files concerning various government and police activities are excluded from the access provisions: see N. Savage and C. Edwards, *Guide to the Data Protection Act 1984* (2nd edn, 1985, Blackstone); and see above, chapter 5.

30 See especially *Council of Civil Service Unions v. Minister for Civil Service* [1985] A. C. 374.

31 E. P. Thompson, *Whigs and Hunters* (1977, Peregrine), p. 265.
32 Ibid., p. 266.

Suggestions for further reading

Introductory works on law

There are various titles currently available which concentrate exclusively on the presentation of legal rules in areas such as contract, tort, crime, property and the legal system. These are not written from the perspective of 'law in context', but generally provide on outline of 'black-letter' legal rules. Among them are P. S. James, *Introduction to English Law* (12th edn, 1989, Butterworths) and Smith and Keenan's *English Law* (9th edn, 1989, Pitman); a comprehensive reference book, written for the lay reader's everyday use, is J. Pritchard, *The Penguin Guide to the Law* (2nd edn, 1986, Penguin).

Law and society: some general books

A number of titles in this area have appeared over the past fifteen years or so: the following are some of the most recent books. R. Cotterrell, *The Sociology of Law* (2nd edn, 1992, Butterworths) is an excellent introduction to the various issues involved in this complex area of study. A. Hunt's *The Sociological Movement in Law* (1978, Macmillan) is a good review of the contributions of social theorists to our understanding of law. W. Chambliss and R. Seidman, *Law, Order and Power* (2nd edn, 1982, Addison-Wesley) is a critical discussion of law in the USA, but has much that is of relevance to the English legal system. C. Campbell and P. Wiles (eds), *Law and Society* (1979, Martin Robertson), and D. Kairys (ed.), *The Politics of Law: A Progressive Critique* (1982, Pantheon) are collections of essays and articles which will be of interest to the student of law and society.

Legal concepts and legal reasoning

On rules and rule-handling techniques, W. Twining and D. Miers, *How to Do Things with Rules* (3rd edn, 1991, Weidenfeld and Nicolson) is an excellent introduction, and is a unique analysis and discussion of this area. J. Farrar and H. Dugdale, *Introduction to Legal Method* (3rd edn, 1990, Sweet and Maxwell) contains much useful material on legal reasoning and legal method, as do two books designed to introduce students to the study of law: P. Kenny's *Studying Law* (2nd edn, 1991, Butterworths) and A. Bradney, V Fisher, *et al, How to Study Law* (2nd edn, 1991, Sweet and Maxwell).

For the student of legal theory, the best introductory works, combining extensive critical commentary and many extracts from the writings of legal theorists and philosophers from ancient times to the present day, are undoubtedly Lloyd's

Introduction to Jurisprudence (5th edn by Lord Lloyd of Hampstead and M. D. A. Freeman, 1985, Stevens) and H. Davies and D. Holdcroft, *Jurisprudence: Texts and Commentary* (1991, Butterworths). A shorter book is N. E. Simmonds, *Central Issues in Jurisprudence* (1986, Sweet and Maxwell). For the more advanced reader, N. MacCormick, *H. L. A. Hart* (1981, Edward Arnold) discusses the work of one of the most influential legal philosophers; and R. Dworkin, *Law's Empire* (1986, Fontana), J. Finnis, *Natural Law and Natural Rights* (1980, Oxford University Press) and N. MacCormick, *Legal Reasoning and Legal Theory* (1979, Oxford University Press) are recommended.

In addition to the works cited in chapter 2, some excellent material on law and morality will be found in L. Blom-Cooper and G. Drewry, *Law and Morality* (1976, Duckworth). As to whether or not law should be used to enforce moral principles, see P. Devlin, *The Enforcement of Morals* (1959, Oxford University Press) and H. L. A. Hart, *Law, Liberty and Morality* (1962, Oxford University Press). For a stimulating discussion of some contemporary issues, see S. Lee, *Law and Morals* (1986, Oxford University Press).

English legal institutions

Introductory general books are G. Drewry, *Law, Justice and Politics* (2nd edn, 1981, Longman) and M. Berlins and C. Dyer, *The Law Machine* (3rd edn, 1989, Penguin). M. Zander's writings on the legal system are critical and informative; titles especially worth of note are *Lawyers and the Public Interest* (1968, Weidenfeld and Nicolson), *What's Wrong with the Law?* (1970, BBC Publications) and *Cases and Materials on the English Legal System* (6th edn, 1992, Weidenfeld and Nicolson). Introductory works include K. Eddey, *The English Legal System* (5th edn, 1992, Sweet and Maxwell), and up-to-date major standard texts include P. F. Smith and S. H. Bailey, *The Modern English Legal System* (2nd edn, 1991, Sweet and Maxwell). For historical accounts of the legal system see J. H. Baker, *Introduction to English Legal History* (3rd edn, 1990, Butterworths); A. H. Manchester, *A Modern Legal History of England and Wales 1750–1950* (1980, Butterworths); and by the same author, *Sources of English Legal History 1750–1950* (1984, Butterworths), a companion volume to the text which comprises a collection of historical materials. Most of these titles are descriptive accounts, and the reader will find many more titles suitable for further reading in the notes to chapters 6, 7, 13 and 14.

J. A. G. Griffith's critical study of the higher judiciary, *The Politics of the Judiciary* (4th edn, 1991, Fontana) is an excellent, though controversial, discussion. R. Stevens, *Law and Politics* (1979, Weidenfeld and Nicolson) is the definitive account of the judicial role of the House of Lords. A. Paterson, *The Law Lords* (1982, Macmillan/SSRC) provides an interesting account of the House of Lords, focusing on the question of how the judges in that court perceive their function and their role; and S. Lee, *Judging Judges* (1988, Faber and Faber), although written in a rather more journalistic manner, offers a useful critical discussion of the various commentaries on the judiciary, an account of topics of recent controversy, and short accounts of the careers of a number of eminent members of the higher judiciary.

Books dealing with the processes of law-making are still comparatively few. M. Zander, *The Law-Making Process* (3rd edn, 1989, Weidenfeld and Nicolson) combines textual discussion with selected extracts from materials from various sources. D. Miers and A. Page, *Legislation* (2nd edn, 1990, Sweet and Maxwell) is a thorough account of legislation in all its aspects. R. Cross, *Statutory Interpretation* (2nd edn, 1987, Butterworths) is a useful and often amusing account of this topic. R. Stevens and A. Paterson, op. cit., deal with, among other aspects of the judiciary, judicial law-making. Some recently published titles fill something of a gap in the literature on the common law: D. Roebuck, *The Background of the Common Law* (2nd edn, 1990, Oxford University Press); L. Goldstein (ed.), *Precedent in Law* (1991, Oxford University Press); and R. Cross and J. Harris, *Precedent in English Law* (1991, Oxford University Press).

Areas of substantive law

This book cannot, by its very nature, deal in great depth with specific areas of substantive law, and in this section some of the most useful titles in the main fields of law are noted. They range from the fairly slim volumes currently available, such as Sweet and Maxwell's Concise College Text (CCT) series, to the acknowledged standard texts, which are substantial and expensive. Students should take care to ensure that the books they use for deeper coverage of the law are up-to-date editions.

It is a matter of personal preference whether G. H. Treitel's *Law of Contract* (8th edn, 1991, Sweet and Maxwell) or Cheshire, Fifoot and Furmston's *Law of Contract* (12th edn, 1991, Butterworths) is used in this field. Casebooks on contract currently include H. Beale, W. Bishop and M. Furmston, *Contract – Cases and Materials* (2nd edn, 1990, Butterworths), which also contains critical commentary on the materials, and J. C. Smith and J. A. Thomas, *Casebook on Contract* (9th edn, 1992, Sweet and Maxwell). It is sensible to have regard to which title is in the most recent edition at the time of choosing. The CCT series has F. R. Davies, *Contract* (6th edn by R. Upex, 1991), and G. H. Treitel's *Outline of the Law of Contract* (4th edn, 1989, Butterworths) is a much slimmer volume than his text noted above. Blackstone Press have T. Downes, *Textbook on Contract* (2nd edn, 1991) in their excellent Textbook series. All these works deal with the law of contract by means of exposition of the legal rules: works which locate law firmly in its commercial and economic contexts are J. P. Tillotson, *Contract Law in Perspective* (2nd edn, 1985, Butterworths) and H. Collins, *The Law of Contract* (1986, Weidenfeld and Nicolson).

In the related field of consumer and commercial law, R. Lowe and G. Woodroffe, *Consumer Law and Practice* (3rd edn, 1991, Sweet and Maxwell) focuses on practical problems and remedies. Texts which lay out the 'hard law' include D. Oughton, *Consumer Law: Text, Cases and Materials* (1991, Blackstone); I. Ramsay, *Consumer Protection: Cases and Materials* (1989, Weidenfeld and Nicolson); and B. Harvey and D. Parry, *The Law of Consumer Protection and Fair Trading* (4th edn, 1992, Butterworths). Titles dealing with specific aspects of consumer law include P. Atiyah, *Sale of Goods* (8th edn, 1990, Pitman); M. Furmston, *Sale of Goods* (1990, Croner); and C. Wright, *Product Liability* (1989, Blackstone).

Standard texts on tort are Winfield and Jolowicz on *Tort* (13th edn by W. V. H. Rogers, 1989, Sweet and Maxwell), Salmond and Heuston, *The Law of Torts* (20th edn by R. F. V. Heuston and R. A. Buckley, 1992, Sweet and Maxwell), M. Jones, *Textbook on Torts* (3rd edn, 1991, Blackstone), H. Street on *Torts* (8th edn, by H. Street and M. Brazier, 1988, Butterworths), and J. G. Fleming, *The Law of Torts* (7th edn, 1988, Sweet and Maxwell). The main casebooks are T. Weir, *Casebook on Torts* (7th edn, 1992, Sweet and Maxwell); R. Kidner, *Casebook on Torts* (2nd edn, 1992, Blackstone);

and B. A. Hepple and M. H. Matthews, *Tort: Cases and Materials* (4th edn, 1991, Butterworths). The CCT series has C. D. Baker, *Tort* (5th edn, 1991). A much more contextual discussion of those aspects of tort concerning compensation for personal injuries is Atiyah's *Accidents, Compensation and the Law* (4th edn by P. Cane, 1987, Weidenfeld and Nicolson).

In the field of property law, the student will find discussion on various aspects of property rights in texts such as those on commercial law noted above. Of the texts on land law, standard works include R. Megarry, *Manual of the Law of Real Property* (7th edn, 1992, Sweet and Maxwell); Cheshire and Burn's *Modern Law of Real Property* (14th edn, 1988, Butterworths); J-A. MacKenzie and M. Phillips, *A Practical Approach to Land Law* (3rd edn, 1991, Blackstone); K. J. Gray, *Elements of Land Law* (1987, Butterworths); and in the CCT series, E. S. Green and N. Henderson, *Land Law* (5th edn, 1988, Sweet and Maxwell). Useful casebooks are E. Burn, *Maudsley and Burn's Land Law: Cases and Materials* (6th edn, 1992, Butterworths) and M. Thomas, *Casebook on Land Law* (1992, Blackstone). Titles on other more specialized aspects of property law and land-use (housing, intellectual property, environmental law and planning) may be found in the notes to chapter 5.

The acklowledged standard texts on criminal law are J. C. Smith and B. Hogan, *Criminal Law* (7th edn, 1992, Butterworths) and Card, Cross and Jones, *Criminal Law* (12th edn by R. Card, 1992, Butterworths). Combining text with contextual material is C. Clarkson and H. Keating's *Criminal Law: Text and Materials* (2nd edn, 1990, Sweet and Maxwell). A newer text is M. Jefferson, *Criminal Law* (1992, Pitman). Shorter books include M. Allen, *Textbook on Criminal Law* (1991, Blackstone) and P. Seago, *Criminal Law* (3rd edn, 1989) in the CCT series. Casebooks include J. C. Smith and B. Hogan, *Criminal Law: Cases and Materials* (4th edn, 1990, Butterworths) and Elliott and Wood's *Casebook on Criminal Law* (5th edn by D. Elliott and M. Allen, 1989, Sweet and Maxwell). Many important titles in criminology are noted in chapter 10. In particular, the following are useful materials on sentencing and the criminal justice system: A. Ashworth, *Sentencing and Penal Policy* (1983, Weidenfeld and Nicolson); I. Taylor, *Law and Order: Arguments for Socialism* (1981, Macmillan); S. Cohen, *Visions of Social Control* (1985, Polity Press); D. Garland, *Punishment in Modern Society* (1990, Clarendon); and for rather more legally oriented approaches, C. S. Harding and L. M. Koffman, *Sentencing and the Penal System: Text and Materials* (1988, Sweet and Maxwell), and M. Wasik and R. Taylor, *Blackstone's Guide to the Criminal Justice Act 1991* (1991, Blackstone).

The main texts on European law are J. Steiner, *Textbook on EC Law* (3rd edn, 1992, Blackstone); M. Sheridan and J. Cameron, *EC Legal Systems: An Introductory Guide* (1992, Butterworths); D. Medhurst, *A Brief and Practical Guide to EC Law* (1990, Blackwell); S. Weatherill, *Cases and Materials on EEC Law* (1992, Blackstone); and T. Hartley, *Foundations of European Community Law* (2nd edn, 1988, Clarendon).

In the area of administrative law, among the standard texts are H. W. R. Wade, *Administrative Law* (6th edn, 1988, Oxford University Press); P. Craig, *Administrative Law* (2nd edn, 1989, Sweet and Maxwell); Hood Phillips' *Constitutional and Administrative Law* (7th edn by P. Jackson, 1987. Sweet and Maxwell); J. F. Garner, *Administrative Law* (7th edn, 1989, Butterworths); C. Turpin, *British Government and the Constitution* (2nd edn, 1990, Weidenfeld and Nicolson); D. Pollard and D. Hughes, *Constitutional and Administrative Law: Cases and Materials* (1990, Butterworths); S. Bailey, B. Jones and A. Mowbray, *Cases and Materials on Administrative Law* (2nd edn, 1992, Sweet and Maxwell); J. Beatson and M. Matthews, *Administrative Law: Cases and Materials* (1983,

Oxford University Press); D. Foulkes, *Administrative Law* (7th edn, 1990, Butterworths); and S. A. de Smith, *Constitutional and Administrative Law* (6th edn by S. A. de Smith and R. Brazier, 1989, Penguin). The main issues and problems are dealt with by all of them; they vary somewhat in length and in price, but perhaps the best advice, as usual, is to consult the titles in the most recent editions. More contextual discussion can be found in J. Jowell and D. Oliver, *The Changing Constitution* (2nd edn, 1989, Oxford University Press); C. Harlow and R. Rawlings, *Law and Administration* (1984, Weidenfeld and Nicolson); and – discussing public regulatory agencies in particular – R. Baldwin and C. McCrudden, *Regulation and Public Law* (1987, Weidenfeld and Nicolson).

Reading in the area of sociology

Apart from the texts noted in chapter 1, the reader is directed to the following selected titles. Good starting points are C. Wright Mills, *The Sociological Imagination* (1970, Pelican), and P. Berger, *Invitation to Sociology* (1967, Penguin). Main themes and perspectives within sociology, many of which are touched on in this book, are dealt with in various recent texts and readers, including M. Haralambos, *Sociology: Themes and Perspectives* (3rd edn, 1991, HarperCollins); A. Giddens, *Human Societies: A Reader* (1992, Polity Press); and E. Cuff, W. Sharrock and D. Francis, *Perspectives in Sociology* (3rd edn, 1992, Routledge). Sociology texts should be consulted on all the sociological concepts and theories noted below.

On social class, see J. Westergaard and H. Resler, *Class in a Capitalist Society* (1976, Penguin); A. Giddens, *The Class Structure of the Advanced Societies* (1973, Hutchinson); and F. Parkin's reader, *The Social Analysis of Class Structure* (1974, Tavistock). The more advanced reader should read something of the works of Marx, Durkheim and Weber – a useful starting-point is A. Giddens, *Capitalism and Modern Social Theory* (1971, Cambridge University Press), and the major works by these social theorists should be noted for further study; E. Durkheim, *On the Division of Labour in Society* (1964 edn, Free Press, New York), *The Rules of Sociological Method* (1964, Free Press, New York), and *Suicide* (1970 edn, Routledge and Kegan Paul); M. Weber, *The Protestant Ethic and the Spirit of Capitalism* (1971 edn, Allen and Unwin), and *Law in Economy and Society* (1954 edn, Harvard University Press); K. Marx, *Capital* (vols 1, 2 and 3, 1976, 1978 and 1981, Penguin); K. Marx and F. Engels, *The German Ideology* (in K. Marx and F. Engels, *Collected Works*, vol. 5 (1976, Lawrence and Wishart)), and *The Communist Manifesto* (in *Karl Marx: The Revolutions of 1848*, 1973, Penguin).

Finally, on power and the state, see S. Lukes, *Power: A Radical View* (1974, Macmillan); J. Hall and G. Ikenberry, *The State* (1989, Oxford University Press); and the excellent collection of articles and extracts in D. Held *et al.*, *States and Societies* (1983, Martin Robertson).

INDEX